Confessions *of a* Hollywood Stunt Man

Confessions *of a* Hollywood Stunt Man

(or It Seemed Like a Good Idea at the Time!)

JESSE WAYNE

Cover Photo by Mary Rondell
From *The Mini-Skirt Mob*, February 8, 1967, American International Pictures, Tucson, AZ. Jesse Wayne stunt double for actress Patty McCormack.

Book cover design by Cal Sharp
Caligraphics.net

Book design by Maureen Cutajar
www.gopublished.com

*Frank & Edee
Thank you for being my guiding light.*

Preface

The Hollywood Stunt Man!!! Contrary to a general misconception, not all stunt men are six-feet-two inches tall. Women, children and short men also needed to be stunt-doubled in action sequences dating back to the earliest silent films. Stunt man Bobby Rose started the ball rolling in 1915, doubling Serial Queen Ruth Roland.

In 1959, at five-foot-four, Hollywood's studios allowed me to begin a 40 year career stunt doubling Tinseltown's most famous short actors, actresses and children. It's been exhilarating knowing a million guys wished they could change places with me in a flash.

Born September 14, 1941, it all began in 1946 when my dad, Frank, took me to see my first moving picture, Walt Disney's *Song of the South*. I was fascinated and knew immediately that I wanted to be in Show Biz. Fortunately, being born and raised in Los Angeles provided the perfect opportunity to appear in the early days of live television production in the late 1940s.

At eight years old, my decision was definite. Few kids know what they want to be at that age, but I knew I would become a TV cameraman. By 12, I had free run of KTLA, channel 5, L.A.'s premier TV station, and was mentored by its founder, electronic/showman genius Klaus Landsberg. TV cameraman, Bill Matheson, on Saturdays between car commercials would train me to operate the RCA TK-10 b&w

camera. At 17, I became a full-fledged KTLA employee, but after nine months soon realized that corporate television was not for me. Three months later Fate stepped in when I became Mickey Rooney's stunt double at MGM at age 18.

My career successes, with its many twists and turns, seemed pre-destined and very appropriate as it delivered me to my ultimate destination as a Hollywood Stunt Man.

Additionally, my creative juices took me behind the camera as a first assistant director, and just about every other job required on a movie set. The assistant director, I believe, is the toughest job on any film was my favorite. You're the problem solver, the psychologist and the father-confessor. You are constantly weighing the production's rigorous shooting schedule, budgetary and crew demands against the director's desire to get his vision up on the silver screen. It's a position where experience in the filmmaking process is a must.

There were many laughs, a few tragic moments, and over the years, I'm thankful for several cherished friendships that have endured for over half a century. Those dear folks still put a smile on my face.

But what a wild and wonderful life experience, meeting and/or from 1959 to 1999, working with the greatest, most extraordinary entertainers, writers, directors and producers of the Twentieth Century:

Mickey Rooney & Judy Garland, Fred Astaire & Ginger Rogers, Tony Bennett, Jerry Lewis, Clint Eastwood, Steve McQueen, Doris Day, The Three Stooges, Karl Malden, Elvis Presley, Michael Douglas, Steve Allen, Dick Van Dyke, Charlton Heston, Nick Nolte, Don Johnson, Kurt Russell, Bobby Darin, Sir John Mills, David Niven, Dan Duryea, Nick Adams, Audie Murphy, James Arness, Mel Tormé, Fess Parker, James Garner, Gene Kelly, Alan Hale, Lee Majors, Barbara Stanwick, Helen Hayes, Leslie Caron, Lucille Ball, Janet Leigh, Ava Gardner, Bob Newhart, Jack Benny, Dick Powell, Bob Hope, George Gobel, James Stewart, Don Knotts, David Niven, Robin Williams, Harry Morgan, Jeanne Crain, Dana Andrews, Glenn Ford, Dale Evans, Coach Jerry Glanville, Gene Barry, Jack Lord, Chuck Connors, Ricardo Montalban, Alan Alda, Robert Blake, Walter Matthau, Tom Sellick, Natalie Wood, Robert Wagner, Ernest Borgnine, Brian Keith, Bill Cosby, Danny

Thomas, Andy Williams, Phil Silvers, Tony Curtis, Frankie Avalon, Henry Fonda, Robert Taylor, Burgess Meredith, Fred MacMurray, Pat Boone, Blake Edwards, Alfred Hitchcock, Stanley Kramer, George Marshall, Billy Wilder, Mark Robson, Robert Aldrich, Joseph L. Mankiewicz, Don Siegel, William Witney, Carl Reiner, Ronald Neame, Richard Donner, Jacques Tourneur, John Carpenter, Otto Preminger, William Asher, William Castle, and so many more.

It's been a remarkable trip with fantastic memories. I hope you enjoy the tour as much as I have.

—Jesse Wayne

Acknowledgements

Valerie Allen, Chuck Amman, Rick Arnold, Jeanne Basone, Rick Barker, Bob Bayles, May Boss, Jan Shepard, Ray Boyle, Brandon Boyle, Freddie Brookfield, Dixie Carson, Fred Carson, Rick Danner, Roy Downey, Dick Durock, Georg Fenady, Sunny Ferrari, Chuck Hicks, Whitey Hughes, Fred Krone, Audie & Fritz Manes, Maurice Marks, Denver Mattson, Frank Messina, Burr Middleton, Bob Miles, Jim Nissen, Treva Orrison, John Parkinson, Diane (Di) Roberson, Alex Sharp, Jack Verbois, John Steinriede, Syd Stembridge and Terry Wooley.

I apologize to anyone I've neglected to mention, but you know who you are and I am forever grateful.

Confessions *of a* Hollywood Stunt Man

CHAPTER 1

The Beginning

It's July 1962—I'm almost 21, in the third year of my stunt career, and again stunt doubling Mickey Rooney, this time in Stanley Kramer's *It's a Mad, Mad, Mad, Mad World*, featuring a cast of America's greatest comedians, with an estimated film budget of $9,400.000.

The stunt action had gone well this morning—Ivan Volkman, the first assistant director called lunch, I ran to Paramount Pictures' Café Continental and was suddenly face to chest with John Wayne. Surprised and thrilled, I blurted, "Hi, Mr. Wayne, I'm Jesse Wayne, Mickey Rooney's stunt man." Duke's massive hand shook mine, "Well howwwya doin'? I thought yaaa were Mick-eey Roo-ney."

John Wayne was my Dad's all-time favorite actor. Fourteen years had passed since 1948 when Dad pointed to the movie screen—America's Greatest Cinema Hero—during John Ford's *Three Godfathers*. Over the years, this was the first of several times I'd meet "Duke" – all moments I will never forget.

It's a Mad, Mad, Mad, Mad World – now revered as one of Holly-wood's greatest classic comedy films, was based out of Universal Studios and had filmed at many Southern California locations, but now we were on Paramount Pictures' Stage 15, home of Hollywood's most advanced rear screen projection system, the best technology of 1962, utilizing two interlocked film images through two projectors.

The film's gyrating fire ladder, constructed on a five-ton, iron-beamed, rotating gurney gave us ten stunt doubles an "E Ticket" ride. For the closer shots, Hollywood's greatest assortment of madcap clowns ever assembled out-mugged each other, as all vied to out-wit Jonathan Winters. None succeeded. Everyone involved with the production knew *Mad World* would be a great success—and were not surprised it became one of Hollywood's most enduring comedy classics.

Veteran New York make up man Dick Smith was brought to Hollywood to work his specialty: the latex rubber facemask. Each stunt double was fitted with a life mask of the actor they doubled. Mike Westmore, of the famous pioneer makeup family, had recently begun his makeup apprenticeship, assisted Smith.

The forming of the mask initially entailed a generous amount of Vaseline applied to the entire face area. This slick coating enabled the dried plaster mask to be removed without sticking. Plaster of Paris was applied and to facilitate the breathing process, plastic straws were placed in each nostril. The process wasn't for the claustrophobic, namely Rooney, who went ballistic when they inserted the straws and first gob of plaster. The entire procedure took only enough time for the plaster to dry, then the mold "popped off" like a dental impression.

Veteran Stunt man/Stunt Coordinator Carey Loftin assembled this group of stunt performers:

Bill Couch (Buddy Hackett)	Janos Prohaska (Peter Falk, Arnold Stang)
Chuck Couch (Terry-Thomas)	Philip Crawford
John Hudkins (Jonathan Winters)	John Daheim
Jack Perkins (Jonathan Winters)	Bob Herron
Loren Janes (Eddie Anderson)	Richard E. Butler
Regis Parton (Milton Berle)	Walt LaRue
George Robotham (Dick Shawn)	Robert F. Hoy
Carl Saxe (Sid Caesar)	Fred Scheiwiller
Helen Thurston (Ethel Merman)	Buddy Van Horn
Jesse Wayne (Mickey Rooney)	Paul Stader
Marvin Willens (Phil Silvers)	

Chuck Hayward	Max Balchowsky
Fred Gabourie	Gary Epper
Tap Canutt	Carol Daniels
Frank Tallman	Bill Shannon
Paul Mantz	Stephanie Epper
Tom Steele	May Boss
Sol Gorss	Alex Sharp
George DeNormand	Dick Geary
Gil Perkins	Paul Baxley
Dale Van Sickel	Wally Rose
Dick Crockett	Harvey Parry

In Universal's tallest sound stage 12, the first shots involved the climax of the movie chase at the deserted office building. The interior shots consisted of the stunt doubles scurrying up the staircase on their way to the roof, chasing Spencer Tracy with the satchel of money. It was every man for him self as we scrambled ass over teakettle to get up the steps. A week later we were on the Universal backlot.

"Holy Shit!" uttered a stunt man under his breath, as we stared at the seventy-foot tall hotel façade, constructed on Universal Studio's highest hilltop. I had been a professional stunt man for three years and had never been asked to do high work, but why not? I wasn't afraid of heights, weighed 125 lbs. and was in great physical condition. Like most aspects of life you become acclimated to your situation, and after ten minutes I was climbing the faux building structure like a monkey.

The chase scene plot had the stunt doubles scrambling over the building's edge like Lemmings. On the fire escape our added weight causes it to break loose and hang precariously. A fire ladder comes to our rescue with Billy Shannon, doubling fireman Sterling Holloway, and one by one, we transferred to the ladder. One of the stunt guys, definitely not a "high man," whined about his position, but only made me think "Shut up, just get on the ladder and hang on."

Later, on Universal's backlot street set, Chuck Couch, Bill Couch, Bear Hudkins and I were the only live members hanging (with six other mannequins) from the fire ladder attached to the 100' telescoping construction crane. Bear remained stationary, doubling Spencer Tracy as me and the Couch brothers moved rung to rung. The next day, just minutes prior to filming, with the ladder in a horizontal position, I inhaled deeply as I checked my position. It sounded like a twig snapped as I suddenly felt something pop in my back, immediately producing an aching, burning pain in my left mid-back area.

For the next three hours I performed as the ladder whipped around, and then, when we wrapped, I rushed to Dr. Charles B. Faranella. While lying on my right side he suddenly twisted me and I heard another "snap." The good Doc explained that a "floating rib" had popped out of its socket. The irritation ended a couple of days later. When you're twenty, you heal fast.

Weeks later, I heard that while Bear, Chuck, Bill and I did our ladder romping a hundred feet up, the crane wheels were bouncing eighteen inches up off the ground during its gyrations.

At Paramount, in front of the rear screen process screen, I scampered from rung to rung, at one point hanging upside down on the jerking, turning, whipping ladder. Suddenly, I was falling toward the rig's counterweighted bucket twenty feet below. Somehow, my foot hooked a ladder rung, swinging me upright. Whoa! That was close: I silently scolded myself for becoming too complacent and confident. The next day, Bear was transferring to a fake tree and almost missed the palm branch, ended up hanging on for dear life as the massive, counter-weighted, apparatus whipped him around like a rag doll.

Between shots, Spencer Tracy appeared sullen and lonely. At times, I found him staring hard at me and I smiled at him. Perhaps my youthfulness caused him to reminisce about *Boy's Town*, the MGM film he and Rooney worked on twenty-five years earlier, in 1938. He seemed so sad. Mickey, on the other hand continued regaling the cast and crew with his many tales of Hollywood's Golden Age when he was the world's top box office star.

Mad World was a fantastic, once in a lifetime, never to be forgotten, experience with virtually every comic and comedian in show business. Laughter abounded as each one tried to best each other with their one-liners. The most sedate of all was Sid Caesar, who missed his family and would arrive on the set at 8am, even though he had a noon call time.

Initially, I met Sid when Carey Loftin called me to double comedian Jackie Mason. Sid verified that I was Mason's size, but the job went down the crapper when Mason became unavailable for the classic gas station demolition scene.

English actor Terry Thomas was charming, but became noticeably irritated and distant when I inquired about song and dance man Norman Wisdom, whom I had always regarded as England's Mickey Rooney. Oh well, I just chalked it up to professional jealousy.

Between takes, Stanley Kramer, being a sporting gent gave the cast and crew participants "gambling lessons" on the portable, green felt crap table provided by the prop department. Phil Silvers was the most intense as he paced anxiously, gripping his horse-choking wad of hundreds. Sig Froelich, Rooney's long-time stand-in since Andy Hardy at MGM, asked me for a quick $500 loan to pay his loss to Kramer. During lunch, I rushed to North Hollywood Savings & Loan still wearing my Latex Rooney mask. When I said "Hi Margie," my favorite teller looked up and screamed, then quickly warded off two guards with shotguns. She later informed me that it was illegal to wear a disguise in public anytime other than Halloween. A week later Sig repaid me.

Jonathan Winters was as zany as imagined. A year prior to *Mad World*, he was removed from the high mast of the tall ship, Balcultha, docked at San Francisco's Fisherman's Wharf and was "detained for observation." Our initial one-to-one meeting began as a joyful, comedic experience as he jumped head-on from one character to another. Ten minutes elapsed before I realized his fantasized characters and their monologues were open-ended, with no ending. Not wishing to offend this comic genius, I searched for a way out and snatched the first guy who walked by to "Listen to this one!" and then quickly excused myself.

That's Jonathan Winters. I'm proud that after viewing his first appearance on NBC's *Colgate Comedy Hour* in 1954, he became the recipient of my first fan letter.

But, I'm getting ahead of the story. So just like in the movies, let's do a "flashback," one of Hollywood's greatest cinematic storytelling devices to tell my story.

To reiterate, it all began in November 1946 when my Dad took me to my first picture show -- Walt Disney's *Song of the South*. The Ninth and Hill Street RKO Theater's flickering marquee lights and colorful one-sheet movie posters presented a whole new world to this five-year-old, as the film's 94 enchanting minutes jumpstarted my lifelong love of the movies.

During the mid-1940s, long before we ever heard the word, "suburbia," downtown Los Angeles was the town's beehive hub of activity. During the Christmas season our family enjoyed the many department store windows decorated with every holiday scene imaginable.

Visiting the ornately decorated Orpheum Theater—constructed in 1926—Dad and I moved along the red velvet rope to witness the last remnants of vaudeville. Show headliner Eddie Peabody, the "King of the Banjo," at 5'5" with a shock of corn-yellow hair, was the world's most famous banjo player of all time for more than half a century. To secure his mark in musical film history, Walt Disney's Donald Duck imitated Peabody sporting a blond schlock of hair strumming a banjo.

Next, Yaconelli & Moro performed a comedy musical act. Dad smiled knowingly when I pointed at the stage to our next door neighbor, Frank Yaconelli, who at this time was also Gilbert Roland's sidekick, "Baby", in the Cisco Kid western features for Monogram Pictures.

On January 22, 1947, we were the first family on our block to have a TV set. My Dad rented a 5" table model with a glass bubble to enlarge the picture, and later purchased the unit. I was captivated from the first moment KTLA, Paramount Television Productions, channel 5, started broadcasting as the first commercially licensed television station west of the Mississippi.

The local programming was primitive initially by today's standards, featuring a plethora of American and English motion pictures from the 1930s and 1940s. On Saturdays, we kids would crowd the TV for our favorite cliff-hanger serials and cowboy heroes. As youngsters, we viewed the same film classics that audiences had enjoyed 15 years earlier in the picture shows.

Though my bedtime was 7:30pm, I would commando-crawl through the living room and hide behind the living room sofa to watch the nightly fare in the den. Four decades later, when I confessed my viewing habits to my Mom, she smiled and nodded, "I knew you were there."

In the late forties and early fifties the picture show became a regular Saturday and Sunday event. Residing in L.A.'s Wilshire District made the Clinton, Embassy and Wiltern theaters easily accessible within a two-mile radius—as we enjoyed two cartoons, a short, a newsreel and two feature films, all for 10 cents. (The Wiltern, at Wilshire and Western, today, is considered one of the finest examples of Art Deco in the country.) Each subsequent movie I saw made me more determined to be a part of the movie industry.

In those days, most kids heroes were cowboys, but school chum Jimmy Sullivan couldn't handle the pain and gave me his brand new, ill-fitting, pair of brown Acme cowboy boots. For me they were a perfect fit. A year later, my Uncle Carl bought me a black second pair and cowboy boots became my lifelong footwear, cementing my cowboy yearnings.

Schoolmate John Blanchard's father worked at North American Aviation, and took us to the 1948 unveiling of the F-86 Sabre Jet. John was the biggest kid in school, built like a moose, and had a predilection for uniforms—showed up wearing a U.S. Army Sergeant's khaki uniform. When I last talked with him in 1963 he was a West Covina police officer, with a goal of becoming a small town Chief of Police: "I'm not out to set the world on fire like you," he said, "but someday I'm going to be a big fish in a small pond. Every month there's notices from small towns around the country recruiting a police chief." We lost touch, but I suspect he succeeded.

While bike riding one day, I heard music—exciting, toe-tapping music—Dixieland Jazz coming from the Beverly Cavern. From the late forties to the mid-fifties the bar at Beverly and Ardmore was Mecca for America's greatest Jazz musicians. At every opportunity, I'd straddle my bike at the club's entrance to enjoy the rhythmic Dixieland sounds of trombonist Edward "Kid" Ory, writer of Muskrat Ramble. Lionel Hampton, Jack Teagarden, Red Nichols, The Firehouse Five plus Two—The Beverly Cavern was their home; and also included Louis "Satchmo" Armstrong, when he visited L.A.

At nine, I decided it was time to step out into the cruel world and start making a buck – selling newspapers. My decision was hastened by my parent's refusal to pay a weekly allowance for doing chores you were expected to do as a family member.

Attending St. Brenden Catholic school had become a dreary bore, where we'd pray daily that the A-Bomb would not obliterate us. It was one hellava way to start your day. In 1951, I recall hearing in class a faint "boom" sound emanating from Nevada's Yucca Flats testing grounds 350 miles away. Regardless, with the vicious, hateful, ruler-wielding nuns, you were more concerned about their omnipresence, invariably eager to pounce on you like a cougar. The only redeeming benefit of a Catholic school is that you are going to be educated whether you wanted to be or not. I just don't believe that bullying and physical abuse is a necessity to teaching unarmed youths.

One day two classmates decided to settle their differences punching and rolling on the school ground asphalt. Sister Mary Frances quickly appeared, I asked, "Aren't you going to stop them?" She replied, pointing, "No. He deserves it!"

Herald Examiner's Pete Price placed me at Third Street and Vermont Avenue, a busy intersection with Ralph's and Safeway markets on two corners, the Monte Carlo Cocktail Lounge and Standard gas station on the other two. It was also a rather famous intersection where the Palomar Ballroom sat on the present Safeway store site in the mid-thirties. Benny Goodman and Glenn Miller played there until the tragic fire of 1939 reduced the ballroom to ashes. Strangely, the Safeway market built on the site also burned to the ground in the mid-1960s.

To a kid in those days, earning $2-$3 a day was a fortune, plus I found meeting people interesting and enjoyable, especially when a customer presented a dime for a nickel paper, and said, "Keep the change!" That made my day, but overall I believe everyone should be compelled to treat their fellow man with respect, consideration and compassion.

Working the busy Third and Vermont intersection was a hustle with a newsboy on each corner to catch the four-way traffic. This included dodging the streetcars, where we'd stand in the *safety zone*, a three by 40-foot lane marked off between the traffic lanes to allow passengers to board. If these zones existed today, most drivers would undoubtedly consider them pedestrian target areas.

Occasionally, before the Herald's five-star-edition arrived, we'd treat ourselves to a 35-cent chocolate shake at the nearby soda fountain located a few doors west on Third, beyond the Monte Carlo cocktail lounge.

My daily paper sales grew enormously when I decided to stroll through the Monte Carlo bar, and wondered who'd want to sit in a dark, smoky bar and drink alcohol?

On a vacant lot at Third and Berendo sat a rust-encrusted tank from World War I, and an adjacent brick garage was home to Pacific Movie Rentals. Enchanted, I saw rows of vintage American and European motorcars dating from 1900 to the forties, everything from a Stanley Steamer, a Ford Model T to a Rolls Royce—all for rent to the movie studios. My imagination ran wild as I sat in each driver's seat. Interestingly, the Rolls Royce emblem went from red to black when Fredrick Stewart Royce died in 1933.

Word spread quickly that Warner Bros. was filming in the Jewish synagogue at New Hampshire and Fourth streets. Checking it out, I found the studio's fleet of blue and white vehicles for the 1952 *The Jazz Singer* remake starring Danny Thomas and Peggy Lee, directed by Michael Curtiz.

During a filming break Danny Thomas exited the synagogue, and bought me a Coke and a doughnut from the roach coach. Danny was a gentle man and was one of my Mom's favorite entertainers, noted especially for his creation of Saint Jude's Children's Research Hospital in Memphis, Tennessee. For many years, I intended to thank him for being so nice to a kid.

Appropriately, in 1958, as a KTLA-TV Page, I would lead the VIP tours through the former site of Warner Bros. first studio at Sunset Boulevard and Van Ness, specifically Stage 6, where Hollywood's first talking motion picture, *The Jazz Singer*, starring Al Jolson was filmed in 1927. This film's success enabled Warner Brothers to move to its present Burbank studio location in 1929.

While at NBC in Burbank in 1967, I visited Danny during the rehearsal of *The Danny Thomas Hour Show* – He remembered me and we chatted over a cup of coffee and a donut.

Still determined to have my own newspaper corner, I hounded Pete Price until he placed me at Third and Alexandria, in front of the Gold

Coast drug store—which included a soda fountain, where a chocolate or cherry coke cost a nickel.

In the spirit of free enterprise and promotion, I dove into my extensive hat collection of sailor, cowboy, race driver's helmet, sombrero, etc.—wore a different one every day to attract the drive-by customers, and it worked. My parents instilled in me a work ethic early on, a sense of responsibility and commitment to "Make hay while the sun shines." as I worked the paper corner for almost five years, rain or shine, including holidays.

I immediately recognized him from his photos and movie appearances, boxing world champion, Max Baer. He had just purchased the Kipling Hotel at Kingsley & 3rd street. Smiling, he gave me a quarter for a 10 cent paper. Ten years later, I would work with his son, Max Bear, Jr. on *The Beverly Hillbillies*, when I would occasionally stunt double Irene "Granny" Ryan.

While bicycling to my newsstand one day I found a wallet in the street containing $86.27. The driver's license revealed the owner's address. A gal about 25 opened her apartment door and was unaware she had even lost her wallet, and quickly counter the bills. Satisfied she had all of her cash, she was blasé, searching the coin pocket, turned to her friend, and asked "Do you have change for a quarter?" Her friend didn't, so she reluctantly rewarded me with the two bits.

Returning to my bike, I had mixed emotions about my good deed. Mom had always preached: "What goes around comes around," something about the *Law of Retribution*, but I wasn't completely convinced. However, several months later when my $1 ticket won St. Kevin's monthly $100 raffle, I became a believer.

Mom's family had owned a hotel, restaurant and saloon in the 1920s. Unfortunately all was lost during the Great Depression. She was the consummate chef and baker, and her expression was worth a million times the $32 I paid when she received her new Dormeyer Power Chef mixer.

Dad was a dapper dresser; I learned at an early age the merit of sartorial importance. John Burroughs Junior High School's Boys Vice-Principal John Hunt said, "If you dress like a bum, you will act like a bum." His comment made an indelible impression on me, as did Richard Bell, a young, 24-year-old instructor who had recently acquired his teaching credentials for the Electric Shop and Stage Crew classes. Each of us can recall a teacher who made a difference. Dick Bell took the time to care and support a determined thirteen-year-old kid's desire for a show biz career. I'm forever grateful for his friendship and guidance.

This day I had eaten my lunch, sat reading a book when I was suddenly confronted by six boys, known as the Jewish Mafia (I heard later), led by Steve Cohen, who said, "You're a sonofabitch!" I slowly closed my book and as I stood, said, "You're not calling my mother a bitch." Instantly, one of the gang whispered in Cohen's ear and they scattered like cockroaches. They never screwed with me again.

A year or two before I had read a Shakespeare *Julius Caesar* passage noting, in act three, Caesar tells Calpurnia "Cowards die many times before their deaths. The valiant never taste of death but once." I have lived by that rule all my life. You gotta go down fighting.

During this time, I brushed elbows with one of America's greatest entertainers, Nat King Cole. Well, not exactly. Actually, it was his elegant English Tudor home that I passed daily to and from school. When Cole purchased the $80,000 prime corner property at Fourth and Muirfield Streets in the early 1950s, Dad mentioned how the irate residents protested a Negro family moving into the exclusive all-white neighborhood. Nat then visited each neighbor, introduced himself and addressed each occupant, "Is there a problem?" "Oooh no, Mr. Cole," they all replied, "Welcome to our neighborhood." Nat King Cole is one of my favorite singers—every song he sang was a gem.

Returning home one afternoon in 1954 from Burroughs, I stood in the street car safety zone at Third and Western with a Negro lady dressed in her white maid's uniform. Looking west, down the hill, we could see the streetcar approaching some four blocks away. Suddenly, she started shouting, "Mickey Rooney! Mickey Rooney! Y'all look like Mickey Rooney!" I smiled, as this was not exactly a new revelation. For as long as I could remember, Mom and many others had mentioned my resemblance to him. Mom told of being a Rooney fan and had seen every Andy Hardy film back in the 1930s, when she was employed in the art departments of 20th Century-Fox, and later at Monogram pictures. When I was born she even parted my hair on the left like Mick.

Adding to the look-alike situation was next-door neighbor Nancy Randall, who appeared locally in print ads, billboards and on local TV. Her ultra-frustrated stage mother fancied her red-haired, freckle-faced daughter as the next Judy Garland. Unfortunately, she knew only one song, a monotonous rendition of *Over the Rainbow*. Regardless, we were considered the neighborhood duo, always ready to stage a show. However, our setting wasn't a barn, but a TV studio I constructed in the Wayne garage, complete with fake cameras, tripods, a sound boom and a control room. Oh, how I dreamed of and wished we had headset walkie-talkies and real TV video cameras like the kids today have, sixty-five years later.

Dad and I would take evening walks past the newsstand at Beverly and Western. Ten cents bought my copy of Daily Variety, and when I declared, "Someday, my name's going to be in here!" my Dad and the news vender chuckled gratuously. It wasn't exactly a put-down, but to an eight year old kid, it made me even more determined. And my name did appear in Daily Variety AND the Hollywood Reproter many, many times. An old Chinese axiom cautions, "Be careful what you wish for—you may get it."

KTTV's Bill Welsh hosted his *Star Shopper* TV show from a different Los Angeles area supermarket daily, awarding winning game participants a shopping cart of groceries. Whenever the show ventured near my home, I was there to carry cable for cameraman John Parkinson. On camera, a smiling Welsh startled me one day when he thanked the local 1950's homemakers in attendance, then looked at me, "including a TV crew member who ditched school to be here today." But those brief moments were euphoric—for those thirty minutes I was in show biz, thanks to John Parkinson.

Yeakel Oldsmobile broadcast their 1955 *Rocket to Stardom* TV show on KTLA. Bob Yeakel's weekend, mid-night to morning talent show was ostensibly the forerunner to *The Gong Show*; unfortunately, without the gong. Utilizing every trick to attract buyers to the car showrooms, his two sons and I gave quarter-midget car racing exhibitions on an adjacent car lot. These spiffy, molded, fiberglass racers resembling the Indy 500 Offenhauser cars of the 1950s, capable of 30mph, and each one was available for purchase. During one race, Bob Jr. tagged me in a turn, propelling me toward a hay bale. I swerved and was heading toward a chain link fence. Luckily, the fence leaned on impact, allowing me to steer through it like I was banking a turn at Daytona Raceway. But that was too close, without a roll bar or helmet; if the car had rolled over I would have been crushed.

Another day, my race car ran out of gas and Bob Jr. quickly filled the small tank mounted behind me, spilling gas over the engine. Restarting necessitated lifting the cars rear-end and slamming the left rear wheel to the ground to kick-start the engine. Junior couldn't lift me and the car so I jumped out, picked up the rear end, intending to run and jump back in as it cranked over. I slammed the tire to the ground and the engine instantly burst into flame. We quickly retreated, fearing the gas tank would explode. The $500 racer melted to a molten mass of metal and fiberglass. My Guardian Angel was with me once again, but boy was Bob Yeakel pissed.

Often in the late forties, our Sunday drive, a family tradition in those days, took us past the RKO (Radio-Keith-Orpheum) Studios at the corner of Gower and Melrose, I'd say to myself, "Someday, I'm going to work in there." And later I did in 1961, on the *Ben Casey* TV series, playing a gun-wielding punk fighting Robert Blake. By this time, RKO Pictures had become Desilu Studios, owned by Lucille Ball and Desi Arnaz, and in 1966 Desilu would be purchased by Gulf + Western, the next door owners of Paramount Pictures.

Los Angeles High school was a vast educational step backward with unruly students disrupting every class, all awaiting their 16th birthday so they could "quit school." This was coupled with indifferent teachers waiting their retirement. My only delight was Jeanne Briggs, a beautiful teenage look-a-like for *Gunsmoke's* Amanda Blake. Her father was an instructor at Hollywood's premiere Don Martin TV & Radio school. We often discussed my TV cameraman desires, and I couldn't wait to begin my career.

At fifteen and a half, I admitted to being 16 and become a box boy for Safeway Markets. No one checked IDs in those days and for a kid in the fifties, it was the best possible job, paying union wages with fringe benefits. Additionally, it provided access to the Local 770 Retail Clerks credit union, which allowed a $750 loan on my signature alone—to "cherry out" my 1949 Oldsmobile convertible, which originally cost me $160.00.

Boxing the customer's groceries became a mental exercise I enjoyed. First, you "squared the bag's bottom," placed the perishables on top and soon learned by repetition, which items fit perfectly – not too bottom or top heavy. I was proficient and honored as devoted customers clamored to my checkout stand. Other duties included cleaning the restrooms, and washing the store's large, plate-glass windows. Disney's *Zorro* series was TV's big hit and using foaming Windex, I would form an enormous backward "Z" which invariably brought smiles from the customers inside. Even then I was a frustrated comic!

When the assistant manager mentioned they were "grooming" me for management, I was somewhat stunned. To the right person, a 1958 grocery store manager enjoyed a very inviting salaried career at $12,000 a year. But, in my youthful impetuousness, I blurted out my desire to be in "Show Business." The Safeway bosses were not principled and I was instantly ostracized; my work hours were cut back and the "dirty" duties increased. The mere thought of going to work produced a sickening, unbearable pain in my gut—until one Saturday, the store's busiest day, when I didn't show up. That day I vowed no job, situation, or person would ever give me a stomach ache again.

I've come to believe that much of what happens is destined to be—set in place by a higher power. My theory was confirmed in September 1958 when Dad suggested I "Join the Navy and see the world. I later realized that it was he that placed me on the Navy's mailing list." Mostly, it was the "girl in every port" (or port in every girl) I'd heard about that produced erotic visions in this hormonal peaking 17-year-old kid. Of course, "Mister Roberts" and "The Caine Mutiny" helped to create far away visions.

At Hollywood's U.S. Navy recruiting office I graded well on the 45-minute exam, and eagerly looked forward to the next four years tarveling the globe. The Navy petty officer presented papers for my parent's signature and said, "I'll see you at nine tomorrow morning."

At six that evening I received a phone call from Guest Relations boss

Chuck Walker, "Jess, we've got a job for you here at KTLA." The Navy papers were ash-canned, and I've often pondered the results if Walker's call had come 15 hours later.

Fate had now placed me at KTLA. I had quit the unionized box boy job at $1.22½ per hour for KTLA's $1.00 minimum wage, but I would have worked there for free—this was the moment I had dreamed of and prayed for since I was ten.

My first day at KTLA, got me a ride in the world's first Telecopter, which wasn't too surprising as the station had created many TV firsts since its inception in 1947.

Television's *Who's Who* includes many who began as a TV network Page, but at KTLA it was small town versus big city, where opportunities were accelerated within the station's employee chain. From the stage-hands to KTLA's vice president / general manager James Schulke, all were cordial and supportive—possibly recalling their own entrance into television. Or, maybe it was because I wasn't a threat to them, not bucking to take their job—at least not yet.

In addition to ushering TV show audiences for the Big Band sounds of *Russ Morgan, Freddie Martin, Orrin Tucker* and their orchestras, other varied duties placed me in the mailroom, newsroom, publicity, art and production departments. I even spelled the operators on the plug and pull PBX switchboard, where I practiced my "radio voice." Each position was a magnificent educating experience. You learned by doing it. You can't get it all out of a book. However, I still wanted to be a cameraman, and knew that finding my exact niche in television was just a matter of time—and reveled knowing that as an employee of the nation's finest independent commercial TV station was the opportunity of a lifetime.

"Whether you think you can or think you can't, you're right."... Henry Ford.

Additionally, the cushion of living at home shielded me from the everyday financial burdens of rent, mortgages, car payments, etc. My excitement peaked and fell when TV commercial announcer Tom Brenneman said he was selling his maroon 1937 Cord 812 Phaeton and the price was $1500, today (restored) it sells for upward of $250,000. At $1 minimum wage it was indeed out of the question.

A threatening fire had started in Griffith Park near The Los Angeles Observatory. KTLA's smallest and fastest TV mobile unit, a 1957 Ford Fairlane station wagon, sped past me as I entered the station's main gate. Two cameramen jumped in my Oldsmobile convertible and yelled, "Follow the mobile unit!" Racing, we caught the TV unit at the Barnsdell Park, at the Western Avenue entrance, and all three of us jumped onto the mobile unit's trailer-mounted generator as it took off up the winding canyon road. We hung on for dear life as the two-wheeled trailer became airborne on the dips and turns—we screamed for them to slow down. The mobile unit pulled over as a surprised engineer and veteran newsman Clete Roberts exclaimed, "We heard the yelling and figured a bunch of kids had jumped on the Jenny." (Clete Roberts, aside from being a famed international reporter-journalist, is best remembered outside of Los Angeles as the mustached, trench-coated, reporter on the *M*A*S*H* TV series.)

Two RCA TK-10 cameras were quickly set up on the famous observatory lawn. Someone handed me a coiled reel of microphone cable on a wind-up jig. I worked feverishly to untangle it—knowing we had to get on the air as fast as possible. But the more I pulled on the cable the more it got snagged. Clete, realizing my predicament, rushed to my aid: "Relax, take it easy." Carefully, he grasped a cable end and in moments had the coil unraveled.

Relax. It was a word and a lesson I would never forget—one that has enabled me to get through many life situations, especially stunts. If you relax, you can do anything.

The KTLA newsroom's United Press International and Associated Press wire service Teletype machines fascinated me. The yellow paper rolls churned out the latest news reports, and copy writer George Lewin schooled me in TV news copy writing. Often I noticed the news copy was vastly different from what I had read on the teletype machine earlier that day. Even in 1958 the forces were slanting the news. However, that didn't happen to Clete Roberts—his news copy was supervised and written by his son-in-law.

It's December 30 and an executive order decreed the yearly KTLA Christmas party would be celebated during the scheduled musical shows telecast from TV Studio 1 at 8pm to sign-off. This gala event began with the station's employees, in front and behind the cameras, enjoying a boundless buffet and flowing magnum bottles of Korbel champagne. Behind the cameras everyone appeared to be bombed, and I was asked to man one of the TV cameras. It was wild. This was my first "Christmas office party," and everything I had ever heard about these shindigs proved to be true.

The next night, at 3am, January 1, 1959, two remaining KTLA mobile units set out for the Pasadena Tournament of Roses Parade telecast. My wish had come true—I was now part of the KTLA crew—carrying the camera cable for Bill Matheson. My parents weren't worried when they hadn't heard from me all night, but were surprised during the Rose Parade's 6am pre-show when Bill's camera caught me standing next to KTLA's veteran newsman Stan Chambers. The day's greatest thrill was a smiling wave greeting from President Dwight D. Eisenhower and his wife, Mamie, at the Valley Hunt Club mansion.

The *Bozo the Clown* TV series debuted January 5, 1959, starring Vance Colvig, a local kiddie show host, best known previously as KNXT's *Buck Shurshot*. Bozo was an immediate TV success as many film celebrities brought their children to the show for fun and games, including Rosemary Clooney and her young son, 5 year old, Miguel Ferrer.

A later Bozo contest winner was scheduled to receive the grand prize during the show's special remote telecast from Marineland of the Pacific, located on the Palos Verde peninsula near San Pedro, California. The mother and her two children lacked transportation, so I was elected to transport them from their San Bernardino home to Marineland in Jim Schulke's new 1959 Ford Fairlane. After depositing them home safely, I returned hours later to the station after driving almost 250 miles that day, contented that KTLA's trust in a 17-year-old kid was proven.

In Griffith Park, I assisted Mary Henderson Parker – Miss Mary of *Romper Room* at an outing for her many faithful children viewers. What a beautiful, vivacious, caring lady she was.

Veteran TV news cameraman Tex Zeigler was a diminutive bundle of energy kind of guy. "C'mon, help me load up my camera gear for a Los Angeles Press Club meeting." At the Ambassador Hotel's L.A. Press

Club's Eight Ball Room, Tex set up his Bach Auricon 16mm sound-on-film camera as I strung a sound cable to the podium microphone. "How's it going?" said a Boston-accented voice I recognized from TV news broadcasts. Looking up, I was face to face with Massachusetts Senator John Fitzgerald Kennedy. A year later he would announce his candidacy for President, and was the second of three U.S. Presidents I would meet.

Completing the shoot, as we returned to the KTLA newsroom, Tex confided, "If Nixon gets elected I'll be his chief White House photographer."

KTLA produced several Hollywood celebrity TV talk shows, including one hosted by Pamela Mason (James Mason's ex-wife) with Tinseltown's former elite, including the debonair Adolphe Menjou (always on Hollywood's Best Dressed List), silent film matinee idol Francis X. Bushman and actor Mischa Auer. The show's producer, Marvin Paige, was a demanding complainer. My buddy, floor director Bob Kraft, suggested, "Well, he probably has a corncob up his ass." A few weeks later, while in the director's control room, Paige rolled his chair across the room next to mine, proceeded to describe his rented apartment overlooking the Sunset Strip, costing $130 month. To me, earning a dollar an hour, the rent appeared astronomical. When I later mentioned the conversation to Kraft, he blared, "The guy's a fag," which explained Bob's corncob comment. Subsequently, that Paige found his niche as a Hollywood casting director.

My first duty as an integral part of a TV production team was during *The Guy Mitchell Show*. In November 1958, fellow page Bob Sherwin and I were assigned to hand-letter the "idiot cards." Guy's poor eyesight necessitated that the song lyrics be printed three inches high. We used Cato Flo-Master felt-tipped pens—to refill each pen the metal housing was unscrewed, carefully filled with bottled India ink and reassembled. I still have mine, 60 years later. The Sanford Sharpie permanent marker had yet to be invented.

My parents were non-smokers and I never sneaked behind the barn to smoke a cigarette, but Sherwin offered me a filter-tipped Kent. With our neckties loosened, sleeves rolled-up and a cigarette dangling from the corner of our mouths, we worked through the day and night—

twenty-six hours straight. Truly, I thought, this is Show Biz. We were absolutely positive that if we didn't complete our assignment the show wouldn't go on. When you're seventeen, it's funny what goes through your mind.

The Mitchell show featured three stuntmen, Lennie Geer, Ronnie Rondell and Dave Perna, performing a picture-fight that culminated in a twenty-foot high fall. Veteran stunt man Geer is best remembered as "Ollie" the ranch hand on Mickey Mouse Club's *Spin & Marty* series, with his horse, Sky Rocket. Ronnie and Dave were congenial, but reserved in their answers when I quizzed them about entering the stunt business.

Years later, Ronnie explained that at that time he was trying to break into the business. However, his road to hoe was somewhat easier than most—his father, Ronnie Sr., a former stunt man, was a first assistant director at Universal Studios. At this time in the business, the assistant director hired the stunt men, so it was a perfect open door. Regardless, Ronnie's exceptional talent and abilities made him one of the best, all-around stunt men to ever hit the ranks.

With my stunt juices flowing, KTLA's *Bozo the Clown*, Vance Colvig, offered to call his friends at Knott's Berry Farm and Ghost Town, figuring my playing a gunslinger, holding up the park's steam engine train, might get me started. Unfortunately, the hiring guy at Knott's didn't agree. I then visited the Corriganville Movie Ranch in Simi Valley, talked with the show manager/emcee, Country-Western singer Walkin', Talkin' Charlie Aldrich, and agreed to work the stunt shows for free.

One comedy bit entailed the entire hoard of twenty stunt folks; one gunshot and everyone dropped over dead. When I hit the ground, I whipped out a plastic bouquet of flowers from inside my shirt. Aldrich immediately picked up on my action and the audience laughed when he pointed to the dead guy "pushing up daisies." Aldrich made me his assistant and driver at $6.00 a day and a free lunch—a hamburger or hot dog (not both!), fries and a Coke. During a fight scene a strained leg muscle raised my salary to $15 a day for the Saturday and Sunday performances, happily augmenting my KTLA $1.00 an hour wages. My grand total per week was $40-$50.

The Corriganville Movie Ranch performers reacted to the blaring loudspeakers of pre-recorded tapes—I portrayed Billy the Kid and other nefarious Western characters. Teaming up with Steve Lodge, a 16-year-old budding actor, we created a fight routine based on every old Western movie we had ever seen. Playing to a three-sided audience, we perfected a face punch that would by-pass the face and strike the shoulder, thus making the hitting sound and looking real from all angles. Monkey flips, tosses and other athletic moves allowed us to become (we heard years later) "the best fight team to ever hit the ranch." While greeting those wanting autographs, I always admitted to being Mickey Rooney's stunt double. Was it just wishful thinking? Old proverb: "Act the way you want to be and soon you'll be the way you act."

The Corriganville troop appeared at a new market opening in El Monte, a small town east of Los Angeles. Steve and I performed our fight routine and signed autographs for eager fans; one of them was a beautiful, seventeen year old brunette. She and I enjoyed the ancient art of osculation. That's *kissing* to you folks in Arkansas. During the ensuing week I phoned her every evening, and when I later mentioned meeting her, Aldrich became very serious. He knew her from his weekly Riverside Rancho music performances. "She's being raised by her grandparents and if you knock her up, then what? You have dreams of being a Hollywood stunt man, and if you continue to see this girl you'll be kissing it all good-bye." Charlie didn't have to say another word and I never called her again. But, today, I'll bet she's one good-looking grandmother.

Back on the Bozo TV show, to publicize Colvig's Corriganville personal appearances, Elaine DuPont, Ray "Crash" Corrigan's wife, and I presented Vance with a commemorative cake. With a zero-budget for a cake purchase, I stacked bread slices four-high and coated them with whipped cream. It's amazing what can be accomplished when you're forced to improvise. I then "accidentally" tripped and plunged head first into the creamy white slab much to the kid audience's delight.

Every Sunday night I hurried back from Corriganville to KTLA to guide the audience to their seats for *Polka Parade,* a musical variety show hosted by Dick Sinclair. In an effort to ply my stunt talents, as future game show host Tom Kennedy "warmed up" the audience, I would interrupt him repeatedly. Finally, he would give me a forceful shove and I'd do a forward flip off the stage into the aisle. The audience would laugh and a few little old ladies would scream and clutch their chests. Tom would then introduce me as a Corriganville stunt performer.

While on Page duty I was always running, quick and agile, prompting the Polka show's dance choreographer to call to me, "Excuse me. Excuse me! Would you like to become a dannn…cer." Being light on my feet, but not in the loafers, I declined. Years later, while dating several dancers, I would come to respect their dedication and rigorous training, often pondered the boundless benefits of being a straight male dancer among female dancers.

Teens flocked to *The Art Laboe* and *Johnny Otis* shows, featuring major rock & roll artists, including The Platters, Bobby Darin singing Splish Splash, and a friendly Ritchie Valens singing La Bamba. Tragically, a few weeks later on February 3, 1959, Valens, Buddy Holly and J.P. "Big Bopper" Richardson perished in a Mason City, Iowa, plane crash while on tour.

Often, fellow Page Ken Weiss and I traveled down Sunset Boulevard each in our own convertibles, his 1953 Pontiac to my 1949 Oldsmobile. We'd come to a stop light in front of the famous Hollywood Palladium, leap from our vehicles and exchange picture punches. The signal would change and it was back to our cars, drive to the next stop light at Sunset and Vine and repeat the battle to startled drivers. Thank God there were never any cops around. Ken graduated from radio school in 1959, and when last seen was headed for a disc jockey job in Wyoming.

Interestingly, not everyone at KTLA was supportive of my future stunt career. Soundman Lennie degraded me at every opportunity; but years later when we met at Universal he grinned, "I always said you were going to do it." Yeah, right.

As a kid actor, I listened, re-acted and just had fun, appearing on several early local Los Angeles TV shows. My first KTLA TV experience began in 1949, and then segued to KLAC and KECA. Owned by Earl C. Anthony, a Los Angeles Packard motorcar distributor, KECA occupied the old Vitagraph Studios at Prospect and Talmadge.

Dad gave me his Kodak box camera when I was seven, which instilled in me a love of photography. When I was 16, I set up my first darkroom in the family bathroom.

During my 1948 summer vacation, Dad exited his dental laboratory's gold casting room where he made dentures, bridges and partials. This was prior to air conditioning; he looked like he had been caught in a monsoon—dripping wet in the 120° heat. He said something tantamount to, "Someday, this will all be yours," to which I blurted out, "I'm not going to work that hard for my money." It was unintentional, but I didn't realize the devastating effect my comment created. I can still see his hurt expression.

Within two years Dad sold the lab. Those were the days when a son was expected to follow his father into the family business. But what did he expect? From the moment I was born all I ever heard was how much the dental lab was a lousy business. Three decades later my Mom said Dad had made the same offer years before to his brothers and they had also refused him.

Thanks to KTLA cameraman Bill Matheson, I had the run of the KTLA. Bill, a former World War II bomber pilot, possessed a gentle, quiet demeanor, was always more than willing to help. When I was 12, under his watchful eye, he taught me to operate the RCA TK-10 black and white TV camera, and after school allowed me to carry the camera cable or crank the scrolling cue card holder for the on-camera talent during the car commercials. Every kid should have a Bill Matheson.

My big moment came when I formally introduced myself to KTLA's headman, Klaus Landsberg, the vice president-general manager of Paramount Television Productions, the parent company of KTLA. In 1940, Paramount Pictures hired Landsberg to set up the Los Angeles experimental television station W6XYZ. Born in Berlin in 1916, he was an electronic boy genius, having designed an all-wave radio receiver when he was fourteen and at 20, assisted in the 1936 Olympic telecasts in Berlin. When Hitler began his siege of Europe in 1939, the Landsberg family came to the USA.

I was fourteen when I mustered up enough courage to ask Klaus Landsberg for a job at KTLA. He smiled and asked my age, "When you're sixteen, you've got a job here." From that moment on I was in ecstasy, someday hoping to follow in his TV showman footsteps. During my every waking hour (and probably while asleep), I pictured myself working at KTLA. It was where I wanted to be and I counted the days to my sixteenth birthday. Years later I realized I was practicing the *Universal Law of Attraction*, and as the Good Book suggests, "Ask and ye shall receive."

Commercial television officially arrived in Los Angeles on January 22, 1947, when KTLA became the first commercial TV station west of the Mississippi River. Almost two years would pass before another TV station would enter the Los Angeles area. This is a rare known list of the original seven Los Angeles television stations and their start dates:

KTLA – January 22, 1947
KLAC (*KCOP) – September 1948
KHJ (*KCAL) – October 1948
KTTV – January 1949
KNBH (*KNBC) – January 16, 1949
KEAC (*KABC) – September 16, 1949
KNXT (*KCBS) – October 9, 1950
(*) denotes current TV station call signs.

On February 21, 1947, KTLA televised its first TV news remote broadcast – a factory explosion. From this moment KTLA would be the channel all of Southern California would immediately turn to for the latest breaking news events.

Landsberg's sense of showmanship equaled his electronic genius accomplishments – he was first to air the *Hopalong Cassidy* films, and in 1951 his persuasive charm convinced a reluctant Lawrence Welk to give television a chance. The Welk band played at Santa Monica's Aragon Ballroom on Lick Pier, but it was Klaus' proposal to "Let's try it for two weeks to see if we get an audience" that made television history.

KTLA's highly-rated Friday evening *Western Varieties* hosted by Doye O'Dell presented the Maddox Brothers & Rose, a sister brother singing group from Bakersfield, then the west coast bastion of western music. They were an audience favorite, especially the comic brother who always had a joke. This night he stated that he knew that God was in the bathroom. "Every time I go, someone yells, 'God, are you in there again?'" They then played their scheduled musical number. All I could hear from the control room was Klaus screaming profanities, a look at the TV monitor showed Doye, listening to Klaus on floor director John Polich's headset. The Maddox's completed their song and scampered off the stage. Doye then offered an apology to the TV and studio audience concluding that, "The Maddox Brothers & Rose will never appear on KTLA again." From TV's inception, strict moral values and standards were set and enforced by all broadcasters. Obviously, that joke would not cause the blink of an eye today.

Welk's first TV Champagne Lady Roberta Lynn candidly revealed his command to the orchestra moments before each live broadcast, "Pee on your toes, boyz. Pee on your toes!"

The Lawrence Welk Show continually broke all television audience records locally, as it competed with the high budget programming of CBS, NBC and the new, fledging ABC network.

KTLA had a "first refusal rights" contractual agreement with Welk's manager, Sam Lutz, when the American Broadcasting Company offered them a network slot in 1955. "First refusal" meant that the first party, KTLA, had a right to "meet or beat" any offer made by a second party, in this case, ABC-TV. Welk and Lutz immediately packed their bags for the network timeslot, and also took the Southern California Dodge Dealers sponsors account with them. Klaus held no animosity and wished him well, "He's only trying to better himself."

Once again—timing is everything. When the Welk incident erupted, Landsberg was secretly formulating plans to create a fourth television network.

On Sunday, September 16, 1956, as Dad drove us home from a day at the Santa Monica beach, the car radio's Big Band music was suddenly interrupted with a news bulletin, "Klaus Landsberg, KTLA's Boy Wonder has died of cancer at age 40." Seated on the rear seat of Dad's immaculate 1951 Packard, I was numb, frozen in shock. All my life's desires seemed to collapse in those few moments. I had turned 15 two days before and was devastated. I stayed in my bedroom, and didn't talk to my family or anyone for a week, wondering what I would do. The man who had promised to open the door to my career when I became 16 was now gone.

A few days later I attended Klaus' funeral, with Father Montoya from the San Gabiral Mission presiding. Through this all, I still pondered where destiny would lead me. It all seemed so hopeless. At KTLA you could feel the void; it wasn't the same without Landsberg. Several weeks later the Maddox Brothers & Rose would return to perform on *Western Varieties*.

At KTLA, thank God Bill Matheson continued to support my ambitions and, at 17, I submitted an employment application for a Guest Relations Page. Later, I was told Bill had influenced my hiring. God bless Bill Matheson.

Klaus Landsberg's plans for a fourth television network also died with him in 1956. More than twenty-five years would pass before Fox— the fourth TV network—would be created. Today with Cable TV there are hundreds of channels.

At sixteen, I became involved in the 1950's fast draw craze, thanks to fellow high school buddy, John Spitz, who showed me his gun magazine. Later, membership in *The Great Western Fast Draw Club* allowed me to participate in quick draw demonstrations and shoot-outs at local clubs and market openings—every boy's dream come true, "playing cowboy." Of course, every member's desire was to own a genuine Colt .45 single-action revolver, not the replicas available for less than the $125 Colt price. Dad found an original 1873, Colt .45, made in 1881, for $85. Daily, I would practice my fast draw and fancy gun-handling over my bed to prevent any damage should I drop it. I got pretty good, drawing on the gun clock at .25 hundreds of a second.

Since the late 1950s, I've found several particular firearms to be a very stable investment, more so than the stock market. Most of my gun collection has increased in value many times their original cost; including a Ruger .22 cal. Frontier Single-Six I had bought in 1957 for $53, and sold it recently for $400. My 1881 Colt .45 Single Action I paid $85.00 in 1958, sold in 2005 for $1500.

So, every Wednesday night, driving out the Santa Ana Freeway to Bellflower, CA to the 7pm meeting, I knew by the dairy farms odorous aroma I was nearing the Great Western Gun Shop. This weekly 60-mile round-trip by today's standards would be a miracle (the Highway 10/Santa Ana freeway routes through East Los Angeles) and there I was, with my Colt .45 and Arvo Ojala gun belt and holster slung over the front passenger seat of my 1949 Oldsmobile convertible. Gun laws of the 1950s permitted the carrying of firearms, if they were unloaded and displayed in full view. Today, a SWAT team would besiege me as the TV news copters zoom in for a close up.

For an August 1958 stunt show at the Calico Ghost Town, owned by Knott's Berry Farm, northeast of Barstow, we slept under the stars, positive we were living a gunslinger's life. The next day our show was minus a performer, so we allowed the caretaker's son to join us. The gunfire began and, as Billy the Kid, I ducked behind a building hoping to gun down Pat Garrett. Our new troop member tracked me and as I ran from an alley, he jumped out and fired. I hit the dirt to the crowd's applause, but the blast had peppered my face with black gunpowder. When I didn't rise, a buddy lifted my head and cringed at the sight of blood trickling from each embedded pockmark. Without delay, he floored his new 1958 Chevy Bel Air to 120mph to rush me to Barstow's Santa Fe Medical Center. Eye drops blurred my vision, but when the doctor heard I was 17, without a parent or guardian to grant medical approval, the treatment ended.

Somehow, with my eyes dilated and blurred vision, I managed to drive the 160 miles back home to L.A., and made a bee-line to my bedroom. The next morning Mom became suspicious when I wouldn't come to breakfast—Dad immediately drove me to Dr. Vincent Bonfiglio who repeatedly applied and removed the Vaseline to pull out the facially imbedded black gun powder.

Months later, with nary a facial black powder mark, while hanging out at Arvo Ojala's gun belt & holster shop I met Ed Stembridge and accepted his invitation to visit Stembridge Gun Rentals, supplier of firearms for movies, located on the Paramount Pictures lot since 1925.

My KTLA duties often took me to the studio and Ed gave me the Cook's tour. The 7500+ firearm collection outnumbered most museums—with any firearm from a Derringer to a Gatling gun to a pedestal-mounted anti-aircraft gun. And every piece worked – even the pre-cartridge models—regardless of historical significance or value, was converted to fire blanks.

You never knew who might visit the Stembridge gun room. Fess Parker, "Davy Crockett" (1950s) and "Daniel Boone" (1960s), a true gentleman shot a close-up of me with his new Minox 16mm spy camera. And one day there he was, my other boyhood hero, The Lone Ranger, Clayton Moore. He was exactly as I imagined, plus we shared the same September 14th birthdate, though his was in 1914, and mine 1941.

The day after the December 7, 1941, Japanese sneak attack of Pearl Harbor, Stembridge loaned the local L.A. Harbor police and military authorities several hundred firearms. The prevailing attitude was that a Los Angeles invasion was imminent by Japan. Stembridge proudly displayed a letter of gratitude for their patriotic commitment.

During L.A's wartime black-outs Mom answered the door bell, and on impulse hit the porch light switch as the Air Raid Block Warden screamed, "Shut off the light! Shut off the light!" Reports of a Jap submarine firing at oil storage tanks near Santa Barbara made every Los Angeles resident fearful a Japanese attack was possible.

Stembridge trustee Frederick T. "Fritz" Dickie was born in 1899, in St Louis, MO, joined the company in 1927 and, utilizing his mechanical engineering genius, designed the automatic 5-in-1 blank cartridge loading equipment, still in use today.

Immediately, Fritz and I became best friends. A 33rd degree Scottish rite Mason, Fritz was one of the most giving individuals I have ever met. Whenever I needed anything, he was there for me. It sounds cliché, but any words attempting to describe this gentle man and the good he performed for so many would be insignificant. Fritz was Christian Science and his beliefs refused medical care. Sadly, he passed away in 1974 of a heart attack.

Bob Lane was the gunsmith as Gordon Worthington and Fritz, Jr. cleaned the firearms and processed the blanks. Never have I seen anywhere a group of men working together in such harmony and congeniality. All were sports car racing fans—and in Bob's 1956 Jaguar I got my first 130mph ride on Riverside International Raceway's back straightaway. Often, they would travel to Utah's Bonneville Flats, where

Gordon speed tested his immaculate 1957 Mercedes Benz 300SL gullwing coupe, which he sold in 1962 for $7500, exactly what he had originally paid. Today, the car sells for about one million.

At KTLA, I was contented and thrilled, anticipating my future career as a TV cameraman. But yearning to be in TV production also gnawed at me and a live Western Show seemed a most plausible stepping stone. My first effort was to convince Lorne Pratt, general manager of the M. Penn Phillips Land Development Company of Hesperia, California, to allow me to stage Hesperia's 1st Wild West Day on December 28, 1958. Pratt was reluctant to allow a 17-year-old kid tackle such a venture, but relented when I revealed the several KTLA TV kiddie shows I had arranged to plug the event. He was impressed. To give the audience an eyeful, I found two gals at the Hollywood Studio Club to appear as Hesperia Western Days beauty queens.

With my KTLA buddy Ron Burhans' Hi-Fi tape recorder, I wrote the script and he narrated a tape depicting Newton, Kansas, a Wild West town historically more lawless than Dodge City or Tombstone ever was. My Great Western Fast Draw Club cohorts portrayed the cast of live show characters, and a fast draw contest with trophies provided by Pratt topped off the festivities. The one-day event was a great success—as Ron and I split the profits garnered from the fast gun contestant's fees.

Monthly, I'd phone stunt man Lennie Geer with a career progress report. When I mentioned my performances in shoot-outs and western shows, he responded, "Yeah kid, keep at it. You're a good size to double small guys, women and children." His five-minute pep talk was always enough to keep me going.

I was also The Larry Finley Show's substitute talent coordinator for Chuck Walker. Co-hosted by Scatman Crothers, we were KTLA's answer to NBC's *Tonight Show with Jack Paar*, presenting Hollywood's acting and musical talent—Lionel Hampton, Terry Gibbs, Joe Williams. Sammy Davis, Jr. would drop in to plug a movie or club date. The show had a zero budget, so, to keep it legal we would issue the performing talent a check for AFTRA scale. The artist would endorse the check and hand it back to us. KTLA then paid the union's health and welfare benefits, a mere pittance compared to what their appearance would have cost. It was a perfect trade-off—we needed performers and the performers enjoyed the TV exposure.

Finley, constantly on the lookout for talent to fill his hour and forty-five minute show, booked a Tucson, Arizona, father and daughter bullwhip act. With the speed of sound, the father sliced pieces from the rolled newspaper protruding from his daughter's mouth. Larry suggested that Scatman hold the paper stick in his teeth. Reluctantly, Scatman stood motionless—and hardly winced when the whip slashed his baldhead. Ever the trouper, Scat smiled, continued his comic antics, and then held the paper stick at arm's length as blood trickled down his temple, which was unnoticed by the black & white TV cameras. During the commercial break, the Tucson couple was hastily ejected from the KTLA lot. Scat was the consummate professional and never complained for a second about the incident.

Steve McQueen's appearance and demeanor was indicative of his non-conformist behavior that set him apart from his contemporaries. Finley, aware that I was pursuing a stunt career, thought the coup de gras of Steve's visit would be for him shoot me with his *Wanted: Dead or Alive* Mare's Leg. "It's like a Hog's leg, only it kicks harder"—a chopped version of the Winchester '92 rifle. The soundman, concerned that the full-load 5-in-1 movie blanks (they fit: 38-40 cal. Rifle & Revolver, 44-40 cal. Rifle & Revolver, 45 cal. Colt Revolver) would blow out the microphone, suggested we remove the black powder and fire only the cartridge's primer to eliminate the loud concussion.

In the makeup room, Steve and I popped the wadding of a dozen blanks and discarded the black powder into a small, white porcelain makeup bowl. I don't recall why we emptied that many, as he was only going to fire at me once, but Steve nonchalantly picked up the bowl, said, "C'mon." Following him to the narrow hallway between the KTLA's Commercial Stage and TV 2, he placed the bowl on the floor, struck a match and casually dropped the burning ember into the bowl. Instantly, a three-foot white-orange flame flashed upward—Steve recoiled backward, ricocheted hard off the opposite wall into me. His quick reflex saved him from a charred disfigurement – otherwise, he would have been a natural lead in *Phantom of the Opera*.

We quickly retreated to the makeup room as, moments later, crew members screamed about the hallway's rotten-egg, sulfur smell of black powder and the white smoke cloud, so dense, you thought you were in London.

Silently, I applied my makeup as Steve changed his shirt, we didn't discuss the scorched, blackened hallway wall. Instead, our eyes met in the wall-long, makeup table mirror, as Steve proclaimed, "You don't need that stuff; they'll be looking at me." I retorted, "Well, my Mom will be watching and she'll have her eyes on me!" Steve laughed.

After Larry Finley's introductions, Steve and I lined up for the shootout, ala the Marshal Dillon shootout on *Gunsmoke*. I nodded slightly, Steve fired and I did my crash and burn. As for the soundman's concern for the blank's sound blast, the cartridge primer explosion resembled the pop of a kid's cap pistol. Oh, well.

KTLA news director Jim Karayn admired my work (He would become a Public Broadcasting System President who organized the broadcasts of the Presidential campaign debates in 1976 and the Watergate hearings in 1973) and offered me a full time newsroom position. Ecstatic, for the pay increase, and also as a stepping stone to becoming a TV cameraman; I suggested he call Walker to transfer me from Guest Relations. A couple of days later, Les Kandel, Walker's kiss-ass, was working in the newsroom. When I questioned a disappointed Karayn he lamented, "Chuck Walker said you weren't available." I was, at first, shocked and then, angry. I thought Walker was my friend, but his blatant lie had now produced great doubts in my mind about continuing a career in corporate television.

From age ten, my only desire was to be at KTLA, and follow in the showmanship steps of Klaus Landsberg, but now, in a flash, it had all vanished. I couldn't erase my ill feelings of Walker's deception and betrayal, but mostly his vile attempt to control my destiny. My decision was extremely painful, devastating and absolute and life-changing. I quit KTLA.

Walker's self-imposed God-like intrusion to alter my life was possibly what encouraged him to become a minister for the California State Prison system. Maybe the convicts fared better under his control.

Have you ever been passionate about anything in life? Well, I dare say there is nothing more frustrating or more exhilarating than trying to make your mark in show biz. The yearning desire to perform gnawed at me. I knew I could do it. All I wanted was a chance—just an opportunity to prove myself.

And like all the wannabees before me, I knocked on every door, hoping that each was *the* one. When driving past the Screen Actors Guild building at 7750 Sunset Boulevard I would picture myself entering the building to obtain my SAG card.

But Tinseltown was full of naysayers, each plying their discouraging persona on my every move to become a stunt man. "You're too short, inexperienced or you don't know anybody," were the usual comments. Though these comments were aimed directly at me, I suspect these clowns would have forced their negativity on anyone attempting to grab the next rung of life's ladder. Encouragement was not a word in their vocabulary.

Actor/gun coach Rodd Redwing, a mainstay at Stembridge's, called producer Robert Sisk of *The Life and Legend of Wyatt Earp* and writer/producer Frank Gruber of the *Tales of Wells Fargo* TV series. Both men were very cordial, but did nothing to kick start my stunt career. But through it all, there was my Mom, consistently advising me to follow my dream, and that I could be and do anything I wanted to do in life.

Miraculously, or destiny imposed, three months later I was working at Metro-Goldwyn-Mayer as stunt double for Mickey Rooney. I was a month over 18. Ultimately, it all happened exactly as I had pictured in my mind, so many, many times.

The most-often-asked question to every stunt performer is "How did you get into stunts?" Well, ask a hundred guys and gals and you'll get a hundred different answers. In my case, participation in school gymnastics proved invaluable in learning body control, coordination and timing. Next is your perseverance and undying desire to reach your goal, knowing that nothing will deter you. Ultimately, being in the right place at the right time finally opened the Show Biz door for me, but you must be prepared for that moment.

Veteran character actor Ken Mayer portrayed Major Robbie Robertson on early TV's *Space Patrol* series. His daughter, Cindy and my sister, Carole, were schoolmates. Hearing of my yearning to become a stunt man, Ken suggested I visit him on the TV set of *Black Saddle,* starring Peter Breck, Russell Johnson and Anna Lisa.

On this day, veteran stunt man Troy Melton was doubling Ken in a fight scene with Chuck Couch. Troy was impressed with the action photos of Steve Lodge and me, taken during the videotaped pilot presentation for *The Wrangler* TV series. Two weeks later, Troy heard MGM was looking for a double for Mickey Rooney and recommended me to MGM casting director Warren Mace. My good friend, actor/gun coach Rodd Redwing, made an early morning MGM visit to Rooney prior to my 11am interview.

At 11 am, at Hollywood's most prestigious studio, I stood with two other stuntmen, Mike Donovan, a good fight man, and Del Graham, a renowned circus performer. I tried to ignore that Del was Rooney's exact 5'1" height to my 5'4". First a.d. Eric Von Stroheim, Jr., director Charles Haas and Mickey were huddled. Animated, Mick was the loudest, demanding, "I want Jesse to double me!" Anxious moments passed, Eric looked at me, pointed to his bald head (like his famous actor father's. His dad Sr. was the chauffer in *Sunset Boulevard*), and made a scissors-like motion with his fingers. I nodded and suddenly, the job was mine.

My long hair was then cut immediately to match The Mick's crew-cut by one of the stand-ins, Jerry Martin a former barber. Jerry later retired to a cabin in Washington and when Mt. Saint Helens exploded on May 18, 1980 none of his remains were ever found.)

Subsequently, my entrance into Show Biz happened exactly as I had envisioned, walking into the Screen Actors Guild building on Sunset Boulevard, paying my $175 initiation dues and embracing my new SAG membership card.

I'm truly indebted forever to Ken Mayer, Troy Melton and Rodd Redwing, but eternally grateful to my sister Carole for making it all possible.

A year later, a chance meeting of my former next-door neighbor, Nancy Randall's frantic stage mother, allowed me to mention my stunt doubling for Rooney at MGM. Her horrified, face-in-her-hands response of "That's not fair" had me laughing all the way home.

CHAPTER 2

1959-1960

To clarify one aspect of this book some readers cannot comprehend: This book is not a novel. It details my life's desire to become a member of the Hollywood entertainment industry. It is a saga described in a daily, weekly or monthly manner as it takes you through decades of my adventures in Tinseltown. If the tales jump from one to another… that's the way it happens in life.

The irreverent stories, observations and profane comments may ruffle the politically correct, but I offer no apology as what I have written is the truth, exactly as I witnessed or as the participants explained it to me. To quote James Cagney in *The Oklahoma Kid* and *The Strawberry Blonde*, "That's the kind of a hairpin I am."

It seemed like a Good Idea at the Time—seemed to be a most appropriate book subtitle when reflecting on my many personal and business decisions. These nine words have also caused more problems than "Stick 'em up!" or "I do!" Oh, how many times have I spoken that ominous phrase?

Simply, my memoirs are the saga of an 18 year-old kid, though many friends suggest it borders on total recall. Fortunately, my memories of the people, locations and dates is supplemented by my personal daily log, listing everywhere I went, everyone I met and everything I did. It was not a diary or journal, but just a word or two to stimulate my memory. Also, my Call Sheet collection, Cast & Crew lists, plus hundreds of photographs were invaluable to verify historical information that time might have otherwise obscured.

I do recall being about nine or 10 when I asked my Dad about some historic event in the 1930s. He couldn't recall the incident. Having been born in 1901 I couldn't understand how he lived through an event during an era and didn't remember it. From that point on I maintained I was going to pay attention to everything that occurred around me. As a result, I can visualize almost everything that has ever happened in my life. At times it's been a curse rather than an advantage.

My resemblance to Mickey Rooney had provoked comments from as far back as I could remember and as fate would have it, I was now his stunt double. The exhilaration of attaining my goal was indescribable – or as Bogie put it, "The stuff dreams are made of."

The world's greatest studio Metro-Goldwyn-Mayer was a city unto itself with "More stars than there are in Heaven." It was Hollywood's epitome dream factory – where everything was available to create the desired celluloid illusion and effect. The day I had visualized had finally arrived.

On Stage 28, I still recall opening the heavy, foot-thick stage door, with my stunt bag in hand, the cavernous sound stage, the distinct smell of new lumber and the freshly painted diner set. And director Charles Haas on Albert Zugsmith's *Platinum High School*, starring Rooney, Terry Moore, Dan Duryea, Harold Lloyd, Jr., Christopher Dark and rock and roll singer Conway Twitty. Especially, I remember actress Terry Moore, a 27-year-old dream to behold, and the shiny leather belt neatly cinching her eighteen-inch waist into a perfect hourglass figure.

Howard Hughes was known for his astute creativity, business acumen and, particularly, romancing Hollywood's most beautiful women. Obviously, he included Miss Moore (her real name was Helen Koford), who proved years later in court that she had been briefly married to the reclusive billionaire, and received a sizable seven-figure inheritance from his estate.

The Hughes-Moore relationship evidently blossomed during her marriage to Glenn Davis, a Heisman Trophy winner and a Los Angeles

Rams running back. Her secret tryst prompted the irate Davis to locate the billionaire at his Sam Goldwyn Studios office and, as observers reported, "Davis knocked Hughes on his ass."

Charley Horvath, the *Platinum High School* stunt gaffer at 6'2", 200 lbs., was a teddy bear of a guy. Listening to every word and watching his every move, I marveled at his ease to set up the fight, and even more impressed when told that he was the U.S. Marine Corp's World War II Self-Defense Champion, and author of the USMC's Manual of Self-Defense. His acerbic comments and wry sense of humor kept us all constantly amused.

Platinum's M-1 rifle fight in the greasy-spoon diner resembled a form of fencing, with many of the same moves—action, lunge and parry, each move choreographed by the numbers. It was also difficult to suppress my excitement to be working with veteran stunt men Allen Pinson and Russ Saunders. These were two of many stunt men I had seen performing the thrilling daring-do action all my life. These guys were my heroes.

Russ Saunders had worked with many film legends, including Humphrey Bogart, Alan Ladd and Gene Kelly. In *Shane*, he doubled Ladd in the famous fight scene, and for Kelly in *The Pirate, Singin' in the Rain, The Three Musketeers and An American in Paris*.

Allen Pinson had doubled many of Hollywood's greatest stars, including Errol Flynn, Burt Lancaster, Stewart Granger and Tony Curtis.

We rehearsed the rifle fight for several days before the film company moved into the greasy spoon diner set. In the interim, I noticed a reserved attitude among the stunt guys and kept my distance. Everything changed, however, after the first morning of filming. Breaking for lunch, while walking to the MGM commissary I brought up the rear, but was more than flattered when they invited me to join them. Their previous detachment wasn't personal; I was the new kid on the block and until you proved yourself, that's the way it was.

Mickey Rooney was a grand piece of work, performing since the age of two; his acting abilities are boundless. British actor Sir Laurence Olivier once stated, "Mickey Rooney is the greatest actor America has ever produced." On the set, I've seen Mick perform a dramatic scene that brought tears to every cast and crew eye, and when the director said, "Cut," Rooney would tell a ribald joke.

But, as evidenced by many a genius, brilliance is a difficult endowment to tote, which seemed valid in Mick's situation, possibly due to his lack of a strong father figure. For many years, MGM chieftain L.B. Mayer was Mick's pick. This void first caught my attention in 1961, while visiting him during the filming of a *Pete & Gladys* TV episode.

Veteran director Jack Donohue, a large, imposing, gentle man, had worked with Mick in the 30s, placed his arm around Rooney's shoulders, pulled him close, "Now son, you go in there and…" Mick was forty years old, but this was as if Judge Hardy was giving advice to Andy. To my amazement, Rooney immediately became subservient, like a puppy wanting to please his master. This was indeed contrary to the always on, very opinionated, forceful Mickey Rooney we all knew.

While working on Universal's 1960s *Checkmate* TV series, I sat in Rooney's dressing room as he repeatedly dialed a special number for horse race results. Finally connecting, he listened, and then slammed the phone down, exclaiming, "That's another $1500!" He angrily complained that this was the second tip his new bookie had given him, "Three thousand bucks down the crapper in two days." All I could think about were the better uses for the money. Mick most always bet "on the nose," so even if the horse placed or showed, he still had no chance to recoup his "investment." He once said, I lost $2 at Santa Anita and I've spent $3 million trying to get it back.

Later, I again met my first stunt coordinator Charley Horvath at the Starlight Room in North Hollywood. By this time his marriage was over and he took comfort in a drink or two. One evening while walking from the Starlight Room parking lot, two bar patrons were approaching me from the corner. Suddenly, I heard a car horn behind me. Turning, I saw Charley's enormous grin as I leaped from the path of his shiny red MG convertible roadster. Driving on the sidewalk, he had the duo squarely in his sights as they turned, scrambled in retreat. A laughing Charley skidded the sports car to a stop inches from them, just as an LAPD cruiser arrived at the cross corner. The officer's double takes were priceless, "What the hell's that car doing on the sidewalk?" Luckily, Charley had worked with one of the officers on a film and managed to squeeze out of another fine mess.

In November 1959, I attended my first Screen Actors Guild meeting at the Beverly Hilton Hotel in Beverly Hills. I rubber-necked the many actors I'd watched and loved for years. Ronald Reagan was SAG's outgoing president, and my mentor, Rodd Redwing had taught him fast draw, introduced me to the future U.S. President who exhibited his famous smile and firm handshake. Not bad for a stage-struck eighteen-year-old kid.

A year later, the annual SAG meeting was held at the Hollywood Palladium. After parking my 1949 Oldsmobile convertible, I joined the long procession of performers walking toward the entrance. Directly in front of me was my all-time favorite actor, James Cagney. Suddenly, without provocation, he turned and greeted me, "How are you?" I don't recall my response, but I stammered something. What a thrill. What a gentleman.

With *Platinum High School* completed, I was now ranked among the unemployed stuntmen. This was a new experience for me; you have a job and then suddenly you're out of a job. Now, to pay the rent, you had to beat the bushes to find your next stunt gag. Little did I realize that this would become my modus operandi for the next forty years.

I soon discovered my secret of employment was to contact any and all a.d.'s, or assistant directors. They hired the stunt people, so it behooved a fall guy to get (and remain) on the best side of these guys. Constantly bombarded for work by every stunt performer or extra, my introduction always mentioned I was "Mickey Rooney's stunt double," and they usually concluded, "Yeah, I can see the resemblance." It was, I believed, a simple marketing formula to enable them to put a face with the name, and it usually worked. If they needed a little guy and couldn't remember my name, they then asked for Mickey Rooney's stunt double.

Most a.d.s didn't use their job as a stepping-stone to directing and producing as they do today. Their prime concern was that you were a good double for the actor, performed the required stunt within the film's stunt budget, and didn't kill yourself or someone else in the process.

Generally, a.d.s were honorable gents, but as they say "There's always the ten percent." These particular assistant directors filmed the "gag," then would refuse to pay a stunt adjustment. You always remembered those guys—<u>BOHICA: Bend Over Here It Comes Again</u>—and would wait until the stunt was rigged and the cameras were ready to roll, then "negotiate" the stunt adjustment. Often, it was necessary to ask for fifty or a hundred bucks more in an effort to finally settle on the equitable amount you really wanted. Finally, I concluded the a.d.s' predilection for cheapness stemmed from the fact that many resented paying a stunt performer more money in one day than what they earned in a week. Also, kudos was in order for them if they paid you less than what the production manager had budgeted for the stunt.

Teddy O'Toole's Answering Service catered specifically to the stunt performer and most all of Hollywood's stunt performers were on her phone board. The single exception was veteran stunt great Davy Sharpe, who preferred to stay with Nina's Service. Teddy had previously worked for Nina, and then started her own service with financial help from stunt man Paul Stader. Allen Pinson suggested I join Teddy's: "It's the best way to get known in the stunt business." Assistant directors often called her, seeking a certain type, height or size, so it was also wise to stay on Teddy's good side. I usually included a $1.10 pound box of See's candy with my $10 monthly fee, while other stunt guys chose a more romantic approach—dating her operators.

Days after signing on, Teddy's sent me on a Warner Bros. interview for the Colt.45 TV series, to be shot off a horse (saddle fall) and when they pull away his bandana, they see it's a young lad. While waiting to meet associate producer Cedric Francis, a cowboy-attired guy joined me for the interview. He introduced himself as Vince Deadrick, Steve McQueen's stunt double on the *Wanted: Dead or Alive* TV series. I figured either one of us would be perfect for the part, but neither Vince nor I got the job.

Vince Deadrick and I became instant buddies and he invited me to the *Wanted: Dead or Alive* set at Republic Studios. He then ushered me through Four Star's assistant director's "bullpen." Soon, I was doubling child actor Johnny Crawford on the *Rifleman* TV series.

I frequented *The Rag Doll*, a large dance saloon down the street from the famous country-western Palomino Club. At the bar one night I met Wayde Preston, the former star of the Warner Bros. TV series, *Colt.45,* but the series was long gone by 1961, and he was now piloting a cargo plane for a construction company between Los Angeles and Mexico. When I expressed intentions to take flying lessons, he immediately tried to dissuade me: "Don't do it! I wish I had a nickel for every buck I've spent in aviation."

Asking about his TV series cancellation, Wayde explained he had asked for more money, citing "Character actors with only two lines earned more in one day than I did in a week." Those were the studio system days when an actor was a seven-year contract player. When Wayde refused to work for $350 a week, complaining about guest actors receiving $350 a day, the studio promptly tossed his ass out the gate. "Don't think Warner Bros. isn't powerful," he bemoaned, "I can't even get a job as an usher in a theater." I imagine that when Wayde initially signed the seven-year contract, he was probably very happy to accept the $350 a week.

December 1960 was a busy month—I worked two days. The first day was on Blake Edward's *Breakfast at Tiffany's*, doubling Rooney. Mick portrayed a Japanese photographer with buck teeth and thick, Coke bottle-bottom glasses, (now considered politically incorrect) involving him taking a bath, only to be interrupted by Holly Golightly, who repeatedly forgot her key to the apartment building front door. In the shot: hearing his door buzzer, Mickey irately exits the Japanese-styled tub, drops a bar of soap, steps on it, causing it to spurt into his adjoining photo studio (an effects man jerked it on a wire). In a bathrobe, Mick rushes through the studio towards the door, steps on the soap bar and is propelled into a 180° pratfall, crashing to the tile floor on his back.

The scene also required exact timing by the special effects man to trigger the flash bulbs as Rooney hits the hard floor. Unfortunately, the effects guy was having a bad day. Wearing a bathrobe and a swimsuit, one of the falls cooled me when the back of my head made contact with the hard tiles. I hit the tiled floor seven times before the photoflashes matched my fall. Blake was pleased; one of Hollywood's great, nice guy, directors.

Awaking the next morning, I moved to get out of bed, but was para-lyzed from my neck down. Terrified, I didn't know what to do. Then, ever so slightly, I attempted to move my arms. Gradually, I was able to sit up, but very part of my upper torso ached in pain. Slowly, I carefully rolled sideways to plant my feet firmly on the floor, and tried to stand. I could. The seven falls to the hard tile floor had obviously stunned my body. After several minutes of bending and stretching, my extremities began to work again, and the aching pains finally subsided by mid-afternoon. The body recovers quickly when you're nineteen years old. Unfortunately, Rooney's hilarious darkroom scene where he enlarged distorted photos was cut, as was the photo studio scene with my fall.

Filming my slap-stick prat fall would become Blake Edward's forte. He and his buddy/stunt coordinator, Dick Crockett, made the Silent Movie Theater on Fairfax their second home. They studied the silent comedies of Buster Keaton, Laurel & Hardy and Mack Sennett, which explained the zany stunts in Blake's subsequent films; The Pink Panther(s), The Great Race, Darling Lil, The Party, et al, —all modernized versions of stunts performed in the 1920s films.

A few days later Paramount called me for an interview for Jerry Lewis' *The Ladies Man*. About twenty stunt guys were ushered into Jerry's spacious office, formerly occupied by Cecil B. DeMille. Suddenly, his finger was pointing at me and we adjourned to his dressing room for a soft drink. Casually, he explained the opening scene where I'd ride a bicycle through a slapstick chain of events, culminating with my crash into a telephone pole. Jerry knew exactly what he wanted me to do. More slap-stick comedy.

On Universal's backlot, at what is now *The Back to the Future Square and Street*, my collision triggered veteran stunt man Carl Saxe to slide down the pole and become impaled on a pointed ornament. Max Sennett would have been proud.

The Ladies Man's specially lighted, open-walled, three-story set, with over 60 hidden microphones, provided a new dimension in cinematic storytelling. Most movie sets are closed to visitors, but large signs posted on Jerry's stage doors informed, *Visitors ARE allowed on the set*.

Jerry Lewis, actor, writer, producer, director, is a dichotomy. Far from his many zany character creations and antics, he was also an innovative filmmaker. Today's film director now views the actor's performance on a

TV monitor. Jerry's "The Noisy Toy & Video Assist System" was initiated on *The Ladies Man* 60 years ago.

Nevertheless, Jerry's child-like behavior prevailed when a visiting 400 company CEO cringed in horror as Jerry scissored his expensive necktie amid the crew's laughter. The next day the surprised executive received a gross of assorted Italian silk ties from Hollywood clothier Sy Devore.

MGM and other studios continued to call – I was becoming known and doubling kids soon became the norm. For an explosion on a *Combat* TV series episode I doubled a French underground child—directed by a guy named Robert Altman. Twentieth called for a *Dobie Gillis* teenage fight scene with Jerry Summers, directed by Rod Amateau.

Then it was back to MGM for director Abner Biberman on the *National Velvet* TV series, a rearing saddle fall for child actor Ricky Kelman. Meeting Lori Martin, the show's star was enchanting. A blue-eyed blonde, the studio dyed her hair black to resemble Liz Taylor. At 14, with a 140 IQ, Lori projected the wisdom of a 30 year old woman. I was 19 and considered asking her to lunch, but didn't think being perceived as a creepy pervert was a great idea.

Warren Mace, the MGM casting director, who originally signed me as Rooney's double, called me for the *Oh, Those Bells* TV pilot starring the Weir Brothers, NBC's answer to The Three Stooges, who were enjoying a resurgence of popularity. Also called in to double the trio were veteran stunt man Harvey Parry and actor Frankie Darro. Meeting Frankie was a thrill – He was my childhood hero from his 1930's action films and serials with Rin Tin Tin.

The *Oh, Those Bells* pilot sold and twelve more episodes were set. On the first episode, Harvey Parry was there, but Mike Donovan now replaced Frankie Darro. My inquiry about Frankie prompted Harvey, "He's working." I later recalled, that when Mike was absent, he, too, was "working," and John Benson substituted.

One episode required the Weirs to infiltrate a crook-operated ladies club dressed as women, headed by veteran actor Jack Albertson. After several shots, dressed in drag (my first time), I had to relieve myself, so we ventured to the men's room adjacent to MGM's Stage 5. Not giving my feminine attire a second thought, I entered the tiled facility. A studio worker, standing at the fifteen-foot trough was noticeably startled to see three broads walk in, and in his fumbling effort to cover himself, irrigated the front of his pants. We casually ignored him as he attempted to aim the wall-mounted hand air dryer at his crotch.

Back on the set, the shot called for two of the Weirs to harass the heavy, while I got on my hands and knees behind him for them to shove him backwards over me. Veteran stunt man Paul Stader, doubling the actor, described the dangers of falling backward to the a.d. and demanded a pad be placed under the carpet. I watched in amazement as he continued to build this simple three-foot backward fall into what was becoming the *Fall of the Century*. But maybe he was right. We each received a $25 stunt adjustment, but I'll bet Ol' Paul received a $100.

I worked one more *Bells* segment, and then sat at home waiting for the phone to ring. Finally, I called men's costumer Gene Ostler, who asked where I'd been working, "Nowhere. Why?" "Well, every time production mentions your name, Harvey Parry says you're working." I was still new to the business, but never for a moment imagined that Parry would be so treacherous.

A call to Warren Mace in MGM casting revealed the last few shows didn't have any action in them. Later, I heard Parry was instrumental in having Frankie Darro replaced and had brought in John Benson, a stunt man-turned-production manager, who was presently employed by the *Truth or Consequences* TV show. How odd that Parry soon began performing the zany stunts on that program.

Back on the "The Rifleman" set, dressed in Johnny Crawford's "double" wardrobe, I was taken to the backlot's schoolhouse set as filming commenced with Chuck Connors and Johnny filming a scene, as a group of children extras romped in the background. During a break to re-set the shot Connors spied me, his six-foot-six frame moved toward me in stride comparable to a charging water buffalo. Extending his hand, he shook my hand with bone crushing strength as if he was priming a well. Filming resumed until he suddenly began a bellowing diatribe of profanity, all directed to "Manny, Moe and Jack," referring to the TV series producers, Arthur Gardner, Jules Levy and Arnold Laven.

Later, when the company moved to the "cave" set, I was greeted by

Connor's stunt double Fritz Ford, a handsome 6'5", blond, former baseball player, turned actor like Connors. Fritz is best remembered in the classic film, *Mr. Roberts*, as Lindstrom, the sailor outside the captain's porthole, reporting the blow by blow vomiting prowess of the ship's captain, James Cagney.

I mentioned Connor's forceful handshake and Fritz said it was just part of his "macho bullshit." Connors had tried it only once on Fritz and it evolved into an arm wrestling match which Fritz won. Once during a round of golf, a furious Connors wildly slung his club at a tree. Wedged high in the branches, he told Fritz, "Go get it!" Fritz looked at him, "Fuck you! Go get it yourself." Connors climbed the tree and never screwed with Fritz again.

Fritz invited me to join him at his local haunt on the Sunset Boulevard, The Roundelet, located at the "Tip of the Strip," across from the famous Cock & Bull restaurant. The C&B was famous for their *Moscow Mule*; a delightful libation of vodka, ginger beer and lime wedge, served in a frosty copper mug. Few ever left the C&B sober, where their regular drink was a hefty two shots, and their prime rib and roast beef ranked among the best anywhere.

The Roundelet was a quaint cocktail lounge with plush, red leather booths catering to the famous—Jack Webb, Johnny Weismuller, Burl Ives, Robert Preston, Kent Taylor, Robert Lowry and Lorna Thayer.

Lorna is best remembered as the surly waitress taking Jack Nicholson's order in *Five Easy Pieces*, and these famous moments have come to be known as the "Chicken Salad Scene," in which Nicholson's character has a run-in with the waitress, who pointedly informs him that no menu substitutions are allowed. When his attempt to get wheat toast rather than the menu-ordained cottage fries and rolls with his omelet and coffee fails, Nicholson tries a different approach by ordering "a chicken salad sandwich on wheat toast, no mayonnaise, no butter, no lettuce … Now all you have to do is hold the chicken, bring me the toast, give me a check for the chicken salad sandwich, and you haven't broken any rules."

"You want me to hold the chicken, huh?" Lorna spitefully replies.

"I want you to hold it between your knees," was Nicholson's comment.

The scene ends with Thayer pointing to the "No Substitutions" sign. "Do you see that sign, sir? I'm not taking any more of your smartness and sarcasm."

"You see this sign?" Nicholson says, angrily sweeping all the water glasses and menus off the table with a hasty exit.

Other times, during a Roundelet' Men's Room visit, Weismuller would shock the unsuspecting out-of-town customers with his famous Tarzan yell.

And then there was singer Leigh Ann Austin, a statuesque blond, former Texas beauty queen, who would return to the Lone Star state and marry a millionaire (don't they all?!?). This delectable, sweet young lady with a personality to match was every man's ideal dream girl a la Doris Day.

On Paramount's *Walk like a Dragon*, I doubled gunslinger Mel Tormé in this James Clavell production starring Jack Lord, Lilyan Chauvin, James Shigeta and Josephine Hutchinson. Mel and I became lifelong friends and in 1990 I presented him with the personalized gun belt and holster he wore in *Dragon* that Rodd Redwing had given me. The black suede leather rig was the perfect addition to Mel's premiere Army Colt .45 Single Action gun collection, one of the finest in the world.

Years later Mel confided that a divorce had cost him the gun collection. Noticing my pained reaction, he said, "Don't worry, my current gun collection is better than the last one." I can't imagine how that could be. It included an original Colt .45 Buntline Special with the 12" barrel, but knowing Mel I'm sure it was true.

While filming a saloon card game, Jack Lord didn't approve of direc-tor Clavell's multiple camera setups and angrily threw a handful of poker chips at the table. The chips bounced up, striking Lilyan Chauvin in the face, luckily missing her eyes. Lord stomped off the set as the crew mumbled, "That sonofabitch will never work in this town again."

However, contrary to a farmer's premise that "cream rises to the top," Tinseltown's version had Jack Lord starring in the *Stoney Burke* TV series a year later. Then, in 1968, Lord began a twelve-year run as Detective Steve Garrett on *Hawaii Five-O*. He once fired a female crewmember and ordered, "Get off my island!" That guy really took his last name too seriously.

Gentlemen writer-producer-director James Clavell would continue his prolific film career with *The Great Escape, Shogun, King Rat and Tai-Pan.*

Guy Way, a former U.S. Marine and UCLA football player, turned stunt man, frequented The Roundelet and we, too, became good buddies. Guy was one hellava stunt man—never cheated a gag. It hurt just watching him hit the ground.

Six months later, Guy hired me to perform my first fire gag for Paramount's, *Hell Is For Heroes*, starring Steve McQueen, Bobby Darin, James Coburn, Fess Parker, Nick Adams, Harry Guardino and introduced Bob Newhart. The other stunt personnel consisted of Vince Deadrick, Dick Elmore, Fritz Ford, Chuck Hicks, Hubie Kerns and Dave Perna.

This was my first distant location, filming in Cottonwood, 19 miles south of Redding, California. We were housed at the local Travelodge motel and spent our idle time lounging by the Olympic-sized pool. One day, we wondered about the absence of one of the stunt guys. The motel complex rimmed the pool area, so I went to his second floor room to inquire. After several knocks he cracked the door slightly, saying he would join us at the pool later. An hour passed before the stunt guy's motel door opened and out walked a gal that made Rosie O'Donnell look like Twiggy. We all stared in amazement as this massive vision of flabby epidermis waddled down the stairs to her car.

I missed Psychology 101 and can't figure it, but here's a handsome, personable, well-built guy with a beautiful wife and children at home and he's consorting with a gal that, if you saw her on the street, you wouldn't look at her twice. Well, maybe, but only because you couldn't believe what you saw the first time.

It was a fun location with Bob Newhart spieling his cache of humorous stories. A Nazi bunker set was constructed in a pasture that, unfortunately, contained a voluminous rattlesnake population. Bob found this very unnerving as a rattler seemed to greet him whenever he exited his dressing room trailer. Ultimately, two grips with long sticks preceded his every step to and from the set.

Bob's initial film appearance occurs as an enemy mortar shell explodes, causing him to crash his Jeep into a large tree. Dick Elmore was suited up as Bob's double and awaited "Action!" from director Don Siegel. Dick gunned the Jeep and roared up the curved road. Special effects triggered the mortar blast and Elmore jerked the Jeep off the road toward the old oak tree. Someone yelled, "He missed the tree!" We watched as the Jeep raced over the hill, down into a valley and up another hill. Half the crew laughed, while the other half wondered where the hell Elmore was going. Siegel was bewildered, looked to Guy for an explanation, but Guy just stared at the runaway Jeep, shaking his head. This was before walkie-talkies were used on the set, where waving a flag or firing a blank served as signals, so there was no way to communicate with Elmore, who, when last seen, was headed for Canada. Several more minutes passed before Elmore and the Jeep appeared on yonder hill, heading toward us. Arriving at camera, he sheepishly explained to Guy and Siegel that his Army boot got wedged between the accelerator pedal and the steering column. We all doubled up in laughter.

One evening, we were enjoying adult beverages in the Travelodge bar and lounge, when Vince Deadrick discovered the bartender's specialty drink was a Pousse-café. I had heard of this potent, seven-layered rum drink and accepted Vince's dare, "If you'll drink one, I'll buy it!" Well, I did, and was having a fine time table-hopping and joking with the production manager Joe Boehm, sound mixer Phil Mitchell and Dorothy Yutzy, script supervisor. When Guy Way figured it was time for me to leave, he snatched me up under his arm like a sack of potatoes and carried me off backward. I was still talking as we exited through the double doors.

Show biz had its perks: wherever we traveled, we always met the local regal gentry; and accepted an invitation to Lake Shasta for a day of sunbathing, boating and water skiing. Our hosts presented a delicious barbeque buffet and open bar. I was invited to water ski, but declined, not wanting to do anything that might be physically detrimental to my first fire gag. However, Fritz Ford, all six-foot-five of him, after a few drinks, decided to give it a try, nodding as the instructor explained how to handle the tow-line-handle and the skis. And they're off. Fritz was upright for about five seconds, and then did a header into the ski boat's wake. He obviously didn't remember his instructions to "Let go of the tow-line handle when you dump." Like a torpedo, a foot under the lake's surface, Fritz tracked the ski boat around the lake as we laughed and screamed for him to "Let go of the rope!"

At dusk, Chuck Hicks and I were walking the lake's edge when we saw Dave Perna walking toward us with a girl on his arm. Dave was a tall, dark and handsome Italian guy from Chicago I had met in 1958 on KTLA's *Guy Mitchell Show*. All smiles, he introduced us to Laurel Goodwin, a pretty, blue-eyed, freckled, girl-next-door type, about twenty years old, wearing a torn, soiled dress, with hair that looked like it hadn't been combed in days or her bare feet washed in a week. Chuck and I were cordial, bid them adieu and continued on our way. Noticing we were distanced far enough from the young lovers, we looked at each other in disbelief, "What's a nice guy like Dave is doing with a gal so unkempt." Oh well, we figured—to each his own.

Later, back in Hollywood, we learned that Laurel Goodwin was an I. Magnin model-actress from San Francisco and was appearing at a local Lake Shasta theater with actress Millie Perkins in Tennessee Williams' *Tobacco Road*. How lucky for Laurel. A Paramount Studio executive saw the play and signed her to a multi-picture studio contract, her first film—*Papa's Delicate Condition*—with Jackie Gleason. She and Dave soon married, but it was short-lived union.

The fun continued on *Hell Is For Heroes* with Newhart, Harry Guardino, Bobby Darin and his very pregnant, radiantly beautiful wife, Sandra Dee. Chuck Hicks and I were playing German soldiers and our scenes had yet to be filmed, so we continued to party in the Travelodge lounge. We were roommates and would repeat this arrangement on many subsequent film locations.

A Nazi soldier was to attack and McQueen suggested his monkey-flip over the camera would be most effective from the German's POV (point of view). The timing was askew as Steve landed atop the hand-held Arriflex camera. The next day the cameraman sported a beautiful shiner.

Finally, my fire gag was going to be filmed. There were several shots of us Nazis running to the point where I was to be set ablaze by a flame-thrower. Guy Way was meticulous in preparing me for the fire gag. Veteran special effects man Dick Parker and director Don Siegel carefully explained exactly what they expected me to do. This included my position in the foxhole, the ignition of the powder charge to set the rubber cement afire, and my route to a distant water-filled foxhole. I was mesmerized, in an almost trance-like stare, as I concentrated on each and every move I would make. Memorizing his every word, all I could do was nod as Siegel spoke.

We were getting close when, suddenly, Dick Parker met me face to face and pulled a claw hammer from his tool belt, "See this? If you don't hit your foxhole mark, I'm gonna hit you in the head." He mentioned a fire gag in another film when the stunt man panicked, ran up a hillside setting the brush on fire. Dick tackled him resulting in painful burns to each of them. I assured him the hammer wouldn't be neccessary.

Then, with a large 5" paintbrush and a gallon of rubber cement, Dick applied the clear, molasses-thick, paste to my back, arms and legs, from head to foot. A shroud-like asbestos cloth under the German helmet would protect the back of my head and neck from the fire. I wore gloves, but remained bare faced, undoubtedly, in more ways than one.

Self-hypnosis would best describe my mental state, as every move I was to make became indelibly etched in my mind's eye. The moment had finally arrived as Don called "Action!"

Looking forward, I watched as James Coburn triggered the flame-thrower, spewing a jet stream of fire toward me. Another shot hit my foxhole and the squib taped to my leg exploded behind me, triggered by Parker. Instantly, the fire climbed up my back into flames three feet above my head, illuminating the entire area. Staggering from the foxhole, I charted my pre-determined course to my final mark. Falling head first into the water-filled foxhole, I went under. Coming up for air, the water's surface was aflame as Dick Parker and his assistant triggered their fire extinguishers. Gasping for air, I got a CO_2 mouthful—a rancid taste that leaves something to be desired.

Dripping wet, I crawled out to the applause of the cast and crew. Don Siegel shook my wet hand as Dick smiled, patting the hammer in his tool belt. My first fire gag was a success and was later told, at nineteen years old, I was the youngest stunt man ever to perform a fire gag. Two days later I was on my way back to Hollywood.

Several weeks later, *Hell Is For Heroes* returned to the Paramount lot to complete interior filming. When I entered the sound stage, I was surprised and gratified when several cast and crewmembers offered congratulations on the fire stunt. Nearing the camera, I watched a trucking shot of an emotional Steve McQueen, tears streaming down his cheeks. A pssst, pssst, sound emanated from the camera as the atomizer sprayed a menthol mist, obviously kinder than the age-old tear-making custom of pulling nose hairs. Steve's tears flowed like the Mississippi River, but the shot didn't make the film's final cut.

Joining Guy for a cup of Java, Don Siegel asked me to follow him. In a stage corner, a large, six-foot tall box with wheels contained a portable 35mm film projector—a rough cut of my Nazi assault, including the fire stunt had been assembled. I was pleased. It looked real. Well, hell, it was. This was my first *BIG* stunt and a great step toward establishing me as a Hollywood stunt man. Ronnie Rondell called to say he had heard I did a good fire burn. I realized performing a stunt well was only half the battle: but having your fellow stuntmen ballyhoo your abilities was equally important.

Although I enjoyed performing stunts, my desire to work behind the camera still loomed. Carroll Righter, Hollywood's Astrologer to the Stars, was contacted and a meeting was set to discuss my new TV production creation, *It's In The Stars*. Accompanied by my two Jesse Wayne Productions partners, publicist Chief Samuelson and talent agent Harry Lipton (he discovered Marilyn Monroe), our initial meeting was set at the Hollywood Brown Derby.

The meeting progressed nicely as an animated Righter became enthusiastic about the program's potential. Over a Cobb Salad, originated at the Derby by Robert Cobb in 1937, I enjoyed the exhilaration of having a TV project accepted by a known celebrity.

Unfortunately, my plans for a successful television series vanished in a flash when Federal Communications Commission's Chief Newton ("TV is a vast wasteland.") Minow issued an unexpected edict declaring that astrology was a form of fortune telling.

Righter was also known for his monthly zodiac parties at his Holly-wood Hills mansion, never calling you by name, but by your astrological sign. Robert Cummings, Arlene Dahl, Tom Conway (The Falcon, and brother to George Sanders), producers, directors and others mingled over lavish food and drink. Most attendees were interesting, but I soon avoided those who wouldn't open a can of beans without first consulting their daily horoscope.

Late, one night, in a vacuous moment, I agreed to my buddy Claude "Doc" Baum's offer to teach me to ride his 1960 BMW R69 motorcycle. We had been partying, sitting astride the bike, he sat behind, coached me when to "clutch in," "down shift" or "throttle." What a way to learn to ride—at night, in the rain, on a new freeway we had never traveled—after having a few drinks. Well, it seemed like a good idea at the time. But the Sunday rides through the Angeles Crest Forest, past Mt. Wilson to Big Bear and on to Lake Arrowhead was exhilarating – seeing 90% more than you would while driving a car.

Doc said dirt biking was going to be the next big phase in motorcy-cling. Subsequently, many stunt guys began riding dirt and sustained broken bones. And, I still didn't believe in "free" stunts.

CHAPTER 3

1961

Today's stunt business is unrecognizable from the one I entered in 1959, when the last vestige of the Hollywood studio system still ruled. To an eighteen-year-old, it was the perfect outlet to experience every childhood fantasy to release dormant inhibitions of a gunslinger, a racecar driver, or a 1930's gangster. Where else could you whack someone and get away with murder, excluding, of course, a Los Angeles County courtroom?

In 1959, the Screen Actors Guild Hollywood stunt community totaled about 45-50 guys and a half dozen gals. Additionally, there were also approximately 50-100 Two-Card members – those who worked both the SAG and the Extra Guild contracts, many as cowboy background extras, picking up a stunt whenever possible.

Today, SAG's actuary guesstimate (from a SAG exec) is 4,000 stunt performers nationwide with about 2000 residing in Southern California. Of this number, approximately 200 legitimately earn their living as professional Hollywood stunt performers—a number that hasn't varied in the past sixty years.

Hollywood's wonderful Golden Age peaked in 1939. *Gone with the Wind, Stagecoach, The Wizard of Oz, Goodbye, Mr. Chips, Wuthering Heights, Ninotchka, Of Mice and Men, Love Affair, Mr. Smith Goes to Washington* and *Dark Victory* rated so well that all ten films were nominated for a "Best Picture" Oscar.

Rounding out the other classics of 1939 were *The Roaring Twenties, Babes in Arms, When Tomorrow Comes, Union Pacific, Idiot's Delight, Gulliver's Travels, The Great Victor Herbert, The Hunchback of Notre Dame, Drums Along the Mohawk, Intermezzo, Beau Geste, Golden Boy, The Story of Vernon and Irene Castle, The Women, Juarez, The Old Maid, The Private Lives of Elizabeth and Essex, The Rains Came, The Story of Alexander Graham Bell* and *Gunga Din.*

1939: what a magnificent banner year of movies, by the finest actors, writers, producers and directors this business has ever known. Of course, this hallmark year can only be attributed to the tenacity of the studio heads and their system. I expounded on their actions in an October 29, 1991 newspaper article for Nashville's The Tennessean:

"After viewing a movie, did you leave the theater feeling confused and unfulfilled? Possibly angry? Were you forced to create your own ending? Well, if your answer is a resounding yes, don't fret, you are not alone. In fact, in recent years, it's become the general rule for the audience to do what the filmmakers didn't. However, it was different a generation, two or three ago, when the movie-goers didn't have this responsibility thrust upon them. That was when motion pictures had a beginning, middle and an ending. That was also when 'The End' needlessly appeared on the screen to let you know the film was over. Today, when this notice is often a vital necessity, it's missing.

"With few exceptions, today's Hollywood is vastly devoid of the competent writers, producers and directors that created the Motion Picture Capital of the World. Absent is the art of cinematic storytelling. It seems that ninety-five out of a hundred films miss their mark. You wonder just when the experienced and creative moviemakers lost control.

"There's not a single answer, but much of this problem goes back to the 1948 United States Justice Department Anti-Trust decision, demanding the separation of the studios from their studio-owned theaters. This demise of the studio distribution system, combined with the advent of television, served to hammer the final nail into the coffin of Hollywood's Golden Age.

"Long gone also are the autonomous studio chiefs who reigned supreme. Though many of these motion picture pioneers were perceived as uneducated, it was their pristine entrepreneurial instincts that dictated company policy and the films produced. Often, their contention that a short story, in Saturday Evening Post or Collier's, be developed into a feature film provided many box office blockbusters. They *KNEW* what the audience wanted. But mostly they all had one trait in common—*Taste*. Today, 'taste' is the sole ingredient most lacking in Hollywood's new breed of money-driven studio chiefs. To attract an audience, these so-called 'film-makers' will allow any form of verbal or visual titillation to appear on the screen. If you're over sixty, you'll recall that the movies you watched in person or on television as a child—those made in the 1930s, '40s and '50s—were geared to an adult mentality—not to the lowest common denominator of today's youth. No, this isn't youth bashing. It's just that there are two generations of moviegoers that don't know a good film from a bad one. It's not their fault; they have been at the mercy of the motion pictures projected to them. (Augmenting this delimma is that most of today's action films are geared to the pre-teen and teen audience and derived from the heroes of video games, comic books and cartoons.)

"Another wrench in the gears prohibiting the personal enjoyment of motion pictures is reviews. I don't read movie reviews, or listen to the critics on radio or TV. Why? Because when every nuance of the production is revealed, it's tantamount to reading a book and someone tells you, 'The Butler did it.' The thrill is gone. There are no surprises.

[*Today, this is called "Spoiler Alert"*] "Recent films blatantly challenge your mental capability to choose and appreciate a film. In addition to their TV commercials, the producers also present productions detailing 'The Making Of' these movies. Not to be outdone, the 'Coming Attractions' feature the best scenes—the highlights—for their capsule version theater trailers. As usual, every story point is 'telegraphed.' Nothing is left to your imagination.

"If you doubt what I say, give this a try at home. Prior to viewing your favorite TV program, don't consult the TV listing that summarizes the show. And when the program's 'opening teaser' begins, don't look at it. Change the channel for the next minute. You will then find there are no preconceived notions to interfere with your enjoyment of the production. And, as the final scene fades to black, you'll realize that the plot unfolded to you in storybook fashion, much to your amazement and satisfaction. That is, of course, only *IF* the filmmakers have done their job correctly."

Through Hollywood's Golden Age and into the 1950s several attempts to form an association for stuntmen were tried, and all failed. Generally, this was the result of dealing with a professional stunt performer—an individual whose very nature is one of self-reliance and independence. Some might call this stubbornness or ego, and they would be correct on both counts. Regardless, when it comes to performing the gag or stunt it's the individuals talent and ability that is challenged and on the line. No one else can make that sometimes split-second decision between life and death. It's their call.

Sounds ominous, doesn't it, and often it is. However, 95% of the time, I found performing stunts to be a piece of cake—a percentage often prevalent by my contemporaries, and in an occupation where the person performs his duties well. Action is what they do. To the common spectator the stunt looks so easy they suddenly believe they are also capable of performing the same deed. Many might be capable if you're in good physical condition, coherent and have analyzed every aspect of the action to be performed. Also, a basic knowledge of the filmmaking process doesn't hurt either.

A 1930's director didn't like the way the stunt man was swinging on a rope, and grabbed it to show how he wanted the stunt performed. When they got to him, he was lying in a heap with two broken legs.

Again, Monday, February 27, 1961, marked the initial discussion leading to the formation of the Stuntmen's Association of Motion Pictures, Inc. This creation occurred quite by accident during the filming of Columbia Pictures *Everything's Ducky* starring Mickey Rooney and Buddy Hackett.

We were on Columbia Studio's Hollywood Stage 10 set of a naval base cocktail lounge, where Rooney, Hackett and their talking pet duck become involved in a full-blown saloon brawl. Director Don Taylor blocked out the action as stunt guys, Guy Way, Dick Geary, Bill Couch, Chuck Couch, George Sawaya, Loren Janes, Lennie Snow and I watched patiently. Several "both cards" extras were also chosen to be in the melee. "Both cards" described the Screen Actors Guild members who also worked as background atmosphere under the aegis of the Screen Extras Guild.

Director Taylor casually mentioned that he wanted Jack "*Bob-A-Loo*" Stewart Taylor, an extra/stuntmen sitting on the bar, to take a punch and fall backward. Instantly, "Bob-A-Loo" said, "Do you mean like this?" and flipped backward, crashing into the back bar, demolishing four shelves of glassware and bottles. We all stood frozen in disbelief with only one question, "What the hell's he doing?" Especially pissed were the prop men and set dressers, who now rushed to rebuild and redress the wrecked back bar. We later discovered that ol' "Bob-A-Loo" had been sampling beer all morning from the set's beer keg.

We continued rehearsing the fight scene, as the cameras filmed a scene in a nearby set, when Rooney suddenly became enraged at a nervous actor for flubbing lines. Rooney then argued with Taylor over "artistic differences" and profanely fired him. Don handled it well—he simply ignored Rooney, who promptly stomped off the set. Now, without the film's producer-star, the frustrated assistant director Jerry Bernstein called a long lunch. Rooney later returned, rehired Taylor, and we continued filming with a rebuilt back bar full of new glassware and bottles.

It was during the long lunch period that Dick Geary and Loren Janes, sitting on Stage 10's stoop, decided that a professional stuntmen's association should be established—with an organization comprised of SAG stuntmen *only*. This agendum, of course, would serve to weed-out the "Extras" that worked "both cards."

There has always been a caste system in Tinseltown and the "Extras" are the amoeba. Even among themselves, the Stand-Ins – those standing on a mark for your favorite actor as the Director of Photography lights the shot – generally ignored the common Extras. Unfortunately, those "two-card guys" who often performed stunts as well, or better, as the recognized SAG stunt men, were relegated to a second-class status. Many two-card carriers would have made the switch to stunts full-time if their economics permitted it, but chose instead to make background crosses between the stunt jobs.

In the early sixties, the Hollywood consensus deemed it would take three to five years to become an established stunt performer. It was a big gamble and there were no guarantees. Even if you landed a stunt job, it could be weeks or even months before your next stunt workday.

Geary and Janes continued their quest to organize SAG stunt men, arranged an initial meeting at The Villa Nova Restaurant on the Sunset Strip with Fred Krone, Troy Melton and Jerry Catron. For the subsequent meetings others were invited until a nucleus of eminent SAG stunt men was assembled.

In April 1961, Teddy O'Toole's Answering Service notified all SAG stuntmen (those who worked stunts only, no "both cards") about the formation meeting of a new stunt organization.

The first Stuntmen's Association general membership meeting took place in the Screen Actors Guild's James Cagney Conference Room at 7750 Sunset Boulevard. Sixty-one stunt guys became charter members that evening and, at nineteen years old, I was the youngest member of the new group. A Board of Directors was selected and veteran stunt man Dale Van Sickle was named President, a position he would hold for the first three years of the organization.

Fred Krone was elected secretary-treasurer and must be given complete credit for efficiently handling the preliminary business affairs, including the Stuntmen's Association's logo. At a local print shop, Fred searched for "something indicative of the movies," found a motion picture camera in silhouette; surrounded it with the group's name and the SAMP logo was born.

A unanimous vote from the membership declared the 1st Annual

Stuntmen's Association Dinner-Dance would be held at the vintage Club Casa Del Mar in Santa Monica. Built in 1926 for $2 million, this grand old hotel became Synanon, a drug rehabilitation center in the 1960s. In the 1990s the beachfront property was purchased for $200 million, and now the Casa Del Mar ranks among Southern California's most posh hotels.

With my contacts at KTLA, I handled the television public relations. On a June Sunday morning, Reg Parton, Henry Wills and Harvey Parry appeared on KTLA's Skipper Frank Herman's TV show to trigger ticket sales for the event. The interview was tame by today's standards, instead of stunt action film clips, only a few black and white, 8x10 action still photos were displayed.

The 1st Annual Stuntmen's Association's Dinner-Dance projected a new image of the Hollywood stunt man. The underlying motive was that this black-tie event would suggest stunt men were more than just a guy who fell on his head. And it worked—everyone had a fine time, including many directors, who expressed wishes that their yearly Directors Guild of America dinner-dance would be as enjoyable and, especially, as relaxed.

Lee Marvin and Keenan Wynn emceed the festivities and when they completed officiating, I joined them at the massive bar and learned a great lesson: Do not attempt to match drinks with experienced, professional drinkers. How I made it back to my Studio City apartment from Santa Monica, through the winding Sepulveda Pass (the 405/San Diego Freeway was under construction) is still a mystery.

Someone suggested a dinner-dance raffle of door prizes to entice ticket buyers, so I volunteered to procure the main prize through my old buddy, Jim Devine, the West Coast regional head of Colt Firearms. Graciously, he offered a new Colt .45 single-action army revolver, retailing in 1961 for $125. Today, a new Peacemaker model sells for about $1600.

Again, fortuitously, I was present February 27, 1961, when Loren Janes and Dick Geary determined it was time to form a professional stunt organization, The Stuntmen's Association of Motion Pictures, Inc. From 1961 thru 1984, I served as SAMP's Publicity Director, Secretary, Treasurer and Board member—which has also aided in documenting the group's conception along with the history of the Hollywood stunt man.

The Stuntmen's Association monthly meetings continued at SAG's Hollywood conference room as the attendance proved to vacillate. It was a simple deduction. The members attended as long as they believed a job might be gained, but didn't want to travel fifty miles to do it. Even though I lived in Studio City, and SAG was just a brief run over Laurel Canyon, I dreaded the winding drive home, especially after having a couple of after meeting drinks with the guys at the Saratoga on Sunset Boulevard.

After reviewing SAMP's membership roster, my calculations revealed that eighty-seven percent of the members lived in the San Fernando Valley. Obviously, the meeting attendance would rise if the majority of the members didn't have to drive into Hollywood. The SAMP board agreed and the monthly meetings were set at various Studio City and Sherman Oaks restaurant banquet rooms. Immediately, the monthly membership attendance doubled and participation increased, but personal animosities and discord also accelerated.

Prior to SAMP's formation you generally met a fellow stunt performer while working on a production, otherwise while studio hopping you'd see a guy carrying what appeared to be a stunt bag – a ha, a stunt guy! Now, SAMP brought individuals together where an opposing opinion, a voice tone or even a guy's haircut frequently generated personal dislikes. Actually, if the truth were known, one might loathe another member only because of his matching height and weight. Competition was not a favorite ally.

For those who missed a meeting, an inquiring SAMP phone call to their household ceased when their spouses learned they were absent. Somehow, extracurricular activities were involved.

Often, valid moneymaking propositions were brought to SAMP and promptly shot down because it was perceived the member presenter might make a buck on the deal.

A few years later, the purchase of a Studio City two-story office building at Whitsett and Ventura was considered—price: $100,000. The Cartoonist's Guild occupied the ground floor offices and their rent payment sufficiently paid the monthly mortgage. Upstairs was perfect for SAMP, but this property was nixed because members complained they would have to park on Whitsett and walk fifty yards. Max Kleven then chimed in, "If you don't buy it, I will." Well, he never made the purchase, and today you can't touch the property for $1,000,000.

The monthly banquet room plan worked well until a few members began visiting the restaurant's saloon prior to the meetings. "When the booze goes in, the truth comes out" is academic, but the liquor did produce some exciting meetings – profanity, fights and even resignations.

Back on Rooney's *Everything's Ducky* set at the Sportsman's Lodge in Studio City I was attracted to a beautiful brunette extra, playing a Navy nurse. At wrap, this petite former Playboy centerfold needed a ride to her Hollywood apartment and, naturally, I volunteered. Traveling down Ventura Boulevard, she asked if I was "hip." Assuming she was referring to my love making, I assured her there hadn't been any complaints. Immediately, she produced a marijuana joint from her purse and lit up. I had never smoked or, much less, seen dope and quickly cranked opened my driver side window. She got the message, extinguished the butt and returned it to her purse. Instead, we made a detour to my apartment. She was quite a gal and never brought out drugs in my presence again. Years later, while working at Twentieth on *The New Phil Silvers Show*, doubling Herbie Faye, I passed a gal and heard a voice ask, "Well, aren't you going to say hello?" There she was, but I hadn't recognized her. How embarrassing.

While filming *Everything's Ducky*, I ducked away for a quick interview on Four Star's *Stagecoach West* TV series. The show starred Wayne Rogers, Robert Bray (later, of Lassie fame) and Richard Eyer, the child actor from *Friendly Persuasion*. Director Don McDougall almost gave me the kiss-off, when he saw my U.S. Navy seaman's uniform, thinking I had just gotten off the boat, literally. Assistant director Marty Moss assured him I really was a bona fide stunt man, working on a Navy feature for Columbia. Moss then explained the stunt; doubling an Indian boy leaping from a cabin porch to a horse at the hitching post and ride away. Yep, just a piece of cake.

With a day off from *Everything's Ducky*, I found myself in the rolling hills of Conejo Valley, near Thousand Oaks. Stunt man Bill Hart was there to portray "four" of the invading redskins during the Indian raid.

Filming commenced as the Indians attacked and the frontier settlers returned gunfire. Bill's first saddle fall broke his clavicle and pulled all the ligaments in his left shoulder. Behind the barn, one wrangler held the horse's reins as two others assisted the native Texan into the saddle. Bill rode away to perform three more saddle falls that day.

In a business with no secrets, Bill's reputation preceded him as one tough stunt man, which ultimately made him one of Sam Peckinpah's favorite fall guys. Bill was equally a fine actor and it's a shame he didn't receive more acting chores during his career. His left shoulder healed a bit out of kilter, negating him a proper fit from a suit off the rack. Then again, that's assuming you can get a proper fit from a suit off the rack.

That day would not prove to be one of my favorites either. It was now my shot, but Director McDougall changed it. I wasn't leaping to a standing horse by the porch as Moss had stated, but now had to catch a horse running from the corral, swing up into the saddle and ride off. Have you ever run toward a galloping horse? Horses are skittish by nature and this monstrous seventeen-hand equine would gallop past me. Minutes ticked away between the takes while the wrangler out-riders attempted to catch the runaway while McDougall was screaming about "losing the light." Someone suggested we shoot the segment in pieces (I suggested shooting the horse). I attached my "step," a sturdy foot platform hanging from the saddle cinch "D" ring, then tied a short length of rope to the saddle horn. These accessories enabled me to finally pull myself into the leather seat and ride off into the quickly disappearing sunset.

A lesson was well learned that day. The change they made was implausible. How in the hell can a kid run to a galloping horse, mount it and ride away. It may have "seemed like a good idea," on paper, but putting it on film was something else. Of course, with today's computer generated graphics, anything is now possible on the screen.

Returning to the last day of filming *Everything's Ducky*, I watched as Mickey Rooney, Buddy Hackett and the talking duck filmed the final scene, floating weightlessly (by wires) in a space capsule, culminating with all three laughing uproariously. Turning to Sig Froelich, Mick's stand-in and also the film's associate producer, I was exasperated, "Is that the ending?" He nodded and I shook my head, "Well, it stinks!"

That evening, at the wrap party on Columbia's Stage 10, I stared in disbelief as Buddy Hackett chugalugged a full 8oz. glass of Vodka. Swallowing the final gulp, he let out a blood-curdling scream, threw the empty glass at the sound stage wall and ran howling into the night. Who knows why? Maybe it was his own wrap party ritual.

Months later, in a theater packed matinee, when the film's final scene hit the screen there was a moaning "Aaaaawwww" from every kid in attendance.

I later bummed around with Lennie Snow, Hackett's two-card stunt double, who introduced me to a stunning Sunset Strip brunette, named Thumper. During her ladies room visit, he mentioned the $500 per weekend she regularly received from Desi Arnaz in Palm Springs (by this time, Desi was divorced from Lucy). She was intriguing, but I have never paid for sex directly. Regardless, I'd bet the farm this beautiful doll was worth every penny.

A call from *Burke's Law* at Four Star Entertainment to double Rooney was a great thrill for several reasons. The first was obvious, it's a job, but the other was that I might possibly meet Dick Powell, my favorite male singer-actor from the 1930's musicals. Actor, producer, director, Four Star was Powell's baby, having created the successful television production entity with three other stars, Ida Lupino, Charles Boyer and David Niven.

The *Burke's Law* TV series starring Gene Barry was directed by Don Weis, a former editor, who was never troubled with doubt; he knew exactly what he wanted. The scene called for a brief tussle between Gene and Mickey as an enraged Rooney swings a fireplace poker at Gene, who quickly side steps, disarms Rooney and then punches him. Don had filmed the scene up to their struggling clinch, and then I stepped into Rooney's position. In this separate cut, Gene would swing me around, throw a punch, driving me over a French providential sofa. Those familiar with this elegant furniture style will recall the carved, wood ridge along the back top of the couch. Gene and I had slowly rehearsed our moves. I now stood locked in Gene's embrace as he said, "Gee, I'm afraid I'm gonna hit you," just as Weis called "Action!" Gene and I struggled for a beat and as we rehearsed, he swung me into position to take the picture punch. Watching him, I kept my distance as he cocked his arm to throw the punch and BAM! Over the sofa I flew, hearing a "pop" as I topped the sofa's wood lip. Don yelled, "Cut and Print that." Immediately, I went to Don to explain, but he had heard Gene's dumbass comment and assured me everything was okay. He just wanted to see me in motion after the punch, going over the sofa and it would "cut together perfectly" with Rooney's close up. Again, I had bruised a rib and couldn't take a deep breath for a week. 25 years later, a chiropractor's x-ray proved two ribs had been broken, not bruised.

Working with actors in a physical situation always provoked concern among the stunt performers and in most cases, rightfully so. Most actors are not schooled in the varied aspects of performing action sequences. That's not their job, and should they become injured the entire film usually shuts down. Generally, when called upon to do so, their heart rate doubles, their eyes get glassy, their memory vanishes and anything can happen. A few stunt men also had this malady.

A perfect example was when veteran stunt man Jerry Summers performed a fight in *Surf Party* with Rock & Roll star-turned-actor, Bobby Vinton. During the shot, Vinton's first punch to Jerry's mouth loosened several teeth. Continuing the fight scene, Jerry pleaded with Vinton to take it easy and Bam! Right in the choppers, again. Later, Jerry sported a beautiful set of ivories—paid for by the studio. Jerry was a fine stunt man, in addition to being an excellent actor.

A broken nose was a common injury during the fight scenes. On the *Batman* TV series, Victor Paul tagged Fred Carson. Jerry Catron nailed Fred Krone on *Richard Diamond, P.I.* On *Bob Hope Presents the Chrysler Theater*, Aldo Ray swung a punch, brushed my chin with his little finger as I took the hit. It was nothing, but he apologized for the next two hours. On *I Spy*, Bill Cosby fractured Fred Carson's nose, which doctors had to re-break with a hammer and chisel. A distraught Cosby called Fred all night long to check his condition. A variation occurred when

Fred Krone, fighting *The Range Rider* co-star Dick Jones, noticed a wayward punch approaching and dropped his head. Jones broke his hand on Fred's forehead, leaving a four-knuckle bruise. The picture punch in the wrong hand is undeniably an occupational hazard.

Bill Hart, Jack Lord's stunt double and stunt coordinator on the *Stoney Burke* cowboy rodeo series, called me for a fight under the grandstand seats at Saugus Raceway in the Santa Clarita Valley. In supporting roles were Warren Oates, Bruce Dern and Harry Dean Stanton, whom I was doubling. Waiting to film the fight segment, we roared at the salacious, men-only tales spun by Bruce, relating a mentally troubled Montgomery Clift on *Raintree County*, who, during dinner with his close friend Elizabeth Taylor, whipped out his manhood and proceeded to masturbate. Another time, while strolling with Miss Taylor, Clift threw himself in front of a parked bus and screamed for the driver to run him over. Bruce had a million tales to tell.

The costumer handed me Harry Dean's double wardrobe, suggested I wear lifts in my western boots to bring my height up to Harry Dean's. Rehearsing the fight with Chuck Roberson, John Wayne's longtime double, Fred Krone and Allen Pinson, the cameras were ready to roll when the costumer asked me to change back into Dean's chukka boots because my boots would be seen.

The fight ensued and Chuck was the pivotal brawler as he punched Allen, then Fred. His next move was to punch me when I approached him from behind. Spinning around, ready to throw the punch, Chuck looked right over my head. His expression of "Where the hell'd he go?" was priceless. Startled, he looked down and quickly backhanded me. I fell backward through the wood structure and then rejoined the others to subdue Chuck. Director Leslie Stevens called "Cut and Print," and the whole crew broke up, including Chuck, shaking his head.

On another *Stoney Burke* episode, we were shuttled from an old Cahuenga Boulevard West parking site to the location in an eight-door stretch out—just a long sedan. Joining us was actress Patricia Breslin, who had co-starred with Jackie Cooper in the *The People's Choice* TV series, featuring Cleo, the sad-eyed Bassett hound. Venturing out the Ventura Freeway toward Thousand Oaks we all made polite conversation. If an individual had a comedic bent, they usually tossed in a joke or two. Patricia began a tale about a cannibalistic African tribal chief's son who was brought to England and schooled at Oxford. She continued to describe the great education he received, graduating Summa Cum Laude, "but, it was all for naught. With all that education he reverted to his tribal instincts and the first thing he did when he returned to his village was eat his wife." We all sat there, staring at the demure Patricia, not quite knowing how to react, giving "Silence is Golden" a new meaning.

Fred "Krunch" Krone never cheated a stunt. When you hired Fred, you got more than your monies worth. If a saddle fall on Iverson's Ranch cement-hard insert road was required, Fred was the guy to call. Understandably, his association with Jock Mahoney paid off, ranking him as a top, all-around, stunt man and an exceptional actor to boot. Most notably, on Robert Aldrich's *Kiss Me Deadly*, Fred performed filmdom's longest stair fall from L.A.'s Bunker Hill down to Third Street.

In 1957, when Disney's *Texas John Slaughter* TV production aired, I watched as a stunt man took a gunshot and was jerked off his horse in a jack-knife position. He struck the ground in a two-point landing—his head and his toes. Whoa, who the hell did that I wondered, and did he live to tell about it? Two years later, when I "officially" entered the stunt ranks, I found Fred Krone had become the innocent passenger when the jerk-off cable snapped. Indeed, it would have killed anyone else.

Initially, Fred taught me the finer points of a picture fight as he had learned from Jock, and then perfected his own style. In the biz, every stunt guy said they were "fight men," but ninety percent of them should have taken a lesson from Fred.

I returned to Universal for the *Laramie* TV series starring Robert Fuller and John Smith to double a kid at Vasquez Rocks. I changed into wardrobe and did a double take when veteran stunt man Whitey Hughes appeared in the same outfit, explaining he was the kid's photo double, doing the horse backing. He was very gracious and one of my idols, but I was embarrassed. Whitey had doubled kids and women for years and he should have had the stunt job.

Robert Fuller is one of the good guys. We first met at Arvo Ojala's

North Hollywood gun belt and holster shop in 1957. Joseph Kane, the veteran Western Republic Pictures director-producer, explained what he wanted and called "Action!" From his horse, Fuller jerked me by my shirtfront and belt buckle, over his horse, dropped me five feet to the ground on my back. Figuring I'd better do an ass-buster in front of Whitey, Bob did exactly as I had asked. Bob quickly dismounted, I tackled him, and we scuffled, tumbled and rolled over and over under the horses. Finally, Bob yelled, "Hey, how long are we going to do this?" Kane was so enthralled with our action he had forgotten to yell, "Cut."

This night *on It's A Man's World*, director Peter Tewksbury, creator of *My Three Sons*, was very determined and knew exactly what he wanted—a free-wheeling, ass-over-tea kettle tumble, down a 40°, fifty-yard-long hill doubling Michael Burns, and he wanted it fast. On "Action," standing far behind the camera, I ran and threw myself down the hill—letting gravity and my momentum take over. Burns' final fall position had been filmed previously to release him by 6pm—I ended up face down in his final spot, much to the delight of Dee, the script supervisor.

It's not natural to hit the ground, so your first instinct is to stick your arms out for protection. One trick I learned early on was to acclimate my body—going behind a set I'd do a couple of hit and rolls – almost like priming an engine. Now, I was ready to plow in for the camera.

Work continued on *The Rifleman, It's a Man's World, Combat* and doubling Larry Fine on *Snow White and the Three Stooges*, producing total earnings for 1961: the grand sum of $4300. Yep, I was on my way.

CHAPTER 4

1962

1962 promised to be a great year, but I was always very hopeful, which you must be if you're going to be in show biz. I would credit my Mom as the one person responsible for my optimistic outlook, who ranked beside Pollyanna when it came to expressing bountiful confidence that "Everything is going to be all right."

And she was right—January started off vigorously with my doubling child actor Michael Burns on 20th Century Fox's *Mr. Hobbs Takes a Vacation*, starring James Stewart and Maureen O'Hara. This was a second unit filming the action with stunt doubles only, no principal actors. George O'Day, owner of the O'Day Boat Company, was an uncanny look-a-like double for James Stewart.

Exiting Balboa's Lido Island, the camera-tug boat towed our 16-foot O'Day sailboat through the dense pea-soup fog toward a pre-arranged rendezvous point with a Standard Oil Company tanker, en route from Seattle to San Diego. Somewhere between Balboa and Catalina Island the camera-tug cut us loose, figuring their search would be easier without us in tow. "We'll be back to get you," were their last words as they disappeared into the thick fog. We floated aimlessly for an interminable amount of time as George explained the basics of sail boating. I became overjoyed, experiencing man's eternal fascination with the sea. What adventurers had done for thousands of years, I now vowed to pursue with the purchase of my own O'Day sailboat.

Suddenly, the spell was broken as a United States Coast Guard cutter appeared out of the fog like a ghost ship. The USCG officer explained the camera tug's radar had failed and had notified them to find us. Tossing a line, they towed us to meet the Standard Oil tanker.

Just like in the movies, we came through a wall of fog into a clear area about a mile in diameter, with the camera tug fifty yards away. We were handed a bulky Motorola two-way radio, a vast contrast to the palm-sized models of today as veteran Director William Witney took charge. What a charge, my fist opportunity to work with him. With a lustrous career dating back to the 1930s Republic Studio's serials and Western films, he was one of the best action directors in the business. Most notably, he helmed many of Roy Rogers' films.

Witney, with his 10-watt Motorola radio, explained the scene to us from his location atop the ship's bridge. To get the shot from the camera tug the oil tanker needed to make a 360° turn to run by us—and disappeared into the fog. Witney instructed us not to look at the ship until his cue and "Don't worry, the ship will miss you by a hundred yards." The boat, rather ship, required a radius of a mile to make the turn back toward us. Continuing our wait, George and I heard the ominous groan of the approaching tanker's churning forward propellers. I fought the urge to peek. Suddenly, we heard Witney's cue to "Look now!" Turning, I could now see both sides of the enormous oil tanker as it bore down on us. Resisting the urge to take a second look, I wondered how this floating projectile would miss us. Witney's voice again blared, "Look busy!" George and I pulled lines and shifted the boom as the churning water sounds grew louder and louder. A huge black mass slowly appeared in my peripheral vision, I then looked. It towered ten stories above the waterline and seemed close enough to touch. The forward twin propellers whipped through the water like huge eggbeaters, and abruptly disappeared again into the fog as we pitched and rolled in the prop backwash waves. And no, we were not wearing life preservers.

The ship missed us, all right, not by a hundred yards, but by about seventy-five feet. The script girl later commented how realistic I appeared – tying lines and trimming the jib. Strangely, my great urge to own a sailboat had disappeared, like the ship into the fog.

On another show at Warner Bros., Bronwyn Fitzsimmons, Maureen O'Hara's beautiful daughter, nervously stumbled through two takes when the director suggested to her, "Let's rehearse one without camera. Now just relax." Silently, he motioned to roll sound and camera. She was perfect, but stunned when the director yelled, "Cut and Print it!" A lesson well learned, relax!

Billy Rose's *Jumbo*, starring Doris Day, created a complete Big-Top circus tent on 15, MGM's largest sound stage. When I arrived about 11am, the crew was wrapping up, two hundred extras were signing out and the animals were being returned to their cages. A crewmember explained that costumed stunt man Yanos Prohaska, a genius at portraying primates, had leaped into Doris Day's dressing room in his handmade gorilla suit, scaring the bejeezes out of her. Miss Day was so shaken MGM wrapped production for the day.

Venturing through the biz you meet many people on the sets—an extra and I talked one day. I was still doubling Johnny Crawford on *The Rifleman* TV series and received a call from an assistant director asking if I would also be Crawford's stand-in. I explained that I didn't do "extra work" and suggested another individual. Well, I never doubled Johnny Crawford again.

There's an old axiom, "Be careful who you help out of the hole, because once they're out, they'll shove you in it." I've often wondered long and hard about that one: But I've concluded that many people helped me and I still feel bound to pass it along.

Dick Powell, the 1930's crooner, actor, turned producer who headed up the very successful Four Star Productions was diagnosed with cancer. I recall Powell visiting the various sound stages to bid farewell. He would pass away in 1963.

Dick Powell produced and directed *The Conqueror*, starring John Wayne and Susan Hayward. Released in 1956, it was filmed in St. George, Utah, near government nuclear testing grounds.

People Magazine reported that, of the 220 cast and crewmembers who worked on the film, 91 had developed cancer by 1980, and half of them died of the disease.

John Wayne, a three-pack-a-day smoker, died of cancer of the lungs, throat and stomach. Susan Hayward died of skin, breast and uterine cancer. Agnes Morehead also died of uterine cancer. Pedro Armendariz died from cancer of the lymphatic system. Dick Powell also died from lymph cancer.

In June 1962, Group W (Westinghouse) Television was producing a new *Steve Allen Show* and I was surprised to find many of my former colleagues from KTLA were working the show. Bill Daily, the show's first announcer, would soon leave to pursue an acting career as astronaut Captain Roger Healey on the *I Dream of Jeannie* TV series and, later, as airplane Captain Howard Borden on *The Bob Newhart Show*.

Jerry Hopkins, a New York to L.A transplant, was the show's talent coordinator and we hit it off from the start. Writers Mike Marmer and Stan Burns were very receptive to my comedy ideas. Informing them I had been a KTLA Page, I suggested we plant a stunt man in the audience to heckle Steve. Then, as a Page, I would rush in to quell the disturbance and a fight would ensue to the shock of everyone. They bought it.

Money-wise, AFTRA's 1962 principal player day rate of $265 greatly exceeded the Screen Actors Guild daily scale of $112.

I phoned six-foot-four Chuck Bail, feeling the contrast between our heights would help sell the stunt fight. Plus, I knew he needed the job. With his wife, Drew, and two infant children, Mark and Vanessa, they rented a house in Northridge, near actor Jack Oakie's estate. A dusty corral bordered the dirt road leading to the board & batten structure, a scene right out of the Ozarks included his two kids romping around bare-assed. It was obvious he and his family were not living La Dolce Vita—The Sweet Life.

Several times I brought them bag loads of groceries and, one day, while watching TV the electricity went dead. We rushed to the fuse box to confront a startled Los Angeles Department of Water and Power serviceman attaching a lead seal to the box. He explained the electric bill was several months overdue and the seal removal without authorization would cause legal action.

Receiving the *Steve Allen Show* work call, Chuck picked me up at my Studio City apartment. While traveling the Hollywood Freeway through the Cahuenga Pass, he suddenly exited at the Barham Boulevard off-ramp. Soon, I was unexpectedly parked in front of his "girlfriend's canyon house." My only reaction was, "That's just great, a wife and two kids, and he's got a girl friend." We stayed only a moment—he just wanted to "show off" his lady friend to me. Yeah, like I really cared.

We arrived at the Steve Allen Theater on Vine Street in time for rehearsal. The set was lazy L shaped, with shelves for Steve's books, mementos and playthings. I told Chuck that when I threw the driving punch to take it easy and just glance off the wall, so the set wouldn't be destroyed needlessly. He agreed as we continued the fight rehearsal.

In addition to the fight that would, hopefully, shock the home viewers and the live audience, Mike Marmer and Stan Burns thought a funny bit would be to have Steve interview us after the fight. Setting this apart from the usual talkfest, Steve would ask me a question and throw a punch. I'd reply, and then punch him. Steve turned to Bail, continued the same routine.

During rehearsal, Steve asked, "Jesse, how did you get in the stunt business?" and threw a punch to my gut. With that, I replied, "Well, Steve, you might say I kind of fell into it," and shot him a stomach punch. This line was an old retort the stunt guys had used for years, but Steve now glared down at me through his black, horned-rimmed glasses, "I'll handle the jokes around here." During the actual TV taping, Steve directed that question to Chuck.

We continued the rehearsal to the satisfaction of the director, Steve Binder, as he noted my suggestions for which camera to "cut to," insuring that our picture punches would look like "hits." Ultimately, every punch was a perfect hit to the television viewing audience, and for the smacking sound effect, prop man Max Pittman slapped a sandbag with a wood paddle, while viewing a monitor.

Comedy Rule No. 1: The Set-Up. Wearing the Steve Allen Show page's blue blazer, complete with the Group W embossed logo, I accepted tickets and helped seat the audience. The show progressed with Steve at his desk, then Chuck, on cue, began his harassing, "C'mon Steve, bring on the babes!" Rushing down the aisle, I tried to calm him, and turned to Steve as Chuck stood to his skyscraper height—on the slanted aisle he looked ten feet tall. Turning back to Chuck, he threw a punch knocking me backward toward the stage. Rising to my feet, he lunged forward and I ducked under his arms. At this point, a male body rushed by me and grabbed Chuck in a vicious neck chokehold. I tried to release this guy's death grip but, with fire in his eyes, he was determined to save the defenseless Page. Jerry Hopkins, seated nearby, grabbed the man's arm and whispered, "It's a fake fight!" The startled man released Bail as I threw a roundhouse punch, driving Chuck onto the stage. Following him, my next punch drove him backward behind Steve's desk. Chuck then did exactly what I told him NOT to do—he wiped out several wall shelves, but fortunately, missed the fish tank. I knocked him to the floor, dived and he monkey-flipped me onto a breakaway table. Steve Allen then rushed in and laid a well-placed breakaway chair across Chuck's back, thus ending the great melee. The audience loved it.

Steve's shrill infectious laugh subsided long enough for him to call our "other" fight partner on camera. Bill Richards was red-faced with embarrassment – the poor guy was only trying to help. Steve knowingly asked what he did for a living—Richards admitted he was the "public relations man for the Steve Allen Show." The audience again howled. Richards knew there were to be stunt men on the show, but somehow never put it all together.

Changing from the Page's blazer, I re-entered the studio as Jerry Hopkins rushed to me, thanking me for a job well done, and then asked if Bail was a good friend of mine. "No. Why?" "Well, he just told me he could handle the stunts on this show better than you. What do you want to do?" Stunned, I said, "Why don't we make sure he never works this show again?" "That's fine with me," Jerry said, exiting with a smile.

Riding home with Bail, I said little as we approached my apartment. Once again, treachery and deceit had reared its ugly head. Bail's actions substantiated H. Ross Perot's theory of infidelity: "If a guy cheats on his wife, whom he's vowed to love, honor and cherish, what will keep him from cheating you?" Guys like Bail are opportunists and don't screw just one person, but many. Like the guy said, "Trust everyone, but cut the cards yourself."

To Bail, I was just another mark, as stunt man Fred Carson later remarked, who had loaned him money, a truck and even housed the Bail family for a time in his North Hollywood home. Fred even got Bail established at ZIV Productions performing stunts.

Previously, my biggest laugh came when Bail suggested a stunt to shoot an arrow into my back as I loped by on his lame horse. Yeah, right. When pigs fly!

The Bail experience didn't jade me, even thinking back to Harvey Parry's conniving lies on *Oh, Those Bells*. Unfortunately, when great amounts of money are a factor, it's the nature of any business. I'm not making an excuse for their actions, but everyone in Hollywood has a similar story to tell. Appropriately, Bob Miles labeled the three traits necessary to be an unscrupulous, opportunistic, stunt performer: Jealousy, Ego and Greed.

Bail later conned his way into doubling Peter Breck on *The Big Valley*. In fact, Breck even wore lifts to match Bail's height. Years later, Peter lamented that Bail, who had become one of Hollywood's busiest television directors, never reciprocated with one day of work.

The Steve Allen Show videotaped from 1962 through 1965 and for the duration I remained the stunt coordinator. But most exhilarating was being in the presence of Steve Allen, Mike Marmer and Stan Burns, where I learned to "think funny," allowing me to come up with comedy material with and without stunts.

Over lunch one day I related Steve's "I'll handle the jokes around here" comment to Jerry Hopkins. He wasn't surprised, confiding that Steve was in therapy to overcome his extreme shyness and insecurities. However, give him a mike and point a TV camera at him and he was rolling.

Steve Allen was one of the great talents of the twentieth century, appearing in all entertainment venues with a multitude of accomplishments, he excelled as a comedian, actor, musician, songwriter, playwright and a prolific author of countless books. It's doubtful if anyone will ever approach his genius.

Jerry and I bummed around and one New Year's Eve found us at a party in the Hollywood hills. We drank, listened to music, and were generally bored, due to a lack of female companionship, while waiting for the remaining fifteen minutes of the old year to tick away. Suddenly, TV's nature boy, Gypsy Boots, burst in, surrounded by a bevy of hippie young ladies. Jerry and I looked at each other, figured this could be the start of something big. Mingling, we soon found we had nothing in common with these drugged-up young things, regardless of their enticing free-love doctrine. Hell, forget AIDS or HIV, to this day I'm still terrified of herpes—the gift that keeps on giving.

The evening climaxed with Jerry returning me to my Studio City apartment in his 1961 silver Austin Healey convertible. I continued to perform stunt gags on the show, working with Andy Williams, Lionel Hampton, Terry Gibbs, and the most beautiful Polly Bergen, among other entertainment greats.

Andy Williams was guest starring the night I convinced Jerry that Reg Parton and I could do an Apaché dance act, referring to the renowned French cabaret, featuring a beret-wearing Frenchman and his lovely slit-skirted amour, me. Wardrobe ordered the dress, nylons, spiked heels and wig from Western Costume. Evidently, when they ordered the Apaché wig, their hair handler thought they were referring to an Apache Indian.

Andy Williams and I shared the same dressing room in the cramped Steve Allen Theater. His glimpse of me in the girly makeup, wig and slit-skirt immediately caused him to sashay into a riotous, lisping gay bit. He laughed when I suggested he do the routine on his NBC show. I have every LP album Andy ever recorded. To bad I didn't get his autograph on a couple of them.

The Stuntmen's Association was a longtime benefactor to The Los Angeles Children's Hospital. My proposal to include ten stunt men in the Apaché act caused Jerry's blood pressure to rise, proclaiming "We don't have a budget for ten stuntmen." Our discussion continued until we contacted AFTRA to request a special dispensation for an appearance on the show. The TV union agreed to exempt eight stuntmen salaries, allowing two $265 stunt contracts to be paid to the SAMP charity fund.

Reg Parton and I sat in the Parisian cabaret set at a small round table as Steve gave a glorious introduction of having personally discovered us in Las Vegas—a "Direct from Paris adagio dance team." The music began and Reg grabbed my arm and swung me across the stage and over a table, then over another table. Immediately, Steve rushed in to protest my rough treatment and decked Reg. Eight stuntmen had lingered behind the cameras as part of the show's stage crew as the melee erupted, but when I looked up fifty people were fighting in this free for all. Floor director Johnny Wilson had arranged for the show's entire "real" crew to join in the brawl. The unsuspected audience delighted in this comedic donnybrook and the kids were $530 richer.

The stunt bucks continued rolling in and I pursued my life-long love of photography by purchasing a Bolex 16mm Rex Reflex motorized camera with fine Switar and Pan Cinor lenses to augment my Moviscop editing equipment. These instruments complemented my filmmaking studies and I was soon a freelancing cinematographer shooting car races, TV commercials, ball games, travelogues, boxing matches, medical, sports and religious films. Name it and I filmed it.

In November 1962, my Dad suffered a debilitating stroke that left him speech impaired and unable to walk without assistance. The family was devastated and I couldn't help but think back to his 1957 arterial sclerosis-heart attack, and why he didn't remain under a doctor's care.

During my five and a half months on *Mad World* I earned over $15,000, and had built my savings account to $7500. There was a piece of property in Sherman Oaks I had planned to purchase and build on, but those plans vanished when Mom said she had missed a payment on Dad's Mutual of Omaha medical insurance. Without a second thought, I paid my Dad's $5600 hospital bill in full. Years later, an insurance executive friend assured me there was a payment grace period and Mutual of Omaha would have paid the hospital costs. How very comforting to hear this – fifty years too late.

An addendum to *It's a Mad, Mad, Mad, Mad World*: It wasn't until the November 1963 film premiere at the New Cinerama Dome in Hollywood that I realized Harvey Parry had nailed me once again. In the film's opening sequence, he had wrangled his way in to double Rooney, driving the red Volkswagen convertible, a month before I came on the picture.

At that time in the stunt business, Cary Loftin, Dale Van Sickle and Parry were considered the "old guard" stunt drivers, for decades. Even John "Bear" Hudkins was an outsider when Kramer insisted that he double Jonathan Winters, driving the 5-ton moving van, demolish a gas station and swing from the taxi cab door. Bear's intrusion didn't set well with the "good ol' car boys." Parry, et al, resented a "cowboy" entering their long held turf. Rooney's stand-in, Sig Froelich, later admitted he knew about Parry's driving for Rooney, "I figured there was enough work for you, later." I guess he also figured it was enough when he pried his way in as Rooney's double during the taxi cab car chase. Yep, another guy playing God, making decisions that affected my livelihood and my wallet. It would appear that only Bill Gates is immune from such intrusions.

Again, I admit being star struck, and meeting the stars I had watched all my life was overwhelming. Chatting with Ethel Merman was a wonderful experience, but I still can't picture her marriage to Ernest Borgnine, a tempestuous union that lasted a mere month. Then again, Ernie's marriage to actress Katy Jurado (or as she was often called "Karate Judo") didn't fare much longer and are both textbook cases of strong personalities clashing.

I completed *Mad World* filming on December 5, 1962, and at four-thirty the next morning was on my way to Lake Arrowhead, California, for Columbia's *13 Frightened Girls*. How wonderful it was: finish one film and go on to another without missing a day, performing the job you love. Like Confucius said, "Find a job you love and you'll never have to work a day of your life." There is no greater feeling.

Again, I was doubling another young lady, 16-year-old actress Kathy Dunn, who had recently completed an extensive Broadway run in *The Sound of Music*. She had grown up in the production, eventually portraying all the girl roles from the youngest to the oldest Von Trapp daughters.

13 Frightened Girls was another brainchild of showman, producer, director William Castle. His casting of young teenage beauties from around the world stimulated the juices of every male crew and cast member, prompting character actor Charlie Briggs to remark, "Jesse's the only broad over twenty-one and he's in drag."

Doubling Kathy driving the school bus became troublesome. The suspension was shot, chunks of rubber were missing from the tires, plus the engine blew a manifold gasket on the drive from Hollywood. A local mechanic did an overnight patch job, but I still couldn't get the speedometer over 40 mph going downhill. Columbia's second unit director Lawrence Butler belligerently demanded I drive on the Rim of the World Highway's shoulder, with a 2000-foot drop only three feet away, to create a cloud of dust. I refused, detailing the suspension, broken shocks and the potential endangerment of six extra passengers,. He ignored my efforts to explain the vehicle's problems, including my suggestion to drag chains through Fuller's Earth, then became confrontational, "If you can't drive this bus, we'll get someone else." "Be my guest," I countered. It was a stare down and we did it my way.

Returning from the Arrowhead location, the Christmas holidays loomed and the family problems seemed insurmountable. I found solace at *The Playboy*, Troy Melton's newly purchased restaurant and bar, located fifty yards from Paramount Picture's main gate.

My total earnings of $20,000 weren't bad for a twenty-one year old in 1962. A fantastic year financially, all right, but a year that would turn my life around in ways I could never have imagined.

CHAPTER 5

1963

My Dad's incapacitating stroke in November 1962 necessitated a new life direction for me—moving Dad, Mom, a sister and myself into a large, three-bedroom Sherman Oaks apartment for $190 a month in January 1963. Troubled situations bring about moves we wouldn't make otherwise, and I soon found this was not a good idea. Daily, I was reminded of my Dad's frail condition, his instability to walk and inability to talk. My thoughts spanned the three years since my parents had moved from the spacious, luxurious, 2600 sq. ft., six-bedroom Los Angeles-Wilshire District home they had purchased in 1940 for $10,000, and sold for $20,000 in 1960 [*Recently listed for over $1.2 Million*] to a crowded Sherman Oaks apartment in the San Fernando Valley. At 58 years old Mom re-entered the work force after 25 years. Everything seemed turned around, my efforts to "make everything like it used to be" wasn't working, validating Thomas Wolfe's dictum that, "You can't go home again."

Two months had passed since the completion of *Mad World* and *13 Frightened Girls*. Stunt work became nonexistent. Bill Hart phoned me again for *Stoney Burke*, but called back later to say the stunt had been "written out." MGM's Warren Mace called me to meet veteran director George Sidney on *A Ticklish Affair* to play a Jeep driving navy sailor—the part was mine, but I never heard from them. What was happening?

Self-doubt began to set in. Didn't I prove myself on *Mad World*? I performed every stunt as asked on one of the greatest comedy-action films ever produced, and now I couldn't buy a job. This situation was out of control and I didn't know how to cope with it. Friends said this dilemma often affected every performer at one time or another. Maybe so, but it was no consolation to the emotional and financial strain it produced, as I subsisted on my $65 a week unemployment insurance check.

After my misguided attempt to keep the family together, I scrounged up enough funds to have my own apartment again in Studio City, even if I was starting over from scratch. For many single adults in the 1960s the local bar became a second home. Much like the pubs in Ireland and England, it was a local hangout for camaraderie, laughs and, possibly, a stunt job. I was still hopeful.

It was now June, and I had not worked in seven months—half the year was gone. Then, one day upon entering the Starlite Room I saw her. Toni Evans was five-foot-nine, a statuesque blue-eyed blond, and one of the most exquisite visions of feminine class and beauty I had ever seen. A former I. Magnin fashion model from San Francisco (she had modeled with Laurel Goodwin), she was a gorgeous combination of Doris Day and Marilyn Monroe. We conversed only minutes before embracing in passionate kisses, oblivious of all others around us.

A five-generation Californian, with a 160 IQ, Toni had attended boarding school in Zurich, Switzerland. Her father was a former military advisor to Chiang Kai-Shek, and her mother was the first female sales agent with Coldwell Banker Real Estate in San Francisco. I found Toni's combination of intelligence and beauty delectable. She was 23, and I was 21. This was like every romantic movie I had ever seen. She was my Soul Mate, my True Love—the one love you hoped to meet someday, as you both walk off into the sunset.

Our first movie date was *Dr. No*, starring Sean Connery, the first James Bond film, and the second feature was *The Days of Wine and Roses*, which Toni aptly renamed *The Days of Wine and Cirrhosis*. Toni and I were inseparable. It all seemed so natural, as if it was meant to be.

Toni had come to the Valley to visit her aunt who lived in the lavish James Garner-owned apartments at Moorpark & Fulton. In the late

1970s I would reside there in one of the best rental units I have ever live in.

The calendar flipped to July and I was pleasantly shocked when a rush call came from California Studios (now Raleigh Studios) to work on American International Pictures' *Comedy of Terrors*, starring Vincent Price and Peter Lorre. Dashing from wardrobe, dressed in an 1830's English Tuxedo, I was immediately taken to makeup, where I was powdered down to a dead man's pallor—just as a corpse should look. Vincent Price was a charming gentleman and introduced me to his cast partner, Peter Lorre, best remembered as Ugarte in *Casablanca*.

This pseudo-mystery/comedy had Price and Lorre excavating graves to steal valuable caskets from foggy London cemeteries. The film's opening credits played over the scene as stuntmen Tom Steele and Harvey Parry, doubling Price and Lorre, respectively, dumped me into a five-foot deep hole dug into the studio floor. (Many sound stages have false floors to allow sets with downward stairways, fireman poles, tanks, etc. to be constructed.)

Veteran film director Jacques Tourneur, a gentle man approaching sixty, explained how he wanted me to lie in the casket with my arms folded across my chest. On action, Tom and Harvey tilted the casket and I rolled out, and as Jacques instructed, the guys began shoveling dirt into the hole. The soil began to pile up, when I heard Jacques demand, "More dirt! MORE DIRT!" With hands cupped over my face, between each shovel full I'd flip away the layered soil, take a deep breath and cover up again. This went on until Jacques yelled, "Cut!" I crawled to my right, causing a foot of soil to fall aside. Reaching upward, someone pulled me from the hole. My face had sweated and appeared like I'd had a mud facial. Jacques hugged me, looking rather embarrassed, "I forgot you were down there until he reminded me," pointing to his assistant director, Bob Agnew. We all had a good laugh.

Later, as Tom, Harvey and I changed out of wardrobe, Harvey related that Wally Rose had worked the previous day, also playing a coffin corpse—as he was being dumped his left hand gripped the edge of the coffin. Veteran director of photography Floyd Crosby saw his movement and called "Cut!" Rose ranted and raved, declaring he'd been in the business over thirty years and he would never have done that. You don't argue with the chief camera guy and Rose did another take. Fact: If Rose had kept his arms folded across his chest as directed he wouldn't have been able to grip the edge.

The previous twelve months constantly rolled through my mind. After *"Mad World"* I had traded in an immaculate 1956 Cadillac Coupe de Ville for a new 1962 Mercury Custom Monterey convertible and had had a comfortable saving account. Now, I was subsisting on $65 week unemployment insurance, driving a 1948 Buick and wondering if I would ever get another stunt job.

My True Love decided we were meant to be together and had discreetly asked a friend of mine, Dick Jachim, if he would "Loan Jesse $350, so we can runaway to Reno to get married." He gladly agreed, but I declined—my reaction was "Just great! What a way to start a marriage!" That was another *biggest mistake* I would make.

The *Arrest & Trial* TV series provided my second day of work for the year on July 23, doubling kid actor Michael McGreevy at Universal. The following week I did a fight with veteran stunt man Bill Catching on *The American Adventure* and met actor James Hampton, best known as the bugler on TV's F Troop. He's one of the nice guys and his long career has encompassed many facets including directing.

Though Toni continued to entice me to Reno, I still believed our marriage was out of the question until my finances stabilized. Finally, the mother-daughter/love-hate relationship peaked and, at her mother's insistence, Toni married a former millionaire suitor at St. Francis de Sales Catholic Church in Sherman Oaks on August 3, 1963. Standing across the street, I watched, duplicating James Dean's jilted lover stance, just as he had done when actress Pier Angeli married singer Vic Damone in 1954 in Hollywood.

Returning to the Starlite Room I tearfully proceeded to consume a grand total of eleven Stingers, a potent concoction of brandy and white crème de minte, while Doris Day's *"I'll Never Stop Loving You"* played over and over on the jukebox. None of the patrons complained. Thankfully, a buddy had disconnected my car's distributor wires and I slept it off in the Buick's spacious back seat.

Years later, my buddy John Steinriede remarked, "Toni must have loved you. Well, she obviously wasn't marrying you for your money." I must admit that it never occurred to me. All I wanted to be was a good provider as was my Dad.

Flashing ahead to November 7, I accepted a call to double Tony Mordente on *The Outer Limits* TV series, "The Invisibles" episode. The other lead actor was Richard Dawson, best known from *Hogan's Heroes* and the *Family Feud* game show. (Given Dawson's predilection to kiss each lady contestant on the lips, I always believed the Feud's final question should have been: How many cases of trench mouth has Richard Dawson contracted?)

The sci-fi story had Mordente's character being attacked by an eighteen-inch-long mutated bug. Prop man Dick Rubin, whom I had worked with on several AIP films, attached the hairy creature to my back, and helped set the cardboard boxes for my high fall from the warehouse roof. Veteran cinematographer Conrad Hall, seated high on the Chapman Crane, asked where I would land. I carefully explained my planned moves to him. The camera rolled and director Gerd Oswald called "Action!" I scurried up the building's vertical ladder to the top rung, and then as if the creature finally sank its poisonous fangs, I let go and toppled twenty-five feet backward, crashing to the boxes and onto the pavement. It worked as planned and I remained in my final position as the script supervisor made notes to match Mordente for his close up.

The crew applauded, as assistant director Jack Voglin rushed in to ask if I was okay. Assuring him there wasn't a scratch, I glanced at Dawson shaking his head with an expression, "This guy is nuts." Not really. I knew exactly what I was going to do and planned the gag to the nth degree. I have always hated it when a stunt is "telegraphed." You often see the stunt player turn and look toward the fall pads or "catcher." When I started up the ladder, I mentally locked-on to where my catcher was located. With that firmly envisioned, my next move was to reach the ladder's high point, then fall directly backward, confidently knowing exactly where the boxes and pads lay. The trick was not to push off, but do a dead man's fall. No peeking. It was another gratifying day, when you do something someone else wouldn't or couldn't do. How exhilarating.

The day after *Outer Limits* I met stunt coordinator Paul Baxley to double a twelve-year-old Kurt Russell on *The Adventures of Jamie McPheeters* TV series at MGM. Traveling to Twentieth Century-Fox's movie ranch in Malibu Canyon, the stunt called for Kurt to escape from the bad guys by swinging hand-over-hand like on a children's monkey bar beneath an old suspension bridge. When director Jack Arnold looked me over from head to toe and exclaimed, "You're a lousy double for Kurt." I stared at him, "Well, maybe you should have called Billy Barty." With a scowl, he stomped off. What a way to start the day.

The time came for the shot as I lowered myself onto the two 3/4 inch steel cables strung beneath the length of the bridge. Lying prone, with my legs and arms straddling the cables, I waited for the shot. The a.d. asked me to hang down so camera could focus. Finally, I began my hand-over-hand jaunt along the cables, but when I reached the end of the cables, Arnold didn't cut the cameras. Hanging there, I started to pull myself up, but suddenly I had no strength remaining in my arms. What a helpless feeling. Looking down at the ten-foot row of mattress-topped 3x3x3 foot cardboard boxes, I shouted, "I'm coming down!" and plummeted thirty feet. I crashed through the boxes, landed on my left side. The landing felt like a Mack truck had hit me.

Baxley had set the mattresses over the boxes, but allowed a foot separation between the two long rows of stacked boxes. If he had placed them together, I wouldn't have gone through the gap to the ground. Initially, I was going to check the boxes, but figured, "Hell, a veteran stunt man set them up, what is there to worry about?" It seemed like a good idea at the time…

That weekend I stayed at my Mom's Sherman Oaks apartment. That night I could feel my muscles starting to tighten. By Saturday morning my entire body ached with pain. In the course of healing, my bruised left hip changed color from red to black and blue, to yellow, green and purple—commonly called "The Devil's Rainbow." Years later, I was informed this type of bruise is extremely dangerous, and often produces blood clots that cause heart attacks and strokes.

To top it off, Baxley called several times over the weekend, I thought to inquire about my condition, but his ploy was to reduce my stunt adjustment. His recalculation resulted in my receiving $165 less than the amount we agreed on the set. His actions verified what many other stunt men had called him – a liar and a cheat. However, the acorn fell far from the tree—his son, Craig, was an excellent stunt-man-turned-director and is one of the finest gentlemen you will ever meet.

A week later on November 15, I was summoned to the U.S. Army Induction Center in downtown Los Angeles. Helen Sasso, the only psychic ever to accurately predict anything to me, stated, "You will not have to go into the service." As much as I wanted to believe her, a bit of doubt lingered.

The joint was crowded with fellow inductees, including a guy I hadn't seen since the fifth grade at St. Brendan Catholic School. I couldn't recall his name, but I did remember his beautiful sister, Brigitte, her sparkling blue eyes and flowing blond hair, as if it were yesterday.

Anyway, we were all asked to fill out the necessary papers, including a questionnaire form. It became tedious as I checked off the thousand and one squares. Trouble sleeping? Do you drink alcohol? How much? The frequency? Trouble eating? I checked them all, which happened to be true. Then, it was pee in the bottle, bend over, spread your cheeks, turn your head and cough.

As a result of my questionnaire answers, I was told to "follow the yellow line" to the resident psychiatrist. Contemplating the ensuing interview, I ignored the fat, dressed in black creep, wearing rectangle, horned-rim glasses seated next to me. This sonofabitch carried a beige trench coat over his arm. Every couple of minutes he would flip it from one arm to the other, purposely causing it to fall across my knee, then, slowly pull it back.

The doctor thumbed through my file, then asked about my drinking, the amount, the duration, the last time. I would give my reply, and then stare at the floor. I described my father's condition, the family situation, and how the booze helped blot it out. Finally, he asked me point-blank, "You don't really want to be in the service, do you?" Looking into his eyes, I said, "Truthfully, no, sir, I don't." Again, I stared at the floor. He made a notation and handed me the file, "Mr. Wayne, follow the blue line to the Sergeant downstairs." Walking, I quickly peeked at what he had written, "He seems pre-occupied." That was all I could read before handing the file to the Sergeant, who eyeballed the page: "Mr. Wayne, you've been rejected." I was classified 1-Y. This meant I could be drafted only if Congress declared war *Officially.*

I quickly exited the aged South Broadway building, the U.S. Army's West Coast demarcation point without looking back – the site responsible for sending tens of thousands of young men to a war created by the old, power-hungry, money-grabbing bastards in Washington.

Don't misunderstand me, I was a Hawk about the Indo-China war from its inception and believed we should fight Communism to its final defeat—go in and win the war. But as "LBJ's War" progressed, many like me believed this was a no-win situation and began ignoring this tragic debacle as if it didn't exist.

My life has always been filled with ironic blips – when the Selective Service initiated its draft lottery based on birth dates, the first to pop up was September 14 – my birthday! Whew!

Work calls started coming in again. At Universal, I was told about Ward Bond, the wagon master on *Wagon Train*, when he invited his old friend director John Ford to helm a segment of the series. Ford, sitting in his director's chair anxiously waiting for the Director of Photography to finish lighting the set, slowly rose to his feet. Known for his impatience, Ford called a halt, demanding that all the lights be shut off. Pointing to each of three lamps, he said, "Light it!" Returning to his chair he said, "Roll the camera!" Mr. Ford got his shot.

Stunt man Carl Saxe adamantly advised me to "Stay away from horses. Look around, we've got the best horsemen in the world in this business and they're all busted up." He was right. Most of the cowboys limped, walked hunched over and cringed in pain.

However, doubling the kids on the many Westerns was very lucrative, usually involving saddle falls. Seldom was I ever asked to do hard riding over hill and dale. Most importantly, I stayed on the wrangler's good side, playing like I was just starting out. Invariably, they helped me every way they could, even down to attaching my "step" to the cinch strap "D" ring. To reiterate, the "step" is used in place of a stirrup. In a transfer to a wagon, a train or a saddle fall this small platform provided a stable base to push off from.

Always heed your first instincts. Listen to the still, small voice we all hear. It definitely applied when I first saw or, should say, heard, Richard Bartlett in the Starlight Room in 1962, imbibing with Paul Greene, comic Shecky Greene's brother and just as funny. Morry Taich, the most impressionable bartender ever, let it be known that this guy was a former motion picture producer-director. Playing the part to the hilt, Bartlett related his latest production deals at decibels loud enough for the folks in San Diego to hear. Right away I pegged this guy as a loud mouth, blow-hard.

As time progressed, I learned the real story of Richard Bartlett's exit as the fair-haired boy from Universal Studios. By 1959, when MCA—Music Corporation of America—the mega-talent agency, purchased the Universal Studios complex of 423 acres, Bartlett had directed several successful Universal-International features, and then segued to MCA's Revue Television Productions, where he directed every TV series in their camp. With a palatial home in Toluca Lake, money flowed like water, until he stepped on his proverbial dick by calling Lew Wasserman, MCA's chieftain, a "fucking kike." To paraphrase a script direction, Bartlett's next move was a Direct Cut to oblivion. More about him later.

The Stuntmen's Association monthly meeting once again discussed the admission of members. This hotly debated subject never pleased everyone, which explained the yearly By-Law changes for new members. To become a SAMP member an individual had to be sponsored by five SAMP members and have earned X amount of dollars performing stunts. Most SAMP members resented being hustled for sponsorship from guys they had never worked with or even met, though most relented when a stunt coordinator asked them to sponsor a buddy into the organization.

It seemed so obvious. I raised my hand: "The American Society of Cinematographers is Hollywood's oldest fraternal organization since 1919. You can't be born in to it or buy your way in. To become a member, a Blue Ribbon Panel observes up and coming cinematographers, and when they believe the time is appropriate, an ASC membership invitation is extended."

To me, this was a very simple and equitable answer for new SAMP members. The Chair then recognized Gil Perkins, who mockingly laughed, "Well, we're not cameramen." That ended the discussion. Mine was a valid, perfect solution to the present problem, but many wanted the doors left open so they could gain an easy admission for their buddies. The discussion was over.

Though SAMP had a logo, several members decided it didn't depict the stunt man in true grandeur. The search for a new logo began and was soon dubbed the Stuntmen's Patch of the Month club. SAMP co-founder, Loren Janes, designed a patch that appeared more suitable to the USA Armed Forces. Jerry Catron presented a multi-colored psyche-delic version that would have made any Haight-Ashbury hippie proud. Personally, I favored a more visual logo than the group's name surround-ing a silhouetted movie camera—something indicative of a stunt performer, instead of constantly being plagued by those requesting information on how to become a motion picture cameraman.

I contacted artist-production designer Ray Boyle, who formerly ap-peared on TV's *The Life and Legend of Wyatt Earp*, portraying Morgan Earp (as Dirk London), opposite Hugh O'Brian. Ray illustrated a colorful, poster-sized, rendering of a muscular, Oscar award-like-figure holding an "S" strip of film bearing the association's name. This very appropriate design was shot down at a general membership meeting and the camera logo remained. My mistake was not securing the support of certain Board members; the old stunt guard to support this new design to get it passed. Today, after 50 plus years, the original basic camera logo is still used.

In 1974, SAMP President Henry Wills asked Fred Carson to sketch a belt buckle design stressing the Association's "Safety First" motto. Fred's rendition was produced and, as usual, he never received a free belt buckle, much less a thank you.

CHAPTER 6

1964

Dolly Parton once said, "The bigger *they* are, the nicer *they* are," a truism I found to be an accurate evaluation when referring to the "senior" stars of Hollywood.

Though I had worked on James Stewart's *Mr. Hobbs Takes a Vacation*, we never met, but this day he was starring in Universal's *Rare Breed*. Seated in his director's chair studying his script, he casually looked up and smiled, "Good morning."

I have found actors to be some of the most brilliant people I have ever met and, also, some of the most ignorant. I don't mean stupid, just uninformed, virtually living in a vacuum.

In the late 1960's, I was appointed Sergeant at Arms for the Annual Screen Actors Guild General Membership meetings and, when the main agenda was completed, the floor microphones were opened to the general membership for their comments and questions.

Charlton Heston was the SAG President—I marveled at his astute concentration. Often, an agitated member would confront him with a convoluted, multi-part question. Without taking notes, Heston would listen intently, and then categorically address each point of the issues presented. Starting with the fourth point, he would move on to the first, then the sixth and so forth. We stood spellbound as he extemporaneously explained each and every point to the membership's satisfaction.

John Gavin replaced Heston as President and, he, too, performed in much the same manner. Obviously, it wasn't a coincidence years later, when President Ronald Reagan appointed Gavin as the United States Ambassador to Mexico. Gavin, being of Mexican heritage, spoke Spanish fluently.

For centuries, the general characterization of ego-driven, ne'er-do-well actors has been an open debate. A pundit theorized that the best actors were not too bright, "Consider Jill St. John, one of Hollywood's classic beauties with a 190 plus IQ, but I don't foresee her ever winning a Best Actress Oscar." He might be on to something.

I believe he used "not too bright" in the sense that actors are child-like, and not necessarily stupid. When a child is locked-on to something, they have only one thought in mind at that moment. They have no other distractions to break their concentration and, unlike the rest of us, they're not worrying about a troubled romance or any other mind-clogging garbage.

Alfred Hitchcock was once chastised for referring to actors as animals. His inimitable retort—"I did not say actors are animals. I said they should be treated like animals."

Stunt man Dick Geary was running MGM's *The Man from U.N.C.L.E.* TV series, doubling Robert Vaughn as Napoleon Solo, and wanted me to be the regular double for co-star David McCallum as Ilya Kuryakin. This evening's work entailed a fight with veteran stunt man Roy Sickner, doubling the arch villain of the week, actor Theo Marcuse. Roy was also the Marlboro Man; one of several rugged, handsome men to appear in that role during the course of the cigarette's advertising campaign.

However, a dilemma was brewing—McCallum's Beatle-like hairstyle tested the inept hairdresser's ability to match it to my mane. In desperation, she optioned a wig, and when she finished I looked like I had a blond mop on my head.

On the set, Roy and I rehearsed the involved fight that ended when I fired an umbrella rifle shot into his gut. Carefully, we plotted the correct camera angle so that when I fired, the umbrella barrel would be pointed slightly away from his mid-section.

The camera rolled and we performed the fight scene in one take. Again, working with a professional makes your job easy. Returning to my dressing room, a disappointed Dick Geary said I wouldn't be the permanent stunt double, quoting McCallum, "He doesn't look like me!" I had to agree. That wig was ridiculous, plus I was two inches shorter than McCallum. Most actors don't mind if their stunt double is taller, but shorter, that's usually a big no-no. Their egos won't allow it.

In this particular fight scene, McCallum's height difference was relative. Physically, I was a good double for him (barring the wig) because Roy was also shorter than the actor he was doubling. Photographically, our size difference wasn't discernible.

Case in point: On the screen Mickey Rooney's 5'2" height was undetectable from my 5'4" stature. However, another show biz truth is, if someone with enough power wants you on the job, you will be there.

Often, waiting to perform a stunt allowed ample time to people-watch, especially the extras. In the 1960s, several ladies had reputations for providing sexual favors to the assistant directors to get a call back the next day to earn $25. I theorized that if they were going this route, they should become Sunset Strip call girls and make $100 a pop, and eliminate background crosses for the next four days. Conversely, I suspect they would have offset my suggestion with "What? And leave show biz?"

My diminutive height and weight allowed me to shop in most boys clothing departments, specifically, Champion's in Studio City. While sifting through the merchandise one day, I looked up as Mary Tyler Moore and her young son, Richie, also shopped. MTM was radiantly beautiful and… Well, have you ever met a woman so attractive you were mesmerized? I wasn't alone: that's how she affected millions of other men through the years. MTM was the perfect female package of style, class and beauty.

The Paramount Pictures casting office called me to play the boyfriend to actress Lynn Borden, best known from the *Hazel* TV series, on Elvis Presley's *Roustabout*, starring Barbara Stanwick and Leif Erickson. Our scene took place in a college roadside hangout. Elvis appeared rather bored as he kidded and made self-effacing comments while he performed to the playback of his pre-recorded song. He had been through this sing-a-song bit many times before and, as we later found out, didn't much care for the music or the films ol' Colonel Tom Parker had set up for him.

During a break in the filming I mingled around the set. Elvis and his entourage, "The Memphis Mafia," joked and practiced their Karate moves. I was surprised when "The King" came over to introduce himself with a strong handshake. My blue eyes matched his, but mine drifted to his hair, which was a beautiful blue-black hue I'd never seen on anyone before. I tried not to stare. It was many years before I realized Elvis was a natural, sandy-haired blond like me.

One of his Memphis cohorts, Jim Kingsley, expressed his interest in stunt work. Jim was a trim, good-looking guy about 5'10" with an ingratiating smile. We discussed the stunt business, I assured him his Karate training was a great advantage and thought he could have a great future in stunt work.

A year later, Jim had officially entered the movie business, leaving the Memphis Mafia far behind, did well as an extra, stand-in and stunt double.

In 1974, on *Parallax View*, Jim hitched a ride on a stake bed truck back to the company's home base. Stunt man Paul Baxley was driving the vehicle, passed an alley telephone pole and scraped Jim off the side like a bug on a windshield. "Supposedly, Baxley didn't know I was on the truck," Jim said, "and he even visited me in the hospital." Hmmm, Baxley's concern sounded familiar.

From that time on, Jim said he awakened every morning in constant, unbearable pain, unable to go a day without his prescribed medication. In the mid-eighties he returned to Memphis, and found employment at an automotive camshaft company.

We shared a friendship spanning twenty-five years. Jim called to say he was getting married: "She loved the Jerry Lee Lewis band so I introduced her to the group." We continued discussing his new fiancée, when he blurted, "I'll kill her if I catch her cheating on me." Stunned, I suggested that if he had any doubts, maybe he should reconsider taking the plunge, but Jim didn't relent and I wished him well. Three weeks later I received a call that Jim Kingsley was dead.

Without warning, his bride of three days declared she was leaving on tour with the Jerry Lee Lewis band. Returning a week later, she proposed a plan to quick deed her house to Jim, with the stipulation that he care for her two teenage children.

Jim's suggestion of a romantic interlude caused her to barricade herself at a neighbor's home. Jim pounded on the door and she screamed the sheriff's office had been called. Jim returned home, placed a .410 caliber Derringer pistol in his mouth and pulled the trigger. The autopsy revealed his system was free of drugs and alcohol. Before his burial arrangements were finalized, she began selling his possessions and then didn't even attend Jim's funeral.

Hollywood's early seventies drug invasion took a mighty toll on all who succumbed to it. Not until the 1980s did the Los Angeles County Sheriff's Drug Detail begin an investigation of drug use in the Film Industry. Motion Picture Producers Association spokesman Jack Valenti vehemently denied any drug use had occurred at any level, but that's exactly what this former LBJ White House puppet was paid to say via his life-long contract with the MPPA.

Valenti was also instrumental in creating the film industry's movie rating system in 1968, which has allowed the producer to exhibit anything on the screen as long as it has an alphabetic letter and/or number attached.

Everyone in Hollywood's mainstream was well aware of the rampant use of drugs ranging from the crew to the heads of production. At parties, recreational drug use was viewed as the "in thing," often with overflowing bowls of cocaine—resembling mounds of sugar—for all to partake. If you didn't indulge, you were not part of the gang. If you were not part of the gang, then you would not be on the next production with those who did partake. Paul Nuckles admitted that I wasn't hired on his films because "It would make the others uneasy."

Years before, I had made my opinion on drugs clear to Nuckles while we enjoyed musician/actor Bobby Troup at the China Trader in Toluca Lake. While vigorously shaking hands with a guy I saw Nuckles "palm" something; and then quickly exit. Returning a few minutes later, he was glassy-eyed and unsteady on his feet. Confronting him, he admitted the guy had passed him a "joint." Flat out, I told him to never come near me with any drugs, any time or any place.

Any stunt has its own inherent problems, but adding drugs or any other mind-altering intoxicants is disastrous. Legendary tales flourish of early-day stunt men carrying a bottle of booze in their stunt bag, but that was nothing compared to the indiscriminate drug use in the 1970s and 80s Hollywood. It was common knowledge that several top stunt coordinators procured drugs for their producers, directors, actors and crew. I guess that's called job security.

A pretty Canadian model I dated in 1971 moonlighted as a waitress at Donte's in North Hollywood. She mentioned a stunt guy who supplied drugs to the jazz club's musicians, and had just purchased a new Cadillac and an apartment house. Who says crime doesn't pay?

Most tragic is that since 1970, more stunt people have been injured, maimed or killed than in the previous seventy years of moviemaking. Only God knows how many of these incidents were drug-related.

Some will argue that today's stunts are more difficult and dangerous. Aside from the basic "hit the ground," crash and burn gags, little has changed. Today's special riggings, computer-calculated stunts, in conjunction with Computer Generated Graphics (CGI), have eliminated the death defying elements—performers are safer. Many individuals performing simple car stunts are so padded they resemble the Michelin Man, and those fighting hand and feet are gymnasts jumping, flipping and spinning while suspended by wires, which are later computer erased from the film image. This may irk a few, but dare I say the majority of the stunt performers today couldn't handle the action of an average Western film, where hitting the hard ground is required.

Often, the simplest stunt can be the most catastrophic, simply because you tend to lower your guard and take things for granted.

Bell Ranch was located in the Santa Susana Pass, not far from the Spahn Ranch, made infamous by the Charles Manson gang. On this day we were filming the *Marcus Welby, MD* TV series, or as it was affectionately called *Mucus Welby*. Bill Catching, doubling James Brolin, and I stood under a shady oak tree waiting for action. Veteran television director Marc Daniels had set up a motorcycle run-by shot through the beautiful shade trees along a winding dirt road.

Brolin pleaded with Marc to do the ride himself. Bill and I watched as Brolin maneuvered the heavy "street bike" along the road and looked at each other knowingly. The camera rolled as Brolin cranked up the bike's speed. He made it. Marc wanted another take and on came Brolin again, but this time he cut across the corner of the turn. I remarked to Bill, "He's scaring me," and suddenly the motorcycle went down, landing on Brolin's leg. Jim Rawlins, the on-set medic, stabilized the leg fracture with a blowup splint and Brolin was rushed to the Northridge Hospital.

Several years later, on the *Vega$* TV series, Marc Daniels expressed his regrets, continued to blame himself for letting Brolin do the run that day. I reminded him how difficult it is when dealing with actors and their enormous egos: "If Brolin had stayed on the road instead of cutting that corner, the accident wouldn't have happened." Marc nodded, but I could see he was still convinced the accident was his fault.

Gene Law was a TV producer and director for the CBS network on *Where the Action Is* with Dick Clark and *On the Go* with Jack Linkletter. By the mid-sixties, Gene had moved from live and tape production to film as an assistant director and production manager at Universal. We worked many of the Jack Webb TV shows and became best friends. The last Monday of April and October the Scandia Restaurant's Vikings Club on the Sunset Strip held their blood bank drive. It was quite *the* bi-yearly event where 300-400 pints of blood would be donated by a Who's Who of Hollywood and Sports celebrities.

In the early seventies, the donated blood was credited to Notre Dame's football coach Frank Leahy, who subsequently died of leukemia. Gene and I, along with our mutual good friend, CBS's Ken McManus, always made it a point to attend, especially to watch the Navy sailors bused in from San Diego. Some passed out at the sight of a needle and others hyperventilated into brown paper bags. When Gene and I raced to see who could fill the plastic blood bags first, they dropped like flies. To this date I have given over ten gallons.

Scandia donated chits for drinks and the most magnificent food buffet befitting the Mobil Five Star restaurant and thoroughly deserved each sparkling star. When Ken Hansen, Scandia's driving force died, magazine publishing mogul Robert Petersen attempted to pick up the reins. Unfortunately, he couldn't and this fine epicurean establishment disappeared forever.

Ken McManus and I first met in 1961 at the Naples Restaurant at Gower and Sunset, across from Columbia Pictures and KCBS-TV (formerly KNXT) in Hollywood and it was camaraderie at first sight. Ken started at CBS Radio after World War II and rose through the ranks from page, stage manager and TV director to a production executive of the CBS-TV network.

Ken offered me a job at CBS Television City, but the bitter taste of what transpired at KTLA still lingered and I declined. Looking back, CBS was known for promoting from within, so possibly it would have been a prudent path to a network TV camera operator position.

MGM called me to double Robert Morse for a *Quick, Before It Melts*. A peek at the coat label from the gray flannel suit read, "Mickey Rooney, Words & Music, 1948." It was like new and fit me like a glove.

Later, rehearsing the fight scene, along with Patty Elder, Stephanie Epper, Tom Steele, Dick Crockett and a few others, Patty whispered that she and Stephanie were going to pants me during the fight. Evidently, my eager response of "Okay," dashed away their thrill. But during the melee, I caught a glimpse of Crockett as he grabbed a white-haired, middle-aged extra and violently threw him over a table. Later, I heard Crockett hated extras and would go out of his way to hurt them. What bullshit! In large fight scenes, extras worked the background, providing moving bodies to the choreographed foreground stunt action. Crockett's deliberate intention to injure a physically unequipped individual only trying to make a buck is outrageous and beyond my comprehension.

Crockett wasn't alone when it came to causing injuries. On Westerns, the new guy had to contend with loosened cinches, frayed bridles or your saddle tied off to a hitching post when the posse made a quick exit.

Stunt coordinator Reg Parton called me for *Young Fury*, starring Rory Calhoun, Virginia Mayo, Richard Arlen, John Agar and William Bendix. Producer A.C. Lyles was a long-time 1930s Paramount Pictures employee, having started in the mailroom. During that time, Richard

Arlen, star of *Wings* (winner of the first Best Picture Oscar), befriended him and Lyles promised that when he became a producer, Arlen would appear in every Lyles film. A.C. Lyles kept his promise.

Under director Chris Nyby's control we assembled for the first shot, when word leaked that production was a having problem with the leading lady, Betty Hutton. A major Paramount film star in the forties and fifties, Miss Hutton evidently believed nothing had changed in Hollywood. A.C. Lyles deemed her demands were unreasonable and her replacement, Virginia Mayo, was in wardrobe and on the set two hours later.

Again, it was a thrill to meet and work with the stars I'd seen on the screen since I was a child. William Bendix, whom I'd enjoyed in films and on TV's *Life of Riley*, played the blacksmith and was the consummate professional.

Fun times flourished as a young New York actor, initially standing with his horse, would turn to find the reins in his hand were attached to an empty bridle lying in the dirt.

High jinx continued on the set as I stood conversing with stunt man Eddie Hice, s legs outstretched, seated on the boardwalk, with his back against the building, Jerry Summers snuck up behind me and fired a full load 5-in-1 blank into the boardwalk. Eddie, who must have had the strongest ass muscles, and I were suddenly eye-to-eye. He was petrified. This was an ongoing fast draw club prank and I didn't flinch, but I'll bet Eddie had to change his drawers.

Rodd Redwing, a Cherokee/Chickasaw American Indian, was constantly irritated (pissed was more like it) that most Indian film roles went to Italian, Greek and Latino actors. He especially disliked Iron Eyes Cody, famous for the Indian shedding a tear poster, who was actually Espera DeCorti, the son of Italian immigrants. I was a pallbearer at Rodd's 1971 funeral, and watched his casket for any movement as Iron Eyes gave the eulogy.

A call from casting director Dick Ivy at Walt Disney always put a smile on my face; it meant I was going to work at the friendliness studio in town. Early one morning, with my stunt bag in hand, heading to wardrobe, I heard a voice say, "Good morning." It was Walt Disney in his

1965 blue and white 280SL Mercedes. It was well known he disliked being called "Mr. Disney," so my response was "Hi Walt."

On Walt's insistence, the studio commissary operated at a $1200 a month deficit, serving the finest food for the least cost to Disney employees. Unlike other studios, beer was available and you could have as many as you wanted. However, if you got drunk, you were fired. No one ever got fired.

One of the most talented actors, gentle, intelligent and just plain nice was Karl Malden. We met on Disney's *The Adventures of Bullwhip Griffin*, as I stunt doubled child actor Bryan Russell. Karl played a con man during California's 1849 Gold Rush and was a man in complete control. He not only knew his lines, but everyone else's. During our many conversations between scenes, it was clear Karl walked like he talked, believing you should treat "the acting job" as you would a nine-to-fiver, without the Hollywood ego. As for 12 year-old Bryan Russell, he never missed a beat, never flubbed a line.

Working on an adjacent sound stage was dance choreographer Patty Van Patten, wife of actor Dick Van Patten, rehearsing a dance hall scene with ten beautiful and talented dancers. In Hollywood, as on Broadway, the dancer is often the most underrated and underpaid person on a production considering their great contribution. I watched as the enthusiastic ladies performed the dance routine with grace and perfection. Somehow, something was amiss—it was their dance hall outfits. Their "period" costumes appeared cheap and tawdry, hardly depicting the California Gold Rush of 1849. The outfits were cut high on the hips, comparable to the 1990s "French-cut" bathing suits, much too revealing for a Disney family film. Moments later, Walt Disney, surrounded by an entourage of production executives, entered the sound stage to watch the dance rehearsal. A furrowed brow denoted Walt's discontent and when the dance ended his only comment was, "Change the costumes." An hour later the girls returned in different outfits, all colorful and quite befitting the Gold Rush era.

Veteran British actor Tony Hancock was hired to play the other faction in this "Who's got the gold?" yarn. Evidently, in addition to being a fine actor, he was also quite adept at imbibing alcohol. Late one morning, two weeks into the filming of the 50-day shooting schedule, he suddenly fell to the floor, flopping around like a fish out of water, moaning like a sea cow. Bryan Russell was hustled from the set as several grips attempted to control Hancock's jerking body. Taken across the street to St. Joseph Hospital, we later heard he had suffered the D.T.'s—Delirium Tremens. Director James Neilsen remarked that Tony Hancock was the only actor he had ever worked with who consumed a quart of Scotch daily, by noon.

Filming resumed the next morning with actor Richard Haydn replacing Tony Hancock. Too bad—even though Haydn was a very competent veteran actor, Hancock's characterization seemed better fitted to this script's requirements. It called for a Robert Newton-esque "Arrr, Matey" portrayal—a vast contrast to the light, effete interpretation Haydn projected.

Sound Stage 3 was Disney's huge water stage, but Tinseltown's most famous tank was MGM's Stage 30 for the Esther Williams films. Disney's art department had designed a magnificent "side" of a riverboat, seventy feet long, built over the nine-foot deep underwater tank. What a beautiful set. Then again, why wouldn't it be? This was Walt Disney Studios.

I had previously met the assistant director, John Chulay, while visiting *The Dick Van Dyke Show*, and assured him that he'd get his shot even though "I can't swim." I was a swimmer, but my ploy was to have a scuba safety diver underwater just in case there was a problem with the wardrobe I was wearing—sensing the heavy wool shirt and wool pants would absorb water, and the stovepipe boots would fill up like an oak bucket and I'd sink like a rock.

Director Neilsen called "Action." Working with Karl Malden was a thrill as we struggled in a tug-of-war for the gold-filled money belt on the paddle wheeler's upper deck. Karl loses his grip and I was propelled backward into the river's raging, churning waters, twenty-five feet below.

The "churning" was provided by large paddles, courtesy of the Special Effects Department. Falling from the paddle wheeler deck, I surfaced quickly and, though the weight of the wet ward-robe was heavy, I swam in my best Johnny Weissmuller strokes and leaped up on to the tank's coping. Former stunt man Gene Coogan was the first to greet me with "What the fuck do you mean, you can't swim?" Smiling, "I guess I got lucky?" Later, I explained my strategy to him and he loved it, agreeing that you can't be too prepared. Gene, in his heyday, was one of the best water men in the biz (he doubled Franchot Tone in *Mutiny on the Bounty* back in 1935, diving from a 90' ship's mast), and when I asked him how he learned to swim, he said it was easy. At age eight, his dad threw him into New York City's East River.

Between takes, I got to know former major League baseball umpire Art Passarella, Karl Malden's long-time stand-in. Art always had me laughing. His Italian, New York-<u>ese</u> dialogue and stories were classic, explaining the screaming matches that sporadically occur between a baseball manager and the umpire. From the grandstand, with these guys nose-to-nose, the public only receives a silent picture of the yelling, screaming and physical body movements. But on the field, the manager bellowed, "Oh yeah, well, what fucking restaurant do you want to go to tonight? Art would then scream, "I wanna go to Toot Shor's." The manager, now waving his hands and shaking his head negatively, "That's fucking okay with me. I'll be there at eight." "You're damned right you will! And you're buying!" screamed Art. That settled, the manager returned to the dugout and the game continued. "It was a big show for the audience when the game got boring," said Art. That was their trick back in the forties and fifties. I wonder if the baseball participants today continue to operate this way.

After completing *Bullwhip Griffin*, I moved to the *Mickey!* TV series at MGM. Emiline Henry and Sammee Tong co-starred with Rooney in the Bob Fisher/Arthur Marks production. My first day's initial impression upon entering Stage 17 was the chaos. Director Richard Whorf did as much as he could with the actors, but Fisher and Marks constantly intervened. Whenever Dick told me what he wanted, this producer team would corner me to impart their interpretation of the scene, countermanding everything Whorf had told me.

From Day One, I knew the series premise was a losing proposition. The Fisher/Marks concept had Rooney inheriting a luxurious beachfront motel, acquiring Sammee in the process. Sammee Tong was best remembered from the *Bachelor Father* TV series, with John Forsythe and Noreen Corcoran, with Tong playing a wise, Chinese houseman. Conversely, Fisher and Marks had Sammee characterized as a conniving shyster, constantly attempting to extort the motel property from Rooney.

Greeting Rooney one day, "Morning Mick, how's it going?" He declared, "It's all bullsh:t!" "What?" I said. "Everything! It's all Bullshit!" Yeah, somehow, I couldn't argue the point.

One episode featured Mick's nightclub partner, singer-dancer, Bobby Van, guest starring in a slapstick gas station routine. The car hoist went up; Rooney opens the door—I fell out. In another shtick, Bobby squirts oil in Mickey's face. Chocolate syrup replaced the oil and shot right up Rooney's nose. All hell broke loose as Mick screamed, "It's burning! It's burning!"

TV audiences didn't buy it and the show was canceled after 13 episodes.

You may remember Dick Whorf from the Warner Brother's classic film, *Yankee Doodle Dandy*, portraying Broadway producer-partner Sam Harris to James Cagney's George M. Cohan. Dick was a delightful man, and later directed *The Tammy Grimes Show*, only to endure a multitude of problems with his female lead. He succumbed to cancer soon after.

Sammee Tong was a quiet, gentle man. We became friends and he often confided that his son, living in Hawaii, and his daughter, married to a wealthy Hong Kong banker, never called him unless they wanted something. Common to the Oriental yen for gambling, Sammee did more than his share. Whether it was his gambling, his loneliness or the lack of work after this show, Sammy consumed a bottle of sleeping pills.

My old buddy, Paul Greene, Shecky Greene's equally zany brother, lived in Sammee's apartment complex, and we attended the funeral together. The quaint church in L.A.'s Chinatown was filled to capacity as John Forsythe eulogized his dear friend. The service ended as Sammee's daughter and son were ushered past the casket. Suddenly, the daughter put a bear hug on the casket, screaming "Daddy! Daddy!" I silently wondered, "Where were you when Sammee needed you?" The scene was almost comical, like a Roadrunner cartoon, as the attendants tugged and pulled at her torso to free her death grip. Paul and I followed the procession past the open casket, but I refused to look, preferring to remember Sammee as when I last worked with him.

At the church exit we were each given a piece of hard candy in cello-phane and a nickel, both wrapped in a Chinese written note. I looked at Paul. "Damn, this won't even cover the gas to get here!" Paul roared, "Sammee would have laughed at that one."

Hanging out at the Starlite Room this particular Saturday night, Ed Drumhiller, Arvin Parachute Company's ace tester with 849 jumps, invited me to skydive on Sunday. "No way, I'm not going to break my leg," but Jay chimed in, "Hey, I'll go." Monday evening, Ed entered, trailed by Jack Fegan, Tim McDonald and Jay, precariously struggling with his crutches, sporting a cast from his ankle to his hip to support his broken leg. I just shook my head, recalling my "no free stunts" theory. Years later, when I asked Ed why he didn't round off his jumps to 850, he just shook his head, refusing to discuss the subject.

Over the years, I had seen other stunt men become weekend warriors with many resulting serious injuries. Invariably, soon after the injury occurred, they received a work call for eight weeks on location.

Another Starlite Room regular was Colonel Gregory "Pappy" Boyington, World War II U.S. Marine Corps, Black Sheep Squadron, flying ace with 22 hits. Continuing his heavy, life-long, imbibing, he would often lean close, "Do you wanna feel my muscle?" Thankfully, he was pointing to his right bicep. Regularly, I'd laugh when his raging wife would storm through the swinging bar doors and cuss out the bartender "for getting my husband drunk."

Always running, one day I darted across Ventura & Laurel Canyon in Studio City easily, but narrowly avoiding several oncoming cars as an LAPD black & white greeted me with a jay-walking ticket. I noticed the officer had listed my speed as 5mph. Calmly, I said, "Officer, this is BS, I was doing at least 15!" He and his partner laughed and drove away. I gave the ticket to a Judge buddy who "took care of it."

Of all the dominant studio bosses, Columbia Pictures' Harry Cohn was undeniably the most despised and feared. When his elaborate sound-stage funeral service overflowed, Red Skelton quipped, "It just proves that old show biz axiom, 'Give the audience what it wants and they'll flock to see it.'"

CHAPTER 7

1965

Davy Sharpe was coordinating a segment of *Bob Hope Presents the Chrysler Theater*, starring Lucille Ball, Rhonda Fleming, Jill St. John and Aldo Ray. The Western saloon fight had me leaping onto Paul Stader's back. I waited for him to give me the impetus to be flipped forward over the bar. But for whatever reason, Stader began to sway side-to-side, when suddenly I felt a pair of hands grab my shirt collar and belt. Instantly, I was airborne, flying across the set into tables and chairs. I heard "Cut, Print!" and looked quizzically across the room to a grinning Roy Jenson, who said in his raspy voice, "Ya looked too static." Thank God he tossed me. It was a fun trip, I just hit and rolled, but had no idea what Stader was trying to do.

Roy Jenson would later display his fine acting talents co-starring in a bevy of films including *North to Alaska, Telefon, Chinatown, The Way We Were and Paint Your Wagon*.

A big thrill was meeting the still-ravishing Linda Darnell in Studio City's Food Giant market. Months later she would tragically perish in a Chicago fire on April 10, 1965, at age 42.

On The Three Stooges' *The Outlaws Is Coming* we were filming a two-wagon chase at the Janss Movie Ranch in Thousand Oaks. Bobby Rose was doubling Larry, Duke Fishman doubled Curly Joe and I wore a Moe, tunnel-vision mask, zippered up the back—definitely not for the claustrophobic. Tap Canutt, Yak's oldest son, doubling Adam West, had the two-up team in a full gallop as the pursuing armored war wagon neared with its cannon blasting. Our wagon wheels were blown off, and we were sliding on the special effects-rigged skids. I felt the wagon lift slightly as we careened through a sweeping turn, and figured "Naw, it won't flip," but it did, spilling us onto the hillside.

The thundering hoofs war wagon's team pounded in my ears as a limp body pinned me into the plowed meadow. I hoped the war wagon wouldn't run us over. I then heard stunt gal Linda Carroll, who was doubling Nancy Kovak, screaming, "Jesse! Jesse!" She couldn't see my face, cradled my masked head in her lap, "Jesse, are you okay? I didn't feel injured, but I didn't want to know if I was, "I think so…" as Linda unzipped my mask. An un-conscious Bobby Rose was pulled off me, and revived. He had struck his head on a wagon strut—Moments later Fishman and I declared we were fine.

Director Norman Maurer (Moe's son-in-law) looked puzzled about the accident, but readily agreed when I suggested we use the wagon spill film as part of the chase and the pie fight continued.

Back on the Columbia Ranch Western Street in Burbank, Moe signed autographs for several visiting youngsters about eight, "There ya go, son." Turning to me, he whispered with a wicked twinkle in his eyes, "And you know what kind of a son he is." I laughed out loud. That was the first time I had ever seen Moe's gleaming smile. Unfortunately, *The Outlaws Is Coming* would be The Three Stooges' final film.

A part of Hollywood history is the Warner Brother's S.N.A.F.U. (World War II jargon for *Situation Normal, All Fucked Up*) when Jack Warner cast Audrey Hepburn in *My Fair Lady*, instead of Broadway's original Liza Doolittle, Julie Andrews. The reason: screen veteran Hepburn was a bigger box office name.

All was not lost as Walt Disney chose Andrews to play the lead in *Mary Poppins*, which led to a Best Actress of 1964 Oscar and Julie's grateful acceptance speech: "I want to thank the man most responsible for this award… Jack Warner!" Her comment brought the house down. Incidentally, *My Fair Lady* also won Oscars for Best Actor (Rex Harrison), Director (George Cukor) and Best Picture awards.

At Paramount Studios, June 1959, filming began on the pilot of television's first color western series, *Bonanza*, and it was NBC-RCA's maneuver to sell color television to the masses. It worked.

Casually, I sat on the set with the new series lead actors, Lorne Greene, Pernell Roberts, Dan Blocker and Michael Landon. I say lead actors, because previously, they were simply actors seeking their big break, and this was it. *Bonanza* would eventually become one of the finest, longest-running television series of all time.

Still new in the stunt business, I purposely sought out the show's stunt doubles in my quest for employment. I met Landon's double, Bob Miles and Bill Clark, doubling Dan and occasionally, Lorne, also Henry Wills, stunting for Pernell. It was a fun set with a certain excitement regarding the show's success. To assure precise colorization in the film processing and video transmission, technical advisors from Consolidated Film Labs and NBC and were ever present. Chevrolet and RCA were the prime sponsors and NBC was now touted as "The All Color Network." It's no wonder that *Bonanza* was historically responsible for selling more color television sets than any other show.

Over Bonanza's fourteen-year run, I worked on about twenty episodes. On "A Natural Wizard" (#215), I doubled Eddie Hodges, the carrot-topped child actor from Broadway and feature films, portraying *Skeeter*, a troubled, animal-loving kid. Hodges surprised me when he mentioned he had seen my photo at Claude "Doc" Baum's home, an old buddy from my KTLA days. Small world.

Director, writer and actor Robert Totten, a Hollywood wunderkind, carefully explained how he wanted me to crash through the cabin window, get up on one leg and limp away. I placed an apple box inside the cabin to give me a "step-up" and we shot it in one take. Bob was delighted and we became life-long buddies.

We later filmed exterior shots on the rolling hills near Thousand Oaks, California—in the mid-1960s it was open prairie, grazing land. During this period, Paramount, Twentieth Century-Fox and MGM announced a contemplated partial merger to build a studio in this vicinity. Immediately, many ran out and bought real estate to be near this projected studio complex. When the deal fell through, these folks were chided for their impulsive purchases of "Billy-Goat Acres." Today, the luxurious suburban community of Westlake Village stands in place of the grazing cattle and those folks got the last laugh—all the way to the bank.

Dan Blocker invited me to his new home in the San Fernando Valley's Northridge area and explained how he purposely purchased the cheapest home on the block for $50,000. The other residences were priced higher, he explained, and as their value appreciated, his property would gain in parity to the most expensive property.

Curious, when I asked Dan about his neighbors he became livid. Dan was an auto-racing aficionado and figured an invite to an upcoming race would be right neighborly. The next-door-occupant replied, "Sure, I'd love to go. Do you think someone will get killed?" Dan said he almost went over the wall after the guy, "and I haven't talked to the sonofabitch since."

Daily Variety and the Hollywood Reporter headlines bannered the departure of the eldest Cartwright son, Adam. Tinseltown couldn't believe Pernell Roberts would deliberately walk away from one of the world's hit television shows. Rumors suggested his former New York actor colleagues chided him for abandoning his Broadway stage origins. In their eyes, any performance on the boob tube was a sacrilegious desertion of his "thee-a-tah" roots. If you weren't emoting on stage you were prostituting yourself and your craft.

Lorne, Dan and Mike went on to amass millions of dollars from the show, personal appearances and residuals, often openly searching for financial endeavors for their capital. Pooling their funds allowed the purchase of extensive land parcels in Malibu at 1960s prices. This was also when a one-hour episode of *Bonanza* cost $160,000. Quite a contrast to the millions spent on a 30-minute sit-com today.

On the set, we wondered why Pernell walked away from his *Bonanza* paycheck when, had he stayed with the show for the entire run, "he could have built his own Shakespeare Theater," mused a crewmember. However, Pernell was financially redeemed years later when he starred in his *Trapper John, M.D.* TV series.

On another *Bonanza* episode, "Napoleon's Children" (#265), several of us younger stunt guys played wayward kids harassing Virginia City and the Ponderosa. My old buddy, Chris Nyby, was directing and once again we were out in the pre-Westlake Village area. A "bulldog" shot called for Hal Burton and me to hide in the tree branches as Hoss' double, Bill Clark, rides by. Hal and I would leap, taking Bill off the horse. This was the old reliable Western stunt gag where you hoped you wouldn't end up singing soprano.

We were about 15 feet up in the tree, crouching on individual limbs. I would drop first, landing behind Bill, and Hal would then take both of us to the ground. Six other stunt guys would then pile on to subdue poor old Hoss. During rehearsal, without the jumps, Bill rode in and stopped for camera position. I wanted to do this shot only once—during my adrenaline rush—and asked Hal if his position was satisfactory. He assured me there was "no problem."

Director Nyby called "Action." Bill Clark rode to his mark and I dropped from the tree limb, landing as planned right behind him. Bill and I were doing a pseudo-struggle, waiting for Hal, but only heard a thump. Hal had jumped, hit the horse's rump and bounced to the ground. Under my breath I called for the guys to pull us off the horse. What a pile-up, with me on the bottom. We later discovered the horse had moved out of position, causing Hal to miss landing behind me.

Later, we all reposed on a nearby, grassy hillside as the filming continued. Several of the cowboys had Beechnut chewing tobacco in their bulging hip pockets, so I figured I'd give it shot and chaw some tobacco. Taking a pinch, I placed it in my lower lip. However, when chawin', you should always spit out the tobacco juice or you'll be one green, sick sonofabitch. Dammit.

Back on the lot, hardcore chocoholics delighted in visiting Paramount's commissary for their famous Round Chocolate Shake, a scrumptious blend of chocolate ice cream, chocolate milk and chocolate syrup—one giant zit for mankind.

Bob Miles and I bummed around the various joints like the Red Coach, Foxfire and the Top Banana in North Hollywood. His parents were stunt people—his mother, Frances Miles, had created Riding Stunt Girls of America, one of the first stunt fraternities back in the thirties.

Bob's marriage to former wife Vera Miles produced a beautiful daughter or two but, not wishing to open old wounds, I refrained from mentioning Bob's name when I worked with her and Fred McMurray on Disney's *Follow Me, Boys*. The 1948 Miss Kansas and Miss America's 3rd runner-up's real name was Vera Ralston (not to be confused with actress Vera Hruba Ralston of Republic Pictures' fame). With a mischievous grin, Bob related a meeting with Hruba's husband, Republic Studios titan Herbert B. Yates, regarding the same-name problem. Knowing full well that his bride would use her new married name, Bob watched a nervous Yates explain the situation, emphasizing the millions of dollars the studio had invested in his native-Czechoslovakia wife. Bob would have preferred a monetary exchange, but was content he had placed a now comforted Yates in the hot seat.

Bob was a fine stunt man and one of the best picture fight men as any *Bonanza* episode will attest. Growing up in the business, he also found himself in an enviable position with Howard Hughes—from 1948 to 1951, Bob was the eccentric billionaire's personal driver.

A memorable drive took them to the Beverly Hills mansion of Metro-Goldwyn-Mayer's chieftain, Louis B. Mayer. Entering the long winding driveway Hughes insisted that Bob stop the car about fifty yards from the front door. They sat and waited. Moments later, the massive door opened and Mayer appeared. Staring at the parked, four-door, Chevrolet sedan, Mayer waved for them to drive closer. Bob looked at Hughes, who uttered, "Let the Jew sonofabitch come to us." And, Mayer did indeed.

One evening, Bob and I were seated at the Back Stage bar when *The Rockford Files'* assistant director, Bob "B.J." Jones, walked in. I introduced them and casually mentioned that they had a lot in common: both had been married to Vera. They had a good laugh as each had heard of the other, but had never met.

One day I wandered into the *Bonanza* production office as assistant director Charles Scott, with the phone handset cradled on his shoulder, listened intently. Hanging up, his furrowed brow accentuated his frown. "What's wrong?" "That was Lorne, calling from the Lake Tahoe location. He's pissed because he had to roll around in the snow." Shaking his head,

"Hell, for fifteen grand a week, I'll roll around in the snow all day long." What a contrast to the million dollars per episode today's TV series actors now receive.

Charley, a tall, handsome, prematurely gray gentle man, had been an actor under contract to Universal Studios. We first met when he was one of several second assistant directors on Stanley Kramer's *It's a Mad, Mad, Mad, Mad World*. He was a true gentleman and one of the honest, nice guys.

Another Bonanza episode found us in a big brawl in Virginia City. There were twenty stunt guys and a pigsty, but somehow Gary Epper and I ended up thrashing in the slimy, muddy pig pit. We watched every move these piglets made, primarily in their corner of the sty –– where they pissed. They didn't want to be near us anymore than we wanted to be near them.

Gary and I did our fight and staggered from the pigsty, mud coated from head to toe. Production manager-associate producer James Lane had previously balked at the show's stunt budget and had taken the stunt adjustment decisions away from Bob Miles. We elected Ted White, known for his high-side adjustments, to handle our cause. Big Ted, who doubled Fess Parker on *Daniel Boone*, faced first assistant director Nate Barragar, stating we deserved $350 for the day. Nate looked shocked as Ted quickly injected, "Hey, Michael (Landon) did his own stunts, didn't he?" Nate nodded reluctantly, "Well, you're saving $350 right there!" To our amazement, Nate agreed. However, on the next *Bonanza* episode, Bob Miles was again handling the stunt adjustments.

Standing clothed in the shower's streaming water washed the mud from the wardrobe, but cleansing all body orifices took an effort. These showers were located in the gymnasium; formerly, it was the original Lasky Players-Paramount studio –– an old barn, located at the corner of Selma and Vine Streets, surrounded by orange groves in 1915. The building has since been moved and restored on Highland Avenue property across from the Hollywood Bowl. It is now a movie museum and a revered location known simply as "The Barn."

Of the many *Bonanza* episodes I worked, many were fight scenes. Walking on the set, Dan Blocker would spot me and bellow, "I want to fight Jesse!" On several of the shows, we had a running bit—I'd jump on Dan's back and apply a calamitous chokehold. Dan would comically endure my vicious gyrations and casually back into a wall, causing me to gasp in crushing pain and fall to the floor unconscious. Quite a sight – my 130 pounds compared to Dan's 325—I looked like a monkey fucking a football.

Dan and I had many laughs and talks, including the self-destruction of director Richard Bartlett. Bartlett, along with producer David Dortort, gave Dan his first big break in 1958 on George Montgomery's *Cimarron City* TV series.

In 1960, Bartlett was also the first director to complete a Bonanza episode, "*Day of Reckoning,*" in five and a half days, while other directors struggled to complete their shows in 7 or 8 days. His editing experience allowed him to "cut the show in the camera." Dortort invited him to stay with the series, but, with his drinking buddy, William Tallman (the prosecutor on *Perry Mason*) in tow, Bartlett declared their directorial and writing demands and was promptly told to take a hike. Dan was saddened by Bartlett's behavior, but it was out of his hands.

Dan Blocker, a former Texas schoolteacher, was one of the sincerest gentlemen I have ever met. His passing May 13, 1972 at 43 from a blood clot after gall bladder surgery was a tragic, needless, loss.

Stunt men Boyd "Red" Morgan and John Epper decided my diminutive size would be best suited aboard a thoroughbred at Santa Anita or Hollywood Park—they suggested I take a job at their friend's Riverside, California, horse ranch, mucking out the stables, literally learning the racing biz from the ground up. I declined, saying I couldn't afford the pay cut, but primarily that I was too old at 24 to become a jockey. Each countered that Japanese jockey George Taniguchi began when he was 28. Remaining unconvinced, I stood steadfast that ten was the ideal age to begin a jockey career and by 18 you'd be an experienced pro.

While walking toward the Warner Bros. back lot for an *FBI* TV episode early one morning, I was startled as a dapper dressed Jack L. Warner surveyed the wardrobe building's foundation, seemingly checking for termites. When I mentioned my sighting to a long-time Warner employee, she said, "Oh yeah, and sometimes you'll see him turning the lights off on a vacant sound stage."

I had doubled actor Ralph Manza for several years, and now we were filming the *Laredo* TV series starring Peter Brown, William Smith, Philip Carey, Robert Wolders and Neville Brand.

This comedy episode called for a shirtless, knife-wielding Indian Manza, perched on a tree limb ready to leap as Bill Smith passes beneath him—leaps to "bulldog" the cowboy from the horse—but misses. The comedic intent is a bumbling, little redskin who screws up, no matter what he does. Actor Richard Devon and veteran stunt men Fred Carson were the heavies, also intent on causing the Texas Ranger bodily harm.

Fred Carson, from Texas, was one of the best stunt men in the business, doubled Victor Mature, Jeff Chandler, John Carroll, Gene Barry, John Russell, Clint Walker and Anthony Quinn, among countless others. Also, a fine actor, he played Chief Thunder Hawk in Hollywood's first 3-D Western, *Charge at Feather River*.

Whenever I had a stunt to perform alone, and other stunt guys were present, I'd always seek their opinion. Two heads are better than one and, though I might not use what they suggested, it was always another perspective to consider. "How would you do this 'bulldog'?" Fred suggested I jump, land on my feet and roll to the ground. "That's cheating it," I said, visualizing the bulldog leap as a straight dive, with my arms extended, as if I was really trying to take Bill Smith off the horse. The comedy in the stunt was the Indian's miscalculated crash to the ground. Since I wanted to do it my way, Fred agreed, and suggested I build a small pyramid of sand and I was ready to go.

I'd known Director Paul Stanley from previous shows and when I explained my feelings about the stunt he simply nodded. Wise directors let the stunt man do the gag their own way, that is, if the idea coincides with the written scene.

Whenever receiving a work call, I always inquired exactly about what the stunt involved. Once you knew the parameters, you then knew if special equipment was required. With three stunt bags full of gear, it was one hellava load to drag around, especially when you didn't need two of them.

Often, after the director explained what he wanted, I would then recite my interpretation of his words. Interestingly, his verbal description would conflict with his vision simply because of an incorrect word choice or usage.

The late California State Senator, S. I. Hayakawa described this communication problem in his several books on semantics, *Language in Thought & Action, Symbol, Status and Personality* and *Through the Communication Barrier*. If you care enough to sharpen your communication skills, I suggest you read any one or all of his books.

Anyway, back to the "bulldog" stunt. Like a cougar, I sat perched on the tree limb, ready to spring on its prey. The camera rolled as Bill Smith began his ride toward the tree. With a wooden knife clinched between my teeth and bare-chested in leather pants, I leaped at Bill with my arms outstretched, passing right behind him, and plowed hard into the sand mound. I did exactly what I had intended, using my arms as much as I could to absorb the hit, as the area between my nose and upper chest made a solid contact with the sand-topped terra firma.

The crew applauded while I tried to catch my breath. The dive knocked the hell out of me, and the wood knife produced a small trickle of blood at right the corner of my mouth. I was pleased the stunt worked just as I had planned, with the exception of my air speed into the ground face first. Never have I seen ground come up so fast. Regardless, it was a satisfied feeling knowing I didn't "cheat" the stunt.

Kudos should also go to the show's editor who included my entire crash and burn. Often, in action sequences, a stunt is interrupted with a "closer shot," as the "star" is shown landing in place. It's called "going with the money," but this form of editing takes the onus off the stunt. Check out the old silent movie two reelers – where the stunt action goes from A to Z.

A month later, the morning after the show aired, I was on the *Laredo* set for a fight scene when stunt man-wrangler Davy Rodgers entered, very excited, "Who the hell came out of that tree last night?" The other stunt guys all turned, pointed at me and, in unison, exclaimed, "Him!" Once again I had done something someone would not or could not do. It's a wonderful feeling of accomplishment, and thank God for youth. The ground gets harder as you get older.

Neville Brand was a kick. His excessive drinking became a problem to the point that he was virtually held him captive in his on-the-lot studio dressing room. To insure his daily presence on the set, the producers provided a lady companion to keep him occupied so he wouldn't stray.

Nevertheless, the Universal Studios Tour trams proved a constant irritant to him, especially the edict from the "Tower" decreeing that all filming would cease when the trams passed a company filming on the back lot. This was devastating to an actor, when in the middle of a scene they had to stop dead because of a bunch of rubbernecks.

On one occasion, the shocked visitors found Neville pissing on the side of his mobile dressing room. Another time, he flung open his trailer dressing room door and yelled to his tram audience, "My name's Peter Brown and I'm a cocksucker!"

Neville continued his crazed antics when actress Barbara Nichols, the brassy, blond bombshell, guest starred on the series. She had moved to descend from a large work wagon when Neville, with the speed of lightning, reached up under her long-flowing dress, latched on to her crotch in what we can only presume was a "bowling-ball" grip. Screaming like a banshee, Nichols was unable to move in any direction until the other cast members freed her from Neville's vice-like hold.

Once again on a *Bonanza* episode, "Peace officer" (#222), I returned to the pre-Westlake Village rolling hills with veteran Director William Witney. I had first worked with Bill on Jimmy Stewart's *Mr. Hobbs Takes a Vacation* and again, here was a director who knew exactly what he wanted to see on every frame of celluloid. Carefully, he explained how he wanted me to play the fugitive being pursued by Eric Fleming.

I hadn't seen Eric since the *Rawhide* episode when I doubled Rooney, but that's the thrill of the business—you never knew whom you might find on the next set. Be it an actor, director or crewmember, it was one big family and you were proud to be part of it.

Eric portrayed a nefarious sheriff preferring to bring back the wanted more dead than alive. In the scene, Eric enters a desolate line shack—a shot is heard, and then I stagger from the doorway and fall to the ground. Witney set the next camera angle, asked for some blood for my chest wound. Makeup artists Tommy Thompson and Abe Haberman were out of fake blood, so Bill said, "Get some catsup from the caterer."

Well, I figured, it finally happened—they really do use catsup for blood (black and white films used Hershey's chocolate syrup). Carey Loftin and I were terrified of bees and ran like hell to avoid them, so naturally, one hovered around me as I played dead.

Eric asked my permission to kick my hand as he exited the scene, an actor's "bit of business" to reveal his character's contempt for the lawless, and I was happy to oblige.

A year later, on September 28, 1966, while filming location shots for MGM-TV's two-part adventure series *High Jungle* on Peru's Huallaga River, Eric dove from a dugout canoe into the turbulent waters. His body was recovered three days later.

I met Cinema's greatest dancers. When Mickey Rooney appeared on ABC's *Hollywood Palace*, I was thrilled to meet Fred Astaire, the show's host that week. Previously, I had met Gene Kelly when he starred in Universal's *Going My Way* TV series, and discussed his longtime stunt double, Russ Saunders, noted for his famous slide down the ship's sail in MGM's *The Pirate*. Russ would design and practice the stunt before an athletic Gene would perform it.

I later crossed paths with Fred Astaire in Beverly Hills and he remembered me. What a class act.

Reportedly, Fred Astaire, Gene Kelly and Ray Bolger were flying to New York when Bolger exclaimed, "Do you two realize that if this plane crashes, Ken Berry will be the best dancer in Hollywood?"

Several of us, including Buddy Joe Hooker, Von Deming and Charlie Picerni, were called to augment Dick Crockett's stunt crew on Blake Edward's *What did you do in the war, Daddy?* Charlie and I paired up for the Italian village plaza fight. On "Action," we exchanged picture punches with the camera shooting over my shoulder toward Charlie, but I made the mistake of taking a head punch and falling backward to the cobblestones. Suddenly, a body fell across my legs pinning me helplessly to the ground. I cussed at the uniformed soldier's body to move, but he just lay there. Charlie realized the scuffling crowd were close to kicking me in the face, fell to his hands and knees, bridged my head, and warded off the stomping boots. When the scene ended, I was startled to see the body across my legs was veteran stunt man Dale Van Sickel.

Being on the receiving end of a prank takes fortitude, not to mention a sense of humor, but Buddy Joe Hooker pushed the envelope when he defecated in Von Deming's stunt bag. Dragging the bag to an assistant director, Von exclaimed, "Somebody shit in my stunt bag." With a verifying, yet detached glance, the A.D. simply replied, "Yeah, they sure did."

At Warner's, we were involved in a bar fight on the *Mister Roberts* TV series starring Roger Smith. Vince Deadrick doubled Smith as Ronnie Rondell, et al, tore the place apart. Talcum powder sprinkled on the twenty foot long bar enabled me to do the ever famous "slide down the bar" bit.

Between shots I talked with the stand-ins, Paul Nuckles and Scott Wilson. Yes, the same Scott Wilson who later co-starred with Robert Blake in Truman Capote's, *In Cold Blood*. He's a fine actor who has never received the acclaim his talent deserved.

Between takes Nuckles cornered me to express his desire to become a stunt man and invited me for a drink at the Sax Club, a watering hole across from the Warner Brothers studio.

I have always believed in a person's desire to be whatever they want to be. Everyone in life is helped at one time by someone. No one accomplishes anything *alone*, though many conveniently omit any memory of a helping hand. I was aided in every step I have ever taken and dutifully believe it's reciprocal. You have to pass it along.

Over drinks, Nuckles talked about his trek from East Tennessee to Hollywood and how much he wanted to be a stunt man. There was an upcoming U.S. Marine benefit for the families and children of the fighting men in Vietnam. I invited him to the pie fight, figuring this freebie show would give him a chance to meet and work with two other stunt guys, Roger Creed and Vince Deadrick.

In the Sheraton Townhouse Hotel banquet room, the kids enjoyed a fun time as we played waiters delivering the pie desserts. One guy tripped and suddenly whipped cream was flying everywhere—all to the delight and laughter of the kids.

Introducing Nuckles to Roger enabled him to be one of the *two-card* stunt men when Creed became the stunt coordinator on *The Rat Patrol*

TV series. Chuck Hayward and Cary Loftin had filmed the pilot and several episodes in Spain, but now the high desert north of Los Angeles become the sands of Rommel's North Afrika Corps. The World War II series became the perfect training ground for many of the 1960s up and coming stunt men including Jack Verbois, Dick Ziker, Nick Dimetri, Ron Stein, Dick Warlock and Paul Nuckles—the ideal situation to *learn while you earn.*

On *Slattery's People*, at 7am, I was a dapper dressed dead bookie lying in Culver City's cemented Ballona Creek's icy water. My soaked suit and trench coat dripped as stunt man Joe Brooks hoisted me onto his shoulder, climbed up the fire ladder and deposited me on a coroner's gurney. Director Dick Sarafian loved the shot. I retired to my heated honey wagon dressing room wet and shivering, to await the next shot as the prop man handed me a bottle of vodka. He apologized for not having brandy, the usual heart-warmer for a cold, drenched performer. But the second shot never happened. Five hours later, the wet clothes had dried on me and, I was damn near shit faced. For the following week I had one hellava head and chest cold. What we won't do for the arts.

A fun time was always assured on *The Virginian* TV series set, in addition to the wonderful guest stars. Meeting veteran actor Victor Jory was an honor, best remembered from *Gone with the Wind* as Tara's overseer Jonas Wilkerson. At aged sixty-two, he was as tough and feisty as when he was the U.S. Coast Guard's champion boxer and wrestler back in the 1920s and 30s.

Pranks were plentiful with James Drury and Doug McClure leading the troops. The day I visited the set a cotillion scene was in progress. The fiddle and squeeze box played as the square dancers did their do-se-doe your partner. Doug McClure, however, decided the punch needed spicing up so he sent a driver for a bottle of vodka. Several guys stood shoulder-to-shoulder, shielding Doug as he "freshened" the punch bowl. Soon, everyone was having one hellava time and by lunchtime half the extras and several crewmembers were feeling no pain.

On another *The Virginian* episode, an early call for a saloon fight scene had us waiting for the company to move from the adjacent sound stage. We amused ourselves with a game of gin rummy, hearing the swinging doors—I looked up as a delectable dance hall garbed lady entered. She quickly averted her eyes from us, but continued her walk past our table. Her frown and tunnel vision stare pissed me off. This was the one show on the lot where everyone was always congenial and had no room for prima donnas. As she neared our table I became the self-appointed greeter, "Howdy!" She snobbishly responded with a curt, "Hello." I then asked, "What's your name?" With a bored, get lost, eye-rolling glance, she said, "Raquel," "Raquel what?" I demanded in a gruff voice. "Raquel Welsh," she said. "Well, nice talking to you" and I returned to my gin hand amid the laughter of the four other players. Six months later she was the biggest name in Hollywood. Funny, though, I don't recall her chest being as *large* that day as we now know it.

Later, when *The Virginian* went into rerun syndication, audiences must have really enjoyed her *Guest Star* billing and performance within the ninety-minute program—a guest star with only two brief lines of dialogue.

Twentieth Century-Fox casting called me for a *Peyton Place* TV series interview to double Mia Farrow for a car hit. Pepper Curtis, a fine stunt girl and good friend was also called, but director Ted Post panicked when he saw me, "Jess, please hide. If Mia sees you she'll go nuts." Pepper did a terrific crash and burn.

The 4th Annual Stuntmen's Association Dinner-Dance was held at the Ambassador Hotel's famous Coconut Grove and the show biz audience was treated to Liza Minelli's first nightclub stage appearance. Of course, Judy Garland and Mickey Rooney were seated at a front stage center table. Mick was gracious enough to introduce me to Miss Garland, another great thrill of my lifetime.

Liza's debut was wonderful, but this Hollywood audience was awed when Frank Sinatra, Dean Martin and Sammy Davis, Jr. suddenly walked on stage. Bless Robert "Buzz" Henry, Sinatra's longtime stunt double, for asking *Old Blues Eyes* to appear and, naturally, his *Rat Pack* buddies tagged along. Needless to say, the two-hour show was fantastic and—priceless.

I had never worked with Buzz and had only met him briefly at the

Stuntmen's Association meetings. When his daughter, Christina, was born in 1969, I rushed to the St. Joseph hospital nursery to photograph a proud father viewing his daughter for the first time. Buzz appreciated the picture album. Two years later, at forty, Buzz foolishly raced his new sports car against a motorcycle. The bike won when Buzz tragically crashed his car into another on-coming car on Forest Lawn Drive, just yards away from the Warner Brothers backlot where he so often worked.

The following year, I was on the Stuntmen's Association's dinner-dance committee, and had met Joe X. Price, an advertising-publicity executive with Capitol Records. Joe spoke favorably of our yearly shindig, noting the many producers, directors and casting people in attendance, the perfect venue to showcase the record label's talent. His interest to furnish entertainers for our bash was self-serving, knowing well the great exposure they would receive and specifically mentioned a new male singer who "in six months he will be a big star."

Returning to SAMP's Board, I presented Joe's proposal, including Capitol's magnanimous gesture to provide an eighteen-piece orchestra gratis. The Board members debated the free band offer, a grand saving of at least $1000—and it seemed a sure bet until one Board member declared that *he* wanted "established talent, not some unknown singer." After last year's "Rat Pack" appearance, he "deserved" no less. Yeah, right. The chicken-hearted Board went along with him—after all he was a stunt coordinator and he might not hire them.

The next morning I broke the sad news to Price who damned the mistake SAMP had made. Six months later, the male singer did become a major recording star and did sustain a long lasting career. His name was Lou Rawls, who eventually sold over 40 million records..

Singer Jack Jones was guest starring on *Rat Patrol*—so I rushed to MGM's Lot 3 to ask if he would headline the entertainment. Jack was cordial and smiled, "No offense to you, Jess, but fuck the Stuntmen's Association. I was scheduled to appear last year after Liza, but when Sinatra, Martin and Davis popped in, I was bumped from the show. I really needed the exposure that night." I apologized and concurred that SAMP had definitely stepped on their dick, and I didn't blame him for his feeling as he did.

On November 30, I received a call from co-stunt coordinators Hubie Kerns and Victor Paul to work a new series from Twentieth Century-Fox TV called *Batman*. Twentieth had recently purchased the Desilu Culver Studios, formerly the David O. Selznick Studios where *Gone with the Wind* was filmed. Hubie was a former UCLA track star and Vic was a grand fencing master.

My initial visit to the *Batman* set was a surreal experience with sets painted varied rainbow colors. Intensifying the film effect was the angled camera for certain shots, not unlike a comic book. Hey, we *were* filming a comic book. The series starred Adam West, a fine gentleman, whom I had worked with previously when he played the handsome sheriff in the Three Stooges' final film, *The Outlaws is Coming*. Burt Ward, a twenty-one year old kid (Hell! I was only 25!), portrayed Robin.

"The Purr-fect Crime," *Batman* episode was a kick; I was doubling Ralph Manza once again, and Jock Mahoney was playing Leo, one of Julie Newmar's Cat Woman henchmen. I hadn't seen him since he and his wife, Maggie, (mother of Sally Field) were my guests at a Stuntmen's Association Dinner-Dance a year ago. Jock, with his wild wit, continued to ply his playful antics.

While rehearsing the ubiquitous, Wam! Bam! *Batman* fight scene, Jock exchanged picture punches with Hubie, doubling Batman, while Robin's double, Victor, rushes to Batman's rescue—swinging on a rope across the wide set to kick Jock into oblivion, Jock would casually sidestep, causing Vic to crash into the set wall like Wylie E. Coyote. Gathering himself, Victor reminded, "Geeze, Jock, you gotta stay on your mark." Jock, feigning a faulty memory, apologized with sincere concern. Stunt man Alex Sharp and I bit our lips, turned away to stifle our giggles. Another rehearsal and again, Jock moved, as Victor crashed and burned again. Victor crawled to his feet cross-eyed as we finally proceeded to film the fight as Jock, naturally, hit his mark; as well he should, being one of the best stunt men the business has ever known.

The only injury sustained during the fight occurred when Hubie became tangled in his Bat Cape while throwing a punch, struck and bloodied Alex's mouth. Cat Woman Julie Newmar was exquisite with the ultimate proverbial *hourglass* figure and, as unbelievable as it may seem, her stunt double (a model and wig designer) was even more beautiful in body and soul.

It was a thrill to work with Jock, whom I had idolized since I was a kid when he starred in *The Range Rider* TV series with Dick Jones for Gene Autry's *Flying A* productions and, later, in the *Yancy Derringer* series on CBS.

A Marine Corps flight instructor in World War II, Jock had doubled Errol Flynn in *The Adventures of Don Juan* when Charley Horvath said, "Jock's the only guy in Hollywood who can make that 19-step leap," during the climatic sword fight with Paul Baxley, doubling actor Robert Douglas.

At Universal Jock made several western films with director Richard Bartlett. With stripper Lili St. Cyr in *Runaway Girl* – Jock described how she never made eye contact (an actor's cardinal sin), but just stared at his forehead. Later, when he questioned her about her dialogue, she replied, "Oh, I just start talking when you stop." Obviously, Lili was not an Academy of Dramatic Arts graduate.

Jock's 1958-1959 *Yancy Derringer* series was a growing success when CBS demanded a greater share of the show's ownership, but when Jock and his producing partner refused, the program was "missing" from the Big Eye's 1959 Fall TV schedule. Jock later confessed their decision should have been rethought.

During this period, Jock made personal appearances for a new expanding hamburger chain – but chose cash instead of an offered franchise unit called McDonald's.

In 1961, at age 42, Jock became the 13th movie Tarzan and was more physically fit than men half his age. However, on the India location, Jock contracted Dungue fever and almost died when his 6'4" body weight dropped to 130 lbs.

Back on the *Batman* set, I worked the show continually during the first season, never knowing who would be playing the weekly villain—Cesar Romero, Shelly Winters, Liberace, Eartha Kitt, Otto Preminger, Burgess Meredith or Frank Gorshin.

On one episode, I was taken aback by a stunt wannabe Hubie hired who said he had quite a business selling goods on the black market in

Vietnam—items used against our fighting forces. He avoided me after I called him a "Fucking Commie," and I never saw or heard about him in the business again.

A cantankerous Burt Ward was jolted back to reality one day when he was reminded by Adam West: "The name of this series is *Batman*—NOT *Batman AND Robin*.

In one shot, Tony Epper and I were to crash into an eight by ten foot wide bookcase. I was doubling an old KTLA Page alumni buddy, Joe E. Tata. On "Action," we both took off when he suddenly straight-armed me, almost sending me out of the set. I did a quick two-step and crashed into the bookcase beside him. It was a "Print" and I turned to him, "Why did you...?" He got in my face immediately—pointed his finger, "Don't you say a word..." To this day I don't know what caused his dim-witted behavior. However, this may explain his demeaner: A lady neighbor called John, Tony's stunt man father, to mention an affair Tony was having with a goat. John asked her about the color of the goat. She said, "Black and white." John replied, "Oh, that's Tony's goat!"

Hubie displayed a directory of two-card stunt guys, asked me about Erik Cord's stunt abilities, "He'd be a good fight double for Jack Kelly, but I don't know him." "Hire him," I said, "He can do it,"

In 1961 I had met Erik, a Canadian, at a Los Angeles Sports Arena gun show as actor Brad Johnson (Lofty on the *Annie Oakley* TV series), Rodd Redwing and I performed fast draw exhibitions. Erik mentioned his stunt aspirations and I offered encouragement; he later joined the Universal Tours stunt show in 1964. Hubie did hire him and that was the beginning of Eric's very successful, long-standing film career.

The *Batman* company broke for lunch and a few of the stunt guys were lounging around the set, candidly discussing the very demanding Shelly Winters—wondering why a production would cave in to her ultimatums. Suddenly, we heard "Help! Help!"—Sounded like someone drowning at sea. We all jumped up and ran toward the voice. I was the first to find Winters near the sound stage door, sitting in a puddle of water like a beached whale. Hubie and I each grabbed an arm and got her vertical, then to a chair. She thanked us and continued talking as if nothing had happened.

Winters portrayed *Ma Parker*, a take-off on the infamous 1930's Ma Barker and her gang. Tisha Sterling, the beautiful offspring of Ann Southern and Robert Sterling played her daughter. I never understood why Sweet Tisha didn't become a major film star.

Two weeks later, an issue of the *New Zealand TV Weekly* quoted Shelley Winters, "We didn't even get to read the script or rehearse before shooting. No wonder that Adam West and Burt Ward look about dead. You hardly have time to eat lunch." She also complained about unsafe conditions on the set, obviously referring to her prat fall. My only feeling when we lifted her was that she didn't feel like she had missed many lunches. But *Batman* producer Howie Horwitz was outraged. Winters was accorded every courtesy and convenience possible by the cast and crew, but you can't please everyone and some people, never.

With work plentiful elsewhere, I didn't work the final season of *Batman* because of the continuous ten-hour fight rehearsals. One stunt guy mused, "Hubie couldn't remember a two-punch fight." Hence, we would receive a 7am call, rehearse all day, and finally film the fight about 5pm. I always believed over-rehearsing destroyed a fight routine's spontaneity, and by 5 o'clock just about everyone was all played out. Both reasons were a valid cause for accidents to happen.

The last week of December was spent filming *Iron Men*, a TV pilot starring Tom Simcox in Victorville, some ninety miles northeast of Hollywood. Gary Epper and I were playing *Gandy Dancers*. When I received the call my first reaction was, "Hey, I'm not a dancer!" and was promptly informed that a *Gandy Dancer* was a railroad laborer who drove the rail spikes with sledgehammers.

The production company was housed at the Green Tree Motel and, of course, we all ended up in the cocktail lounge the first evening. It appeared that every cowboy extra in the business had been hired for the show. Seated at the bar with Rod Magaughy, Ross Dollarhide and Wag Blessing, I recognized the well-known black character actor, Davis Roberts, (often billed as Robert Davis) sitting alone at a corner booth. He appeared lonesome so I invited him to join us. He quickly mounted the bar stool beside me and we made some small talk. Turning away to converse with Wag, I felt Roberts' leg rub against mine. Moving my leg, I figured it was an accident, but it happened again. With one swift motion I swung my arm around, knocking him off the stool, flat on his ass. His panicked expression was priceless as he jumped to his feet and ran out the door. The cowboys wondered what happened and when I explained, they all howled and heckled me for the next two days.

The following night Gary Epper and I decided we would check out the town's females. Gassing up Gary's Corvette, we asked the attendant "Where's the action in town?" He suggested we go down the road until we spotted a yellow building with a red light. Oh boy, this is it and couldn't wait to get to the babes. The thrill vanished when we opened the door to find a Bikini-clad bartender, a pool table and two guys seated at the bar. We ordered beers. Gary and one guy played pool while I conversed with other—the beer maid's boyfriend. Two beers later we were back at the Green Tree. So much for the "action" in Victorville.

From the early 1930s actor Pat O'Brien starred in many Warner Brothers films and though he didn't engage in battle with Jack Warner, he and his cronies at the Masquers, the venerable Hollywood men's club for actors, would often vent their sorrows. When the drinks peaked, the bartender dutifully phoned all their individual wives, "Come and get him, he's talking about the Jews again."

When the circus came to town, a buddy, formerly with Ringling Brothers-Barnum & Bailey, took me backstage to meet America's most famous clown, Emmett Kelly (1898-1979), better known as *Weary Willy*. Photographing him, holding his ever-present cabbage, compelled me to ask why he didn't substitute the real cabbage for a rubber prop. He looked hurt, replying, "Oh, nooo." It was definitely out of the question.

CHAPTER 8

1966

Work was plentiful on *Bonanza, Branded, F.B.I, Winchester '73,* and on Red Buttons' short-lived ABC TV series, *The Double Life of Henry Phyfe.* Jean Merrick was the head costumer and, hearing her name, I mentioned my CBS buddy, Jay Merrick, the floor director on The *Red Skelton Show,* "Do you know him?" Startled, she looked at me, "Yeah, I do. He's my husband."

Phyfe was the usual spy caper comedy, included my skiing down a carpeted ramp and out the swinging doors. Never having skied before; a grip suggested the correct form—bend the knees and lean forward! I shot down the ramp, through the doors like a rocket and the crash sounds were real as I plowed into a wall of C-stands and lights.

A year or so later a buddy called about a girl he met who wanted to become a film costumer. Figuring he was trying to get in her knickers, I met her, and then called Jean. They had lunch and the girl was in the union two days later. The guy didn't get laid, which coincided with my not receiving a thank you from her. She later married and divorced one of Hollywood's most prolific writer-director-producers, John Milius.

A scene on *The Virginian* TV series scared the bejeezes out of me. It was a simple shot of a mother and her son riding down the road in a small buckboard wagon. The wheel falls off and the mom is thrown out. Veteran stunt lady Evelyn Finley (she had starred in many 1940s B-westerns) handled the buckboard for the actress in crisis, Patricia Breslin, and, of course, I was doubling the kid.

The wagon was rigged with a small hydraulic mechanism to blow the right rear wheel off the axel. On "Action" Evelyn loped the horse to the pre-designated mark and triggered the lever with her foot. The wheel blew off and Evelyn tumbled out backward to the hard ground. Reacting to her fall, my bit was to grab the reins and bring the wagon to a stop. But Evelyn was being dragged alongside the skidding wagon's rear axle. The hem of her 1870's dress was caught on the hydraulic lever and, as if that wasn't enough, the hundred pound wheel was rolling beside her head, ready to lose momentum and topple over—onto her face. I quickly jerked the left rein as the heavy wheel plowed into the ground, missing her head by inches. Nonplused, Evelyn jumped to her feet and dusted herself off. We both just stared at each other and said a silent prayer of thanks.

While working on Paramount's *Caper of the Golden Bulls*, to double Vito Scotti, a *Bonanza* assistant director, George Wall, hired me for 30 minutes to double an actor dunked in a horse trough by Dan Blocker. A very nice, double payday.

Veteran stunt man-driver Carey Loftin summoned me for Sam Katzman's *Hot Rods to Hell*, starring Dana Andrews and Jeanne Crain, to be filmed in Palmdale, California. Carey said several of us would be doubling punk kids in hot rods, "You've got the job, but Katzman wants to see all of the stunt people himself." The second unit action with the stunt people would be filmed first and the actors would be cast accordingly—to the stunt folks hired. This was indeed a turn-about since stunt doubles were usually chosen to match the actors.

Arriving at MGM the next morning, I was decked out in my *Rebel without a Cause* basic outfit, a black leather motorcycle jacket, T-shirt, Levi's and boots. Having lost work previously because the *creative geniuses* lacked vision, "dressing for the part" became a necessity. Alone, I was ushered in to Sam's office as he looked up from his massive desk and exclaimed to his assistant, "Perfect! That's the look I want. Show him to wardrobe!"

Parking my Ford Mustang convertible at MGM, I joined the stunt guys and gals for the journey by studio bus directly to the Palmdale location. It was a long two-hour drive to the Antelope Valley high desert; long before the present day Highway 14 freeway was completed. Disembarking from MGM's relic bus, we were greeted by Al Murphy, a perennial second assistant director, a funny little Jewish guy. Al suddenly became postal when one of the stunt guys asked, "When do we get paid?" "When do you get paid? You just got here! Sonofabitch!" said Al. I'll bet the guy's rent was probably due.

We changed into wardrobe and were assigned our hot rod cars. The vehicles looked slick in every rainbow color and sparkling chrome accessories. Most were show cars built by car enthusiasts who were now thrilled their prized vehicle would be in a movie. Boy, would they learn a valuable lesson.

Beauty is only skin deep. Ugly is to the bone. While you may find these vehicles in your dreams the actual driving produced other problems—Failed brakes, blown engines, clutches, transmissions and rear-ends, but most often, overheating kept the company mechanic and a water truck busy.

I was saddled with a spiffy 1932 Ford roadster, dazzling in chrome and 12 coats of black lacquer, the rod had everything—except a radiator. For one or two takes, it ran at top speed and then it was time to bring on the water truck. Other stunt drivers experienced similar difficulties. In reality, the cars were only for show—to win pretty ribbons, five-foot tall trophies and Bikini Babes.

We had quite an assortment of stunt folks, Carey, Patty Elder, Sharon Lucas, Jack Coffer, Ron Burke, Jerry Brutsche, Bob Herron and Dale Van Sickel. Between shots several of us guys crammed into a small honeywagon dressing room to avoid the sandblasting winds as the group's great storytellers told tall tales, mostly all risqué. We laughed long and hard. And when called back to the set were surprised to find the stunt gals had huddled in the adjoining dressing room, had heard every nasty word—and said they loved every minute of it.

Housed at the Antelope Valley Inn, the stunt contingent and crew spent the evenings relaxing with Manny's Margarita's. This was his delicious creation of the famous Tequila liquid libation and a far cry from the usual potable recipe. Maggie's flowed like water and only when you slid off the barstool to stand up did you realize you couldn't. Thank God the motel rooms were within crawling distance.

Patty Elder was petite, blond and pretty, one of the best stunt gals in the biz and married to Eddie Hice, an equally talented stunt man. One evening as I enjoyed my drink at the bar, Patty waved me over to the booth she was sharing with assistant director, Don Klune, who had gone to the men's room. (His father, Ray Klune, the production manager on *Gone with the Wind*, was presently MGM's production chief.) She insisted I join her, whispering that Klune was trying to "get in her pants."

Don Klune wasn't a popular a.d., as it was widely known that he was solely responsible for erroneously causing stunt man Bob Morgan to lose his right leg and suffer facial disfigurement during the 1961 filming of *How the West was Won*. Morgan, He was married at the time to actress Yvonne DeCarlo, and was doubling George Peppard, hanging from huge logs mounted on the train's flatcar. Special effects had mechanically rigged the logs to swing back and forth over the deep gorges and bridges as the train careened down the tracks.

Overstepping his authority, Klune yelled for the logs to be repositioned and Morgan was knocked beneath three speeding railroad cars, with a clearance of only twelve inches. Bob's arms and legs were broken and wrapped around his torso—he was literally picked up in a basket. During surgery, his fragile condition negated anesthetics, an orderly recalled, "You could hear his screaming in the parking lot."

Stuntmen Fred Krone, Charley Horvath and Bill Catching were at Bob Morgan's bedside when he awakened, "What are you guys doing here? Horvath retorted, "We're here to watch you die." Bob cussed them. Later, Morgan's doctor confided that Charley's comment was Bob's best medicine, provoking his will to live.

Prior to the accident, Bob was a low 80s golfer. Surviving the loss of a leg, he devised a swivel-ball-joint prosthesis, allowing him to continue his passion for golf with a single digit handicap.

Klune returned to the booth—Patty and I out drank him until he finally staggered into night. The Margarita's also took their toll on us, as we carefully navigated a wobbly course to our rooms.

Karma—*what goes around, comes around,* but it's one of life's rarities to see the retribution actually occur – even if it's only a small portion. The large Mitchell NC camera on Gil Caspar's insert car filmed head-on as the lead hot rod roared into a sliding 90°right turn through the T-intersection. This was Gil's cue to accelerate – and truck with the following cars down the road. Klune was seated atop the camera car, tumbled backward and broke his arm.

My disdain for him is obvious, mostly because of his sleazy, conniving demeanor. Over my years at MGM, he was the only a.d. that caused a money problem. Every attempt to negotiate a fair, rightfully deserved stunt adjustment, an argument always ensued. He was not an honorable fellow.

The film's prime story point involved the hotrodder's Corvette convertible (occupied by mannequins) sails off a bridge into a ravine. The special effects department devised a "pull and drag" rigging—the cables and pulleys anchored to the car were connected to a large truck. The ingenious mechanical engineering involved in these shots always intrigued me. Everyone watched as the "half-speed" rehearsal brought the vehicle to the bridge-ravine's edge. Slowly, the car was retracted to the "first position," as the cameras were readied to roll. Curiously, I watched as an effects man quickly ran to the cable-pulley mechanism and made several turns with his ratchet wrench. I questioned this adjustment since the rehearsal worked so well—*if it ain't broke—don't fix it.*

Soon, Klune gave the command to roll three cameras as veteran second unit director James Haven yelled, "Action!" The cast and crew watched as the car slowly gained momentum. Faster and faster the red Corvette accelerated toward the bridge. Suddenly, the cables became rigid and, like it was on a rail, the car made an abrupt right turn and crashed into a lone telephone pole. And I do mean lone. Spaced fifty yards apart, the car severed the pole at the base leaving it hanging precariously, suspended only by the phone lines. Ron Burke burst out laughing as the remainder of the crew reacted in horror. The Corvette's fiberglass front-end carriage had disintegrated almost to the windshield as the teetering telephone pole dangled above. What a mess. Shocked and bewildered, Jerry Katzman, Sam's son, was heard to mumble as a driver rushed him to a pay phone, "What am I gonna tell Daddy?"

To learn the business, I found it wise to stay close to camera because that's where the production problems were discussed between the director, the assistant director and the director of photography. If they couldn't find a solution, then it was time to call the production manager and producer. Chances are if it went that far, some heads might roll.

We completed the seven days of action and headed back to Hollywood and I had never been happier to leave a location – the worst I'd ever been on. The "High Desert" lived up to its name in more way than one—you could set your watch by the daily 2pm winds. We all ended up windblown, sandblasted and sunburned.

In 1962, while I was working *Mad World*, stunt man Fred Krone touted land parcels near the proposed Palmdale Airport, painting breathtaking pictures of land baron possibilities. The Palmdale Airport has yet to become a reality, although there is still talk of it almost 60 years later. True, you wouldn't have lost any money on a Palmdale land purchase as *they don't make it anymore*, but as far as I'm concerned, it's still a damn desert. Personally, I prefer green and lush terrain around me. I was advised to "Get a lot while you're young." It was years before I realized they were referring to real estate.

Three and a half weeks had passed since we wrapped *Hot Rods to Hell* and, after countless calls to payroll, none of the stunt performers had received their paychecks. Somehow, I became the spokesman for the group, so I called SAG and filed a late pay grievance. We received our checks in three days, but for almost six years I didn't work at MGM. A while later I mentioned this to my old buddy, Jim Nissen, who was SAG's number three man in command. Candidly, he cautioned, "Jess, even though your claim was supposed to be anonymous, MGM knew your name 10 minutes after you called. They have their spies here at SAG, don't ever do that again!"

The Stuntmen's Association's monthly meetings continued at various Ventura Boulevard restaurant banquet rooms at a nominal cost. As a SAMP Board member (later secretary & treasurer), I believed it was foolish to pay a restaurant $75-$100 for a monthly meeting room and arranged for the free use of The Sherman Oaks Fashion Square La Casita Community Room. Many shopping malls and financial groups provide facilities gratis for non-profit clubs and organizations. We met there for a year until the room was demolished during the mall's expansion.

I then moved our monthly meetings across the street to the Lincoln Savings Community Room, which, like the La Casita Room, graciously provided free coffee, tea and hot chocolate. The use of this location was cancelled abruptly when Lincoln Savings found two podium microphones missing after the meetings. I should have taken them home and returned them the next day, but who knew? At that point, I said the hell with it. Some of these guys would steal your eye teeth if you left your mouth open.

My script writing yearnings prompted me to team up with assistant director Lester William Berke to write a *Bonanza* script, based on a story idea I had long pondered—Where did Hop Sing come from? Jackie, a girlfriend of John Hawkins, the show's story editor, and I were Foxfire Room drinking buddies, offered to open the proverbial "door" for us. Les and I wrote laboriously, detailing how the Chinese—Hop Sing was shanghaied to America to build the railroad. A subplot had Little Joe falling madly in love, but the lady died tragically. *Bonanza* Rule #3 All *Bonanza* women must die. Les was having trouble with the Antoinette Evans/Little Joe love scene and went ballistic. This was before computers, so with a razor blade, I cut, rearranged and taped the dialogue pages together until the scene played perfectly, basing much of it on my personal love relationship with my True Love, Toni Evans.

The script was now cohesive and we were proud of our efforts. Our meeting lasted forty-five minutes as Hawkins and producer Richard Collins extolled our writing talents, but they didn't purchase the script. Standing outside Paramount's main gate I grumbled, but Les was exuberant, "This is the first time in twenty-four years anyone has ever said I was a good writer." Yeah," I said, "and that and five bucks will buy you a cheap bottle of vodka."

Years later, when I mentioned the Hawkins/Collins scenario to Bob Miles, Michael Landon's stunt double, he asked, "Why didn't you let me take your script to Mike?" Who knows? It seemed like a good idea at the time.

For a couple of weeks at a time my apartment became a "Home for the Marital Dispossessed," when Les Berke, then Fred Krone found comfort on my living room sofa.

Mini-skirts were a late-sixties rage as a beautiful Foxfire Room waitress modeled her latest creation, bartender Frank Legoo uttered, "Well, it'll keep the flies out of your face." The doll face became infuriated amid the laughter and stomped out. Frank suspected her destination and phoned the nearby Red Coach lounge bartender. Ten minutes later, Frank answered the phone and and held the receiver at arms length, All we could hear was a female voice screaming, "You sonofabitch!"

On the *Destry* TV series at Universal, I had a couple of lines as a hotel clerk for director, production executive Frank Bauer. The next scene entailed a card game with five players. Frank established the table—the players and we then broke for lunch. Returning, Frank proceeded to complete the scene, but a veteran actor drank his lunch and couldn't remember his dialogue. Take after take it was "Cut, print, pickup." Going as far as he could, Frank dismissed the actor and had a stand-in wear the actor's clothes. The actor had been established before lunch walking to the card table. Frank shifted his lines to the other actors, and in the final cut all you saw of him was his opening lines and his stand-in exiting the scene. The actor didn't work much after that.

The *My Favorite Martian* TV series had me as the messenger delivering the Magna Carta to the King of England. I had played a jockey on a previous episode and had already met Ray Walston, admired his work since I'd first seen him in *Damn Yankees* and *South Pacific*. Bill Bixby was fun. Both actors were consummate professionals and a joy to watch.

Back to merry old England—Costumed in the obligatory tights, I was to be waylaid by a 350 pound, six-foot-six hulking giant, portrayed by the producer's personal jeweler. Always leery of non-professionals performing stunts, I reluctantly gave him the benefit of the doubt. We rehearsed the broadsword fight routine, culminating in my fighting off his vicious half-Nelson neck hold. It was obvious this fellow had never participated in picture action, so I carefully explained every move as we continued the routine at half-speed. During the broadsword segment I was to be slapped across the butt with the forty-one inch sword. I showed him where to place the metal blade and prayed he understood. Figuring, this was as good as it was going to get, we returned to the set to shoot it.

On "Action" we began our routine and he nailed me squarely on the coccyx, commonly known as the tailbone. Enduring the pain from his wayward hit, I ran to the horse to make my planned get-a-way. He grabbed me in a Half-Nelson, we struggled, and then the horse suddenly sidestepped, mashing my right foot into the soft laid dirt on the sound stage floor. It was like being on "the rack" as the Big Guy pulled and the horse stood his ground. Anyway, I got loose, mounted the nag and rode off. For the next three days my foot and tailbone ached, making walking and sitting a royal pain. So much for working with amateurs.

Nice guy assistant Director Tommy Thompson (Is every Thompson you've ever met named Tommy?) called from *The Lucy Show*, wanting me to double a little old lady on a motorcycle. It was a three-camera show, filmed in front of a live audience, tantamount to performing a Broadway play—Lucy wouldn't tolerate retakes.

Watching Lucille Ball in action was fantastic. She knew everyone's job and did it better than them. Taking me aside during a rehearsal, she suggested that since my speed while traveling across the set was relatively slow, I should lean forward to simulate a look of greater speed. She was right.

For the show, I rented stunt man Gary McLarty's metallic blue Triumph Bonneville motorcycle for $50 for the rehearsal and shoot days. During each rehearsal the bike never started with the first kick. The prop man and I agonized over this, wondering if the bike would actually start the night of filming.

The show began and we were ready. Hidden from the audience view by a section of the set, we nervously awaited our cue. It came and I hit the kick-starter. Miraculously, the bike roared to life and, in a leather jacket and helmet, I traveled to the other side of the set. During the entire time I had the bike in my possession that was the first and only time the motorcycle ever started with one kick. Lucy later thanked me. What's the old Hollywood axiom? God protects children, drunks and movie people.

A friend recommended me as the Publicity Director for the Miss San Fernando Valley Beauty Pageant and during the process I began dating the 1965-1966 reigning queen, Diane Stanley. During the preliminary Miss North Hollywood Pageant, I suggested the probable winner would be Barbara Ferrell, which didn't set well with Diane, also the incumbent Miss North Hollywood. Very insecure and jealous, Diane was not a happy camper when I suggested the pageant photographer shoot the three of us together.

While 16mm filming the pageant's swimsuit competition, I concentrated my attention on Barbara. Though I wasn't a judge, she did become Miss North Hollywood. Suspiciously, my extensive film footage of her makes it appear the contest was rigged, but it really wasn't—she was just the most beautiful, demure and classy contestant of them all.

Subsequently, Barbara Ferrell didn't win the Miss SFV Pageant, but was offered a contract at Warner Bros. She declined their offer and later married her boyfriend.

Former producer-director Dick Bartlett was still playing the part as he sat in the Red Coach cocktail lounge exclaiming the many projects he "had in the fire." I worked steadily performing stunts, but yearned to get into film production, still a first love of mine. Bartlett made me his assistant as he attempted to re-enter the business. I burst in one morning greatly enthused about an L.A. Times article on Red Adair, the Texas oil well firefighter, figuring it would make a fabulous action film, but Bartlett brushed me off, "They did that on the *Empire* TV series at Columbia." Well, evidently, John Wayne figured the idea wasn't outdated and a year later, his Batjac Productions released his very profitable *Hellfighters* film. It was great to be right.

Bartlett and I pitched a movie idea to actor/director Fernando Lamas in his palatial Bel Air mansion. Two cups of coffee later, Fernando directed me to the bathroom down the hall. Passing an open door, my glance revealed a radiantly beautiful, night-gowned Esther Williams sitting in bed reading a book.

I later worked with Fernando when he directed episodic TV. His easy on-the-set demeanor made him a joy to work with, saying "We're not doing Cancer research here!" Incongruously, years later he would succumb to the disease.

Bartlett and actor-writer John Mitchum, Bob's brother, joined forces to write a feature script, *The Men of the Green Beret*, based on the U.S. Army's elite corp. Together, they dictated the scenes as I feverishly typed the words into a screenplay. Though relegated to my typewriter, I would often chime in with my thoughts whenever something seemed out of kilter. Bartlett was a tough taskmaster who nailed me when I said the scene, "Just isn't right." He admonished me that it wasn't enough to say something was wrong, but you must present a solution to the problem.

Though Bartlett had a proven grasp of the filmmaking process, he seemingly had a thirty-word vocabulary when dictating a scene description and action. Unbeknownst to him, I became his personal Thesaurus to prevent the same word from being used ten times in one paragraph.

Finally, with the completed script in hand, we met with Bartlett's former partner, producer Earl Lyon of United Pictures. Located in the old California Studios, near Paramount Pictures, his company was small, but turned out three or four low budget features a year, and they all made money. Earl liked the script and immediately made arrangements to meet the Department of Defense officials in Washington, D.C. It was essential that military cooperation be obtained to reduce the production costs. Without a DOD alliance the film would not be produced.

Bartlett decided I would direct the second unit for a parachute jump sequence. U.S. Army Lt. Colonel Alfio Bernardi, head of the West Coast Green Beret operations, arranged the military clearance for us to film 150 members of the Special Forces at the U.S. Marines Corps' Camp Pendleton, in Oceanside, just north of San Diego.

Kicking it off on June 5th, 6:30am, I hired two cameramen to handle the 35mm filming, and I had my trusted 16mm Bolex Rex-Reflex. My footage would be blown to 35mm for a special effects sequence within the film.

Upon our arrival, a Green Beret Pathfinder greeted me and explained his duty in combat was to be the first parachute into uncharted enemy areas to set the ground markers for the incoming air troops. He asked where I'd like to have the troops land. Pointing, I suggested that since the planes were to fly toward us in this wide valley from the Pacific Ocean, I preferred to see the troops leaving the planes, float toward us and land in the foreground. "Fine," he said, "I'll put'em right in your lap." In a Jeep, he raced toward the beach, about a mile away, he set two, twenty-foot, vinyl fluorescent orange arrows, pointing in our direction. Returning, he placed a similar sized "X" about fifty yards in front of our cameras. We were all set.

Thirty minutes later, a large, Royal blue, 10-ton truck pulled up and an Air Force Captain forcefully announced he would coordinate this parachute jump. Politely, I informed him the Green Beret Pathfinder had set the marks and everything was A-Okay. He repeated his intentions and moved the Pathfinder's "X" a hundred yards behind our cameras. The Captain then launched a weather balloon and a smoke bomb to check the windage.

Watching, what appeared to be a "Dog & Pony Show," I turned to the Pathfinder and asked if the Air Force had the authority to over-ride what he had already set up. He simply stated the jumpers were using U.S Air Force C-130's and it was their jurisdiction. Damn, I trusted him, plus his markings made more sense.

Minutes later we heard the moaning drone of the C-130's approaching from the sea. The two planes began to fill our viewfinders—we rolled cameras. The aircraft continued, but there were no jumpers as I yelled, "When the fuck are they going to jump?" All three cameras were vertically tilted skyward as the planes went out of frame. Suddenly, my camera battery-carrying assistant screamed, "There they go!" I jerked my head from the camera eyepiece as the first chutes appeared, floating in all directions—behind us; over the new "X" position. We all snatched our cameras and ran toward the descending silk mushrooms. Planting the tripods, we'd roll some footage, and run again, as the many chutes continued their wayward, earth-bound paths.

In five minutes the jump was all over, and I do mean *all over*. Soon, reports of injured soldiers, landing in streams, fields and on service roads was verified by the ambulance sirens. Everywhere, bodies were being treated. Soldiers received broken arms and legs, another suffered a concussion when his chute snagged. A chute and its occupant dangled precariously, thirty feet in the air from a tree branch, awaiting rescue. One participant mused how he glided over a fence, hit and rolled and came face-to-face with a cow. Another soldier suffered severe burns when he landed in a power station, shorting out a portion of Camp Pendleton.

Afterward, I was disgusted, especially with those who maintain there is no military inter-service rivalry. These soldiers risked life and limb all because of an overblown ego.

Ultimately, this exercise was in vain. Earl Lyon returned from his DOD Washington meetings and repeated their matter-of-fact statement, "We'll give you all the cooperation you need *after* John Wayne makes his picture." They were referring, of course, to the Duke's film, *The Green Berets*.

The Green Berets was prepping at Warner's and veteran stunt man Cliff Lyons was the film's second unit director. After twenty minutes with him, I thought I had a pretty good chance of being a stunt man on the film, but I was wrong.

Months later the company returned from Fort Benning, Georgia, and continued filming on the Warner Brothers back lot. John Wayne smiled and waved to me as he conversed with visiting director/buddy Mervyn Leroy. Talking with John Wayne's longtime stunt double Chuck Roberson, he asked why I didn't call him? While driving home I asked myself the same question.

On July 19, I met a budding actress, June, through a local clairvoyant. Yeah, I know, but some of us still attempt to understand our existence. She was a "Hollywood Starlet" and every man's dream, just what you wish for.

She lived at the Hollywood Studio Club, a residence famous for a previous tenant in Room 334 named Marilyn Monroe. To showcase my Tinseltown image, we lunched at Paramount Picture's Cafe Continental. Immediately, we hit it off and the following night we hit the sack. This romance continued hot and heavy as we wined and dined in Studio City and Sherman Oaks restaurants. Two weeks later, she proclaimed she was pregnant. Figuring, if you're going to dance, you have to pay the fiddler, I offered to marry her. She, instead, vehemently insisted on an abortion.

Putting out feelers, I was soon contacted by a local Italian restaurant owner's son who "knew a doctor." I paid him the $450 fee and he delivered her to the doctor on operation day. Interestingly, he returned in an hour to the Foxfire and drank himself into a stupor. I later found the actual cost of the abortion was $350. You would think that when a guy cops a $100, he'd find a better use for it, but maybe his Catholic guilt got to him.

Many years later, when I mentioned this situation to my Mom, she asked why I didn't call her. Well, simply, because I never troubled her with my situations, contrary to a sister who would lay every problem on her, then go merrily on her way while Mom sat and cried for the next hour. When Mom said a gal wouldn't know she was pregnant in two weeks, I wished I had talked with her.

For whatever reasons, this gal proceeded to harass me with phone calls for the next two years. During a chance meeting, I confronted her, saying a psychic reader said I wasn't the father of her aborted child. I lied, but the look on her face said it all. Immediately, the annoying calls ceased and I never heard from her again. A Hollywood Starlet, huh? Again, "Be careful what you wish for, you might get it."

Work continued on *Gunsmoke, Batman, Bonanza, Laredo*, and features at Universal and Paramount. How honored I was meeting James Arness as he leaned back in his canvas director's chair, telling jokes, and hearing his infective laugh. He was one of the greatest and as an actor so underrated.

Directing a *Batman* segment was Larry Peerce (Tenor Jan Peerce's son); we first met when he was a staff director at KTLA. Larry called "Cut" and Director of Photography Howard Schwartz chimed in, "Print that! It was perfect." "You liked it?" said Peerce. "Oh yeah," smiled Howard. "Great, we'll do another take," said Larry, "I will say when we print a scene." Howard did overstep his bounds, but once again the Hollywood egos were on display.

One evening while imbibing in the Fox Fire with Dick Bartlett, I started to converse with George Gruskin, a talent agent. I figured he could be the most important guy Bartlett could ever meet, but Bartlett kept shining me off, until I damn near dragged him into meeting Gruskin.

Gruskin personally re-opened the MCA/Universal doors that had been closed to Bartlett for seven years. He and Lew Wasserman were friends for decades, and Bartlett was signed to direct an episode of the *Laredo* TV series. Gruskin also arranged for his agency, Goldstone-Tobias, to advance Bartlett the back-dues funds to regain his Directors Guild membership.

In Universal's Black Tower, Bartlett and I prepped the *Laredo* episode, "The Small Chance Ghost," for a week. While reading the script, a character described fit "The big guy who played *Lurch* on *The Adam's Family*," but I couldn't recall his name. Bartlett and the producers agreed with my suggestion and Ted Cassidy got the role. When I related the story to Cassidy on the set he angrily stomped away. Oops, I had violated Dale Carnegie's, *How to Win Friends and Influence People*, Number One Rule: *A man's name is his most important possession.* Cassidy would later gain fame in *Butch Cassidy and the Sundance Kid*, when Paul Newman would kick him in the nuts.

Filming commenced, I continued to run the lines with the actors. Bartlett and Neville Brand hit it off, comparing World War II stories as Peter Brown, William Smith, Phil Carey and Robert Wolders did their bit. When the A.D. introduced Bartlett to the tall, dark and handsome Wolders, married to actress Merle Oberon, Bartlett confided, "When we met I didn't know whether to shake his hand or fuck him."

Between shots, Bartlett sipped vegetable soup from his Thermos, and later admitted to spiking the vegetable soup with vodka, but he couldn't taste the alcohol. It wasn't until he bit into the carrots, which had absorbed the vodka that he then started to get a buzz. Nothing had changed, years before he had injected oranges with vodka to suck on while directing.

Seems the creative juices flow freely when a guy wants to conceal his need for alcohol. Costumer Steve lodge stuffed his briefcase with two Listerine bottles; one filled with scotch. After a morning of imbibing Lodge needed a quick nip, he unscrewed a bottle and quickly took a healthy swig and almost chocked—it was Listerine. Then there was another fellow with a major hangover who brushed his teeth from a tube of Ben-Gay.

Bartlett, however, appeared to be in control, asked the director of photography, Andrew Jackson, his camera operator when he got bounced out of Universal years before, to "Give me a forty [lens] over here." Bartlett didn't "ride the camera" – meaning, to check the shot's composition or go to dailies—so his former associate used instead the lens he preferred. Bartlett wouldn't find the lens discrepancies until the show aired a month later.

During the filming of the saloon earthquake scene, special effects dropped a large wagon wheel with eight kerosene lamps. The hundred-fifty pound fixture crashed and catapulted a glass lamp across the set, passing just inches from actress Jeanne Cooper's head, crashing into the back bar. The other seven shattered lamps sat amid puddles of kerosene. When I asked the A.D. to declare a no smoking order, the prop man Ace Holmes, another Universal panic, became testy. Well, why not, because of his incompetence, those lamps should have been replaced with breakaways.

Denver Mattson was hired to double Ed Binns for a 56-foot high fall from atop Alfred Hitchcock's "Psycho House." Stuntmen Rick Arnold, Jon Thorguson, Chuck Waters and I watched Denver as prop man Holmes set his 10x20x3 foot Port-A-Pit in position. The pad, I thought appeared to be too far out from the building. Bartlett suggested I discuss the pad's outward position with Mattson, but I declined, maintaining it was always the stunt performer's decision.

Bartlett was always queasy about stunt action and would never watch any stunts he directed. He called "Action," and quickly turned his head away as Denver started the fall. Mattson then realized the pad *was* out too far and with his body at a 45° angle, he was already committed, but gave an extra push with his toes as he left the roof. Rick reacted and shoved the pad in about four inches. Denver crash landed with his upper torso hanging over the edge of the foam-stuffed pad, his head only an inch from the ground. That was too close. I then vowed that the next time something didn't look right to me I would definitely speak up.

A week after the *Laredo* episode was completed Bartlett received his $7,000 Director's fee and casually handed me $150. Again, no good deed goes....

A year later when the final *Laredo* TV episode aired September 1, 1967, I was seated at the Fox Fire bar with John Russell, who had co-starred with Peter Brown in the *Lawman* TV series. Suddenly, he broke into an irate diatribe when I mentioned Peter Brown and the canceled series, "What'da think he's a has-been… that he'll never work again?" Seemingly he was referring to himself, as I moved my drink to the other end of the bar.

In November 1966, the *Ironside* TV pilot brought me my first visit to San Francisco, the City by the Bay, or as the late, great columnist, Herb Caen termed it, *Baghdad by the Bay*. Exiting the Mercer Airlines charter flight from Burbank, the burning smell and white smoke from the front landing gear caught my attention immediately. Cheated death again, I thought, as a crewmember quipped, "That's why they're called 'Mercy Airlines' and 'We fly you *almost* there' is their motto"

The *Ironside* TV pilot starred Raymond Burr, Don Galloway, Barbara Anderson and Don Mitchell and I was doubling actress Geraldine Brooks in a fire gag. Regardless of the talent and abilities of stunt women, production often preferred to hire me, Whitey Hughes, Jerry Brutsche or Jerry Summers to double the actresses. Production's male preference prevented a guilty conscience should a stunt guy became injured as opposed to a stunt gal.

To the consternation of Barbara Anderson, *Ironside* co-star, Don Galloway and I joked as the limo took us to San Francisco's Golden Gate Park location. She didn't know what to make of our humor. Later, back in Studio City, I would visit Don and his wife, Linda, at their home or we'd have a drink now and then at a local pub. Don was one of the good guys, without an actor's ego.

San Francisco's fine restaurants, preserved buildings, both public and private, museums of *The City* was a contrast to Los Angeles' lack of historical relevance, where a "tear it down and rebuild" mentality prevailed. L.A.'s attitude, however, might possibly be attributed to Southern California's major earthquake every twenty years or so. Since the Long Beach quake of 1933, others have occurred at seemingly regular intervals—Tehachapi 1952, Sylmar 1971, Whittier Narrows 1989 and Northridge 1994. You don't have to be a brain surgeon (or even a seismologist) to deduce a certain shake, rock and roll pattern from these dates, which in recent years has become more frequent. As the earth's movement within the Los Angeles basin continues, my theory may eventually corroborate the predictions of Nostradamus and Edgar Cayce – that California's coastline will submerge and West Coast ocean front property will be available in Arizona.

My *Ironside* days were open because of the night filming, so I phoned my True Love, Toni, still married and now employed in San Francisco's financial district. She suggested lunch at Domino's, a famous local haunt located in an alley, luxurious with its massive, 100 year old mahogany bar. However, the joint's charm was the red-flocked walls, decorated with countless nude paintings of every size. Now, these were not the usual buxom ladies on velvet, but magnificent artistic masterpieces you would expect to find in a museum. Every painting was an elegant work of art, admiring the female form. In particular, an eight by ten foot photographic "painting" on the rear wall depicted a beautiful lady reclining on a couch, ala Francesco Goya's *The Naked Maja*. The image was mesmerizing, as the back lighting changed from a glowing sunset to a sensual night scene, an enchanting controlled effect.

Toni was still radiant, vivacious and charming. I still wasn't over her—and I never would be. My dating was a constant search to emulate everything we had, but it didn't prove likely. In 2000 I sent Toni a copy of George Jones' classic hit, *He Stopped Loving Her Today,* considered to be the quintessential country music love song of all time.

Sausalito, the quaint, small hamlet across the bay was the chosen location site for the Brooks character's houseboat art studio. This converted barge sat on the end of a row of hippie decorated floating residences. When I asked a local resident how the area became known as *Shit Alley*, my question was soon answered when we suddenly heard a swishing sound—an amplified toilet flushing noise. Turning toward the source, we focused on an old houseboat duct as waste streamed into the dark waters. He looked at me, "And you're going into THAT water?"

James Goldstone was directing this MOW/pilot, created by Producer Collier Young. I hadn't worked with Jim since the critically acclaimed 1961 TV series *It's a Man's World*. My old KTLA buddy, Joe Cavalier, was the assistant director. Goldstone carefully explained what he wanted, which was a continuation of a houseboat interior shot they would later film back in Hollywood at Universal Studios.

Goldstone's fire gag shot had me busting through the houseboat doors aflame, crash through the porch railing into the cold, dark Sausalito waters and be rescued by Jeanne Coulter, Barbara Anderson's stunt double. Cavalier said I would also do the interior portion of the fire stunt back at the studio.

For the night shot, the flames emitting from me would be spectacular in the pitch blackness of *Shit Alley*. It has a nice ring to it, doesn't it? Anyway, I was taken aback to find that special effects man Bob Warner had never supervised a fire gag before—plus, his two assistants had never even seen a fire stunt. After mulling it over I wasn't fearful, but cautious, hoping this just might work out.

The constant, icy cold wind had everyone bundled up as we watched Carl Saxe, doubling the wheel-chaired Raymond Burr, steer the rolling chair down a steep hill to the water's edge. Jeannie Coulter, the stunt double for Barbara Anderson, in a flimsy knee-length skirt, would swim out to save me after I hit the water. Anticipation, combined with the normal adrenaline rush of a pending stunt, helped me combat my cold wind shivers.

Finally, we were ready to film. Inside the houseboat, Warner and his assistants nervously ran about like chickens with their heads cut off. I would later determine their heads were actually stuck in another part of their anatomies. They were making me nervous as they painted the rubber cement on my back, arms and legs. Warner understood that he would light me and wait until my entire back was afire—with the flames high above my head—before cueing me. I had him repeat the procedure to me. I prayed he understood my every word.

On "Action!" Warner touched the torch to my back—I heard the swishing sound fire makes, when he suddenly yelled, "Go! Go! Go!" I thought the cue was premature, but Warner could see the flames and I couldn't, so I busted the doors open, crashed through the railing and into the water. Jeannie swam out and pulled me to shore. Her knee length dress had shrunk to a mini-skirt. We both conceded that we'd never been that cold in our lives. Jeannie would go on to prove her exquisite stunt talent and abilities, including doubling Farrah Fawcett and Cheryl Ladd on *Charlie's Angels*.

Goldstone was not pleased, in fact he was pissed. He expected to see more flames and he was right. I changed into dry wardrobe and we did the shot again. And, there still was not enough flames, but they weren't about to go for a third take. As I walked back to the honey wagon dressing rooms the 30° icy wind was almost unbearable. Geraldine Brooks rushed to me with her pair of thermal underwear and dried my hair. What a beautiful, sweet, caring lady.

Later, I confronted Cavalier, reiterating that fire gags were my specialty, and this was the first time I ever had to do two takes because of an incompetent special effects department – plus, he balked when I mentioned my stunt adjustment. What an eye-opening experience—my first opportunity to see my old buddy in action and he wasn't too honorable.

The two Sausalito detectives assigned to the film company were very concerned, asked if I had ingested any water during my plunge into *Shit Alley*. I was still so keyed up by this time that I didn't recall, but suggested it was a probability. Immediately, they marched me toward *The Ark*, an old paddlewheel boat converted to a restaurant bar, moored at the entrance to *Shit Alley*. In true seafaring character, the ship was moored at a 10° angle.

Now very serious, the guys insisted I wash my mouth out with whiskey, explaining how one of their officers had been scuba diving at the *Shit Alley* location and became deathly ill—the infected water caused sores on the inside his throat, with swelling so severe he required a tracheotomy.

Ushering me to the bar, one ordered three double shots of Jack Daniels and, with glasses in hand, we moved to an outside balcony. To eliminate the germs, they suggested I take a big gulp, swish it around and spit it overboard. Complying, with a big slug, I rinsed my mouth as one cop slapped me on the back, causing the overpowering liquid to warm my innards. They laughed uproariously; explaining that their fellow officer did have a health problem, but it wasn't caused by the contaminated *Shit Alley* water—a virus had necessitated his emergency treatment.

When *Ironside* returned to Universal Studios, Cavalier didn't call me for the fire gag interior shot as promised, but instead hired veteran stunt gal, May Boss. The rubber cement Bob Warner neglected to apply on me, he used on May, causing the flames to shoot six feet above her head. Luckily, stunt men Chuck Courtney and Bill Davis, May's boyfriend, were visiting the set as the local county fire marshal froze in horror. Chuck quickly leaped into action, grabbing the marshal's fire extinguisher and doused the flames, as Bill used a wet blanket to prevent the flames from burning her face. May was very lucky that day.

I later realized this fiasco was business as usual at Universal, known throughout the industry for paying its crewmembers only union scale. The workers accepted this pay rate to establish their required work days and would later move on to another studio or independent production where they could negotiate a greater salary. Guys like Bob Warner never left Universal.

Universal had used this same ploy against the stunt folks in the early sixties when their production managers, most all Columbia Pictures alumni, simply stated, "The stunt is a hundred bucks. If you don't want to do it, we'll get someone else. Take or leave it." SAG's scale in 1959 was eighty dollars a day. I turned them down repeatedly, and then later realized the stunt guys who were telling me to keep my price up were working at Universal, often performing two and three stunts a day.

Veteran stunt man Fred Krone had met Universal's chieftain Lew Wasserman in the early 50s, with Jock Mahoney, when Lew was the head of MCA. Fred, always ready to right a wrong, explained the $100 Rule to Wasserman and we were then allowed to negotiate for stunt adjustments.

Four or five years later, I bumped into Raymond Burr and remarked that I hadn't worked *Ironside* in a while. *Ironside* wasn't a true action show, but more of a psychological who-done-it cop series, but there was an occasional need for a stunt performer. Surprisingly, a month later, I received a work call for the show. Arriving at the 110 Freeway overpass location near Chinatown, I found that Burr was directing the episode and he had requested me. It was one of those times when someone remembered.

It was the usual San Fernando Valley 98° summer day, where the Sun attempted to shine through the Los Angeles basin's brown smog layer. I wasn't a beer drinker, but a cold beer sounded refreshing. For years, I had passed a small, canary yellow log cabin beer bar on Studio City's Ventura Boulevard. Settling on a stool I could see two doll faces dancing together, when the female bartender approached, and said, "I don't think you want to drink in here." Beyond her stood two menacing bull dykes prompting my reply, "I think you're right," as I dashed out.

On American International's *Wild in the Streets*, a 1960's youth rebellion film condemning "anyone over 30," I fought Dale Van Sickel, and was the first to be shot in freeze-frame, after I pushed past Walter Winchell, once America's most influential columnist. Filming on MGM's Lot 3, we broke for lunch: co-star Ed Begley, whom I had known and worked with previously, saw my bloodied face and torso, yelled, "Dammit Jesse, I told you to behave." Ed was a kind, fine actor and a gentleman with a great sense of humor.

Alfred of the Amazon, a TV pilot starring Wally Cox made *Gilligan's Island* look like Shakespeare. The vapid story line had Wally inheriting a cotton plantation in South America. While checking out the vast property he meets the caretaker, a short, German accented, mustached fellow, strangely resembling the Third Reich's fuehrer.

My old buddy, Charlie Rondeau was directing as I thrashed about a lagoon, with an old, ten-foot rubber alligator. As rubber ages it becomes hard and sharp. During this wrestling match the inside of my right forearm was rubbed raw. The gator's old rubber skin literally sanded layers of epidermis off my arms. Tough, those damn rubber gators.

The show's shooting schedule spanned the Thanksgiving holiday and, once again, I'd be paid while enjoying my Mom's turkey dinner. After wrap Wednesday night, I met Charlie at the Culver House for a drink. He was having a brief meeting with the show's producer, and said he would meet me at the Sax Brother's new cocktail lounge in Encino. Paul Nuckles joined me at the club and as time passed we wondered what was detaining Charlie. After two hours we each headed to our own barns.

Returning to the set Friday morning, I was anxious to know why Charlie was a no-show. Seated near camera, studying his script, his right arm was in a plaster cast, "Charlie, what happened Wednesday night, a car accident?" He explained that the producer wanted to go to dinner and one drink led to another, until he arrived home in the wee hours of the morning. Pulling back the covers to get in bed, his wife said, "You're not sleeping here." He tried again and she shot him a kick, fracturing his arm. "Where'd you end up sleeping?" He sheepishly replied, "On the couch in the den."

Fred Stromsoe was the stunt coordinator when I had last worked the *I SPY* TV series, but this time the call came from the first assistant director Mark Sandrich, Jr. ((his father directed several Fred Astaire-Ginger Rogers musicals at RKO) I'd worked with Mark on the *Alfred of the Amazon* pilot with Wally Cox and would again be doubling the former *Mr. Peepers*. The episode's workdays spanned December 7, 1966, marking the twenty-fifth anniversary of the Japanese sneak attack on Pearl Harbor. The cast and crew listened to my transistor radio of our nation's *Day of Infamy*, as radio station KDAY aired the actual radio recordings of that fateful day.

The Culp-&-Cosby-to-the-Rescue shot had me leaning under-the-hood of a damsel's European sports car engine as Wally recited his dialogue into an off-stage microphone. As he spoke, I reacted to his words when suddenly the car's front-tilted hood crashed down on me. Culp had delivered a well-placed hit. Bill Cosby then dragged me from the scene. It was a "Print" and all was well. Later, as I changed out of wardrobe, the men's costumer said, "Boy, were you lucky." I replied, "Oh, it was a piece of cake, especially, with the rubber padding lining the inside of the hood." "No, you're lucky Culp didn't decide to Karate kick the hood, then the hood would have really nailed you, rubber padding or not. Shit, he seldom does what he rehearses." I just shook my head and finished dressing.

This reminded me of the first time I had doubts about a fellow stunt guy. It was during the bar fight in *Everything's Ducky*, when after jumping on Dick Geary's back, George Sawaya was to throw a round-house punch to knock me off. Two days previously, during the season's first rain, I had flipped my pristine 1956 Studebaker President on the Hollywood Freeway, resulting in a six-stitch cut under my chin. I probably over-reacted, but my chin was still throbbing when I told George "If you hit me, I'll find you whenever I get up off the floor." Of course, he missed me by a mile, but like the mule and the two-by-four, first, you have to get his attention.

It seemed like the job of a lifetime when The Mary Webb Davis agency called me for a TV commercial interview. "You've got it. They're looking for a young Mickey Rooney. Can you sing and dance?" Emphatically, I replied "No!" "Well, don't worry, you're perfect."

Entering the cavernous Century Plaza Hotel banquet room, I was impressed as 50 or so transplanted Broadway singers and dancers rehearsed. The TV commercial was for Google, an all-in-one-jar, peanut butter and jelly combination—a novel idea still on the market shelves. Seated at a piano was my buddy Dick Winslow, whom I had met with Rooney, translating the musical jingle to paper. Dick was a musical genius, former child actor with Rooney, a one-man band and a great guy. In the 1960s he entertained airline passengers aboard the Hacienda Hotel's Burbank to Las Vegas flights.

This Chicago advertising agency had held auditions in the Windy City, and had now extended their search to Hollywood. Apparently, the ad agency execs just wanted a Tinseltown vacation, as their final choice was a fellow they originally auditioned in Chicago. The selected singer-dancer wore purple tights and a large peanut with bulging eyes costume. You could have put a moose in that outfit and no one would have known the difference.

Tim Rooney called me to double dear ol' Mick for a Chicago area sulky racing TV commercial. Videotaped at a doctor's ranch in nearby Sunland-Tujunga, the stable and racetrack location was a world away from L.A.'s downtown hustle and bustle. The sulky trainer coached me once around the track and we got the shot in one take.

1967

With the overwhelming success of *Batman*, ABC-TV quickly doubled their bet with another comic book hero TV series, *The Green Hornet*, starring Van Williams and an unknown Karate expert named Bruce Lee.

During the lunch breaks the stunt guys from each show would get together. Bruce Lee was incredible as he displayed precise timing and agility with two "hits" on me. With complete control and split-second timing his first kick stopped a quarter of an inch from my nose, another just slightly touched my crotch—a touch I *almost* felt, otherwise today I'd be singing soprano in the Vienna Boys' Choir.

Though Bruce Lee performed with lightning-fast speed, his martial arts skills were admired, but was generally pooh-poohed by the other stuntmen as just a passing fad. None of these stunt seers will ever be accused of being a Nostradamus incarnate.

CBS, yearning to prove that "Imitation is the sincerest form of flattery," made their move to cash in on this high-rated, comic book programming style, created *The Original Yellow Tornado and Dickie Boy*. Starring Eddie Mayehoff and Mickey Rooney respectively, it was a *Batman* and *Green Hornet* variation of two 1920s retired crimefighters, recalled to duty in their 1927 Buick Touring car, driven by their Japanese chauffeur, Hibachi—Morey Amsterdam played

Krumholzt, the mad scientist. The hilarious, half-hour pilot, final edit timed out at forty-three minutes, but unfortunately didn't make the network schedule.

Harvey Parry, the stunt coordinator on Clint Eastwood's *Hang 'Em High*, called me to double an actor in a hanging scene, directed by Ted Post. This was Clint's first American film after making his "Spaghetti Westerns" for Italian Director Sergio Leone.

On MGM's Lot #3 in Culver City, the thirteen step gallows loomed ominously for the multiple hanging. Carefully, I checked out the scaffold, the tripping mechanism as the special effects man triggered the lever. Sand bags, matching my weight, plummeted through the trap door. It worked well and I was then fitted for the hanging harness and wardrobed for a perfect and comfortable fit.

Hang 'Em High would film in two days, so I trekked back to Studio City to await my work call. However, Fred Stromsoe, running the *Dundee and the Culhane* CBS-TV series, called me to double Sir John Mills (Juliet and Hayley Mills' father) for filming at the Corriganville Movie Ranch in Simi Valley.

Quoting Yogi Berra, "This is deja vu all over again." I had worked at the movie ranch in 1958 for $6.00 a day and this job would indeed be an event, returning as a full-fledged Hollywood stunt guy and earning fifty times that amount.

I phoned Harvey to explain the job conflict and asked to be replaced. He wasn't pleased, but considering his past behavior and what he would do under the same circumstances, I didn't particularly care.

Meeting Sir John Mills was a great honor. Casually, we conversed and he surprised me when he mentioned how much I resembled his good friend, Sir Richard Attenborough.

On *Hang 'Em High*, Janos Prohaska replaced me in the gallows plunge through the trap door and suffered a broken ankle. I never learned what occurred to cause his mishap, but I marveled how destiny had once again stepped into my life.

Often, booze had nothing to do with it. In 1967, the Academy of Motion Picture Arts and Sciences notified SAMP that veteran stunt man Enos Edward Yakima "Yak" Canutt would receive a special Academy

Award Oscar for his contributions to the motion picture industry, especially, his creation of the chariot race in Ben Hur.

Yakima Canutt was a stunt pioneer from the first day he stepped on a movie set. This award befitted the Washington state native, who ranked as the World All-Around Rodeo Champion in 1917, 1919-1920 and 1923, and starred in many silent film two-reelers. Combining his extraordinary horsemanship abilities and ingenuity, Yak devised many innovations that are still filmmaking basics of action today.

Take the picture fight, for instance. Originally, the actors and stunt-men threw aimless punches, with many connecting on purpose or otherwise. The result was nothing more than windmill-like arm waving, tackling and rolling around. Yak devised the art of throwing a punch past a person's jaw-line with a corresponding reaction of being punched in the face. When sound arrived in 1927 the sound effect of fist-to-jaw contact was added.

Later, Republic Pictures director William Witney, after watching veteran musical director Busby Berkeley rehearse dancers, would choreograph the fight routines into shorter segments and varied camera angles.

Yak stunt doubled many leading actors, including John Wayne and Clark Gable. His most famous stunt occurred during the Indian attack on 1939's *Stagecoach*, when he leaped from his horse to the stage coach's galloping six-up running team. John Wayne shoots him and he falls between the team to the ground as the coach continues over him. FYI: Yak had performed this same stunt on several Bill Witney films prior to *Stagecoach*.

In *Gone with the Wind*, Lila Finn doubled Vivien Leigh as Yak, doubling Clark Gable, drove the wagon through the "Burning of Atlanta" scenes. Later, on a lone bridge, Yak appeared as the vicious marauder attacking Miss Scarlet in her wagon, only to be thwarted by Big Sam, one of her faithful, former slaves.

To commemorate Yak's Oscar, Daily Variety and The Hollywood Reporter called SAMP proposing an ad purchase for this historic event—the first time a stunt man was ever honored by the Academy. The SAMP Board of Directors discussed the rates and decided to allow the general membership to vote on the ad size to be purchased.

President Roy Sickner opened the floor for discussion and immediately, Joe Yrigoyen (pronounced ear-going) shot his hand to the ceiling. From the mid-1930s, Joe was an extraordinarily talented cowboy stunt man and among the fortunate to have a regular gig—doubling Gene Autry and Roy Rogers at Republic Studios. Recognized by the chair, Joe jumped to his feet with a pained expression, "Why is he getting the award? I've been in this business a long time and I don't think that he…" Several members rolled their eyes, some shook their heads and the others simply didn't care to acknowledge such an inappropriate comment.

I don't wish to impugn Joe Yrigoyen; his stunt abilities and contributions to the stunt world speak for themselves. God knows he was the best at what he did. This is only to illustrate a prevailing attitude and mindset among the stunt performers.

After a lengthy discussion, the membership's final vote opted for an embarrassingly small, quarter page ad in Daily Variety. The Hollywood Reporter advertisement was ignored because the trade paper had supported the producers during the 1960 Screen Actors Guild strike. Often, subjects and their discussions rambled on, but stunt veteran Jack Verbois often brought everything into focus to settle the many disagreements.

Those in the Hollywood mainstream were privy to its stars peccadilloes, though much was unknown to the casual moviegoer.

Joan Crawford, a mega-movie star for five decades, had appeared in several adult stag films in the 1920s. Harvey Parry related his visit to Crawford's set. She greeted him warmly, noticed the 16mm film can under his arm, and ordered, "Go to my dressing room." She soon entered. "All right, you sonofabitch, how much do you want?" Parry handed her the film print, "Joan, I don't want anything." Crawford broke down and cried, "Oh Harvey, if you only knew how much these prints have cost me?" For years, she had purchased every film copy she could locate.

Warner Brother's veteran casting director Jim Martell called me for a favor—perform a live surprise fight for a prestigious Pasadena men's club shindig. They would pay the tuxedo rental and an additional fifty bucks. He also invited Denver Mattson to be my fight partner.

I had never worked with Denver, though we did meet briefly in 1964 at the Starlite Room. He was a construction cement worker, having just arrived from Washington to become a singer, but now, four years later, he was a legit Hollywood stunt man.

In my new 1967 Acapulco Blue Mustang convertible, we ventured out the Pasadena Freeway (L.A.'s first, built in 1940) to the Valley Hunt Club, one of Pasadena's oldest men's organizations and originator of the Tournament of Roses Parade in 1890. Eugene Metcalf, the club's chairman, explained how the surprise fight should be staged. Since Denver towered over me, I suggested we take precautions should a caring club member be inclined to rescue the little guy.

I related a staged fight I'd performed in 1959 with Steve Lodge at a socially elite Los Angeles Breakfast Club bash. It was Wild West night with the city's local gentry garbed in their finest "Drugstore Cowboy" Western attire. On cue, I loudly proclaimed to Steve, "You can't shove me!" and threw a right round house punch, knocking him to the ballroom floor. Immediately, I was on him and drew back to throw the next punch when a huge hand grabbed my right arm. I looked up as a guy was rearing back to strike me in the head with the butt end of a snub-nosed .38 revolver. Suddenly, a voice yelled out, "It's okay, Sarge!" He released his vice-like grip as Steve and I fought our two-man melee to applause. We later met the invasive undercover LAPD cop and laughed how the uniformed rent-a-cops cowered behind the potted palms at my first punch. Anyway, it was too close for comfort and I didn't care to repeat that experience this night.

Eugene assured us that a couple of the members would prevent anyone from interrupting our fracas and since we were an hour or so from the fight, offered us a drink at the bar. I requested a plain Coke, but became concerned when Denver ordered a hard drink. Suggesting he should have all of his faculties during our performance, he then had another drink and another.

Finally, we received our cue and our fight ensued. All went well with the battle ending with one guy in a prone position—Me! The crowd applauded and, as a live show veteran, the response was music to my ears. However, Denver misinterpreted the applause as a cry for more and suddenly snatched me by my tuxedo lapels. Before I could get my feet planted, he said, "Take a knee," and swiftly kneed me in the solar plexus. I collapsed like a sack of potatoes. Doubled up and gasping for air, I crawled behind a nearby partition. It was ten minutes before I could get my breath. I found Denver having another drink at the bar, and on the way home I proceeded to tell him what the Lord told John. We've remained friends for over forty years, but at times it wasn't easy.

Denver fancied himself as a serious participant in the "Sport of Kings" which prompts the question—if horse racing is the "Sport of Kings," is drag racing the "Sport of *Queens*?"

Regardless, Mattson had John "Bear" Hudkins tutor him in the art of horse racing. Scion of the Hudkins Bros. Stables, one of old Hollywood's supplier of livestock and wagons, Bear knew well his way around the horsy set as Mattson proclaimed, "Someday I'm going to win the Pick-Six."

Denver's wish was granted in the early 1980s, when he won the Pick-Six at the Santa Anita Race Track, winning over $600,000 in a three-week period.

From his Club House box seat, Denver attempted to emulate the rich lifestyle of his racetrack millionaire doctor cohorts. He purchased two thoroughbred racehorses for $70,000—a minimal cost, since these steeds also needed to be fed, groomed and stabled. A trainer and a veterinarian also became part of his racing enterprise.

Next, we visited a spacious $200,000 hillside home he was contemplating for purchase in the San Fernando Valley's West Hills area. I suggested he purchase the property out right, or at least make a hundred grand down payment, saying, "After all, this was a gift and its money in the bank." Instead, Denver only placed a $40,000 down payment.

His accountant Leonard Lizzi asked, "What kind of a car have you always wanted? Excited, Denver replied, "A Corvette!" "Well, get it, the government's gonna buy it for you." (I never have figured out how that works!) Denver promptly plopped down $29,000 cash for the luxurious, metallic brown sports car.

Within the stunt biz, Denver's fellow stunt men now perceived him as wealthy and he didn't need to work anymore. (They love to pigeonhole you.) His on-camera appearances dwindled, but his high lifestyle continued. The $40,000 house down payment produced a hefty monthly mortgage payment, as did the Corvette's $5000 a year car insurance. And, like most gamblers, Denver continued to "place an occasional wager on the outcome of an equine sporting event."

A year and a half later the Corvette was street valued at $16,500. Denver eventually lost the house and moved into a $600 a month motel room on Sepulveda.

Mattson's stunt career continued on the downward slide. He mentioned his new CDL (commercial driver's license) so he could perform truck stunts. My only thought was how could he, with virtually no experience, compete with veteran stunt men Carey Loftin and Jim Wilkey, who could slide, swap-ends or flip a 40-foot trailer on a dime? Denver was desperate and just drawing at straws.

The Red Coach in Studio City remained my regular watering hole, rubbing elbows literally with Los Angeles Mayor Sam Yorty, George C. Scott and Los Angeles Rams football legends Bob Waterfield and Elroy "Crazylegs" Hirsch. Representing the stunt ranks were Carey Loftin, Bill Hickman and Bob Miles.

One evening Hickman decided to show me his Studio City-Berry Drive home, racing his Chevy Corvair coupe around the hillside hairpin turns at 40 mph – completely disregarding the possibility of meeting another vehicle, bicyclist or pedestrian head-on. A card in his wallet may have spawned his invincible, devil-may-care, behind-the-wheel attitude. He had aided an LAPD officer and this official document prevented him from ever receiving a traffic citation. Nevertheless, this was the first and last time I ever rode with him. His recklessness blatantly fell into my "No Free Stunts" category and I wanted no part of it. Hickman would later be remembered as the driver escaping from Steve McQueen in *Bullitt*, and later coordinated and drove the car chase in *The French Connection*.

Football Hall of Fame, Los Angeles Rams quarterback, Bob Waterfield (formerly married to actress Jane Russell), a quiet, gentle giant, surprised me when we discussed player's salaries in 1951. Bob's highest, single season, earnings totaled about $30,000. However, his involvement in the oil industry amassed him millions. When Bob passed away March 25, 1983, Stu Nahan, the impetuous local L.A. sportscaster, erroneously stated Bob's age as 69, instead of 62. When I phoned the KABC-TV news director about "Nahan's flub," he responded, "Okay, what's he done now?" Bob would have loved it

Seated beside Noah "Pidge" Berry, Jr. in the Red Coach, I was in awe, recalling his many roles, including the 1930's *Tailspin Tommy* serials, aired every Saturday during TV's early days. I was still attempting to produce my *Butterfield Stage Depot*—a daily kid's show featuring the old serials, special guests and hosted by a Stage Master, hopefully, Pidge. He turned serious, "You're not going to make fun of the serials, are you?" "God no, Pidge, I grew up watching them, they were my favorites shows and you were my hero." He smiled. Later, when I pitched *Butterfield* to KNBC, NBC's local owned and operated Los Angeles TV outlet, they liked the concept, but passed because "We're now the all-color network."

In actuality, live-host kiddie shows had become extinct as the broadcasters found cartoons more profitable, and cheaper to air without a kiddie show host.

Saddling up to the Red Coach bar one day, we were stunned to hear that Bill Hickman, while driving home the previous night, had been hit broadside at Ventura and Whitsett by a drunken sailor on leave. A month later, we were again shocked when Carey was involved in a car crash at the same intersection. Each ended up at St Joseph Hospital across the street from Disney Studios. It was now two out of three and I cringed when they began eyeballing me suspiciously – as if I was a jinx, a "Jonah".

Several months later, after an evening of bar hopping with Denver Mattson and Jon Thorguson, I exited the Park View coffee shop in Universal City, crashing through an unmarked four by eight foot plate glass window beside the entrance door.

The next morning, from my St. Joseph Hospital room, lying naked on a gurney, adorned with only a sheet, awaiting surgery to my left lower lip, a nun passed my door, stopped, came in and lifted the sheet. She smiled and quickly exited. Guess that peek got her juices flowing. Later, finally stitched up, I called Carey Loftin and Bill Hickman, exclaiming, "I made it! I made it! I'm in St. Joe's!"

One evening from the Red Coach, I called Teddy's to check for messages and was told stunt man Ronnie Rondell wanted to speak with me, moments later we were connected. Ronnie said he had heard I had been drinking to excess. I was grateful for his concern, but was curious and asked where he got his information, "Dick Bullock told me." That was interesting, since Bullock was seated at the bar and feeling no pain.

This scenario reminded me of the guy who said, "Every time I see Harry, he's in a bar." The moralizers shake their heads and never ask what this clown is doing when he sees "Harry." There were few who drank more than I, but I never took a drink while I was working. But after I wrapped, hold on to your hat.

However, through it all, I always wondered why a drinker is never asked why he or she drinks?

Projecting the right image didn't fool anyone, as one regular drinker's policy was never to go to the same bar two days in a row. Another buddy would only order two drinks and leave, giving the impression he was homeward bound, but would visit one or two more saloons before hitting the barn, sh:t-faced.

Most interesting were the delusional chest thumpers who proclaimed, "I haven't had a drink in twenty years," but they smoked a joint every chance they got.

I doubled Ralph Manza on the *McCoy* TV series starring Tony Curtis, on *Hill Street Blues*, and again when he portrayed George Peppard's chauffeur on the *Banacek* TV series.

On this particular *Banachek* episode, Andrew McLaglen, 6'7" son of actor Victor McLaglen, was directing. I had worked for him on Disney's *Monkeys, Go Home!* His favorite joke was to catch two people talking, walk toward them, while pretending to be engrossed in a conversation with an assistant, and walk right over their feet. Actually, I guess it *was* funny if you were not the unsuspecting guy, who danced like a chicken with a hot foot, tyring to escape being stomped. Laugh and the world laughs with you. Yeah right, until Andy crunches you with his size 14, triple E, clodhoppers.

When George Peppard walked on the set, I greeted him, reminding him of *Breakfast at Tiffany's* when I doubled Rooney. Smiling, he assured me he didn't need to be reminded. Shaking my hand he recounted the many falls I made to the hard linoleum flooring, "It was painful just watching you."

George, seated in the limousine rear seat, as I doubled his chauffeur Ralph Manza during the moving shot. I crowded against the driver's door as the camera operator aimed his hand-held Arriflex at Peppard. McLaglen sat away from George as the crew readied the shot. With a break in their conversation, I asked Andy how fast he wanted me go? McLaglen didn't reply, and I knew he heard me as I was only three feet away. I repeated the question. Again, receiving no response, I muttered, "Shit," under my breath. George chimed in, "Jesse, go 20 miles an hour." McLaglen, immediately countered, saying "Make that *15* miles an hour!"

Accelerating the long, black Cadillac limo up to speed, I carefully watched the speedometer. We traveled the three blocks and I pulled over to the curb. "Cut! Print! That was perfect!" cried McLaglen. "How fast were you going?" I shot back, "Twenty miles an hour!" He jumped from the back seat, slamming the door. I exited the limo driver's door as a grinning George Peppard grabbed my hand, "Jesse, thank you. That was terrific!"

A local pub continued to beckon. On this particular day, Carey Loftin and I imbibed at the Red Coach and at 2am found us closing the Zomba, a Studio City strip joint. We had actually drunk ourselves sober, and then attempted to date the two strippers. What a day and night.

From time to time, the studio backlots of Universal, Warner Bros. and the Columbia Ranch would become ablaze. Televising the Universal backlot inferno, a KTLA Telecopter pilot later said the fire was burning backward from three locations, contrary to the wind direction and the fires reported point of origin. We nodded our heads knowingly, having never ever recalled a studio announcement to demolish their backlot sets to construct new ones.

During the sixties, I was a member of the Academy of Television Arts and Sciences when they presented interesting monthly programs, seminars and meetingsat the Director's Guild auditorium. Yearly, ABC, CBS and NBC presented their lineup of new fall shows. Often, these capsule presentations were an accurate barometer of the three networks future rating positions and existence.

A snippet of Producer-Director Jack Webb's new *Adam-12* TV series starring Martin Milner and Kent McCord had everyone on the edge of their seats as the black and white police cruiser chased the baddies into the Los Angeles river viaduct, culminating in a spectacular crash. The audience overwhelmingly predicted the new show would be a great success.

During the filming of the show's pilot I had visited the Laurel Canyon & Moorpark in Studio City location while veteran stuntmen Dale Van Sickel and John Dahiem, playing the baddies, prepped the cars for the chase. Another stunt man had been hired to double actor Milner in the *Adam-12* car. Jack Webb viewed through camera mounted in the cruiser's back seat for the ever popular "over the shoulder" shot. He noticed the stunt man's hair was too long to match Milner's, and called for a hairdresser. Then Ron Burke flatly announced, "I'm not cutting my hair." Webb turned to the assistant director, "Send him home."

Some of the guys inhabiting this business were difficult to understand. Hair grows back, so why would you refuse to cut it? Especially, on a show that can potentially become a great source of income for many years. Your prime mission in this business is to get hired and, if at all possible, find a steady gig. It's nice knowing where you're going to be working tomorrow—as opposed to the constant pounding on doors looking for work. I'd often heard, "You're only as good as your last job," but Guy Way countered, "No, you're only as good as your *next* job, because you don't know when that will be." At any given time, there are only so many jobs available in front or behind the camera. And you pray that a job will coincide with your talents.

I was invited to preview the *Adam-12* "Christmas reel," a collection of scenes, consisting of out-takes, flubs and general cut-ups by the actors, viewed at the yearly TV series Christmas party. Dick Clark made a fortune calling them *Bloopers*.

A porch scene involved Marty Milner and Kent McCord interviewing a gal in her mid-twenties. Standing in the doorway, it was obvious her mind was elsewhere. Finally, Marty said, "Well Ma'am, my partner and I are going to get a cup of coffee and when we return we hope you'll know your lines." In her comatose-stare she replied, "Thank you very much, Officer" and closed the door.

Another out-take showed the *Adam-12* police cruiser, towed by the camera car, as driver Marty and passenger Kent conversed about this episode's running bit regarding Kent's efforts to find homes for a litter of kittens. The ending credits and music theme played over their dialogue, so the audience couldn't hear Marty say, "Well, partner, I hope you find a home for those little pussies." "Well," said Kent, "you know how it is with stray pussy." Their banter continued until Marty conceded, "Anyway partner, regardless of what happens, I still love you," and disappeared out of view into Kent's lap. A grand smile soon graced Kent's face as the driverless police vehicle continued to cruise the streets of Los Angeles.

Unlike most in the Industry, I didn't get in it for the money—I was just doing what I loved and figured the money would be forthcoming. I always tried to be fair and equitable. But found my background in production has also been my misfortune. I refer to the historic attitude of most stunt men, actors and crew to "screw" the producer.

I'm not suggesting that producers should be considered for sainthood, but I've always maintained that if it were not for the producer there wouldn't be work. Someone has to create the job and this applies to any business.

Stunt man Fred Krone recommended me to the *Lassie* TV series for a fall down an old deserted mineshaft, doubling actor Bobby Diamond, formerly of the *Fury* TV series. This faux shaft was constructed on Stage 3 at the old Selznick Studios in Culver City. Fred had suggested $150 adjustment for the stunt to production manager, Bill Beaudine, Jr. (son of veteran director Bill Beaudine), but explained to him, "If the shaft timbers stick out too far outward, the gag price should be $175." The timbers did protrude and when I pointed to the extended beams, tears began to well in Beaudine's eyes. We stood silently, face to face, eye to eye. He was amazing. I couldn't believe it. This guy was getting emotional over twenty-five dollars. I figured I'd wait him out and maintained eye contact. After, what seemed an eternity, he said, "Well, you'd better do the fall in one take." I quickly replied, "I only do one takes!" I began to wonder, do all these assholes have the same line? But, this was astounding, *Lassie* had made millions upon millions of dollars for The Wrather Corporation, and here stood this clown quibbling over 25 bucks.

The gag called for me to fall through the decayed planks covering the mineshaft and grasp the edge before the fall. The exterior shot of Bobby Diamond's foot stepping on the boards had been previously been filmed on location.

To rig the stunt, I wrapped a section of seat belt webbing tight around my right wrist and had it securely riveted by the effects man. Measuring, I tied off the other end to a sound stage girder, allowing for the six inch stretch in the webbing my weight would cause while droppin/hanging. Veteran director Jack Hively (former editor/director from RKO's 1930s hay day) mentioned the small birdcage with a live white dove in my left hand as I crashed through the boards. Nearby, an American Humane Association checker watched my every move, blinked nervously when he heard "live white dove."

To capture the height of the fall, an Arriflex camera with a 20mm lens was set, looking up the shaft. This wide-angle lens, and the dim lighting, meant you could have stuffed your Aunt Fanny in the birdcage and not know what it was. I insisted on a stuffed bird and Jack agreed.

The fall through the balsa wood boards worked just as I had anticipated. The webbing stretched just enough to make it appear I had grabbed the top edge with my right hand, while frantically flailing the birdcage with my left hand. Had I allowed a live bird to be used in the cage, it surely would have suffered an unnecessary injury. More so, it was just one less factor for me to worry about.

For the second part of the shot, I cut the webbing from my wrist and now hung on the shaft's edge. On "Action!" I again struggled trying to escape, and then fell backward, twenty-five feet, to the boxes and mattresses below. The applause from the crew was, as they say, most gratifying, but not as much as receiving the 25 bucks that had made a grown man cry.

After performing a stunt, the adrenaline is still surging through every corpuscle, so, naturally, I'd drop by my local watering hole. There were several to choose from, and I usually chose the one closest to home to wind down. A favorite haunt was The Back Stage, located across from the CBS Studio Center, formerly Republic Pictures, in Studio City. At evening wrap time it was stargazing at its best, as the casts and crews from *Gunsmoke, Gilligan's Island, Big Valley, Wild, Wild West* and *The Mary Tyler Moore Show* gathered to relax. Several days a week, movie heavy Jack Elam held court in the corner booth playing Liar's Poker with assistant director Paul "Tiny" Nichols and other *Gunsmoke* staff. Jack always won.

I had been a *Gunsmoke* fan since the show's debut in 1955 and wondered long and hard how Ken Curtis' *Festus Hagen* could ever replace Dennis Weaver's *Chester Goode* character. This was all wasted energy as Ken proved to be an extremely talented actor, with an enduring career, including vocalist with the Shep Fields, Tommy Dorsey orchestras and The Sons of the Pioneers. He was also a member of John Ford's stock company, and married to Ford's daughter.

A fellow imbiber said he was "On the wagon." I asked, "How long?" He replied, "The day after tomorrow will be three days."

Warner Brothers casting director Jim Martell usually pulled out all stops to get a laugh at his annual Kentucky Derby party. He removed the bathroom lights so that when a gal closed the door and flicked the light switch without results we would all hear a blood-curdling scream. The door would swing open to see she had grabbed the doorknob, draped with a mayonnaise-smeared condom.

After a day of filming *Code Name: Heraclitus* at the Janss Ranch near Thousand Oaks, the Universal Studio driver navigated the country road toward California's Highway 101. Carey Loftin, Fred Krone and Buddy Van Horn occupied the back seat as May Boss and I sat forward with the driver. While reading the Hollywood Reporter, I sensed May was staring at me. Our eyes met, and then her look drifted to my left shoulder. Following her eyes, I suddenly let out a girlie scream and ended up on the station wagon's floor, under the dash. Everyone roared uncontrollably, including the driver, who was trying to keep the vehicle on the two-lane highway. The laughter subsided as I crawled back onto the seat. Carey knew I feared spiders and bees as much as he and had placed a wadded-up piece of black camera tape on my shoulder. He got me good.

But most unexplainable was how my right boot wrangled its way through the two straps of May's purse. If I had deliberately tried, I couldn't have done it.

With my yearning to become more than a fall guy, I conjured up a W.C. Fields project. I had been a fan since I'd seen him perform his famous juggling tricks in several Hal Roach comedies aired in the early days of television. Eccentric, to say the least, William Claude Dukenfield arrived in Hollywood in a chauffeur-driven Lincoln with $700,000 in a suitcase. He was one of Broadway's biggest earners, starring particularly in *Ziegfeld's Follies*, and the most insecure. It's impossible to estimate the many bank accounts he secured in fictitious names while performing in vaudeville from coast to coast. When Fields passed away December 25, 1946, he took the locations of his many bank account locations with him.

My tribute to him was to categorize the many one-liners from his films for a record album. MCA/Universal Studios had recently purchased Paramount Pictures film library and, with the exception of MGM's *David Copperfield* and the Hal Roach two-reelers, all of Fields' films were now under one roof.

Paramount Pictures publicity assistant Terry Wooley gave me several W.C. Fields photographs from the studio "morgue" to enhance my record project presentation. Hundreds of thousands, of still photos, dating back to the inception of the studio, were stacked to the ceiling of this isolated room. Months later, under studio guard, the entire "morgue" contents were taken to the construction mill and run through a band saw. Even at fifty cents a photo the studio would have accrued a sizable buck.

Evidently, destroying entertainment history was becoming endemic. When Gene Autry's Golden West Broadcasters purchased KTLA in 1963 from Paramount, all 16mm film kinescopes from the "First Commercial Television Station West of the Mississippi" were dumped off to a film salvager for their meager silver content. The monetary compensation received was paltry in terms of preserving Hollywood's television history for posterity.

I mentioned my record album concept to Tip Corbin, a former KTLA director, now a production contract coordinator for MCA/Universal, who suggested I meet Gil Rodin, Decca Records chief (now MCA Records): "His office is next to mine." Energetically, I pitched the popularity and financial potential of a W.C. Fields record album to Rodin, suggesting Dean Martin as the narrator, because of his and Field's mutual love affair with the bottle. Rodin was attentive and two days later called to ask if I had a detailed format for the album. I didn't, but promised to have it for him Monday morning. Over the weekend, I diligently designed each record track according to Fields' philosophies, his likes and dislikes. Rodin was pleased and we agreed on my salary of $500 a week for ten weeks to co-produce the album.

I was in Hog Heaven—five thousand bucks and I was officially a Hollywood record producer. Though this was a record deal, it could conceivably open doors to other production phases of the business I knew best. I loved performing stunts, but I was now seeking a new plateau and there was no telling where it would lead.

The following week my balloon burst. Rodin refused to accept my calls or answer my letters. "I place your letters on top," said Marilyn, his secretary, "and he puts them on the bottom." At our initial meeting, I could not see Rodin's eyes through his dark glasses, which should have been a tip-off. At my request, Marilyn returned my original presentation and I placed it, unopened, in attorney Doug Smithers safe. Informing Tip Corbin that legal action was imminent, his face turned ash-white when I suggested he would be my star witness. Well, so much for my good old buddy, Tip.

October 1968, the W.C Fields album was released with *Laugh In*'s Gary Owens as the narrator, a fine talent, and obviously less expensive than Dean Martin. The album was a great success and Rodin, utilizing the same principle, also produced albums from the Marx Brothers and Mae West films. All three albums became great hits and I never received a dime as the album's creator. I purchased it for $3.98. As for legal action, their attorneys maintained "Decca had planned this record album for several years."

A year later, MCA Chieftain Lew Wasserman, recognizing Rodin's creative efforts, rewarded him with a $125,000 Palm Springs home.

In 1971, Universal's main commissary was crowded as a buddy and I opted to sit at the lunch counter. Looking up from my menu, there sat Rodin two seats to my right. In four years he had become a shriveled up old man, crouching over half a grapefruit and a cup of creamed soup. The skin on his pale face was flaky, resembling scales on a fish. With a spoon, shaking like a dog shitting razorblades, he attempted to remove a grapefruit wedge. Sensing my stare, his eyes met mine as I said, "How's it going, Pal?" He nodded as I watched the trembling spoon approach his chapped lips. About a year later he began enriching the soil. Unfortunately, I never got around to it, but I seriously contemplated pouring a bottle of Scotch whisky on his grave. Of course, I was going to run it through my bladder first.

MGM called and this time it was for *Where Were You When the Lights Went Out*, starring Doris Day, doubling Broadway actor Robert Morse, noted for his Tony Award winning role in the stage and film versions of *How to Succeed in Business without Really Trying*. Directed by Hy Averbach, the script was based on the famous November 1965 New York City blackout, when exactly nine months later every hospital in the five boroughs was filled to capacity with pregnant women.

Working on this picture was my dream come true—meeting Doris Day. I had loved and admired her since the first time I heard her honey-sweet voice singing with Les Brown and his Orchestra on the radio in the mid-1940s. But, on the silver screen, she was the proverbial girl-next-door every red-blooded kid hoped to partner up with someday. As when I saw Mary Tyler Moore, I was mesmerized by her beauty, rendered speechless.

One evening on MGM's Lot #2 New York Street, while watching the crew set up the next shot, an unexpected set of soft lips kissed my right cheek. Turning, I was face-to-face with a Carol Morse, "Oh, Jesse, I thought you were Bobby." When you can fool the actor's wife, it's a stunt man's ultimate compliment.

Between takes I listened to the witty storytelling of Jim *"Mr. Magoo"* Backus, whom I hadn't seen since *Mad World*. This wonderful gentleman was on hiatus from his Thurston Howell III character on *Gilligan's Island*. He was a true gem and a laugh riot.

Location manager buddy Jim Mohlmann invited me to his apartment for a spaghetti dinner, his specialty. While reading a magazine, his new neighbor, Kathy, a cute, nineteen year old brunette came bouncing in. My "Hi" barely acknowledged her grand entrance as I continued to focus my attention on the magazine article before me. But, somehow, before long, she and I were rolling around Jim's living room floor. It was a spontaneous animalistic coupling, as we "ate and ran," much to the chagrin of ol' Jim.

After a blissful night of love making in her apartment, Kathy said she had a court appearance the next morning. Bashfully, she confessed her involvement in a Sunset Strip call girl-prostitution ring, and she was the star witness. Also, she confided that "Kathy" was an alias because there was a contract out on her. Whoa, I just love surprises.

We remained an "item" and spent many happy times together. She moved on with her life a few months later, and I often wonder where life's path took her. She was a sweet gal.

December 8th found me at Morey Amsterdam's party, surrounded by many Hollywood notables, including Pat Boone, Henny Youngman and my old cohort from *The Double Life of Henry Phyfe*, character actor, Fred Clark.

The next morning Paul Nuckles, Steve Lodge and I drove to Bakersfield, California, to catch a blacked-out L.A. Rams football game. As my 1967 Mustang convertible and two other cars, anxious to catch the game, sped down Highway 5's Grapevine, each vying for the lead position, we were amazed when two California Highway Patrol cars pulled all three cars over for speeding. Recalling my speedometer at one point had read 103 miles per hour, I was relieved when the CHP officer stated, "I clocked you at 80." Happily, I said, "Yeah, you got me!"

Did my favorite team win? I couldn't say, but when a touchdown was scored an enthusiastic male patron seated at the bar jumped up, lost his balance and fell backward, wiping out a table booth. That alone was worth the $78 speeding ticket.

Production manager Willard Shelton called from Universal regarding *The Perils of Pauline* TV pilot, directed by Don Taylor. I would double actress Pamela Austin, a pretty blond from a Dodge TV commercial fame. Two wardrobe ladies were fitting me for a dress when

Grady Hunt, the department head, appeared and had a hissy fit because I didn't have my own bra. I glared at this idiot, and then blurted, "I do this for a living, not because I enjoy wearing women's clothing." The ladies stifled their laughter as he sashayed back to his office.

The stunt was switching from a rope suspension bridge as it falls away, to a rope ladder dangling from a biplane. The bridge spanned the backlot's 450-foot deep canyon as a hundred foot crane on a side road prepared to swing in the rope ladder, creating the illusion it was hanging from the plane. Willard asked if I wanted a circus net rigged down below? "Are you kidding? From this height, I'd go through it like an arrow." The gag worked and Willard kindly embellished the stunt adjustment we had initially discussed.

The original *The Perils of Pauline* films dated back to 1914, starring Pearl White, with many thrilling, cliffhanging stunts, but this TV version didn't sell.

Veteran stunt man Fred Carson's sense of humor was as wicked as mine and while doubling Victor Mature on *Escort West*, he had to handle a large Diamondback rattlesnake. One of the rattlers got loose and as it scurried past Fred just reached down and snatched it up. The relieved and grateful snake wrangler said he wanted to mention Fred's able talents to production. Fred quickly told him to clam-up; as he couldn't make any money if production thought he wasn't afraid of the creatures. Often, making a stunt "look too easy" caused the assistant director to reduce or even eliminate a stunt adjustment. Then, the arguing (negotiations) would begin.

For the shot, the wrangler "milked" the snake's fangs of the poisonous venom, and then its mouth was sewn closed with nylon thread. The scene required Fred to sling the snake at actor X Brands (*Yancy Derringer* TV series co-star). Director Francis D. Lyon advised Brands, "I want a big reaction when Fred throws the snake at you." Brands was confident that he was safe with the snake's mouth sewed shut. The camera rolled and as Fred slung the snake from off-camera, and yelled, "The thread broke!" Brands gave an Academy Award performance as the cast and crew scurried for the nearest exit. Director Lyon got his "Big Reaction" and Fred got his "Big Laugh."

Another time, while working at Warner Brothers Fred told of a horsebacked actor waiting for the crew to finish lighting. Slim, a tall Texan electrician was moving a large arc lamp when the actor blared, "Don't spook my horse or I'll get down and kick your ass!" Slowly, Slim turned, "If you don't fight any better than you act, you better stay on the horse." The actor took his advice.

A November Sunday afternoon found me at the Hollywood Palladium as Sergeant of Arms for SAG's annual membership meeting. With several SAMP assistants, we coordinated the security with the LAPD and State Police for our unannounced guest speaker, Governor Ronald Reagan. The unsuspecting membership enjoyed the future President's appearance, including SAG Board member Nick Adams, whom I hadn't seen since *Hell is for Heroes* in 1961. He winked, greeted me with an endearing smile. As an actor, Nick was underrated, a true original and one of the good guys. His inexplicable medication overdose death a few months later on February 6, 1968, shocked us all.

In an effort to ease my Mom's life I'd often drive her home from her daily Hollywood Universal Tours managerial duties, and this day invited Steve Lodge along for the ride. A bit early, I gave him a tour of the exhibits, shops and quaint art galleries—was dumbfounded to see four linebacker-sized college students standing on the wing of a vintage World War II fighter, unscrewing the side panels using their quarters. I shouted, "Get off there! But, first, screw everything back together." They quickly complied and scurried away, but I couldn't imagine why they ignored the no trespassing signs to vandalize property. I turned to Lodge—but he was gone, nowhere to be found. I finally found him in an art gallery fifty yards away, "What the hell happened to you?" He then lashed into a tirade about how my interceding was none of my business. He was always a gutless prick, afraid of his own shadow. Looking at paintings? The only painting this SOB had ever seen was "Bulldogs playing poker."

CHAPTER 10

1968

A great start for the New Year—working on *The F.B.I.* TV series at Warners. Doing what you love is life's nourishment.

A week later, Nuckles reported he was the stunt coordinator on a low budget film called *Changes* for producer/director Hall Bartlett, and promised plenty of action for all of us. (At this time Bartlett was married to actress Rhonda Fleming.) Paul was the new breed of stunt men who would wangle their way in as a stunt coordinator, after serving a brief, if any, apprenticeship. Previously, there was an unspoken formula employed to attain this position: Tenure (i.e. experience). But now the doors were thrown open to any and all wannabees, if they could *CON*vince someone to hire them. Some failed as quickly as they started, while others were smart enough to hire the best performers for the job to make themselves appear creditable.

Nuckles did just that on *Changes*. In a park scene on a Harley "Hog," I rode behind Dick Ziker as we terrorized the local picnic goers. Roger Creed wore a harness under his shirt and as we roared past him, I grabbed the noose behind his neck. On paper this stunt must have read well, but when a 130 lb. guy grabs a two hundred-ten pounder... Well, suddenly, I was horizontal, stretched out, hanging with a one-handed death grip on the motorcycle seat strap and Roger's neck harness with the other—dragging him on the grass behind us. In the film, you only see me snatch Roger and it's a cut to the other action.

In another shot at Disney's Golden Oak Ranch location, I sat behind Nuckles as he executed a forty-seven foot motorcycle jump. My butt cheeks kissed the inside of my lips when we hit. I had considered standing on the rear pegs, but didn't want my possible weight shift to affect our jump. Paul was ecstatic, and rightfully so, he did a good job.

George Dockstader, a veteran two-card stunt man, supplied motorcycles and camera mounts to the movie business, was miffed because he wasn't coordinating the stunts on this show and didn't hide his feelings.

Nuckles related how Roger Creed had tried to roll a Porsche coupe, but the vehicle's low-center of gravity wouldn't allow it. After seven takes Dockstader approached a frustrated Hall Bartlett, saying he would roll the vehicle and guarantee the shot for X amount of dollars. Bartlett had financed the film with his own money and at first refused to pay George's costly demand, then relented. The company stood ready to shoot as Dockstader took off down the road and around the bend. A curious Nuckles ran to a nearby hilltop to see Dockstader releasing air out of the Porsche's right side tires. On "Action," Dockstader accelerated to his mark and slid the car into the soft burm. The right side tires mashed in and the car rolled over. There are many tricks of the trade and Dockstader knew which one to use that day.

Nuckles was a master opportunist and parlayed this stunt coordination job into others, primarily on low budget films. During this time Nuckles frugality showed through. There are several profane words to describe his thrifty manner, but you have to hand it to a guy whose entire wardrobe consisted of T-shirts, Levis and cowboy boots. His one-room bachelor apartment had only a closet and a bath, but wise investments in land and the stock market were his first steps on a path to becoming a millionaire.

My visits to Arizona always found the azure blue skies and cumulus clouds intoxicating, though I prefer lush landscapes of trees and foliage to burning sand and scorpions. Evidently, my predilection for greenery stemmed from my parents land purchases in the California desert communities of Apple Valley, Hesperia and Victorville. Years later, the property produced generous profits, but had they spent those same dollars seventy miles further to the southeast, they would have been ranked among the Palm Springs list of millionaires.

Veteran stunt man and buddy Fred "Krunch" Krone called me to double actress Patty McCormack in a fire gag for producer-director Maury Dexter's *The Mini-Skirt Mob*. This low budget epic joined the then current plethora of terrorizing motorcycle gang films. Jeremy Slate was the male lead and the mini-skirted Sherry Jackson and Diane McBain provided the eye candy.

Sherry caused a panic when she disappeared a couple of days later The search ended when Miss Jackson casually appeared after hopping a jet back to Hollywood to visit a boyfriend.

Exiting the Continental Airlines terminal, I hand-delivered Fred a 4"x4"x4'long balsa wood plank for the ubiquitous "belting a biker off a bike" shot and was rushed to location.

The fire gag was scheduled for filming early afternoon in a valley near the Old Tucson Movie Ranch. Changing into the fire suit and wardrobe, it was five o'clock before they were ready to film the scene. By now a breeze was blowing through the canyon. Veteran special effects man Roger George exploded the small travel trailer, sending debris a hundred feet up, amidst the mushroom cloud. In the next shot, I was to run from the burning trailer shell aflame, which was rather ludicrous since no one could have survived such an explosion. However, it's called "taking an artistic license." Stunt man Ronnie Rondell torched me and out I ran, turning and falling to my knees as the late afternoon wind whip-flashed the flames across my face burning my right eyebrow and lashes. On my feet again, I moved out of frame to a wet blanket as Roger and Fred manned the CO^2 extinguishers.

That evening Fred, Ronnie & Mary Rondell and I enjoyed a steak dinner at Pinnacle Pete's, a rustic steakhouse that sold your favorite prime beef cut by the pound. Catering to the casual, an unsuspecting gent wearing a necktie soon found his prized silk creation lopped off and nailed to the ceiling along with thousands of others—kind of a customer's rite of passage.

Fred Krone's voracious appetite peaked as he ordered a 32oz. Porterhouse steak. Finishing it off, he then ordered a 16oz. T-Bone. Obviously, this was his ploy to irritate every self-respecting vegetarian.

The only photographer to capture the stunt in flaming color was Ronnie Rondell's wife, Mary. The company still man missed the shot and had used black and white film. Go figure. Also, my cry for air triggered Patty McCormack's scream as she embraced her new husband.

Seven days later, as a result of the flash burn, a couple of layers of skin peeled off my face like a woman's facial mask.

Call it fate, being in the right place at the right time or just plain luck, when veteran assistant director Jack Voglin told Ronnie Rondell to call him when he returned to Hollywood. Jack was prepping a TV pilot and thought Ronnie would be a perfect double for one of the three leads, Michael Cole. *The Mod Squad* was the first TV series sale for the Aaron Spelling television dynasty and Ronnie would spend the next thirty years coordinating every series the company produced.

As usual, picture work slowed down in the spring as the networks chose their shows for the fall season, but if you were fortunate to land a feature film, it would take you through to the TV season start in July and August. However, those working on *Paint Your Wagon* in Bend,

Oregon, complained, "We're not making any money," referring to a lack of stunt adjustments. For six months, (while looking a gift horse in the mouth) they were glorified extras on weekly stunt contracts while the rest of us in Tinseltown scrounged for a day of work anywhere.

The F.B.I. TV series called again, and this time the filming took place at Fort MacArthur (named for General Douglas MacArthur's grandfather), located on a bluff overlooking San Pedro, California, and the Los Angeles Harbor.

In a scene of the townspeople versus the military, Nuckles was an Extra, but would garner additional bucks participating in the action with the stuntmen. The high-cover shot captured a mob of angry towns folk advancing on the military. Nuckles was leading the pack wielding a lead pipe as I stood in the front line of the opposing military. Step for step, he was trying his damnedest to look menacing. Actually, he was damn laughable. With my back to the camera I silently mouthed to him, "I love you" and puckered my lips in a kiss. He almost broke up, biting his lip and stared at anything, but me. The director yelled, "Perfect, Cut," and Nuckles howled in laughter. I wasn't trying to jeopardize the scene or Nuckles, but with the camera's 25mm wide-angle lens establishing shot our faces were indiscernible on the largest twenty-one inch TV sets of the day.

The movie business has always been known for its eccentric characters. Be it in front or behind the camera, some of the most unique individuals were the Extras, or as some preferred to be called, background artists or atmosphere. They came from all walks of life, a grand assortment of attractive young ladies and gents, retirees, former businessmen and just plain con men. Many complained when they worked and bitched when they didn't. Most all had an unrealistic vision of fame and fortune.

Always jovial, Lew Smith worked MGM almost exclusively, standing-in for Gable, amid small acting roles. One evening, while in the Retake Room near MGM's East Gate, he was invited outside by a guy who had borrowed money from him, who then shot Lew to death.

On the set, between shots, I admired one extra diligently studying a law book with grand hopes of becoming an attorney. Twenty years later, his nose was still buried in a legal text book and maintained he was "going to pass the bar soon."

Being an extra or background player is an easy way to make a buck without much talent. I don't wish to paint an unsavory picture, but after years of observation, it was obvious many would have stabbed their mothers in the back for a "Whammy," a $10 adjustment for doing a "little business" on camera—like merely being pushed aside as the star moved through a crowd. If you wangled a "Double Whammy," you were really in tall cotton. The Whammy was eliminated in the early seventies when the rules for extra "business" were modified.

A fellow 6'4" stunt guy asked about my recent jobs. When I mentioned recently doubling Rooney and Wally Cox, his jaw muscles tightened and his eyes became slits, his attitude changed like I had stolen his jobs. A buddy later quipped, "There are guys who hate you simply because you're successful, and many have never met you!" I found that reaction difficult to comprehend. Overall, I found that the money-based mind-set of extras and stunt performers differed only by the dollar amount involved. Don't think I'm a "woe is me" complainer. Just ask anyone who has been in the business more than a year and they'll agree that jealousy, envy and greed reign supreme.

Columbia's casting director Ernie King called me for a delivery boy interview on *Cactus Flower*, starring Walter Matthau, Ingrid Bergman and Goldie Hawn, which earned her a Best Supporting Actress Oscar. On the set, I met the beautiful Miss Bergman, whom I had loved since *Casablanca*. Director Gene Saks, the bilegerous husband of *Maude* actress Bea Arthur, got in my face, asked, "What have you done?" I blurted out, "About what?" Needless to say, he didn't appreciate my humor and a dorky-kid with glasses was cast in the part. Actually, I really was too old for the part.

During the interview for Universal's *The Hell with Heroes*, starring Rod Taylor and Claudia Cardinale, several of us were dressed as Bedouin terrorists wearing a burnoose, a one-piece hooded cloak, revealing only our eyes. Director Joe Sargent carefully studied me as a radiant Miss Cardinale remarked about my "beautiful eyes." I noticed Sargent's expression, who quickly countered, "He's got blue eyes. We can't use him." My old buddy producer Stanley Chase, watching, quickly jumped in, "We're filming from a copter—and you'll never see Jesse's eyes." I got the job.

On this blacker than black night, *The F.B.I.* series was filming in San Dimas, a small town forty miles east of Los Angeles, and I was doubling Kurt Russell again, escaping from bad guy actors Ed Asner and Wayne Rogers. Veteran director Jesse Hibbs, a former USC All American football player, described what he wanted me to do: Dash in front of an oncoming train.

We rehearsed the on-coming train at speeds of 10mph, 20mph and finally decided 30mph was the ideal speed. Cameras rolled and I ran toward the oncoming locomotive. It was disconcerting; all I could see was a bright, rotating, headlight approaching in the blackness; making the train speed was imperceptible. However, my plan was obvious: It's better to be early than too late. I made my run and purposely tripped and did a lay out, hit and rolled in case I was too early. But as I rolled to a stop, the local newspaper photographer I had asked to take photos of the stunt was kneeling beside me. The train continued roaring past as he vowed that he would "be my witness" to the accident. What? Was this guy *nuts*? We had discussed this stunt in detail an hour before. Suddenly, he disappeared into the crowd of 300 sightseers.

A week later at Warners, I bumped into director Jesse Hibbs, "The train hit your foot didn't it? I was surprised he knew, "Yeah, I felt a little touch." "I know you did," he said, "We ran the shot over and over in the projection room, and I won the bet." Jess bought me lunch at the Warner commissary.

Roger Creed and I were scouting jobs possibilities at Paramount and entered the *Rosemary's Baby* stage to see veteran assistant director Danny McCauley. Immediately, a male assistant to Roman Polanski asked, "Do you want to see Roman?" I don't know whom he was expecting, but it wasn't me. Later, in the wake of Polanski's exile to France, his involvement with a thirteen-year-old girl was matter-of-factly rumored on his behalf; she had a body of a nine year old.

Much like Jock Mahoney, Rick Arnold had a fantastic set of legs. At the Left Bank, Rick accepted the bet that standing flat-footed; he could leap up into a standing position on the bar. The bar's four-foot height didn't factor as Rick performed the astonishing deed without breaking a sweat. Apart from Rick's exceptional physical abilities, he later realized the stunt business was often in flux and became a Teamster driver coordinator.

Doubling Barbara "Missy" Stanwick on *The Big Valley* TV series as she fought her way out of a burning basement where she was being held prisoner was a kick. Von Deming doubled actress Julie Adams as we fought and fell down the wood stairway and through the railing. Rushing to a window, high up the wall, Von was to grab me and throw me backwards onto a breakaway table. Again, I didn't want to telegraph my crash and I wasn't going to look. It was all up to him to place me on the mark. To make him more conscientious, I warned him that if I missed the table I was going to get up and kill him. Well, Von couldn't have done better. One take and director Virgil Vogel was happy.

Stanwick, at fifty-nine, was a trouper and a professional, rolling among the flaming debris for her close-ups. Her balls-out, no bullshit manner reminded me of a photo Bill Hickman smuggled from MGM's *To Please a Lady* set in 1950—Stanwick, Clark Gable and Bill "flipping off" the camera. In those kinder times the picture would have flipped out Louis B. Meyer.

Between the *Big Valley* scenes I sat with Missy, Linda Evans, Richard Long, Lee Majors and Peter Breck. Peter and I were old drinking buddies and always enjoyed a bit of jest. Eyeing me in my Stanwick wardrobe he performed his best gay prancing routine, I countered, "Hey Peter, I remember when you used to kid about *THAT!*" Everybody broke up, including Missy. Peter stopped dead in his tracks, flustered, without a comeback, stomped off the set and didn't talk to me for six months. Oops, I had broken another Cardinal Rule: *Never upstage an actor.*

However, getting back to the characters, if you asked who the most outrageous men in the background were, I'd have to say it was the cowboy extras. Some came from the rodeo circuit; others were just good old boys off the farm, oil rigs, with a few ex-cons thrown in for flavor. Needless to say, they were wild, and partying was a main priority. One inebriated fellow named Taylor managed to chalk up 16 DUI's. He had an attorney on a retainer. "Crazy George" Tracy, a talented country-western harmonica player, succumbed to pills and booze. Jack Torneck, with his trimmed, black, moustache, was impeccable in his elegant Western wardrobe for every occasion. At the wild Sky Star saloon, an unsavory *Gunsmoke* fellow urinated in a gal's drink while she visited the ladies room and roared when she later remarked, "This drink tastes funny."

"OK Freddie" was famous for his "Super-sized" manhood—twelve silver dollars could be placed in a row, edge to edge. His notoriety continued years later in the George Segal starring vehicle, *The Black Bird*, an updated parody of *The Maltese Falcon*, when a film character was referred to as "O.K. Fredrico."

For a gala party, Ann Sheridan hired Freddie as a waiter, to circulate among the guests with a tray of hors d'oeuvres at crotch level, permitting his "Johnson" to be displayed like a sausage to the unsuspected. To enliven the festivities Sheridan pricked him with a fork, sending the tray and contents flying.

Other cowboys preferred to fight, whether they could or not. The saloon hang out of choice was the notorious Hitching Post, located near the stables on Riverside Drive in Burbank. Much like the Palomino, you had to fight your way in and fight your way out. The Hitching Post was gone by the early sixties, so many of the cowboys made their way over to the saloons near Warner Brothers Studios.

Located across from Universal Studios' main gate, prop man Eddie Keys' restaurant-bar, Keys, dangled thousands of hotel keys from its ceiling, donated by devoted customers returning from film locations around the world. What a collection!

Art imitates life. Fred Carson, Brando's double on *The Wild One*, rode his cycle into Keys one night after work. The next morning when assistant director Paul Donnelly heard about Fred's bar stunt he suggested Brando do the same in the film. Bill Hickman, while also riding through another doorway at Columbia Ranch, kicked the door, got hung up and broke his leg—played the rest of the movie in a plaster cast painted black.

Opposite Warner Brother's main gate was the Riverbottom Inn, next to the El Chiquita Mexican restaurant, up the street from Lou & Mack's (these gin joints have been replaced by a Warner Brothers parking structure), became a popular meeting place for actors, crew and extras. Customarily, we all made the rounds, I've often said, "I wish I had the money I made from the jobs I got out of a bar." Conversely, some of those drinks probably cost me a few jobs.

As usual, we were having a fine old time at the Riverbottom Inn, when a ruckus started between stunt man Denver and Gil, a large affable fellow—we occasionally chewed the fat over this and that. In four words, Denver was *drunk on his ass*—fancied himself a boxer and was out to prove his expertise to Gil.

Gil's reputation as a street fighter was no secret, having been a member of the old fighting troops of Bob Terhune, Fred Carson, Al Farley, et al, at the notorious Hitching Post saloon. Also, Gil had recently been released from San Quentin, was short on money, asked me the previous day if there was anyone I wanted roughed up, "Ya know, broken arms, legs, the normal routine for $150." I declined with "I'll keep you in mind."

Denver was still mouthing off to Gil as I pulled Gil aside, asking him to ignore Mattson's drunkenness. Gil grinned, "Just let me give him a little tap." My pleading continued as Mattson taunted him.

Finally, the two exited to the parking lot followed by the bar patrons. Denver wobbled, circled Gil in a fighter's sparring fashion. Gil, with hands at the ready, watched Denver's every move. Mattson swung a wide right—Gil adeptly sidestepped and pushed him on by. The shove, aided by his forward motion, took Denver crashing into two-card cowboy Tex Lambert's full dress blue Harley. Everyone laughed and retreated back to the bar. I thanked Gil, who grinned, "He shouldn't do that when he's drunk." Shaken and barely able to stand, Denver admitted he "come to" while circling Gil. Prior to that moment he was lost in an alcoholic black out.

The Denver Mattson saga continued. Denver drove a purple "Plum Crazy" 1968 Dodge Charger, one of the late 1960's hot muscle cars. After closing The Left Bank saloon at 2am, he found himself being chased by a police cruiser in Studio City. Exiting an alley near Vantage and Ventura, he failed to negotiate the turn, missed a telephone pole by inches and crashed into a Baskin Robbins ice cream store. Imbedded ten feet into the store, Denver attempted to start the car, but a cop's voice and cold gun barrel at his temple warned, "Don't even think about it." Denver slurred, "I just wanted a chocolate shake!"

The next morning Paul Nuckles called to suggest I photograph the crash scene. Approaching the disaster area, the irate Baskin Robbins storeowner surveyed the damage, spotted my Stuntmen's Association jacket. His anger spewed "Are you the stunt man who did this?" Adamantly, my "Hell, No!" still produced a suspicious glare.

The store looked like Nagasaki as "Plum Crazy" sat amid the ice cream freezers crushed against the rear wall—The two huge shattered plate glass windows were mere memories – with only a chain hanging sign proclaiming Flavor of the Month: Plum Nuts.

However, as strained as our friendship had been at times, I will forever be grateful to Denver. When my Dad died in 1971, he loaned me "Plum Crazy" to attend the funeral services.

My fervent love of movies continued with Sir Carol Reed's film *Oliver!* based on Charles Dickens' *Oliver Twist*. I was overwhelmed by all the actor's performances, the magnificent sets, the period costumes, the lyrical music and Onna White's fluid choreography. In all, after viewing the film three times, I found it to be an excellent film in every respect, however, Winifred Blevins, the Los Angeles Herald-Examiner's Entertainment Editor, panned the film unmercifully.

I couldn't believe the demeaning comments from a so-called professional film reviewer could be so far off base. My feelings were based on every movie I had ever seen and vowed to write her a Wayne Letter, but, unfortunately, I never did.

The Academy of Motion Picture Arts and Sciences members would later award *Oliver!* six Oscars, including Best Picture and Direction by Sir Carol Reed, uncle to actor Oliver Reed.

Cap Somers was a large, powerful man, and one of Hollywood's most notorious background characters. We were filming A.C. Lyles' *Young Fury*, in 1965, at Paramount and Cap was one of several passengers loaded in a team driven work wagon. The shot called for the passengers to exit. The others made their way out as Cap moved head first, right into the long 2 by 4 wagon brake. The thud sound was like hitting a mule between the eyes to get its attention. Cap rose back and nailed the board with a hard right. The six-foot oak timber quivered like an arrow. The director yelled, "Cut" and the scene was re-shot without Cap.

Mostly, Cap was known for his intimidation of assistant directors—threatening bodily harm, if they didn't hire him. He worked all the time.

For Thanksgiving, Cap invited one of his buddies over for dinner, watched the TV football games as Cap's wife, also a movie extra, prepared the multi-course dinner. Happily, she announced, "Cap, dinner is served." Cap and his friend continued to watch the game. She again asked them to come to the dining room, but they didn't move. Several more times her requests still went unheeded. Finally, in desperation, she marched into the living room, turned off the portable TV set, Cap turned it back on. His bride switched it off, but Cap again hit the on switch. Mrs. Cap grabbed the set, opened front door and heaved it onto the front lawn. Infuriated, Cap jumped up, stomped to the dining room table, grabbed the turkey platter, and heaved it also unto the front lawn. His wife walked calmly to the bedroom and slammed the door. Cap, also very calm, walked to the den and slammed the door. Alone, the invited buddy looked around, sauntered over to the table, grabbed a stalk of celery and pondered his Thanksgiving Day dinner at Denny's.

There were gentlemen like Mickey Golden, Mario Lanza's stand-in, and the Sunday drives through the San Fernando Valley, chauffeuring Mario's convertible, being serenaded by the great operatic singer. Proudly, he sported the engraved gold watch from Lanza.

Charlie Cirillo, a former vaudevillian, always with a smile on his face. For years, whenever we'd meet on a set, I'd give him, "Hi Charlie, a-one, two, three" and Charlie would jump into a soft shoe dance routine. He was wonderful, gentle man.

When not performing stunts, Guy Way worked extra, not for the $25 a day, but for the on-the-set card games. My most vivid vision was Guy, puffing a cigar, entering the Warner Brothers gate in his luxurious Rolls Royce (a gift from his wealthy second wife.), being waved through by an unsuspecting studio guard, and parking in a reserved space by the sound stage. Studios have since banned card playing.

Then there was Jack Berle an Extra, Milton Berle's brother, always the distinguished, white haired, mustached gentleman in every shot. From across the set I'd yell, "Hey Jack, ya heard from Milton?" He always replied, "Not a dime."

May 6th found me at Columbia for Jerry Lewis' *Hook, Line and Sinker.* Jerry was a big money maker for Paramount where his pictures never lost a dime, but when Howard Koch became Paramount's studio chief, a falling out caused him to move to Columbia. Jerry had full autonomy at Paramount simply because he had diligently learned every aspect of filmmaking, plus his films never lost a dime.

On the Columbia Ranch set in Burbank, I looked for Jerry—we hadn't worked together since December 1960, and he greeted me like it was yesterday. Veteran Director George Marshall, a gentle man, and his easy manner made my job easy—he knew what he wanted.

Jerry was as playful as always, between takes tossing a baseball or played one-on-one basketball. Columbia Pictures, however, didn't understand Lewis' carefree filmmaking modus operandi and, while his many films had made Paramount millions of dollars, Columbia's *Hook, Line and Sinker* was not a box office blockbuster.

My particular scene involved playing a newspaper boy on a bicycle, colliding with a milkman. George Marshall gave me free rein after I explained how I would hit the ground while still on the bike, roll and take the bike with me in one swift motion. The shot worked perfectly and George loved it.

There had been a six and a half year lapse between my Jerry Lewis films, so the following day I sent this Telegram: "Dear Jerry: In December 1960, I worked with you on "Ladies Man" when I collided with a telephone pole. Now, in May 1967, I again worked with you in a collision with a milkman. I look forward to 1974 when I again ride a bike and collide with a ?????"

The next day I received a call from Hal Bell, Jerry's long-time friend and assistant director, relating Jerry's enjoyment. In November 1969, Jerry's next film was Columbia's *Which Way to the Front?* Hal called to hire me, but I was on location in Nassau, The Bahamas, on CBS Films' *Darker than Amber.*

There are many stories about Jerry Lewis, most all written by those who don't know him and have never worked with him. He's one of the most talented men I ever worked with, one who took the time to relate and talk to me.

Hollywood's assistant directors and casting directors all knew my size, so when it came to stunt double Arnold Stang in *Skidoo*, an Otto Preminger film at Paramount Studios, I was there. Greg Amsterdam, comedian Morey Amsterdam's son, assistant to super-agent Jack Chertok, representing Jackie Gleason called earlier to ask if I could recommend a stunt double and stand-in for Jackie Gleason. Naturally, I named my buddy Guy Way, a perfect double for Gleason.

Our first night of filming was on Paramount's *New York Street* to film Gleason and Carol Channing. I was in awe, having watched Gleason since the early days of television, when he starred in NBC's first version of *The Life of Riley* in 1949, a short-lived series. William Bendix would later portray the bumbling Riley in a later *Life of Riley* NBC television series from 1953-1958.

Gleason strode arrogantly onto the set, scowling, looking at no one. Conferring only with Preminger, he moved from his director's chair, to his scene and back, still ignoring one and all.

Carol Channing, beaming and radiant, from her magnificent Broadway run of *Hello, Dolly*, was most charming. The scene rehearsal began when suddenly Preminger began shouting, "You call yourself an actress? You don't belong in Hollywood. You don't belong in movies." Channing began to cry. I couldn't believe it. With his German accent, this prick was using Gestapo tactics on one of the Broadway's great stage stars.

At 10:30pm assistant director Eric Von Stroheim, Jr. dismissed several of us, saying they would film our action the following night. After changing out of the wardrobe, I quizzed Preminger's longtime costume designer, "What should I do if ol' Otto starts screaming at me?" "If he starts on you and you're right, give it right back to him." I returned home cautiously contemplating my next night with this tyrant.

Later that night on the set, which had now become early morning; stuntmen Carl Saxe and Johnny Indrusano were playing cops in a 1948 flashback scene within the film. The shot called for them to run from a police station front door, down the steps and around the corner. Otto called action, and Carl lead the way, but Indrusano didn't run fast enough for Preminger and he started screaming in his Germanic accent. "You're no stunt man? You're nothing but an extra." On the second take, Carl and Johnny tried it again with Johnny right on Carl's tail as they rounded the corner. Suddenly, everyone heard aching, groaning screams. In the darkness, Johnny had crashed into a massive, ornate 1920's cast iron street light standard. Injured and agonizing in pain, Indrusano was removed by ambulance as Preminger continued filming as if nothing had happened.

The next evening I returned in my little old lady outfit to double Arnold Stang. After dinner, while returning to the New York Street, I practiced my slow, short stepped, little old lady walk. I had walked fifty yards or so when I heard footsteps behind me. Turning, there was Preminger, his wife and veteran cinematographer Leon Shamroy approaching me. Preminger uttered, in his best Nazi officer accent, "Very good. You look just like a little old lady."

A half hour later we began to rehearse the shot for camera. The premise, as part of the film's heist plan, was for Stang, dressed as a little old lady in a crosswalk, causes a speeding police car to skid to a stop, allowing his cohorts to escape.

For rehearsal, Otto yelled "Action," I began my slow, short-stepped walk into the crosswalk. Out of the corner of my eye I could see the 1948 Ford police car, driven by Victor Paul, was going too fast to stop. Sure as hell, Vic hit the brakes and the car skidded through the crosswalk, but not before I jumped out of the careening car's path.

Immediately, Preminger was at my side with his intimidating accusing accent, "Are you afraid he's going to hit you?" I looked at him eye to eye, "Yes, I am. I don't want a broken Leg." "Well, you didn't hit your mark!" he snorted. I snapped, "You never gave me a mark!" He looked around the crosswalk and pointed, "There!" I made a scuffmark on the pavement with my heel. The police car occupants, Charlie Percerni, Hubie Kerns and Victor Paul, rushed to console me, thinking his bullying was upsetting me. No way, I assured them. Cameras rolled and Vic was right on the button, skidding up to the crosswalk's white line. I didn't flinch a muscle, completed my walk. Preminger yelled, "Cut" and extended his hand for a firm handshake, thanking me. I went home pleased for another job well done, feeling that he might have upset the rest of them, but not me.

Ol' Otto years later admitted to "using LSD – to experience the drug's true effects" so he could relate to the film's basic hippie theme. For whatever reason our segment never made the film's final cut.

Later, while filming in San Francisco, two of the *Skidoo* prop men had heart attacks, some praised Otto's benevolence for picking up their hospital bill tabs. Sure, why not, he aggravated their heart problems. Months later, Indrusano hung himself with a thin garden hose, leaving $83,000 and, without surviving relatives; the Great State of California quickly stepped in to confiscate it.

A classic Hollywood story was when Robert Mitchum had signed to do a film with Preminger. Prior to filming, Otto cautioned Mitchum, "Bob, sometimes on the set I get tense and if I call you a son-of-a-bitch, I really don't mean it." Mitchum smiled, "Otto, that's all right. If I knock you on your ass, I really don't mean it, either." Otto never raised his voice to Mitchum.

To hone my stunt driving skills, I would often rent a car to practice skids, spins and swapping end maneuvers and, after eight hours, returned the vehicle with near-bald tires and 10,000 miles worth of road wear. When the western TV series and features faded in the early seventies, every cowboy stunt man suddenly became a "car man." When an A.D. questioned their driving ability, "Can you drive?" they boldly replied, "I drove to the studio, didn't I?"

My old friend, Chris Nyby was directing a *Lassie* segment, recommended me to double veteran actor Steve Brodie's young son, Kevin, in a quicksand scene at the Thousand Oaks Janss Ranch. Lassie pulled, saved me from this sucking quagmire and I returned to the wardrobe trailer to be hosed off and sent home. Suddenly, the second A.D. wanted me in a clean outfit to double Kevin again for several galloping run-bys. Seems the cunning nag traveled under a low-hanging branch, scraping the young actor from the saddle, leaving him bruised and shaken up.

Soon after, I received another call from *Lassie* for a rearing saddle fall and hurried out the old Selznick Studios' "Forty Acres." The a.d. Bill Derwin, a wrangler and I discussed the hillside burm location for the fall. The wrangler saddled up to me, "Stevie Myers' horse will be used and Stevie really should do this fall." His "recommendation" set off an alarm as I then suggested that Stevie should perform the stunt. The disappointed Derwin finally agreed, and I left knowing I wouldn't have to screw with a wrangler who could make you a hero or a bum. Mostly, I didn't care to negotiate the stunt adjustment with their teary-eyed production manager.

Ladies continued to flow in and out of my life, but Patty Dwyer, a legal secretary, still brings a smile to my face. I was 27 and she was 52—a delightful May-December romance.

Like other mature ladies I had dated, there was always mutual respect, a love of life and no game playing. For no apparent reason, my preference for older ladies began at 19, when I dated a thirty-year old doll from Paducah, then a 26 year old at twenty-one, and a thirty-seven year old when I was 30. Each had confidence, maturity and admired a younger man's dreams and desires. They were lovely ladies and it's to my detriment for not marrying any one of them instead those several years my junior.

Ben Franklin said it best in his *Poor Richard's Almanac*, "Always go with an older woman. They don't tell, they don't swell and they're grateful as hell."

A call came in to double actress Kathy Nolan, star of the *Broadside* TV series at Universal. George Robotham was doubling actor Edward Andrews, the commanding officer on this female version of *McHale's Navy*. Entering the set, I was greeted by Nolan's beautiful, young stand-in, the niece of stunt man/actor Frank McGrath, played Charley Wooster on *Wagon Train*, and was one of John Ford's favorite fall guys. She gave me the once over in my form fitted jumpsuit, complete with padded bra, "You've got a better body than Kathy." I didn't know whether to say thanks or slap her.

Veteran director Charles Barton (several Abbott & Costello films) explained how he wanted me to give George an "airplane spin"—wrestling jargon for someone laying across your shoulders as you spin around—a "cut to" shot with George already spinning. George weighed 210 pounds and was positive I'd drop him on his head. We were ready to film and, as I bent over to allow George to lie across my shoulders, he didn't push-off as I lifted. I thought I'd gotten a hernia when he didn't budge—it was like trying to pick up a rooted oak tree. Cameras finally rolled and we got the shot. When Barton called "Cut!" I gave George a couple of extra spins, just to let him know I was in complete control.

I didn't have a hernia, but the next day stunt gal Jeanne Epper cornered me about the job. Her on-going attitude was that every stunt double job for any actress, anywhere, was hers by divine right. Simply, I told her I didn't particularly like dressing in *drag* and anytime a girl qualified for any stunt job, including spinning a 210 pound guy, they could have it with my blessings. Still, she was pissed because she didn't get the job. In forty years, she was the only stunt girl to ever question my doubling a female; a job I never solicited.

Maybe the other guys enjoyed dressing in drag, but I found the up-draft chilly to the male anatomy and an invitation to injury. The major occupational hazard when doubling ladies and kids are the clothes, they are usually tight and short sleeved, which make it impossible to conceal stunt padding. Invariably, I always got bruised and banged up.

For the *There's Always One* file, whenever I'd walk onto a set in a female double outfit, invariably among the crew jokes, there was always one guy who got his jollies patting my ass or squeezing my padded bra. Freud or Jung might have described these fellows as having latent homosexual tendencies, but my guess is they were just vicariously living their desire to squeeze a breast and not getting knocked on their ass for doing it.

Hollingsworth Morse directed the *Adam-12* episode when I played a drugged out marijuana junkie on fire in bed. The fire suit was borrowed from Columbia Pictures' wardrobe boss, Tommy Dawson, who had made it for me on the film, *The Dying Room*. At the last moment, the film's fire gag was written out of the script, but not before the studio had invested $1000 for the asbestos-cloth jumpsuit. Tommy was a nice man, apologized because he couldn't give me the fire suit outright, but said I would have access to it anytime I needed it.

Heading to Universal's Stage 4 ready to be set aflame, I met special effects guy Al Henley and immediately thought, "Ah ha, another Universal Studios panic," recalling the Bob Warner fire debacle on the *Ironside* pilot.

This was September 25, 1968 and I had checked everything with Henley. Eddie Dodds, a former assistant director, was now associate producer on *Adam-12*, Harry Hogan, Jr. and Don White were the first and second assistant directors, respectively. Gathering them together while filming on the backlot, I emphasized that I only wanted to do this fire gag once or it would cost them double. Holly had previously agreed to use a second Arriflex camera and suggested I clear it with Dodds, who consented to the additional camera.

We were ready to film as I checked everything, including the fire extinguishers. Everything, that is, except Henley. While applying the rubber cement on the top of my legs, he moved to paint the flammable glue over my crotch, "Hold it, on the legs only." He looked like a deer caught in the headlights with his cherry red complexion framed by snow-white hair.

Hogan called for a "Roll," as Henley, with a flaming torch in hand, suddenly lit me, then turned to light the rest of the room on fire. I couldn't believe he lit me before lighting the set. I didn't call "Cut" because we'd then have to start all over again. However, I was burning 20 seconds before he exited the set and Holly called "Action." On cue, Marty Milner came through the door into the smoke-filled room, as I lie in bed aflame. I could feel the growing heat as it began to penetrate the fire suit. Through gritted teeth and squinting eyes, I quietly pleaded, "Marty, hurry up, it's getting hot." The fire was becoming unbearable, but it was like a runner's second wind—I was suddenly able to withstand the pain a bit longer. Still, Marty was "acting" and maintained his slow pace. I almost screamed, "Cut," but, again, knowing that we'd only have to reset the shot, I didn't.

I thought that *there must be an easier way to make a living*. Never had this thought ever occurred to me while performing a stunt. Finally, Marty tossed a rug across my legs, smothering the flames and carried me out of the room.

But the damage had been done. I was in pain and didn't know how bad the burns were until I unzipped the fire suit to see the blistered skin on my upper thighs. Director Holly was very concerned. Assistant director Hogan then came over to say they now wanted to shoot a close up of the fire. "What?" I said loudly as I grabbed his arm and pulled him to Dodds, who was standing with producer Bob Cinader. "Eddie, you said we'd have a second camera for this shot this morning?" Eddie played dumb and didn't answer. It was typical MCA/Universal Studios bullshit, constantly cutting corners at everyone's expense.

The pain from the burns was increasing, and with the prop man's assistance—I wrapped towels, then aluminum foil around my legs and we hurriedly filmed the closer shot. Hogan told me to change wardrobe and a driver would take me to the studio infirmary.

Changing into my street clothes in a flash, I could feel the burned area rubbing painfully against my pants as I rushed back to stage 5. I flung open the stage door to a dark and vacant sound stage. Never have I ever seen a crew wrap a set that fast. I couldn't have been gone for more than ten minutes

Struggling with my heavy stunt bag, I walked toward the infirmary a hundred yards away. I could feel the burned skin tightening. The lone nurse on duty cleaned the burn areas, applied a salve and wrap-bandaged each leg wound. The medical report noted I had suffered second-degree burns.

I received double the bucks from what we had originally discussed for the fire gag. But it still wasn't enough. A burn healing process is slow and it's no wonder people leap from twenty story buildings to avoid being burned alive. Fortunately, my legs weren't scarred. It would be the first of four injuries I would suffer performing stunts in a forty year career span. I guess, overall, that's not too bad a record.

Rising early the next morning, I drove to Disney's Oak Tree Ranch near Placerita Canyon, in what is now called Canyon Country. With my legs still bandaged, I changed wardrobe to double veteran actress Irene Tedrow, who was playing Dick Van Dyke's mother in Columbia Pictures, *The Comic.*

Director Carl Reiner and producer Aaron Ruben wrote this fictitious compilation tale of a silent movie comic star, based on Buster Keaton, Stan Laurel, Charlie Chaplin, et al. Rounding out the cast were Mickey Rooney, Michele Lee and Cornel Wilde. It was a fun show. Carl knew what he wanted and the cast and crew was more than anxious to deliver.

Doubling Tedrow, the shot called for me to "bull dog" Van Dyke's double, Walt Davis, as he rushed from a cabin. Walt confided that he had a bad back and begged me not to tackle him in that area. I suggested a lower hit from the knees down, and assured him the "grab" would be light, so he could take his own forward fall.

On "Action," my run and leap—a layout caught him around the shins as I crashed to the ground. My contact with Mother Earth was more direct; a "goose egg" suddenly appeared on my right forehead. I wasn't aware of it until Carl pointed at the bump and produced a fifty-cent piece from his pocket. "Cold metal is good for it," declaring it was an old wives-tale remedy.

My subsequent work on this film was joyous. Doubling Rooney leaping out a window, to portraying various characters in the many silent movie vignettes was the thrill of my life. From the Keystone Kops to Laurel & Hardy and Buster Keaton, I was duplicating the silent film stunts I'd watched all my life.

One shot called for Dick Van Dyke to be caught in hurricane-like winds, causing him to grab a vertical pole. The strong winds have him clinging for dear life. With great physical control, Dick braced himself into a horizontal, flag-waving position as the prevailing winds continued. Starting from behind camera, my bit was to roll past Dick like a tumble weed into a hedge, twenty feet behind him. Struggling against the roaring wind, provided by three Ritter (airplane engine) fans, I repeatedly staggered to my feet, only to be blown backward into the bushes. Finally, Carl called "Cut, print." Dick immediately relaxed his straining grip and asked Carl how he looked. Carl replied, "I don't know, I was watching Jesse."

Another silent bit had Dick trying on a jacket, taking with him the long board it was hanging on. Like B-47 airplane wings extending from his shoulders, he creates havoc as he innocently strolls along the city street, knocking and batting everyone.

Once again, I was in "drag" and would have to walk in the scene. Donna Roberts, the set costumer, taught me how to walk as an unaware demure lady who luckily manages to avoid the wrath of the swinging board as it creates mayhem. Finally, the broad gets nailed, again and again. Dick and I rehearsed the routine a couple of times for timing, and then we shot it. It was perfect, but what else can you expect when you work with Dick Van Dyke.

Actor Mantan Moreland, best known from the Charlie Chan films, as *Chauffer Birmingham Brown*, "C'mon feet, don't fail me now!" had a couple of lines in our film's opening minutes. He beamed when I mentioned the laughter he had brought to me during his wonderful career.

The Comic didn't fare well in the theaters, but has since become a cult classic on cable TV and just recently been released on DVD. Regrettably, the silent movie vignettes we laboriously filmed proved to be a greater waste of film than my wedding pictures.

The term, *Multimedia*, reared its ugly head in 1968 as a screen of multi-pictures of 20 or more individual "thumbnail" images on one movie screen. It doesn't take a brain surgeon to realize you cannot watch more than one scene/image at a time. *The Comic* vignettes played on the wide screen for a few seconds, and then each image would *zoom* to the far upper left corner of the screen—creating a row of minute images, as a new vignette appeared. It was impossible to view each clip, only to have it reduced to Lilliputian-sized images in a flash.

The Comic's spectacular 1920's Carthay Circle Theater movie premiere scene would be the famous landmark's last appearance. It was demolished on March 18, 1969 and replaced by an office building-shopping complex.

Another cinematic lesson I learned was the fine-line separating comedy and drama. During certain dramatic scenes the audience laughed when it should have been deeply concerned. Much of this, I believe, was derived from audiences watching years of Dick Van Dyke's comedic antics. DVD made them laugh and that's what they wanted and expected.

The Comic was one of the most enjoyable films I'd ever worked on, but when you're on a movie more than a few days, it's like leaving your family when the production ends. Sadly, you realize that the old and new friends you worked with will never again be together again under these exact circumstances. Always, we would vow to get together for lunch, but it rarely, if ever, happened as we moved from show to show.

Work continued on Disney's, *The Love Bug, Felony Squad* and the *Bonanza* TV series. *Bewitched* was a pleasant set, Elizabeth Montgomery was even more beautiful in person than she photographed. Agnes Morehead was delightful, and meeting George Tobias, the stalwart Warner Bros. character actor, sidekick, was a blast.

This day, Director Bill Asher made my doubling a Leprechaun actor in a Texas-switch a breeze – leaping from the ten-foot ceiling to behind a sofa. Most memorable was Dick York, agonizing in back pain, seated in his director's chair, where the canvas seat had been replaced with a piece of thick plywood.

My buddy, Claude Binyon, Jr., the *Star Trek* TV series first assistant director, helped my being chosen to double actor Walter Koenig as Chekov. Like any business, ability is invaluable, but knowing the boss doesn't hurt either.

One day, while standing outside Oblath's restaurant, across from Paramount's main gate, I bumped into veteran actor/film writer Bill Leicester. We were old Fox Fire Room drinking buddies and discussed my parting as Dick Bartlett's assistant. Bill knew of my production desires, and said he was the new story editor on NBC's *The High Chaparral* TV series, "I know you have some great story ideas, so please come up and see me. I'm lonely in that damn office!" We laughed and I promised him I'd come by, but I procrastinated, and a month later Bill died of a massive heart attack in that office.

Bill Leicester would have made sure I received a writing assignment, plus his mentoring would have countered the many promises and lies Bartlett had made. The moral of this story: *When opportunity knocks— Answer the door.*

CHAPTER 11

1969

My first production of the New Year was *Jack Cassidy's St. Patrick's Day TV Special*, videotaping at my old alma mater, KTLA, in Studio 6, *The Jazz Singer* sound stage. It was like old home week seeing my former compadres from ten years prior, especially, my mentor, TV cameraman Bill Matheson.

This Irish musical extravaganza co-starred actor Mickey Shaughnessy, singer Jan Daley, Mickey Finn and Marie Wilson (radio, film and TV's *My Friend Irma*), produced by her husband, Robert Fallon. It was a fun show, performing a comedic Irish pub fight with Shaughnessy to "Clancy Lowered the Boom."

The handsome Cassidy was delightful and became embarrassed when I said, "Jack, if I looked like you, I would have been dead ten years ago," referring to his chiseled, handsome, good looks. Tragically, Jack died in a house fire seven years later on December 12, 1976.

Jan Daley was a beautiful, talented singer and when Dick Geary and I co-chaired the 1973 Stuntmen's Annual Dinner-Dance, I called her to headline the show. Her performance so impressed Bob Hope's producer, she appeared with Hope on his final USO Vietnam Tour.

The evening's unpublicized guest was John Wayne and I was the first to greet him when he entered the Hollywood Palladium. Seeing my tux, he questioned his entourage because he would have preferred wearing a tux instead of his dark gray suit. Nevertheless, his appearance captivated the audience when he received SAMP's Life Membership plaque.

Brother-in-law stunt man Roger Creed was prepping a Warner Brothers-Seven Arts production of *There Was a Crooked Man....* This would be the first Hollywood-produced film for the prolific, multi-talented, writer-producer-director Joseph L. Mankiewicz *(All about Eve, The Barefoot Contessa, Guys and Dolls)* in 14 years, since *Cleopatra.* In the early 1930s he wrote films for the Marx Brothers.

And what a cast—Kirk Douglas, Henry Fonda, Hume Cronyn, Burgess Meredith, Alan Hale, Jr., Warren Oates, Victor French, John Randolph, C.K. Yang, Michael Blodgett, Lee Grant, Martin Gabel and Barbara Rhodes, plus twenty stunt guys and another sixty extras to the 100-man motion picture crew.

The selected stuntmen were a varied bunch, chosen for their particular look—that of a circa 1870s prisoner in the West's most notorious prison. Bill Hart, Carl Saxe, Jack Perkins, Gene Lebell, Chuck Hicks, Fred Carson, The Great John L, Tony Brubaker, Chuck Courtney, Jimmy Casino, John Sistrunk, Paul Nuckles, Bud Albright, Ron Stein, Bob Morris, Len Felber and Jerry Rush were among the fall guys. The remaining chosen "stuntmen" were extras also hired for their particular appearance.

Creed, for whatever reason, didn't declare my presence on the film until the very last moment. But I was happy to be anywhere for twelve weeks and found myself in one of Indio's several motels, paired up again with Chuck Hicks. (Later, the 1970s the Screen Actors Guild contract would stipulate single rooms for each guild member.)

Chuck and I tolerated the motel for a week before deciding twelve weeks in one room would cramp our style. Pooling our $180 each motel allowance, we added ninety bucks and rented a spacious two bedroom Palm Desert home with a pool for $450 a month.

The evening before our move I had a question for Roger, who occupied a room far across the motel parking lot. Approaching his door with my knuckles poised to knock; I heard a woman giggle as Creed quietly shushed her. My mind worked overtime, and quickly determined that my sister Carole was on the road for Revlon cosmetics and wasn't due to visit her cheating husband until the coming weekend.

Retreating, I reluctantly mentioned what I'd heard to Chuck, who simply said that Roger and Leah had been an item for quite a while. Evidently, their tryst was common knowledge, and my renting a distant Palm Desert home with Hicks was Creed's idea to keep me isolated.

I never mentioned my surprise visit to my sister, preferring to heed Ann Lander's advice: A spouse probably knows about or suspects a partner's infidelity, so keep quiet. My sister later admitted I was right.

Married at 17, Carole became Roger's fifth bride, and divorced him five years later in 1970. Yes, she had known of Roger and Leah's liaison for more than two years. Roger later married Leah, and their union lasted until his death in November 1997. Maybe it's the sixth and not the third time that's the charm.

For *There Was a Crooked Man...*, a re-creation of Arizona's infamous Yuma Prison was constructed at the Joshua Tree National Park. To build this elaborate $500,000 set, the government required that the acreage be extensively photographed, including each and every tree, bush and shrub. This procedure was to assure that any foliage removed during the set construction would later be replaced exactly where it was previously planted.

Hicks and I would drive from our rental house to the motel each day, then board the "stunt bus" for the forty-five minute ride to the location. Daily, we'd enviously watch the Bell Jet Ranger copter land after the fifteen-minute trip with Kirk Douglas, Henry Fonda and Mankiewicz from their luxurious lodgings in Palm Springs.

Again, we had an interesting assortment of stunt fellows. While on a Creed film the stunt adjustments were virtually non-existent. Roger believed you should do something for your weekly salary besides just showing up and, for the most part, I agreed. The film was being shot in continuity—as the story line progressed. Essentially, we were glorified extras and would not be involved in any action until the final prison break segment.

I was anxious to participate in some minor action scenes, but Carl Saxe and Jack Perkins advised me, "Let the new guys do it. We're on a blanket!" Translated that meant: "We're all going make the same bucks whether you hit the ground or not."

Jack Perkins, Charley Horvath's U.S. Marine Corp Commanding Officer during WWII, kept us laughing doing his drunk act. Jack, in the staggering footsteps of filmdom's Jack Norton – the 1930's and 40's top hat-tuxedoed, pencil-lined, mustached, imbibing scene-stealer. Perkins' teetering antics on countless shows included *The Good Guys* TV series, starring Bob Denver and Herb Edelman. Jack enjoyed my drunken rendition and wanted to suggest that I play his stumbling younger brother to the *Good Guys* producers, when the series resumed production in a few months, but the show was too soon canceled.

It's advisable to maintain a reasonable relationship with the Production Office staff. Assistant Director Don Krantz had asked Roger to hire stunt man Walter Scott. Roger didn't and, subsequently, his most meager request was usually refused.

One day I looked at Chuck Courtney and it suddenly dawned on me—Chuck had played Dan Reid, the Lone Ranger's nephew in the early fifties TV series, but when I confronted him, Chuck whispered, "Don't tell anyone." Geeze, here was my hero—every kid wished his uncle was the Lone Ranger. Chuck did the series when he was twenty and, now, at thirty-nine, I surmised, he didn't want to become a pawn in the Hollywood age game.

At times, the movie set resembled a stunt school as several stunt neophytes practiced high falls from the twenty-foot high prison wall during lunch. To the stunt veterans this was considered professional suicide. How can you ask for a stunt adjustment when the production folks see you do these falls for free? You're supposed to know how to perform the stunts *BEFORE* you arrive on a set.

A few days later during lunch, I heard a commotion—someone screamed that Bud Albright had fallen from the wall, missed the stunt pad, and they needed a bench for a stretcher—we rushed to Albright, mangled and moaning in the desert sand. Creed pushed his way through the crowd, stared down at Albright, and uttered through gritting teeth, "Die, you cocksucker, Die!" I began laughing so hard I almost fell next to Albright. No harm, no foul, Albright was back the next day having had only the wind knocked out of him.

Word got out that 1964 USA Olympics star, C.K. Yang, would need a stunt double for a twenty foot leap at Fonda's double, Bob Morris. All during the morning bus ride, Tony Brubaker, one of the best black stunt performers the business has ever seen, pleaded that he was the best physical double for Yang. Roger argued that Tony was much too dark to double the light-skinned oriental. The "stunt bus" arrived at the prison set and I called out, "Hey Rog. Let Tony do it. When he gets up on the ledge and looks down, he'll be the right shade to double C.K." The guys roared as Tony yelled, "You sonofabitch," and chased me off the bus.

Between scenes Tony grabbed a football and casually tossed a Hail Mary pass from the prison yard over the main gate, flying like a bird, easily seventy yards. I was amazed, "Why aren't you playing for the L.A. Rams?" Tony had no regrets—a pro-football player's salary in 1969 was a fraction of today's astronomical figures and, ultimately, the stunt biz was enhanced by his presence. Tony is still a best buddy and one of my favorite people.

Several times, Kirk Douglas yelled my name, requesting that I stand beside him in several shots, "Geeze, what a great guy, he wants me to have more screen time." Suddenly, I realized that this friendly gesture made him look taller. Hollywood egos never cease.

Another day, we were all standing around talking, Kirk was crouched, squatting on his heels. Michael Blodgett settled next to him, tried to assume the same position, lost his balance and tumbled backwards on his ass. Looking at Douglas' cowboy boots with the two-inch dogging heels, he blurted out, "Ahh Ha! You're wearing lifts!" Everyone froze as Blodgett was nailed by Douglas' piercing stare. Swiftly, we all drifted away.

Our evacuation prompted visions of a previous fight routine Douglas performed with one of Creed's boxing buddies, Craig Peterson, when Douglas really got into it, screaming repeatedly "You sonofabitch," as he forcefully shoved Craig's face into the prison's urinal trough.

In a climactic scene where Douglas and his jailed cohorts blow a hole in the three-foot thick prison wall to escape, Roger said he wanted me to leap on top of the convicts as they scramble for the hole and be carried out by the mob. Letting the other stunt guys in on the plan, we went for a rehearsal. It all worked perfectly, exactly as Roger ordered, re-entering the set I heard a booming voice, "Who the hell are you trying to be, Joe Stunt man?" It was Mankiewicz, seated atop an eight-foot ladder. I wondered who he was referring to, then realized it was me. Instantly, the entire set became silent as he continued his diatribe. My eyes darted between the director and Creed, who stood beside the ladder, head down, staring at the floor. I kept asking myself, why doesn't Creed explain that I was following his instructions? Still, he just stood there and said nothing. Subsequently, the scene was filmed with me scrambling on foot with the rest of the prisoners.

Afterward, the stunt guys said my face became cherry red during Mankiewicz's tirade. I have always believed that you have to stand up and be counted—*It's not who is right, but what is right.* Still, I couldn't believe Creed was that gutless. It wouldn't have cost him anything to address Mankiewicz, and say, "Sorry, Sir, that was my idea. We'll change it for the shot." I was reminded of four years earlier when we were filming, Bob Hope's "I'll take Sweden," when after doubling Hope for over thirty years he still addressed Bob as "Mr. Hope."

The next day, Joe Mankiewicz hugged my neck, smiled, "How's it going?" I was startled, yet pleased by his graciousness. I later suspected that assistant director Don Krantz had explained the real situation to him. I didn't know Don, but we would later become great friends.

Working with this stellar cast was fun, complemented my access to one of the world's greatest locations, Palm Springs. I soon became known as "The Roadrunner of Highway 111," with nightly visits to "The Springs" finest restaurants and saloons. One in particular was the Rim Rocks, featuring Ted Fiorita and his Orchestra, playing his Big Band music of the thirties. By candlelight, it was an elegant setting for dining, drink, music and dancing.

Another night I spent a delightful dinner with Alan Hale and Burgess Meredith at the *Bessimé Mucho*, a mother-daughter owned Spanish restaurant in Rancho Mirage. This was my first taste of Spanish food—so delicately seasoned, refined and delicious, a vast contrast to the ordinary enchiladas, rice and beans associated with regular Mexican fare. Alan bought dinner and months later, I later attempted to reciprocate at his Los Angeles' *Lobster Barrel* restaurant on La Cienega's

Restaurant Row, but he wouldn't allow it. Alan "The Skipper" Hale was another one of life's genuine nice guys.

During a prison night scene, three of us are seen playing cards with Burgess "Buzz" Meredith. When Krantz rolled the cameras "Buzz" whispered every profanity in his effort to break us up. We didn't.

Maybe it was an act of contrition when Director Mankiewicz featured me throwing a rock at a prison wall guard. In rehearsal, the balsa wood rock struck the guard like a rocket, but the filmed shots weren't as effective, again proving the old maxim: "Shoot the rehearsal!" Script supervisor Marvin Weldon later mused, "I haven't seen anything like that since Cagney in 'White Heat.'" Yeah, right. Thanks, Marv.

We had a few weekends free, so rather than endure the two-hour plus drive back to L.A. we chose to fly into the Hollywood-Burbank airport. This service was provided by a since-defunct airline using a German Hunza, a thirteen passenger jet plane. Each stewardess was no taller than five feet, due to the five foot three inner cabin height. Comfortably, just as the small jet leveled off at ten thousand feet, you could feel it tilt downward for the Burbank landing. It was a joy ride, arriving from Palm Springs in twenty minutes at a cost of $19.42. Who wouldn't spend forty bucks to save over five hours of driving time?

Pam Tucker, actor Forrest Tucker's beautiful daughter, was Barbara Rhoades' stand-in and during a production lull we broke into a spontaneous foot race across the burning desert sands. Pam was tall, slender and fast and I was giving my all, but suddenly found myself losing my forward balance. Beyond the point of no return, I tried to do a forward tuck and roll and instead buried my head in the sand as I flipped over. Chuck Courtney laughing, "I knew what you were trying to do, but you just didn't get all the way over." He was as right as Pam was fast.

I first met Gene Lebell, a former wrestler, and martial arts expert, in 1960, when he operated a Judo-Karate school near Paramount Pictures main gate. For years, Gene had a standing offer; He would fight anyone in any form of self-defense. If he lost, you'd take home $10,000. Gene never had any takers.

On a Sunday afternoon, Chuck Hicks and I returned to the Indio motel film production office for our weekly per diem, as Gene La Bell and others worked out around the swimming pool. Gene said, "C'mon, try to take me down." I ran at him and suddenly I was upside down and lying on the mat at his feet. I couldn't believe how fast it happened, but mostly how he set me down like a feather. Then I heard a voice ask, "Well, aren't you going to say hello?" It was veteran stunt woman Sharon Lucas in a neck brace, relaxing on a chaise lounge. She had been injured on "Paint your wagon," during the collapse of the gold mining town scene. She and Dar Robinson were in a room and were ejected as the building façade falls away. Dar, unfortunately, landed on Sharon.

On a set with this many participants, there's always a poker game. A black extra, Eddie Smith, evidently decided to enhance his gaming odds with a marked deck, to which Gene retaliated by holding him by his neck, and feet off the floor, against the wall, demanding, "I want my money." Smith complied immediately. Fearing for his safety from several other gambler extras in the game, production insisted that Smith ride back to Indio in the "stunt bus." He was then fired, and shuttled back to Tinseltown that evening in a prop truck.

For the prison break, the "reverse" shot of the exploding wall was being readied to include statuesque actress Barbara Rhoades making her escape across the desert. In the previous interior scenes, Barbara is partially stripped of her dress by the escaping prisoners, but by the time we see her running from the great hole in the wall, she is naked as a Jay Bird. Of course, when the film was released in 1970, Americans never saw the shot, which was included only in the foreign release prints. Today, that shot would probably be G rated.

A Bell Jet Ranger helicopter provided the high cover shot of this great escape. Stunt man Jack Perkins, a devote Catholic, attempted to make gentlemen out of this horde of horny extras and stunt men—requested they not look at Barbara's naked body double, Ilona Wilson.

Jack, I, and several others were chosen to chase this tall beauty in a fifty-yard dash through the soft sand. Our cue came and we started the run, passing the littered bodies of prisoners—all lying, conveniently, on their sides, staring at us through squinting eyes. The copter got the shot and banked away, sandblasting us with the prop wash. Immediately, I whipped out Ilona's silk robe stashed in my prison uniform. I was temporarily blinded as Ilona, too, stopped to shield her eyes, and I promptly got a face full of her right breast. (As Rooney once said, "Who wants to be tall?") Impulsively, we embraced each other to keep from falling. Ilona quickly donned the flowered robe and we had a great laugh. Hey, somebody's gotta do it.

Once again, *There Was a Crooked Man…* wasn't assembled as it was written. Somewhere, between the fine completed script and the final edit, it took a wrong turn. Gone was much of the suspense of Kirk Douglas' prison escape. Often, the vision of the writer becomes the director's interpretation and the waters soon become muddy. Many collaborated variables exist and this is not Filmmaking 101 so, if you're so inclined, study and make your own films. Experience is still the best teacher.

Finishing *Crooked Man*, with a nice wad of cash in Bank of America's Studio City branch, I often ventured to the nearby Sav-On drug store. Taking a hankering to one of the attractive checkout cashiers, I asked her to dinner. In a whirlwind relationship, we became engaged and planned a September wedding.

Susie Cleary was a five-foot-nine blond with, I soon found, definite problems and most were anger-based. One day while grocery shopping, a laughing little boy about 4 years old came scampering down the aisle toward us. She turned and screamed, "Get away from me, you little bastard!" What a lady. Today, that kid is probably looking for a clock tower with his rifle.

During her "time of the month," she was a roaring bitch three to four days *BEFORE*. Then there was a week of *HELL*, and then another three to four days of *AFTER*. You don't need a calculator to figure two weeks of every month she was on the warpath.

Her propensity to gargle and swallow Scope mouthwash (20%+ alcohol) twice a day conceivably contributed to her erratic outbursts.

Still, stunt work was plentiful on *The Virginian, H.R. Pufnstuf, Run, Baby, Run, Adam-12, The Bold Ones, The Grasshopper* and the *Herb Alpert TV Special* starring Petula Clark.

Director Hollingsworth Morse was still upset about the burns I received on the *Adam-12* fire gag and, particularly, the drunken special effects guy. In his effort to throw some bucks my way, he called me to stunt coordinate the new Sid & Marty Kroft kids TV series, *H.R. Pufnstuf* and to double actress Billie Hayes as *Witchiepoo*.

It was a fun show working with former Mouseketeer Sharon Baird, comic/writer Lennie Weinrib and a delightful Jack Wild, who had scored big as the Artful Dodger in Director Sir Carol Reed's *Oliver!* Jack was a polite kid, but unfortunately was quickly overcome by his teen idol status with many female companions and a foray into the Hollywood booze and drug scene. A 2001 TV interview revealed the additives had taken their toll. In horse stable jargon, "He looked like he had been rode hard and put away wet."

At Disney, I doubled Wild's *Oliver!* co-star, child actor Mark Lester and met Parley Baer, the wonderful veteran actor as Dorby on *The Adventures of Ozzie & Harriet* and Mayor Stoner on *The Andy Griffith Show*. In all, he appeared in sixty motion pictures, 1600 TV shows and an amazing 15,000 radio programs. On radio he was Chester on *Gunsmoke* to William Conrad's Matt Dillon.

Candidly, I mentioned my pending wedding in a couple of months. Parley listened thoughtfully, staring at the floor, and calmly responded, "Don't do it." I don't know if Parley was a psychic, but on September 7, 1969, I made one of the biggest mistakes of my life and, it's to my everlasting regret that I didn't heed his advice.

During a passionate lovemaking session with my new bride, I reveled in the enjoyment of satisfying my new partner. Unfortunately, her response wasn't mutual, "I'm embarrassed," she said. I instantly queried, "What are we on Candid Camera?" This prompted the old bromide "You should always take a test drive before you buy the car.

While employed at Sav-On Drugs (she later became a Bank of America teller), she mentioned that she had lunch with one of her customers. I was so stunned I didn't say a word.

Roger Creed called once again and I was off to Nassau, Bahamas, to film *Darker than Amber*, a John D. Macdonald action-packed mystery novel starring Rod Taylor as Travis McGee. Macdonald's titles always reflected colors, which made for an interesting connection between the title, the story, and the characters.

Rod Taylor, shadowed by Fred Hakim, his Mafia-looking bodyguard, was living the Travis McGee detective role with a bottle of his favorite brew at hand. Feeling no pain one evening, Taylor confronted first assistant director Ted Swanson and his beautiful wife and declared, "I'd like to fuck your wife." Swanson did nothing to defend his wife's honor. Regardless of the odds you gotta man-up. You must go down fighting. Win or lose.

In junior high, we were required to study Shakespeare's *Julius Caesar,* and among the most memorable quotations is "Cowards die many times before their deaths; the valiant never taste of death but once." Those 15 words have had an everlasting, life-long effect on me.

In 1969, the Bahamas was still a British colony (they received independence in 1973) and Nassau was everything you ever expected to find on a Caribbean island. Never, have I seen sea water so crystal clear. The friendly black, white-uniformed, Bobbies, with their very precise vocabulary, and refined English accent was an interesting contradiction I wasn't used to hearing in Los Angeles.

At the time, I was a two-pack a day Tareyton cigarette smoker and was warned to properly dispose the empty pack or face a $25 fine if you toss the empty wrapper in the street. Rumor suggested the British Empire considered Tareyton a traitor. However, this same cigarette pack in the Bahamas, with the same logo and colors was imprinted *Tennyson*—another case of crass commercialism over-riding national sentiment.

We were housed at the Royal Queen Victoria, a magnificent rambling, 1880s Victorian-styled hotel with louvered doors and shutters. Anticipating the next day stunts, I was lying on my bed reading up on the local lore when I saw something move in my peripheral vision. Zeroing in, I slowly turned to see a six-inch long lizard scurry across the wall. A call to the front desk assured me that this was a normal occurrence—the four-legged guests were cultivated for their insect devouring appetites and occupied all the rooms.

Frank Phillips, a director of photography I had worked with many times, was delighted to see a familiar face on his first day of filming, having just flown in to replace the previous cinematographer. Director

Robert Clouse was very congenial and would later direct Bruce Lee's *Enter the Dragon*. He and Frank were old friends, hence Frank's appearance on the film.

Rounding out the cast was English actress Suzy Kendall, Theodore Bikel and my buddy, William Smith, from the *Laredo* TV series. Bill, in one of his best roles, portrayed a hit man pursuing McGee to a docked passenger cruise ship. In my purser's white uniform, I was one of several bodies that Bill bowls over like ten pins in his chase to get McGee.

On "Action," I ran up the gangway and Bill tossed me over the railing to the wharf. Confronting him at the base of the gangway, he nailed me with a kick to the chest, and then continued down the wharf battling other stunt guys. The action worked fine and we re-set for take two due to a faulty camera dolly move.

Sitting on an apple box next to camera was the film's producer, Walter Saltzer, who had obviously enjoyed a multi-Martini lunch, waved me over, "Hey kid, this time really go splat." I went to Roger and mentioned Saltzer's directive, "Fuck'em. Do what you just did. It was fine."

Nevertheless, every performer wants to make the scene better and I began thinking about what I could do to go "splat." In the first take I controlled my over-the-rail speed with my arm. On Take Two, I loosened my grip, which accelerated the speed to my eight-foot drop. Wardrobe had saddled me with a pair of white Italian loafers with laminated leather heels and I can only equate the slamming of two bricks together when my right heel hit the cement wharf. I wasn't able to stand up for Bill's chest kick and the fight continued down the wharf without me. "Cut and print!" said Clouse, who was delighted with the shot.

Bill Smith was very concerned about my injury, believing it was his fault, but I reassured him it was my call because I didn't control the speed as I had during the first take.

Afterward, while sitting on the set, I knew I was severely hurt. The mere touch of my toe to the ground produced excruciating pain, but Creed insisted it was just a sprain. When we wrapped Jimmy Casino carried me on his shoulders up-hill to the hotel.

Later, in my room, Roger and Jimmy soaked my swollen right foot in Creed's menthol-alcohol concoction of Bigeloil horse liniment to no avail. Repeatedly, I told Roger this was a serious injury, but he countered with "Don't fuck me up. You have to do the gangway close up tomorrow." It was a rough night without a painkiller.

The next morning, as Jimmy Casino again carried me the quarter mile to the wharf set—you could almost see my foot throbbing. As the crew set up for the first shot, I asked Frank Phillips to give me thirty minutes notice before they would get to my shot. Soon, Frank signaled me and I hobbled over to the on-set medic. I explained the situation and requested something strong for pain. She produced a bottle of Demerol, I took two capsules with water and thirty minutes later I ran up the gangway like Jesse Owens. Bill Smith grabbed me, flipped me over the railing onto the stunt pad, and a minute later I was on my way to the local hospital.

Limping only slightly, thanks to the medication, the hospital workers and nurses were blasé, as I entered the ER, thinking I was just an injured ship's purser. But when word spread that a movie stunt man was in the emergency ward, I became an instant celebrity. The X-rays showed a fractured oscalcis—a crack straight up my round heel bone. One hour later, I was back on the set with my right foot wrapped in light gauze cast and teetering on crutches.

Production supervisor Frank Baur suggested I remain for another five days since I was on a weekly stunt contract, or at least stay another day to enjoy the cruise ship captain's invitation to dine at his table. But no, not me. Instead of accepting this honor, I chose to return to my blushing bride of ten weeks. Another one of those, It seemed like a good idea at the…

The next day I flew into LAX and and a day later ventured to an appointment with Dr. Danny Levinthal, the noted Beverly Hills orthopedic surgeon to the stars and the Los Angeles Rams football team.

I had met Doctor Danny a year before when I'd drive Chuck Hicks to his appointments for an injury occurred while playing a Saturday game of touch football game. Receiving the ball, Chuck took a step as someone stepped on his heel, ripping his Achilles tendon loose. Again those damn those free athletic activities! Now it was my turn to lug around a plaster cast.

On a previous visit to Levinthal's office with Chuck, Fred MacMurray and his former-actress wife, June Haver, arrived to see the good doctor. Holding a dime, Fred leaned close and asked if she had change for the parking meter.

MacMurray Money Lesson #28: *Do not give a parking meter a ten-cent coin when a nickel will do.* Chuck and I grinned at each another, realizing we had just witnessed a prime factor of how Fred MacMurray had become one of Hollywood's wealthiest residents.

Though I was in Nassau only three days, it was ample time for the bride to run my credit cards to great new heights, purchasing clothes for several girlfriends and her mother, but nothing for herself. That's another one of life's mysteries. However, Christmas was a month away.

The wife and I stopped battling long enough to see the highly touted, Peter Fonda-Dennis Hopper low budget film, *Easy Rider*. The next day the bride mentioned how she and her co-workers "felt sorry" because Hopper got blown away by the two good ol' boys in the pick-up truck. I exclaimed, trying to restrain my angst for such stupidity, "Those guys were drug smugglers. Did you forget the opening scene in Mexico, when they concealed the drugs in the motorcycle gas tanks?" Her eyes widened as she gasped, "Oooh yeah."

Easy Rider represents the ultimate power of a motion picture. This wasn't a new revelation. Hitler and even our own U.S. Forces became equally adept in film usage for propaganda and persuasion.

The bride had found an affectionately autographed photo from an actress I had doubled. Immediately, her accusations of my infidelity spewed forth evoking the old axiom – *The best defense is a good offense.* Little did she know this actress appreciated the female sex as much as I do.

One evening she asked, "What did you do today?" I mentioned visiting several production offices and playing golf with a couple of buddies at Kirkwood's (Studio City Golf Course), whereas she declared, "I resent the fact that I'm working and you're out playing golf." Regrettably, I, again, didn't say what I was thinking. That I earned more in ten seconds than she did in a month. That she had all the comforts of home, restaurant dining every night, and a maid's visit every other week. There was no satisfying her any way, shape or form, including sexually. That was the final nail in the matrimonial coffin.

The year was drawing to a close and my excursion into matrimony had become a disaster. As a stunt professional, where analyzing and split-second decisions becomes second nature; I wasn't troubled with doubt, and chose to pull the marital plug after the New Year. I had tried everything in my power to save this union, but you don't have to be kicked in the head by a mule eight times to realize it hurt the first time.

She had recently left Sav-On to become a Bank of America teller. When I suggested she return to her Mother's home, a week later I received notification of $1500 in bounced checks. She had emptied our joint checking account with a post-dated check. My complaint to the B of A manager produced shrugged shoulders. In those non-litigious years it never occurred to me that a lawsuit was feasible.

Seeking legal representation, I sought out Doug Smithers, a former Screen Actors Guild attorney. Later, I was subsequently amused to find the divorce court had granted an annulment for my 4½ months of aggravated marital assault. Shortly thereafter, the Ex married the guy she was "lunching with" behind my back, moved to Utah, and was later divorced by him.

Several stunt buddies, including Denver Mattson, helped me move to a new Studio City apartment. After a sudden love affair with my Jim Beam bottle Mattson became useless, so I suggested he guard the smaller items while we moved in the couches and refrigerator. Minutes later, when Mattson staggered into the kitchen I realized he had abandoned my belongings. Rushing to the front lobby, sure as hell, my stunt bag was gone, filled with every stunt tool I had accumulated for eleven years, including my wedding pictures with the negatives. I had interlaced three photo light stands through the stunt bag handles, and the thief obviously believed it was camera gear. When I confronted Mattson about his misdeed, he was so shit-faced he couldn't understand a word I said.

CHAPTER 12

1970

In 1961, an aimless Hollywood male stunt populace experienced an incredible change with the formation of the Stuntmen's Association of Motion Pictures. From the 1920s, several attempts to organize the stunt ranks had all failed. To facilitate their needs in the late 1930s, Paramount Pictures had Jimmy Dundee as their "Stunt Gaffer," while Jack Palmeroy handled those duties over at Warner Bros.—bringing in stunt greats Jock Mahoney and Charley Horvath after the War in 1946. Others he mentored were Terry Wilson, Bob Morgan, Paul Baxley and Glen Thompson.

The Stuntmen's Association of Motion Pictures, in the sixties, became the single most enduring source when production executives chose a male stunt performer. Becoming a SAMP member gave you validation—the equivalent of receiving "The Good Housekeeping Seal of Approval," deeming you as one of the best.

"Someday, I'm going to be the biggest stunt man in Hollywood and I don't care who I step on," bragged Hal Needham to stunt man Fred "Krunch" Krone in 1958. I'm unaware if there's a list of those Needham tromped on, but he did make good his promise. During the ensuing twelve years, Needham evolved into Hollywood's most famous stunt man and top-earning stunt coordinator. Also, with Burt Reynolds as a friend and roommate didn't prove to be detrimental.

Needham's loner demeanor can be seen during a group photo from Blake Edward's *The Great Race* (1965) as he stands distanced from the other stunt performers.

Unfortunately, Needham's bold, ego-based declaration would ultimately create an even greater transformation that would affect every stunt performer on several levels.

Burt Reynolds was Hollywood's #1 box office champion of the mid-1970s and Needham became his film director. In tandem, they were propelled to the astronomical heights of Hollywood stardom and financial independence and, like the perfect timing of a well-executed stunt. Needham was at the top of the heap.

But, let's go back to the night when Needham was not elected SAMP President. He was pissed, and so were many SAMP elder members when they heard of his rumored intention to charge the stunt people he hired a ten per cent commission. This rumor of truth, exacerbated by Needham's arrogant manner, came to a head at a Valley Hilton SAMP monthly meeting. He faced the ire of many veteran members, who hadn't been to a meeting in years, to protest Needham's hiring proposal. Cornered, an angry Needham resigned, followed immediately by Ronnie Rondell, Glen Wilder and fourteen other SAMP members.

Deliberately, Needham now had the nucleus to create a second Hollywood stunt group. Lennie Geer had performed live stunt shows under his "Stunts Unlimited" banner for many years, and granted Needham permission to use the moniker.

In retaliation, a committee of SAMP stuntmen petitioned the SAG Board of Directors, who promptly issued an edict stating a Screen Actors Guild member may not function as an agent or collect an agent's fee. This 1970 SAG proclamation killed Needham's commission plan, but didn't deter his professed desire for fame and fortune. When it came to on-camera interviews and stunt demonstrations, Needham made Jesse Jackson, Al Sharpton and Obama look like camera-shy introverts.

In a jet-propelled car Needham jumped a ravine only to be hauled away on a stretcher after supposedly suffering a broken back. He almost swallowed the microphone, proclaiming this to be the norm – that he had previously broken 47 bones. Broken 47 bones? Maybe you should find another line of work.

Years later, while having a drink at Monty's Steak House in Encino with Needham's ex-wife, Arlene mused that she was with him during those years and maintained those injuries were news to her. Regardless, one can not deny Needham's stunt abilities, ranking him as one of Hollywood's top stuntmen.

Needham's notoriety became a double-edged sword, providing publicity for him and Stunts Unlimited, but forever removed the mystique surrounding the Hollywood stunt performer.

From the inception of motion pictures, moviegoers were aware their favorite star was being doubled in action sequences. Even though Douglas Fairbanks, Sr. performed the majority of his own stunts, it was Richard Talmadge, one of Hollywood's all-time greats, who rigged and perfected the stunts for Fairbanks.

Before Talmadge changed his name from Ricardo Metzzeti, he and his two Metzzeti brothers comprised their famous Austrian acrobatic circus act. In the early 1920s, he starred in many Hollywood two-reelers (each reel was 10 minutes), creating some of the best stunt action ever filmed.

Hollywood was aware of those select few who performed the action. But the studios wanted their stars to be bigger than life and between the studio's publicity department and/or an actor's ego, a stunt performer was denied any notoriety. Harvey Parry had doubled Harold Lloyd since the 1920s, but was sworn to secrecy until Lloyd's death March 8, 1971.

In the early 1960s, stunt man Bobby Hoy warned, "In our anonymity is our security." Burt Reynolds' 1978 blockbuster hit, *Hooper*, directed by Needham, blatantly ignored Hoy's admonition and depicted fictitious Hollywood stuntmen in all their glory.

Now, the genie was out of the bottle and the mystique was gone as the public learned the behind-the-scenes tricks of the stunt trade. Wannabes came from everywhere and from all walks of life, seeking Hollywood's "easy money, glamour and fame." Veteran stunt man Troy Melton lamented, "Every guy who ever fell off a bar stool in Paducah is now out here trying to be a stunt man."

Unfortunately, the one factor most wannabees had in common was their misconception of the movie stunt performer. Needham's publicity machine created the impression that the industry harbored super human daredevils who would do anything for a buck. Consequently, the guy from Paducah, getting off the Greyhound at Hollywood & Vine, was willing to do anything to make a name in the biz.

On the *BJ and the Bear* TV series, a stunt to ride a motorcycle off a high Monterey, California, seaside cliff and pull a parachute enticed the show's novice stunt coordinator. Local experts warned him about the fierce prevailing offshore winds that would most certainly slam his carcass into the face of the bluff. Undeterred, he wanted to attempt this daredevil act knowing that injury or even death was likely. This is not the mindset of a professional stunt performer, but that of an idiot with deranged priorities. Ultimately, wiser minds prevailed and this gag was completed with a construction large crane and cables.

In 1980, on the *Escape from New York* St. Louis, MO, location, stunt coordinator Dick Warlock was confronted by a stunt wannabee who wanted to dive head first from the roof of a Union Station railroad car to the cement landing to prove his stunt abilities. Warlock was going to let him do it, until I asked him if he could live knowing full well he caused the kid permanent injury or death? Warlock recanted.

Often, I'd meet a wannabe and marvel at his stunt photos of a high fall, car crash and a fire gag, "Hey, this guy is really something." Then I'd discover he had no film credits, and had hired a photographer to shoot his pictures. Okay, you did the gags for a still shot, but can you do it on a real set, in conjunction with other performers, and hit your mark? In several instances, the untalented and unscrupulous used action shots from legit stunt performers as their own.

It's a dreary sampling of those who have entered the stunt ranks in the past thirty years or so. Unfortunately, this caliber of individual also accounts for the fact that more stunt people have been seriously injured, maimed and killed since 1970, than in the previous hundred years of motion pictures.

Years ago, the stunt men and women had a different state of mind—individuals who treated stunt work as a job you do, then you go home, ready to work the next day. Few had aspirations toward an acting career and most were satisfied knowing they performed physical activities that others would not or could not do. But never did they ever perceive themselves as super human.

Overall, they realized the money was good when you worked, but often it was feast or famine. You could be in great demand one year, but twelve months later you couldn't buy a job.

The animosity between the Stuntmen's Association and Stunts Unlimited accelerated the competitive job market. Naturally, some studio production departments took advantage of this feud, playing both ends against the middle to reduce their action budgets. More so, the rivalry escalated, extending to the stunts themselves. If one group performed a car chase at sixty, the other was sure to do seventy, but the facts proved that Stunts Unlimited wrecked more vehicles off camera than on.

Stunts Unlimited, however, thrived on its difference from SAMP—a profit making organization versus SAMP's non-profit status. While the Association membership numbered over a hundred, Unlimited maintained only 35-50 members, with a philosophy of unity that set them apart: *We hire our own members first.* Only after everyone in their group was employed would they consider hiring a non-member. Originally, "hire our own" was SAMP's unofficial policy, but was never enforced and only randomly practiced by the coordinators—"It's easier to control 35 members than a hundred," but if you screwed up at Unlimited, you were history.

A wag commented, "When you quit Stunts Unlimited it will cost you $150,000 a year, but if you quit SAMP you'll save $1500 a year [in dues]!" I laughed, but it was true!

Another contributing factor to affect the stunt ranks in the mid-1970's occurred when the assistant directors voluntarily relinquished the stunt hiring duties to Stunt Coordinators. Now, it was no longer the A.D.'s responsibility, and if a stunt went awry their collective response was "It's not my job."

Now the Stunt Coordinator was in control. This hiring shift also drastically limited a stunt performer's job possibilities. Previously, you got the job when the assistant director chose you. Theoretically, you had an even shot as anyone else of being hired on any Hollywood production. Today, each stunt coordinator has their own stable of performers and if you aren't part of his/her clique, you most likely will not be hired regardless of your talent and abilities.

Based on this premise, your job possibilities are now down to a meager 10%. However, this figure is based on the assumption that your door pounding will get you in a side door via a director, producer or even the craft service guy. But that may not work for you either, as the stunt coordinator might balk at any outside hiring interferences. So, in reality, you don't have a snowball's chance in hell of being hired.

This now brings us to the current over-population of the stunt business. From the sixties and ensuing decades the film industry supported about 200 stunt performers comfortably. That figure has not changed much, but the wannabe numbers continue to rise. Those are steep hiring odds and my suggestion to anyone considering a stunt career: Keep your day job.

Stunt guys are, for lack of another word, *interesting*. Then again, that's the word you use when you meet someone's ugly child.

The Hudkins, John, Dickie and Acey: All brothers were kin to the great prizefighter, Ace Hudkins. From the early 1930s and into the 1950s, the Hudkins Bros. Stables provided much of the livestock and wagons for the studios.

Acey, Jr.'s stutter made Mel Tillis sound like Sir Laurence Olivier. Acey, this evening addressed a subject at a monthly Stuntmen's Association meeting. SAMP President Bobby Herron gave him the floor. Acey laboriously attempted to convey his deepest feelings regarding an obviously heart-felt issue. He seemed to go on forever, struggling to form each syllable as every member politely hung on his every word. Finally, he finished and took his seat. Herron looked at him, and said, "Yeah, easy for you to say." The place fell apart.

Ready to film a saloon fight, Herron quickly volunteered when the director needed someone who spoke Italian to yell, "Hey, that's my buddy" to start the donnybrook. On action, when Bobby proclaimed, "Hey, thatsa maa buddy!"

SAMP's most productive years appear to be the formative first three, from 1961-1964, when Dale Van Sickle was president. Several like Bob

Herron, Chuck Hicks, Rock Walker performed admirably (pardon me if I have missed someone), but others went through the motions (pun intended). One particular evening a subject was debated for 3½ hours, stretching everyone's patience, with several members vowing never to attend another meeting. Finally, President Reg Parton made a valid point and the subject was resolved immediately. When I asked him why he didn't speak up sooner, he quipped that "I'm only here to referee." I said, "Bullshit. You were elected for your supposed leadership abilities, and now you've wasted 3½ hours of our lives we'll never get back."

Terry Leonard once described the stunt trade as "The only business you can come into with a third grade education and make $50 thousand a year." Today, that dollar amount has escalated to a hefty six figures.

Stunt man John Sistrunk, doing his civic duty, organized a rock & roll band for a Pacoima city park dedication and asked me to film it. I arrived early to set up, entered the parking lot and saw a carload of Mexican gang members. And said to myself, "Get the fuck out of here," and sped out the exit. Two days later I received a call from Sistrunk, but could hardly understand him. He was in the hospital—I rushed to his side. His broken jaw was wired shut; his face was cut, bruised and swollen. He strained to talk about how he and the band were attacked by the Mexican gang. All of the musical instruments and sound equipment had been destroyed.

Another time, I was asked to film the Watts Festival. Mom's black friend, Millie, said, "Jess, don't you dare go down there." And I didn't. God bless Millie.

Work resumed on *Bonanza* and a new TV series at Columbia, *The Young Rebels*, starring Rick Ely and Lou Gossett, Jr., and my ex-brother-in-law, Roger Creed, was the stunt coordinator.

The program theme was the American Revolutionary War and the constant torment of the British by a band of "Rebels." The network-studio geniuses hoped to capitalize on the youthful rebellion against the Vietnam conflagration to garner an audience. It didn't work and the series was canceled after twenty-some episodes.

While filming at Disney's Oak Tree Ranch, it was a crapshoot whether I would be a "Rebel" or a "Red coat." This day Orwin Harvey and I were British soldiers as the encampment is attacked, the stored munitions explode and were set to run "fleeing" through the area. Chuck Gaspars was the head special effects man and when we asked him about a safe distance from the multiple explosions, he simply replied, "I donno." He personally rigged the powder charges and doesn't know the safe distance, well who does know? Finally, Orwin and I planned our own route, purposely avoiding the "pots" filled with cork, balsa wood scraps, black powder and gasoline. Again, we asked Gaspars about his timing of the explosions, he promised to let us pass the large wagon on our right before triggering the pots on our left. Orwin and I were relieved the blasts would be behind us instead of in our faces, but we still didn't trust him.

On "Action" Orwin and I took two running steps as the pots on our left exploded. Instantly, it became Dante's Inferno as fire, smoke and burning debris rained down upon us. Stopped dead in our tracks, not knowing where to go, we made a dive and rolled under the large wagon for shelter. The Fire Marshal, fifty yards from the set, ducked for cover as chunks of burning debris fell near him. "I'll be damned, he lied to me," said the fireman about Gaspars.

The shot was finally over and we crawled out to view the destroyed set. Orwin and I just looked at each other and shook our heads. I wanted to "talk" to Caspars, but Orwin, always a gentlemen and a gentle man, suggested we forget it and treat it as a lesson learned. Indeed it was.

We later surmised Director Sutton Roley more than likely instructed Gaspars to load up the explosions. For years, we knew of Roley's intimidating ploys to induce stunt men to take that extra chance. Jack Verbois was his favorite stunt guy and many of us warned him to be careful, because "One day that sonofabitch is going to get you killed."

Over the years I can recall only a hand full of special effects men (Roy Downey, Dick Parker, Nick Carey & Roger George) I worked with who could be trusted implicitly. Whatever these gents told you to do you could take to the bank.

For the next *Young Rebels* episode I scouted the Twentieth Century Fox's Malibu Ranch location (now a California state park) with Roger Creed, the director and an effects man (not Caspars). Roger suggested I attack a British work wagon and perform a fight with George Orrison. "How about a shot like Errol Flynn's *Adventures of Robin Hood*, where his Merry Men swing out of the trees." I figured this would make a great shot, sweeping across the screen. He agreed and I pointed to a tree limb mark where I wanted the rope attached.

Early, the next morning with Roger and the effects man, I again pointed to a specific tree mark and hurried off to wardrobe and make up. Returning an hour later, the rope was ten feet short of the mark I requested. When I mentioned this discrepancy to Creed, he replied, "C'mon, we gotta get this shot."

Not wanting to delay production, I climbed a ladder to the tree's lofty position, knowing the rope should have been mounted further up the limb. To do this stunt correctly, the rope must be taut, allowing me to swing—like a pendulum. Instead, the rope hung in a lazy arc to my hands. On "Action" I swung from the perch, but my downward momentum spit me off when I reached the arc's apex, slamming me into the side of the seven-foot high work wagon. I stuck there for two beats then collapsed to the ground in a heap. Crewmembers later remarked that I looked like Wile E. Coyote colliding with the solid cave entrance. After a few profane words to Roger, I tried it again. For the second take, I vowed they would have to pry my hands from the rope. Again, I swung down, perfectly, landing behind George and we proceeded with our choreographed fight routine, from the wagon, falling between and rolling under the horses. This was my first picture fight with George Orrison and I delighted working in perfect rhythm. He made it easy. When it's right, it's great.

Several years later, I reviewed *Robin Hood* again and noticed that the Merry Men sequence was a cinematic illusion I'd seen as a kid. It was actually two separate shots – the Merry Men leaving their perch, and then another shot hitting their mark. The fine editing made it appear it was one complete shot.

Back on *Rebels*, Roger said I would be driving the same "two-up" (that's two horses) wagon in another shot at a gallop. I had driven buckboards, but never a huge work wagon with a team resembling Clydesdales. With the reins in my hands, I sat in the wagon's seat musing how I was going to get through this shot, or out of it, when Jim Spahn, the head wrangler, rode up. "Everything Okay, Jess?" "Yeah, Jim, except for one thing," I said, "I've never handled one of these wagons before." "Sonofabitch!" screamed Spahn, "He's doing it to me again," as he rode away to find Creed.

Minutes later, stunt man Jack "I'll do it" Tyree, an affable, nice guy, climbed onto the wagon seat declaring he was going to drive the wagon in the shot. "Jack, have you ever driven one of these before?" I asked. "No," he grinned, "but it looks easy." With anticipation, I reluctantly handed him the reins, thinking "Oh, shit."

This run would take us down a dog-legged road to the right with the horses at a full gallop. Adding to this accident-waiting-to-happen scenario was the camera position, located on our left, smack in the middle of the sweeping turn. If Tyree loses control of the horses or takes the turn too fast, the wagon could roll and the camera crew would be wiped out. Jack assured me that he could handle the horses. He looked big and strong enough, but…

We got our cue and off we went, hell-bent for election. I sat high in the bench seat, prepared to jump if the wagon started to slide. We came through the turn at full speed and I was thrilled when two outriders pulled the team to a stop. Years later, on *The Sword & The Sorcerer* film, Jack wouldn't be so fortunate; while performing a high fall at the Bronson Canyon cave, he would miss his fall pads and plunge to his death.

Working with Roger Creed had become troublesome. I couldn't forget my swing from the tree and resented being placed in situations where I had no control. A stunt performer must have complete command of his stunt. It's the individual's responsibility and he must feel comfortable. If there's a screw up, you know where the fault lies. Roger had a propensity to force his will on others; what might work for him might be detrimental to another. I didn't trust him.

A case in point: The following week Roger called me for another wagon stunt on *Rebels* at Disney Ranch. This time he and I were to jump from a runaway wagon before it sailed over a cliff. I declined when my inner voice suggested I should. He was pissed, and replaced me with Orwin Harvey.

Tinseltown is and always will be a small town. A day after the wagon stunt I heard all the details. As the wagon careened toward the cliff's edge, Orwin, with Roger crouched behind him, hung on as the wagon gathered speed. Orwin attempted to jump, but Roger had latched onto the back of Orwin's belt. Frantically, Orwin fought himself loose and jumped—Roger leaped a beat later. The wagon hit and rolled—Creed missed being crushed to death by a foot or two.

Once again, my inner voice had spoken, and that did put a smile on my face. But the big No-No is: Never touch, grab or impede anyone during a stunt.

Clint Eastwood said it best: "You gotta know your limitations." The old-timers warned me to never take a stunt job if I had any doubts. You might be the best swimmer, horseman or fight man, but if you screwed up a stunt beyond your ability. Your credibility would be questioned from then on about your other abilities.

On the *F.B.I.* series at Warner's, Director Jesse Hibbs got me my first screen kiss—smooching a cute extra gal in a park as Richard Kiley steals my car. Howard Curtis, doubling Kiley, roared away as I hung on the door, skidded left through an intersection, tossing me to the street, as the right rear wheel slapped my left hip. No, I never did get the extra's phone number.

Kiley was kind and congenial when I mentioned my vain attempts to see his *Man of La Mancha* at the Dorothy Chandler Pavilion, "We could have gone another six weeks in L.A."

Robert Aldrich's *The Grissom Gang*, a 1930's gangster-kidnap yarn, starring Robert Lansing, Scott Wilson and Kim Darby, was filming in Fiddletown, an 1849 gold rush burg east of Sacramento. This was a three day gig—a fall through a second story window and off the roof. I'd travel to the location, perform the following day and return the next. During lunch, production suddenly announced they wanted to film the stunt as soon as makeup could put a skullcap on me to match veteran actor Alvin Hammer's baldpate in the 110° heat. So much for three days in Fiddletown: one take and I arrived back in Burbank at 6pm.

At the Janss Ranch in Thousand Oaks, Dick Durock and I continued on the film, racing the vintage 1930's vehicles through the winding country roads, though much of this film footage was obliterated by the superimposed opening titles. What a waste.

For the kidnapping scenes at the Malibu Lake Lodge, my Ford Model A, four-door sedan, was no match for his elegant super-charged Duisenberg roadster. My load of white-knuckled gangster-actors tensed as a bridge abutment loomed, but a quick jerk of the steering wheel kicked the rear end around enough to propel us over the wood structure. For the second take, I firmly admonished Dick to check his rearview mirror and car speed so we'd both remain in the same camera shot.

Oscar Rudolph later directed the second unit action chase on Universal's New York Street as stunt vet Chuck Waters did one hellava motorcycle crash and skid, while Roger Creed hurt his knee on a window crash attempt. Paul Nuckles stepped in and crashed his speeding police bike head-on into the storefront, which propelled him through one large corner breakaway window and out the other. Immediately, Nuckles jumped to his feet and bragged, "If you want it done right, I'm the…"—I rushed to tell him it was wise to let others say how well the stunt went, but it was very revealing that he would ridicule Creed, whom I had introduced him to, who gave him his first regular stunt jobs on *Rat Patrol*. When Creed died in 1997, Nuckles exclaimed, "Good!"

One day, a buddy rushed in The Back Stage, announcing, "Earl Graham died." "What?" I responded, "Earl Grant died?" "No, no, Earl Graham, the laborer across the street at CBS." "Oh, I thought you said, Earl Grant." Grant's name brought back pleasant memories of my days at KTLA, when I was a Page for his musical TV show. He was a Nat King Cole sound-a-like, and no less a fine entertainer. Strangely, the next day – on June 11, 1970—Earl Grant, 39, was killed in a Lordsburg, New Mexico car crash. Don't ask. I can't explain it.

Stunt man Dick Butler called me for the *Police Woman* TV series starring Angie Dickinson to back a car out a driveway, and broadside the police car blocking my escape. On the first take, doubling a teenager, I floored the convertible, but the other driver was fearful about the hit, and I had to slam on the brakes to avoid crashing into Eddie Hice's new van parked across the street. Eddie, doubling Charles Dierkop, screamed at the driver, "Hit the fucking mark!" On the second take the car was there and I camed to an abrupt stop. My head whipped-lashed and I fell across the seat, and it was a "Print." Immediately, the set medic was at my driver's door to check me out, she filed a medical report listing a possible neck injury. For three days, I could barely move my head and neck, but what hurt most was that the assistant director, Jon Anderson, never included my $25 stunt adjustment.

I wasn't surprised as this was Columbia Studios modus operandi, practiced to the hilt by their notorious production head, Jack Fier (appropriately pronounced, "Fear"). When a performer's meal penalty crossed his desk, he would toss it in his desk drawer. He would endorse the voucher for payment only when SAG or an agent confronted him, demanding payment. I should have called the cheap prick.

LAPD Detective buddy Steve Rogers invited me to a party at a Studio City hillside home rented by four fellow officers. We talked and drank when fifteen nurses suddenly appeared. One doll face caught my eye and we hit it off. An hour later we heard, "LAPD Vice! Open the door or we'll break it down!" Ten cops entered. Laughing, they had heard about the party and wanted a drink.

The nurse and I decided my apartment was our next stop and were joined by her girlfriend, and her newly found cop friend. We secured my bedroom while the other couple found my living room couch comfortable. A cop's party is the only way to go, after all, who's going to arrest you if it gets too rowdy?

John "Bear" Hudkins and I flew to Prescott, Arizona for Stanley Kramer's *Bless the Beasts and Children*. Once again, I fell in love with a distant location, which seemingly happened every time I ventured from Hollyweird. Prescott, the first capital of the state or territory, preceding Phoenix, was quaint, complete with a bronze statue in the courthouse square. Naturally, the airline lost my luggage, which is why I now only use carry-on luggage. That evening Bear and I joined camera car owner Gil Casper for dinner, and were delighted when Stanley Kramer came to our table to welcome us, then picked up our dinner tab.

Later, I met A.J., the key grip, who suggested we visit The Palace for a drink. This vintage saloon was located across the square from the courthouse and had been in operation since the 1890s. Replete with local cowboy guys and gals, the twenty-foot high, tin stamped ceiling and the four and a half foot tall bar was a picture study of the Old West. This bar was perfect for my height; I refer to how my arm fit on the bar while standing. My only movement for a scotch and water was to slide my hand a few inches to move the glass to my lips. The massive bar held me in place. I couldn't have fallen over, even if I was pushed. A.J. and I enjoyed the country music and finally headed back to our rooms.

Bear's snoring was an experience, comparable to a runaway locomotive, and I was happy for the few drinks that enabled me to fall into a sound sleep. The next morning, I showered, but couldn't shave, then found I was working with kid actor Billy Mumy of TV's *Lost in Space* fame. Kramer looked at my unshaved face like I was nuts – he didn't know my luggage was lost and instructed prop master Max Frankel to get me an electric razor.

I drove an olive drab World War II weapons carrier truck, as Bear, driving a fastback Mustang runs me off the road. While waiting for the shot, I overheard Mumy badmouthing Stanley Kramer to the other kid actors. You shouldn't judge a book by its cover, but this sixteen-year-old punk always looked like an asshole so I made an exception. Immediately, I related Kramer's extensive film background, successes and talents to this baby brat, but he ignored my every word. Mumy persisted, but I had captured the attention of the other kids. And finally suggested he keep his mouth shut or I would do it for him. We got the shot, and then Bear and I waited another day until the lab approved the film footage.

My biggest laugh was at the Prescott Airport, or meadow, as it was surrounded by lush, green rolling hills. What a beautiful place to learn to fly, I thought, nothing but open space.

Suddenly, the loudspeaker blared—a pilot was requesting landing permission. Immediately, a man, gripping a hard hat and binoculars, ran from the small coffee shop counter to a ten-foot ladder, leading to a platform atop a red and white, eight by eight foot, building. In position, he searched the sky for the in-coming aircraft. Bear said, "Watch this!" and yelled, "Over there!" The man looked at Bear pointing, and whipped his body around in that direction, lost his balance and almost tumbled over the railing as his hard-hat fell into the tall grass. I stifled my laughter as Bear innocently surveyed the horizon.

My missing bag finally arrived the day Bear and I returned to Hollywood. In all my years of traveling to locations in 36 states, Canada, the Caribbean and Mexico, this was the one and only time I ever lost luggage. This must be a record.

Denver Mattson had just moved into another North Hollywood apartment with his buddy, Jon Thorguson. As Denver and Jon were dressing for a brunch at Los Arcos, I picked up their heavy L.A. Times Sunday paper and screamed, "Mad Dog! Mad Dog!" With full force, I slammed the paper down on their massive coffee table. Squealing the high-pitch yelping sound of an injured dog, I continued yelling, "Mad Dog! Mad Dog! Kill the Sonofabitch!" and kept slapping the coffee table.

Jon came running and was so confused he was actually looking for the pooch. Denver rushed in, took one look at Jon and began laughing wildly while I continued slapping the table and yelling. The next morning Denver received a notification from the apartment manager that the complex did not allow pets, much less condone animal abuse. Denver had a hellava time explaining that one.

On *Sixth Sense*, a TV film directed by Sutton Roley, stunt man Jack Verbois was to perform a 25-foot fall through a breakaway plate glass window. Nuckles and I had been indulging in adult liquids and visited the set on Goldwyn Studios backlot. Jack was checking his position when a self-appointed Nuckles placed the fall pad in position. I walked to the side, visualizing Jack's trajectory; it didn't seem right, "Jack, I don't know about this." Jack yelled, "Jess, put the pad where you want it." Nuckles had the pad flat against the building and I pulled it out about six or seven feet. I clicked off a shot with Jack's camera as he landed smack dab in the pad's center. Nuckles didn't appreciate my intervention.

While driving my 1967 Mustang convertible through Cahuenga Pass toward Hollywood at 65mph, I tapped the brake pedal as I switched to the right lane. It felt spongy and I hit it again, plunging it to the floor. Nearing the Vine Street off ramp, I had no brakes as I ducked in between two vehicles entering from the on-ramp. When I first started driving at 15½, I had often thought of what I would do if the brakes ever failed and, in effect, had preprogrammed myself. It all seemed automatic as I popped the transmission lever into low and slowly pulled the emergency brake to reduce my speed. Skidding to a stop on the shoulder, I used the freeway phone to call the Auto Club.

The tow truck driver marveled at how I had maneuvered the car safely, compared to a guy with his family aboard, who might not have reacted accordingly. Checking the undercarriage, he discovered the hydraulic hose to the front right wheel brake cylinder had burst. I found this situation suspicious for a car less than three years old. More so, because the hose was easily accessible, anyone could have damaged the pressured line with a simple slash from a razorblade or knife. I had no proof, but wouldn't have put it past the ex-wife to get her pound of flesh. Regrettably, for my own edification, I never checked with Ford or notified Ralph Nader for a count of how many Mustangs that might have experienced this same malfunction.

The Left Bank had many of the regulars' photos on the wall, and I roared when a stranger asked about the *Star Trek* photo of Dick Durock's huge Latex forehead and facial appliances, "Who's the Moon Fag?" Durock had the picture removed when his buddies started calling him M.F.

Dick, the local USPS postal carrier would shout, "Airmail" and fling the daily mail toward the bartender. A few drinks and an hour or so later, he continued on his mail route.

On Universal's *Senator* TV series starring Hal Holbrook, I had a bellman role with actor Gerald O'Loughlin. We rehearsed my knock on the door—Gerald opened the door to my "Room service." On action, he only cracked the door an inch, so I stood there waiting for him to open it wider. We just stared at each other. Finally, he asked, "What do you want?" "I want you to open the door like you did in rehearsal." The crew busted up as gaffer Gene "Woody" Woods yelled, "That's my Jesse, trying to keep his kisser in the camera."

Universal production manager Abby Singer called me to coordinate a fight scene between two actors on *The Counterfeit Killer*, a TV movie. Stunt performers sell punches with body-English, action and reaction.

But, a diminutive actor's climatic, double-handed rabbit punch to the leather-jacketed big guy looked phony. Finally, after multiple takes, I took the little guy aside, explaining how he needed to strike the big moose harder, "You're slapping-leather and it sounds worse than it is. Besides he's wearing a pad under his leather jacket." There was no pad, but Bam! It was a good hit and even brought tears to the big guy. That's all it took to sell the hit and we had a great shot. That's a wrap!

CHAPTER 13

1971

Warner Bros. casting director Jim Martell called me to an interview on the *Chicago Teddy Bears* TV pilot, starring Dean Jones, Art Metrano, Marvin Kaplan, Mickey Shaughnessy, Jamie Farr and John Banner. Rounding out the cast was the ever popular, former Eastside Kid, Huntz Hall.

Entering the Warner's lot through the casting office, I was greeted by Denver Mattson and a crowd of stunt men so thick you couldn't have swung a cat by the tail without slapping them all in the puss. Great!—A Cattle Call, but figured I'd stay and take a chance.

And a good chance it was. We all entered the sound stage and were greeted by director Hy Averbach, whom I had worked with on Doris Day's *Where Were You When the Lights Went Out?* Shaking my hand, Hy turned to the assistant director, "I want Jesse for the newsboy." Thanking him, I was off to the wardrobe department where a white-haired costumer asked, "What's your waist and inseam?" "My waist is twenty-eight, but why do you want my inseam? It's 1931 and shouldn't a newsboy be wearing knickers?" His telling expression registered an, "Oh yeah, that's a good idea." It's not like he wasn't around in 1931 and didn't know, but possibly he just stayed too long at the fair.

My shot with Denver had us standing at a newspaper stand as it's demolished by a vintage 1930's touring car, driven by George Sawaya—

didn't sit too well with Denver, who considered himself as Hollywood's Greatest Stunt Man -- and once again we had *cheated death*. Anyway, Hy was pleased, but the show's anemic, one-note, storyline caused the show's demise after a dozen episodes, defining an old Broadway axiom "If it ain't on the page, it won't get on the stage." But meeting Huntz Hall was kick.

While exiting Warner's inner courtyard, the door to the administration building swung open and there was a smiling Bill Cosby, "Hi Jess." I was amazed, it had been four years since we had worked together on *I Spy*, and Cos remembered my name. Obviously, he had also read Dale Carnegie. Class will tell.

I was called for *Chrome and Hot Leather* to double actress Kathrine Baumann, Miss Ohio 1969, in a motorcycle crash riding with Bud Ekins. Bud, a champion motorcyclist, had doubled Steve McQueen in the famous motorcycle jump over the fence in *The Great Escape*, so I knew I was in good hands.

While in the Red Coach, I recalled overhearing a conversation describing the *Bullett* car chase. To his drinking buddy, this fellow adamantly maintained the motorcyclist who lost control as the vehicles whizzed by was an innocent bike rider on his way home from work. Wrong. It was Bud Ekins, but I didn't have the heart to burst this guy's bubble – who probably wouldn't have believed me anyway.

Hot Leather had no hairdresser, so with a bit of gauze from a first-aid kit, thread from wardrobe and bobby pins borrowed from the female extras, I fastened the wig tightly to my head as many previous hairdressers had done to me. Seated behind Ekins, ready to be side-swiped by a 1961 Lincoln convertible, I was curious what Bud had in mind—would we go down on our right or left side? "Who knows?" he grinned. That got my juices flowing and during the simulated sideswipe hit, Bud dumped the bike into a slide to our right—and I bounced like a rubber ball. "That was really easy," I said. "Shusssss," Bud whispered, "or everybody will want to do it." He was right—it was the easiest $250 stunt adjustment I ever picked up.

Kathrine Baumann continued her cinematic career and today is a renowned Beverly Hills apparel designer.

Bellying up to The Casting Office bar near Barham Boulevard early one Saturday afternoon, I was startled to see a Catholic priest chugging down a beer. Paul, a retired Army Colonel buddy, introduced me to the Irish-brogued, Dublin, Ireland native. They had just visited Paul's good friend, actress Rosalind Russell in the hospital. Paul believed the good Father could offer support and comfort in her weakened condition. However, my chance meeting with this priest produced mixed feelings in me, recalling a rumored Roman Catholic Church credo that bragged, "Give me a child until he is seven and he'll be a Catholic for life." Wrong. I was 13 when Father Noonan died, soon after I told them to kiss off and never looked back. Still, after a few drinks, I had unanswered questions and offered my business card in hope we might meet again.

A week later, Teddy's called late at 10:30pm saying the priest was calling. Something didn't seem Kosher, and I told them to say they couldn't reach me. Two months later I bumped into Colonel Paul at the Coral Reef and asked about the good Father. "Don't mention that cocksucker to me. He's a phony sonofabitch." Paul angrily described how this priest imposter had burgled him and his friends. With an offer to "bless your home," then would steal jewelry from their bedroom dressers.

Another late night visit to The Casting Office had me feeling no pain and in a frisky mood. So much so, I went from stool to stool asking each lovely lady, "Do you mess around?" Several replied, "No, I don't," but a pretty, young, new arrival from Jacksonville, Florida, answered, "Yes." When I suggested my apartment, she said her two traveling companions didn't have a place to stay either. This was too good to be true, as I suggested they join us. An hour later, we cuddled in my bedroom as her girlfriends bunked on my living room couch and floor. "That's a hard living room floor. Maybe we should ask your friend on the floor to join us?" "Oh, no you don't, I know what you're trying to do." Dammit, that blew every Man's Favorite Fantasy, ménage a trois – a threesome.

At 3am, my doorbell sounded. Peering through the glass peephole stood The Casting Office's exotic, brunette bartender. When it rains, it pours. I motioned for the three sleepovers to be silent and she soon walked away. The next morning it dawned on me—she might have made Man's Favorite Fantasy come true.

Once again, I was back at Warner's with James Garner. With Jim, it's very simple—what you see is what you get. He's just a great guy. His longtime stunt double, Roydon Clark called me for an interview for Garner's new TV series, *Nichols*, set in the early 1900's. Several of us were ushered into writer, producer and director, Frank Pierson's office for the Second Scully brother part. From behind his desk, Frank jumped up and pointed at me, "That's him!"

On an interview, it's said an actor is judged during the first three seconds. In this case it seemed plausible, but then, too, you again had a director who knew exactly what he wanted.

When *Nichols* filming began, I found myself paired with character actor John Quade, the First Scully Brother. Story wise, Garner and the townsfolk didn't appreciate the Scully's saloon brawling and wild hillbilly antics. In one scene, riding to our homestead Sheriff Nichols confronts Quade, who countered with a dissertation that brought tears to everyone. Pierson shot our close ups as an off-camera Garner flipped us the bird. We didn't break up, but after "Cut and Print," we did. Later, in the saloon brawl, Jim was a stunt man's dream as he jerked me up and over the massive saloon bar with ease. He was easier to work with than most stunt guys I had worked with.

To repeat, action involving an actor is often a stunt performer's nightmare. Granted, there are skilled actors who are physically able to handle themselves, but most are not qualified. Some can, and most can't, but Jim could.

Unfortunately, the series, also starring Margot Kidder, just didn't gel. Garner, you would think, wrangling a town full of people would ideally lend itself to many wonderful, personal stories of the characters. The basic turn-of-the-century concept, examining the changing society and the character of a new century was lost. The Industrial Revolution was in full gear and the story possibilities were endless, but there was no cohesion to hold the vapid stories intact and the series vanished after 24 episodes. A few years later, I worked Jim's *The Rockford Files* TV series and he was the same gracious guy, a true star in every sense.

This story traveled fast—Garner cornered TV producer Glen Larson at Universal's main gate, accusing him of pilfering music from the

Rockford show and knocked Larson on his ass. Larson screamed to the gate guards, "He hit me, he hit me. Did you see it?" Jim chimed in, "In case you didn't, watch this," and punched Larson again. A month later, Jim was brutally attacked by an "irate motorist" at Coldwater Canyon and Mulholland Drive. Coincidence? I doubt it.

Harvey's Coral Reef at Laurel Canyon and Riverside became my saloon du jour. Harvey was a good ol' Southern boy from Alabama and was presently building the largest house in Frasier Park, up Highway 5, where the exterior scenes for *The Waltons* were filmed.

He came to the Valley after WWII and talked about the rising land values. I mentioned my 1948 Sunday family drives to the San Fernando Valley, particularly Woodland Hills and the Harry Warner Ranch bordering Ventura Boulevard between Canoga Avenue and Topanga Canyon. My parents checked out the commercial land parcels on Ventura selling for $400 to $900 with $100 down and $10 a month. My Mom and I pleaded with Dad to make a purchase. Often, when an opportunity presents itself, lack of money is usually the prime factor, but not in this case –- after the War, Dad was bringing home $1500 a month from his dental laboratory.

Finally, Dad exclaimed, "The freeway's going to come through and it'll take all the traffic off the street." Harvey smiled, "I remember those parcels well. I bought a few of them."

Like any saloon, Harvey's Coral Reef had its cast of characters and Joyce Cunningham was a delightful, shapely blond bartender, who shared my passion for kissing. Somehow, she and I, along with furniture refinisher Max and his date, ended up on his 36-foot cabin cruiser. After a night of amour at the Wilmington Marina, our foursome found ourselves each sipping a Bloody Mary—the Hair of the Dog, in a dingy San Pedro longshoremen bar. The joint resembled a film's Barbary Coast dive where guys got shanghaied. Fortunately, the inhabitants that morning only enjoyed ogling our ladies.

Bill Hart called me to double James McCallion on *Cade's County*, the Twentieth Century-Fox series starring Glenn Ford. The job offer caused some consternation due to a tragic accident two weeks prior. The series rural setting necessitated using Jeeps as sheriff's vehicles, which, of course, included the obligatory chase. This time, two Jeeps were required to jump a ravine. One Jeep made it, but the other, driven by Hal Needham, with stunt man Roy Sickner seated in the rear, nose-dived in and flipped forward. Roy had a death grip on the side support bars when the tailgate caught him across the forehead. We can only surmise that had Roy been tossed free he might have experienced only bruises. The head injury caused permanent brain damage to a fine writer, stunt man and former TV commercial Marlboro Man.

Then, there was Boyd Cabeen. He was Robert Mitchum's stand-in and the combination of them together sent shivers up the spines of their producers and directors. Once, their pranks caused MGM to issue an order that they not be permitted to work together on the same film, an edict that began with a dispute between Mitchum and MGM's Louis B. Mayer. To get even, late one night Mitchum and Cabeen drove a panel truck onto the MGM lot and went directly to the Make-Up & Hair Department. Accomplishing their mission, they exited the main gate, waving to the guard. The next morning, an alert was sounded when it was discovered that all of the large, floor standing, hair dryers were missing. Mitchum and Cabeen eventually returned the dryers and Mitchum received his demands.

June 1971, stunt man Erik Cord invited me to Carmel for the filming of *Chandler*, a Leslie Caron-Warren Oates film for MGM. Having heard that Boyd Cabeen now owned a Carmel cocktail lounge, I decided to drop in on him. A tall, handsome, blue-eyed ladies' man, Boyd's Hollywood reputation was legend—to win a bet at The Coach & Horses on Sunset Boulevard; he orally pleasured a lady on the bar amidst smiling patrons.

So, here I was on Carmel's main drag, looking every bit like a lost tourist, spied a cop in his parked cruiser and asked for directions. He was quite congenial when I said a friend owned a local bar, but when I mentioned Boyd's name, his reply strangely changed to an angry, "Down the block, on your left!"

The small cocktail lounge was located among several art galleries. Entering through the Dutch doors I found a seat at the bar. After the bartender served me a Screwdriver I asked if Cabeen owned the bar. He replied with a curt, "What'd ya want with him?" Relating we were old buddies and that I was in town on a film to double Leslie Caron, he seemed relieved and quietly said Boyd was in the hospital, recuperating from serious injuries. Assuming a car accident was the cause he quickly corrected me, but didn't volunteer any additional information. I later heard ol' Boyd was banging somebody's wife and her husband had made an unscheduled appearance.

Chandler filming continued and I managed a visit to Boyd's bar again, but never got to see him. Interestingly, the husband who administered Boyd's bone-breaking treatment was the Carmel Chief of Police. Boyd died a few years ago, probably with a smile on his face.

Director Paul Magwood, one of USC's wunderkinds, was a congenial guy attempting to film his vision, but the on-set MGM production executives wouldn't give him the reins. He blocked out a scene and the crew trudged through the soft beach sand to set the rails for his dolly shot. Forty-five minutes later, the MGM watchdogs insisted the rails be moved "five feet to the right." This readjustment took another thirty minutes for the exasperated grips to complete. Again, it's one ship, one captain. Magwood was last seen working as an assistant director in television. Too bad, he was a nice guy and maybe *that* was his problem.

Mitchell Ryan (*Dharma & Greg* TV series) played the lead bad guy on *Chandler*. He completed filming *The Honkers*, and had flown directly from the New Mexico location to the Monterey airport. Mitch is a nice, fun loving guy Lee Marvin once called the best actor in Hollywood, and yes, Mitch was also known to enjoy a drink. In the ensuing ten-minute trip from the airport to Carmel's Holiday Inn, Mitch managed to get into a squabble with the studio driver, a teamster's wife, and called her a "cunt."

I arrived on the next flight and her driver husband was there to deliver me to the hotel. He needed to talk to someone and I was the one. Visibly upset, he complained there would be a problem unless Ryan apologized: "My wife is a cunt, but I'm the only one who can call her that."

Mitch apologized and a few days later, quit drinking. I suspect his decision of sobriety was influenced by my antics in the Holiday Inn lounge. Guess you could say I was a good "bad example" for Mitch.

My attention-getting saloon stunt was to lean back on the bar stool and let go. Crashing to the floor usually produced shock and often, near heart attacks among the older patrons. But, to a frustrated comic, it was a great way to get a laugh. I always maintained that while the other stunt guys kept in shape working out in gyms, my physical fitness technique was "truer to the art since I was performing for an audience."

On May 1, 1971, Amtrak officially assumed America's railway passenger system and an MGM executive decision was made to film several scenes aboard the Los Angeles to Monterey train. However, the filming would take place while returning the entire crew to Los Angeles. I can almost hear this suggestion during the pre-production meeting, "Hey, we can shoot all the scenes, plus save thousands in air fares." As well intentioned as this genius may have been, the southern direction of the train, traveling along the beautiful California coast, placed the Pacific Ocean on the wrong side of the train -- when the script had the train traveling north to Monterey. In the editing room, if someone caught this faux pas, they probably commented, "Don't worry. The audience will never notice it." Yeah, right, Einstein.

In the Ontra Cafeteria at Vermont & Ninth, Reg Parton, Chuck Hicks, Louie Elias and I attended a meeting extolling the virtues of not paying income tax. Irwin Schiff and a Twentieth Century-Fox grip named Terry Oaks lectured that since the USA was no longer on the Gold Standard, our monetary system was illegal. When he asked us not to be concerned about guys in the parking lot listing license plate numbers, "They're only the FBI," Parton and I were out the door. Hicks stayed and went along with their program. He later complained when the IRS nailed him for back taxes, penalties and interest totaling over $90,000.

Universal called me to work with Johnny Daheim on Anthony Quinn's *The Man and the City* TV series. We did a car chase near the San Fernando Mission, but the greatest thrill was meeting the director, actor Paul Henried. For you film trivia fans, Henried played Ingrid Bergman's husband, Victor Laszlo, in *Casablanca*.

Hustling stunt work required visiting a studio and checking out the production offices, where the production managers and assistant directors prepped their shows. Usually, I just said hello and moved on, not wishing to infringe upon their busy schedules—Just being seen was enough to let them know your availability and often resulted in a "We'll need you next week." From there, it was customary to drop by the shooting sets to catch a director or anybody else you've worked with who might need your services.

Entering a stage quietly, a camera rolled on a love charged scene between a guy and his paramour. Tightly embraced, they exchanged tender dialogue as the director, completely caught up in the moment—mouthed each word, devouring their every nuance. The crew watched in silent anticipation as this romantic spell was shattered by a "buurrrrap"—that unmistakable sound of breaking wind. Everyone knew when what they heard, looked up toward the catwalk to see a seated electrician, whose flatulence had jarred him awake. His startled expression caused the set to roar with laughter.

I had met Howard Chappell in the mid-sixties through director Richard Bartlett. Chappell's military background was truly impressive—during World War II he was a member of the O.S.S., the Office of Strategic Services, in what would later become the Central Intelligence Agency. Under the O.S.S. head honcho, General "Wild Bill" Donovan, Howard's behind-the-lines exploits were well documented and published.

One tale had him avenging atrocities by tracking down a Nazi officer's girlfriend and leaving her severed breasts on the German officer's doorstep.

Chappell was now the president of the City of Los Angeles' Board of Public Works and requested my assistance, along with Jock Mahoney, to create a One-Stop Permit Office, Mayor Sam Yorty's effort to facilitate the filming needs of the motion picture industry, for a token $1.00. A dollar I never did receive, but Jock received his. Up to now, a studio or production company had to contact each city department individually to obtain the necessary filming permission for each location, street or city facility. The time involved was pervasive considering the restraints common to the immediate, ever-changing, schedules of a production. This revolutionary office was long overdue.

Then the politicians became involved. The Los Angeles City Council was ambivalent regarding the needs of the motion picture industry, "If we give concessions to the movie industry, then the aerospace industries will want special treatment."

The Hollywood film industry had put the town on the map and only through the concerted efforts of councilmen Joel Wachs, Robert Stevenson (a former actor), John Farraro and Donald Lorenzen did the One-Stop Permit Office finally become a reality.

The One-Stop Permit Office was well received and my calls to the studio production heads proved eventful—all favored streamlining the film permit process. Paramount's Sam Strangis (we met on *Batman* and my Mom had known him since he was ten) was eager to mention a local film location where a guy fired up his noisy gas lawnmower and sat with a five-gallon gas can, waiting to receive $50 to shut it off. Today, L.A.'s municipal laws now prevent deliberate film company interferences.

A studio needed to park their equipment trucks on a vacant lot at Wilshire and Kensington and a property check revealed the owner was the Catholic Archdiocese of Los Angeles. A side note: The New York Catholic Archdiocese is the largest landowner in NYC.

Built in 1893, Los Angeles' ornate, wrought iron trimmed, Bradbury Building lacked parking space for a film company's vehicles, and the adjoining pay parking lot owner demanded $1000 per day. We issued a permit to allow parking in one of Third Street's two traffic lanes—and the ecstatic production company gladly paid the city permit fee of $25.

L.A.'s senior helicopter pilot Cliff Welsh gave Jock and I a Cook's Tour of the city facilities. At 5000 feet, while hovering over the 110 and 405 Freeways interchange, Cliff demonstrated the copter's auto-rotation capabilities by disengaging the engine from the transmission. Calmly, he explained our falling speed could be slowed from 80mph to 50mph. Sensing, probably by our pained expressions that we understood the demonstration he reengaged the trans and we continued our trip.

Passing over MGM I was shocked and saddened to see the condominium construction on MGM's Lot #3. I had not heard the studio land had been sold to a developer. Near the lake, the grand Cotton Blossom paddle wheeler from *Showboat* had been reduced to a pile of lumber, as were the major sets from MGM's many epic films.

Continuing to the Hyperion Treatment Plant in El Segundo, south of LAX, we toured the complex where the city's waste was processed and pumped out to sea through two 36"—five and eight-mile long tubes.

Jock and I didn't fit well into the city's suit and tie regime, with him in his custom-made Western suits by Nudie and me in a sport coat, slacks and turtleneck shirt. The day a playful Jock kissed an irate councilman's (Don Lorenzen) forehead really put us over the top. Don became a good friend and would later, at my request, present to SAMP, a Los Angeles City Council proclamation commemorative plaque at our annual dinner-dance. Troy Melton later snatched it from the SAMP office and destroyed it because his name was not listed on it.

A trip to inspect the county morgue was overpowering amid the formaldehyde odor and the naked bodies. Only when the clothed body of a male heart attack victim, who had just died 20 minutes earlier on an L.A street was wheeled in, did I almost up-chuck.

Jock and I mulled over the L.A. city bureaucrats lifestyle and their grumbling about the rival Department of Water & Power employee's elitist status, their attitude and salaries, which exceeded the common city employee rates for the same job classification.

The City clowns had their personal salaries and finances honed down to a science, anticipating a fiscal pay increase every July 1st, weeks of paid vacation determined by tenure, paid national holidays and 13 paid sick days. Simply, with eight weeks yearly vacation, holidays and sick leave, many were paid a year's salary for nine months of employment.

Mostly, we laughed when they punched in at 7:30am and immediately went to breakfast in the City Hall's cafeteria. Returning to their desks by 8:15am, then took a break at 10am, and went to lunch at 11:30am. Back from lunch at 12:30pm, a break at 3pm, return at 3:30pm and punch out at 4:30pm. Jock and I figured that if you induced only one third of the 12,000 city hall employees to do the work they were assigned to do for eight hours, the other eight thousand could park cars somewhere.

Our biggest question regarded city politics—when multiplied to county, state and federal levels, we wondered us how anything equitable was ever accomplished. Well, occasionally, even a blind pig finds an acorn.

But most astonishing was the condescending attitude. From the City Hall janitor to the Mayor's Office their perception seemed to be, "Screw John Q. Public. We're running this town. They'll do what we tell them."

An Economic Development Department manager then declared the *One-Stop Office* should justify its existence to the City Council, which was never a council concern. His new guidelines doubled all filming related fees and costs. The increase occurred not because of the Council's financial concerns, but at the whim of an individual trying to boost his bureaucrat image and his salary. That sounds familiar.

CHAPTER 14

1972

While visiting the *Deadly Dream* production filming at the City of Burbank Water and Power plant, I spotted actress Janet Leigh. Introducing myself, I mentioned how she was robbed of an Emmy for her poignant portrayal of an alcoholic actress on the *Bracken's World* TV series—a truly memorable award winning performance.

Janet Leigh was such a dear, sweet lady and suspecting her vibrant sense of humor, I whipped out a picture of my "so-called" girlfriend. Actually, it was a police mug shot of a guy, with a face only his mother could love. Janet took one look and howled as her co-star Lloyd Bridges walked by, "Lloyd, come see Jesse's girl friend." Holding the picture, he stared at it, looked at me, then handed me the photo, said, "Very nice," and walked away. Janet and I again roared. To his passing day, Lloyd probably believed it really was a photo of my girlfriend.

When Janet received my copy of her book, *There Really Was A Hollywood* to autograph, along with the infamous picture, her grand sense of humor came through once again when she inscribed, "Dear Jess, Love from your 'other' girlfriend!"

When SAMP members Al Wyatt, Sr. and Reg Parton rented an office across from CBS Studio Center for their new independent production stunt service all hell broke loose. Though this was a viable entrepreneurial enterprise, it violated SAMP by-laws, which forbade such endeavors. After much hand wringing, Al and Reg were persuaded to merge their operation with SAMP—thus the SAMP office was created and now became a physical presence instead of a post office box. This new office provoked increased membership dues to subsidize a full-time secretary, rent and merchandizing, comparable to Stunts Unlimited's operation on Cahuenga Boulevard West. SAMP was always inclined to imitate rather than innovate.

SAMP's later move to a larger North Hollywood location at Riverside Drive and Whitsett Avenue included room for a pool table and coffee maker. The secretary's main duty was to find future productions for members to bird dog. In the past, this information was unearthed from word-of-mouth, studio production office visits or a blurp in the trade papers.

From day one, per SAG's stipulation—new SAMP members were instructed that SAMP was not a hiring hall—a SAG member could not hire another SAG member. Historically, this had been a gray area as stunt gaffers only "recommended" stunt performers, but it was the casting office or assistant director who gave the actual work calls.

I attended John Burroughs Junior High School with Tony Curtis' brother, Bobby Schwartz (Tony's real name was Bernie Schwartz), we met again at Paramount in 1960, when Tony was costarring with Debbie Reynolds in *Rat Race*, showing off his new Rolls Royce Silver Cloud. A group surrounded this magnificent $20,000 convertible, priced $5000 above the regular Rolls. All I could think was, "Geeez, I could buy a house for twenty grand." With the hood popped, Tony removed a small roll of wire, explaining that if a fuse blows you can re-wrap it with new wire. I asked, "Tony isn't a blown fuse a safety valve for the real problem?" His enthusiasm vanished instantly and I was sorry I asked. Rumor had it that this car purchase was the impetus for their divorce. Years later, when I told Janet Leigh of this incident, she roared.

Veteran stunt man Paul Stader was coordinating *Towering Inferno* at Twentieth, called to pick my brain about fire gags, saying I would be very busy on the film. Contacting several special effects buddies to verify the latest pyro-techniques and equipment, I sent Stader several fire gag photos, the information he requested and waited for my work call. I'm still waiting.

Veteran stunt man Fred Krone, the business mind behind SAMP's formation, was doubling a heavy on the *Banyon* TV series starring Robert Forster. Taking a gunshot, Fred fell forward into an empty nine-foot deep indoor swimming pool. I watched the shot on TV. It was a brutal dead fall—it hurt to watch, as he landed on his head and shoulder. This was Fred's stunt swan song. "My timing was off, I didn't get over," explaining his multiple injuries, including a concussion and a broken shoulder.

In the previous ten years, Fred had studied to become a master clock maker and, having considerable more gray matter than most stunt guys, determined that clock parts from a single New York source was absurd, so he created a West Coast clock parts distribution center. Fred later sold the parts house, made wise land investments, grew avacados and became a richly deserved multimillionaire.

I was hired as the lone assassin on *Melinda* at MGM. Hiding behind a curtain, I suddenly appeared and emptied a snub nose pistol into the speaker at the podium. Vicariously, these actions definitely alleviate your inhibitions.

Tom Sawyer was a co-production of 20th Century-Fox and Reader's Digest, starring Johnny Whittaker, Warren Oates and Celeste Holms and a nine-year-old, Jodie Foster. I was chosen to double a 14-year old Jeff East, who would later play Christopher Reeve as a boy in *Superman*. Once again, it would be fun to work with director Don Taylor and Warren Oates.

Stunt girl Gerry Coffer (stunt man Jack Coffer's sister) and I boarded the Trans World Airlines champagne flight from LAX for the Missouri location. Seated in first class, per the Screen Actors Guild contract, the flight attendants apparently believed we were honeymooning and persistently replenished our glasses with the bubbly. Arriving in Kansas City en route to Columbia, Missouri, we were feeling no pain and having a ball. From the Ozark Airlines counter, we were escorted through the double doors for the final leg of our flight. Spotting the majestic Lear Jet, Gerry and I made a staggering beeline for the gleaming bird. The pilot quickly steered us 180o toward a small, single engine plane. Neither of us had ever flown in a four-seater and if it hadn't been for the champagne we'd still be standing on the tarmac discussing the flight.

Our preference for a multi-engine plane might have stemmed from the stunt process. When setting up a stunt, the main objective is to be comfortable with the chosen plan of action. Next, you look for a "Plan B"—just in case. In this baby, when the one and only engine quits, I don't care how well they say the plane will "glide," I want a "Plan B" or, in this case, another engine, two or three.

Nevertheless, we followed the beautiful Missouri River and truly enjoyed our flight to Columbia, home of the University of Missouri. We even spotted a paddlewheel boat and later found it was the Julia Belle Swain, traveling to our film location from its base in Peoria, Illinois.

The next day we were driven to the Missouri River location. Jodie Foster's mother said she was considering a script from Martin Scorcese, called *Taxi Driver*, and thought it could be a career-boosting film for her daughter. History proved she was correct.

Our stunt called for Tom Sawyer and Huckleberry Finn to accidentally crash their log raft head-on into a paddlewheel boat. Viewing the river site, Gerry and I agreed that everything seemed in order, with one exception—The River current. Moving at eight knots, a crew member tossed a ten-foot log into the water and it immediately disappeared in a sucking whirlpool. Moments later, fifty yards down river the log suddenly emerged like a Nike missile fired from a submerged nuclear submarine.

We then watched as Warren Oates, Whittaker and East lip-synchronized a song to playback. Years later, I was informed that Warren's voice was dubbed by my old buddy, singer-musician-composer-arranger Billy Strange. Having known both guys very well, it's the greatest voice matching of all time.

Mark Twain's 1840's fictional home of Tom Sawyer, St. Petersburg, modeled after his childhood in Hannibal, Missouri, was recreated in magnificently preserved Arrowrock. The art department made only minor changes—simply covered the paved streets with dirt and removed the television antennas and window air conditioners.

Unfortunately, much of this creativity went unnoticed via the poor choice of camera angles and over-use of the zoom lens. The film's "look" was strictly "TV"—tight shots and close ups. I can only imagine how this location would have appeared with John Ford's *High Cover Establishing Shots* to capture the town's full flavor. With the exception of the flowing Missouri River scenes, the rest of the movie could have been filmed on any Hollywood studio back lot.

On Saturday afternoon, July 22, 1972, Gerry and I arrived at the location and as usual, the stunt was the last shot scheduled. Eventually, at five a.m., Sunday in the darkness, Gerry and I were placed on a studio crafted log raft. The river's normal current of eight knots was now moving at 12 knots, caused, we were told, by a rainstorm several days earlier in North Dakota. Up river, a safety boat held us as we awaited the cue to set us free on our collision course.

The Julia Belle Swain approached from down river and "took aim" on the raft to assure a hit. "Action!" blared from the safety boat's radio and we swiftly drifted toward the steamboat. From the bullhorn aboard the Julia Belle, Director Don Taylor yelled, "Jump!" Gerry leaped out and away into the dark water—I jumped a beat later causing the raft to duck out from under me, plunging me into a swirling whirlpool—I was sucked under. Struggling to the surface for air, I found the left—port side of the Julia Belle Swain in my face. I attempted to swim away, but the strong current held my head to the wood hull, also as the ship's captain steered starboard toward the rivers mainstream. Suddenly, I was sucked under water again. In the pitch-black water, my head continued to bounce off the ship's keel. My vision was zero as the wood hull continued scraping along my back—I went limp into a "Deadman's Float."

Then it flashed on me that this paddle wheeler might have been converted to screws (propellers) and any moment I was going to be chopped up. All I could think of was my Mother and, oddly enough, who was going to complete the environmental film I was producing, directing and photographing for the City of Los Angeles.

Still limp, I didn't know how much longer I could hold my breath. After attempting every move to surface, I accepted the fact it was all over – as a great feeling of calmness enveloped me. A two-pack a day smoker, my lungs felt like they were going to burst when suddenly, in the blackness, I received a hard hit to my left shoulder. It was the paddlewheel. I tumbled end-over-end, in a vertigo-state, into the paddlewheel's churning backwash. With no idea which way was up, I pulled the cord to my CO^2 inflatable diving vest. Instantly, it ballooned and shot me toward the river's surface.

A voice yelled, "There he is!" Moments later a safety boat, steered by Teamster driver captain Jim Foote, arrived as prop man Gregg Bilson latched on to my bib overalls strap. My first question was about Gerry— Jim assured me she had made it to the other safety boat without a problem. Gregg produced a flask of brandy and insisted I partake. He didn't have to twist my arm. All told, they estimated I was underwater well over a minute, but it seemed like an eternity.

Don Taylor greeted me with a big bear hug. The morning sun was now rising as the company rushed Gerry and me back to our hotel in Columbia. Hurriedly we showered and changed to catch the next flight out and we touched down at LAX at 1:04pm that afternoon. What an adventurous day.

The raft-paddle wheeler collision was not as effective on the big screen as it should have been, as evidenced later by the still photographer's photo – He had the perfect camera angle from the riverbank. Often, a mediocre stunt will look fantastic when filmed correctly. Conversely, a spectacular stunt becomes ineffective when photographed with a wrong lens, angle or camera speed.

Forever it seems; one of my greatest interests has been the paddle-wheel boats of the 1800s. Possibly, it was Mark Twain's romanticized written images of Southern Belles and Mississippi Gamblers traveling on what was then America's greatest waterway system. However, it was also actress Helen Hayes' passion that prompted her to enjoy more than nineteen Delta Queen and Mississippi Queen paddle wheel boat voyages on ol' man river.

While in Nashville, I became good friends with Captain Edgar Allen Poe (his real name, but not a descendent of the literary genius) of Opryland's General Jackson, a $12 million showboat built in 1985.

Captain Poe often invited me to the ship's pilot house as we cruised along the Cumberland River. When I related my Julia Bell Swain story he said he knew the boat well, and had been its pilot on occasion. He then mentioned how lucky I was to survive, and I happily agreed. "No, I mean you were *REALLY* lucky." Now, very serious, he explained that, "98% of the guys who get swept under a paddlewheel boat never make it out. They get hung-up on one of the three, very sharp, rudders. You went right between two of them."

Whew! I'd always known I was fortunate to get through that stunt, but never realized just how much, especially, if the paddlewheel had struck my head instead of my shoulder. This stunt just validated what I have always suspected—when it's your time to go...

I recently heard the good Captain Poe had died of cancer. He was such a gentle man—a five-generation riverboat captain with so many hilarious stories of the river. I miss him and his stories.

Returning to Tinseltown, stunt work continued on *Superfly, Love: American Style* and *Emergency!* On July 4th, for *Unholy Rollers* I was doubling a mini-skirted Claudia Jennings, Playboy magazine's 1970 Playmate of the Year, during a motorcycle chase on Culver City's vacant Venice Boulevard. Later, during a 2am car/police-car chase, we observed a red stop signal as an imbibed, blurry-eyed gent in the right lane, slurred, "Hey buddy, there's cop with his lights on behind you." I yelled, "Are you bullshittin' me?" and burned rubber as the light changed, with the cop car hot on my tail.

Chief Samuelson, my former production company partner from the early sixties, was handling the public relations for Hollywood's Annual Santa Claus Lane Parade. Years before, Gene Autry had heard some tots scream, "Here Comes Santa Claus!" and promptly wrote the Christmas tune of the same name.

Samuelson believed the Stuntmen's Association of Motion Pictures deserved to participate in this televised event, with Erik Cord, Vince Deadrick, Chuck Hayward, Dean Smith, and George Wilbur. Vince and I moved to grab a drink at Nickodell's on Argyle, but the Wells Fargo Bank stagecoach was ready to load, and we soon found ourselves flashing our six-guns. The Stuntmen's Association logo was in full view when actress Joanne Worley waved to us from her KTLA TV hostess booth, giving us a fine introduction.

Traveling the world-famous Hollywood Boulevard, from Argyle to LaBrea, was a personal thrill of a lifetime. My Dad had first taken me to the parade in 1946, lifting me up to shake hands with *Red Ryder* actor "Wild Bill" Elliot. Of course, we all remember his sidekick, "Little Beaver," played by Robert Blake from the *Baretta* TV series. A year later we visited the Hitching Post Theater, where every young cowpoke was required to "check" his six-shooter at the door. Evidently, 300 kids firing their cap pistols at the movie screen annoyed some parents.

Along the parade route, our "Wild West" presence was greeted warmly, though small children were often timid and we enjoyed winning them over. Conversely, there was the teenage stud, holding is babe tightly, flipping us the finger. You can't please everyone.

Arriving at the end of the parade route, we climbed down from the stagecoach. Expecting a ride back to our parked cars, we were informed there was no return transportation. That was par for the course, re-calling several reasons for dissolving my previous partnership with Samuelson.

With no other choice, we began our trek back along the two and a half mile, sardine-packed Tinseltown's Street of Dreams (my apologies to Broadway). Single file, with George Wilbur leading, we snaked our way through the sidewalk's moving mass of humanity, flowing like a river in each direction. We were all in a good stride, when George suddenly turned and threw a punch at one of the passer-bys. The grinning male deftly avoided the flying fist and evaporated into the moving crowd. George angrily screamed the guy had fondled his crotch. I laughed all the way back to our cars.

A buddy's connection set me up at Cal State Northridge's FM radio station, where I worked briefly as the early morning news broadcaster. What a wonderful experience to exhibit my many speech and voice classes stressing diction, enunciation and news copywriting. What a thrill.

Blooper LPs were popular during the sixties, so I figured a SAMP motion was in order—"When a stunt doesn't work right during the first take, have the director print it and SAMP would pay any the costs. In five years we could accumulate enough bad stunt/good stunt footage to have our own stunt blooper TV special." The Board agreed and the motion was passed. To this day not one clip has appeared. This concept was many years before Dick Clark began his long running *Blooper* TV series.

Hit! stunt coordinator Everett Creach invited me to Seattle for the Sidney Furie production starring Billy Dee Williams and Richard Pryor. The film, with the ubiquitous car chase, included fellow stunt players, Vince Deadrick, Larry Holt, Bill Lane and Bob Minor. We were housed at SeaTac, mid-way between Seattle and Tacoma, with beautiful rooms overlooking a flowing stream—so close you could fish it from your balcony.

One quiet evening, the SeaTac cocktail lounge approached a near riot when Richard Pryor took center stage to perform his bawdy nightclub act. His profanity and lewd remarks came to an abrupt halt when several offended male patrons rushed the stage. Fortunately for him, a film company grip quickly enabled Pryor's escape through an emergency exit.

For many years, John Wayne presented his cast and crew with a colorful, personalized coffee mug from each film they worked. Stunt man Chuck Hayward's mantle proudly displayed his ceramic collection of 26.

I, too, had coffee mugs made up with the SAMP logo on the front and "Thanx from Jesse Wayne" on the backside. Word got back to me that Dick Warlock, whom I had considered to be one of my best friends, had complained to the SAMP Board of Directors that I was in violation for using the SAMP logo for my own personal publicity. After a lengthy discussion, sanity prevailed and a reprimand against me was denied. Jealousy, along with Ego and Greed, had reared its ugly head again.

CHAPTER 15

1973

The year 1973 bloomed as Jock Mahoney and I departed from the innards of the Los Angeles City Hall and the One-Stop Permit Film Office. We were pleased to have produced a viable entity to aid the film industry, but couldn't help but feel we had also created a monster. The bureaucrats had seized the permit office and, regardless of film industry needs, now made it a "City First" operation. However, the previous fifteen months had provided me with an invaluable "hands on" insight to the city government's inner workings, something my high school civics class never accomplished.

One of the most troubling aspects I found was the general attitude of a City employee. Each exuded a lofty, self-anointed position of importance. A case in point: One day I needed to check the Records Department for a prospective film location address and owner. Approaching the counter, I watched as several male and female City personnel "joked and played grab ass," purposely ignoring me. Finally, I yelled, "Hey!" and held high my gold embossed Mayor's Office identification card. Immediately, a guy rushed from the group, "Oh, I'm sorry. I thought you were someone off the street." The public be damned.

Moving on, the *Emergency!* TV series was Jack Webb's baby and was instrumental in the creation of the EMT – Emergency Medical Technicians. Nation-wide, in every city and town these units have saved countless millions of lives since 1972. Initially, Jack had contacted the City of Los Angeles Fire Chief Raymond Hill to use the city's facilities, but when Hill refused, the County of Los Angeles Fire Department gladly extended their complete cooperation.

Through the years a stunt performer often gravitated to one studio more than another as the production personnel shifted from job to job. At this point in time, Universal had become my home, working virtually every TV series the studio filmed. However, a call from Disney's resident stunt coordinator, Dick Warlock, took me to the San Francisco location of *The Love Bug Rides Again*, the sequel to the studio's successful, *The Love Bug*, which I had also worked on in 1969.

We departed the Hollywood-Burbank Airport at 1:15pm, arrived in the Bay City at 2:00pm and were on the set by three, ready to film the night shots. Disney Studios always ran a tight ship.

This *Love Bug* sequel starred stage and screen star Helen Hayes, and I would stunt double her later on *The Snoop Sisters* TV series for NBC.

Our driving shots consisted of a fleet of 20 Volkswagens following Number 53, as *Herbie Rides Again*, through the streets of the City by the Bay. To create the illusion of the driverless VWs, the stunt drivers wore black shirts and hoods. Black makeup was applied around our eyes. Standing around, waiting for the camera set up, we resembled an NAACP chapter of the Ku Klux Klan. Ingeniously, the special effects crew had removed the backs of each driver's seat, allowing the black shrouded driver to simulate the up-right seat back, and then grip the steering wheel at arm's length. Ahhh, the phony tinsel of Hollywood— what we need is real tinsel.

My main concern was maintaining vision through the hood's eye-holes as the slightest movement, either way, would shift the peepholes to the side of my head. Seeking a solution, I remembered a wool navy watch cap stashed in my stunt bag. Aha! Course cloth to cloth solved the problem – many years before the hook & loop connection – now commonly called -- Velcro.

Herbie led us through several run-bys. Walkie-talkies in each car notified us of "Cut," and we would then reassemble at the "Number One Position," ready for the next shot. Some one noticed that veteran stunt man David Sharpe was missing from our entourage. Second unit director, Art Vitarelli, immediately radioed, "Davy, where are you?" Davy instantly responded that he was at the corner of Lombard and Van Ness streets. Art told him to stay there and a Teamster would arrive to lead him back to our location. Minutes passed as we awaited Davy's return. Several more minutes later, we listened as the driver explained that he was at Lombard and Van Ness, but there was no Davy. Suddenly, Davy's voice cut in saying he was parked right under the street signs and didn't see any studio driver. Thirty minutes passed and we're all laughing as this radio banter continued between Davy, Art and the driver. Where the hell is he? We can hear him, but nobody can find him. Then we heard the driver's voice, "I got him!"

It seems that when our pack of VW's made a series of right turns to return to "Number One Position," Davy mistook a passing "civilian" Volkswagen for one of ours and followed it. Ultimately, he found himself parked under street signs placed by the art department to cover the real street names.

Vitarelli told me to switch cars, pointing to an old, dilapidated VW— seemingly rescued from the junkyard. There wasn't a square inch of metal without a dent. With its bent, flopping hood and broken head- lights, this little VW was to bring up the rear, always trying to catch up with Herbie and his troops. In motion, the collapsed, knock-kneed wheels caused the car to gyrate and jerk in spasm-like movements.

Vitarelli cued me and around the corner I came. Lying in a prone position allowed me to align myself with the street's telephone lines. Staying parallel with them permitted me to maintain a straight course as I passed through the Chapman camera crane high shot.

Naturally, kids packed the movie theater when *Herbie Rides Again* was released. Interestingly, when the little beat-up VW appeared, chugging along as best he could, many of the small children began crying—feeling sorry for the little guy. This was just another example of the emotional force that a film can create.

Now and then I tossed down a few with Lindsey, Bing Crosby's youngest son, and later worked with Gary Crosby on the *Chase* TV series. Both were tragic examples of living in their father's shadow.

In Calabasas for Universal, we shot *SNAFU*, a WWII pilot directed by Jackie Cooper with Bill Couch as stunt coordinator. Jay Leno had a bit comic-relief part. It didn't sell. Carey Loftin and I were foot soldiers getting shot or blown away.

On another show, a congenial Van Johnson caught me staring at his scarred forehead and candidly revealed how it happened in a car accident, just after he had been cast in MGM's *A Guy Named Joe*. The studio wanted to replace him during his four-month hospitable stay, but his co-stars, Spencer Tracy and Irene Dunne, went to L.B. Mayer and refused to do the film until he returned. Ultimately, the role made Van Johnson a major star.

The *Emergency!* TV series, starring Robert Fuller continued to be fun with always some sort of hi-jinx going on. Often, I felt like their resident victim and patient. While portraying an injured disaster victim, I was placed on a gurney and inserted into an ambulance. The stationery vehicle rocked gently by two grips with leveraged 2x4s on the bumpers, as the camera shot past my feet to the show's co-stars Kevin Tighe and Randy Mantooth. Randy monitored my blood pressure as Kevin performed a "Babinsky" (that's a test where a sharp object is scraped along the bottom of the foot causing the toes to curl indicating nerve reaction). Administering emergency care, each recited my age, weight, blood pressure and other medical jargon, then Randy suddenly looked down and exclaimed, "Aw geez, it's him again!" With the crew's laughter, director Christian Nyby, II (Chris Nyby's son), yelled, "Okay, Cut! We have enough footage."

Another time, as a victim in the emergency room, the great, veteran song writer-musician, Bobby Troup ("Route 66"), Dr. Joe Early on the show, introduced himself. From my reclined position on the operating table and the Airway in my mouth, he didn't recognize me, "Bobby, it's me, Jess." Greeting me like a long lost brother, the former U.S. Marine hero reminisced about his former days playing piano at Whittinghill's in Sherman Oaks, and later with his combo at The China Trader in Toluca Lake.

Bobby and singer Julie "Cry Me a River" London, Nurse Dixie McCall on the series, were married. Julie was also the ex-wife of Jack

Webb, producer of *Emergency!* Obviously, animosity didn't reign in this relationship.

Meeting the CIA pilot shot down over Russia at his *Operation: Overflight* book signing was a thrill, especially when he inscribed (at my suggestion) "To Jesse, Best Wishes from one stunt man to another. Francis Gary Powers." Years later, while flying the KNBC Telecopter (formerly owned by KTLA), the craft plunged into the San Fernando Valley flood control basin. Official Cause: Out of fuel. There's something dreadfully wrong with this picture. In Powers' book he suggested there were those in the government who preferred to have him dead. Seems the U2 pilots were instructed that should a problem occure they should use the ejection seat. The pilots believed the seat was rigged to blow the plane to smithereens. Well, Gary was captured by the USSR and later exchanged for a Russian spy. Out of gas? I don't think so. My guess is someone had tinkered with the fuel guage. And they finally got their wish.

A day here, a week there kept me well employed. On *Rhinoceros*, starring Broadway actor Zero Mostel, I was a supermarket box boy, pushing a shopping cart in a crosswalk. From out of nowhere, a speeding car nails the cart, drenching me in milk as an oblivious Mostel struts on by. The milk was spoiled and I couldn't wait to get home to take a hot shower.

At 4:30am, a day later, I was in a makeup chair at Twentieth Century-Fox's ranch in Malibu Canyon (It's now a California State Park) for the *Battle for the Planet of the Apes*. The largest team of makeup men I had ever seen assembled on one film carefully applied the primate latex rubber appliances to each actor, stunt man and extra. Three hours later our simian faces were ready to be photographed. Initially, we believed it would be impossible to recognize each other in these full masks, but we were astonished to find *The Eyes Have It*—identifying each other was easy. However, our lunch consisted of sipping liquids through a straw—and certainly, not much nourishment for the big battle scenes.

Back at Universal on *Columbo*, Chuck Waters and I performed a late night, back lot car chase doubling Ray Milland and Bradford Dillman, respectively, and both over six-feet tall, proving once again, if you're wanted on a show, you'll be there.

Quinn Martin was a name synonymous with quality television—it was always a pleasure to work for this first class production company. The 3:00pm call brought me to the Sam Goldwyn Studios in Hollywood for the *Cannon* TV series starring William Conrad to double actress Marlyn Mason as two thugs throw her down a cement stairway. I was happily surprised when my old buddy, costumer Pat McGrath, said, "Wear this," and handed me a SCUBA divers wet suit. We had met on Columbia's *Here Come the Brides* TV series, and he was always ahead of me. Under the wardrobe, this quarter inch of rubber was the ultimate protection from the usual stair fall bumps and bruises. Pat was one of the great guys.

The cement stairway to the QM production offices became the *Cannon* set. Assistant director Lloyd Allen, whom I'd met at Four Star, still he had that negative expression, like someone was going to steal his wallet, nervously explained the stunt.

Veteran director Leo Penn (Sean Penn's father) was terrific as always, a gentle man. Jack Swain was the director of photography and Vince Martinelli was his camera operator for the hand held shot (I later worked with Vince after he became Director of Photography on the *Simon & Simon* TV series).

In what had become my normal piece of business, I stood at the camera lens position, looking up the stairway, carefully visualizing every movement I would make during the fall. Some might call it a mindset or self-hypnosis as I visualized the stunt, as the camera would see it. Then, from the top of the stairway, I slowly walked my intended path for Jack and Leo.

The camera rolled and down I tumbled, head over heels, bouncing like a rubber ball. Landing at Leo's feet, he said, "Print it." Dusting myself off, McGrath saddled up to me, "How was it?" Happily, I grinned, "Perfect, I didn't feel a thing."

Leaving the *Cannon* set, I smiled at Lloyd Allen's vapid stare. Once again, I can only assume his attitude was provoked by the fact I had earned in ten seconds what it took him a week to take home. A few days later, at the Stuntmen's Association's office, Jimmy Casino, William Conrad's stunt double, bragged that D.P. Jack Swain (*The Twilight Zone,*

Rawhide) had said my stair fall was "the best he'd ever seen." The compliment put a smile on my face and, maybe, even on Lloyd Allen's puss, but I doubt it.

The key to a stair fall is to do it at "speed," using your momentum. If you try to slow it down, you'll hit and feel every point of contact. A stair fall is by its very nature an involuntary action—whether the victim trips or is pushed, it must look like the action it is intended to be—a body plummeting uncontrollably, end over end, down the stairway.

I once hired a young guy about 20 to do a stair fall, seemingly rendered semi-unconscious by a toxic gas. It was a sight to behold as this poor kid staggered side-to-side, step-by-step, railing to the wall, and finally crawled to his final mark at the bottom step—all at half speed. It wasn't a lack of communication—he just didn't have his mind set. We needed an out of control stair fall, but it wasn't going to happen and I definitely didn't go for Take 2. Hell, if he had performed the fall at speed, he would have probably broken his neck, and I didn't want that on my conscience. Under my watch no one was ever injured. With any stunt you have to be comfortable and have a plan of action—some physical ability and a bit of heart won't hurt either. He was a nice kid and eventually made a career change. He became a bread baker in Wisconsin.

Universal called with work on Dan Dailey's *Faraday and Company* TV series. It was a thrill to meet one of Hollywood's great song and dance men I'd watched since childhood. Stunt coordinator Dick Dial set up the "bulldog" with Nick Dimitri, who got his stunt start on *Rat Patrol.*

I explained to Dimitri that the "bulldog" should not be telegraphed – meaning, I was not going to turn to see him or try to catch him; he was to leap and nail me. I was prepared to take a hard hit. Dick Dial heartily agreed and the rehearsal worked fine. In the shot, I moved to my mark and then heard his body hit the ground behind me. Dimitri's timing was off as Dick Dial concurred. In Take Two, Dimitri got to me and we hit the pavement. It's a small business, so it didn't take long to hear that Dimitri had blamed me for his incompetence.

Roger Creed had me doubling a midget on *Little Cigars.* My so-called buddy Robin Clark was the production manager and was so tight—

when he blinked, he got a hard on. Roger was set to slide a car into me as I bicycled down the road. From the camera angle, it would look like a hit, but Roger repeatedly missed his mark. I hit the pavement twelve times and my stunt adjustment from Clark was only $100.

Our so-called friendship dated back to 1953 at KTLA, but most distressing was the time I helped him paint the home he was selling. Five minutes later he was gone and didn't return until four hours later. Also, don't believe that lightning doesn't strike twice in the same place. Later, at his new home, while digging an endless trough for his backyard lawn sprinkling system, I turned around and he was gone again. When he returned hours later, his only comment was, "I'm putting in sprinklers, not a sewer." Not even a thank you. Clark was not an honorable person and during my last marriage the bride angrily bragged he "visited her" while I was away on film locations. You could say he had it "in" for me. He had hired her for *The Master Gunfighter* film and she was promptly fired.

Little Cigars featured several of the most famous "little people" in the business. Among them was my old buddy, Jerry Marin, the lead Lollypop Kid in *The Wizard of Oz*, and later as Little Oscar, touring the country in the Oscar Mayer Weinermobile. 1958, when I was a KTLA page, I'd drive him to his Hollywood apartment after his Lil' Oscar TV appearances.

Billy Curtis, with his ubiquitous foot-long cigar, starred in the 1940's, all-midget film classic, *Terror of Tiny Town*. Felix Silla was Cousin Itt on *The Addams Family* and Twiki on the *Buck Rogers in the 25th Century* TV series.

The finale had the film's femme fatale, Angel Thompkins, being hauled off to the pokey. The police car's rooftop light bar had no switch, so I hid beneath the dashboard to connect the hot wires. We rehearsed it once. After the shot, "Cut!" blared from the walkie-talkie, I popped up asking, "Was that a take?" Thomkins suddenly enraged, screamed a barrage of profanity I'd only heard when I hit my thumb with a hammer. Laughing, I opened the door as A.D. Foster Phinney mentioned our next location. Only then did the bitchy blond realize I was joking.

Speaking of pranks, a stunt guy placed plastic wrap over the toilet bowl in an actress' mobile dressing room, the crew howled when they heard her blood-curdling scream. Now that would really give Thomkins something to scream about.

Speaking of toilets, what is it with the female preoccupation of having the toilet seat in the down position? The tales I've heard of women falling into commodes is astonishing. How in the hell does anyone stick his or her "business" anywhere, without looking first? I don't understand the problem. It's another one of life's mysteries. However, it took a lovely lady, Sunny Ferrari, to resolve this great dilemma, "Whoever uses the toilet last, put the lid down. That's why there's a lid—to cover the commode." It's so damn obvious it's kinda frightening.

The Wolper Company invited me to an interview for their new television documentary, *Primal Man*. I exited the production office feeling confident I'd be on the project. Several weeks passed before I heard that stunt man Janos Prohaska and his son, Bobby, had been chosen and brought in several of their friends.

Janos, a circus performer, escaped the 1956 Hungary-Communist invasion, was certainly qualified to do the ape-man. He had passionately perfected the man in a monkey suit routine. With his hands and feet in unison, he could climb up any building drainpipe. Through the years, several others performed the Gorilla-Chimpanzee imitation, including cowboy star Ray "Crash" Corrigan and muscleman George Barrows, but, Janos was the best. Ingeniously, he constructed his costumes on SCUBA divers wet suits, with each hair hand-sewn in place. He painstakingly researched and photographed the primates and had their every movement down to a gnat's ass.

On MGM's *Jumbo*, starring Doris Day, he sent the actress screaming from her dressing room, causing the film company to wrap early. We worked together playing a group of chimps in Rooney's 1964 TV series *Mickey!* While wearing one of his outfits for six hours, I was surprised at the amount of fluid I lost from perspiration. After disrobing, the wet suit slippers wrung out like a dish rag. Later, weighing in at home, I was six pounds lighter. Later, Janos would become the "Cookie Bear" on the *Andy Williams Show*. But I was still pissed, thinking about the beautiful, long location shoot in Lone Pine and Bishop, California I had lost.

Several months passed and I had all but forgotten about *Primal Man*, until a news broadcast reported the plane returning the cast and crew to

Hollywood had crashed, killing all 36 aboard. The overloaded aircraft had departed from the Bishop airport and slammed into a mountain.

Makeup man Rolf Miller, whom I'd worked with on *It's a Mad, Mad, Mad, Mad World*, along with Janos and Bobby, was among the victims. I then realized that had I gotten that job as promised, I, too, would have been on that aircraft. The crash shocked the stunt community, causing us all to recall the many times we were rushed from a distant location in an overloaded charter plane to avoid going into overtime. The Screen Actors Guild pay schedule has since changed to eliminate production's need to get you off the clock as soon as possible.

From that day on I ceased being disappointed at losing a job. Every bromide fitting this incident ran through my mind—*When it's your time to go*—*It's God's will*—*Everything happens for a reason*, including Doris Day singing "Que Sera Sera"—*What will be, will be.*

Deep Throat, the triple-X rated adult film, was a huge financial success, subsequently rumored to have earned over $600 million—I was surprised when Steve Lodge and Dave Cass called to say we were going to make an adult film. We had often talked of making our own films, but I never figured it would be of this genre. Also, since I had left the L.A. City Hall and was "between pictures," the $100 a day rate as a cameraman with a bevy of beautiful, erotic women sounded intriguing.

The California Connection script, later released as *The Erotic Adventures of Peter Galore*, written by Lodge and Cass, was basically a James Bond-type spy film with explicit sex. Early on, we decided to give this film every production value possible, since most of these films looked shoddy—usually lit with a couple of photofloods. To us this was just another film to utilize our filmmaking talents.

Cass had some Texas friends, so off we went to Terlingua, the site of Carroll Shelby's original Chili Cook-off Capitol of the World, near the Big Bend Country, southeast of El Paso. At the Villa de La Mina, a budding resort, we set up shop with cameras, lights and plenty of erotic action for this $7500 budgeted epic.

Porn actor and adult film business spokesman Bill Margold rounded up the reigning adult stars of the day, Barbara Bourbon, Rick Cassidy, Talie Cochrane, Dalana Bissonette, Cyndee Summers, Lee J. O'Donnell and Shari Kay. The rotund, arch-villain was portrayed by a rotund Tony Lane. His father, my buddy, George Lane, had headed up the makeup team on *It's a Mad, Mad, Mad, Mad World*, and was now the department chief at CBS Studio Center studios.

Tony worked as a film extra, primarily on *Gunsmoke*, and later attempted to follow his father into makeup, though he'd never come close to filling his shoes. George had a wonderful wry sense of wit and could tell you to screw yourself and you'd thank him. Tony's botched efforts to imitate dear ol' Dad had folks lined up to punch him out.

Thank God, his film role didn't require him to perform any sexual acts. That would have been a vision I would have had to live with forever. During filming someone screamed we had a gas leak, and we all headed for the exits. It was Tony.

Filming began on this six-day epic with Frank Q. Dobbs directing, and operating a second camera. Contrary to what you may think, the nudity and the sexual activities become very clinical after ten minutes. It sounds strange, but it was really like any film set except for several individuals moving around nude.

The script called for one more actress than we had, and everybody was in a quandary until I suggested putting a red wig on Dalana. No one ever noticed she's the same girl playing two roles. It was another time when you make do with what you have or don't have. Improvise.

The cast and crew were housed in several one and two bedroom brick bungalows scattered throughout the craggy Texas terrain. Steve and Tony were awakened one morning to my blood-curdling scream. I'd gone to the bathroom, switched on the light and found spiders everywhere—in the sink, shower and toilet. Steve, knowing my dislike for arachnids, quickly cleaned them out. Years later, he asked what scared me the most and I naturally replied, "Spiders." He had just sold his first screenplay for *Kingdom of the Spiders*, starring William Shatner.

During the *Connection* filming, Talie Cochrane, the pretty Southern lass from Memphis, expressed her desire to "get together later." Filming this beautiful, blue-eyed blond vixen making passionate love all day stimulated my visions of a hot shower together. Later, we heard a broken water main eliminated any chance of bathing and I politely declined her most alluring offer. Regrettably, that's like losing an hour of sleep—you will never make it up.

The catered food left much to be desired—deep fried goat. A small bite produced a bulging mouthful, expanding my cheeks like a blowfish before I spit it out.

Observing these beautiful, $100 a day, Love for Pay performers proved an insight into the human condition. What, I pondered, provoked them to get into this line of work? Was it was a lack of marketable skills? Were they molested as a child? Was it a rebellion against parents or religion? Was it to pay the rent, or buy drugs? The answer could be *yes* to any one or all of the above, but basically, in all probability, it came down to one word—Money.

Although the completed film appeared a many times more expensive than its $7500 budget, it took several years to get the film distributed as unmentioned, gravel voiced, bent nosed factions controlled the multi-billion dollar adult film industry.

Returning to Hollywood, Lodge remarked, "Do you realize that we are the D.W. Griffith's of porn films?" What a claim to fame—like I really want that epithet carved on my tombstone.

We continued to congregate at our favorite haunts, the Red Coach, Left Bank, Starlite Room, Foxfire, Players, Riverbottom Inn, Money Tree, O'Briens, and on this day, the Back Stage. I occupied a corner booth with Peter Breck, Guy Madison, Steve Lodge and Tony Lane. All of us were feeling no pain as Breck decided Tony's cowboy hat needed reshaping and pouring his bottle of beer into it was the best technique was to give it a "beer bath." Guy looked stupefied when I asked him to "Say something in buckskin," referring to his *Wild Bill Hickok* TV series wardrobe. Two beats later Breck fell out of the booth, laughing hysterically.

On another day, a bubbly young blond student from FIWI—Film Industry Workshop Inc. enthusiastically raved about her numerous Show Biz classes. John Mitchum listened, and then using his best John Carradine baritone, Shakespearean tremor, and enunciation, remarked "My dear young lady, I suggest you take a class in cock sucking. Because that is the only way you'll get a job in this town." Horrified, she was last seen running out the door.

In San Francisco, while filming Clint Eastwood's *The Enforcer* as Dirty Harry's detective partner, Frank DiGiorgio, John was invited to a lavish Nob Hill party. After several drinks, John confronted a gay guest, "Why do you think you deserve special privileges just because you suck a cock?" Figuring his question created more destruction than the 1906 earthquake, I asked, "Then what happened?" John grinned, "A couple of minutes later the hostess suggested I leave." She made a wise decision—otherwise John, known for his pugilistic talents, might have leveled Nob Hill.

McDonald's was prepping a TV commercial—I was hired as the production coordinator. Traveling to the City of Industry industrial business area east of Los Angeles, a ubiquitous McDonald's come into view. Belying its normal appearance, the Golden Arches interior housed a complete film production center.

The sixty-second ad needed a Chevrolet Blazer, a Schwinn tandem (two-seater) bicycle and allotted $300 for the rental costs. I suggested product placement—companies supplied their products gratis just for the exposure. Schwinn bicycles agreed immediately. Then I contacted International Harvester about their Scout. Ranking third to General Motors and Ford in rough-terrain vehicles, I figured IH would be receptive to my request because they were "trying harder."

The IH exec, said, "Sure, the last time we loaned a vehicle for a TV commercial, the Scout was so prominently displayed, the ad resembled an IH commercial." I personally picked up the bike and the Scout, and wasn't even asked for my ID or to sign an agreement. I doubt if this handshake agreement would ever happen today. In all, everyone benefited and I had saved the production company at least $300. In production, I always figured that I should save the production company ten times as much or more than what they were paying me for my services.

A few days later, Reggie Parton and I traveled to San Francisco for another segment of *Streets of San Francisco*. Leaving at 7:15am, Reg was subbing for Karl Malden's regular stunt double, Al Wyatt, who was working elsewhere. It was an easy day, just a foot chase and we returned at 6:15pm to the Hollywood-Burbank airport.

Days later, I was a dead body hanging from a commercial laundry's conveyer belt in John Frankenheimer's *99 44/100% Dead*, starring Richard Harris and Jack Palance. A disaster almost occurred when one of the stunt guys innocently flung a conveyer belt hook along the rail to clear our headway. The 10-pound cast iron hook took off like a bat out of hell along the well-lubricated track. Suddenly, a second assistant director appeared on our high perch of girders as the hook rocketed toward his head. We all yelled, but the laundry washers drowned out every word. God was with him as he miraculously stooped to give someone a message just as the iron hook sailed an inch over his head. Actor Richard Harris and I just looked at each other—there are Guardian Angels among us.

Individually, Steve Lodge and I continued to bang out screenplays on our Remingtons and Underwoods. He needed a typist to retype his Western drama in correct script form—I recommended a gal I used at Universal, who charged $100 a script. Several weeks passed when an agitated Steve came bounding into the Back Stage. Seems he figured to save the hundred bucks and used a CBS Studio Center secretary he had banged to do the retyping. Unknowingly, she corrected his syntax, the Old West colloquialisms and dialogue, all of which he had to painstakingly rewrite.

Universal called me to double actress Helen Hayes on her new limited-run TV series, *The Snoop Sisters*. Veteran actress Mildred Natwick portrayed her counterpart. Forever star-struck, it was a thrill to meet and work with these stalwart stars of stage and screen. Miss Hayes, dubbed "The First Lady of the Theater," was no stranger to film having first appeared in silent films in 1917, not to mention *Farewell to Arms* with Gary Cooper in 1932. Miss Natwick was a full-fledged member of John Ford's stock company, appearing with John Wayne in *The Three Godfathers, She Wore a Yellow Ribbon* and *The Quiet One*.

Carol Daniels doubled Natwick and Fred Lerner doubled actor Lou Antonio, playing the sister's detective nephew. Miss Hayes had a 6pm filming limit and I was rather startled when director Leonard Horn asked me to double her in a thirty-yard walk. I'd doubled ladies many times, but never walking that distance. It worked and on the screen it was impossible to tell us apart.

Another shot had Carol and me transferring from the roof of the 1930s Lincoln to a home fire escape ladder. Rung by rung, I slowly duplicated the movements of a 73 year-old lady climbing a ladder, but wondered what happened when Horn yelled, "Cut, Print!" amid the crew's laughter. Climbing below me a few rungs, Carol's quicker pace allowed her head and upper torso to disappear up under my dress. That shot was no doubt saved for the Christmas reel.

The lead heavy on the first of four episodes was actor Bo Svenson, so I was able to bring in my old buddy Dick Durock to double him. Dick, at six-foot-six, became Bo's regular stunt man and credited me for getting him in the business in 1966. Actually, I only suggested he visit veteran stuntmen Paul Stader's gym in Santa Monica. A year later, when he called to say he had his SAG card, I was pleased my advice had paid off.

In two *Swamp Thing* feature films and TV series Dick played the frightening monster, 100 lb. costume, et al. Though he received $5000 per episode, the series, unfortunately, was broadcast on the USA cable network. If the show had aired on any one of the three major networks he might have become a millionaire.

Dick called me while I was living in Nashville complaining about the friends and relatives he hadn't seen or heard from in twenty years. "Terrific", I said, but he said "No, they all want money!" I then suggested he first pay off his Agoura Hills condo and then tell everyone you have a business manager who has control of your funds. He did and it solved his problems. When I returned to Studio City Dick tried to place two $100 bills in my hand. It was a nice gesture, but I refused.

Veteran director Boris Sagal (father of Katie Sagal from *Married, With Children...*) was an amiable fellow and very focused in his concentration, so much so that he was often unaware of anything or anyone in his immediate vicinity. This idiosyncrasy would reach its peak a few days later when we filmed inside Universal's main auto gate, near the studio's infamous Black Tower.

Wearing Helen Hayes' two piece dress outfit, gray wig and veiled hat, I sat in the Lincoln touring car with Miss Natwick's photo double, patiently waiting for my turn at bat. Boris walked to my driver side window to describe where he wanted me drive in the shot and walked away.

The cameras were almost set up, when I heard assistant director Gil Mandelik yelling, looked over my left shoulder as he frantically waved his arms for me to back up. The grand old Lincoln cranked over, sounding like a John Deere tractor. I checked the rear view mirrors, turned, peered back through the small rear window, shifted into reverse and slowly let out the clutch. We moved a foot or two when I felt the vehicle's rear end rise and fall. Suddenly, Mandelik is screaming, "Stop! stop!" I stopped, shut off the ignition and jumped out to see what the problem could be. Boris was on the pavement, massaging his left ankle—I couldn't believe it. I just ran over the director. Ripping off the wig, I threw it at his feet, "I quit!" Boris pleaded, "No, no, please stay. I'll get it wrapped and be back in twenty minutes," as he was hustled off to the studio infirmary.

I put the wig back on and sat on the Lincoln running board, contemplating another line of work. Why didn't he hear the Lincoln? It was loud enough to be heard a block away.

Scotty, was the the venerable Universal Studio's main gate senior guard. He knew everyone and was loved by all. He ran to me, "Jess, I saw it all. It wasn't your fault. Boris was just standing there, and he (pointing at Mandelik) could see him standing there." Mandelik was a nervous A.D., so who knows what was in his mind. Anyway, Boris returned in twenty minutes with a diagnosed bruised anklebone.

We completed the shot and I removed my wig again as three black "suits" from *The Tower* confronted me, "Are you the stunt man that ran over Boris?" I was dubious—thinking these fellows were the official committee to ban me from ever working at Universal again—and cautiously answered, "Yes." Instantly, all three were vying to shake my hand, commenting "Great!" "Fantastic!" "Beautiful!" Veteran stunt man Victor Paul, my buddy from the *Batman* TV series, had rushed from the backlot, "Is it true you ran over the director?" I nodded, and Vic doubled up laughing. Before leaving, I went to Boris and again offered my apology—graciously, he waved it off.

This "incident" didn't affect my employment at Universal, as I was soon again working on *Faraday and Company, Adam 12, Chase, Banacek* and *Kojak.*

Inside the Make-Up Building entrance was a large bulletin board displaying the call sheets of every show filming that day, on and off the lot. At this point in time, Universal was my "home lot," providing me with steady employment.

During a casual visit through the production offices I was stopped by production manager assistant director George Bisk. Always with a pleasant demeanor, George was now very serious when he asked, "Do you remember the guy who sued Universal, MGM, 20th, Paramount and Quinn Martin Productions? Well, he's trying to cause problems here, again.

He evidently saw your name on two call sheets and complained that we were hiring you too often." That sonofabitch," I said, "I was 'on hold' on one of those shows." George nodded, "I have always hired who was the best for the job, and no goddamned nigger is going to tell me who to hire." I was astounded. In all the years I'd known and worked with George, I had never seen him this angry. What right did this SOB have to dictate who should be hired? His endeavor was ignored and Universal's production department continued to function as they had for decades.

The old Shell Oil cracking plant at 190th Street and Vermont produced synthetic rubber during WWII and was a popular location for many Universal shows. This *Adam-12* segment had me doubling child actor Moosie Drier, who had climbed out onto a girder, fifty feet up. Doubling a six-year-old kid who came up to my navel? Are you kidding? Well, with the use of the correct lens, angles and my crouching made it work.

Police Story at Columbia always excited me because I got to play a "Cop." On location in Hollywood, at the corner of Yucca and Vine Streets, a block north of Hollywood and Vine, we sat in our cruiser with red lights flashing. Rush "Serge" Adams, manned the radio as we waited for the cameras to roll a block away to be set. Casually, I looked over to a car making a left turn onto Vine Street. The driver stared viciously at me and was mouthing every name-calling profanity you've ever heard. I did a double take, "Serge, look at this asshole." "Jesus!" he replied, as I whipped out my rubber pistol—the driver panicked and burned rubber through the red light, almost T-boning another car. Then it dawned on me, what if this idiot had pulled a real gun on us?

We completed the chase—I quickly corralled our LAPD traffic control officers and related the incident, they nodded, "It happens all the time. They even spit on us." "Spit? What do you do?" "Well, we take that individuals aside and try to teach them some manners," he said, smiling. I decided then and there that I had made the correct career choice as I probably wouldn't have lasted ten minutes on the force.

Another time a *Police Story* car chase took us through a vacant dirt lot in East L.A., and as I neared the paved street my vehicle stalled. Bobby Hoy was behind me and sensed my predicament—I shifted into neutral and Bobby pushed me bumper-to-bumper on through the shot. Director Virgil Vogel yelled "Print" and no one knew otherwise. Again, working with professionals makes it easy.

For Universal, we locationed at Crocker Bank's, 6th and Grand Street skyscraper for *The Elevator*, to double Barry Livingston, formerly of the *My Three Sons* TV series. Jerry Jameson directed the stellar cast including Craig Stevens, Teresa Wright, Myrna Loy, James Farentino, Carol Linley, Don Stroud and Roddy McDowell for producer William Fry. I was in seventh heaven – I had loved Teresa Wright since *The Best Years of Our Lives*, one of the finest films ever made, directed by William Wyler. What a thrill meeting her and Myrna Loy, the beautiful lady from MGM's "Thin Man" features.

Just like the Army, moviemaking is "Hurry up and wait." It's not a deliberate ploy to waste a producer's money, but it takes time to rehearse the actors, light the sets and a million other tasks to get a film made. Don Stroud and I, drinking buddies from the Left Bank, were relaxing in one of the empty offices on the 28th floor, and joked about his uptown three-piece suit—a far cry from the T-shirt, jeans and cowboy boots his wayward characters usually wore.

A female stunt member entered with a small glass vial of white powder, "Want some?" "Sure," replied Don. Placing the glass spoon to his nostril, he snorted the substance, jumped up and ran out the door. The gal also took a snort, screwed the black cap on the cocaine vial, and exited as swiftly as she had entered. Two lady extras nearby and I just stared at each other, shook our heads.

This was the first time I had ever seen anyone use coke. I was never into the drug scene, having found enough enjoyment and companionship with my buddy, Jack Daniels. My position has always been that you drink or you don't drink. Alcohol has never been a problem for me, and I have never lost a day of work because of booze. I've always believed that if it affects your life in any adverse manner, don't do it. I stopped drinking at the outset of both marriages, musing that should the matrimonial bliss end—alcohol would not be named a co-respondent.

Humphrey Bogart believed, "The trouble with the world is that it's always one drink behind." President Harry S Truman said; "Only one thing worse than a drinking man is one who doesn't." Someone once theorized, "You can't drink it faster than they can make it." "Yeah," I said, "but I've got 'em working three shifts."

The brilliant comic Sam Kinison, taken from us way too soon, put it succinctly upon hearing complaints from San Quentin's prisoners, "If you don't like the way you're treated, DON'T GO THERE!!!" This also applies to many aspects of life.

As in the past, there were times when it was nice to be in demand, working days on *The Snoop Sisters*, then at night on *Faraday and Company, The Elevator* and *Kojak.*

It was then over to Warner Brothers for the *Cowboys* TV pilot to double Clint Howard, Ron Howard's younger brother. Henry Wills was the stunt coordinator, wrangling Loren Janes, Jack Verbois and myself in a fight around the campfire set. After several rehearsals, I could see the possibility of not getting to my mark on time if the fight accelerated. We commenced to film the melee and as I suspected, after falling to the far side of the covered wagon, it did speed up, so I tucked and rolled under the wagon to my spot in time to continue the brawl. Henry Wills exclaimed, "I didn't know you could do that." What, again? That was his same response four years earlier on *The Master Gunfighter*. Evidently, ol' Henry *still* found timing, experience and ability difficult to accept from me. It's not unlike a sports fan's emotional involvement when their favorite athlete performs an incredible play. That's terrific, but what's the big deal? That's what they get paid to do.

Erik Cord called me for *Twice in a Lifetime*, a TV movie and pilot starring Ernest Borgnine, Della Reese, Arte Johnson and lovable, good ol' boy Slim Pickens played their nemesis.

Meeting Ernie Borgnine was a great thrill after his never-to-be-forgotten role of Fatso in *From Here to Eternity*, and in *Marty*, which brought him a Best Actor Oscar.

Naturally, the free-for-all in Della's Cajun restaurant set brought hilarious results, not only in the fight but also among the background participants. Props had dished out bowls of fresh shrimp jambalaya and beer, real beer. Many of the extra players readily enjoyed the feast before the cameras rolled; leaving empty plates when the filming began, but a few enjoyed the free-flowing beer even more.

Returning from wardrobe and makeup, the actors and stuntmen gathered on the set to rehearse the big fight. Erik Cord had assembled quite a group of stuntmen including, Dick Butler, Hank Calia, Dick Durock, Bob Herron, Chuck Hayward and Chuck Hicks. Herron and Hayward had a hearing loss, so, always looking for a laugh, one of us would begin talking to their impaired ear and as they turned their good ear toward us, we would move, continue talking into their bad ear as they turned. Soon, we'd have them going in circles, like a dog chasing its tail.

Bob Herron had also experienced an errant rifle's blank cartridge blast. While filming *Major Dundee* in 1965, he spent a week in a Mexican hospital for intensive back surgery to remove debris after being accidentally rifle shot at point-blank range.

Doubling Vito Scotti, Della's excitable Italian waiter, required a black mustache and my blond hair sprayed black and slicked down. Stunt buddy Dick Durock, playing one of the crazed longshoreman, looked at me, "All you need now is a monkey and an organ grinder."

We rehearsed the fight and part of the action called for Durock to pick me up and threw me through a breakaway table. I watched as the special effects man, Dick Parker, the same fellow who assisted my first fire gag on *Hell Is For Heroes*, carefully scored the table legs. Parker had spent the last twelve years in Spain and Italy working the "Spaghetti" westerns."

Having performed this breakaway gag more than a few times, I told Durock the importance of giving me the momentum to hit and roll, "Don't just get me to the table, throw me through it." Well, Dick tossed me—but the real, hard wood tabletop knocked the proverbial fart out of me, followed by the unyielding crash to the floor. It hurt and I knew my left shoulder and side was going to hurt the next day.

Confronting Dick, I asked him why he didn't do what I asked. "I didn't want to hurt you." Dick was six-foot-six, two-twenty, and I understood his concern about injuring me, but it's a stunt you must visualize and do correctly to prevent injury.

Again, it's a judgment call and often doubly difficult when working with another. Most stunt people will say they prefer working alone. You analyze your stunt and perform it. If it gets screwed up, you know exactly whom to blame.

The *Twice in a Lifetime* company moved to the San Pedro harbor for the exterior action shots. Steve Lodge was the on-set costumer aboard and was ailing. The second day, Bobby Herron, Borgnine's longtime stunt man, and I became ill. Rather than return to our San Fernando Valley residences, only to return the next morning, we opted for the Travelodge in San Pedro. Mustering just enough strength to grab a couple of McDonald's Quarter-pounders and fries to go, we called it a night. By morning, the twenty-four hour flu bug was gone.

The harbor water was still as we passed Franklin Delano Roosevelt's 165-foot "Floating White House" yacht, the *USS Potomac*. Steve remarked, "I'll bet a lot of people got screwed on that ship." "Yeah," I said, "The entire Country." Lodge repeated my comment for years.

The stunt-action continued as Herron pulled me, doubling Arte Johnson, to safety a moment before Slim Pickens sideswiped Borgnine's tugboat. To retaliate, Ernie decides to use his ship's hoist to swing a three thousand pound boat engine at Pickins. Dick Parker was again scoring wood, but this time he used a chainsaw to assure the tug's wheelhouse would disintegrate on impact. Three cameras rolled as the engine swung like a pendulum toward the tug—watching as the ton and a half engine bounced off the wheelhouse like a rubber ball. Adding insult to injury, the heavy welded-link chain suddenly snapped, plunging the engine to the depths of Los Angeles Harbor. The usual exclamation uttered during a stunt or special effects mishap is "Oh Shit!" and this day was no exception. Parker searched for another engine and continued scoring the cabin. The re-shoot worked the next day and we all went home. The show had a good premise and the chemistry between Borgnine and Reese worked well, but it wasn't picked up as a TV series.

On another show, a stunt man said, "I hear you're interested in guns." "Yeah sure, I'm always looking for a good deal." He popped open his car's trunk to reveal a cache of firearms that would rival many guns shops. 25-30 revolvers and automatic pistols, and the 15-20 rifles and shotguns—were $50.00 each. I checked a pistol and noticed the serial numbers had been filed off. An expensive Wetherby scoped rifle revealed similar results. After wiping my prints from the weapons, I told this guy to take a hike—it's a felony to possess a firearm with filed off serial numbers. Nevertheless, those stolen arms undoubtedly found their way to the criminal underground, to guys who never go to a gun shop or gun show to buy a weapon.

Closing out the year, Bob Hoy called me, Mickey Gilbert, Bob Minor, Dar Robinson and Walter Scott to be the musical members of "Jack Benny and the Pips" band on *Jack Benny's Second Farewell Special*. Hoy played the escapee chased by policeman Fred Lerner and I was the gum-chewing drummer, who became air-borne when Dar crashed headfirst into my bass drum. It was fun, especially meeting Jack Benny, one of the great icons of radio, film and television. He was relaxed and disarming as we sat on the steps between the vacant audience seats chatting.

Breaking for dinner at the NBC Burbank cafeteria, made infamous by Johnny Carson, all eyes watched as Jack nonchalantly enter the crowded dining room. Two stagehands immediately insisted he move in line before them. Graciously, he accepted, approached the cashier and paid for their dinners. Everyone smiled at his generosity. I chimed in, recalling his tightwad persona, "Well, there goes the image!" Jack smiled and nodded, "Yeah, image." Another privileged moment to remember and cherish.

CHAPTER 16

1974

The New Year opened with work on *Barnaby Jones, Emergency!* My career was in high gear and I was pleased to be a part of the Hollywood stunt community.

And. again on *Ironside*. San Pedro's hilly streets often doubled for San Francisco and the expansive Vincent Thomas Bridge subbed for The Golden Gate Bridge. Though the green finish hardly matched the Gate's famous golden orange tone, it become a silhouette in the afternoon sun and tricked many a viewer.

On "Action" *Ironside* guest star actress Elizabeth Ashley steered the four-door sedan around the corner with a camera shooting over her shoulder. George Sawaya and I, driving our own cars, were told to aim at her vehicle and swerve away. We performed the near misses and regrouped at home base. A visibly shaken Ashley said she wasn't told of our vehicle gymnastics. Just Beautiful! This scenario had all the ear-marks of a disaster—had she panicked, there might have been an injurious crash. The fault lay with the assistant director for allowing this to happen, and as the "watch dog" it was his responsibility to be on the lookout for *anything* that can run amuck.

TV mogul Dick Clark approached SAMP about a Stuntmen's Award TV show, offered $2000 to secure the rights, but a San Francisco producer-director team offered $5000 and the SAMP Board opted for cash over experience. Dick Durock and I favored Clark's reputation and guaranteed network affiliation, voiced the only two dissenting votes. Regardless, the *Stuntmen's Association—Richard Talmadge Awards* became a syndicated TV production with Efrem Zimbalist, Jr. as the emcee.

During the show's rehearsal at Warner Brothers, SAMP President Henry Wills and I watched the monitor as the camera slowly zoomed back as "Zimmie" descended the Tara-like staircase. Very diplomatically, I asked the Frisco director to change the shot to an opening close up of the SAMP logo—then slowly zoom back to include Zimbalist on the staircase, as "the logo had cost over two hundred dollars and it seemed a shame not to feature it." His response "I can't do that" made my blood boil. His unspoken reason was that he didn't want to change his shot list. "What?" I said, (Thinking of my camera experience)"They can put a man on the moon and you can't change this shot to include the logo?" Wills quickly moved me aside, suggested I get a cup of coffee, and the show's opening title shot was changed to include the SAMP logo.

Historically, it was a grand evening with appearances by several of Hollywood's greatest action directors, John Ford, William Wellman, Henry Hathaway and George Marshall. Richard Boone and Joel McCrea were among the presenters. It was a true piece of Hollywood history never to be repeated.

Former SAG attorney Doug Smithers personified John Arbuckle's proviso, "You get what you pay for." Since SAMP's inception, Smithers had endeared himself to several Board members by providing *pro bono* (Latin "for the good") free legal services – and was chosen to create the award show's production contract. In error, his contract stipulated that the program's ownership would revert to SAMP after *one rerun*, instead of *one run*—a major screw-up. Additionally, Smithers' agreement also neglected to cover any financial production overages. The syndicated show producer accrued added production expenses of $4000, which were paid out of SAMP's initial $5000 payment. Ultimately, SAMP received $1000 less than what Dick Clark had offered, and after Smithers' submitted his bill, SAMP was in a deficit hole.

Smithers' faux pas would continue to mount. A new stunt group, The

Hollywood Stuntmen's Association of Motion Pictures had been formed. However, when SAMP was incorporated and registered by the State of California in 1961, Smithers neglected a common legal practice to protect the original organization's name by also registering possible name variations to protect any similar identity infringements. Thus, the HSAMP continued in operation for many years, and was often confused with, and a constant embarrassment to SAMP.

Several years ago, I initiated a search for this program's master videotape with hopes to interest an entertainment cable channel for its historic value. The tape was never located.

In 1972, when Karl Malden began *The Streets of San Francisco* TV series for Quinn Martin Productions, many stunt folks enjoyed an early morning flight out of Burbank to the great City by the Bay. Pacific Southwest Airlines planes left on the hour for the fifty-five minute flight north, cost: $25 round trip. On arrival a QM driver would ferry us to that day's particular film location. Whether it was a high fall, a car chase or a fight, we'd complete our scenes and return to Burbank before sunset that evening. Often, I'd stay overnight and catch the sights of North Beach, enjoy dinner in a classic restaurant at Fisherman's Wharf and return the next day.

My favorite San Francisco restaurant was Alfred's. Opened in 1928, this fine eatery was a local haunt and proudly served Chicago corn-fed beef, while the Italian-based menu featured a delectable Lazy Susan of antipasto. The massive hundred-year-old mahogany bar, red-flocked wallpaper and chandeliers provided a relaxed dining setting decrying the usual tourist traps.

Art Passarella continued as Karl's stand-in on the series and occasionally had a speaking role, portraying Officer Sekulovitch. Karl Malden's real name was Mladen George Sekulovitch and in most of his films you will hear him call another actor Sekulovitch. Thinking of Art still puts a smile on my face. Just having known him was one of life's joys.

On one overnighter, I met a lady in the hotel bar who had never been to Finnocchio's—a taxi soon delivered us to North Beach's most famous female impersonator showplace. I had seen the show previously (during my first honeymoon), and always enjoyed the female audience reactions more than what was paraded on stage. Somehow, the visiting ladies could not comprehend that these voluptuous, beautifully quaffed, elegantly gowned damsels were men. Their clinched-jaw and furrowed-brow stares, unmistakably revealed their displeasure. A lady seated a foot away suddenly screamed at her embarrassed husband, "You sonofabitch! Get me out of here!"

The stage show was well worth the price of admission. A Doris Day look-a-like, with a voice to match, appeared center stage—at the song's conclusion, the blond wig came off and the dress top dropped to reveal a manly chest. Next, a brunette with one of the most beautiful faces and bodies I've ever seen appeared on stage—that face should have graced every magazine in the world. I was in love twice that night. Sadly, Finnocchio's recently closed its door.

In the 60s and 70s, Pacific Southwest Airlines, or PSA, as it was affectionately known, was always a fun experience. The "regulars" soon discovered that the twelve rear seats were served cocktails first, so we would enter through the plane's rear ramp, while the uninitiated scrambled for the front entrance ramp. Often, we were served cocktails before the plane hit the runway.

The PSA flight attendants were the most beautiful ladies you could ever imagine. Decked out in hip-hugging hot pants or mini-skirts with white shinny knee-high boots, each young lady resembled a beauty queen. Well, close, anyway. PSA co-sponsored the Miss California Beauty Pageant and (bless the guy who came up with this idea) offered PSA flight attendant positions to the contest "losers." Losers? No way. Each lady was more stunning than the other. What a wonderful way to start the day and get those morning juices flowing.

John Daheim was the stunt coordinator on Universal's SenSurround Sound disaster epic, *Earthquake*. Veteran director Mark Robson and John had first worked together in 1949 on Stanley Kramer's *Champion*, starring Kirk Douglas, Arthur Kennedy, Ruth Roman, Marilyn Maxwell and Lola Albright, when Daheim played a fighter defeated by Douglas.

Mark and Johnny were at the far end of the set when I noticed Robson staring at me—then confer with Daheim. Ignoring the looks, I nevertheless checked my zipper. Finally, Mark then remarked on my resemblance to his close friend, Sir Richard Attenborough. I cited past comparisons to him, and also to Mickey Rooney. He smiled and mentioned working with Rooney on *The Bridges at Toko-Ri*, starring William Holden, Grace Kelly, Fredric March and Charles McGraw.

McGraw was looking forward to meeting Rooney, having worked as a hoofer (dancer) on Broadway with Rooney's Dad, Joe Yule. Rooney's response was "Yeah, and my old man said you weren't very good." Incensed, Charlie replied, "Well, fuck you, and fuck your old man." Mark said you could only see the tops of Bill Holden and Grace Kelly's heads, doubled over as they tried to control their laughter. McGraw never took any prisoners.

In *Earthquake*, Gary Epper and I scampered down a sweeping, spiral staircase, which was rigged to move a foot or two on its axis. We swayed and fell as the camera moved and jerked, when the entire set shook by electric motors, strategically hidden under tables and chairs. Additionally, the motors produced the rumbling sounds of a real quake. Gary and I did our routine with much of it inspired by the actual movement of the set. I had experienced Los Angeles quakes all my life and these effects were as horrific and as realistic as it gets.

Later, Charlton Heston remembered me as his Sergeant at Arms at the yearly SAG membership meetings, and then introduced me to a radiant Ava Gardner, stunning in her pink Edith Head two-piece suit. Her eyes sparkled when I mentioned I had been Rooney's longtime stunt double.

Veteran stunt man Bill Catching was coordinating *The Story of Pretty Boy Floyd*, starring Martin Sheen and Kim Darby and I was doubling Sheen's brother, Joe Estevez. The opening scenes had Floyd's gang drunk and recklessly following him in his Model T Ford on horseback. My mount was a mule with a halter and no saddle—almost an uncontrollable runaway. At one point, I was hanging around the mule's neck, staring into his left eyeball. Stunt man Chris Howell belly laughed, "The only part of you that didn't touch the mule were the soles of your boots." Well, Dammit! Horsemanship had little to do with it—you had to be an acrobat. Catching said, "If you're going to fall off, try to do it 'on camera.'" I never did fall, but wish I had just to boost the stunt adjustment. Because of that damn mule's backbone and pile-driving gait, I couldn't stand erect for two days.

At the Stuntmen's Association office, Dick Durock fielded a request from a tabloid paper, *Star*, for two small stunt guys to play space aliens visiting a remote farm country location. Dick tossed the call to me and I suggested that former jockey, veteran stunt man Freddie Brookfield join me. The checkout stand rag said we would be outfitted in shiny jumpsuits with blinking helmets. It sounded like fun and we agreed the SAG stunt daily rate would be fair compensation for three days, that is, until they suggested we wear bulletproof vests. The Star then said they couldn't divulge "the unnamed rural area" that had reported several UFO sightings. But, at five in the morning, the startled farmers just might grab their firearms. I questioned the vest's safety protection, not to mention the possibility of receiving a shot to the head, legs or crotch. Star upped the ante to $2500 for each of us. After analyzing every aspect we declined their insane offer, figuring the tabloid would have had a scoop either way; "Farmers see Martians" or maybe "Startled Farmers Kill Hollywood Stunt Men Posing as Martians," an even bigger story.

Mel Brooks' *Young Frankenstein* film beckoned stunt coordinator Roger Creed. The location was the vintage Mayfair Theater in Santa Monica, filled with two hundred extras and eight stuntmen, including Gil Perkins, doubling Peter Boyle as the Monster. Rounding out the stunt ranks were Rush Adams, Fred Lerner, Conrad Palmisano, Sonny Shields, Jimmy Casino and Chuck Waters.

Brooks, realizing he had a captive audience clowned it up and was hilarious. But when Gene Wilder and Peter Boyle performed a "buck & wing" tap dance to Irving Berlin's "Puttin' on the Ritz," Brooks had to cut the camera several times because everyone was laughing so hard.

Plot-wise, the theater audience revolts and throws raw vegetables at the dancing duo. Again, without considering the consequences, the prop men indiscriminately handed the tomatoes and cabbages to the male atmosphere. On "Action" Wilder and Boyle were pelted with the veggies and were now fighting for their lives. Several Extras were throwing the projectiles with a vengeance, especially the guy who caught Gene in the crotch with a cabbage. "Oomph" was all we heard as Wilder doubled up, holding his groin, but, courageously, kept dancing. He was a trouper, but does Blue Balls ring a bell?

Between scenes at the craft service table, I recognized the set nurse from Universal and began discussing on-the-set injuries. I described how a Universal Studios special effects man, Al Henley, was responsible for my second degree burns on *Adam-12* three years before. Disturbed, she interrupted saying that Henley had died and had been a dear friend of hers. I retorted with, "The sonofabitch should have died before I met him. I was in constant pain for three months because of that drunken bastard."

My feelings have always been that just because someone turns room temperature, it doesn't make them a Saint. If you're an asshole alive, you're still an asshole when you're dead.

Again, it was always exciting to see who would be on the set of your next film. Dale Hennessy, one of Hollywood's premiere production designers, whom I'd worked with many times, regretted that *Young Frankenstein* wasn't being photographed in color, especially, the elaborate laboratory set, aglow in color, but would only be filmed and viewed in monochrome – black & white.

Between stunt jobs, my desire to work behind camera came to fruition as assistant director on several low-budget, non-union productions. It was always difficult working with the first-time "directors" who had "possibly" read a book on filmmaking. The $1000 weekly salary wasn't union scale, but my years of on-set experience to get every buck up on the screen were personally gratifying.

Don Krantz, *There Was a Crooked Man…* first assistant director, was now the production chief for Twentieth Century Fox, called to discuss director Sam Peckinpah's new film, *The Killer Elite*. We had last talked during the formation of L.A.'s One Stop Permit Office. He was now concerned about the studio's reluctance to allow the wild director to shoot his film in San Francisco—alleging they would have more control if Peckinpah remained in Los Angeles. Candidly, I stated that Jock and I had created a monster "and I wouldn't make a film in this town." Suddenly, I heard a voice exclaim, "Sonofabitch!" "Who was that?" I asked. Don, on his speakerphone, said it was Gordon Stulberg, President of the studio. "I'm sorry," I continued, "but the One Stop office we created has been taken over by the bureaucrats, and I don't believe you'll receive the filming cooperation you will find elsewhere." I don't know whether my comments had any bearing, but Peckinpah filmed *The Killer Elite* in San Francisco.

Two years later, Don Krantz called again, this time to check my availability to leave immediately for Tampa, Florida, to take over the assistant director reins on the Lee Majors, Mel Ferrer, Cornel Wilde vehicle, *The Norseman*. Seems the director and the A.D. had come to fisticuffs on the set and Don would get back to me in an hour. Vince Deadrick, Sr. was doubling Majors and I immediately phoned his Tampa hotel room, his suggestion—"Don't come down. This film is a mess." Don phoned later to say the situation had been resolved. I don't recall the entire Daily Variety film review except to say these were the only Norsemen they had ever seen with "blown-dried" hair.

At Universal, assistant director Howard Kazanjian and I had become friends on Billy Wilder's *Front Page*, starring Jack Lemmon and Walter Matthau, based on the Ben Hecht-Charles MacArthur play. I doubled Austin Pendleton, portraying the convicted killer, Earl Williams, crashing through the pressroom window, landing at Lemmon's feet. Is there anyone who doesn't love Jack Lemmon? What a nice guy. I fondly recall him on the set relaxing between takes playing the piano.

The police chase for Killer Williams entailed my climbing fire escapes and driving a speeding police car through the dreary streets of L.A.'s skid row, doubling for the late 1920's Chicago. In the various shots I'm a cop seen breaking in a street level door and in the next cut kicking in a second story window on a fire escape. At night, in a blue police uniform, everybody looks alike.

A speeding ambulance carrying Martin Gabel (he was married to *What's My Line?* panelist Arlene Francis) spins 180°, spilling his hospital gurney out the rear door and continues on down the street. Another shot was a "run-by"—where the filmed subject enters and exits the picture frame. Veteran stunt man Carey Loftin directed the second unit action and, God knows, he was the best.

Nick Carey and his special effects department at Universal ingeniously created a steering mechanism to control the gurney. The unobtrusive lever fit perfectly in my right hand, as I lay prone. The cameras rolled as Carey called "Action." Nick gave me a hearty push, sending me down Fifth toward Los Angeles Street. Moving at a good clip in a straight run toward the bottom of the hill, but a slight indentation in the road running diagonally across Fifth Street went unnoticed. The gurney's front wheels hit the rut, instantly propelling me 45° toward a parked 1929 Lincoln touring car. I tried to correct the gurney's wayward path as the massive, chromed, spring-steel bumper neared. The crash was unavoidable as I rolled to the right, dumping the gurney, a split second before it struck the bumper and bounced away. My forward momentum carried me under the bumper to the rear axle.

Carey Loftin yelled, "Was he out of the shot?" Translated: Did Jesse crash and burn *after* he exited the camera frame? I had, so it was a "Print." However, from the crew's perspective, the collision looked as if my face had smashed into the bumper. It *was* close. The next day my sternum and upper chest area ached from glancing off the bumper.

On the Universal backlot, while rehearsing the *Front Page* scene where Jack Lemmon rushes to meet his girlfriend at the train station, we were momentarily concerned when Jack jumped from the truck, slipped and fell hard to the wet pavement. He had been sipping his favorite libation and luckily wasn't hurt, as he slowly stood up and laughed it off.

Billy Wilder's *Front Page* was the third remake of the Ben Hecht-Charles MacArthur play and didn't play well at the 1974 box office, despite the casting of Lemmon and Matthau. Carol Burnett played Williams' hooker girlfriend. However, I believe Wilder should have been considerably more diligent in his direction. Far be it for me to second-guess one of Hollywood's greatest writer-directors, but Carol Burnett is a delightful lady and deserved a better venue.

Up until the late sixties, a black man could generally only be found employed at a studio as an actor, extra or in the barbershop shining shoes. In the 50s, white stunt guys doubled black actors; Fred Krone doubled Willie Best climbing a tree. I even doubled a young black man on fire in *Blacula*.

In 1968, when Mod *Squad* stunt coordinator Ronnie Rondell needed a black acrobatic stunt double for actor Clarence Williams, III (his grandfather, Clarence Williams, was the early 1900's jazz pianist, vocalist, theatrical producer, and song publisher), he found Alan Olney in UCLA's gymnasium. During this same period, Tony Brubaker, Wayne King and Bob Minor began to establish their stunt careers.

The early seventies were turbulent times, and also produced unrest among the black stunt performers. The Black Stuntmen's Association was formed and several black SAMP members joined their ranks, contrary to SAMP by-laws prohibiting membership in another stunt group. SAMP's Board of Directors, however, turned a blind eye fearing racial connotations and lawsuits. Immediately, the BSA adopted a stance, sanctioned by the Screen Actors Guild that minorities should comprise ten percent of stunt performers hired on a production. This "You're going to do what I tell you" edict rankled many white stunt coordinators. Many did choose to abide by the "minority" rule—they only hired Cajun, Oriental, Hispanic or female stunt performers.

A meeting was set at Universal Studios to discuss minority hiring practices. Hispanic stunt man Tom Rosales was refused admittance, and became infuriated that "minority" applied to *blacks only*. It would be several years before all minority stunt performers would be represented equally.

As always, the untalented inept will strive to profit in these situations. The no-talent black wannabe stunt man that brought lawsuits against Paramount, Universal, MGM, Twentieth Century-Fox and Quinn Martin Productions in a quasi-attempt to enter the same stunt ranks. Stuntmen Tony Brubaker, Greg Elam, Wayne King, Bob Minor, Alan Olney and John Sharrod, etc., had accomplished with unbridled talent, ability and perseverance what this clown could not. To appease this nefarious individual, he was briefly appointed as an assistant to MGM President Dan Melnick. That didn't last long and it was this wannabe's final step to oblivion.

Paul Nuckles was gaining momentum as a stunt man and coordinator, worked a car commercial in my favorite town—Carmel, California. The film company stayed at the Carmel Holiday Inn and, while having a drink in the lounge, Nuckles took a liking to a nautical cocktail table, uniquely constructed from a ship's brass propeller. Slipping into his orange race driver's jumpsuit and cap, he returned to the jam-packed bar that evening and removed the heavy, one-inch thick, beveled glass top. After two trips the table base was snuggly hidden in his car's trunk. The next morning at the hotel's front desk to check out, Nuckles stood nonchalantly beside two Carmel police officers as they wrote a theft report. He smiled to himself as the agitated hotel manager disavowed the officer's theory that it was "an inside job by one of the hotel employees in overalls."

Darktown Strutters, a quickie, low budget Roger Corman film, was shooting in the vacant LAPD Wilshire Division at 4526 Pico Boulevard. To quote Yogi Berra: "It's deja vu all over again." It had been twenty years since I had been a member of the DAPs—Deputy Auxiliary Police. Like a bird dog, I went directly to the room where I had roared at the crazy antics of the monthly Abbott & Costello films. Standing on the building's front stoop, I remembered waving to Mom and Dad as I left for LAPD's Camp Valcrest, in the Angeles Crest Mountains behind Mt. Wilson, at a grand cost of $7.00 for the entire week.

Director Bill Witney had come from his home in Mexico to take-over this production and it was wonderful seeing him again. Bill was a director's director, loved stunt folks, and just watching him set up a shot was a great education.

Suddenly, the site became edgy when the LAPD mentioned a nearby shoot out involving the Patty Hearst kidnappers—the Symbionese Liberation Army, subsequently killing the SLA members.

I doubled a gal who is shot, blown backward through the swinging doors. Without a jerk-harness, a half-inch rope was tied around my chest and extended to a couple of grips in the next room.

Don Taylor was Liz Taylor's groom in MGM's *Father of the Bride*. Moving later into directing, we first met on Columbia's *Everything's Ducky* in 1961. But, as if ordained by fate, it appeared our business relationship was to be a tumultuous one, spanning the next fifteen years. It wasn't deliberate, but whenever I was hired to perform a stunt on a production he was directing, there was always a mishap.

Universal Studios called me to double actress Dana Wynter driving on *The Name Of The Game* TV series. I arrived on the Malibu beach location and there was Don Taylor, "Oh, God, here we go again." Though I hadn't seen Don since the *Tom Sawyer* film, he greeted and hugged me like a long lost brother.

The Ferrari convertible roadster was a bright canary yellow, once owned by actress Jane Mansfield and everything checked out—tire pressure, the suspension, tied down battery, even though the camera shots just called for speedy run-bys.

In the wardrobe and a wig matching Miss Wynters, I made several run-bys. The next shot called for a run-by on a bluff, high above the beach. For rehearsal, I drove slowly past camera, but on "Action" I passed the camera at 30mph in a cloud of dust and applied the brakes. Under normal conditions this would have been sufficient, but now I was on sand and gravel and the car was sliding. I pulled the emergency brake. The rear wheels locked and with a thunderous crunch I came to an abrupt stop on the Chapman Titan camera crane's front bumper. Fortunately, the crane was there—otherwise I would have traveled off the cliff to the beach 20 feet below. I wasn't injured, moved to survey the damage—a foot-long gash to the left rear panel. I was sick to my stomach. The camera operator attempted to console me, but the sound of "You'll never work in this town again," screamed louder in my ears. Most unexpectedly, I was back working at Universal the following week.

Joe Cavalier, aware of my love of photography (I shot his wedding photos), suggested I call Camera Union 659 (now International Cinematographers Guild Local 600 IATSE). The female voice asked if I was a minority. "Yeah, I'm 5'4." "No, I mean are you black, Oriental, Mexican or American Indian?" Having been rejected previously, I said, "In 1961, I had to be born into your union and now I'm not the right color. I'll call you in twenty years and you can tell me I'm too old."

The Streets of San Francisco called me to double Michael Burns, whom I'd first doubled in 1961 on the *It's a Man's World* TV series and in 1962 on *Mr. Hobbs Takes a Vacation*. This time I brought, Cheri Stewart, a sweet lady, along for her first airplane flight and first trip to the Bay City. With the stunt action completed, we stayed a couple of extra days to see the beautiful sights of The City; Fisherman's Wharf, the Balcultha ship, Ginsberg's Irish Pub, Top of the Mark, The Fairmont Crown Room and topped it off with a fine dinner at Alfred's. We had a fun time at The Buena Vista, the first USA saloon to introduce Irish Coffee, where you may be seated next to a high society matron or a Hell's Angel. The next day we checked out Ghirardelli Square, grabbed a cable car ride to Union Square and lunch at the Sir Francis Drake Hotel before our return flight to Studio City.

Those three days with Cheri were some of the most enjoyable moments I had spent with any female companion since Toni. But chalk it up to my naivety (or stupidity)—we were well into our relationship before I accidentally discovered her attempt to pocket a joint. She admitted smoking marijuana daily, "I can't get through a day without it." We went our separate ways.

The *Manhunter* TV series starred Ken Howard and Dick Durock became his double. I reveled in this early 1930s show, wearing the period clothes and driving the fine, vintage, automobiles.

One segment had us filming in Piru, a small agricultural town, an hour north of Tinseltown. Doubling the bad guy, I was to drive a 1932 Packard roadster during the getaway. Smiling, I cranked up this beautiful old relic, listened to the engine purr and thanked my Dad for instilling my love of the vintage vehicles. Without power steering to ease the maneuverability of this three-ton beauty, I mounted a 1950's "necking knob" on the large 18-inch steering wheel.

On "Action," I crashed through the breakaway picket fence, narrowly missed a head-on crash with Guy Way and sped away. It was a "Print." Returning to camera, driver captain Jerry Johnson came to retrieve the car but stopped at the left front fender. A six-inch, pencil-sized, piece of balsa wood had pierced the chromed fender-mounted running light lens like an arrow. It was a freak accident and the Packard will always be ranked as one of the greatest specimens of American automotive craftsmanship.

The *Manhunter* series journeyed to Longmont, Colorado, to film Dick Durock's leap from a trestle to a moving 1930s train. His target from the 36-foot high bridge was a 4x8 sheet of plywood supported by

Styrofoam cups to break his fall. Dick did a great jump, but the editor chose to cut before he landed to Ken Howard landing in place. Unfortunately, this type of editing, usually in TV, takes the onus off the stunt and diminishes the intended action effect.

Another *Manhunter* episode, helmed by veteran actor-director Lawrence Dobkin had us filming at 1633 N. San Pablo in L.A.'s Lincoln Heights, a perfect 1930s location. A personal request prompted Larry to hire Wally Rose to play a "stunt guard." Standing on the two-tiered roof, Larry explained how he wanted Rose to take the bullet hit, fall down the three steps to the roof, landing with an arm hanging over the edge. Howard Curtis, Bob Miles and I were casually seated, watching and waiting for our time at bat in the ensuing scenes.

The camera rolled and Larry fired a .38 cal. blank to give Wally the impetus to take the bullet hit. Wally jerked slightly, *slowly* moved to the three steps, *slowly* grabbed the railing, *slowly* stumbled down each step, *slowly* lowered himself to the asphalt-tiled roof, *slowly* rolled over and then dangled an arm over the roof's edge. Howard, Bob and I stared in disbelief. I leaned close and whispered, "Was he fucking shot or was he poisoned?" There was a beat, then, Howard and Bob doubled up. Larry yelled, "Cut! Let's do one more."

Again, Dobson fired the pistol, and again Wally repeated each previous move verbatim. We three again stared at each other, shaking our heads in amused disbelief. A frustrated Dobson said, "Print it" and quickly moved to the next set up.

Tom Sutton had doubled Stu Whitman on the *Cimarron Strip* TV series. During the run of the show he courted and married its co-star, Jill Townsend, daughter of Robert Townsend, the brilliant car rental CEO who turned Avis around with his "We Try Harder" motto. This gene pool of intelligence included his other daughter, Clair Townsend, a former production executive for Twentieth Century-Fox.

On this particular afternoon, Tom came to the Stuntmen's Association office to find Henry Wills, Reg Parton, Denver Mattson and myself lingering. We were all "between pictures" and surprised when he asked us to be at Disney Studios Stage 4 at four p.m. to rehearse for *The Apple Dumpling Gang*. We gratefully accepted the job and promised to be there.

Three hours later, with the exception of Denver, we rehearsed the Meeting Hall scene to be shot the following day. We wondered what had happened to Mattson, but figured he had other plans. During the rehearsal, Tom was demonstrating a quick move to an actor and accidentally stuck his finger in the actor's eye. Immediately, Parton turned on him like a snake, accusing him of being unprofessional, belligerent and, to top it off, drunk. I saw the incident and cannot say for certain that Tom had been drinking. He was always a gregarious character, and unless he was administered a Breathalyzer test, I'll defend his innocence. Nevertheless, Sutton was fired and Parton later persuaded the Stuntmen's Association board to bring charges of "conduct unbecoming a member" against him.

The next day, Harry Morgan held court in the Meeting Hall set as Bill Bixby, Susan Clark, Don Knotts, Tim Conway, four stuntmen, forty extras and most every character actor you've ever seen. Between the shots, it was a thrill to meet veteran actress Iris Adrian, playing Poker Polly, but was better known as the wise-cracking telephone operator from the Jack Benny radio and TV shows. Disney veteran Norman Tokar, always a fine gentleman was directing. The day went well as old buddy Harry Morgan called me "Elmer" during the scene.

Back at the Stuntmen's Association office, we found that Mattson did come to Disney and had waited outside the main gate. When I asked why he didn't ask the studio guard or casting office about us on Stage Four, he just shrugged his shoulders.

A Teamster met Bill Hart and I as we arrived in Statesboro, Georgia, to film *The Greatest Gift*, a TV movie-of-the-week starring Glenn Ford and Julie Harris with Boris Sagal directing. I was anxious to see Boris again, but the driver said, "Boris told me to tell you, that if you apologize to him one more time, you're going home."

This was my first visit to the South in years and I loved it. The people in Georgia were gracious and accommodating, but Statesboro was a dry county, so an order placed with our driver soon brought our favorite beverage from an adjacent county. In the motel lounge, fifty cents bought a *set-up*, a glass of ice and choice of mix, and we were off and running, although some didn't run as fast as others.

A visiting New Jersey salesman had finished off his bottle, so I offered him my half-gallon of Vodka, as I sure as hell wasn't going to drink it all. Unfortunately, this simple courtesy put him well over his limit. The next morning word circulated that he had flipped out, threatened someone with a .45 caliber automatic and the local constabulary had hauled his ass off to jail.

The following evening it was my turn at bat, not planned, but when you pour for yourself, the tendency is to pour either too light or too heavy. I chose the latter. The morning after, I sat in the coffee shop, reading the local paper, enjoying my ham and cheese omelet. Glenn Ford and his fiancée, Cynthia Hayward, entered and moved to a back corner table. Smiling my morning salutation, I had noticed their odd look, but simply disregarded it. However, her ten-carat engagement ring sparkled, causing me to speculate that the batteries were extra. A few minutes later, Cynthia returned to ask how I was doing. "Just fine," I said.

She was concerned because the previous night she and Glenn's stand-in had found me wandering the motel's hallway, going door to door, with my room key in hand. They then led me to my room and locked the door, she said, and were amazed at how chipper I was after such a festive night. I then confided my imbibing technique, "Four Bayer aspirins… and the glass bottle on my pillow is always a good reminder when my head hits it. The next morning, when the alarm rings, you jump out of bed like a milk-fed calf." I have often wondered what Glenn Ford thought of my methodology.

The Greatest Gift filming progressed slowly for a week before Bill and I were told our stunts would be performed back in Hollywood. Returning to Universal, I was startled to see Universal's backlot "Southern" set. The art department's truckload of Spanish moss hung from the trees and the set actually looked better than it did in Georgia. I'm forever amazed by Hollywood's artistry.

But Boris Segal was still inclined to envelope himself in deep concentration. On May 22, 1981, while filming *World War III*, a TV miniseries, he exited a helicopter, tragically walked into the tail rotor, and died hours later. He was a nice man.

Universal TV's production manager Mel Bishop served gratis as a Los Angeles County Deputy Sheriff Reserve motorcycle officer. When the LACS needed a thirty-minute *Hit & Run* training film, Mel produced it. Early on a Saturday morning, studio artisans from every department assembled on the studio's back lot to offer their services gratis. Mel asked me to take a bicycle hit from a car and I called George Fisher to nail me. On cue, George roared around the corner in a white Volkswagen bug and struck my rear wheel, catapulting me over the handlebars. Evidently, the crash was impressive one of the extras, as a deputy sheriff's daughter began crying and screaming, "He's dead, he's dead." That put a smile on my face, as did the film's total cost of $1900, contrary to $50,000 were it a studio produced film.

Work persisted on *Manhunter*, *Get Christie Love*, *Shazam* and also a rush call from assistant director Claude Binyon, Jr. to coordinate a scuffle on *The Virginia Hill Story*, starring Dyan Cannon and Robbie Benson, directed by Joel Schumacher. Hill was the girlfriend of the notorious gangster, Bugsy Siegel. The scene involved an actor I'd known for years, mostly from The Left Bank saloon, who had a knack of getting injured on the set. After every job, he would file a medical claim and go on state disability, allowing him to convalesce at Santa Anita and Hollywood Park racetracks.

During rehearsal, I watched his every move, especially where he was to fall after being conked on the head by Cannon. He was eyeing a chair behind him, and as the camera rolled I removed the chair from the set. He took Dyan's hit and actually stretched without looking to reach the spot where the chair had been. Oh, he was good, and he had it down to a science, but Voila! No chair.

Again, I always prided myself on never having anyone injured while I functioned as a stunt coordinator, and he wasn't going to be the first.

An inner urge made me phone David Whorf, the assistant director on *Streets of San Francisco*. He sounded started, "Jess, we just finished a production meeting and I just mentioned we needed a *Jesse Wayne-type*." "Well, the real Jesse Wayne is available," I said, but David explained "I need a kid around 18 who could act and do his own stunts like you." Damn, no way could I appear to be eighteen again.

Henry Wills, the 1974 SAMP president, lost his wife, Alice, in a tragic heart attack-auto accident. He was taking it hard (as I did when my Dad passed in 1971). While attending to the myriad of funeral details, he was informed her favorite audio music tape cassette would not play on the mortuary's sound system—their system tape speed had been altered, rendering regular recordings unplayable. Naturally, mortuary-recorded music was available at an exorbitant *additional* fee.

At the SAMP office, Hank was still recovering from his loss, when I received a call from production manager Robin Clark to instruct *Billy Jack* actor, producer, writer and director Tom Laughlin in the art of fast draw and gun handling. He also wanted a *cowboy* stunt coordinator for *The Master Gunfighter*, Laughlin's new film. Wills was seated next to me, so I handed him the phone. Wills got the job, as did Victor Paul, the 1973 Senior Olympics Sabre Champion, whom I'd also recommended with Buddy Van Horn, to coach the swordplay. Clark later admitted he chose Victor's 5'9½" height over Buddy's six-feet-two, because Victor would be less intimidating to Laughlin. It's called CYA—and he ran scared as usual.

My initial visit to Laughlin's Brentwood palisades mansion, located behind the proverbial iron gates, was to discuss his firearms wants for his 1840's Early California film. Historical accuracy was obviously not a great consideration; I cringed while his "artistic license" prevailed. Reluctantly, I had no other choice than to recommend the Colt Navy 1851, which had not yet been invented, as the film's main pistol. Gulping hard when he said he wanted to "fan" the pistol, I played down "fanning" as a false fixation perpetrated by Hollywood Westerns to fire rapidly. Still, he insisted he wanted to "fan," like a whining kid for a piece of candy. Finally, my resigning retort was, "I think you should 'fan."

Laughlin then said he wanted to wear a shoulder holster, and I recommended the smaller .31 cal. Sheriff's model version of the Navy Colt. He also wanted a hide-away Derringer and two knives. To enable him to carry this armament comfortably, I designed two special gun belt & holsters and contacted Alfonso Pineda in North Hollywood to build the leather rigs. I'd known Alfonso since 1957, when he worked for fast draw king Arvo Ojala (pronounced, O-ja-la), the Finnish gunfighter, seen each week opposite James Arness on *Gunsmoke*, as he draws down on the Marshal. Alfonso did an excellent job and, after all the years, I could still only understand every fifth word he said. He was a sweetheart and a fine craftsman.

Ray Aubert, the film's property master, shook his head in disbelief as I detailed the armament of this human arsenal. I facetiously mentioned that the only weapon Laughlin wasn't carrying was a slingshot. Quickly, Ray put his index finger to his lips and whispered, "Shhhhh, he might hear you."

The Master Gunfighter was to be filmed in Carmel's Big Sur area and is truly one of the most beautiful places on earth. Three years had passed since I had been there on *Chandler*. Carmel, it's said, is one of several high-energy points on our globe. I don't doubt this theory; it always seemed so rejuvenating and invigorating.

The fifty-minute United Airlines flight to Monterey allowed Billy Shannon and me two quick Screwdrivers, enough to eliminate our white-knuckle flight jitters. Arriving in the production office for per diem and contracts, I was greeted by production manager Bill Davidson, who had replaced Robin Clark. I had known Bill since 1960 from Paramount, and it was like old home week to see him again. As for the production personnel change, Bill said, "This is the third time I've replaced him [Clark] on a show. I guess all I've got to do to keep working is follow him around."

We were no sooner unpacked at the Holiday Inn's Highway 1 and Carmel Valley Road, when the entire cast and crew was invited to a pre-filming party, contrary to a film's wrap party. This was a novel idea, a chance to get to know each other, but mainly it would allow Laughlin to expound on his filmatic procedures. Specifically, when a bell sounded on the set, whether it was a rehearsal or actual filming, *EVERYONE* was instantly ordered to freeze in position and not move a muscle. He was more than adamant about this rule and would later fire crewmembers on the spot for not complying.

In addition, we were notified that we were required to see *Goyo Kin*, the Japanese film Laughlin had used for his *Gunfighter* script. In a multiplex movie theater across from the Holiday Inn, I attended the screening with a cute cocktail waitress from the hotel lounge. We both fell asleep halfway through the film.

Goyo Kin was an artsy-fartsy Japanese film, an anemic version of Akira Kurasawa's, 1954 *Seven Samurai,* later to be Americanized as *The Magnificent Seven.*

In Laughlin's depiction, he chose to cast himself as a lone "Samurai" gunslinger, thus replacing all seven warriors. *The Master Gunfighter* was not so much a remake, but a vapid duplicate of the original film. Laughlin literally re-filmed each scene, shot for shot, angle for angle, cut for cut. Though Laughlin's son, Frank, went through the directorial motions, it was dear old Dad making the decisions.

Regardless, I still wondered what happened to Laughlin's vision for this Americanized film version. Beautiful Barbara Carrera, from Managua, Nicaragua, was the one and only bright spot in front of the lens. Though Barbara's scripted material was mediocre at best, her beauty and talent will forever be immortalized as James Bond's Fatima Blush in *Never Say Never Again.*

The show became a first and second-generation stunt bonanza with Henry Wills hiring his son, Jerry, to double Laughlin and Victor Paul, bringing in his son, John Romano, as a swordsman.

During pre-production, at Laughlin's demand, Victor Paul was required to study the *Goyo Kin* sword fights, frame by frame on a Moviola to duplicate the film's action. Interestingly, he found that seeing was not believing, but careful editing of individual film frames to create an illusion of precise sword movements.

On the set, Laughlin maintained his insistence on absolute silence, as the view off-camera resembled time-frozen mannequins in every configuration. It was unlike any movie set I had ever seen and the inadaptable were fired for a first offense.

The stunts moved fast and furious. Jerry Wills doubled Laughlin rearing a horse when the steed slipped and fell over backward. Luckily, Jerry was wearing his large rodeo buckle under the wardrobe which prevented the large Mexican saddle horn from crushing his stomach. He was sore and opted for a Demerol from my stunt bag's medicine cache.

Several of us were running in the deep sand as Buddy Van Horn galloped past us. Suddenly, his horse stumbled and they both went down. A hoof to Buddy's head caused over thirty stitches and three months later his bouts of dizziness finally subsided. Buddy is one of my favorite people and best remembered as Guy Williams' double on Walt Disney's *Zorro* TV series. In 1968 he began doubling Clint Eastwood on *Paint Your Wagon*, and since has directed Eastwood's *Any Which Way You Can, The Dead Pool* and *Pink Cadillac.*

Another *Gunfighter* shot had me as an escaping Indian, running afoot, then bulldogged by Billy Shannon on horseback. An area of soil was spaded to cushion our hit on the hard ground. Billy and I were fed up with Laughlin's explosive personality and wanted to get the shot in one take. The camera was panning with us, so I told Billy to nail me regardless of where I was; plowed soil or not. Well, as I knew he would, Billy found me and as he later put it, "I rode you like a sled." He didn't really, but it got a laugh. Again, a job's easy when you work with professionals and Billy was one of the best there ever was.

Nightly, Billy and I returned to our regular bar seats before cleaning up for dinner, while the other stunt guys said they didn't imbibe. An hour later these so-called teetotalers would return from their rooms glassy-eyed and half in the bag. A peek into their rooms revealed enough booze to stock a liquor store.

Laughlin spared no horses in gathering a top-notch crew, including former Warner Brother's hairdresser Jean Burt Reilly, who had worked on *Yankee Doodle Dandy* and *Casablanca*, two of my all-time favorite films ranking behind *Gone with the Wind*. She was a charming, beautiful, delightful lady.

Gordon Dawson, son of Tommy Dawson, head of Columbia's wardrobe department, handled our outfits, and would later become director Sam Peckinpah's protégé, writing Sam's action scripts. His extensive future credits would include executive producer and writer of Chuck Norris' *Walker: Texas Ranger* TV series.

Again, call it fate, destiny or whatever, but one evening while getting spruced up, I suddenly had an unstoppable nosebleed. Little did I know how great a bloodletting this would later become?

Sprawled across the king-size bed, head over the edge, nostril plugged with tissue and an ice pack bridging my nose, proved a futile effort to stop the flow. My door was ajar, and in walked, Suzy Schor, Laughlin's executive assistant. Concerned, she called the production office and was granted permission to take me to the local emergency room to cauterize, what I believed was a broken blood vessel. We returned to the hotel, and like a bear with a thorn removed from his paw, I gratefully asked her to dinner, but she declined, but said she'd be available another time. While sitting with Billy at the bar an hour later we noticed her fondness for Laughlin's co-producer.

The stunts continued as I played a Vaquero bandit at a rooftop window, posed to shoot Laughlin. Script-wise, his innate sixth sense of danger tells him I'm up there as he suddenly fires a shot through the ceiling, striking me in the gut. As in *Goyo Kin*, Laughlin wanted me to react to the bullet's impact with a slight flinch, fall backward, slide to the roof's edge and fall seven feet to the muddy ground, landing on my back. The fall was easy enough, but camera technical problems occurred and we did the stunt again.

Initially, I had questioned Wills about me taking a bigger "hit" from the bullet, get airborne from the initial shot and bounce from the roof to the ground. Like everyone else on the film, Laughlin's ceaseless intimidation prevented Henry Wills from suggesting any variation from the original film. We got the shot and Wills saddled up to me, "I didn't know you could do that." What? I thought—that's what I get paid to do—perform action in the movies! Like many stunt men, he lived in a vacuum with only a vague idea of what was going on around him.

Wills then asked me to play an Indian—take a shot and tumble head over heels down a sand dune. A piece of cake, I had performed this fall many times down hillsides, mountains, stairways and sand dunes, allowing my momentum and gravity to take over.

Just off Carmel's picturesque Seventeen Mile Drive, I tumbled down a sloping fifty yard, forty-five degree dune. This time the soft sand caused me to stick with each hit. To maintain the tumbling, I had to purposely *help* each roll over to keep me propelled in motion. The camera operator said he could do it "a little better," meaning he screwed up the shot. Again, I threw myself down the dune, exerting as much of a flip as I could without making it look acrobatic, after all, I'm supposed to be a dead body. Injuries usually happen on the second take—and the slight bulge and aching pain stretched from my groin to my chest proved it. I had pulled my right stomach muscle and according to the emergency room intern would take ten days to heal.

Returning to the hotel, the first guy I bumped into was production manager Bill Davidson and being honest to a fault, I mentioned the doctor's projected recovery time frame. The next morning I returned to L.A. after three and a half weeks with many more weeks of action to be filmed. Henry Wills and Victor Paul's tenure on the film amounted to over five months each.

At my suggestion, *The Master Gunfighter* film credits listed S.A.M.P. after the stunt players, a motion I had also made, and was passed by the SAMP Board. These initials would identify association members as they do for the director of photographer, editors and makeup. To my knowledge this would be the only occasion SAMP was ever listed in film credits after a stunt member's name.

Stunt performer screen credits were rare prior to the 1970s, and generally considered "to be at the discretion of the producer." Today, the screen credits read like a phonebook, sometimes listing hundreds of names, including the producer's gardener.

Invariably, much of what the SAMP Board voted in over the years was sacrosanct until the next monthly board meeting, and by then the item had become buried in the minute's files to be ignored and forgotten forever. Unfortunately, in the mid-80s all of SAMP's records from its inception in 1961 were deemed useless and ordered destroyed by certain foolish individuals.

Chalk it up to my thirty-three year old resilience, and two days later I was back to work for veteran stunt man Bob Minor, a former Mr. Los Angeles bodybuilding titleholder, on *Jezebels*. The following day I was doubling Jose Feliciano on *Kung Fu*.

The *Kung Fu* episode had the script's bad guy shoving Jose backward over a chair as a fight ensued. During the free-for-all, vases are pitched past the blind singer-actor—it was obvious I shouldn't react *until* they actually struck the wall. So, I played the entire scene with my eyes closed behind the dark glasses, reacting only to the breaking ceramics sound. Director Barry Crane commended me on my reactions, but I never mentioned my "method stunt man" acting technique to him or to stunt coordinator Greg Walker.

Again, it will get you killed. Beware of the take-two mentality—it's invariably the second take that always gets you hurt, maimed or killed. On Robert Aldrich's *The Flight of the Phoenix*, starring James Stewart, Sir Richard Attenborough, Peter Finch and Hardy Kruger, the film was beset by this malady when veteran director Oscar Rudolf helmed the second unit action sequences near Yuma, Arizona. An Amelia Earhart contemporary, veteran stunt pilot Paul Mantz flew the film's makeshift plane as it rises above the crest of the sand dunes. The first take was perfect, but there's always the "Let's do one more for protection." On take two, one of the plane skids caught the tip of the sand dune, somersaulted the aircraft, breaking it apart as it tumbled. Mantz was killed. Veteran stunt man Bobby Rose was catapulted over one hundred yards and survived with a broken back.

The more times you perform a stunt, the greater the possibility of an injury—you're contending with *The Law of Averages*. The body may tire, the concentration may drift, but the one element that always concerned me more was a mechanical failure. Equipment, like humans can be pushed only so far. I have performed my stunts correctly, in one take, ninety-eight percent of the time. This isn't an extraordinary accomplishment as most professional stunt performers maintain this number.

A call came again for *Get Christie Love*, and then it was over to the *Hearts of the West* feature with Alex Sharp (no relation to Davy). Alex was James Arness' stunt man for 13 years on *Gunsmoke* and was doubling Herb Edelman, whom you'll remember as Stan, husband to Bea Arthur on *The Golden Girls*. I was again wardrobed to double English actor Donald Pleasence.

Suzi Schor from *The Master Gunfighter* called and we made a date for dinner at her apartment. However, a small voice later screamed at me to avoid this situation, so I pulled a George Jones and became a No Show. I have stressed the importance of listening to that still, small inner voice, but a stiff prick has no conscience and we again set another date.

Her invitation to a home cooked dinner actually fascinated me, re-calling the ex-wife who couldn't boil water and ranted, "I don't like to cook, I don't want to cook and I'm not going to learn how to cook." That was the only marriage vow she kept.

The evening was mutually charged and after dinner we each became the dessert. She later mentioned her anger when I didn't show up for the first dinner date—and how she drove to a nearby residential street and flung the entire spaghetti dinner on someone's lawn. She also mentioned being fired from *The Master Gunfighter,* and received three speeding violations while returning to L.A. If I hadn't been drinking I'd have realized she was a loose nut.

A week later she arrived at my Studio City apartment with one suit-case containing her every possession. In a whirlwind romance (or whatever it was), two weeks later we were exchanging marriage vows in Carmel's Highlands Inn wedding chapel—the second biggest marital mistake I would make. Possibly, it can be attributed that "Pain has no memory." Otherwise no woman would ever give birth to a second child.

My unabashed advice to anyone remotely contemplating matrimony is to hide the Scotch, and be completely sober when making one of life's most important decisions. You wouldn't purchase a car smashed. Secondly, don't rush it—be engaged at least one year, and know that even with these precautions you still have a less than a fifty percent chance of a successful marriage. However, I do believe the best bromide is "Familiarity breeds contempt."

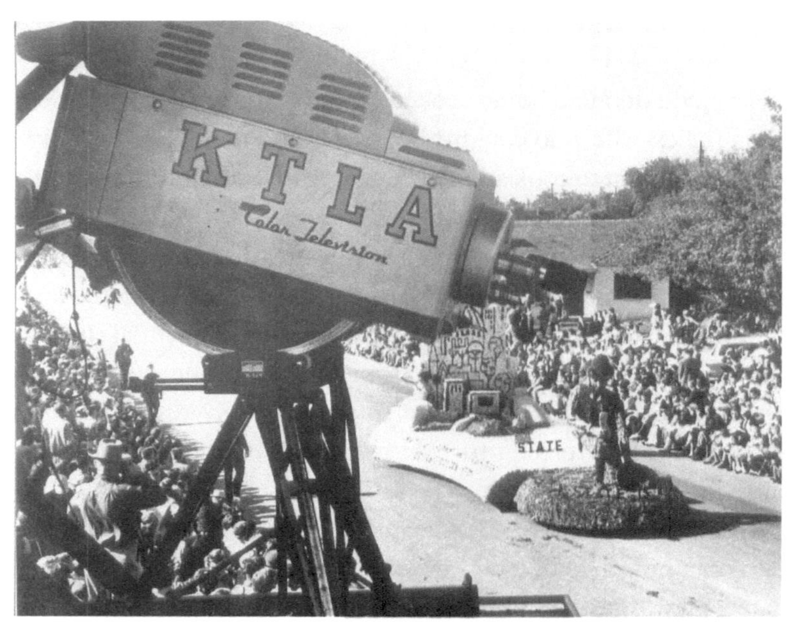

ABOVE: KTLA televising Pasadena Rose Parade in Color (1955)
BELOW: Actor/Gun Coach Rodd Redwing

Everything's Ducky (1961) Columbia Pictures

ABOVE: Cameraman Bill Matheson – My KTLA Mentor
BELOW: *The Wrangler* TV Pilot – First videotaped western series.

ABOVE: Actor/Friend Ken Mayer
BELOW: My trusty 16mm Bolex Rex camera above Palm Springs (1969)

ABOVE: Mickey & Jan (1968) Grand Marshalls Hollywood Santa Claus Parade
BELOW: My 1949 Oldsmobile "Starlight Mist" convertible

ABOVE: KTLA Telecopter - First in the World (1958)
BELOW: *Darker than Amber* (1969) Bahamas

Hangin around on *It's a Mad World* piano wires

ABOVE: Harry Morgan, one of the nicest guys I ever met
BELOW: *Marineland of the Pacific* (1976) Hanging unconscious

ABOVE: *Battle for the Planet of the Apes* (1973)
BELOW: Bob Newhart

More photos may be found at Jesse's website: jessewayne.net

CHAPTER 17

1975

Work-wise, 1974 had been a very good year, culminating in my committing matrimony on December 21, a decision that proved I should have been committed to the insane asylum in Camarillo.

The few days into January 1975 the bride abruptly ended a phone conversation with her father, angrily slammed down the receiver and screamed, "Why doesn't he die and leave me all his money?" referring to dear old Daddy's million dollar estate. "Honor thy Father" was the first of several Ten Commandments she would violate.

When I told her, "I don't deserve you," she thought it was complement.

The marriage was almost a month old as I was leaving to watch Super Bowl IX at the Left Bank with the guys. She asked who else would be there, "Oh, Denver Mattson," I said, "Dick Durock and probably Roger Perry with JoAnne Worley." With a devious grin, she said, "Ask Roger if he remembers when we were in bed and the bed frame broke." I couldn't believe what I heard.

Never to her or any other amours have I ever divulged my previous love life, nor inquired about theirs. I believed that it was all in the past and neither of us was a saint. Conversely, she bragged about her many college and Tinseltown conquests.

Actually, I preferred to abide by radio's *Feminine Forum* host Bill Ballance's warning that "Anything you tell someone you love will eventually be used against you."

I have always derived my greatest satisfaction from my work, whether it was in front or behind the camera, and was pleased to double Arte Johnson again, this time on *Get Christie Love*, starring Teresa Graves. On location at the Hollywood Universal Studio Tours we awaited the arrival of the first unit, which had been filming on the lower lot. The equipment trucks soon arrived and a dinner break was called. The not-ready-yet caterer feverishly arranged the salads, drinks and condiments as the hungry cast and crew of eighty waited patiently in line. Impetuous Arte suddenly rushed to the salad table, picked up a huge two-foot wide stainless steel bowl of tuna salad and flipped it upside-down on a nearby park bench, ran to his Mercedes Benz sedan and sped away. A few crewmembers laughed, and then one angrily yelled, "Hey, the sonofabitch just dumped our food." Why Arte dumped the tuna bowl is still a mystery. Maybe, as a child, he was scared by a fish.

January 21, 1975, would mark the 100th birthday of D.W. Griffith, director of *Birth of a Nation* and *Intolerance*, the Father of the Hollywood Film. Wondering what Los Angeles had planned for this officious occasion, I phoned Los Angeles Mayor Tom Bradley's office. His young field representative had never heard of Griffith, and suggested I submit a written description of his cinematic achievements. Two Months later, I was surprised to receive a hand-lettered City of Los Angeles proclamation commemorating David Wark Griffith's 100th birthday, signed by Mayor Bradley. The large laminated-walnut framed certificate is proudly displayed in my office, but it really belongs in a film museum.

D.W. Griffith died in 1948 in the Hollywood Knickerbocker Hotel lobby. Louis B. Mayer, Jack Warner, Harry Cohn, et al., gave solemn eulogies; expressing regrets that they hadn't worked with him. Oh, really? Griffith made his last film in 1931 and for the ensuing 17 years, in Hollywood jargon, "He couldn't get arrested."

Production manager Hal Klein called from American International Pictures to invite me to be stunt coordinator on *Return to Macon County*, a sequel of sorts to capitalize on Max Baer Jr.'s successful, low budget film, *Macon County Line*. When I inquired about the cast, Hal said they were just couple of young unknown actors—Nick Nolte and Don Johnson. Hal also said Terry Leonard would be sharing stunt coordinator credit with me. He was a likable guy, a good, no holds barred stunt man, and I looked forward to working with him.

Terry had performed a spectacular fall from the Hollywood Holiday Inn's tenth floor into their swimming pool. I filmed it with black and white loaded in my 16mm Bolex, D.P. Ron Brown cornered me, "Don't you ever shoot film on a set unless you use color film." He was right. In 1958, during the filming of *The Buster Keaton Story*, starring Donald O'Connor, stunt man Russ Saunders filmed a boat launching scene and the "master shot" camera failed. MGM paid him well for his hundred feet of 16mm film.

The *Return to Macon County* script involved a couple of young guys off to the drag race nationals in their souped-up sedan. The 1957 Chevrolet Bel Air brought wonderful memories of the first new car I ever drove. Realizing a lengthy car chase and crashes were required, I was concerned about the quality of the vehicles Terry and I would be driving. From past experience I knew you couldn't leave anything to chance and must check it out yourself. Hal referred me to the film's transportation captain, Paul Casella, who vowed the picture cars would be fully equipped with whatever we requested before the vehicles left Hollywood, and promised to call when the cars arrived so Terry and I could check them out. A week passed and my calls to Casella were not returned. The production office finally informed me that Casella and the vehicles were on their way to the Georgia location.

A pleasant Delta Airlines flight took Terry and me to Atlanta, where a driver drove us sixty miles to Forsyth, Georgia. The motel production office was packed with Hal Klein, producer Elliot Shick, assistant directors, Bob Dijoux, Mike Kusley and production coordinator Andrea Nachman. Hovering nearby was Louis Arkoff, son of AIP founder, Sam Arkoff. After the obligatory signing of contacts, W-4s and receiving our per diem, we went to our assigned rooms to unpack.

Checking out the motel premises, I noticed a void—no cocktail lounge; Forsyth was a Georgia dry county, just like Statesboro. No loss, I thought, as

I had again gone on the wagon two weeks previously, on Super Bowl IX night. For whatever other reasons that might occur I didn't want alcohol to be a factor if my new marital union went down the tube.

Early Monday morning, January 27, 1975, filming began under the direction of Richard Compton, a competent writer-director who spoke with the dulcet-tones of a radio or television announcer. Jacques Marquette was the director of photography, the best and fastest in the business. I had worked with Jack since the early 60s on many features, and most recently on *The Streets of San Francisco*.

The crew readied the first shot as Nick and Don leaned on the hot rod, garbed in the de rigueur costume of the fifties—Levis, white T-shirts and boots. Immediately, Terry and I checked out the Chevy Bel Air. Actually, it was a Chevy 2-door coupe, adorned to resemble the famous Bel Air. Of course, none of the safety preparations I had discussed with Casella had been made. Terry then went with a driver to the speed shops in Atlanta for the needed safety equipment. Along with special effects man Roy Downey we installed seat belts, battery tie-downs and inner tubes. These were basic safety precautions, especially, the tubes in the tubeless tires, a procedure to prevent a tire from dislodging or air escaping during a slide, spin or jump.

Per the script, Nick and Don pick up a girl hitchhiker. Actress Karen Lamm was typecast for this wild, run-a-way role and personified the no-bullshit kind of gal writer Compton envisioned. We exchanged pleasantries and a moment later said she was living with Mike Love. Staring at my blank expression, she obviously expected my screaming exaltation of "Holy shit!" In desperation, she blurted out, "He's one of the Beach Boys! Ya know, 'Good Vibrations,' 'California Girls.'" "Yeah…?" I knew of him and the band, but didn't acknowledge them, as she indignantly stomped away. Place this one in the "Who gives a shit?" file.

My favorite music has forever been The Big Bands, featuring the honey-sweet voice of Doris Day with Les Brown and his Band in 1946. I was weaned on it, but much of the 1960's music never appealed to me, as I preferred Frank Sinatra, Tony Bennett, Andy Williams, Johnny Mathis, Nat King Cole, et al. The Beach Boys were an exception, however, and I've since collected all of their CD albums.

Lamm's attitude, albeit perfect for the script's character she portrayed, didn't fair too well with the film's executives. Two weeks into the filming her tardiness had Elliot and Louis knocking on her honeywagon dressing room door repeatedly, politely requesting her presence on the set. Screaming "Fuck You" awarded this impetuous diva an immediate return trip to Hollywood and a forever passage to oblivion.

Enter actress Robin Mattson, who went on to become a soap opera mainstay. Robin is a fine actor but in this part she lacked the raw grit and spunk that Lamm projected naturally. It's nothing critical of Robin's talent; it's just that some roles fit some actors better than others.

In a "game of "chicken" sequence, I doubled a kid run off the road in a 1954 Chevrolet coupe, and again had no choice in vehicle selection. Terry doubled Nolte in the pseudo-Bel Air as we raced side-by-side down the highway as a truck car carrier loomed head-on. With the accelerator floored, I was only traveling at a top speed of forty-five when I careened off the road into a ditch; 65mph would have been the ideal speed.

My old buddy, veteran cinematographer Jacques Marquette shot the film postcard perfect with his crew from Hollywood, augmented from Chicago and Atlanta. Chicago camera operator, Lutz Hapke, was a tall, handsome, white haired gentleman about 55, with a profound German accent. I facetiously remarked, "You look and sound like a German tank commander." He looked down at me and smiled, "I vass." It was 1975 and WWII had ended thirty years ago and I thought it was now the time was to say, "Welcome!"

Because Forsyth County was booze-free, allowed the transportation department to make liquor runs to the adjoining county. The cast and crew placed their orders, so it didn't hinder anyone's drinking habits, but unfortunately, I was on the wagon. My evenings were spent calling the bride and reading the books I'd brought with me.

Late one night, Andrea Nachman called my room for an ice bag from my stunt bag of tricks for Nolte's head. It seems Nick and Don were entertaining the local lasses and, while bouncing on his motel bed, Nick ricocheted into a wall. The next day scenes had Nick's forehead donning an unexplained Band-Aid.

The Allman Brothers and their drummer, Dickie Betts, lived thirty miles away in Macon, so the partying continued through the production. What a lousy time to be on the wagon.

Script supervisor Shirley Ulmer asked a female hairdresser about Nolte exposing himself, "Why would anyone want to show something that small?" she asked, holding up her index finger and thumb. Several laughed, conceding, if you're going to be a "Weenie Waver," at least have something comparable to John Holmes to wave. Hey, it was February and thirty-some degrees.

The script's vengeful State Trooper pursued Nick and Don, calling for them to spot a roadblock and "swap-ends"—slide the Bel Air into a 180° turn to escape. Terry doubled Nick and I sat in the front passenger seat doubling Don. Prop man Gregg Bilson, who fetched me out of the Missouri River on *Tom Sawyer*, was in the back seat doubling Robin Mattson, but in the reddish-blond wig, resembled Harpo Marx. Two vintage police cars were set-up for the highway barricade.

Terry clamped off the hydraulic hoses to the front wheel cylinders, causing only the rear wheels to brake. In previous car stunts I had made the same adjustment as it allows you to keep both hands on the wheel, but it leaves you without front brakes. The walkie-talkie blared it would be a few more minutes before the cameras were set. Terry said he wanted to do a practice one-eighty, so we headed back down the road away from camera. At speed, he hit the brake pedal and cramped the wheel. The car swung around perfectly, end-to-end. "Great!" I said, "We're all set." Terry insisted, "I want to do one more." I adamantly reminded him that the car was "eighteen years old and a piece of shit. Casella put it together with spit and chewing gum. This car can't take it." Terry glared at me, stomped the pedal and swapped ends again.

Most stunt players can relate tales of a sixth sense, experiencing feelings, so powerful—you're compelled to react. I had those feelings and sat silently with clinched white-knuckles as Terry did yet another one-eighty. The car came to a stop as "Action" screamed from the walkie-talkie.

The Canary yellow Bel Air roared toward the roadblock at 50 mph. Terry stomped the brake pedal. Suddenly, the left rear wheel locked, throwing the vehicle into a left 90° turn, propelling us off the high hog's back road. Sailing seventy feet through the air, I said, "Oh Shit!" and tried to dive into the back seat. But Gregg and I bumped heads and bounced around like ball bearings in a boxcar as the car continued mowing through a sapling forest of six-inch tree trunks.

When we finally jerked to a stop, the cracked windshield was resting on Terry's hands as he gripped the busted steering wheel, now bent downward, resembling Brahma bull horns. Crawling out the windows, it appeared we were all without injury, though Terry had a small head cut above his hairline where the windshield had struck him. The "V" shaped front bumper and grill was imbedded into the gushing, steaming radiator.

Second assistant director Mike Kusley got the worst of it—he looked like he had fought a wildcat and lost. When our car sailed off the road, he started running into the woods, but didn't see the three-strand, barbed-wire fence. Luckily, Mike had beautiful Andrea Nachman to soothe his lacerations.

Elliot Schick suggested a hospital checkup, but I declined, however, the next morning, as I exited the shower an accidental glance in my motel mirror proved startling. The back of my upper legs had a black, three-inch stripe across them. The muscle bruise occurred, I figured, when my legs slammed up against the metal dashboard as I attempted to get to the back seat as we crash-landed.

Whether you label it a premonition or what, afterward, I had no intention of doing an "I told you so" to Terry. He knew what happened. Anyway, what else was there to say? Fortunately for us, he was tough enough to muscle the car and keep it upright with a full tank of gas. However, Terry avoided me and didn't talk to me for three days. To this day we have never discussed our off-road journey.

In another era, a Shakespearian actor might have reported the Georgia weather conditions as "The precipitation descended like a bovine urinating upon a prostrate mineral mass," compared to a guy in Texas yowling, "It's raining like a cow pissing on a flat rock." A cloudburst caused the cast and crew to huddle in the lube bays of an old, abandoned gas station—with the visibility so limited we couldn't see across the road. A half an hour passed, I asked Elliott if we were moving to the cover set, "I'm saving it until we really need it." Geeze, I thought, the animals are pairing up. If we don't need it now, when will we need it? Five hours later we resumed filming.

This scene reminded me of Robert Lippert, undeniably the early 1950s most successful independent film producer with budgets of only $100,000, only allowing his directors to film only master shots and an occasional two-shot. On location, when rain was imminent he would cue an actor to say, "It looks like rain," and continued filming without a moment of downtime. On the final day, all actor close ups were then shot accordingly against a powder blue or black background to be edited into the film later. It was crude, but it worked.

Another time on *Macon*, while relaxing between shots, I sat in the black and white Forsyth County patrol car chatting with Deputy Sheriff John Bittick. 1975 marked forty-two years that his father, uncle and grandfather had reigned as the Forsyth County Sheriff. Come September he would be off to Auburn for four years. Moving from location to location we would often stop and target practice with his .357 magnum pistol. John later became the Sheriff of Forsyth County to maintain the family tradition.

Our truck caravan of filming equipment lined both sides of the country road as we sat in John's patrol car telling war stories when a car approached at a swift speed, crewmembers scattered to avoid being hit. John said, "Hang on!" He did a one-eighty, and off we went red light and siren. A mile down the road the speeder pulled over on the shoulder, John unlatched the shotgun and tossed it to me, "Cover me, it's cocked." He approached the car, ordered the driver to exit—I carefully removed the safety and watched their every move. John gave the speeder a ticket, but retained his driver's license—a Georgia State procedure insuring the violator will pay the fine for the return of his license.

Another day, the camera insert car towed the Bel Air past camera where the film's fanatic Trooper fires at the Bel Air's passenger-side window, causing Terry, Gregg and myself to duck low. For two takes Roy Downey fired the pellet rifle to shatter the passenger side breakaway window. I thought we had the shot, but they wanted one more take. So, as we again approached camera, I realized it wasn't Roy firing at us, but the Trooper, with the camera shooting over his shoulder. I don't know why, but I suddenly yelled, "Sonofabitch, Duck!" The actor fired, missed the breakaway window and splintered the Bel Air windshield, sending shards of glass flying.

I was pissed as we returned to camera, "What the hell happened? Why didn't you tell us you changed the shot?" I didn't receive an answer, but first assistant director Bob Dijoux looked at my forehead, "You're bleeding," jerked the door open, shattering the breakaway window the actor had missed. Poor Bob had forgotten about the breakaway window. Thank God, only a few glass slivers got me, but as usual with facial cuts you'll always bleed like a stuck pig.

During a filming break in the beautiful Forsyth town square, replete with the War for Southern Independence cannons, statues and plaques, I complemented director Richard Compton on his dulcet, deep-toned, voice with my tongue-in-my-cheek suggestion, "In case you're interested, I can always get you an announcing job at KTLA." He suddenly appeared dazed and replied, "No, Noooo. I'm a DIRECTOR!!!"

Prior to its release, AIP held a preview showing of *Return to Macon County* in their office theater. A month later, I met Richard Compton exiting Universal and mentioned I had seen the film. Anxiously, he inquired how many were in the theater audience. "About ten," I said. Obviously believing the film wasn't doing any business; he grimaced and burned rubber in his white VW bug. I neglected to mention I'd seen the film in AIP's private screening room, which only had a seating capacity for 20. Once again I had made the wrong comment to Compton. As Strother Martin advised in *Cool Hand Luke*, "What we've got here… failure to communicate."

A year later, Don Johnson co-starred with Jim Davis in *The Deputies* TV pilot for Quinn Martin Productions, basically, a *Streets of San Francisco* in the West. Filming at the CBS Studio Center, I later found myself with Nick Nolte, Don Johnson, Darlene Carr, Melanie Griffith and drummer Dickie Betts at the Back Stage. It was one of those nights when we all drank until closing and no one got drunk—just chalk it up to the stimulating conversations and one of the most enjoyable nights I have ever experienced. The pilot didn't sell, but that would not be the last we would see of Don Johnson.

Veteran actor Jim Davis was a gentle giant, and would later find success as Jock Ewing on TV's *Dallas* series. We'd knock down a few in the Back Stage, but Jim was a quiet, gentle man and never quite recovered from his daughter's tragic car accident.

I received a call to be Woodsy Owl, in a U.S. Forestry Department's public service announcement, commonly referred to as psa's. Unlike TV commercials, where one could reap thousands of dollars in residuals, this gig only paid the SAG daily rate.

Snow covered the beautiful Arrowhead Lake location; a group of seven year olds were brought in from a local private school to romp with Woodsy. While waiting filming, I suddenly felt a sharp pain in my right shin. Reeling, I peered through the eye netting as a seven-year boy was doing his damnedest to kick me again. With Woodsy's wing, I backhanded the little bastard on his ass, "Get out of here, you little sonofabitch!" Just amazing, what goes on in their heads? Conversely, we later used children from the local public school and they were terrific AND well behaved.

I wasn't warned of the area's snow report and arrived, naturally, wearing my western boots instead of Woodsy's webbed feet. I don't know if I appeared lethargic, but a black crew member asked how I was doing, especially, about my cold feet. He immediately removed my boots and began massaging my feet. I started to feel better. God bless him for his thoughtfulness preventing me from frostbite.

In February 1976, *Rich Man, Poor Man* aired, and Nick Nolte was on his way to becoming a major star while Don Johnson worked sporadically. A few years later, I personally delivered *San Francisco Rip-Off*, a script Bob Louden and I had written to his home in Santa Monica. After a week I phoned, expecting to hear his reaction, but Don apologized, saying his dog had chewed it up and requested another copy. Aha! The old "My dog chewed it up" bit, I thought, and promptly regarded it to his disinterest. A couple of years later Don was starring in his *Miami Vice* TV series. Yeah, I know, *it seemed like a good idea at the time!*

Six Million Dollar Man production manager Ted Shiltz asked me to stunt double Buddy Foster, Jodie Foster's estranged brother. Portraying

Wolf Boy, Buddy attempts to avoid Lee Majors, which, of course, becomes a chase. My double wardrobe consisted of a loincloth fashioned from a khaki shirt and a blond Afro wig. The wardrobe man was adjusting my exaggerated loin cloth, when suddenly a brash guy wearing a floppy tennis hat stuck his face in mine, nose to nose, "Do you know what you're gonna do?" "Yes. I'm going to fall off that cliff over there." He just walked away. Turning to the wardrobe man, I asked, "Who the fuck was that?" "The director, Jerry London," he said laughing. This was a first, I guess I was spoiled having worked with so many great directors, who would introduce themself and discuss the shot, but this bozo didn't even say hello.

I did the cliff fall into a pad, and the company then moved down to Falls Lake on Universal's back lot for a continuation of my fall into the cement-based lake.

Vince Deadrick stunt doubled Lee Majors as he had since the *Big Valley* TV series. A 20-foot high scaffolding was set up in the water about thirty feet from shore. The camera was mounted on the top tier, shooting downward toward the water. On "Action," I threw myself off the tower in the same position as in the prior shot, into the four-foot depth of this man-made lake. At Universal it was understood, "They don't shoot a script, they shoot the clock!" so everything was being rushed as production wanted to call lunch in eight minutes at noon.

Diving from the scaffolding, Vince was in perfect Olympic form, but London didn't like it, claiming he wanted a "straighter dive." What? A six-foot man into four feet of water didn't compute, but moments later Vince dived headfirst again, straight as an arrow, into the murky water. Surfacing, he looked stunned and dazed. Suddenly—his head seemed to explode as gushing blood drenched his upper torso. Not waiting for an ambulance, a station wagon rushed him to nearby Saint Joseph Hospital, across from the Walt Disney Studios.

I joined Vince, Jr. in the hospital waiting room and was assured ol' VD was going to be all right. Later, I heard he had died for ten seconds on the operating table, but Vince was tough and, to coin the old line, "It would have killed a normal guy." Vince had always worked out and, with a dislike for hospitals, literally got up and walked out of St. Joe's days before he was to be officially released by his doctors. A week later, he visited the Stuntmen's Association office; his red faced, swollen head resembled ground hamburger. When the TV episode aired, yeah, they used Vince's first diving shot.

Stories circulate just as they do in any other business. One involved a lady that had been "seeing" several production executives at Paramount. On a trip to "visit her sister in New York City," she later phoned her paramour to say she was pregnant and requested he send her $2500 for an abortion. Married, he quickly ran to the nearest Western Union office to wire her the money. It appeared she was also "seeing" nine other gentlemen and called them, too. Months later she reappeared, elegantly slim and trim, which didn't apply to her bulging $25,000 bank account.

The sound mixer hears it all. Generally, upon entering the set, actors have a wireless microphone concealed under their wardrobe. In moments, the actor usually forgets that their every sound is being monitored, including their trips to the rest room. A soundman once told me the female lead was banging her married co-star, so what else is new? Occasionally, when several mikes are activated, it's difficult for the sound mixer to ascertain who's talking unless you're in his view. Wired up, hiding behind the set, I would comment that the best boy is banging the sound mixer's wife. Suddenly, the mixer would leap out of his chair, "Who said that? Who said that?" I always got to him before he could get to the best boy. Also, any mention of his sexual preference would also cause a rise.

I received a rush call to work at Twentieth Century-Fox's Malibu Canyon Ranch on the *M*A*S*H* TV series. Gary "Radar" Burghoff was mowing his home lawn, when a propelled pine tree needle struck his eyeball. This was the "Welcome to Korea" episode that introduced BJ, played by Mike Ferrell, to the series, replacing the departing Wayne Rogers. Over the many dirt roads, I drove the Jeep bringing BJ and Hawkeye to the base. Both Alan Alda and Mike were delightful. When the North Koreans attacked, I became a non-descript soldier who was shot and blown up. When Burghoff returned to the set, I noticed he eyed me suspiciously. Finally, in what appeared to be a surge of courage, he confronted me with questions about a baked beans TV commercial with a "Radar" look-alike and he was pissed because, "It's my character!" When I explained to him that I was first, and foremost, an established stunt man, he still wasn't convinced. The next day I showed him my stunt photo album, but he still bore a belligerent, angered expression of disbelief. Finally, I figured, "Who cares what this asshole thinks."

Later that day, the show's producer and director, Gene Reynolds, gave me a sly look and called, "Radar," I answered, "Yeah, Gene." Burghoff began screaming, "You… You… You can be replaced." Instantly the entire crew became silent and focused on him. Like Bogart's Lt. Commander Queeg in *The Caine Mutiny*, he nervously relented, "Ah, aah… Just like McLean Stevenson." The crew glared at him for a moment, then resumed their work. Gene Reynolds had a grin from ear to ear.

M*A*S*H writer Burt Prelutsky wrote, "Although nobody wanted to be quoted for the record, the feelings about Gary Burghoff's leaving were fairly unanimous: loved Radar, hated Burghoff. As summed up by one of the principals: 'Gary had personality problems. He always felt there was a conspiracy against him. He was rude to everyone, but if anyone ever said anything back to him, he'd throw a tantrum. He had frequent spats with his cast members, particularly with Alan Alda. Once his other cast member, Mike Farrell, told him that his problem was that he could dish it out but he couldn't take it. Gary said, "And I'm getting real sick and tired of dishing it out." The poor fool didn't even realize what he'd said.'"

The rest of the cast was a joy. Jamie Farr, with or without his dress, was a gentle man and Harry Morgan, whom I also doubled, was always the epitome of professionalism.

A few years after the series ended Twentieth Century-Fox's 8200-acre ranch location for many of the most notable films ever produced, was deeded to California and became the Malibu Creek State Park.

At Universal, *Rooster Cogburn* assistant director, Richard Hashimoto, asked me to double a kid riding a raft down Oregon's Rogue River with John Wayne and Katherine Hepburn. Whoa, what an opportunity to finally work with the Duke. But don't worry, he said, "We'll have a net strung across the river." Yeah, right. I declined, still wincing from my

Julia Belle Swain paddlewheel incident in 1972. Jerry Summers did a hellava job.

One evening, my panicked bride phoned Steve Lodge, "Jesse's watching *Casablanca* on TV and he's crying." Calmly, Steve replied, "Oh, he always cries when he watches *Casablanca*." It was reminiscent of my True Love experience. I first viewed this classic film in 1960, and taped the audio in 1962 – I knew every line. It's still one of my two favorite films, along with *Gone with the Wind*.

Walt Disney Studios kept me busy working on *Now You See Him, Now You Don't* and on *GUS*. Doubling Charles Martin Smith on *Now You See Him*, I had to step into a noose and get yanked upside down. But, my biggest thrill was meeting David Niven, as suave and debonair as you'd expect—his congeniality and sense of humor kept us smiling. Vic Tayback, an old buddy, was a Disney bad guy and would later become Mel, of Mel's Diner, on the *Alice* TV series. He, too, died much too young.

Growing up with the films of the forties and 50s, I admit to being star struck. To meet and have worked with the great screen stars I watched for years continued to excite me, though fewer remained every day.

On Disney's *GUS*, Dick Warlock, Wally Brooks and I doubled several of the lady cheerleaders, but most hilarious was Wally, who looked like Don Rickles in drag. Damn, that's still a vision hard to erase. I also reunited my friendship with Ed Asner. It had been seven years since we first met on *The F.B.I.* TV series. Informing him I had married a JAP (Jewish American Princess), he solemnly commented with a "WTC" (welcome to the club), which I ultimately found was more of a curse than congratulatory. I also learned why husbands of Jewish wives die first? Because they want to! Six months later, a chance meeting at Warner Bros, Ed seemingly took the news of my divorce harder than I. But then, he is an actor.

On the Angeles Crest Highway, located behind Mt. Wilson we assembled for the second unit car chase filming of Alfred Hitchcock's last film, *The Family Plot*. Everett Creech was the stunt coordinator and Buddy

Van Horn, John Bear Hudkins, Bennie Dobbins and Bob Harris were among the stunt drivers. After lunch, while waiting to resume the chase, and seeking an audience for my one-liners, I mentioned a book I had recently read, *Nobody Knows You When You're Down And Out* by billionaire J. Paul Getty. The guys knew I was going for a laugh, but Bennie had a pained expression, then blurted out, "Well, what the hell does *he* know about it?" We all roared.

Bennie also didn't quite grasp a reputed book, *How to Play Tennis without Balls* by Dr. Renée Richards, referring to Dr. Richard Raskin, a 1960s male-to-female transsexual.

Minutes later, my pager beeped, thinking another job was in the offing, I called Teddy's from the Forest Ranger's station. It was the JAP with some menial problem that I couldn't have solved, if I'd wanted to. Bennie took me aside and said that any wife disturbing a stunt man at work was an idiot, "Suppose you were doing a dangerous stunt? Ya gotta stay focused." Bennie was right, of course.

An old buddy, makeup artist Lynn Reynolds from *It's a Mad, Mad, Mad, Mad World* was working on Chuck Tamburro, one of the top copter pilots in the business, but Chuck today was wheeling a land vehicle, when I asked Lynn for his famous hand lotion. Politely, Lynn said he only had a small amount left and couldn't spare a drop. I walked away, but returned a few minutes later begging him for the lotion. Again, Lynn adamantly refused. Chuck, meanwhile, has listened to this banter and now asked Lynn about the lotion. Reluctantly, Lynn agreed, cautioned, "But don't tell Jesse," carefully poured the solution into Chuck's right palm, "Now rub your hands together, massage it in." *It* was spirit gum—and Chuck's look of complete frustration was hilarious, as a concerned Lynn, said, "Here, use this solvent." Squirting a gob of surgical adhesive, he then handed Chuck a dozen Kleenex, "Now, wipe it off." Chuck's eager expression had now turned to agonized disparage and disbelief as he waved his white, tissue-coated, glued together hands in total helplessness. The group roared, just as they did when Lynn had suckered me – and them, years before. After this incident, I believe Chuck preferred to fly copters and avoid the nut cases running loose on land.

The Jack Webb production of *Mobile One* TV series starring Jackie Cooper called me to double Sidney Miller, reprising the drunken character he had created on Webb's *Dragnet* TV series. This particular scene had him smashed and staggering, atop a thirty-foot high billboard walkway. The director was Alan Crosland, Jr., whom I'd worked with many times (his father, Alan Crosland, directed the first talkie, *The Jazz Singer* with Al Jolson, in 1927, and I wondered why connections with this film kept popping up in my life?). Carefully, he described how he wanted me to drunkenly stagger to the end of the walkway, climb down the ten-foot ladder, switch over to the I-beam girder, and slide to the ground, landing in a sitting position. He then gave me the script, and pointed to Sidney's lines he wanted me to recite during my journey. Returning the script to him, I asked the A.D. for a bullhorn, then suggested that Sidney say his lines on the bullhorn and I would react to them. In one-take, it all worked perfectly, including the I-beam slide to the ground.

A few days later I bumped into Jack Webb at Barnaby's Studio City hot dog stand, casually mentioned doubling Sidney, bid him adieu and went on my way. The following week, during a routine visit through the Universal production offices prompted Mel Bishop, the show's production manager, to ask, "How do you know Jack Webb?" "Oh, we're old drinking buddies from the China Trader, why?" Jack had requested to see my billboard stunt footage, "Oh, I guess he was just curious and wanted to see what I did."
Jack evidently appreciated my work and had me back on the show a month later, this time playing a hit man after a Senator, portrayed by Tom Bosley of *Happy Days* fame. Joe Pevney was directing—we had met on a *Wagon Train* segment, when I did a saddle fall for a kid. A former actor, Joe was the only director ever to take the time to explain my TV character to me. However, the dramatic tension Pevney created in my scenes was no match for the pressure on the set. Jackie Cooper was not a happy camper, which may explain the series short three month run before the network canceled the show.

Speaking of tension, it was building to great heights on the home front. For many months the JAP bride remained homebound and, unbeknownst to me, had conned three doctors to keep her drugged up on Valium and Librium.

Six months into this marital mess, I attempted a conjugal coupling, only to suggest she take a shower. The shower water flowed like Niagara Falls and when she returned, nothing had changed. Checking out her bathroom, the wet shower, the hamper, I couldn't find a wet towel, "What'd you do, just run the shower for ten minutes?" She countered, "Well, my parents only bathe once a week." From that point on, I never laid another glove on her. A sage once proclaimed, "Cleanliness is next to Godliness." Well, with her it was next to impossible.

When I said, "I don't deserve you," she thought it was a compliment.

On Sunday, October 27, at Denver Mattson's invitation, I arrived in Toronto, Canada, for the filming of *The House by the Lake*. This was my first visit to this beautiful, immaculate city on the shores of Lake Ontario. A studio driver identified me immediately as I entered the Air Canada terminal. Traveling from the airport toward the impressive Toronto skyline and the CN Tower, I was curious to know how he recognized me, "Oh, Denver said to look for the best dressed guy getting off the plane."

Best dressed? I hope so. Thanks to my Dad, I've always taken pride in my appearance, and through the sixties to the 90s; my yearly dry cleaning bill was always around $400. Still, it's interesting though how others perceive us.

In the lobby of the Waldorf-Astoria Hotel, Denver and I laughed how this shabby Toronto version was a far cry from its New York counterpart. This Canadian production was the *Woman Terrorized* genre and starred Brenda Vaccaro and Don Stroud. You may remember Don from the many psychotic roles he played with Eastwood, Shelley Winters, etc. He was a regular at the Left Bank, so it would be like old home week seeing him again.

The next morning an early call had us leaving the hotel at six for the Kleinburg Studios, about thirty minutes north from downtown Toronto. The script had the usual assortment of action—nothing Denver and I hadn't done before. I would stunt double Brenda in the car chase and another actor in a fire gag. First off, the blatant use of weed and booze by the cast and crew amazed me. Some of these folks were drinking brandy and smoking pot at 7am. At wrap, I hopped in to drive the passenger van back to Toronto, when a crewmember lit a joint. It was about 33° outside and I suggested he lose it or get out. That's all I needed, to get stopped driving in a foreign country with a guy-smoking pot.

Denver and I performed the car work and started to plan the fire gag. The script called for the flaming actor to flee from a boathouse built at the end of a dock and run toward the shore. We checked out the lake location and the existing dock, where the boathouse was to be constructed. The strong offshore breeze caused me to rethink the logistics of this stunt. The unrelenting off-shore wind would whip the flames around me if I turned my back to them. I then suggested the boathouse be built closer to shore, so I could run from the boathouse, down the dock toward the water, with my face in the wind all the way.

But Denver and I differed vehemently as to how this fire gag was to be performed. I decided not to do the stunt and returned to Hollywood. Denver hired a local Canadian stunt man, Bobby Hanna, for the fire shot. Hanna ended up in the hospital with third degree burns. Also, I still can't imagine why Bobby wasn't wearing fire-resistant gloves.

It's now December 2, 1975 and Don Taylor is directing *The Great Scout & Cat House Thursday* in Durango, Mexico. This turn-of-the-century western epic starred Lee Marvin, Oliver Reed, Strother Martin, Robert Culp, Sylvia Miles and Kay Lenz. I was there to double Kay, driving a run-a-way horse and wagon. Since my first day in the business I had been warned that, "Sooner or later, you'll be on location in Mexico and if you're going to patronize the local saloons, don't piss anyone off. They all pack pistols and they'll blow you away as look at you."

It makes sense, look at the California Latino gangs and the astronomical crime rate. This modus operandi has been their way of life for centuries. Just because the illegal aliens step across the border isn't going to change their inbred way of life. Yeah, I am a cynic—one, who has watched Los Angeles, my hometown become a diseased, crime-ridden, Third World Country.

Departing LAX on AeroMexico, twenty minutes later we were aimed at the Tijuana Airport for a customs check. And, I do mean aimed. It was as if the pilot proclaimed, "There it is!" and, like a dive-bomber, went for the runway, touching down for a bouncing nine-point landing. It was then on to La Paz on this milk run. The many landings helped him to finally make a perfect three-point landing in Durango. A driver took us to the Mexican Court Motel. I exited the car and was suddenly plunged into darkness and I mean pitch black.

To this day, with the exception of my photo darkroom, I've never been anywhere that dark, but within thirty seconds the motel looked like a Vatican High Mass as flickering candles produced isolated spots of illumination. Obviously, these blackouts were a frequent occurrence.

I was also warned about Montezuma's Revenge, the Mexican equivalent of our Outhouse Trots or the old Texas Two Step. The main cause was the water, so to combat this malady; I decided to limit my diet to what I found in the motel lobby office—a package of Fig Newtons made in Houston, Texas, and two beers a night. That was it.

On the fourth day into my self-imposed diet, stunt coordinator Jerry Gatlin asked me if I was finally going to eat. Declining, I opted for an iced bottle of Coca Cola. Finishing lunch, Jerry said, "C'mon." I followed him to the Mexican caterer's truck. Finding the cook, he said, "We had goat for lunch?" "Si, Senor." "I bet I can tell you what color it was ... black and white." "Oh, si, Senor. How you know?" Jerry opened his hand to reveal a one-inch square cube chunk of meat covered with black and white hair and dripping with gravy. "There is a God," I thought. The cook must have just taken a machete to the animal and just tossed it in the pot.

Chapman camera crane driver, Kenny Reed, was hospitalized, and almost died after a disentary bout caused excretions from every orifice in his body.

In the coffee shop I found myself seated across the table from Lee Marvin. Flanking my right was Strother Martin and my left, Oliver Reed. Many actors are wonderful storytellers and these three were unmatchable. Lee related a tale when he and Keenan Wynn were diehard bikers. In the early sixties, Big Bear, California, hosted a week of motorcycle races, attracting thousands of bike enthusiasts, including the infamous Hell's Angels. Admired by the gangs for their macho personas, on and off the screen, Lee and Keenan were made honorary members of the clubs. The festivities, the races and the booze produced a lively week in this beautiful mountain resort an hour and a half from Los Angeles. So much so, the San Bernardino County Sheriff's Department arrested thirty of the gang.

Hearing about the incarceration, Lee suggested to Keenan that their appearance in court might be beneficial to the "Boys." The next day Lee and Keenan entered a crowded courtroom as the thirty Hell's Angels were ushered into the defendant's area. Dressed in cycle boots, jeans, T-shirt and vest the first member was brought before the judge. The judge eyed the biker from head to toe, "Nice outfit you have there. What does the MF mean?" referring to the monogrammed vest. "Awww Judge, you know what it means." "No, I don't. What does the MF mean?" repeated the judge. The biker spied a "Don't be chicken, Man" stare from his comrades, turned back to the judge, "Mother Fucker!" "Thirty Days!" said the judge with a rap of the gavel. Two bailiffs quickly hustled the biker to the slammer as the next defendant, wearing an identical vest, stepped up as the judge addressed him with "Nice outfit you have there. What does the MF mean?" This biker turned toward his twenty-eight remaining buddies, all staring at him, slowly twisted back toward the bench, "Your Honor, it means Motorcycle Fan!" The judge rapped the gavel, "Ten dollars. Pay the clerk." The judge continued as the other twenty-eight bikers each repeated, "Motorcycle Fan." Lee said, "Can you imagine how pissed-off that one sonofabitch was when he got out thirty days later?" I laughed so hard my jaw hurt.

Turning to Oliver Reed, I mentioned how much I enjoyed his portrayal of Bill Sykes in *Oliver!* Also his mid-sixties British film called *The Box.* Politely, he replied, "I wasn't in that film." Turning to Lee, I described one of Lee's most famous films. With a raised eyebrow, Lee interrupted, "I wasn't in that film." Oliver Reed was now looking at me like I was crazy and quickly excused himself. Lee's eyes twinkled, and then he and Strother busted up laughing. After returning home, I found *The Jokers* was the Reed film I had seen years before.

To Johnny Carson on NBC's *Tonight Show*, Lee played down his own US Marine Corp Iwo Jima heroics during WWII, but described TV's

Captain Kangaroo's Bob Keeshan as the bravest soldier in the War. Lee told one hellava story and years later it was revealed that Keeshan had completed boot camp as the War ended, and had never served in combat duty. Lee's sense of humor knew no bounds.

In a wig and billowing dress, doubling actress Kay Lenz, I surveyed the area where the run-a-way wagon would sail off the two thousand foot cliff. My duty was to jump before it did. Production manager Pepi Lenzi drove up in his new, red, Chevy truck, exited through the passenger door. Staring at the proposed path leading to the deep ravine, I glanced back as Pepi's truck was slowly moving toward the cliff's edge. In bloomers et al, I ran past Pepi and dove head first into the truck's cab through the open right door. With both hands I plunged the brake pedal to the floorboard. The truck skidded to a stop as I shoved the transmission lever into park and pulled the emergency brake. I crawled out of the cab as a shaken Pepi ran toward me. All he could do was silently point to the edge of the cliff, ten feet away. Later, I thought to myself, "What the hell are you doing?" With that wig and wardrobe, a simple miscalculation would have sent the truck and me on a nice two thousand foot high fall. Well, it seemed like a good idea at the time.

Posing for a photo with Strother Martin, he whispered, "Watch this" as his wife stood next to the photographer. I stood motionless as his hand almost grabbed my crotch. He was wild.

I never worked with Don Taylor again; in fact, Don didn't work much after that film, although we did talk on the phone a couple of times. Also, I have never have returned to Mexico, per the pact I made with God and I prefer it this way.

Returning on December 6 the marriage manure hit the fan. In my absence, the mad JAP gave away every item, gift or otherwise, that linked me to any previous female, including the ravaging of my fifteen-year-old restaurant matchbook collection. She destroyed every matchbook noting any female companion's name and date. Sadly, 98% of those Los Angeles Restaurant Row and San Fernando Valley dining establishments from the forties through the 80s no longer exist.

Previously, during this wedded discord, we would take a weekend jaunt to Ventura's Pierpont Inn. Rather than dine in the elegant restaurant she always insisted on room service. Between courses she'd flip through the Gideon bible because she'd heard there was a $5 bill in each copy. During a movie, she would leave the theater seat—sit in the lobby, smoking a cigarette, waiting for the film to end. In the apartment, I watched more TV during this union than in my previous twenty-five years of my life.

Months before, a lengthy conversation with her father produced no solution, although he offered to send us on an all paid, two-week trip to Hawaii, "to work everything out." I declined, but later regretted my decision. As in the *Heartbreak Kid* film starring Charles Grodin, she obviously would have stayed in the Maui condominium and I could have enjoyed the island with newfound friends.

Chivalrously, I paid off all of her outstanding bills, including a $1000 tab at Georgio's of Beverly Hills, and provided maid service every other week. Though she admitted a desire to continue her career, she worked a total of 12½ days, citing several reasons for quitting; the job wasn't challenging, it was too far to drive, she didn't like the people, and finally, (drum roll, please!) they're all trying to get in my pants. She then spent the remainder her time watching TV, sleeping and desecrating our marriage vows. (The maid would later tell of having to vacuum around her.)

My futile attempts to appease her constant complaining about "being closed in" accounted for the four address changes in eleven months from a comfortable Studio City one-bedroom to a spacious three-bedroom apartment—one block from Bob Hope's Toluca Lake Mansion. Apropos, I recalled the line about "Why women have two set of lips—so they can piss and moan at the same time!"

Later, self-analysis made me realize that I had created the problem; I had caved in to her every whim, giving her no reason to do anything but lie around, watch TV and eat bonbons.

Suspicions of her infidelity prompted me to ask the bride of 11½ months to "swear on your father's life that you never cheated on me." Like a cornered rat, she faked crying and didn't know whether to shit or go blind – she wouldn't pledge her word, so I told her to take a hike. An enormous load had been lifted from my shoulders. Leopards don't change their spots, so you change leopards.

A year later, while viewing Johnny Carson's Tonight Show, a guest therapist discussed Agoraphobia, the fear of open places. This was the first time I had ever heard of this condition, which wasn't even mentioned during my candid discussion with her psychiatrist while we were married. I wanted to know what her problem was and after the visit, I knew less than when I entered. Most shocking was an $80 charge for his consultation.

Regardless, if that really was her problem, it was no excuse for her lies and infidelity. To quote Confucius: "Never get involved with any girl with more problems than yourself."

Unequivocally, I want it understood that I never accused her of having an extramarital affair at Disneyland; I only said she was *fucking goofy*.

Early in December, Dick Dial called me for a fire gag on Columbia's *Helter Skelter*, directed by his buddy, Tom Gries, whom I hadn't worked with since *Rat Patrol*.

It was a simple shot, Dick pulled me from a van with my back and arms ablaze, threw me to the ground to extinguish the flames as the van's gas tank exploded. My old buddy special effects man Roger George rigged the scene and it was perfect. Dick and I received $350 and $500, respectively, but Lorimar was a notoriously slow pay. When the check didn't arrive after two weeks, I phoned and announced I'd sit in their payroll office until I received my check – and I did, for three hours on December 24. I quickly hammered the check and drove to the Pierpont Inn for Christmas.

While enjoying a drink in the Pierpont Inn lounge I made another pact with God – please get me out of this wedded debacle and I'll be content to forever spend the rest of my life in a saloon.

Seven days remained of 1975 and I was more than happy to place this year as far behind me as possible.

CHAPTER 18

1976

January 1976 opened with a visit to attorney Ben Waxman to begin my divorce proceedings. Stunt man Jimmy Casino served the divorce papers to the soon-to-be-ex, and then apologized to her. Oh well.

California's divorce law was swift and I was pleased the ball was in motion. However, when Waxman said, "No problem, I once had offices next to her attorney on Wilshire Boulevard," I swallowed hard. Hearing, "No problem," made me recall Ivan Volkman's directive. For me, every lawyer I have ever known, whether hired by me, for me or against me, have screwed me royally.

A friend, Albert Baxendale said, "In the Bible, Christ speaks better of the prostitutes than he does of lawyers." Shakespeare's Henry VI also declared, "First, you kill all the lawyers." The Three Stooges frequently confronted the dastardly legal firm of Dewey, Cheatham & Howe. However, my favorite line comes from veteran character actor Henry Hull in *Jesse James*, starring Tyrone Power and Henry Fonda, as he portrayed a newspaper publisher, "If we are ever to have law and order in the West, the first thing we got to do is line up all the lawyers and shoot'em down like dogs."

One day, Albert's always skeptic, bible-toting wife, Jane Baxendale, challenged me, whereas I said, "It's in the Good Book." Instantly, she was on me like a duck on a June bug, mocking, "Really, just where in the

Bible?" I smiled, "The Book of Fred." Albert burst out laughing and Jane didn't talk to me for six months.

Previously, the ex-wife was briefly employed as Joan River's personal secretary and related the gory tales of the bitchy comedienne's infidelities with her male hairdresser. Incongruously, when River's husband, Edgar, committed suicide, ol' Joanie suddenly became the grieving widow. Rumor has it; Joan Rivers had so many face-lifts she ended up with a goatee.

For two months, Wally Rose had promised to loan me $4000 to cover my divorce proceedings. Finally, a call to him from the SAMP office proved he didn't walk like he talked. Bear Hudkins had heard my conversation, "Where ya going now?" "Household Finance," I answered. "Wait a minute." Bear dialed the phone and moments later said, "C'mon, you're driving."

Entering the Great Western Savings & Loan office at Ventura and Reseda Boulevards in Tarzana, we were greeted by the smiling manager, "Good morning, Mr. Hudkins," then presented Bear with a $4000 check made out in my name. I was shocked and gratified and a month later I handed Bear $4400 cash. He refused the ten percent interest, but I insisted, "Bear, take the $400 to Santa Anita and parlay it into another four grand." Bear was a lifesaver and a true great friend.

Norman Mailer put it succinctly: "You don't know anything about a woman until you meet her in court." Attorney Waxman, an Agent of the Devil, received his $4000 fee and after our final court appearance billed me for an additional $2000. Infuriated, I sent him a *Wayne Letter** and never heard another word from the phony, lying sonofabitch.

*Wayne Letter: A detailed description of the situation, listing dates, times and the bullshit perpertrated on me. My writing partner Bob Louden once suggested: "Forget your book; just publish your Wayne Letters."

Six months later, the dissolution of marriage divorce papers arrived. In total, I had amassed an annulment and a divorce: but legally I had been married only once. This seemed a farce. Nevertheless, I concluded that my track record to choose a life companion rated a big zero, and to this day have refrained from pursuing such an arrangement.

The JAP, however, promptly married the guy she was banging while I was on my film locations. That union lasted 4½ months and, at last count, she had been married and divorced five or six times.

Continuing her life of lies and deceit, she wangled her way on to a TV quiz show, proclaiming she had been a dancer on a Bob Hope USO show. What bullshit. The closest she had ever been to Bob Hope was five feet from a TV set.

The following articles appeared in the California Bar Journal in April and May 2003.

LOS ANGELES—A San Fernando Valley woman who assumed the identity of an attorney with a similar name, then practiced law for about seven months in 2002, pleaded guilty today to one count each of identity theft and grand theft, the District Attorney's office announced.

Deputy District Attorney William Penzin of the Justice System Integrity Division said the plea from Suzi Schor, 56, came before the start of her scheduled preliminary hearing before Los Angeles Superior Court Judge David Horwitz. The defendant will be remanded into custody on April 29, 2003, and held in the county jail until sentencing, Penzin said. He said a sentencing date would be scheduled at a later time.

The prosecutor said that in April 2002, Schor assumed the identity of Susan Schorr, a real attorney who is working for the United Nations in Switzerland. The real Susan Schorr had placed her State Bar of California membership on inactive status while she was out of the country. The State Bar is the licensing organization for California lawyers.

The defendant discovered the similarity in names, contacted the State Bar and asked that the status be reactivated, Penzin said. She paid the required dues and was sent a bar card necessary to practice law in state courts, he said.

Penzin said the defendant worked for two law firms in the San Fernando Valley. She was fired from the first job after about six months and had joined the second law firm when the charade was discovered. The prosecutor said the defendant had joined a San Fernando Valley bar association and a friend of the real Susan Schorr saw the named listed. The friend contacted the real Susan Schorr in Switzerland and as a result, the case was turned over to the Justice System Integrity Division for investigation.

Phony lawyer pleads guilty to two felonies

Suzi Schor, a nonlawyer who impersonated an inactive California attorney with a similar name, pleaded guilty last month to grand theft and identity theft.

Schor was sentenced to nine months in the Los Angeles County jail, and was ordered to repay two law firms who hired her nearly $50,000.

As part of her probation, she also was ordered to use her real name at all times.

Deputy District Attorney Bill Penzin said Schor was paid almost $50,000 in wages by law firms in Calabasas and Encino who hired her as a workers' compensation attorney in 2002.

But she was not a licensed attorney and had conscripted the legal background of a colleague and presented it as her own on her resume. As her legal career evolved, Schor changed her name to Susan Schorr, an inactive lawyer who is licensed in California and works in Switzerland. Investigators believe she found Schorr by surfing the net.

Shortly before being hired by Adelson, Testan & Brundo in Calabasas, Schor changed the State Bar status of Schorr from inactive to active, paid bar dues, changed Schorr's address to her own Woodland Hills address, received a bar membership card and ultimately changed the spelling of Susan Schorr's name to Suzi Schor.

Penzin credited State Bar investigator Michael Henderson with breaking the case and tracking Schor down. "He did a good job," Penzin said.

I thought long and hard about including the previous account of the ex's illegal antics, but believed, as I have for five decades, that Karma's a bitch. Or could it be that her pendulum of evil just swung back to slap her in the face? It's your call.

Moulin Rouge (Red Windmill) was the classic 1953 film biography of French painter Henri de Toulouse-Lautrec, directed by John Huston. Jose Ferrer, brilliantly portraying the genius artist, said it best: "The wise woman patterns her life on the theory and practice of modern banking. She never gives her love, but only lends it on the best security and at the highest rate of interest."

An intelligent man also proclaimed, "Most of the troubles we face come from saying 'yes' too soon and 'no' too late. During my 34th year I had an epiphany; I began saying "No" to requests I didn't want to do. So often we acquiesce to others demands, knowing full well we're making a mistake. Suddenly I felt relieved, and soon these requests stopped coming. I haven't become a recluse, but just contented to do whatever I want to do without any encumberances.

Unlike most individuals who have a job to go to every Monday morning, I didn't, and was flat-ass broke, relegated to eating peanut butter and jelly sandwiches. To reiterate, most movie folks have no idea when their next job will be. During this marriage interlude, I had filmed on locations in Georgia, Canada and Mexico and, while in absentia, the ex-wife's spending habits managed to deplete our joint bank accounts of over $50,000 in eleven months. Later, a buddy reprimanded me for not having a separate bank account, emphasizing the need for stashed cash. Well, live and learn, hopefully.

Reevaluating 1975, I mused what the $50,000 would have produced had I hired certified young ladies. I figured, if you're going to get screwed, get the best. At least you're dealing with a true professional. During my formative years, Mom reminded me to always treat my date with respect, warning that you wouldn't want someone to mistreat your sisters, or something to that effect. I've often wondered if it was an admonition or a curse?

Each bride was named Susan, from Chicago, and both of these societal misfits arrived with only a single suitcase of possessions. Each time, I paid off their outstanding bills, also personifying two age-old adages: "A fool and his money are soon married." and "Kindness is often mistaken for weakness."

My marital concept was to give each bride everything my mother didn't have. But, I guess I'm a slow learner. It later dawned on me that it took my parents decades to attain all they amassed, and these two had a fully furnished abode, immediately after the "I do's."

And if I sound cynical, I am. These two marriage endeavors were choices I made, and I have no one else to blame. It's unfortunate it's taken decades to reach this conclusion, but I now realize it was a futile search to find a replacement for my True Love, Toni Evans was the one and only, and I dare say there would never be another.

I'm not a Mama's boy. But for every occasion, holiday or otherwise, Mom always topped my list. She was the one I could turn to for advice, and for the emotional boost I needed.

Happily, I was now alone again, but not lonely. My opening question to the ladies was, "Are you married or are you happy?" or more apropos, "You're not a cop are you?"

Thank God, for his divine timing, I received a work call for Mel Brooks' *Silent Movie*, a "unique" excursion into creating a modern film without sound.

Filming a movie, *MOS – With Out Sound*, on the University of California at Irvine campus in Orange County, a mile from the John Wayne Airport, was odd as the jet planes flew overhead and not hearing the director yell, "Cut." *MOS* was derived from the early talkies, when Germanic film directors immigrated to Hollywood and couldn't pronounce "W." Hence, "With Out Sound" became "Mit Out Sound."

Traditionally, noisy aircraft is a movie company's greatest nemesis. However, even though this was a "silent movie" the soundman recorded a *wild track*—probably as protection should Brooks later decide to include sound effects. Brooks' films have an open door—the decisions, whether individual or by committee are hard to come by.

At the wardrobe trailer, I was pleased to see Patricia Norris, the film's costume designer (and one of director Dick Bartlett's four out of 5 former wives named Pat), again. We hadn't worked together since *The Master Gunfighter.*

My particular film scene required me to be an injured victim arriving at the hospital by ambulance. Patricia meticulously wrapped me in rolls of gauze bandages from head to toe. When she finished, I resembled King Tut's little brother.

The expansive walkways surrounding the UCI medical building involved Paul Newman driving a souped-up wheelchair, pursued by Brooks, Marty Feldman and DeLuise in their motorized chairs. We were discussing the various aspects of the shot when suddenly I was face to face with Paul Newman. Extending his hand and with the baby blues peering down at me, he said, "Jesse, Hi, I'm Paul Newman." I almost said, "No Shit!" Without going into all the complementary platitudes, I'll just say I was very impressed—Paul Newman was a class act.

Marty Feldman was congenial and candid when I asked about his zany TV comedy episodes for the British Broadcasting Company I had watched for years; "Oh, the BBC provided a camera crew and off we went," he mused.

During the rehearsal I was the injured, bandaged patient on a stretcher, carried from an ambulance by two white-uniformed attendants, stuntmen Dick Warlock and George Wilbur, toward the building. When Newman roars toward us, Dick and George drop the stretcher and all three of us leap over the cement railing and hang there. After the chase participants pass, I returned to my reclined position on the stretcher with my two attendants. Newman once again appears and we repeated the previous moves.

"This is ridiculous," I said, "Doing this same bit twice is repetitive," and proposed that after the second pass, Dick and George should just "toss me and the stretcher over the railing, and then rush into the building." Dom DeLuise heard my suggestion and immediately went to Paul Newman, who then loudly proclaimed the idea to an agreeable Brooks. A two-tier parallel with pads was set beyond the wall for me to land on and we then did the shot in one take.

If Brooks had known this suggestion was my idea, his caustic, demeaning reaction would have been, "What the hell does a stunt man know about comedy?" Fortunately, I was weaned on the Buster Keaton, Hal Roach and Max Sennett comedies, and I do know.

Once again, freed from the bonds of unholy matrimony, I returned to the bar scene, and traveled with a former girlfriend for a quick getaway to Solvang, a quaint Danish community of gabled buildings and windmills, shops and restaurants north of Santa Barbara in the Santa Inez valley. Cruising along California's picture-perfect coastal route, this lovely lady's amorous desires prompted me to adjust my El Camino's tilt steering wheel, which added a whole new meaning to a car's "headroom." Well, the title is "Confessions of a…"

Several of us adjourned from the SAMP office to lunch at Studio City's Albion's restaurant when Steve McQueen with Ali McGraw entered. Steve greeted me, "Glad to see you're finally getting older." Seventeen years had passed since we had first met on *The Larry Finley Show* when I was 17.

Stunt man buddy Chuck Hicks called me to San Francisco to double David McCallum on the *Bert D'Angelo/Superstar* TV series starring Paul Sorvino. My first reaction was, "Ah Ha!" after twelve years I'm doubling him again. At San Francisco's oldest building, the Delores Mission, built in 1776, David cordially greeted me as if I were his long lost brother.

Tony and Frank, the SFPD cops I'd known from *The Streets of San Francisco*, were again ably handling the traffic and crowd control, as Chuck and I performed the ubiquitous car chase. Often, many of the vehicles we drive in films are on their last legs and this production was no exception. My white, battered van checked out for what we had to do, but I wouldn't have given it another hundred more road miles.

One shot called for the van, speeding down a steep San Francisco hill, through an intersection, continuing down the street and career into a 90° skid around a corner. Instead of hiring a legit stunt woman, my female passenger was the show's local-hired stand-in, undoubtedly placed there to make some extra bucks by a production friend.

The walkie-talkie squawked, "Action" and we sped downhill toward the intersection. SFPD's Tony, took one look and began motioning for me to slow down, but I wanted to get airborne, and that we did, as all four wheels left the pavement. The van's rear wheels landed first, followed by the front, hitting hard, as both sun visors plopped down. This caused my young lady passenger to burst into a shrill, nervous laugh, which continued until we skidded around the corner to a stop. I wouldn't have been surprised if she ran for a change of underwear, and I'll bet that day was the beginning and end of her stunt career.

That evening, Chuck suggested we have dinner at *The Gold Spike*, a quaint Mom and Pop Italian restaurant in North Beach. A small blackboard listed three main entrees and, at once, before ordering, we were welcomed with a tureen of Minestrone soup, a basket of Italian bread, butter, followed by a huge salad. Without a doubt, this was one of the most delectable dinners I have ever devoured and gladly placed a five dollar tip with the tab's total of $6-$7.00. Chuck, frugal as usual, cautioned that I "shouldn't spoil them," "Are you kidding?" I said, "This dinner, would have cost five times as much in L.A. and not taste half as delicious." I grabbed my ten bucks and replaced it with a twenty. *The Gold Spike* disappeared forever in 2006.

Actor Bill Bixby directed the next chase sequence at the San Francisco International Airport, involving Chuck, doubling detective Sorvino, as he makes a valiant effort to stop a criminal from escaping in a two-seater aircraft.

On "Action," the plane taxied from the hanger as Chuck raced the unmarked police sedan to block its path. Chuck explained to the local pilot that because of the camera's point of view the plane could stop ten feet from the car and it would look close. The shot was fine, but Bixby wanted the aircraft closer to the car. On take two, Chuck skidded to a stop, again blocking the escape route; but the plane continued its path. The propeller sliced through the vehicle like a giant can opener, as Chuck steadfastly held his position amid the shattering glass shards and sheared metal.

All aircraft mishaps require the immediate notification of the Federal Aviation Administration, stipulating that the accident scene must not be disturbed. So, the crash was written into the story and filming continued around the immobile vehicles, providing an even better scenario than what was originally scripted.

Chuck Hicks always had a good sense of humor, "It must be great to be a bisexual, you walk down the street and everything looks good."

Later, at the SAMP office, I quoted Chuck, who immediately denied saying the line.

I didn't blame him, like a bunch of old ladies the rumor mongers were ready to pounce. A minor work bruise or injury that healed in a week had these revelers declaring you were still laid up six months later. If you added a few extra pounds over the holidays, they had you wearing Orson Wells' hand-me-downs. Any innocent comment could be misconstrued, distorted, exaggerated and used against you. These clowns had me married and divorced as many times (8) as Rooney.

A director buddy asked me to shoot glider footage for his film's opening credits. Flying out of Palmdale's El Mirage airstrip, the glider pilot pulled a lever to cut us loose from the tow plane at 5000 feet. We then performed several figure eight turns before a final left wingover. I suspected his "I don't think we have enough altitude to return to the airfield" was a ruse to get a rise out of me, but I figured if we ditched, we were relatively safe in the flat open desert, sparse with scraggly Joshua trees. Flying silently like a bird was an exhilarating experience, and I rolled the camera again as we set down on the runway with a perfect three-point landing.

Dave Cass, stunt coordinating *Robbers and Sinners*, a Tom Sawyer-Huck Finn movie-of-the-week, said I was too tall to double the kid actors, but he wanted my opinion, "There's a card game and the lads are spying on the gamblers from above. The old rafters give way and they crash onto the table." Cass was in a quandary, so I advised using two dummies (the stuffed kind!) to eliminate any injuries, "It's a dead fall and there's no way for protection. Just drop the dummies with some debris and Fuller's Earth, and your next shot are the actors on the floor in the rubble." Cass agreed, but supposedly the director insisted on using stunt doubles. Little Bobby Porter was brought in and Cass found a local stunt gal in Atlanta. They did the fall and the girl broke her arm. On the screen, all you saw was "something" fall through the frame in a cloud of dust. You could have dropped a sack of potatoes and never noticed the difference.

It was a cut-a-way shot during a car chase and I needed a guy to ride a bike into a two-foot high brick wall and sail over the handlebars. Like a stair fall, the faster to go the easier it is to hit and roll. But this terrified fellow performed one level above slow motion. On the second take he was a bit faster, and I suggested that the cameraman shoot it at 20 frames per second instead of the normal 24fps to speed up the action, and it worked.

On *Griffin and Phoenix: A Love Story*, starring Peter Falk and Jill Clayburgh, between car chases, I watched as costume supervisor Kent James zapped another crewmember during a spray bottle water fight. Suddenly, the assistant director called him to "spritz Peter"— Hollywood's method to show beads of facial perspiration with the water mixed with glycerin or mineral oil. Holding the spray bottle eight inches from Falk's face, he gave the lever a quick squeeze as Peter flinched, and exclaimed, "Sonofabitch, right in the good eye!" Kent had forgotten to turn the bottle's nozzle to *spray*.

For me, Falk's funniest line came from *The Cheap Detective*, a parody of *Casablanca* and *The Maltese Falcon*, as he imitated Bogart, "I'll meet ya at the corner of Third and Bull Dyke."

Baretta stunt coordinator and double for Robert Blake, Ronnie Rondell, called me to double a Japanese ninja, actor John Fujioka hanging down an elevator shaft. We did the shot and I grabbed a cup of Java. Blake sat in his tall director's chair and our eyes met. Joining him, he quizzically asked, "Don't I know you?" I had been warned to not address him as Bobby, as he was called when he was *Little Beaver* back in the 1940s *Red Ryder* westerns starring Wild Bill Elliot. "Yeah Robert, we did a fight on *Ben Casey* fifteen years ago." He suddenly beamed and we conversed for ten minutes without his usual Brooklynese persona of dees, dems and dows. A second A.D. appeared, "Mr. Blake, we need you on the set," and Robert immediately resumed his New York street talk dialect.

The Universal Studio "suits" seemingly ignored Blake's $65,000 dressing room renovation demands. *Baretta* producer Charles "Diz" Dismukes confided, "He'll eventually get the dressing room, but if we gave it to him without a fight he'd be back next week for something else."

Robert Blake was found not guilty for the alleged murder of his wife. When this first hit the news in April 2001, I received a call from an old stunt man buddy who related a lunch with Blake six months previously, who asked him to perform a certain deed. Taken aback, the veteran stunt man said, "Hey, that's not what I do," quickly finished his salad and exited. I then asked him what he would have done if the prosecution had subpoenaed him. "Oh, I would have denied everything. I first met Blake on *PT 109*, and he's given me a lot of work on *Baretta* over the years."

Subsequently, Blake had allegedly made the same request to three other stunt men who were witnesses for the prosecution. These three turned "states eveidence" volunteering to testify as a precaution should they be accused as co-conspirators in the murder.

Stunt coordinator Ted White called me for the *Black Oak Conspiracy*, an independent, low budget, film shooting in Auburn, a gold-rush community, east of Sacramento. Effects had built a plaster composition head impression of the great veteran character actor Douglas Fowley, best known as the frazzled movie director in *Singin' In The Rain*, and filled it with two pounds of ground meat and a baggy of fake blood. The head sat anchored above my head and shoulders, set to explode when veteran actor Albert Salmi fired the shotgun. At that point I was to be jerked backward on piano wires. The head exploded, but the backward jerk motion by two grips was off cue. Had we used an air ratchet or filmed it in separate cuts the shot would have worked. Furthermore, Salmi was rightfully angered – after a piece of shrapnel from the exploding head narrowly missed his face.

Erik Cord was set to do a Black Oak fire gag, for the movie scene within the movie, playing a stunt man. He was suited up, but there was a delay until cameras finally rolled. I was playing a camera operator and heard a muffled Erik, "Ummuuuaaarrr." An actor next to me whispered, "What'd he say?" I leaned close, whispered, "He said he's out of air." The actor yelled, "Oh shit!" We ran to Erik and stripped open his facemask as others sprayed him with a fire extinguisher. The filming delay had depleted his three and a half minute air supply.

I got my biggest laugh when the production coordinator told the producer there was a problem with the dailies "end slate." He replied, "What's an *end slate*?" The business had indeed changed.

Byron Quisenberry invited Dave Cass, Gary Jensen and me to the

London Bridge's Fifth Anniversary celebration. From LAX's Imperial Highway terminal we joined a planeload of L.A.'s local TV celebrities, including Ralph Story and Kelly Lange, for the hour flight to Arizona's Lake Havasu on the Colorado River. Relocating the famous English landmark, brick by brick, was the brainchild of Industrialist Robert McCulloch. His beautiful wife, former actress Joanne Dru (game show host Peter Marshall's sister) was the perfect hostess.

A shindig official decreed we should perform our stunt fight during the lavish barbeque dinner, but gave a stern warning to avoid the main table of guests, Arizona's Governor, the Lord Mayor of England and their wives. I suggested we perform *after* everyone had eaten, just prior to the stage show, so we would have the audience's complete attention. That idea was nixed by Quisenberry, so on cue Cass and I did our routine, while Byron and Jensen mixed it up. The elite diners thought it was a real donnybrook and, as I suspected, took one look, figured it was a real fight and promptly buried their faces to ignore us,. Jensen, then, as if he were on a rail, plowed into the main guest table, toppling a carafe of red wine into the Governor's wife's lap, drenching her strapless, lime-green gown. Pissed off didn't come close to describing her rage.

For the stage show, cowboy actor Chill Wills performed an emotional, tearful soliloquy as Dave and I blended into the buffet line to enjoy a generous supply of delicious barbeque ribs and Margaritas before returning to LAX that evening at 10pm.

The Left Bank once again was jumping as we celebrated a producer's new production deal at Universal Studios—tossing a wad of bills on the bar, he shouted, "Green Lizards for everyone." Most of us had only heard of the drink, and were more than willing to share his joy—watched as bartender Lori, a pretty brunette, mixed this potent potable concoction consisting of vodka, 151 rum and Green Chartreuse, and served it flaming.

We were all into our third or fourth Lizard, but no one was counting. With hormones raging and enough booze to eliminate all inhibitions, I whispered to the blonde seated next to me, she smiled, "Okay!" Leaping from her bar seat, she hurried to the nearest red-leather booth, scooted off her slacks and black lace panties. Moments later, in the adjoining booths, five or six other couples were engaged in all forms of sexual activities. Lori's bright smile beamed as our eyes locked, sparking the proverbial electricity. Two days later this 5-foot-9 doll face moved in with me for a three-month stay. Lori was a sweet lady and I'm sorry I let her getaway.

Bill Couch called me for Dino De Laurentiis' ballyhooed remake of *King Kong*. I had seen the original 1933 version in 1948 in re-release, and was anxious to see this version of one of my favorite classic films.

Arriving on MGM's Stage 26, the first face to greet me was my old buddy, Joe Sawyers, the film's transportation coordinator. After Carl Reiner's *The Comic* was completed, Joe invited me to his spaghetti party, "I made up a little batch." The "little batch" was ten gallons of spaghetti and five gallons of meat sauce, and it was delicious, including the garlic bread. Had there been a contest, Carey Loftin would have won after refilling his plate five times.

Bill Couch explained the *King Kong* shot and the hydraulic rigged subway car that the gorilla would grab and shake. For two days we bounced around like rag dolls. Most impressive was the twenty foot, hydraulic-controlled, hand of Kong, used to grab and hold actress Jessica Lange. It was a jovial set; especially one morning when Dino entered the sound stage. Well, simply put, when Kong gives you the finger, you really know it.

While enjoying a drink at the Left Bank, a Teamster approached me, "Jess, I hear you're into cameras. Would you like an Arriflex with lenses, motor and magazines for a $1000?"

"Well yeah, but that's a hellava deal worth at least fifty grand. What's the story?" "Well, next week, Universal's got a show going to Santa Barbara and I'm driving the camera truck. The gear will just show up missing and I can get it to you by Saturday." I couldn't believe this guy would think he could get away with this heist and suggested he take a hike, but not in those words.

Paul "Tiny" Nickols from Disney's *Herbie Goes to Monte Carlo* called me to blind drive the number 53 yellow Love Bug, while stunt coordinator Dick Warlock, Jerry Brutsche and his wife, Kevin Johnston, were filming the European establishing shots in France with Art Viterelli's second unit.

Blind driving was originated with the Western films runaway wagon or stagecoach, where a hidden driver controlled a second set of reins.

"Tiny" began his film career as Jim Arness' stand-in on *Gunsmoke* in 1955, and later became a first assistant director on the series. At 6'5" and weighing in at three-fifty, he was indeed the "Gentle Giant."

The Laguna Seca Raceway near Monterey, California provided the perfect location for the famous Monte Carlo road race. On the second day of filming I arrived on the set with my stunt bag in hand as Win Phelps, the second assistant director, said, "Jesse, you're going back to L.A." "Well," I said, "this is the first time I've ever been fired off a picture." "It's not that," he smiled, "You're needed back at the studio to double Mickey Rooney on *Pete's Dragon*." A driver drove me to the motel to gather my bags, then to the Monterey airport as another Disney driver awaited at LAX. "Boy," I thought, "what star treatment. It's great to be in demand."

The next morning on the *Pete's Dragon* set a makeup man applied a full beard to match Rooney; I chuckled recalling the extent some stunt guys would go to avoid having hair applied to their faces. Sure, having your face smeared with spirit gum isn't the most pleasant experience, especially after a morning shave, but many of these guys would go ballistic. I never understood their problem. It's part of your job description and if you don't like it, get into another line of work.

Director Don Chaffey, a charming English gentleman, carefully explained the shot he wanted of me doubling Rooney, standing in the lighthouse tower when a large wave crashes through the windows and he's knocked backward, down the steps. Special effects man, Davy Lee (his brother, Danny Lee designed the special effects on *It's a Mad, Mad, Mad, Mad World*), showed me the two, fifty-five gallon drums of water that would spill down the slanted chutes into the breakaway glass windows. Together, we then arranged the large kapok stunt pad and smaller mattresses in the fall area. It was close quarters, but we carefully covered all of the sharp protrusions and were ready to shoot.

Al Wyatt, Sr. was the film's stunt coordinator. We had worked together many times over the years and I was looking forward to seeing him again. On the set I found he had moved on to another production and had turned this show over to this stunt wannabe.

Obviously new and inexperienced to stunts and stunt coordinating, he believed he had to exert his authority; suddenly jumping into the lighthouse set's recess and began moving the pads Davy and I had meticulously placed in position. "Everything's fine," I said, "We're ready to film." He ignored me and continued to stomp the padded area, compacting the pads we had carefully placed like pancakes. A stunt performer sets their catcher and anything else related to the stunt he/she is about to perform. Finally, I couldn't take it any longer, "Get the fuck out of here." He just looked at me and didn't move. "If you don't leave, I will. Get out." He still didn't get it as Davy Lee shook his head in disbelief. I then profanely related the manner in which stunt coordinators hire the right person for the job and the importance of each stunt performer to rig their own stunts. He slowly reacted. My words seemed to make sense to him. He left the set and we got the shot in one take.

One day while scanning the Stuntmen's Association's wall of stunt photos, I questioned Denver Mattson about the two fellows leaping 30 feet into a European castle's moat. It was George Robotham and this wannabee. Surprised, I said, "You're kidding, who the fuck pushed him???" Denver roared, "Those were my exact words when I heard it was him!"

Eventually, this clown's opportunistic route made him one of the town's busiest stunt coordinators and second unit directors. One said, "He spends more wining and dining than you earn in a year." Another proclaimed, "He is to the stunt business what a kazoo is to a symphony orchestra." Even Bear Hudkins summed him up, "I'd like to buy him for what he's worth and sell him for what he thinks he's worth."

Director Don Chaffey thanked me, and a Disney driver drove me to LAX for the return trip to Monterey to continue *Herbie Goes to Monte Carlo*. My grand entrance to the Laguna Seca track brought laughs when I arrived in a shiny, black, stretched Cadillac limousine. George Shorey (a buddy and my best man at the last debacle) owned the limo service. The levity ended shortly when I found I only had partial vision in my left eye—everything was blurry. Dick Warlock took me to a local hospital emergency room. The intern doctor on duty observed the condition, but seemed at a loss to make a diagnosis and simply performed an eye wash. The next morning I returned to the set and still couldn't see, but I recalled meeting a senior citizen couple who followed the race circuit in their motorhome—he was a retired medical doctor. The white haired gentleman took one look and produced a miniscule tube of ointment. "Conjunctivitis" he said, as he applied the salve beneath the eyelids, "and the water in those 55 gallon drums was dirty and contaminated." In less than an hour my vision returned to normal. Experience will always tell, I later called the emergency room and left a message for the intern describing my cure.

Second unit director Art Vitarelli had set up a ground level shot of the oncoming cars using a 35mm Eyemo camera within a crash-proof housing, resembling half a basketball. Professional race driver Max Balchowsky took one look at its position on the track and said, "I'll probably hit it." And he did, not intentionally, but simply because he forgot about his Porsche's protruding, side-mounted chrome mufflers.

Interesting mindset difference between race car drivers and stunt men: One is trained to avoid accidents and the other to create them.

The *Herbie* film company returned to Hollywood and the San Gabriel Mountains, forming the greater Los Angeles Basin, and was used to duplicate the winding roads of the Italian Alps.

I wrapped the picture on a Monday and received a work call from my buddy Gene Law at the *Emergency* TV series for Wednesday. I immediately phoned Warlock to verify I wasn't needed at Disney and accepted Gene's job. Naturally, Warlock called me the next morning to say he needed me Wednesday, but I was already committed to Gene.

The *Emergency!* stunt had me hanging unconsciously from the three hundred foot space needle at Marineland of the Pacific. With my repelling harness cinched up, it was a joy to work again with my old friend, director Georg Fenady.

We first met while he was an assistant director on Nick "Johnny Yuma" Adams' *The Rebel* TV series in 1959, produced by his brother, Andrew Fenady. We often joked about Nick's portrayal of a post-War for Southern Independence Confederate soldier sporting a "New Joisey" accent.

For years I have questioned the commonly used expression, The Civil War. Every dictionary defines *civil war* as "Two factions fighting for one government." Every informed War historian is aware the South seceded per the rights and conditions of the *then* U.S. Constitution. The *State's Rights* issue can be traced back to the United States Congressional debates of 1820-1822, an argument that continued to 1861. If you're really interested in the truth, read the memoirs by Southern writers who were in the War of Secession. And always remember: *The victors write the history books.*

Hollywood's premiere helicopter pilot, Jim Gavin and Georg Fenady mapped out a plan to photograph my precarious perch, which allowed me to look down upon the patrolling Coast Guard copters. With slow zooms and sweeping camera movements, augmented by the sad violin orchestration, the rescue unfolded as the stunt doubles, Angelo "Angie" DeMeo and George Orrison climbed the slippery pinnacle to rescue me. These more-than-capable two-card stuntmen proved membership in a stunt organization was unnecessary as they performed 90% of the *Emergency!* TV series stunts, most notably the high work.

Figuring I'd be hanging for the duration, the elimination of my morning coffee allowed me to stay in the same position for over five hours.

DeMeo, the newly appointed stunt coordinator on the show, suggested I lie in the Stokes (stretcher) as the rescue crew lowered "the injured victim" to the roof of the observation deck. By this time, the strong, afternoon, off shore winds prevailed, and I declined his offer and suggested a dummy, weighing 30 pounds, would be easier for the guys to handle in the wind, and photographically would not be discernible. It worked perfectly.

Later, I requested a $750 stunt adjustment, but DeMeo didn't agree and offered $500. Obviously, he wanted to secure his new stunt coordinator position, and also keep his budget expenditures to a minimum. A later call to Gene Law allotted me the $750 for the stunt.

When the show aired, Melinda, Gene's five-year-old daughter, asked, "Daddy, why are they playing that music?" She was right. The violins had also brought tears, to my Mom's eyes.

Dick Warlock called regarding the *Herbie Goes to Monte Carlo* shoot saying he had replaced me with stunt man Freddie Brookfield to double

Don Knotts. The shot required them to jump the VW over a picnic table, but the vehicle bottomed out when they landed. Freddie broke his back, screamed in agony as the paramedics worked for thirty minutes to extract him from the vehicle.

Precautions were taken to prevent injuries with an inflated tire tube mounted under each front seat. Normally, this device would have been enough to cushion a hard hit, but after all these years I'm still mystified as to why it happened. I don't know of anything I would have done any differently to prevent Freddie's injury.

I imagined I'd be working on Universal's *Rollercoaster*, but didn't know exactly where as my old buddy Howard Kazanjian was the film's production executive. A couple of months before principle photography started, several of us gathered at the Stuntmen's Association office. Former stunt man-turned actor, Richard Farnsworth's son, Diamond, relatively new to the business, was excited that he'd been cast as a passenger in the careening rollercoaster car crash.

The shot called for the car to be propelled down a twenty-six foot ramp, sail over the ten-foot boardwalk and crash into a breakaway building. Billy Shannon and I answered spontaneously, in unison, "You gotta stay with the car when it hits the building and it'll spit you to your pads." Diamond didn't agree. He believed it was necessary to jump as the car left the ramp to avoid being trapped in the car. Again, Billy and I argued his analogy, stating the physics of motion, momentum and the breakaway building, but Diamond was not convinced.

The *Rollercoaster* work call came through Teddy O'Toole's, at that time, the premiere answering service handling the industry's stunt performers. Stunt Coordinator Johnny Daheim set up the stunt roster to include, in addition to Diamond and myself, Pam Bebermeyer, Jade David, Bennie Dobbins, Ralph Garrett, Vic Hunsburger, Rosemary Johnson, Branscombe Richmond, Tonya Russell, Russ Saunders and John Sherrod.

The Atlantic Ocean's bone-chilling wind proved that Hollywood would once again adhere to its age-old practice to film a warm, summer scene in the 38° coldness of the fall. It was October 28, 1976, in Norfolk, Virginia, and the Ocean View Amusement Park was chosen as one of the namesake locations for *Rollercoaster*. Like other disaster films of the 1970's, an all-star cast consisting of George Segal, Richard Widmark, Henry Fonda and Timothy Bottoms was assembled.

The entire film company was housed at Norfolk's Scope Holiday Inn. The parking lot forced by the downtown area's high crime rate, resembled a concentration camp with razor wire topping the tall barbed wire fence surrounding the entire complex.

On the beachfront stunt location I was pleased to find Nick Carey was the special effects supervisor. We'd first met on the *Batman* TV series (1966) and he was one of a handful of effects men I trusted unequivocally. His meticulous concern through the years had saved me from injury and possible death in countless stunts. He made my job easy, all I had to do was listen and follow his directions.

That's how it was this day as he explained the rollercoaster car's construction, speed and trajectory. I carefully inspected the ramp from every angle. Nick's rigging looked good to me, even though I was to be one of the non-descript stunt people strolling on the boardwalk and not a rollercoaster car passenger.

Pam, Rosemary, John, Vic and Diamond had been on this location for two weeks and had previously witnessed a trial run of a rollercoaster car sailing down the ramp. For that test, Nick had his crew build a makeshift car, consisting of plywood and two-by-fours on wheels. He had explained to them that this model was bottom-heavy and the actual car to be used in the shot would act differently as it became airborne. When Nick released the car the stunt folks were aghast as it soared from the ramp, flipped and crashed, landing upside down on the sandy beach. Immediately, the hand wringing began as the stunt folks decided, as Diamond did previously, that their only chance of survival was to jump as the car left the ramp.

Adamantly, Nick continued to explain (as Billy Shannon and I did) that a breakaway, balsa wood, building would be constructed beyond the ramp to "catch and stop" the careening rollercoaster car. There was no way that car was going to turn over after colliding with the building. Through all of this, the anxious stunt group remained unconvinced.

The *Rollercoaster* shooting schedule required night filming so many of us had the evenings off, knowing that we would work before the week ended. This prompted the not-on-call cast to convert the Scope Holiday Inn hallways into a nightlong party causing its participants to sleep late. For those involved in the upcoming big stunt, this was possibly their way of releasing their tension.

However, Russ Saunders and I were American History buffs, realizing that we might never visit Virginia again, decided to take advantage of this wonderful opportunity to see the area. Conveniently, the Greyhound Bus Terminal was across the street from the hotel and, while the others partied all-night and slept late, we would rise early and grab a bus.

Williamsburg presented a wonderful insight to experience Colonial Virginia. Sitting in the pew seats of William and Mary College, arguably America's first university (though Harvard also claims this title) was an exciting and humbling encounter. So many of our nation's creators sat in those very seats.

Especially memorable in Norfolk was the elegant Roman-columned burial tomb of General Douglas MacArthur, displaying his memorabilia, dark glasses and pipe, including his olive-drab WWII staff car.

The morning of October 30, word filtered down that "tonight was the night" of the big crash. Diamond, Pam, Jade, Rosemary, Vic and John, discussed the stunts monetary worth and arranged to meet with Dayheim. They demanded $2000. Johnny balked at this figure, saying $1600 was all anyone was going to receive for the stunt, "Take or leave it." Unified, the group maintained their stance for the two grand. Later that day, I was surprised when Daheim phoned to ask if I would do the roller coaster car stunt for $1600. For months I knew exactly how this gag would work and had no reservations about it and eagerly replied, "Sure!"

Diamond, Jade, Vic and John also accepted Daheim's counter offer of $1600, but Pam and Rosemary declined. Maybe, declined is the wrong word. In the Holiday Inn lobby, Farnsworth and several others consoled Pam, who wept hysterically, while Rosemary looked on, relieved. A driver took them to their return flight to Hollywood. Personally, I believe they refused the stunt, not primarily for the money, but because they were spooked by the trial run of the flipped roller coaster car. To reiterate, if you're not content with the stunt… don't do it!!!

We had a 6:00pm Work Call and I eagerly anticipated a night of action. Scenes were being filmed prior to the "Big One," so I decided to phone my Mom, as I always did whenever I was to perform a major stunt. She was my good luck charm and it was always comforting to have her rooting in my corner. Searching, I spotted a lone phone booth at the far end of Norfolk's long carnival boardwalk. Opening the folding door, I looked down to see a large owl staring at me. It stood over a foot tall. Startled, I jumped back and called for someone to come see what I had found. When we returned to the booth seconds later, it was gone. During the long distance call, Mom assured me the owl was indeed a good luck omen and everything would go well for me this night.

The "Big Shot" was being readied. Two EMS ambulances were parked beside the midway, ominously standing-by. Having these units near-by during a stunt is S.O.P. – standard operating procedure, but nonetheless unnerving when you consider the next passenger might be yourself.

Dick Colean, one of the four camera operators, asked me to frame the shot for him. His side-angle camera would pan with the roller coaster car as it sailed down the ramp, and into the building. I had known Dick since he first tried out for the Universal Studios Tour Stunt Show in 1964. Instead, he wisely chose to go behind the camera as did his father, assistant director Chuck Colean, also a first class gentleman.

Hairdresser Lorraine Roberson worked feverishly to ensure my brown wig wouldn't come off, as I ended up doubling Rosemary Johnson, fitting perfectly into her white jumpsuit. On the set, five cameras were in place, including a 35mm Eyemo mounted in the roller coaster car's front frame. We patiently waited at the top of the ramp as Farnsworth, Hunsberger, Sharrod and Jade still maintained they should jump the moment the speeding car leaves the ramp. Screw it. I was tired of arguing about this stunt. I knew what I had to do and was prepared to do it.

Director James Goldstone yelled "Action!" and Nick released the car. Swiftly the car rolled downward, gaining speed. I was posed in a low, semi-standing position and watched as the others jumped when the car cleared the ramp.

Diamond Farnsworth, exerting his powerful legs, leaped forward and out, away from his seat in the careening roller coaster car. He landed on his knees in the sand, directly in front of the low camera on baby sticks. He toppled over like *Laugh-In*'s Arte Johnson on the tricycle. Diamond suffered a fractured pelvis and remained in traction for eight weeks.

Jade David also jumped, landing feet first in the soft sand, intending to hit and roll. Instead, she stuck like an arrow, breaking her back and was laid up for almost a year in a full body brace. Vic and John jumped into the balsa and pine wood-framed building and received a wrenched knee and a minor blow to the head, respectively.

The roller coaster car plowed exactly as I expected into the top corner of the breakaway structure. Instantly, I was propelled through the air, toward a two by four, which caught me in the stomach. I went limp, which caused me to flip over and out, toward the cardboard boxes below.

I never heard Goldstone call "Cut," so I just lay there not moving. Stunt man Bennie Dobbins reached me first and I assured him I didn't get a scratch. However, the area was strewn with bodies lying everywhere. Paramedics placed Jade and Diamond on gurneys, while John and Vic were disentangled from the debris, and then all were hustled to a local hospital.

I was ecstatic and grateful to have come through the stunt unscathed. It happened as I had pictured and predicted. As one stunt lady said, "Such instinctive responses are brought about from years of experience." Ultimately, I've maintained it must be the prerogative of the individual stunt performer to make a choice: if you're not comfortable with a stunt, don't do it.

I was still adrenaline-charged when a local TV news reporter interviewed me about the business, the actors I had doubled (Mickey Rooney), and this stunt, "Did your life pass in front of you?" "No, my life didn't," I said, "but Mickey Rooney's life did!" I was still trying to be a comedian.

We remained at the Norfolk location another couple of days, until the film footage was processed—to assure the shot was "in the can."

With little else to do before our return flight to L.A., Benny Dobbins, Tanya Lee Russell, Ralph Garrett, Branscombe Richman and Sherrill, the assistant location auditor, decided we would indulge ourselves to some fine Italian cuisine. We enjoyed an exquisite dinner, accompanied by drinks and later, after-dinner drinks. The location auditor and I were growing closer, getting cozy, when someone mentioned that Ralph had overstayed his rest room visit. Excusing myself, I went to find our wayward friend. Swinging open the men's room door, there was Ralph on his knees, with his head in the commode—worshipping at the porcelain altar.

Returning to the Scope Holiday Inn lounge, we all found a large, padded corner booth and continued our celebrating. After a few more drinks, none of us were feeling any pain. Sherill and I continued to find each other interesting. At one point I rested my head on her lap, out of view from the others in the booth. With her eyes closed and a smile she was enjoying my manipulative attention. After a few minutes, I slowly moved from beneath the table to an upright position to see the shocked stares of Bennie Dobbins and Tanya Lee Russell. Their expressions were priceless as I assumed my place next to a still smiling Sherrill. Soon after my return to Hollywood, tales of this "incident" had circulated through stunt land. To quote the old show biz adage: "As long as they spell your name right."

Though I came away from *Rollercoaster* unscathed, down the road John Sharrod and Vic Hunsberger wouldn't be so fortunate. A few years later, John would die in a traffic accident and Vic, while performing a thirty-foot high fall, would succumb to a head injury, after missing his pads.

Rollercoaster wrapped the Norfolk location to return to Hollywood for additional filming at Six Flags Magic Mountain in Valencia, California. I looked forward to Sherrill's promised visit the following week and planned a surprise get-a-way weekend for us at the Pierpont Inn. Unfortunately, she took a detour and was delayed a week. Still anxious to leave town, even for a day, Steve Lodge and I decided to drive to Santa Barbara for lunch.

I'd passed the Newbury Park turn-off to the Stagecoach Inn, north of Thousand Oaks, for many years, always promising to stop. In the 1880s it was a stagecoach way station on the route between Los Angeles and San Francisco. Forever, the history buff, I grabbed my trusty Minox 35EL camera and proceeded to shoot an exterior shot of the Inn. Suddenly, I felt a hit to the right side of my head, like someone had decked me with a baseball bat. A guy in a station wagon had backed out of the parking lot in the wrong direction and hit me. My head had struck the wagon's rear window as the bumper hit my right leg and I went down. Then, looking up, realizing the car was still moving toward me, I began rolling and kicking off the back bumper to avoid being run over. Lodge turned just in time to see me hit the ground and yelled for the driver to stop. The hospital emergency room doctor confirmed a wrist injury and suggested I check with my own orthopedic doctor.

A buddy suggested that Lodge was a Jonah. A Bad Luck Jinx! He said Lodge was also present when Dave Cass, Neil Summers and Bruce Barbour were injured. Coincidence?

Two days later, Encino, California, orthopedic surgeon, Lester Cohn, revealed a fractured novicula—one of the seven wrist bones. While preparing a new plaster cast, the first of several I'd wear for the next six months, he casually remarked, "Your stunt career is over." "Bullshit," I said to myself, trying desperately to ignore his pompous, presumptive prognosis. However, I left his office thinking he might be right. Now, it was my life that really flashed in front of me.

A week later, I ventured out to Six Flags Magic Mountain to visit the *Rollercoaster* set. Dayheim introduced me to Daily Variety's ace reporter, Jim Harwood, who wrote:

"Stunt man Jesse Wayne was one of those aboard the car as it sailed 26 feet through the air and crashed into a balsa building. And there's a vivid memory of Wayne around the set in a cast.

But true to stuntmen's crazy luck, Wayne wasn't hurt at all – not a scratch – in the coaster car incident. But a few days later, he was taking photographs, intently pursuing his hobby.

And while Wayne's eyes were glued to the camera, a car ran over him."

An actor stopped me as I was leaving Six Flags and recommended "Comfrey, an herb, better than calcium, that healed my wife's broken back." I thanked him and decided to try it, as I wasn't about to let Cohn's career-ending prediction come true. Months later, Cohn studied my x-rays and just shook his head, "I can't believe it. Your wrist should have been bone-grafted and pinned." I then related my taking four Comfrey capsules a day, but his response as he walked away was a disbelieving, condescending, "What the hell's that?" I then shot back, "Well, how do you explain it?" Of course, a few years later the FDA would ban Comfrey.

Stevie G's cocktail lounge opened December 2, 1976. Steve Gallo had purchased the liquor license from Hank Zitelli, who managed to run the Back Stage to extinction. Zitelli had mentioned he had been married to billionairess Doris Duke, whom he met while he was a hairdresser in New York City. Funny, somehow her obituary never mentioned him as one of her ex-husbands. As usual Bullshit Runs Rampant.

So here I was… in Stevie G's, a Screwdriver, my left wrist in a cast and a doctor's echoing declaration that my stunt career was over. Wonderful. Just wonderful.

In typical pub talk, I countered someone's verbal absurdity with, "That's like taking a shower at Martin Borman's place." A waitress, cum brain surgeon, queried, "Wasn't he an astronaut?" "Yeah, right," I said, "and so was his brother, Frank. Martin Borman was Adolph Hitler's buddy." She just shrugged her shoulders and moved away to take a drink order. What can you expect, another victim of the USA's UN-educational system that began its downward spiral in the early 1960s.

Steve Gallo was comically gullible and difficult to ignore, so to keep him jazzed up, I ran from the Men's Room, with my face and chest drenched as if I were caught in a monsoon, screaming, "Stevie! Stevie! The urinal's exploded!" Gallo almost had a heart attack. Another time, Kent Pendleton, a CBS Studio greens man, maintained this theme exiting the Men's Room, "Hey Stevie, look what some sonofabitch did," holding the fiberglass commode he had sneaked in the bar's side door. Gallo eventually sold the gin joint and it's now an optician's eyeglass salon.

The proverbial "Hollywood Party" occurred at Caruth Byrd's hillside house in Studio City when three attendees streaked the bash. Minutes later, Dave Cass yelled, "Jess, c'mere, look at this." Rushing down the long hallway to the bedroom door, I stopped dead in my tracks – On the largest king size I'd ever seen, at least five couples were entangled – like a bucket of worms, in every sexual configuration imaginable. Joining other festivities on the pool level rumpus room, we skinny-dipped as our naked Producer-host played his keyboard.

When Dave Cass tossed a smartly dressed babe into the pool, she was pissed, complained about her expensive watch—Cass then tossed her back in. Not a very nice guy.

In our favorite pub across from CBS Studio Center, the Back Stage, a handsome actor Richard Lapp, resembling a young Audie Murphy, suddenly appeared. Wearing a tailored suit, dazzling rings on four fingers, smiling from ear to ear, he invited us outside to view his new Cadillac. He then told of a wealthy Texan who financed his new career as an evangelist about a year earlier, "You're the perfect image we need to spread God's word," tossed him a bible and said, "You're an actor, memorize every word." With that, he jumped into the Cad and sped away. I guess you can find him somewhere in Texas.

CHAPTER 19

1977

1977 began with my left wrist still encased in plaster and the orthopedic surgeon's ominous prediction reverberating in my ears that my stunt career was over. Bob Louden and I continued to hone our *San Francisco Rip-Off* script. We'd discuss the plot and characters, and then I'd run off to the Pierpont Inn to write the script.

Family-owned since 1928, Ventura's Pierpont Inn provided an ideal environment for a writer. Especially inviting was the quaint cocktail lounge, overlooking the great Pacific Ocean's golden sunsets. With my yellow legal pad, felt-tipped pen, I wrote the scenes longhand, and then returned to my room to edit and type each page. This was my perfect hide-away and only fifty minutes from Studio City. Years later, I'd write again at the same bar using a notebook lap computer.

Often, at the bar I'd sit with legendary veteran actor John Carradine, a local resident and stalwart member of John Ford's stock company, with roles in eleven of his films, including *Stagecoach*, *Grapes of Wrath* and *Cheyenne Autumn*. I'd kid him about playing Bob Ford, "That dirty little coward that shot Mr. Howard" in Twentieth's *Jesse James*, starring Tyrone Power. More so, I sat spellbound as he so eloquently related tales of his many classic films from Hollywood's Golden Age.

Assistant Director Jack Roe called me to double Richard Dreyfuss on *The Goodbye Girl*, but I explained my broken wrist. Nevertheless, he insisted the stunt involved a simple pratfall and how we could hide my cast. Size-wise, I was perfect for Dreyfuss, but foolishly mentioned the job to my attorney, who promptly nixed it. I should have accepted the job, as it would have had no adverse effect on the final lawsuit settlement.

Six months later, I returned for my final office visit and Dr. Cohn's first words were, "Do you ever get to Chinatown?" I curiously answered, "Yeah?" "Well," holding up his pinkie finger tip, "they charge $700 for a piece of an herb this size." I almost fell over—a *medical doctor* who believes in Chinese herbs? This was blasphemy and undoubtedly made him a prime candidate for the American Medical Association's Hit List.

My first returning stunt was for Al Wyatt on *The Manitou*, starring Tony Curtis, performing a stair fall doubling veteran actress Lurene Tuttle. I had first seen her in 1954 at CBS Television City when she starred in "Life with Father" with Leon Ames. I was invited to this new broadcast center by a school buddy, Jack Housley. Lurene was so gracious when I mentioned I was in the audience.

For this stunt, the director wanted a sideway fall which would take out the stairway banister spindles. On "Action," I threw myself toward the breakaway railing and went through it like a rocket, dropping seven feet, landed on my head and left shoulder. Al waved an ammonia capsule under my nose and my next stop was the St. Joseph Emergency Room to re-set my dislocated shoulder. Al called Chuck Waters for the re-shoot; I called him to suggest he drop one knee at the top of the stairs. Afterward, Chuck said, "I dropped both knees and almost crashed through the railing like you did."

Returning to Toronto, Canada, it was a humid 98° as we filmed *The Black Stallion*. Between takes, Mickey Rooney and I discussed our rocky marital pasts and the combined ten attempts at wedded bliss between us. Mick had recently chosen Jan Chamberlin as the eighth Mrs. Rooney, whom I casually referred to as "The Incumbent."

Adding to the mystique as the King of Matrimony, Mick's marriage to Jan was preceded by her romance with Mickey Rooney, Jr. As the story goes, Mickey, Jr. had taken his rock and roll band on the road, only to return a month later to find Jan was now cohabiting with dear old Dad.

Continuing our banter on this hot and muggy July day, Mick suggested we take our food trays to his air-conditioned motor home. His stored up energy was remarkable as he ate and talked about his many matrimonial experiences and opinions on the perfect mate, concluding, "You have to be friends, first."

Friends laugh when I say Mickey Rooney was my marriage counselor. Well, who was more qualified? Here's a guy who has been in the trenches, with a vast personal and practical knowledge of the subject:

Ava Gardner (January 1942—May 1943) (divorced)
Betty Jane Rase (1944—1948) (divorced)
Martha Vickers (1948—1951) (divorced)
Elaine Mahnken (1952—1958) (divorced)
Barbara Ann Thomason (1958—1966) (murdered)
Marge Lane (1967—1967) (divorced 100 days later)
Carolyn Hockett (1969—1974) (divorced)
Jan Chamberlin (1978—permanently separated from his 8th wife, Jan Rooney, in June 2012.

Mickey Rooney put it succinctly: "Behind every man is a woman. Behind me is a group!" He also advised it was advantageous to always wed in the morning because if the marriage didn't work out the entire day wasn't shot. No one ever told Mick that he didn't have to marry them.

Stunt coordinator Glenn "JR" Randall, Jr. had finally brought me to the Toronto location after several attempts to use a local jockey to double Rooney failed. Call it boasting, but I was the best stunt double Rooney ever had. Co-producer Tom Sternberg related, "We couldn't tell if the shots were of you or Rooney." Mick passed away April 6, 2014 at 93. I still miss him.

The Black Stallion principle photography spanned eighteen months, which explained their filming procedure. After viewing dailies, if production didn't like what they saw, the scene was re-shot the next day. Most filmmakers would cherish that luxury.

Corky Randall, J.R.'s older brother trained the beautiful black Arabian stallion, Cass-Olay. Corky made my job easy. My first shot required Rooney to be kicked in the shoulder when the "startled" horse rears at the sound of approaching vehicles. I was standing beside co-star, Kelly Reno, a terrific lad from Colorado, as Corky stood off-camera in Cass-Olay's line of sight. With a buggy whip, Corky visually cued the horse to rear up. It all worked and it's impossible to recognize me as Rooney during the kick in the shoulder.

When I later went to discuss stunt adjustments with J.R., he referred me to Sternberg, "But you're the stunt coordinator," I said, "you should be handling the stunt adjustments. Besides, Sternberg wasn't even on the set when we filmed, so what would he know about what the stunt is worth?" Randall sloughed it off. It just verified what many had said about this no account prick.

Several years later, I received a call from the Screen Actors Guild TV residual department about *The Black Stallion*. The lady asked how long I was on the film. "Two weeks. Why?" She had the film's production report and Sternberg had listed me for one day of work. This informed lady knew the film was shot in Canada and figured the travel to and from Canada alone was two days. She changed the numbers and the subsequent residual payments reflected my actual work on the film, otherwise I would have been screwed out of thousands of residual dollars.

Meeting veteran character actor Clarence Muse, a former attorney, was a great thrill—He and Rooney had worked together at MGM in the thirties. A rare fact—known primarily among Dixieland Jazz aficionados—Clarence wrote, "When It's Sleepy Time Down South," Louis Armstrong's signature song. I cherish our conversations—as brief as they were.

I figured my pristine *American Cinematographer* magazine collection dating from January 1961 to July 1976 deserved a permanent home, and the University of Southern California's Cinema Arts Department was pleased to accept the donation. Many issues are now worth $100 each – featuring articles written by many legendary Hollywood cinematography pioneers.

Joe Cavalier was a staff director at KTLA in 1958—eight years earlier he had directed NBC's *Broadway Open House*, precursor to *The Tonight*

Show. He, like many of his New York live television colleagues, migrated to Hollywood's film industry. After I joined Tinseltown's stunt ranks we continued our friendship. He was a longtime DGA member and, years later, when I mentioned my being rejected for their 1965 Assistant Director's Trainee Program, he said, "You should have asked me, I could have gotten you in." Yep, there's always someone—who could have gotten you in or get it for you cheaper.

Cavalier bragged about his budgeting prowess when dealing with crewmembers. With $1500 a week budgeted for an electrician, he would admit only to $1000. To those who balked, "I'll try to get you $1250. Those needing the job would accept the $1000, while others reluctantly agreed to the $1250. Regardless, they all came to work feeling they've been screwed by production. Nothing's worse than an unhappy crew and in the long run it will cost you more than you think you've ever saved.

At five-foot-two, Cavalier looked up at a six-foot-five-crew member, "Do you know what your problem is? You're too tall." Now how do you respond to that one? And who really has the problem?

A Monday morning visit to Cavalier, the *Kojak* TV series unit production manager, greeted me with, "That sonofabitch. Jennings Lang had a party Saturday and I've gotta deduct $10,000 from this episode." So there he sat, redlining the extras, transportation vehicles and additional stunt performers from the show's budget. Lang was a successful Universal producer and I'll bet that if Cavalier had been invited to the $10,000 bash he wouldn't have complained.

On August 19, Cavalier called me to an Encino location and take over the assistant director reins of a low budget, non-union film called, *Every Girl Should Have One* (referring to a Diamond pendant). The young cast leads were unknown, but I found the veteran cameo appearances overwhelming. Robert Alda, a radio, film and stage actor (Alan's father) was charming and best known for his starring portrayal of George Gershwin in *Rhapsody in Blue* in 1945. Perceiving his wry sense of humor, I asked if he "still played the piano?" Immediately, our eyes locked, "Oh, yes," he beamed, pleased that someone remembered the role that brought him to film and fame.

When I mentioned working with Alan on *M*A*S*H* doubling "Radar," he said, "You're the first and only to work with all of us, Alan, Antony and myself." This film was his youngest son, Antony Alda's first film acting job.

Then, there was Zsa Zsa Gabor—arriving in her elegant black Rolls Royce Corniche convertible, who thought, for some unknown reason, that the first assistant director was also her butler. It was a constant, "Dahling," get me this or get me that. But after the first day, I'd hide behind a flat until she spotted my second assistant director. What a pain. She also insisted on the hiring of veteran hairdresser Sidney Guilaroff, at a great cost to this low budget film—and would meet him at 5am to be ready and on the set by 8am.

When her daughter, Francesca, visited the set, she and her mother retreated into the on-stage dressing room. Hardly sound proofed with the louvered air vents, during their mother-daughter tirade, the names they called each other would have made a longshoreman blush.

However, my real joy was meeting Hollywood's Musical Queen, Alice Faye. From the first moment I viewed her Twentieth Century Fox musicals as a child, I was in love. (Fickle me, I also adored Doris Day and June Allyson).

Alice was a friend of producer Robert Fridley and delighted in playing a cameo role. Between takes she sang and practiced her tap-dancing routines at 65 and sparkled when I gave her a cassette of the songs she introduced, many from Irving Berlin—she was his favorite singer. She later presented me with an autographed copy of *The Alice Faye Story*, the keystone of my prized first edition, personally autographed, book collection. We often lunched in Palm Springs.

Arriving at the San Fernando Valley location, the company was readying an exterior apartment complex scene. I was pleasantly surprised to find Reg Parton's daughter, Regina, had been hired to stunt double the lead actress.

Coping as well as I could under the circumstances, having not read the script and without a "shot list" from the neophyte "writer/director." I was flying blind, hoped I could catch up.

We were nearing Regina's scene and I suggested she change into the double outfit in the motor home, also housing the wardrobe. While filming another shot, I was suddenly face to face with her father, who was curious as to how I came to be the assistant director on this film.

To regress a couple of months to May 1977, the DGA had sent a letter to their nation-wide membership—reporting a shortage of second assistant directors in the Hollywood branch. Simply, if any DGA members in live or tape television chose to relocate to Los Angeles they would be transferred to the Guild's film roster. One of my closest friends, Gene Law, a production manager at Universal Studios had called me about this notice, "Jess," it's a shame you're not in the Guild." I mentioned John Liberti, a DGA floor director, now a Stevie G's bartender, whom I had met in 1961 at Los Angeles' KHJ-TV, channel 9. Gene suggested they do the "Ameche" bit that evening.

At 6pm I found John at Stevie G's, but he was reluctant to speak with Gene even though I pleaded, "You're in the Guild and you're already in town, call Gene right now!" "But I don't know anything about film." "Look, anyone who's been in live or tape TV can do film standing on their head. Call him!"

Liberti went to Universal Studios the next morning and hasn't missed a day of work since. His longest term of employment was on the *Dr. Quinn: Medicine Woman* TV series as producer-production manager from the first episode through the ensuing movie-of-the-week productions spanning six years. Some guys just can't keep a job! And, how about the perks? He hasn't purchased a carton of cigarettes since May 1977, thanks to each production's prop man.

Back on *Every Girl Should Have One*, Regina had changed into the double wardrobe when I noticed her huddling with her father. Their sneaky leers had all the earmarks of a conspiracy, but I discounted it. We got her shot and she was on her way home.

After a full day of playing catch up, we wrapped and I drove to my favorite watering hole (at the moment), The Left Bank. Over drinks with assistant directors John Liberti and Ed Milkovich, we discussed the eccentricities of our respective productions. Like most businesses, there was much to learn by comparing notes, mainly noting that common sense wasn't often all that common.

A week later at The Left Bank, stunt man Denver Mattson mentioned he had worked on *Rockford Files* with Reg Parton, "Isn't it great that Jesse's working as an assistant director?" Parton replied, "Yeah, well we'll see about that." I was dumbfounded, having considered Parton a good friend for many years, and I had thrown a lot of work his way, including hiring his daughter on one of her first stunt jobs for the Mickey Rooney-Eddie Mayehoff-Morey Amsterdam TV pilot, *The Return of the Original Yellow Tornado & Dickie Boy.*

Parton had reported me to the DGA, stating I was a non-DGA member employed on a DGA film. He then went two blocks down Sunset Boulevard to the Screen Actors Guild and filed a claim because his daughter did not have her own private dressing room. Yeah, this guy was a real, good friend of mine.

This was a first class case of jealousy and just four months after he had received the same DGA letter Gene Law had mentioned. At that time, I encouraged Parton to accept the DGA offer because it was also extended to existing director members. He had joined the DGA in the late fifties when he directed one second unit action scene on Rory Calhoun's, *The Texan* TV series.

Parton found the DGA had no jurisdiction because *Every Girl Should Have One* was a not a DGA signatory. Fridley had simply let the writer direct his own script.

Now the pieces started to come together. On Monday, August 22, three days after Regina had worked, SAG representative Frank Bettger, actor Lyle Bettger's son, appeared on the set. We had known each other for several years and I was happy to see him, though I silently questioned his visit. He was a SAG troubleshooter, a "Checker," but he assured me all was in order and soon left. A month later, I casually related Parton's comments to Cavalier, who said our production company had been reported to SAG and Bettger had been sent to investigate the violations. Now, it all made sense.

Back on the set, actors will be actors. Rather than lunch at the studio commissary, three actors decided to venture to a Sunset and La Brea restaurant, a ridiculous notion for a one-hour lunch. We were ready to film and had no actors, then they called saying their car had stalled and wanted me to send a driver. We were now in the studio and the transportation department had been disbanded. When I suggested they were in violation, and SAG would be notified. Also, I suggested they call a cab, they stuttered and returned to the set in fifteen minutes. It was all BS.

None of the actors or crew allowed this film to interfere with their personal needs. It was exhausting being the father confessor, counselor and psychiatrist. When we set up a "TV interview" shot, the soundman complained about where to place his boom mike. "Why, aren't you using lavalieres?" I asked, referring to the small clip-on microphones. Started, "Oh yeah," then he whispered, "Please don't mention that you suggested the lavaliere mikes." It's CYA. Again, it's imperative that the A.D. know everyone's job.

Daina House, *Playboy* magazine's January 1976 statuesque blond centerfold, sobbed uncontrollably in her dressing room because "the director didn't film my close-up." For twenty minutes I used every ounce of psychology and sweet-talk I could muster, explaining the filming process, to convince her that the director would eventually get to her close up. And later he did.

Confirming that an assistant director's job is never done, a 1:30am phone call jolted me from a sound asleep. Veteran character actor Herb Vigran was worried because his son hadn't come home. That day I had noticed the virile 22-year-old drooling over the wardrobe gal and suggested he was probably getting laid. The next morning on the set at 7am, Herb admitted his kid arrived home just as he was leaving for the studio.

With the film finally completed, I bumped into Reg Parton at the Stuntmen's Association office, confronted him, and his only reply was, "You don't scare me." "Well, cross my path again and we'll see how much I scare you." I never talked to the phony sonofabitch again.

Of course, the real star of *Every Girl Should Have One* was the Diamond. When Producer Robert Fridley initially mentioned his need for a diamond, Zsa Zsa graciously volunteered her glittering cut-glass, pendant replica, valued at $10,000. It was a magnificent piece of glass and only a jeweler would have recognized the difference. We were very grateful and filmed the scenes to establish the fake jewel. Fridley phoned

Zsa Zsa, who promptly said he could have the diamond pendant for $400 a day rental. Fridley was furious, until I suggested that a smiling Alda could just say, "I've got it right here," as he patted his suit breast pocket. It was a cheat, but it worked, and for Alda's action scenes I brought in Troy Melton to double him.

Overall, Fridley was fed up with the myriad of production problems and the Golden Goose was now dead. Robert Fridley, a multi-millionaire, movie theater-chain owner from De Moines, Iowa, with aspirations of becoming a major film producer, was only too happy to return home and forego any future plans to produce a film again in Hollywood.

Joe Cavalier had an illustrious career, but on *Every Girl*, he created more problems than he solved. His belligerent, on-the-set, "This is the way it's going to be" speeches, didn't inspire the actors or crew, but annoyed them all. I was constantly putting out the fires he obnoxiously started.

Over the years, Cavalier had alliances with Clint Eastwood, director Don Siegel and worked on several Universal TV series, including *Kojak* and *Marcus Welby*.

Taking his production manager duties to a ridiculous extreme on Eastwood's *The Gauntlet*, Cavalier rationed the milk to one small carton per person during lunch. Like an army, a movie crew moves on its stomach, and to deny them is unconscionable. Appropriately, the aggravated crewmembers tossed him fully clothed, including his wallet and alligator loafers, into the hotel pool.

Later, believing he was in the industry's mainstream, the Loop and had access to folks who funded film projects, I pitched my *San Francisco Rip-Off* script to him. He received the copy at 3pm, and called at nine the next morning to say how much he liked it. This was amazing; unheard of in Hollywood—a script was actually read the moment it was received. Cavalier sent it to Warner Brother's producer Fred Mintz and "He loved it and will secure the production funding," said Cavalier. I was elated. But time passed and when I asked for an update, Cavalier always said Mintz was still "working on it." Fed up with months of promises, I called the studio and was given Mintz' private home phone number in

New York. Mintz answered, I introduced myself, and then had to remind him of the script's title, the plot and who had sent it to him. "Oh," he said, "I told Joe six months ago that your script wasn't my cup of tea." Thanking him, I was stunned, and then pissed, mainly because another six months had been wasted. But the biggest mystery was why Cavalier had lied about Mintz. What could he gain? Why didn't he tell me Mintz wasn't interested?

During an idle moment filming the action at a Studio City film location, an attractive new mother approached us pushing a stroller. We complimented her sleeping tot amid the noisy city sounds and she casually volunteered that a little wine in the baby's milk bottle always produced a sound sleeper. Oh, well, a new degeneration.

It's November and Roger Creed, my former brother-in-law, invited me for twelve weeks work on *Meteor*, a $22 million epic starring Sean Connery, Natalie Wood, Karl Malden, Brian Keith, Henry Fonda and Martin Landau. The story depicted the space projectile striking earth, causing worldwide destruction and havoc as concluded to be a conceivable possibility in an MIT—Massachusetts Institute of Technology—paper.

With a disaster film concept and colorful one-sheet posters in hand, the would-be producers ran to Cannes, France, to pitch their project to the multitude of film distributors. Hong Kong's mega-producer, Run Run Shaw, purchased distribution rights for his Asian domain, and then American International Pictures became involved in the production. Ronald Neame of *The Poseidon Adventure* fame held the directorial reins.

Once again, it was nice to know where I was going to be working for three months. Contrary to the usual manner of filming, we shot in continuity – progression, because the meteor would devastate the master command center set.

The ingenious production designer painstakingly created the flooding of a New York subway tunnel with the East River. Aided by the special effects team, thousands of gallons of oil driller's mud (a viscous mixture of minerals, polymers and water) were pumped into the huge set built on MGM's Stage 30 tank, which was also the stage where Esther Williams filmed her many aquatic extravaganzas. Trudging through the four-foot deep, molasses-thick, synthetic substance was not so much an athletic accomplishment as it was to keep this invasive substance out of every body orifice. At "Wrap" we all rushed to a bank of showers to hose ourselves off before handing in the saturated wardrobe for cleaning.

To pictorially enact our quest to survive this disaster, several were asked to slip and sink into this muddy-brown quagmire and another would quickly pull us to our feet. At "Cut," those of us who submerged were led, like the blind, to the set nurse to have our eyes washed out, an irritating cleansing process that took an excruciating five to ten minutes.

During the shots, I was a safetyman for Natalie Wood. I had loved her since her appearance in *Rebel without a cause,* with James Dean. Notably, this lovely lady endured this film's "water" stunts, but would tragically drown off Catalina Island a few years later.

Steve Rogers, my LAPD detective buddy, was a great fan of Karl Malden and *The Streets of San Francisco*; I invited him to the set to meet Karl for an autograph, pose for photos. A young Mexican extra about twenty saddled up to me and motioned toward Steve, "He's a cop, isn't he?" When I nodded "Yeah," he joyously exclaimed, "I knew it! I knew it!" Obviously, this guy had extracurricular activities we didn't care to know about. Later, Steve's West L.A. Division detective partner was Mark Fuhrman. Together, they had attended many of O.J.'s parties.

Nightly, I'd meet Brian Keith at Stevie G's and marveled at his beer capacity and his bright-eyed demeanor the next morning. Brian simply remarked, "Experience, Jess, experience."

Veteran Director Charles Barton had first introduced me to Brian and on the *Family Affair* set in the late sixties, and later Columbia Pictures TV Producer Christopher Morgan (son of actor Harry Morgan) called me to give Brian a quick draw lesson. Brian's dexterity was no less than amazing, having been self-taught years earlier during his starring role as TV's *The Westerner*, directed by Sam Peckinpah.

Meteor was a textbook case of too many chefs in the kitchen. The script was rewritten by a succession of writers, but it still missed its best bet. Sean Connery and Natalie Wood, two of the world's most famous motion picture stars, never became romantically involved on the screen. It's like baking a cake and omitting the icing.

CHAPTER 20

1978

The Stuntmen's Association office in North Hollywood provided an oasis in the never-ending quest for work. Stopping by for a cup of Java or a game of pool could be advantageous—you just might run into job.

The newest crop of stunt guys visually confounded veteran stunt man Bob Terhune, son of Max "Alibi" Terhune of *The Three Mesquiteers* westerns from Republic Studios. Decked-out in Gucci loafers, colorful leisure suits, love beads and driving a Mercedes, this was the "new breed" now taking root in the stunt business. Bob was the quintessential stunt man in snap-button western shirts, jeans and cowboy boots, often encrusted with horse residue. Shaking his head, he muttered, "These guys are so lucky they didn't meet me when I was drinking," brought a round of laughs from those who remembered when he and Fred Carson terrorized the local saloons.

The turning point in Terhune's life occurred in 1962, when a shotgun loaded with blanks accidentally discharged in his face on the *Rawhide* TV series. The doctor's prognosis was grim – as Bob recalled the blast that "It blew the corner of my upper eyelid away, shredded the eye's cornea and ruptured the eyeball itself." Bob prayed to God that he would change his wayward life style forever if his sight was restored. God obviously heard him and Bob kept his word – soon after Bob and his wife Lila went on to become ordained ministers.

While on a picture location in Louisiana, Bob preached Sundays at a local black church. John "Bear" Hudkins was advised by a local wrangler working on the film that Bob would be wise to stop his weekly sermonizing, "Otherwise," said the Ku Klux Klan member, "Beaaarr, we gonna have ta kill'em." Bear talked with Bob and his preaching in Louisiana ended.

Bear Hudkin's devil-may-care, sometime caustic demeanor, often placed him over societies legal edge—a cagey, wheeler-dealer. When his brother, Dickie Hudkins, visited his older sibling during WWII, Bear, a U.S. Army Sergeant stationed in Australia, flipped open a footlocker full of greenbacks, grinned, "Help yourself!"

After the war, Bear was L.A. mobster Mickey Cohen's wheelman. At Wrigley Field, 42nd Place and Avalon Boulevard, home of the old Pacific Coast League's Los Angeles Angels, Bear revved the four-door sedan's engine, several shots rang out, his passenger leaped into the backseat and Bear burned rubber. The morning papers reported another L.A. gangster killed, satisfying LAPD's "Let'em shoot it out, just one less hood to contend with" policy.

A few years later, Bear would hold court each morning at the El Chiquita restaurant across from Warner's main gate to settle his bookie operation accounts—his partner was the Burbank Chief of Police.

Bear and the Chief had stashed $400,000 in a Burbank safe deposit box, but a fink informed the FBI, causing it to be "red-tagged" – not to be opened unless FBI agents were present. For years, Bear mused over plans to recover the money from an outright bank robbery to paying off the bank employees. Figuring an "insider" approach to be most viable, he enticed a bank manager from another branch to replace the vacationing bank manager for a week. Ultimately, Bear conceded any plan was too risky and would result in a lengthy prison term. At last report, the safe deposit box remained tagged and unopened.

Years later, when Bear owned a liquor store on San Fernando Road, word circulated that he was going to run a big western on location. Bear wasn't impressed when a stunt guy pushed an overloaded shopping cart of booze to the register. Bear bluntly exclaimed, "Put it back, you're not going!"

Another time, Bear was prepping *The Domino Principle*, starring Gene Hackman and Mickey Rooney, answered his front door to Bob Yerkes, "I heard Mickey Rooney is in your film and I wanted to let you know that I double him." Bear snarled, "Jesse Wayne doubles Rooney. Get the fuck out of here," and slammed the door.

When Bear related this story I was stunned. Yerkes, a Bible-totin' "Born Again Christian" (Didn't you get it the first time around?) was a party guest when I was married, and now he was trying to move in on an actor I had doubled for twenty years. I then remembered a call from Universal in 1961 to double Rooney in a *Wagon Train* circus scene. "I'm a stunt man, not a high wire walker," I said, "Get somebody from a circus." Evidently, they must have called Yerkes, who at 5'11"—nine inches taller than Rooney—now figured it was his God given right to double him. Yep, Jealousy, Ego and Greed!

It's interesting how the male machismo causes a guy to reason with an organ other than the one located between his ears. Mostly affected are the would-be studs like Paul Nuckles, who remarked every time an attractive lady passed, "She wanted to fuck me." He was God's gift to woman all right, especially when he philosophized how wise it was to marry a homely gal because then the other guys would not hit on her. Yep, another brain surgeon has spoken.

During my prowling for the female species, I discovered that very few Errol Flynn's exist. To those of you who have never heard of Flynn, I suggest a library visit (or abebooks.com) to fetch a copy of his book, *My Wicked, Wicked Ways*. Personifying Flynn, one of Hollywood's greatest womanizers, you were "In like Flynn" if you, too, were lucky in lust. He was one of a kind and, to us mere mortal males, allowed me to arrive at one conclusion. If you're planning on bedding a lady, you will only succeed on her terms, when and where she wishes. If she don't wanna, you ain't gonna.

One night, while trawling in Stevie G's, a gal and I were soon in the "throes of a beautiful friendship." As usual, my booze enhanced charm and wit was achieving the desired effect and it became obvious we'd soon perform the horizontal mambo. Just why, I don't exactly recall, but I decided to call off this evening's hunt and head to my abode, alone.

Early, per my daily schedule, I sat in Studio City's Dupar's coffee shop with my morning coffee. Fearing I'd miss something if I didn't, I began each day reading *The Los Angeles Times, the Van Nuys Daily News & Green Sheet* and beginning in 1984, *USA Today*. Interestingly, I watched as the amorous lady from the previous evening, wearing the same clothes she wore the night before entered with a guy. The point is—she was going to fulfill her carnal desires with someone—anyone. I believe they now call it equal rights.

The first assistant director has many responsibilities—a seemingly minor task is to sign the food caterer's invoice after the location lunch is served. I stared in disbelief, "What do you mean 115 lunches? We only have a crew of 35 and with the actors and visitors you couldn't have served over 50 lunches today." The caterer was stammered, "Well, the production manager said you'd sign this." "No way, pal." The next day he repeated this scenario with 75 lunches above the actual people present. When I confronted the production manager, he just sat there and stared at me. Bingo! The light went on. This guy was pocketing $300-$500 cash a day for the bogus lunches at $7.50 each. Do the math. On a 40-day shoot that's a nice chunk of undeclared cash. I continued to refuse to sign the invoice and never worked for him again.

One evening at the Red Coach, while awaiting the arrival of my latest paramour, an English lady telephone operator from the Sportsman's Lodge, I was cornered by a barfly I'd seen around for several years, mumbled, "You're a faggot stunt man and I'm in the Mafia (seems every Italian I've ever met said he was a Mafia member). I've got a .45 in my car and I'm gonna blow your ass away." I attempted to dissuade his threat, even asked the bartender to intercede, but he did nothing. A quick jab would end this, I thought, but his trajectory would have placed him in a booth occupied by a Teamster buddy, Jack Grant, and his lady friend. Suddenly, "Joe Mafia" grabbed my shoulder—I pivoted and instinctively slapped my drink in his face. The glass shattered, carving a deep, three-inch gash on his left cheek, gushing blood. He just stood there, stunned and motionless. I then threw a John Wayne-roundhouse punch that sent him over a table into the booth next to Grant. He lay there with a crooked neck, eyes in a frozen stare—I thought his neck was broken. Someone yelled, "Jess, get out of here." The next day I phoned Ray, the Red Coach owner, to apologize, "Well, I'm damn sorry too," he said, "because I've wanted to punch out that prick for two years." Ray sold the Red Coach a few months later.

A week later, while sitting in Monty's Steak House, Rocky Rymond entered, saying "Joe Mafia" was looking for me. "Tell him," I said, "I'm here every day and if I ever see him again I'll put a bullet between his eyes." He never did show up.

Dick Ziker, stunt coordinator on the *Vega$* TV series called me to double veteran actor Strother Martin. It was like old home week not having seen Dick in years, or Strother since 1975 on *The Great Scout and Cathouse Thursday*, or director Don Chaffey since *Pete's Dragon* in 1976.

Strother, a champion state diver in his youth, enjoyed "smoking the weed," but while he sat in his honey wagon dressing room I remained far enough away to avoid a "contact high." Ziker soon had me hanging precariously from the *Circus Circus* rafters as he, doubling Robert Urich, rescued me from my lofty perch. Shot in one take, I returned to Strother, still in his same position, puffing on some weed, "How'd it go?" "Great," I said, "but it's going to look like Mickey Rooney is hanging up there." Strother's quizzical, dazed expression made me laugh.

A month later, Dick called me again for *Vega$*, saying he needed me again for a couple of days. Those two days grew to eleven and all that time I remained on a daily check. The folks in production weren't paying attention; after three days, per the SAG-Producers Agreement, they had the opportunity to convert me from a daily to a weekly contract. Their neglect allowed my $2777 final paycheck to be one-third more than had they placed me on a weekly contract. Nevertheless, I was very grateful.

In this segment, I was doubling Bob Urich's wife, actress Heather Menzies, posing as a disguised bearded male killer. Vivian Blaine, musical film star of *State Fair* and *Guys and Dolls*, was this episode's guest star. My fondest recollection of her was on early TV's *The Pinky Lee Show*. She was still a beautiful, charming lady.

While on "Hold," I sat at the Desert Inn's Raffles Bar, modeled after its Hong Kong namesake, enjoying a Compari and soda, overlooking the casino as the filming progressed. Posted signs warned those who didn't want to be photographed to stay out of the area, but suddenly there was a commotion—a dapper, high-roller, with a voluptuous blond on each arm, was ranting about being seen and the shot was re-filmed. A few years later, I realized the gent was the multi-termed Governor of Louisiana, Edwin Edwards, who proclaimed during one re-election campaign about his opponent, "Sure, I'm going to steal, but I'm not going to steal as much as him!" And he got re-elected.

Compari liqueur is a derivative of "bitters" and you'll get sick before you get bombed, but I was bored, asked second A.D. Chase Newhart if I could be an extra in the scene, "Sure, sit with those two couples," he said, "but, keep your back to the camera." With Compari in hand, I joined the charming foursome and in moments had them laughing for 20 minutes at my repertoire of ex-wife jokes. The men later introduced themselves; they co-owned a casino on the strip and invited me to perform at their Monday night open-mike comedy showcase. Unfortunately, my *Vega$* stint ended on Sunday, but it was nice to be asked.

Once again, while enjoying a Compari, a "plain Jane" slid onto the barstool beside me, and asked, "Do you want to party?" Immediately, I heard a loud voice say, "No, he doesn't," and the hooker quickly moved on. The voice belonged to a Raffle's waitress I'd met, a grandmother, who had sent her two sons to college on her earnings. One had become a lawyer and the other a pharmacist. Retired, she missed her job, and returned to now send her granddaughter to school. She then divulged the hooker's plans to drug and rob me in my room or the parking lot where her boyfriend would mug me. In all, I never paid for their services directly, I always married them.

But, what was disappointing is that this hooker was a not the beautiful, svelte, stunning "Lady of the evening," as always depicted on the silver screen. Damn, how disillusioning.

Stunt man Steve Boyum was working the show's second unit filming a chase scene, "I'll probably flip the ambulance." My feelings about what a person says made me warn him that he might attract disaster to himself. A half hour later, word filtered back to the set that Steve had dumped the ambulance on its side in downtown Las Vegas. Steve is now an established, successful TV producer and director.

I never considered or was involved in the drug scene of the sixties, seventies and eighties. Unfortunately, this virus is still painfully prevalent in our society today. An acquaintance once boasted, "With a little coke, I can get any girl I want." Well, baring rape, I guess that's another way to do it.

The Valley Inn opened in February 1947—the Sherman Oaks restaurant became a hangout for Hollywood's most famous stars, including John Wayne and Clark Gable. From the early sixties, I enjoyed their famous slab of baby back pork ribs, so deliciously fall-off-the-bone-tender, the best I have ever eaten anywhere, and that includes The South.

In late 1979, I questioned Valley Inn owner Al Hesseltine's comments in an American Express TV commercial when he said W.C. Fields had also been a customer along with John Wayne and Clark Gable, "Al, W.C. Fields couldn't have come in here, he died on December 25, 1946, a month and a half before the Valley Inn opened in February 1947." "Shhhhh," he said, "they needed another famous name and, dammit, only you would have picked up on that."

The Valley Inn's twelve stools seated bank, insurance and real estate executives, and most notably, a Jet Propulsion Laboratory scientist, Robert "Olie" Olson, one of Lockheed's original "Skunk Works" U-2 aircraft designers. Occasional show biz luminaries like George Gobel also held court.

On Saturdays the Valley Inn opened at 4pm, so our group would meet at Monty's Steak House for lunch and TV sports. For over a month, I mentioned my music lessons and the fabulous $1200 guitar I bought for $500 from a hard up musician. To hear me tell it, I was the next Chet Atkins. Finally, on this day, I offered to showcase my musical talent and exited to get the guitar from my car. Returning, running as always, I tripped and fell; crushing the instrument into a thousand splintered pieces. Everyone froze in disbelief, stared broken hearted as I brushed myself off, "That's it, I'll never play the guitar again." I gave the busboy $5.00 to clean up the mess as the bar regulars consoled me. I never told anyone my fall wasn't an accident or that the $1200 guitar had only cost me $10 at a discount store. Anything for a laugh!

NYPD's Eddie "Popeye" Egan, of *The French Connection* fame was a Monty's regular, a great guy. This day he met with two characters, and later said they were film producers interested in a script he had written. To me, they looked suspicious, like the crooks he nailed, and I told him so. A couple of weeks later Eddie admitted they were a couple of con men and "full of shit."

Another time, Monty's bartender Steve Skinner's shift was nearly over on a day when he consumed more booze than he had poured his customers. Fuming, he mumbled, "That cocksucker," referring to an allegedly belligerent bar patron. While mixing the customer's drink, he unzipped his pants and used his dick as a stirrer. We all quickly exited and never hit his shift again.

George Fisher was coordinating the action and also directing the second unit on *Racquet*. Over the weekend we scouted the Van Nuys locations. I made a shot list and about 20 call sheets. Assembling early Monday morning with the company, I laughed when a crew member exclaimed, "Geez, we don't even have a call sheet on the first unit!" This omission, a small part of a larger problem, might explain a film reviewer's comment that *Racquet* "Could be the worst movie ever..."

Regardless, the film's stunt action can't be faulted—George brought in Buzz Bundy, known for skiing cars on two wheels – driver-side-high. On *Diamonds Are Forever*, Buzz was hired after Everett Creach, doubling Sean Connery, attempted to ski a red Mustang through an alley and wrecked several vehicles in the process. But oddly the film's final-cut shows the skiing vehicle entering driver-side-high (Buzz) and exiting the alley driver-side-down– which, obviously, was one of Everett's shots.

One *Racquet* shot had me as a little old lady learning to drive as Buzz wheeled around me at an intersection, so close I could have reached out and touched his car's drive shaft. On another shot, I'm bicycling as Buzz nails my rear wheel, and was right on the button but, boy, that pavement came up fast.

CHAPTER 21

1979

January 4th kicked off the year employed on the *CHiPs* TV series as a last minute replacement for Denver Mattson, who had told Paul Nuckles to kiss off, saying, "He's the only guy you can work for and still collect your unemployment insurance check," referring to Nuckle's proclivity to seldom give a stunt adjustment to anyone, but himself.

This would be one of only two days I would work on *CHiPs*. The other day would occur two years later when Gene Law, now an assistant director on the series, and director Phil Bondelli, whom I had met when he was a second assistant director on *I Spy*, requested me. In the scene, my old buddy Don Stroud steals my car and the chase is on.

When Nuckles received his Director's Guild membership for reining the *CHiPs* second unit action filming, Steve Lodge enviously exclaimed, "That's not fair." Well, if life were fair, Garth Brooks would still be selling cowboy boots in Brentwood, Tennessee.

Obviously I am not a Brooks fan, nor of infidelity. While on tour Brooks' opening act was Trisha Yearwood and a torid affair ensued. His wife heard about it and demanded a divorce, he cryed, begged forgiveness and she relented. She soon gave birth to two daughters and promptly filed for divorce and walked away with a several hundred million dollar settlement. Years later this bum would marry Yearwood.

Yep, work was plentiful; although I knew well from experience the bottom could fall out at any time.

A week later, I spent four days on the Alan Arkin-Peter Falk comedy, *The In-Laws*. It was fun working with veteran director Arthur Hiller again—the last time was 1961 on *Ben Casey*—and for assistant director Jack Roe in 1962, on William Castle's *13 Frightened Girls*.

Reminiscing with Jack, now seventeen years later, we had a good laugh when he told me to drive the school bus, which was in excellent condition. Class will tell, as we were served "Turf & Surf"—steak and lobster for lunch. Alan Arkin was a gentleman and it was nice to see Peter Falk again.

Call it old age or a previous stunt injury but, at 38 years old, I began to have an aching neck pain, a pinched nerve, extending from behind my left ear, down my left arm. It became so excruciatingly painful I would awake from a sound sleep moaning. Office visits to my general practitioner produced no pain relief, a chiropractor's treatment was only temporary, and the L.A. Ram's orthopedic surgeon did nothing but prescribe painkillers.

So potent and dangerous was the medication, I fell asleep at a Valley intersection while waiting for the signal to change, causing my car to roll forward and gently bump the car in front of me. Immediately, the Mexican illegal alien jumped out, screaming I had rear-ended him, and demanded $200 cash to repair the bumper. Yeah, his bumper was crunched, but the rust and corrosion negated any possibility that the damage happened only moments ago. When I grabbed my cell phone and suggested we call the cops, he made a hasty exit. But thank God this fellow was there; otherwise I would have rolled into the intersections cross traffic.

Al Hesseltine, the Valley Inn's owner, witnessed my daily agony and suggested I make an appointment with Dr. Hon Cheung Poon, his acupuncturist. The Taipei-born doctor spoke little English at his private practice, and also headed up the UCLA acupuncture unit with his brother. Mom had a lifelong affinity for Chinese culture and, I, too, became enthralled.

Actually, at this point, I was ready for anything. My first office visit was $50 and subsequent visits were $35, but I would have paid $10,000 to eliminate my suffering. Reclining on my right side with my left arm comfortably resting on a pillow, I watched as the good doctor produced tiny needles of human hair thickness. Between my wrist and elbow, Poon inserted five or six needles, none of which produced the slightest irritation, speck of blood or even a pinprick. Five minutes later, he returned and gently swirled the uppermost pin between his thumb and index finger. Instantly, it seemed as if a bolt of lightning had zapped the back of each eyeball. "Geez, I don't know what you did, but something happened." He smiled, spun the other pins, which had no effect like the first pin, and exited. Twenty minutes later, ninety-five per cent of my pain was gone and to this day have never been bothered by what I believe was a pinched nerve. Well, why not? The Chinese have practiced Acupuncture for over five thousand years and I'd say they have it perfected.

Further studies of this ancient science taught me that Acupuncture doesn't work for everyone or for every ailment. With two people suffering from the same disorder it's possible only one may be cured or relieved of pain. I was fortunate to find a true professional.

My further research suggests we should adopt China's former doctor-patient formula to good health. The relationship decreed that the patient pays the doctor to keep them well, and if the patient becomes ill the doctor's revenue stops. The plan makes sense to me, but I doubt if the American Medical Association will agree to it.

February 1, 1979 found me on location in a foggy, rain-drenched New Orleans as stunt double for Mickey Rooney in *My Kidnapper, My Love*. The CBS movie-of-the-week was being produced by actor James Stacy. Jim had starred in the *Lancer* television series for Twentieth Century-Fox in the late sixties and was regarded as one of Hollywood's young, up and coming, leading men. Then, a tragic accident occurred. Stacy and his date, Claire Cox, were motorcycling through Beverly Glen Canyon's winding road from Beverly Hills when a drunk driver struck them—head-on. Jim lost his left arm and leg. Claire was killed instantly.

Through a difficult rehabilitation period, Stacy's determination resulted in this tailor-made script collaboration with his brother, stunt man Louie Elias, who also served as associate producer on this production. The family affair continued with their sister, Carolyn as the hairdresser, and her son also had a small part in the film. After all, what good is nepotism, if you don't keep it in the family?

I watched in an amazed disappointment as the production slowly progressed in an uneasy manner as the participants vied for artistic control. Stacy and veteran actor/director Sam Wanamaker constantly argued over "creative differences." You haven't lived until you've experienced the Hollywood ego in bloom. However, the set's tension-filled atmosphere proved tame for what was to happen later.

During a week of night filming, several of us wrapped early and quickly made our way to the Vieux Carré Hotel Bar for a bit of social imbibing. Replete with history and the ever-present cockroach, the local lore of this saloon proclaimed the carved oak back bar was the bed headboard of New Orleans voodoo queen, Marie Laveau.

Since we hadn't eaten dinner, Hollywood special effects man, Roy Downey, born in Baton Rouge, and having worked several films in Naw'lins, suggested we go to Manuel's, famous for their delicious, finger-sized, tamales. At $1.80 a dozen, this seemed like a delicious idea and too good a deal to pass up. Also, as an amateur historian of the South, I reveled in the heritage of the Crescent City and didn't want to miss any of it.

Jack I. Daniels, one of the local teamsters hired for the film, offered to drive. Roy had worked with him previously and cautioned that Daniels was a Ku Klux Klan member and not one to be reckoned with. I was apprehensive, but then figured, what the hell, what could happen? I'll just stay out of his path. So Roy, his girlfriend Wende Weil, and I jumped into Daniel's twelve passenger van and off we went.

Manuel's was located south of the city, so we headed down Canal Street, arguably the widest street in the United States. Soon, we came to where the thoroughfare shrinks to two lanes each way, with a grassy area dividing the road. The median, called "neutral ground," is derived from the days when the whites and the Creoles battled. To travel through the city, you were safe if you stayed on the "neutral ground". Pivoting in the front passenger seat, I listened and watched intently as Roy pointed out the many historical sites of the city he knew so well.

Casually looking ahead down the street about a block I could see a black youngster, about eight to 10 years old, vigorously peddling his bicycle. He was in the right lane, directly in front of us. Not thinking anymore about the kid, I again turned back toward Roy and Wende when I heard Daniels say, "I'll get that son-of-a-bitch!" Immediately, he stomped the gas pedal to the floor, accelerating the van. The roaring vehicle sped forward. The boy moved into the left lane and, as if in a gun sight, Daniels tracked with him. In the past, I had found many studio teamsters to be frustrated stunt men. Thinking Daniels was showing off for us, I couldn't believe this was happening as we continued to approach the bike at a rising speed.

Then, there he was. From my passenger seat, less than three feet away, was the boy's face, wide-eyed, looking over his right shoulder. Suddenly, the boy disappeared. We bounced upward in our seats as if hitting a speed bump at sixty miles per hour. I was paralyzed in disbelief. Wende screamed and buried her head in Roy's chest. Through the rear window, I could see the boy struggling, crawling with every ounce of strength remaining in his broken body to reach the grassy neutral ground. Unruffled, Daniels drove for another block before pulling over, parked at the curb. He exited the van, quickly followed by Roy.

This seemed like a nightmare—the one where you can't wake up. I attempted to console a hysterical Wende for what seemed an eternity. Trembling, I finally exited the van and steadied myself in the brisk midnight air between the headlights. Lighting a cigarette, I contemplated this strange, inconceivable situation. My eyes drifted downward. Protruding from beneath the front bumper was the boy's mangled bicycle. Wrenching it free from the van's undercarriage, I placed the tangled mess on the sidewalk. Straightening, I felt a strange presence behind me and turned. There stood a black kid, I figured to be about twelve. His dark, watery, eyes reflected an anger and hatred. If only looks could kill. He swiftly jerked the wrecked bike into his arms and moved away into the darkness of the night.

A black New Orleans Police officer arrived in his cruiser to record our version of the incident for his report. Wende volunteered that we had seen the boy peddling his bicycle down the street. Instantly, the officer interrupted to say that he too had seen the boy on the street, "about 10 minutes ago—riding erratically." When asked to sign the police report, I noticed the officer had described the boy and his bicycle as "the striking vehicle." It then hit me; life was cheap in New Orleans, especially, if you're black. Just as the cop left, Roy returned saying the boy, Tyrone Johnson, was "D.O.A." I didn't want to believe it, but Roy insisted. Minutes later, Daniels returned and matter-of-factly lamented, "Now, his fucking parents will probably sue me."

Not a word was said as we continued on to Manuel's, where Roy purchased several dozen tamales. Wende and I had lost our appetite and stared silently into the night. Returning to the hotel parking lot, Daniels broke the silence when he asked for my home address and phone number, "Just in case I need a witness." Staring into his lifeless eyes, I realized this was a veiled threat for me to keep my mouth shut.

Entering the Vieux Carré bar, I quickly ordered a double Courvoisier—hoping to erase the horrible visions of the past hour. Two more doubles and this was indeed a first—the drinks had no effect on me. Nothing would obliterate the atrocity I had just witnessed. It was nothing but an outright murder.

Daniels found his way to the bar seat next to me and produced an envelope of photographs. One by one, he proudly handed me a photo and described each scene. The "scene" was his collection of Nazi memorabilia. Shot after shot revealed Hitler's Third Reich — mannequins dressed in the finest SS Officers uniforms, then officers, regular infantry, pilots and flags. Next, were the armament -- rifles, engraved daggers, and German automatic burp guns. As a firearm instructor to many actors, I stared in disbelief at the many footlockers filled to the brim with Luger pistols. Daniels lovingly caressed each photo and spoke of each article as if it were an offspring from his loins. As he returned the last photo to the envelope, I asked him how much this collection was worth. Jutting his chest, he proudly said it was valued at more than $500,000. He then advised me that if I ever wanted *any* type of firearm, he knew all the sources. At this point, all I thought about was my next flight back to Los Angeles, safely.

With my stunt duties completed, I returned to Hollywood and immediately called a Los Angeles Police Department detective buddy, Steve Rogers. I related the entire murder saga to him, searching for some means to bring Daniels to justice. After carefully considering every aspect, his decision was for me to walk away from it. He believed that absolutely no cooperation would be forthcoming from the New Orleans Police Department, and then suggested that Daniels and his friends would probably seek retribution.

It was more than six months before this tragic vision finally stopped flashing on me. But even today I can still see the boy's face as if it were yesterday. I later asked Roy if he'd heard anything about "the accident." He said Daniels had signed over all of his assets to his parents, in the event the black boy's parents would file a lawsuit.

Roy said the kid snatching the mangled bike was James, the slain boy's older brother, who with their father was to meet Tyrone Johnson at the gas station across from where they had witnessed the murder. Daniels later paid $500 for Tyrone's funeral and gave his parents $500. There is no statute of limitations on murder, so maybe someday justice will be served.

Idaho's October 72° climate reminded me of the San Fernando Valley, as did the mountain range surrounding Boise. Ideally, it's easy to find your bearings—as opposed to Florida, which is pancake-flat and the tallest structure is 350 feet – where a pilot can fly at an altitude of five hundred feet without fear of crashing into anything.

Stunt veteran Chuck Hicks said he was weary seeing all six-foot-two saloon brawlers and wanted me airborne during the fight scenes on Clint Eastwood's new film, *Bronco Billy*. Clint's longtime, stunt double and coordinator, Wayne "Buddy" Van Horn was still working on the Wyoming location of *Heaven's Gate*.

At LAX, the stunt troops, comprised mostly of Hearts and poker players assembled for the Boise, Idaho, flight. The next morning we discovered the Lonesome Pine Saloon location really was a "Bucket of Blood" watering hole with dried blood puddles blotting the pavement. Soon, two luxurious, custom-designed busses arrived with Merle Haggard and his band. And the filming began.

Clint directs with a deft hand, knows exactly what he wants in every shot, and brings in each film on schedule and in budget. Again, any job on the set is easier when the head honcho has a vision and does his homework. The performers know what is required of them and the crew appreciates a set pace that flows, without any screaming or indecisions.

Twenty stunt guys and gals joined the fray started by George Orrison, also included producer Fritz Manes, who took a punch, crashed hard, sideways through the drywall, right between two 2x4s—hitting an inch either way would have broken his shoulder. Six-foot-six Dick Durock tossed me around like a rag doll as Merle Haggard's band played away. Unfortunately, over fifty percent of the fight scene ended up on the cutting room floor.

Clint is a true gem among the rubble. I had first worked with him on the *Rawhide* TV series, doubling Mickey Rooney. It was a fun show to work, still one of my all time favorite Western series. Mickey played a former circus performer, so there was a lot of falling, jumping and a saddle fall. I'd practiced saddle falls many times—the most under rated stunt in the business—but this would be my first on film.

When the scene calls for you to be "shot off" the horse, I always believed you should not telegraph a saddle fall. You're supposed to look like you're shot out of the saddle. Often, you'll see a stunt man leaning toward the plowed up patch of dirt he hopes to hit. But when the saddle fall is performed correctly, there's no way to fake it. Certainly not landing on your feet and rolling.

This *Rawhide* episode featured Rooney doing horse mounts, so in came Ralph McClutchen's horse, Beaut (shortened from Beauty), featured in the *Fury* TV series, starring Peter Graves and Bobby Diamond. Between takes, Ralph would say, "Now Beaut, go back 50 feet, turn left, go 20 feet, stop and paw the ground three times, come back here and nod your head. We were amazed as this beautiful black equine did just that. Horses are creatures of habit and Ralph had trained Beaut well.

Veteran director Tommy Carr of countless Republic Pictures westerns carefully explained the plot—Mick's horse was supposedly an out-of-control runaway—I was to release the bag from my shoulder at one point, then slide out of the saddle at the next mark. Head wrangler Ivan

Connors took great care of me and on "Action," I yelled "Yaaaaa" and galloped into the shot. The bag hit its mark and I slipped out of the saddle, landing on my left hip, flipped over and rolled into a sitting position. Clint rode up, eyed me suspiciously, "Are you all right?" It was a fart-knocker and I think my eyes were crossed, but I was fine. The next morning my left hip had "The Devil's Rainbow."

Later, as the station wagon returned us to the studio, Tommy Carr remarked how wonderful it was to get the shots he wanted and, specifically, how much he liked "Rooney's double." Tommy didn't know I was in the rear seat, I interrupted, thanked him for making it easy. When you know exactly what a director envisions, you just lock in and do it. Sure sounds simple, doesn't it?

Roger Creed called to say he landed the stunt coordinator job on *The Electric Horseman*, and wanted me as a car chase participant. He had a substantial stunt budget, though from past experience with him, I knew it would be a struggle separating him from the dollars. He described the police cars chasing a horseback rider and, in particular, the crash of two speeding police cars ending up roof-to-roof. It sounded like an interesting stunt, and might pay a substantial stunt adjustment. But when he said Robert Redford and Jane Fonda were the stars, the hair on my neck bristled, "Hold it right there. I'll have to beg off. I have trouble living in the same town as 'Hanoi Jane', much less working on the same film. If you or I did what she did, we'd still be hanging from a tree." Roger couldn't believe it, "You'd turn down an action film because of her?"

Creed performed the upside-down police car shot with Conrad Palmisano. Roger said my refusal to work the film cost me $20,000, but years later his subsequent retelling of the story had escalated my loss to $40,000.

Ace stunt man Mickey Gilbert doubled Redford on horseback off-road, while the other car drivers worked to avoid being sand bogged. After the initial chase was completed, one of the drivers, who had risen from the Extra ranks, demanded a hefty stunt adjustment. An angered Roger protested, "What the hell do you mean? Mickey didn't even ask for an adjustment… and he was on a horse!" This guy then went over Roger's head to the production manager, who also denied his request.

Again, with Roger, you knew stunt adjustments would be rare and this guy knowingly accepted the job. But complaining to production was a big no-no and this clown never worked for Creed again.

Roger later confessed his dislike for the treasonous Fonda and exclaimed, "You were right, she is a bitch."

Stunt coordinator Conrad Palmisano called me for *The Lady in Red*, starred Robert Conrad, filming at the old Lincoln Heights Jail, now a popular film location. I was doubling Nancy Parsons, a diesel dyke prison matron character, bent on giving the heroine a severe thrashing. Dottie Catching, stunt man Bill Catching's ex-wife, doubling actress Pamela Sue Martin, was apprehensive about the fight. Actually, she was terrified, noting the battle concluded with my kick to her groin.

During the rehearsal we choreographed our every move, including her final position backed against the bars where I was to deliver the debilitating kick. Carefully, I explained to her that she would not be injured because there was a cross bar directly behind her crotch. "I won't touch you because the bar will stop my shoe. But, you have to stand up straight. If you don't, you're going to get hurt." Her nervous giggle suggested she wasn't fully convinced, but was going along with it because she had no other choice.

We did a final rehearsal for the director, Lewis Teague, and smiled his approval. Forever seeking an audience for my distorted sense of humor, I suggested to him, "How about after the kick, I pull back my foot and my shoe is imbedded 'there'?" Teague thought for a moment, seriously considering this bit of business, and then said, "Ahhh No, I don't think that will work." The crew howled.

On "Action," Dottie and I made our moves and performed the entire fight without a mishap in one take. When Dottie heard "Cut," her facial expression of relief said it all. The film's gaffer, Mike Katz, later admitted thinking the new generation of stunt women was something else, "The one doubling the prison matron was the toughest looking bull-dyke I've ever seen."

At the Valley Inn, romance reared its head again when I met Valerie, a real estate agent. Our romance grew hot and heavy. While at my apartment, I excused myself to take a shower and was pleasantly surprised when the glass door opened and she joined me. At her Woodland Hills home, I was flattered when she asked me to be the "first to christen her new hot tub." At midnight, naked as jaybirds, we cavorted in the bubbling warm water filled fiberglass tub. Moving into a climatic position, she stopped me and pointed, "No, it's much better if you're over there." First, huh? Yeah right.

This romance became troublesome. After several drinks Valerie became antagonistic as the evenings always concluded with an argument. When I asked about her problem, she admitted her divorce of ten years ago was still gnawing at her. Gnawing? It was eating her alive. My Psycho 101 question to her, "Well, how much longer are you going to let this affect your life?" didn't sit well and I never heard from her again.

Nevertheless, she taught me a lot about the horrors of the real estate business. Simply, it's *caveat emptor*... Let the buyer beware. From her prospective, I learned to equate her sales ploys with a hooker or bartender – They'll say and do anything to make a sale.

Again, work continued on *The Bad News Bears, The Incredible Hulk* and on *Airplane*, hired by Conrad Palmisano, where I was closest to the large airport lounge window when the 747 crashes into the terminal. Roger Creed was the only casualty, receiving a slight cut from a tempered glass sliver to the top of his head.

With Lou "The Incredible Hulk" Ferrigno, I expected to be manhandled, but he couldn't have been easier to work with or more concerned about my safety. He's a gentle man.

I entered the set one day as Lou did the Hulk's growling, "trap pose" – short for trapezoid, and almost choked trying to stifle my laughter during the take. His pose just hit my funny bone.

Hart to Hart, starring Robert Wagner, or R.J., as he preferred, was a fun set working with stunt coordinator Howard Curtis and makeup artists, Frank Westmore and "Shotgun" Britton. I was doubling a rotund Mexican female officer who had imprisoned R.J. and Stephanie Powers (a natural beauty via her Polish ancestry). Wearing a full body pad, I resembled a fireplug, and then again, so did the real actress.

Waiting my turn for make up, I casually watched as Layne "Shotgun" Britton (he wore Shotgun Britches as a child and the name stuck). Bob

Hope, Jane Russell and Frank Sinatra's longtime makeup man, applied pancake makeup to a bit actor. Winking at me, "Shotgun," using a guttural throat-clearing sound, faked spitting on the pancake makeup (while squeezing a wet sponge) and dabbed the moist sponge on the actor's face. Studying his script, the actor suddenly realized what was happening, leaped out of the chair, ready to punch Shotgun. The makeup trailer rocked with laughter.

On the set, Howard was in R.J.'s double wardrobe and I was startled when Regina Parton appeared as Stephanie's stunt double. I had not seen her since the *Every Girl Should Have One* filming, when her father reported me to the DGA and the company to SAG. I detest loose ends and I confronted and explained how he had tried to sabotage me. Her distressed expression seemingly revealed she had no knowledge of her father's scheming actions. (Still, I'm not sure.) She said nothing, looked apologetic, but what could she say regarding her deceitful father. Blood is thicker than water. I didn't push it any further.

We wrapped the action in the small Mexican jail set and changed back into our civvies. In the parking lot, Howard and I talked about the weekend. He was going to participate in a sky diving, eight-pointed star in Elsinore, California. All I could do was look into his eyes, silently wonder why one of the best high stuntmen in the business would risk his life for a blue ribbon. It was a knowing look almost like Howard knew what I was thinking. We bid adieu in the Twentieth Century-Fox parking lot Friday night.

My weekend plans seemed tame by comparison—Saturday morning I traveled to Santa Barbara to serve as the grounds manager for the two-day Arabian horse show at the Earl Warren Show Grounds, sponsored by my San Fernando Valley Arabian Horse Club.

Monday morning, I was enjoying my coffee and newspapers at Denny's in Sherman Oaks. Half way through the L.A. Times first section, I read that two skydivers had died in Elsinore. A miscalculation occurred as one diver collided, breaking his neck on impact, rendering the other diver unconscious in the mid-air crash. At first, it didn't register, and then it hit me. There was Howard's name. Knocked out by the first diver, Howard plummeted two thousand feet to his death. My stomach flip-flopped.

Later, Dar Robinson, also a top high man, mentioned he had witnessed the collision and was the first to discover Howard was one of the divers. "His body bounced twenty feet in the air after he hit," Dar said, sadly. Days later, Robert Wagner, with his wife Natalie Wood, attended the funeral and gave a moving eulogy. Tragically, two years later, Natalie Wood would mysterious drown off Catalina Island.

Work continued on the *Benson* TV series, playing a hit man disguised as a little old lady. It was a fun show starring Robert Guillaume, James Noble, Missy Gold, Inga Swenson, Caroline McWilliams and Lewis J. Stadlen.

Stadlen was personable and had received great acclaim playing Groucho Marx in *Minnie's Boys* on Broadway starring Shelley Winters, but quit this steady TV gig for greener pastures on the Broadway stage.

Seven year old, Missy Gold was a delightful, brilliant, young actress. This became a mini-reunion, since I had doubled her father, Harry Gold, several times before he became a top Hollywood talent agent.

My big scene was sparring with Inga Swenson (she played Eric "Hoss" Cartwright's mother on *Bonanza*, then died, as do all Ponderosa women), who subdues me by striking me across the back with my cane. During rehearsal, she was reluctant to swing hard fearing she might injure me. I revealed my back pad and her next wallop brought tears to my eyes. However, during the taping she found the middle ground and it all worked perfectly. Just another one of those times when you dread working with actors not trained in action.

John Wayne died June 11, 1979, and I cried almost as much as when my dad passed away.

Stunt coordinator Roy "Snuffy" Harrison on *Fantasy Island* called me to double Arte Johnson again, to exit a shack before it explodes. Veteran director Earl Bellamy, another one of the best, described what he wanted. Roy and I discussed the timing, as he had to pass a window a moment before the explosion. We rehearsed it and the cameras rolled. "Snuffy" walked by and I waited a beat and then pushed the double doors to escape, but they didn't budge and I bumped my forehead. Knowing the blast was another beat away I flung myself through the doors and BOOM! I could feel the heat of the rolling fireball on my neck as I hit the ground. "Cut," yelled Earl, "Are you okay?" "The damn doors stuck!" I muttered. "The fireball looked terrific and close, too." he smiled. "Too close," I said. At that point, a beautiful young lady about eighteen rushed up and planted a kiss on my right cheek. I didn't get her name, but later heard she was producer Michael Fisher's daughter. Ah, the perks of cheating death.

Again, another lesson learned. Don't take anything for granted. Effects had closed the doors, sagging in their frame, for the shot, but they should have been "set"—just barely touching.

On another *Fantasy* episode, a stunt wannabe finagled his way onto the show through production much to Snuffy's chagrin. Filming at Disney's Golden Oak ranch, Snuffy had scheduled this guy to race a car into a 90º slide, and stop at a barbed wire fence. A car slide entails locking the rear wheels with the emergency brake and cranking the steering wheel. Doubling Arte, I was a front seat passenger, noticed the crew had a pool on how far through the fence—into the plowed field this wannabe was going to go. On "Action," the wannabe accelerated toward the fence. Right on course, I waited for him to grab the emergency brake handle, but he didn't—he just made a casual u-turn in front of the barbed wire. We had lost the light and that was a wrap. Snuffy was livid, confronting the driver, he asked, "Did you use the emergency brake?" The bewildered kid pleaded, "No way, man, I didn't touch it!"

Idyllwild, California was commonly called "The Poor man's Big Bear." Sure, it lacked a lake, but a true a paradise nevertheless and only a brief two-hour drive from Studio City.

So, here I was on *Prey*, a low budget, teenage-hikers-killed-in-the-woods epic, made by a former adult film, husband and wife team Summer and Edwin Brown. My job was to help them film an actress hanging upside down in a foot-noose from a tree. Actress Lori Lethin was patient as I positioned her, but looking around, it appeared the crew was lackadaisical. "Hey folks, let's get this shot or she's going to pass out!" I said, loudly. We quickly got the shot and I was ready to return home when D.K. Miller, the production manager, asked me if I would take over the production as the assistant director. "Sure, but I have to return home to pack enough clothes for the remaining two weeks of filming."

Returning to the mountain location two days later, I was surprised to see Ted Hayden, an old buddy I had worked with at KTLA in 1958. He had strived for years to create an acting career and now was about to be killed by the monster. In the campfire shot, he poured himself a cup of coffee and moved to sit on a large log. As he sat, he farted. Hearing this short report, I immediately looked to the sound mixer, who greeted me with a wide grin. Usually, extraneous set sounds warrant another take, but, evidently, we were the only two who heard the sound and watched as the scene continued under the director's watchful eye. A flubbed line then caused Ed Brown to re-shoot the scene. There must be a moral here somewhere.

On November 25, thanks to a recommendation by special effects buddy Roy Downey, I was on my way to Savannah, Georgia, as stunt coordinator on *Hopscotch*, starring Walter Matthau, Glenda Jackson, Ned Beatty and Sam Waterston. Directed by Ronald Neame, the company had returned from filming in England and Germany.

This was an Edie and Eli Landeau Production, the first motion picture production made through the United States Small Business Administration (SBA) and, unfortunately, to my knowledge, the last.

I'm not a Harvard Business School graduate and can't explain the financial intricacies involved, but this was creative financing at its highest level. In Europe, the initial funds were shifted from bank-to-bank and country-to-country, ultimately producing the greatest possible dividends on the money. Again, beyond this, I have no idea how this money manipulation was accomplished, except that they had doubled the original investment by the time the first foot of film rolled.

It had been two years since I had last worked with director Ronald Neame on *Meteor*. London-born Neame's distinguished film career produced such classics as *The Man Who Never Was*, *Prudence and the Pill*, *The Odessa File* and *The Prime of Jean Brodie*, though his most notable acclaim would be the commercial-financial block-buster, *The Poseidon Adventure*.

Neame and I discussed his vision of Matthau's get-away car chase. With Savannah's Assistant Police Chief Major Jim Stevens at my side, I mapped out the action at a T-intersection. Determining that one FBI chase car would slide off the road and roll over, a trench, eighteen inches deep and thirty feet long was dug. Safety barriers and lighted lanterns marked the area.

With our business completed, Major Jim and I retreated to Oliver's, a chrome and fern saloon located at the Savannah Sheraton, on the banks of the Wilmington River. Built in 1928, this 12 story edifice was owned by the Teamsters and had been newly refurbished. Our jokes included the speculation of how many cement-shoed bodies were in the flowing waters, including the current mystery surrounding Jimmy Hoffa's whereabouts.

Soon, Major Jim's lovely wife, Elizabeth, joined us. We had a lot of laughs, but the next morning brought the biggest knee-slapper. Major Jim cornered me, "How'd you do that? We've got huge potholes we've been trying to get repaired for six months and you guys dig one trench and it gets filled up overnight. Who do you know?" Jim and I roared. Apparently, an over-zealous Savannah Transportation Department inspector saw our newly dug open trench and called in a crew.

From Hollywood, I brought in veteran stuntmen Roger Creed and Dick Geary. Dick and I would hoist a few at days end, admiring and conversing with the beautiful bartenders and waitresses. Interestingly, one of the bartenderettes chided our drinking, but openly discussed her use of cocaine, bragging that her drug dealer was a local attorney. I do believe her personal values needed to be tweaked.

Roger and Dick performed their stunts admirably and with Sunday off, we checked out Hilton Head, South Carolina. Driver Coordinator Jim Taylor suggested we take one of the FBI picture cars, a typical drab, unmarked vehicle, devoid of chrome and amenities. In our enthusiasm, none of us noticed that the car had no plates or registration until we returned. When I later mentioned our blunder to Jim, he stressed how lucky we were that the South Carolina Highway Patrol missed us, "You guys would have gone straight to jail." "Yeah," I quipped, "but I would have called you at home to come get us out," "You're right," he grinned. Major Jim Stevens was one of the finest gentlemen I have ever known. He passed away in 1994.

The *Hopscotch* script was written by Brian Garfield (*Death Wish*), and also served as the film's associate producer. His contract stipulated that NOT a word of the script could be changed without his approval. At the historical Savannah River front area, Brian and I coordinated the second unit filming for several of the film's establishing shots. While checking my $400 Pulsar LED watch, a remnant from the last marriage, I noticed the dimming numerals. Calling Brian, I motioned for him to follow me to the river's edge. Unbuckling the metal band, "I've had it," and threw the watch into the fast moving current, "I got rid of her and now the watch." Brian grinned in disbelief, and then pointed to my right hand as blood dripped from my index finger. "Sonofabitch, she got to me, again." We both laughed.

Again, I was delighted to be in the South where hospitality reigns supreme. Roy and Wende compiled a list of the finest restaurants in Savannah, specifically, The Pirate's House and Watson's, but the shining gold star went to Mrs. Wilke's Boarding House.

Her Jones Street eatery, located in a quiet residential area, is indistinguishable amid the other homes to suggest that you are about to savor the best home cooking since leaving home. The delicious vittles are served family style, in bowls, tureens and platters to the five tables, each seating eight voracious customers. From the first bite, only the "Hmmmmmm" sounds of gastronomic satisfaction may be heard. When the last morsel is devoured, her steadfast rule to bus your own plate is dutifully obeyed by each contented diner.

At her kitchen door, I peered in at her cooks, hard at work. Wearing head bandanas, the three heavy-set black ladies resembling actress Hattie McDaniels, busily prepared the next platters of epicurean delight. I still salivate whenever I just think about Mrs. Wilkes Boarding House.

The Pirate's House was reputed to be the hideout for the notorious pirate, Blackbeard. Quaint, the house just rambled on as the many dining rooms were added over the centuries. The Sunday Brunch with Filet Mignon and seafood was an elegant delight to the eyes as well as the palate. On the other hand, Watson's was a rustic, river front seafood diner with the daily newspaper subbing for a tablecloth. Actually, you wouldn't want it any other way, given the mess after devouring the best shrimp you will ever eat.

Working with the English film crew was a grand experience I'll always cherish. Sound mixer Derek Ball was an erudite gentleman, always nattily dressed in a three-piece suit on the set. Elaine Schreyeck, the script supervisor, was the most meticulous lady I had ever worked with, as she thanked me for matching each shot in continuity. Director of Photography Arthur Immetson and sound boom man, Ken Nightingall taught me the age-old skill of darts, but the following morning my right forearm muscle was excruciatingly painful to the lightest touch. Most surprising was the gala wrap party in Oliver's, as each department head was presented with an envelope containing one week's salary in cash. Once again, class will tell.

Roger, Dick and I returned to Hollywood, anticipating the new decade. The movie business was changing, but I still wasn't sure I could cope with these changes.

CHAPTER 22

1980

On January 1, 1980, I accepted an invitation from my stockbroker, Floyd O'Gorman, to attend the Rose Bowl game in Pasadena. The end zone seats provided an excellent view only when a team was within scoring range—otherwise, I watched the game play on a guy's portable TV next to me as USC beat Ohio 17-16. This day I learned a valuable lesson from O'Gorman: You can enjoy the game better on your home TV set. Months later, he would teach me another lesson: Don't trust your stockbroker.

While on a San Francisco location for a Canadian film, I gave O'Gorman explicit instructions to sell a particular stock when it hit a certain level. It did, and he didn't. Unbeknownst to me, he was controlling the stock price (his friends owned the company). This cost my Mom and I enough money to buy us each a new Cadillac.

Like I told the two ex-wives, "Nothing is forever." This undeniable fact was becoming increasingly evident as many of the Valley's famed restaurants began to disappear. Many old timers will remember Whittinghill's, Jason's, Rondelli's, Jack La Rue's, Charley Foy's, Crazy Legs, Don Paul's The Ram's Horn, Pump Room, Queen's Castle, Blarney Stone, The Doll House and Jimmy O'Brien's (I dated his daughter, Kelly).

The venerable king was the Tail O' the Cock, located in Studio City at Ventura and Coldwater Canyon, with their vigilant black waiters, where fine food and supreme service reigned. Individual brass name plaques marked George Gobel's and other show biz luminaries place at the bar. The Wild Goose, Ben Payson's Ruddy Duck, Alphonse's, Bill Story's, near Universal Studios, became Merrick's, then the Maison Gerard. The Moskva Cliff served a magnificent seven-course Russian dinner. Kover's Bull Pen, Larry Potter's, La Ronde, Chadney's, Sorrentino's and the Fireside Inn were delectable. My personal favorite was Hawley's "tough steaks and tender gravy," famous for their mouth-watering, two-times, stuffed baked potato – long before baked potatoes became the "in" entree.

There were plenty more, actor Benson Fong's, Ah Fong's, in Holly-wood, Beverly Hills and Encino served the best Sweet & Sour Duck and egg rolls. The Ginger House, Fiore D'Italia, China Trader, Barone's, Travaglini's, Café Alma, Rand's Round-Up, the Samoa House, the Hungry Tiger, Pucci's, Chuck's Steak House, The Oak Room, Diamond Jim's, Rainbow Inn and the King's Castle. The Smoke House operated a second restaurant in Encino and is still going strong in Burbank, across from Warner Brothers Studios.

In the sixties and seventies, those that craved nightlife, traversed the San Fernando Valley's fine establishments from Studio City to Wood-land Hills. After dining at one, it was on to another site for live entertainment, and it wasn't unusual to visit two or three venues in one evening.

Once again, I happily reverted back to one of my first loves in the business—production. Though my stunt work had prevailed through the years, I continued seeking the path that would take me behind the camera.

Producer/production manager Bob Manning recommended me as the assistant director on a low budget feature called, *Boxoffice*. When I mentioned my new gig to Gene Law, he pleaded with me to hire his son as my second assistant director, "Gary has worked as a grip, a half-assed actor and I think he might do well in production." Gene was one of my best friends and I needed no prodding to hire Gary Law immediately.

Not to be confused with veteran Director Peter Bogdanovich (differ-ent spelling), *Boxoffice* was written and directed by Josef Bogdanovitch, who had enrolled in a "How to Make a Movie" course at UCLA, but didn't graduate, as evidenced by his vapid, so-called *script*. I read the transcript four times and still had no idea what the hell the story was all about.

The origin of this mumbo-jumbo would later be explained when Gary discovered the director and cast leads snorting cocaine between setups in their motorhome. Gary had spent his early twenties living the drug induced, hippie life-style and I regarded him as a creditable expert witness when he later discovered the film budget included $25,000 for drug purchasing.

Bogdanovitch's pre-production high-strung antics should have been a tip-off, but it wasn't until the filming began that I fully realized the mistake I had made. Bogdanovitch would attempt to explain the shot he wanted. I don't know if cocaine causes halitosis, but this guy's breath could have brought a mule to his knees. Nevertheless, two weeks into filming, I had had enough of this amateur movie making after my every attempt to help him resulted in a heated debate. It was painfully obvious the book he had read on filmmaking didn't include any experience-based advice, so naturally, my every recommendation made no sense to him.

I had recommended D.K. Miller, the production manager on *Prey*, for this project and he soon became acquainted with the problems, but his attitude was simply, "Take the money and run." When I asked to be replaced, he matter-of-factly stated, "Oh no, as long as I'm here, you're gonna be here."

Reluctantly, I attempted to make a film as Bogdanovitch remained irrational and completely ignorant of common filmmaking procedures. And they really are very basic. It's not brain surgery, but a step-by-step process. There's nothing mystical to make a film, though many would have you believe it is.

I later discovered the D.P. had an overtime clause in his deal memo, while his camera crew was on a flat weekly salary. Against my objections, he proceeded to light an LP turntable spinning an overplayed record – "Ssshhhhh, ssshhhhh." This was an insert close-up shot usually reserved for the last day of filming, but he took 45 minutes to light and film the 10-second shot. My talk with the producer did nothing to prevent several reoccurrences as this clown continued to collect mucho extra bucks every week.

My experience with DPs on low budget films was usually tumultuous, stemming from the fact that they were going to take their own sweet time to light the picture regardless of the production time constraints. Whether the film reviewed was a flop or a hit, they were not about to be faulted for their photographic artistry.

Bogdanovitch hired a sketch artist to storyboard the film. My first sight of the four-inch thick, three-ring binder was all I could do to stifle my laughter. Hundreds of drawings not only depicted every scene, but multiple frames of each shot to be filmed. We could (actually, we should) have filmed the binder.

Later, while studying a page of the drawings, Bogdanovitch bellowed, "I can't shoot this scene, the door is on the right and the window is on the left." I asked him to remove the page from the binder. I then flipped it over, reversing the image, and held it up to the nearest light, "Now, can we shoot the scene?" We did and I never saw that binder again.

This clown was still out of control. Finally, I refused to speak to this cokehead, and would send Gary to inquire about the next shot. We would then set it up with the crew. What a way to make a film. Just further proof of how the business had changed.

While filming on the twelfth floor of the Santa Monica Twin Towers, a high-rise condominium community, Bogdanovitch berated our excellent film crew. Discarding all thoughts of diplomacy, I said, "You wouldn't know a good crew from a sack of cow shit." Instantly, he changed the subject, saying he wanted the two-piece sectional sofa moved. Turning to make my request to the crew, he suddenly heaved half of the sectional across the room, pinning the script girl to the grand piano. I yelled, "You sonofabitch!" and lunged at him, only to have six-foot-four Gary Law, shove me into the hallway and lock the door.

Reportedly, Bogdanovitch was from a San Pedro, California, commercial fishing family, supposedly the source of the film's funding. Often, the payroll wasn't there and his wife, a charming, beautiful lady some years his senior, would travel out of town. A few days later she would return with the additional payroll funds.

While filming continued at the Twin Towers, I found the assistant art director, a beautiful girl about thirty, leaning against the hallway wall, crying her eyes out. I had only been gone five minutes while the crew set up the next shot and wondered, "Now, what the hell happened?" Sobbing between her words, she stammered, "The director didn't like the lamp I put on the end table." Well now, there's a situation where we can all shed a tear over. I rushed her back to the set, pointed at the lamp and announced to the cokehead, "That's the only lamp we have." He just looked at me and continued playing director.

My only pleasure derived on this Santa Monica location was meeting the very gracious, beautiful actress Jean Simmons in the elevator, who had just returned from her early morning run. At 53 she was still as elegant and beautiful as always.

Finally, I convinced Miller it was best for all concerned for me to leave this fiasco, while Gary Law stayed on for the remaining two weeks of filming.

I wasn't invited to the *Boxoffice* screening at the Nu-Art Theater in West Los Angeles, nor did I expect or want to be. Gary reported that when the film ended and the lights slowly came up, "Everyone just sat there in silence until someone got enough nerve to head for the exit, then it became a stampede."

Usually, I ignore movie reviews, but *Daily Variety* nailed it:

"'Boxoffice' is a no go at the b.o. A pretentious, implausible and unreal look at showbiz, pic was shot more than two years ago and just received its local preem in a one-nighter at the Nuart revival house. Unintended laughs and walkouts at the screening tell the whole story – it's one of those films that has no conceivable audience."

Gary Law continued to use his father's contacts to secure the four hundred workdays required to enter the Directors Guild as a second assistant director. Gene Law passed away in 1982, and would not see his son rise through the production ranks to become a producer raking in $300,000 a year.

On the *Profiler* set in 1996, he sat smugly in his "Producer Gary Law" director's chair surveying the crew at work. "I'll bet you never thought you'd see me like this," he said. "No," I said, "I sure didn't." He thought it was a complement. For 16 years I had kept track of him, and my sources all said he was a lousy assistant director, which reminded me of when I first hired him.

On a Laurel Canyon mansion location, he was nowhere to be found until I found him fast asleep. I had the still man take shot of his snoozing. And now he was a producer. It just verified that the "Peter Principle" still applied; where you advance to your highest level of incompetence.

Serving as the production manager, he was also bestowed with the "producer credit" as leverage when dealing with the cast and crew. This combination role of producer-production manager historically controls the monetary and physical making of a show, and is usually devoid of any creative input. Basically, he was a bean counter and, most often, the company hatchet man.

I still miss Gene, his smile, his wonderful sense of humor, and most of all, his friendship. Strangely, Gary Law fell short of all these qualities, succumbing to Hollywood's most famous malady, amnesia. Never did he hire me to coordinate or perform stunt work on any production he reined. Could it be he didn't like the "sleeping beauty" photo I gave to Gene?

Gary Law further revealed his true colors when his mother requested a $5000 loan and he viciously told her to kiss off. A loan? Shouldn't you give your Mother anything she wishes with love and kisses? That's a rhetorical question this prick wouldn't understand.

Boxoffice was one film experience I didn't want to repeat, and to lessen or eliminate problems on future productions I created a list of rules for the entire crew to read and initial:

"On behalf of the entire production staff, I'd like to welcome you
to the crew of

(Enter movie title)

"Since you are now a member of our team, you are again about to experience the exciting, hectic, unpredictable days of movie making. I say 'again' because all of you have been employed in film and have been handpicked for this project. You know the job that has to be done. We're all here for the same purpose so let's do it. "PREPARATION is an essential ingredient of picture making. With this word in mind, I say now that I expect all of you, regardless of your position, to READ the DAILY CALL SHEET, READ the SHOOTING SCHEDULE and insist that you READ the SCRIPT.

"You will then know in advance what is required, when and where. There will be no secrets. You will have no surprises. In essence, you will be and feel closer to this project. But, most importantly, you will be part of a team where your participation is expected and highly valued.

"Every production has its own inherent problems. Should you find yourself in a difficult situation, my only request is that you talk to me. We are all in this together. Only with mutual cooperation will the problems be minimized and solved.

"THESE GUIDELINES WORK WELL WHEN WE'RE ON THE SET:

"WORK CALLS If the work call is 7AM, work will begin at 7AM. If you're the type who needs that cup of java to get the old heart pumping, fine. Do it before your work call. This production, more than most, has been tightly budgeted and scheduled with little or no leeway for error. There will be days when we may have to work longer than expected. By the same token, when it all flows and we get ahead of schedule, we'll have a shorter day.

"FIRST SET-UP & REHEARSAL At the work call, the Director, 1st A.D., DP. Gaffer, Key Grip and Props will rehearse the first shot with the actors involved. After this shot is established, it's then off to makeup, hair & wardrobe for the actors while the crew readies the first shot.

"QUIET We have found that a hushed environment is most conducive to creativity. Anything more than the normal din of working sounds will not be tolerated. When the cameras roll, it means Quiet AND Stand Still. Often, the slightest sound or movement, even out of the actor's line-of-sight, will cause a distraction and necessitate another take. All cell phones and pagers must be turned OFF. Make your phone calls during lunch.

"NO ALCOHOL OR DRUGS This is cause for immediate dismissal. What you do on your own time is your business. But when we're on the set and there's a job to perform, it becomes MY business. This also applies to the morning-after-hangover when the eyes are difficult to uncross. However, after "wrap" is called I may even join you for a beer.

"NO SMOKING This applies definitely to any interior set. When we're outdoors do it far away from camera and, above all, use the butt cans.

"LOCATIONS Even though we "rent" the locations, there's no reason to leave the areas in any lesser condition than the way we found them. In other words, remember THE GOLDEN RULE. "You are professionals and you know the game plan. So now let's get on with it and make a film that will rival any production Hollywood has ever made.

JESSE WAYNE
1st Assistant Director"

I was flattered when several Directors Guild of America A.D. friends requested copies to use on their union productions.

I was assistant director on a ballet film short and humorously declared to the 20 year old prima ballerina that "The finest dancers in the business were male – and named Fred Astaire, Gene Kelly… and *Cyd Charisse*." Her blank expression revealed she had never heard of these *guys*.

Stunt coordinator Frank Orsatti called me often for *The Incredible Hulk* TV series starring Bill Bixby. Past experiences working with musclemen, including former football players, resembled grabbing a bull's tail in a China shop. Most didn't have body control, knew their own strength and were out of control, but again, working with Lou Ferrigno was an unexpected pleasure as he snatched me up and threw me into a crowd of rioters. Lou couldn't have been more gentle or professional. Everything we ever did was always one take.

Dick Warlock invited me to St. Louis for *Escape from New York* as Donald Pleasence's double and as one of the street people. I'd not seen Ernest Borgnine since *Twice in a Lifetime* and what a class act he was.

Generally, the wise producer endeavors to make sure every buck he spends ends up on the screen. However, for a hundred years, Hollywood has written the book on creative bookkeeping, involving not two sets of books, but probably three or four. Department heads receive petty cash, but the reins are loose when the receipts are submitted.

Prior to the St. Louis location, I visited a Beverly Hills wig salon with the hair and makeup supervisors. After selecting several items, the merchant presented a receipt for $38.00 and asked them, "Shall I put a "1" in front of the "38"? Sounds like the Federal Government.

On the St Louis location the Teamster driver coordinator presented $10,000 in gasoline and oil receipts to Jack Buckley, the production accountant. Jack stared at the stack, "What the hell are you doing? Selling the gas on the black market?" We had filmed for less than a month within a one-mile radius of the Sheraton St. Louis hotel. Another three-day location involved a bridge twelve miles away. Every film vehicle on the production could have idled 24/7 for a month and the gas and oil costs would not have amounted to anything close to $10,000.

During the scene when Kurt Russell fights a huge gladiator, hundreds of extras applauded like they were watching a ballet at Carnegie

Hall. I told Warlock that they should be signaling their approval with fists in the air. He went to John Carpenter, returned a few moments later, "How's it feel to be right again?" Actually, it felt great, but it was just dramatic common sense.

Another night we were filming through a windshield with the camera in the car's backseat. A stunt guy was to leap on the hood, get knocked off. In rehearsal, he almost broke his neck. I suggested he take the hit, but just slide off on to his feet, as he would be out of frame and didn't have to hit the ground. It's always advisable to check the camera viewfinder to know what's being filmed. He ignored my suggestion, did the shot his way and knocked himself unconscious.

Sightseeing in St. Louis was fun, especially the Arch, a true American landmark with a spectacular view. LaClede's Landing was a former waterfront warehouse area and now housed fine restaurants and shops. When I asked one of our St. Louis cops how long it took to walk to LaClede's he replied, "I don't know. So far nobody's made it!"

John Carpenter's wife, Adrienne Barbeau, found the antique shops of West St. Louis and needed the prop truck to bring her aged bounty back to their Studio City home.

Returning to Hollywood, bouncing back and forth between stunts and assistant director work, I met two LAPD motorcycle cops, Ron Venegas and Jack Ryan. Often, I found myself in a production time pinch, in need of a filming permit, and they would run interference for me. Many times they saved me when I would have had to find a new location or call a "wrap." However, little did I know these two men in blue had a darker side?

LAPD's Hollywood area had been plagued by rash of video store break-ins and burglaries. Suspicions aroused, the LAPD staked out several stores and discovered our uniformed duo would sling shot a ball bearing into a store's plate-glass window, then await the "459-Burglary" call. Parked nearby, they would arrive on the crime scene, kick in the back door, load the VCRs in the police cruiser and drive to their own vehicle parked a few blocks away to transfer the merchandise.

LAPD'S Internal Affairs delved further into this situation and found other improprieties in the Hollywood Division; several officers were involved with under aged female interns. Ryan offered to turn state's evidence, but while driving from his Simi Valley home, he suspiciously lost control, flipped his SUV over a ridge on the 118 Ronald Reagan Freeway and was pronounced dead at the scene. Venegas clammed up and is probably parking cars somewhere, having lost his job and his lucrative LAPD pension.

While doubling Harry Gold on Donna Summer's *Thank God It's Friday*, I stood with Officer Jack Ryan as he controlled traffic along La Cienega's famed Restaurant Row. A car pulled up and a beautiful, buxom, red head cheerily smiled, "Hi Officer Ryan. How are you?" Jack burst out, "Keep moving, you dirty sonofabitch!" Assuming she was an ex-wife or girlfriend, I asked, "A former lady love?" With fiery eyes, he angrily blared, "That's a fucking drag queen I arrested one night near Columbia Studios on Gower and we ended up rolling in the street. I had to call for backup. The cocksucker ripped my uniform." Well, it fooled me. The He/She was absolutely stunning.

Los Angeles and New York have played tug-a-war for decades to be the nation's top TV media market. Judging by the many Los Angeles news personalities that have become network morning hosts, New York has the edge. But, not all of them make it.

News hen Connie Chung began her career at Los Angeles' KNXT (now KCBS), Channel 2, a CBS-owned and operated TV station. However, not all of her co-workers were enthralled with her personality and journalistic abilities. Particularly, KNXT Sportscaster Ted Dawson, a tall, dark and handsome Texan, always nattily dressed in fine western wear suits. During a live news broadcast, while engaged in an agitated tête-à-tête, Ted suggested that Connie "go do the laundry." Ms. Chung obviously had more clout than ol' Ted, as he was gone the next day.

Moving over to L.A.'s KABC, channel 7, his next confrontation involved "punching out" the news director. At last report, Dawson had returned to local broadcasting in his home state.* His fuse may have been short, but I found his quip to be a funny, politically incorrect line. Just chalk it up to the wicked sense of humor I received from my Mother.

---

*Latest reports reveal Ol' Ted is a TV sports broadcaster in Montana.

While enjoying adult beverages with George Gobel at The Valley Inn, a snobbish, regular customer stormed in complaining about her dining experience in Beverly Hills. George and I looked at each other, knowing that the main entrée at the Last Supper would not have satisfied this chronic whiner. Suddenly I blurted, "Dottie's walked out of more restaurants than Duncan Hines." Everyone laughed knowingly. George smiled, complemented me on my sense of humor, and asked, "How'd you like to be my writer on *Hollywood Squares* next season?" I anxiously accepted, thrilled and overwhelmed to be a comedy writer for "Ol' Lonesome George."

Writing for "Squares" would be a challenging experience; I would be filling large shoes vacated by the recent passing of George's longtime writer, "Packy." The show's process was simple: Each Square guest received a complete set of questions and answers, not knowing which question they would be asked. Accordingly, each would respond with a memorized comic quip for each question asked by emcee Peter Marshall:

Q: True or false—a pea can last as long as 5,000 years.
A: George Gobel: Boy, it sure seems that way sometimes.

I knew working with George would be a blast, placing me again into the "Think Funny" mode I enjoyed on *The Steve Allen Show*. Unexpectedly, a month later George called to say *Hollywood Squares* had been cancelled.

At the Lakeside Country Club in Toluca Lake, a member of George's golf foursome agonized about slicing his ball out of bounds and was so angered he tossed his driver club into the water. Hooking his next ball, he furiously threw his second club into the drink. When the third ball went astray, George was so overcome with compassion for his fellow golfer; he walked to the member's golf bag and flung it into lake.

George's repertoire usually included a comedic reference to "spooky old Alice," but never understood why his fans referred to his wife as "dirty old Alice." I had my suspicions. The first time I drove George home from the Valley Inn, I accepted his invitation to a game of pool.

Alice met us at the door and her less than cordial expression inferred I had poured demon rum down "Ol' Lonesome George." Bidding them goodnight, I made a hasty exit. As for my being a bad influence, I dare say George's elbow bending began several years before I was born—in the 1930s when he traveled a hundred miles a night to play his guitar for $5.00.

After the tragic Challenger Space Shuttle explosion, I told George a sick joke, regarding the Captain's last words: "Is it hot in here or is it just me?" George said, "Jess, we used that line in 1937 when the Hindenburg exploded." George Gobel passed away February 24, 1991 at 71. TV's Larry King kindly remarked that George was so underrated. How very true.

Universal's *Magnum, P.I.* TV pilot returned from Hawaii for one night of filming on the studio's backlot. Fred Lerner was the stunt coordinator and had me doubling John Hillerman. It was a simple shot: Selleck bulldogs me and we fall behind a parked car. Doing the Texas Switch, he and Hillerman then pop up into frame. One take and it was over, but I was impressed with Selleck. He personified every girl's dream guy of tall, dark and handsome and the rest is history.

CHAPTER 23

1981

Each New Year produced a Spring-like effect on me, a great, new awakening, and I was ready for anything. But every year it was a crapshoot. Though the industry generally suffered a seasonal economic downturn, I was frequently in demand while others were unemployed. Often, this situation was reversed.

We kicked off with a couple of days on the *Lobo* TV series, starring veteran actor Claude Akins, one of the nicest guys in the business. His double and stunt coordinator Bill Lane called me to "blind-drive" a police car backward down 5th Street, while Bobby Herron, doubling actor Mills Watson, death-gripped the flashing light bar. Once again, I crouched low in the seat and the floorboard. Bill had a multi-paneled rear-view mirror installed, but it distorted my view, so I opted to gauge my position with the street's power lines, as I had done on *The Love Bug Rides Again*. It all worked perfectly, however, each time I braked and skidded to a stop, poor ol' Bobby had to hang on for dear life to keep from being catapulted from the car's roof.

This same day, as a sound man rigged a microphone in a picture vehicle, his buddies noticed his reclined position on the car's front seat, joked about him falling asleep, "He must have had a rough night." A nudge revealed he had died of a heart attack. His body lay on the bare asphalt, covered by a furniture pad from the prop truck. Several crewmembers wept, demanding that a mortuary be called, but county coroner laws prohibited his removal until a medical examiner filed a report. He arrived six hours later. Needless to say, filming continued—as "The show must go on."

Then came *Leave 'Em Laughing*, a TV movie starring Mickey Rooney, a heartwarming tale about a Chicago gent and his wife who raised 40-50 foster children, directed by Rooney's longtime contemporary, Jackie Cooper. One shot, filmed thirteen stories above Los Angeles' Pershing Square, had me doing a tippy-toe-dance on a narrow 16 inch ledge. From a construction site a block away the ironworkers waved to me. The irony was those fellows could walk the girders in their sleep, risking their lives daily, but I was earning as much in a minute as they did in a week.

Later, I cornered Rooney to ask a question that had bugged me for years. "Mick, is the story about you and the Las Vegas show girl true when you supposedly asked, 'What would you say to a little fuck?' and she answered, 'Hi, Little Fuck.'" Rooney became serious, placed both of his hands on my shoulders and looked me squarely in the eyes and said, "Do you think I would ever say that to a lady?" I then stammered, "Oh no, Mick." Quickly moving away to keep from busting up, I dare say that during Mick's hell-raising days he just might have said it.

Director Cooper, assistant director Bill Scott and I traveled to Chicago to do exterior filming. Housed at the luxurious Ambassador East, I was surprised when my door opened to a luxurious suite. Later, Bill and I visited several bars on State Street, reveling in the remarkable difference between a Chicago Lass and the Hollywood Bimbo. Mrs. O'Leary's kin didn't request a financial statement before engaging in a conversation. These ladies were exhilarating and could not have been more congenial. However, with our early call, we retired to the Ambassador East; Bill asked if my room was sufficient. I assured him it was. Entering the spacious suite, I was pleasantly surprised to find my bed covers turned down, a chocolate mint on the pillow and a small bottle of Grand Marnier in a snifter—the perfect night cap.

Leaving the following morning I met Bill at his room and found it to be the size of a broom closet, and refrained from discussing my suite when he again asked if my room was "Okay?"

A brisk 16° wind blew in from Lake Michigan as we commenced filming. While waiting for a set-up, a black man asked me how I liked walking the ledge. "Oh, you heard about it?" I replied. "I'm the producer, Julian Fowles." Later, over lunch, I found him to be a very interesting man, a Harvard graduate and a former MCA vice president, who had originated this project with Charles Fries Productions.

After filming several run-bys, Julian handed me a pair of size 30 clown shoes I would wear in the next shot, belonging to the show's real main character – "He died of cancer and if Rooney knew these were the guy's real shoes he never would have worn them."

Cooper filmed me walking across a hospital parking lot imitating Rooney's jaunty swagger. While filming *A Midsummer Night's Dream*, fifteen-year-old Mick broke his left leg. Somehow, the injury caused his plaster-casted left leg to heal an inch and a half shorter—producing his oscillating gait.

Makeup artist Charlene Roberson, daughter of stunt man Chuck Roberson, provided me with Rooney's make up and red clown's nose, saying I could return it the next time I saw her. Carefully, I studied the Polaroid shot of Rooney and applied my clown face.

Bill Scott had Cooper's shot list and timetable. By noon, we were two hours ahead of schedule and by 7pm I was back on a jet flight returning to Los Angeles. It was a fun twenty-four hours in Chicago.

Work continued, doubling Donald Pleasence on *Halloween II*, and here and there on *Under the Rainbow, Hill Street Blues* and *The Sword and the Sorcerer*. For this medieval-fantasy, we filmed among the tall pine trees of Franklin Canyon, overlooking the reservoir above Beverly Hills, the same terrain where *Combat, Bonanza*, and most notably, the opening of *The Andy Griffith Show* were filmed. I wore a false face-head appliance above my head as Eddie Hice galloped by and lopped it off with his sword. Leaning forward headless toward camera, the makeup man triggered the wireless, remote controlled, mini-pump under my robe, spewing a quart of blood skyward from the arteries, just as I tumbled down the steep hill.

Producer-production manager Hal Klein called me to be the stunt coordinator on Norman Mailer's *The Executioner's Song*, a Lawrence

Schiller TV mini-series filming in Provo, Utah. They filmed at the actual sites where serial killer Gary Gilmore had perpetrated his infamous crime spree.

My flight from Burbank arrived in Salt Lake City, a company driver picked me up and off we were for the thirty-minute drive to Provo. In the production office, Hal introduced me to everyone, including the supervising producer, John Thomas Lenox. He was an affable guy and we hit it off at once.

At the Rodeway Inn lobby I met *The Executioner's Song* co-star Christine Lahti, playing Gary Gilmore's sister. Funny, when working with an actor, you'll often sense a quality that makes them special. Christine was one of them.

Later that evening, I joined Hal and other crew members for dinner at a local Japanese restaurant. Removing our shoes and sitting cross-legged at twelve-inch high tables, this was indeed a new experience for me, mainly because I'm still pissed off about Pearl Harbor.

An advocate of the great adage, When in Rome, do as the Romanians... err, Romans, I attempted to feed myself with chopsticks. The others had no trouble, but I was determined to master these damned overgrown toothpicks. Previously, using chopsticks never presented a problem, perhaps because a couple of drinks usually placed my fingers into a relaxed mode. That was my theory anyway, but a drink was near impossible to find in this Mormon principality. Hal, obviously aware that starvation was imminent, summoned the kimono dressed waitress, who then presented me with a metal fork, a very useful utensil common to the Western hemisphere.

The next morning, I met director Larry Schiller as he rehearsed a backyard barbecue scene with Tommy Lee Jones, playing Gary Gilmore and Rosanna Arquette, his wife. The scene called for Rosanna, sitting on Tommy's lap, to playfully jump away from him, continuing the dialogue. On "Action", Rosanna in her tank top and cutoff jeans, teasingly played grab-ass with Tommy Lee. Intense, she jumped up and out popped her right breast. She was a beautiful sight to behold as we all stared silently with ear-to-ear smiles. I looked at Larry. You could see the wheels turning, can I salvage this shot or do I "cut" it? Larry called "Cut."

Rosanna turned to question Larry as he pointed to her chest. Looking down, she nonchalantly flopped her ample right breast back into her tank top and went for Take Two.

A frugal producer-production manager, Hal had me bouncing like a ping pong ball, back and forth, from Burbank rather than house me for the filming duration. Also, Hal mentioned a local guy who had done some stunts, "Talk to him, I don't want to bring any stuntmen from Hollywood."

Hal was taking advantage of a major transformation affecting the stunt business; simply, there were now stunt men in every region of the country. Typically now, when a stunt coordinator arrived on a distant film location he was bombarded by résumés from every local stunt wannabe. Again, this influx can be attributed to Needham's publicity-crazed agenda.

Rick Barker had worked several Sun Classic productions including *Gentle Ben*. He was responsive to my questions, so I decided he would work well in the driving stunt. Still in need of another stunt driver, Rick said his buddy, thrill show stunt man Rick Seaman, had completed a film in Colorado and was coming through town to visit him. I had known of Seaman's fine reputation as a stunt driver – he could do anything with a car. So it was set, he would stay with Rick and Hal Klein would get his action sequences filmed without having to pay lodging, per diem or airfare for two stuntmen.

Rick Seaman doubled Arquette and Rick Barker and I drove the other n.d. (non-descript) vehicles. Seaman's 1965 Mustang kept logging up, so Frank "Cat" Ballew swapped it with the second Mustang double car. The car-crunching gag worked fine as Bondo chunks rained like hail when we broadsided each other. The director loved the shot, but Tommy Lee Jones went ballistic—he had made a deal with "Cat" to buy the double Mustang.

Six months later Rick Barker moved to Hollywood from Utah. Rick Seaman already resided in Reseda, and for the next couple of years they both worked every show I coordinated. For Barker it was the beginning of an illustrious career as a stunt coordinator and second unit action director. Seaman is still one of the best car men (not to mention auto mechanic) in the business and continues his legacy with a prestigious stunt driving school. You might as well learn from the best.

On one of *The Executioner's Song* return trips to Utah, at 7am, I walked into the Hollywood-Burbank Airport and found assistant director John Liberti setting up a shot for a new TV series called *The Fall Guy*. It was like old home week seeing many of the crewmembers I'd worked with over the years.

While talking with a makeup guy buddy, we were joined by a beautiful, breath-taking blond. Wearing a demure light blue blouse, tight fitting jeans and cowboy boots, she was radiant, and to top it off, very cordial. The clock was ticking and I felt like a mummy; pressed for time. I asked Liberti if Lee Majors had arrived. Having worked with Lee on *Big Valley* and *Six Million Dollar Man*, I just wanted to say a quick hello. "He's down the hallway," pointed Liberti, rolling his eyes. Rushing through the concourse I spotted Lee leaning against a wall, "Morning Lee, how's it going?" "Ahh oooooohh aggghh gaguga," he slurred. I couldn't understand a word he mumbled and quickly exited with a "Nice talking to ya." Rushing to board my plane, Liberti asked if I talked to Lee. I told him what happened and he just shook his head. Seems several folks on the show had "nose candy" cocaine problems.

Later, when the series aired, I realized the stunning blond I had talked with was the series stunning co-star, Heather Thomas. I've often wondered whatever happened to her. But, as for Liberti, he found the situation unbearable and soon moved on to other productions.

Again, while filming in Provo, backdropped by the Wasatch mountain range, I stared curiously at a local movie theater's marquee featuring their current movie, *George Burns II*. Then, it hit to me; this was the *Oh God! Book II* movie. I guess the local Mormon fathers evidently believed the original title was blasphemous.

Again, *The Executioner's Song* saga continued, one of the thrills in this business is that you never knew where or what your next job will be or who will be working with you.

Eli Wallach was always one of my favorite actors, appearing in *The Misfits, The Magnificent Seven, How the West Was Won* and so many other classic films. The November Provo area weather was nippy and would soon provide some of the best skiing conditions in the world. What the hell, it was downright cold, with a snow flurry every now and then. Eli came to the set sporting a classic trench coat, a la Bogart in *Casablanca*. He graciously accepted my compliments and said he had bought it in Poland. Well, folks, forget the Polish jokes, this was one fine piece of workmanship. The cloth, the cut, the styling and the stitching were impeccable.

When I mentioned working with his wife, Anne Jackson, on *Leave 'Em Laughing*, the Mickey Rooney TV movie, Eli discreetly described the difficulty she experienced with Rooney in various scenes. Eli Wallach was a gentleman.

The crew was preparing to film a fight scene between Tommy Lee and actor John Dennis Johnston. Great casting, as John personified the perfect redneck hick. The store was cramped with filming equipment as British director of photography Freddie Francis carefully lit the set. Schiller thoughtfully contemplated the fight scene, slowly walked to Tommy Lee and casually mentioned the neck hold he wanted Johnston to use. Then, without warning, Larry grabbed Jones in a tight headlock, "This is what I want to see." Larry jerked Jones back and forth violently with a vengeance then spun him loose. Massaging his neck, Tommy Lee resembled an escaped bull, "What the hell are you doing? Larry just grinned. With clenched fists Tommy moved toward Larry as Freddie and I jumped between them. This was one of those times when a director had a chance to wring an actor's neck and gleefully seized the opportunity.

Entering the production office, I scanned the room looking for Hal, and didn't notice a guy seated against the wall. All of a sudden he jumped into my face and wanted to know why I didn't say hello to him? "Oh, Hi Tommy," I said, continuing my search for Hal. Killer Gary Gilmore was a beer alcoholic who sucked 'em down every morning. Crewmembers reported that Jones was also indulging at 7am. His Method acting obviously worked—Tommy Lee Jones received a Best Actor Emmy Award for *The Executioner's Song*.

My soon-to-be-ex-stock broker, Floyd O'Gorman, invited me to The Silver Dollar Club luncheon at The Sportsman's Lodge. The guest this day was Gene Autry, with his old movie sidekick, Pat Buttram, as the Master of Ceremonies. The many accolades of Gene's wondrous career concluded with the presentation of a beautiful, engraved plaque. Taking his position at the podium mike, Gene was grateful, "I really don't deserve this honor, but then, I got a dose of clap once and I didn't deserve that either."

Unfortunately, Gene's longtime passionate desire for his Anaheim Angeles baseball team to win the World Series never happened and Pat didn't help the cause when he suggested, "Gene, instead of playing the national anthem at the stadium, you should play "Send in the Clowns." Sternly, Gene retorted, "That's not funny, Pat," and Pat never used the line again.

Production Manager Al Nicholson called me to take over the stunt coordinator reins on the *Jessica Novak* TV series at 20th. Ron Stein, the producer's stunt coordinator choice, moved on to another show, had hired the Jeanne Epper to double the series' star, Helen Shaver.

Epper was told to drive a vintage 1965 Ford Mustang convertible around a street corner, skid and crash into the curb. That is, from the camera angle, to make it appear to crash into the curb. She was told the Mustang was privately owned and must not be damaged, not even scratched. When the cameras rolled she careened directly into the curb. Everyone rushed to inspect the buckled-under right front wheel. The A.D. couldn't believe she did exactly what he told her not to do. Her explanation was that the director had told her to crash into the curb. That, of course, was never corroborated and, when I heard about it, I vowed never hire anyone who would purposely wreck a car when they were emphatically told not to do so. There was no reason to damage the vehicle when it was decided the camera angle and crashing sound effect would create the effect.

I relented while breaking down the show's next script, thinking about how the business is so quick to condemn. Word about her crash could cost her work and my rehiring her on the same series would defuse any tales of the incident. Plus, her brother, Gary and I were good friends. After much pleading, Nicholson reluctantly agreed when I assured him that she couldn't get into trouble since the shots were just run-bys. With the shots completed, Nicholson called, "Okay, you made your point, now hire someone else to double Helen. I never want to see Epper again." On the next show redhead Mary Peters became the perfect double for Shaver.

Seems I was never rid of her, bumping into the infamous Epper again when I was running *Having It All*, starring Dyan Cannon, Barry Newman and Hart Bochner. Immediately, she said she was Dyan Cannon's double. It was too late to contact Cannon to verify, and I figured she couldn't get into any trouble as a passenger. I hired her, and later thought of the many times she said she was "so and so's" double, but who knows? To hear her talk, she doubled everybody, but John Wayne.

Rick Seaman was driving and consisted of one 180° spinout with her in the rear seat. Up front, I told her "There will be no stunt adjustments." None of these stunts were death defying and, as I've maintained, you have to do more for your daily rate than just show up, a fact also emphasized by the show's producer John Thomas Lenox. Of course, when the day's filming was completed, she was visibly upset because she didn't receive a stunt adjustment.

When coordinating a show, if I didn't have a substantial stunt budget, I always mentioned these limitations – up front—to every prospective stunt performer. It was now their decision to accept or decline my job offer. If they accepted, there's nothing to more to discuss—unless the action gets out of control and does warrant a stunt adjustment. Should this occur, the fault is easily determined—a director may have insisted on multiple takes, or there's a technical or mechanical malfunction of a camera, vehicle, special effect, prop or firearm – only then, an equitable stunt adjustment would be negotiated.

Weeks later, word funneled back that Epper had bad-mouthed me because I didn't give her a stunt adjustment. She was a disappointment, a vast contrast to her sister, Stephanie, one of the best stunt women, and stunt double for Gunsmoke's Amanda Blake. Yes indeed, "No Good Deed Goes Unpunished."

Another segment of *Jessica Novak* required a van to back into another vehicle with the crash sound effect added later. Once again, Nicholson said, "Do not scratch the vehicles," so I brought in my old buddy, Bob Miles. On "Action," Bob accelerated the van in reverse, slammed on the brakes and rocked it to an abrupt stop. The shot looked great and from the camera angle it appeared a devastating collision had occurred. When I inspected the bumpers, neither had touched, but was so close I couldn't slide my little finger between them. This happens when you hire a talented professional who does what is requested and expected.

December 15, 1981, was a memorable day. While walking into my dining room, I experienced a slashing, knife-like pain from the left top of my head to my ear. I saw stars, almost blacked out, staggered a step and grabbed a chair to keep from falling. What the hell was that? Smoking two-three packs of Tareyton cigarettes a day was a start and was, obviously, a lack of oxygen getting to the brain.

Well, that was it—I didn't need to be zapped twice to realize I had pushed the envelope. For several weeks I had experienced a light feeling of pressure on the left top of my skull. You don't have to be a brain surgeon to figure that a heavy smoking habit, especially during the previous divorce – when I chain-smoked four packs a day – might cause a problem. Mostly, I recalled my father, a non-smoker, who had suffered a debilitating stroke, leaving him unable to speak and barely able to walk with a stroller.

Days and weeks passed when George Gobel, who had stopped cigarettes a year before, asked if I had yearned for a smoke. Shaking my head, he said, "You will." Several months later, George's prediction came true. Out of nowhere, I suddenly had a voracious desire for a cigarette. I could feel it between my fingers. It was as if I had never stopped smoking, even the taste had returned. I couldn't believe this compelling desire and actually said aloud, "No man, woman or thing is going to rule my life." Oddly enough, after uttering those words, the craving vanished instantly and has never reoccurred.

Friends often admire my having "stopped," praising my great willpower and character. Well, it wasn't a difficult decision to make. What do you want to do? Smoke and suffer a stroke or quit? My only question is where is all the money I've saved by not smoking? In 1981 a pack cost 65 cents. Today, for a top brand, you'll pay $6-$7.

CHAPTER 24

1982

Producer John Thomas Lenox, newly hired by Hill-Mandelker Productions, brought me in for their latest project. Executive producer Leonard Hill, a former ABC network executive, mentioned how much he "appreciated my work" and welcomed me to their company's first television pilot. Hmmm, "appreciated my work"— while he was an exec at ABC. Hollywood really is a small town.

The pilot for *Tucker's Witch* starred Kim Cattrall and Art Hindle with Peter H. Hunt directing. Peter and I hit it off immediately, especially when I heard he had helmed Mark Twain's *Life on the Mississippi*, starring Robert Lansing. My interest in Twain and America's paddle-wheel boats made it one of my favorite films. Peter truly captured the antebellum era and smiled when I described the film's many facets and scenes using the antiquated, mid-1800s colloquialisms and river language. Coincidentally, of particular interest to him was the Julia Belle Swain, featured in Peter's film, the same paddle wheeler that ran over me in *Tom Sawyer*.

Tucker's Witch action included a fight scene between Cattrall and the script's villain. Kim absorbed my every word as I explained the techniques of throwing picture punches. An actor named Ted Danson receiving her punishing blows reacted appropriately and it was a "Print." Surprisingly, Kim threw a better punch than many male actors I trained over the years. To reiterate, picture fights are simply action and reaction and Danson's timing, combined with Kim's, was perfect. Come September, I would work with Ted again, when he starred as Sam Malone in a new TV series called *Cheers*.

Once again, *Tucker's Witch* had the obligatory car chase and I brought in Rick Barker and Rick Seaman to do what they did so well, plus the years Seaman spent performing in car thrill shows had also made him an ace mechanic. His auto garage on wheels, "Big Blue," more than proved its worth when the lead picture car, a Fire Engine Red 1968 Chevy Camero convertible, blew its water pump. Aside from the production time saved, the repair more than pleased Director Hunt who was to purchase the car after the show was completed. Peter also wanted the car to stay in one piece and was ecstatic when Rick ran the ragtop into a Griffith Park embankment without producing a scratch.

CBS bought the *Tucker's Witch* pilot and Lenny Hill thanked me, crediting the exciting car chase and action for the sale of their first TV series. "You're part of our team and you'll be there when we start filming." Oh, oh. There it is again, The Producer's Kiss of Death.

Well, I wasn't there and neither were Kim Cattrell and Art Hindle, who were replaced by Catherine Hicks and Tim Matheson. Again, it was just another time you don't count your chickens. Everyone in this business, with an iota amount of common sense, soon realizes that show biz is a crapshoot and you just keep tossing the dice. It's appropriate that Kim found greater success on HBO's *Sex and the City* TV series.

I was still looking to get *San Francisco Rip-Off* produced. After he read the screenplay, producer John Thomas Lenox and I had lunch in the Twentieth Century Fox commissary. He had just signed a multiple movie-of-the week deal with NBC and, over the best Cobb Salad I've ever tasted, John proceeded to cite the script's elements he enjoyed. Without notes, I was impressed until he mentioned the ending. He believed it was immoral that Troy and Edee should escape with the cash. I countered, "They got away in *The Thomas Crown Affair* and *Topkapi*, and it will have everyone saying, 'I wish I was them.'" He was unrelenting and didn't offer an alternative idea. I later suspected his notion was based on his Texas Southern Baptist upbringingand I should have exerted some force. I walked away. Friends said I should have acquiesced, changed the ending, and I would have found a new career as a TV Producer. For several years I gave it much thought—the O'Henry ending was part of the film's charm. Well, in retrospect, just maybe I should have rethought my decision. It seemed like a good...

Well into the 1980s, I continued to pursue independent film funding including a Louisiana multimillionaire who vowed to provide full financing when he returned from the hospital, but he died on the operating table. It's amazing what some guys will do to get out of a deal.

Later, when Congress, in their infinite wisdom, began eliminating interest deductions from car loans, credit cards, etc., they included the independent TV and film production tax shelters. Consequently, many stanch investors vanished and seeking independent film funding became a hopeless cause.

A musician buddy, Burr Middleton, was performing at Sterling's, a small dinner club in Santa Monica, when Jane Fonda attended with her 1960's then husband, radical-politician Tom Hayden. They invited him to a party at their Victorian home on Eighth Street. While mingling with the guests, the booze flowed and nature soon called. Relieving himself at the half-bath commode, Burr found himself staring face-to-face with a large, framed poster of China's head Commie, Mao Tse Tung. He confronted Mr. Hayden-Fonda, who replied with a wink and a grin, "Well, we are a *little* pink." Yeah, and that's like being a *little* pregnant.

Another old buddy, diminutive stunt man, Bobby Porter invited me on *The Toy*, a Richard Donner film for Producer Ray Stark and Columbia. I was thrilled to be returning to Louisiana, in Baton Rouge, but still felt cautious about the 1979 incident. We filmed on a multi-millionaire's private estate, The Chardonnet, with Richard Pryor, Jackie Gleason, Teresa Ganzel, Ned Beatty and Scott Swartz starring in this updated version of a French film.

Bobby assembled a varied group of action performers to wreck Gleason's garden party. Orwin Harvey and Greg Elam doubled Gleason and Pryor, respectively, as Cheré Bryson, Bill Couch, George Fisher, Donna Hall, Bill Hart, Bob Herron, Henry Wills, Jerry Wills and I completed the stunt troop.

Initially, we were told the filming would take two weeks, but soon heard that Pryor was "under the weather" and our stay would be extended to a month. Rumors of drug abuse abound, and soon became evident via "Gypsy," a gregarious Memphis caterer supplied Pryor's "medication." His low profile was actuated by his periodic appearances in a fire-engine red, 1976 Cadillac convertible, an obvious attempt to throw the Feds off his trail.

While waiting for our action scenes to begin we became tourists, visiting New Orleans and the luscious, age-old, plantations surrounding the Louisiana capital. A particular interesting visit to the Baton Rouge Capital building's narrow hallway revealed where Governor Huey Long was assassinated in 1935, with .45 caliber bullet holes in the marble walls large enough to insert your pinky finger.

After one of our many sightseeing jaunts, George Fisher (a transplanted New Yorker) and I were crossing the garden party lawn area when he asked, "What does antebellum mean?" Before I could respond, an exquisitely dressed lady member of Baton Rouge's elite politely said, "It means before the war." A puzzled George then queried, "What war?" Like a rising thermometer, the lady's face turned crimson, emphatically blurted, "What War? There was only one war and you damn Yankees started it!" George's look of bewilderment had me doubled up.

Stunt gal Cheré Bryson was a stunningly beautiful, tall, intelligent blond with a wicked sense of humor. At 38 years old, a former Playboy bunny, and hostess on Elvis' jet, she maintained her perfect figure running daily—possessed an exquisite set of Casabas that matched her age in inches. When I suggested, "It must be difficult—when you meet a guy, all you see are his eyelids," she roared with laughter. We became friends and would have after-work drinks nightly in the Bellemont Motel lounge. One evening, her tiny, kinky curls, caused me to remark, "Your hair looks like shit!" Casually, sipping her drink, she replied, "Yeah, I keep hearing that!" At once, I could hear what the late comedian Sam Kinison might have screamed, "Well, CHAAAAANGE ITTTT!!!"

Cheré and I were chosen to fall into a fountain during the garden party melee and one hour later I had an excruciating pain running between my left ear and neck. Even with wadded cotton in my ears as a precaution, I surmised it was caused from the stagnant fountain water. A production driver drove me to a local doctor who produced a syringe—"I'm going to give you a shot of Cortisone in your neck." I jumped off the examining table, "You are like Hell!" "Oh," he said, scribbling a prescription, "then take this." It was for Dimetapp, which is now a current over-the-counter medication which had nothing to do with the pain I was experiencing.

The next-door pharmacist filled the prescription, I took two pills immediately and 30 minutes later I was perfectly well. To this day, I have never experienced another neck pain, but damned if I was going to have him shoot Cortisone into my neck and find it in my big toe the next morning. Ya gotta watch them ol' doctors. If it doesn't seem right, don't do it—which, again, applies to stunts and to life.

Between takes Cheré and I continued our verbal sparring as I responded to her invasive personal question, "Are you writing a book?" "Yeah!" she said very determined. "Well, call it a hidden mystery and stick it up your ass!" Richard Pryor roared, "Hey, that's a good one. Can I use it?" Surprised he hadn't heard the line, I grinned, "Richard, be my guest."

Our all day trek to New Orleans was fun, walking the French Quarter, the many shops, culminating with music, dinner and dancing to Woody Herman and His Thundering Herd aboard The President paddlewheel boat.

Back on the set, the biggest disappointment was Jackie Gleason. Nothing had changed in the 15 years since Preminger's *Skidoo* at Paramount—he was still aloof and demanding. We watched daily as he arrogantly strolled from his motorhome, followed in lock step by his wife, stepson and entourage, including his aged manservant, Mel Spear (whom I suspected was related to Sammy Spear, Gleason's former orchestra leader on his Miami TV show).

This day, Gleason settled in his tall director's chair, glaring at Spear, sarcastically demanded, "Where are my glasses, Mel?" Spears, looked befuddled, fumbling, checked his sport coat pockets, pulled open the director's chair pockets as Gleason continued his chiding, "Where are they, MEL?" Then, finally, "They're on the kitchen counter in the motorhome, MEL. Right where YOU left them, MEL." We looked at each other, wondering how much old Mel was earning to take this abuse.

Later, I asked Director Dick Donner, whom I'd known since the 1960's *Felony Squad* TV series, "What's his story?" Dick just shook his head, "I don't know. I can't get anything out of him [acting-wise]. He certainly doesn't need the money."

Overall, *The Toy* location was one of the best, and more of a vacation than a location, but the film was a box office flop. What happened? Theoretically, it had all of the elements: One of Hollywood's prime producers, a fine director, name actors and a seemingly good story premise. Studios will pay millions for the answer.

Producer John Thomas Lenox called to say we had a movie-of-the-week to do, *Having It All*, starring Dyan Cannon, Barry Newman, Hart Bochner and Melanie Chartoff. Again, I assembled Rick Seaman, Rick Barker, Roger Creed, Bob Miles, Ransom Walrod and, as previously mentioned, Jeannie Epper.

Director Edward Zwick, an intense, fast rising talent, explained the chase elements he desired, especially, a long lens shot of a car racing toward camera as another car enters side frame, causing a near miss. (Why isn't it called a 'near hit'?) I assigned a driver to enter off-frame as Rick Seaman headed toward camera, but this driver panicked. Veteran stunt man Bob Miles was in the passenger seat and I should have asked him to take the wheel – but I didn't. How stupid. I really missed the ball on that one.

I drove the taxicab during an interior shot of Cannon and Newman – and as our traffic lane moved along we heard one hellava crash. Seems a right lane driver was too busy watching our filming and didn't see the stopped car in front of him. I've often wondered how the driver explained the accident to his auto insurance company. A sleazy lawyer (a redundancy) might have accused the film company of causing an attractive nuisance.

The July 23, 1982, morning papers shockingly described the tragic death of actor Vic Morrow and two Vietnamese children during the filming of *Twilight Zone: The Movie*. Renee Chen slipped from Vic's grip as he carried the children across the Santa Clarita River. Suddenly, the copter fell crushing Renee. Vic and Myca Dinh Le were decapitated by the craft's main rotor.

Vic voiced his premonition to his motorhome driver, Norman Northam, "I really have a funny feeling about this. I don't want to do it."

Vic and I had worked on the 1961 *Combat* TV series and later became drinking buddies at the Back Stage a decade later. I was incensed by the reported "accident" and wanted answers. Something was dreadfully wrong with this picture.

When filming action it is customary to rehearse a scene by the numbers so everyone involved – in all departments—knows exactly what to do. Many times I have watched directors, during the actual filming, ignore what was rehearsed, become excited and scream into the radio, "Faster! Faster! Closer! Closer!" At that moment, I would shut everything down. When somebody does the unexpected, something not rehearsed, that's when a disaster happens.

A day later, Bill, a former LAPD detective buddy now a California Occupational Safety and Health Administration (Cal/OSHA) investigator on this case phoned for my opinion. Simply, I related, once the first assistant director rolls camera, the set then becomes the director's domain; he or she is in charge – period. The film director is responsible until he or she yells, "Cut!"

As always, film industry rumors ran rampant with fictitious tales, but I found my former writing partner, Bob Louden, was a crewmember and had witnessed the helicopter crash. He heard director John Landis demanding the copter pilot to go "Lower! Lower! Lower!"

During a multi-camera shot, the director views the scene from one angle, one perspective. The other cameras may also be filming the "perfect shot", but an excitable director may give counter-commands detrimental to the crew or performer's safety.

These wayward instructions, coupled with a copter pilot unfamiliar and inexperienced in filming were a perfect formula for disaster. If veteran Hollywood chopper stunt pilots James Gavin or Chuck Tamburro had been flying that copter they would have shut down the shot as soon as Landis opened his mouth.

Twilight Zone stunt coordinator Gary McLarty was a copter passenger during the crash, standing right behind pilot Dorsey Wingo. A special effects explosion sent a fireball into the cabin, "I ducked," said Gary, "Then I heard Wingo scream, 'My neck is burning!'" and then we crashed. For two days prior I had had a premonition about a copter crash."

John Landis and four production personnel were charged with involuntary manslaughter. The ensuing litigation forced Landis and Warner Bros. to bring in the big legal guns.

Tennessee Attorney James Neal was Chief Counsel to the Watergate Special Prosecution Force. His other famous cases include the criminal defense of Ford Motor Company's Pinto's exploding gas tank; the successful defense of Dr. Nichopoulos and his Elvis Presley prescriptions; and the defense of Louisiana's colorful governor, Edwin Edwards.

In the very visible trial spanning five years, Landis was acquitted in 1987, proving once again in a Los Angeles courtroom you receive the best justice you can buy.

Foot Note: Several camera crewmembers were witnesses for the prosecution and have not worked a day in Hollywood since. Their careers were and are over!

Ed Asner, the caustic, loveable, WJM boss of *The Mary Tyler Moore Show*, became the President of the Screen Actors Guild. I had known Ed casually when he was a guest heavy on the various crime shows I'd worked. His Screen Actors Guild presidency soon revealed one of his many hidden agendas, specifically, his rumored intention to make a $26,000 donation to the Sandanistas in El Salvador—riled SAG's Hollywood conservative rank and file, caused them to form:

AWAG

ACTORS WORKING FOR AN ACTORS' GUILD

A non-partisan association of Screen Actors Guild members dedicated to preserving the Guild's historic function
To protect, preserve and enhance wages, working conditions, welfare and employment of professional actors.

STEERING COMMITTEE
Chairman & SAG Board Member Morgan Paul
Co-Chairman & SAG Board Member Marie Windsor

Anthony Caruso, Don Dubbins, Bob Herron, Charlton Heston, Don Nagel & Renee Wedel

All Former or Present SAG Board Members

Leon Ames, SAG President Emeritus
James Cagney, SAG President 1942-44
George Murphy, SAG President 1944-45
Walter Pidgeon, SAG President 1952-57
Howard Keel, SAG President 1958-59
George Chandler, SAG President 1960-63
Charlton Heston, SAG President 1965-71
Bill Baldwin, SAG, Form. AFTRA President
Tyler McVey, SAG, Form. AFTRA President
Bob Easton, Former SAG 1st VP
Ricardo Montalban, Form. SAG 3rd VP

FORMER or PRESENT SAG BOARD MEMBERS

Ann Doran	Ernest Borgnine
Richard Jaeckel	Pat O'Brien
Gary Collins	Iron Eyes Cody
Mary Ann Mobley	Claude Akins
William Fowler	Don DeFore
Gil Perkins	Alan Young
Jack Ging	Gene Raymond
Don Randolph	Robert Stack
Richard Crenna	Lloyd Nolan

* * * * *

Jeb Adams
Gary Adler
Patrick Alan
Lane Allen
Elvia Allman
Pat Anderson
Tige Andrews
Joe Anthony
Arliss Dimitra
Bob Askey
Gene Autry
Roger Bacon
William Bakewell
Parley Baer
Jeanne Baird
Socrates Ballis
Billy Barty
Anita Bayless
Mabir Bedi
Bruce Bennett
Frances Bergen
Marie Berry
Barbara Billingsley
Rhio H. Blair
Roger Borden
Iain Bodkin
Jane Boldizar
Gary Bonart
Peter Bourne
Leo Gordon
Bob Gormley
Coleen Gray
Virginia Grey
Monte Hale
Colin Hamilton

Gene Hartline
Orwin C. Harvey
Elois Hardt
Eileen Heckert
Trevor Henley
Mike Henry
Art Hern
James R. Hess
John Hillerman
Robert Hodge
Fred Hoffman
Les Hoffman
Wendy Hoffman
Jonathan Hole
Tom Holland
Bob Hope
Peter Horton
Rosetta Howard
Tom Howard
John"Bear"Hudkins
Sidney Hutchinson
Dean Jagger
Norma Jean Jahn
Frank Jamus
Baby Jane
Loren Janes
Harvey Jason
Pamela Jason
Justine Johnson
Dean Jones
Charles R. Jumps
Eddie Kafafian
Kim Kahana, Sr.
Debbie Kahana
Kim Kahana, Jr.

Rick Kahana
Tony Kahana
Richard Karlan
John Kelly
George Kennedy
Terry Kingsley Smith
Ted Knight
Josie Knur
Ron Kowall
Paul L'Amoreaux
Reese Lane
William T. Lane
Mary Lansing
Sonny Landham
Bruce Boxleitner
Tom Brent
Kate Brocker
Becky Bronson
Foster Brooks
Carlos Brown
Nacio Herb Brown, Jr.
Anthony Brubaker
Owen Bush
Henry A. Calia
Jimmy Casino
Jean Carson
Lynne Carter
Mike Cassidy
Dottie Catching
Tony Cesere
Diane Chambers
Dan Chandler
David Clover
Emily Cobb
Rhodie Cogan

Michael Cohen
Frances Colland
Mike Connors
Sharon Connors
Joanna Conrad
Nancy Conrad
Robert Conrad
Carolyn Conwell
John Leuger
Carey Loftin
Thomas Logan
Jack Lord
Rosemary Lord
Vincent Lucchesi
Billy Jack Ludwig
Mafa Lyons
Malna Lyons
Patricia Lynn
George Maharis
Ann Mandra
Fritz Manes
Catherine Martin
Denver Mattson
Virginia Mayo
Mike Mazurki
Stephen Mandel
Harry Middlebrooks
Arthur Monde
Ed Morgan
Alberto Morin
Scott Douglas Morrow
Simon MacCorkindale
Joel McCrea
Jim McKrell
Connie Stevens

Ron McPherson
Edward E. Ness
K.C. Nichols
Robert Noel
Mayf Nutter
Frank Oberschall
Margaret O'Brien
Jeanette O'Connor
John O'Leary
Raymond O'Keefe
Janet Lee Orcutt
Harvey G. Parry
Dorothy Patterson
Sidney Paul
Richard Peel
Cynthia Pepper
John Bennett Perry
Penny Peyser
Liana Pierce
Steve Potter
Phil Poulos
Mala Powers
Wayne Powers
Charmian Pratt
Sorin S. Pricopie
Ronald A. Prince
Benito Prezia
Lynn Redgrave
Charles Courtney
James Crear
Richard Crenna
Sondra Currie
Bill Culpepper
Linda Dales
Ray Daley

Vince Deadrick, Sr.
Cesare Danova
Dianne Davis
Bud George Davis
Robert Dannon
Larraine Day
Lynda Day
Richard Deacon
Douglas Dean
Sandra de Bruin
Paula Dell
Pilar Del Rey
George Di Cenzo
Shane Dixon
Elinor Donahue
Robert Donner
Marta Dubois
Dick Durock
Clint Eastwood
Ron Ely
Clifford J. Emmich
Corinne Entratter
Clive Revill
Burt Reynolds
Glenn Robards
Walter P. Robles
George Robotham
Dinah Rogers
Roy Rogers
Wayne Rogers
Mic Rodgers
Cesar Romero
Rex Ryon
Russ Saunders
Ephram Schaffer

Fred Scheiwiller
Lizabeth Scott
Max Showalter
Frank Sinatra
Fred Slyter
Mary Sinclair
Penny Singleton
Dean Smith
Janice Lee Spitzer
Peter M. Spitzer
Ann Stanwell
Barbara Stanwick
Laraine Stephens
Sandy McPeak
James Stewart
George Stover
Beatrice Straight
Robin Strand
Gloria Strook
Randy Stuart
Thomas W. Sutphen
Mike Swann
Joe E. Tata
June Whitley Taylor
Vallie Ullman
Wayne "Buddy" Van Horn
Jack M. Verbois
Dominick Leo Verducci
Fred Vinroot
Jesse Vint
Clint Walker
Giselle Walker
Lila Waters
William C. Watson
Jesse Wayne

Jack Webb
Robert Webber
John Stuart West
Wallace Whipple
Kenneth White
Thelma White
Jack C. Williams
Nicol Ericson
Michael Ehrlich
Dale Evans
Chad Everett
Herbert Edelman
La Velda Fann
Midge Ferrell
Melinda O. Fee
Marina Ferrier
Lila Finn
Steve Fisher
Susan Flannery
Med Flory
Art Frankel
Pamela Franklin
Helen Funai
Ginny Gagnon
Don Galloway
Leonard P. Geer
Chris George
Richard Geary
Larry Gelbmann
Stuart A. Germain
Edmund Gilbert
Joseph Gilbride
Linda Hoy Gill
Kay Gillian
Hugh Gillin

Robert Ginty
Jonathan Winters
Christina Wioch
Joe Witherell
Robert Word, II
Millie Wright
Maris Wrixon

Tracy Keenan Wynn
Bob Yerkes
Brayton Yerkes
Efrem Zimbalist, Jr.
Alan Young
Betty White

An AWAG fund-raising event at the Tail O' the Cock in Studio City assembled a contingent of conservative actors, including Charlton Heston, all vying to keep Asner's agenda in check. While standing with my old buddy Don Galloway from *Ironside* enjoying show biz "war stories", I received a sound bump to my left arm by someone rushing by. The hit almost knocked the drink out of my left hand, but being a pro, I didn't spill a drop. We all looked toward the perpetrator and it was *Wild Wild West*'s Bob Conrad (real name Konrad Robert Falkowski), who had now whipped around into a boxer's stance. Unassuming, I said, "Hi Bob" and turned back to Galloway to continue our conversation. I didn't realize until the next day that Conrad had attempted to provoke an incident. Why? Who knows the motive behind his actions? It's anybody's guess, but this wacko was always off plumb and when you check any dictionary under "asshole – noun. A fool, a stupid or foolish person," you'll see his photo.

Conrad's condescending demeanor came to a head one evening in the Back Stage when he mouthed off to *Wild Wild West* stunt coordinator Whitey Hughes. "You work for me," Conrad bellowed, prompting "one-punch" Whitey to utter, "Not anymore," and knocked Conrad through the Back Stage kitchen's swinging doors.

AWAG worked as intended. Yet, the biggest thrill of the evening, aside from lending a helpful hand to curtail Asner's political interests, was receiving a delicious kiss on the lips from actress Marie Windsor.

Producer Hal Klein called from Vicksburg requesting a good water man to double Ralph Waite on his CBS-TV series, *The Mississippi*. Dick Geary had doubled Waite previously and I also called Marcia Holley to double the female guest star. The gag involved being knocked from a barge into Ol' Man River. Dick and Marcia performed admirably and Geary later related a river tale. Seems a barge had sunk after colliding with a bridge at the confluence of the Mississippi and Yazoo rivers. Reportedly, divers made a quick exit when they "discovered a mammoth catfish weighing 500 pounds"—capable of swallowing a man whole.

Months before Dave Cass started *Smokey and the Bandit III*, and I gave him a copy of *San Francisco Rip-Off*, hopeful that he would present it to the film's director Dick Lowry, who just might want *Rip-Off* to be his next production.

Cass returned from *Smokey III*, invited me to his Sylmar home to see the stunt photos. Well, there, in the 8x10 black and white glossy photos was the prime stunt Conrad Palmisano had devised for MY script—a speeding car traveling under a forty-foot tractor-trailer. I also couldn't believe the sequential photos of another car crashing through a milk tanker. When I mentioned he had stolen the stunts from my script, he bald-faced lied, saying Everett Creach had created all of the gags.

Cass was supposed to be a buddy, who had bragged his earnings jumped from twenty thousand to $80,000 the first year after I sponsored him into SAMP.

Makeup man Tony Lane became livid when I related Cass' story, and mentioned how Cass had stolen his *The Witch of Laurel Canyon* tale, which had the identical storyline of the *Tucker's Witch* TV series I had stunt coordinated. Cass and Bill Bast were buddy-buddy; Bast wrote the *Tucker's Witch* script.

Months later, I chance met a congratulatory Dick Warlock, "Hey I hear you're now a Producer." Taken aback, I said my projects were in need of funding and you're not a producer until the completed film is in the can—then asked where he got his information? "Oh, Dave Cass said you're now producing movies." Seems Cass had seen Daily Variety's list of recently incorporated production companies, my Diamond J Entertainment. This rumor also explained my recent decline of stunt work. Now, like Denver Mattson, I was pigeonholed and no longer considered for stunts because I was now a Producer. This was the first nail in the coffin of my stunt career.

Reverting to square one, Steve Lodge had introduced me to Cass in the late sixties. A year or so later, Lodge complained that Cass has stolen his idea for a Saturday morning cowboy cliffhanger TV serial, called it *Deputy Dan* and had shot a 16mm film pilot in Texas. "Your idea?" I said, "That was my idea, and we were going to film it with my 16mm Bolex camera equipment." "Oh yeah," mumbled Lodge. In retrospect, Lodge was a no good SOB from the moment we met.

Almost every time Cass attempted a stunt he came away injured as evidenced on the first day we met, he had knocked his front teeth out diving at a stagecoach while doubling Robert Mitchum in Tucson. Aspiring to be an actor, he adopted Lodge's advice to "Lower your voice and squint like Eastwood," and relied on his six-foot-four height to carry him, never realizing it takes acting talent to convincingly perform a role.

On September 21, the *Cheers* TV series filmed its fifth episode on Paramount's Stage 25, as I doubled the "Coach", actor/director, Nick Colasanto. I had worked with Nick years before when he directed Tony Curtis' *McCoy* TV series at Universal.

Several days earlier, the *Cheers* rehearsals had just begun as I entered the sound stage with my stunt bag in hand. Producer-Director James Burrows (son of Broadway's great guru, Abe Burrows) gave me full reign to do the fall as I wished, but I knew exactly what he wanted. In rehearsal, on cue, I fell backward down the stairs. Nice guys George Wendt and John Ratzenberger commended me as Rhea Perlman and Shelly Long practiced a soft shoe, two-step tap dance. Looking toward me, Shelly said, "I have to piss" and repeated it two more times. All I could think, "Does she need my permission?" Finally she walked over and I mentioned that the bar background is an interesting touch to the show's storyline. Instantly, with a condescending snarl, "Well, I don't go to bars!" Eagerly grasping her caustic attitude, I retorted, "Well, maybe you should, you might have some fun."

History would later prove she was not a favorite among her fellow cast members or even movie audiences. After leaving *Cheers*, she would vie with Parnell Roberts and David Caruso for Hollywood's "Worst Decision I Ever Made" award.

Cheers production manager Penny Adams and I negotiated my weekly salary, including the stair fall. Initially, she wanted me to be present during all rehearsals, performing a stair fall each time. Four camera shows are notorious for their rehearsals and when I mentioned an additional $250 per fall, she suggested I return on filming day.

I knew how to do stair falls and didn't need the practice, plus I firmly believed in the age-old question, "Why tempt the Gods?" Over the years, you realize that every time the same stunt is performed the probability of an injury increases proportionately.

Filming with a full studio audience, I did the stair fall, landing behind the carved cigar store Indian and a partition. A hole in the adjacent wall allowed Nick and me to change places as the cast rushed to his aid. The audience howled when he appeared with tousled hair, brushing himself off. Once again the old "Texas Switch" worked. This classic scene would later become part of the Cheers 200th Episode Anniversary show.

Charlene Roberson, the makeup artist on Rooney's *Leave'em Laughing*, now handling Danson, greeted me. She was startled when I returned the shoebox of clown makeup we used in Chicago, "Gee, the rubber clown nose is still like new after all this time."

On *Hill Street Blues*, while having my hair sprayed white to double Ralph Manza, costar Veronica Hamel asked me for a light. I was a fan of the series and was awed by her acting ability, radiant beauty and grace. As my lighter moved toward her cigarette my hand began trembling. Our eyes met and we both broke up. Another beautiful had lady gotten to me, but in a delightfully nice way.

1983

Steve Lodge wrote and would direct a 90-minute documentary on the Salt Wells Villa, a Fallon, Nevada, bordello sixty miles east of Reno, recommended me as associate producer. We traversed California 395 north to Reno, stopped off at Harrah's Automobile Museum in Sparks, Nevada, the best $5.00 I ever spent. For almost four hours, we enjoyed a magnificent collection of vintage vehicles dating from 1900. When I inquired the value of a 1920's Bugatti roadster, the white-haired mechanic shook his head, "Name any price, it's the only one in the world." Unfortunately, when Bill Harrah died, most of the collection was sold to private collectors.

The Salt Wells Villa, like the infamous Mustang Ranch, was comprised of several adjoining mobile trailers. Every Monday morning at 9:00, the ladies assembled at a Fallon doctor's office for their weekly examination. When I questioned the possibility of the ladies contracting a disease during the ensuing six days the doctor just shrugged his shoulders.

Videotaping commenced and nightly we retreated to our Fallon motel for dinner and libations. One of the lasses asked me to see her later, and I must admit I was flattered, even tempted, until the producer said, "There are no freebies here." However, our camera operator decided to sample the Villa's merchandise, spent an entire night and $600, two-thirds of his salary for the entire shoot.

The Villa's lady owner wanted a videotape of several girls performing their specialties, but Lodge panicked, screamed like a 12 year old girl, declined to direct the explicit sex scenes. So, like the trooper that I am, I directed the cameraman from a 5" monitor. Later, when I tried to explain what we'd shot, the producer said, "I was watching from behind the two-way mirror. There's one in every room." When we wrapped I traveled Highway 80 west from Reno, past Truckee to Sacramento, then on to San Francisco.

In the City by the Bay, I connected with producer Jonathan Bernstein, who wanted me as his stunt coordinator on *Partners in Crime*, starring Lynda Carter and Loni Anderson, a TV movie-of-the-week/pilot. The ladies played detective agency partners and the excellent who-done-it script was an Agatha Christie: American Style. I loved it. However, Lynda Carter had the clout and soon fired executive producer Leonard Stern, Bernstein and the entire production staff, then brought in her own stunt coordinator. The insipid scripts became tedious and the series only lasted thirteen weeks.

Moving on, through a mutual friend, I met Richard Robinson, a writer-turned-producer for the Orlando-based, Florida International Film Corporation. Immediately, I was elated by his offer to join the budding production company, lured with a round-trip ticket to explore their new facilities. De-planing the Delta jet from L.A., a black limousine delivered me to a luxurious hotel. Not bad, I thought, a bit extravagant, but if they've got the money, why not? Later, Robinson had a local production exec Rodney Cavin give me the grand tour. I agreed to the $2500 week assistant director's salary, returned to L.A. to pack for four months of production.

Returning, the Florida humidity hit me like a belt in the chops, so thick I couldn't take a deep breath as Cavin drove me to a small motel on the far outskirts of Orlando. Evidently, in the week I was absent, a financial austerity program had begun—this room was a dump and Cavin quickly relocated me at a major hotel. That small voice was talking to me again.

In the ensuing two weeks I scheduled and budgeted the proposed film with Cavin. While we were within realistic budget guidelines,

Robinson would then want the budget reduced again. It became obvious the film funding wasn't forthcoming and he was attempting to budget the film according to the money he could raise—a ruse that seldom works out.

My first week's salary arrived, but by week two, Robinson asked us all to take reduced amounts, vowing the balances would be paid when the funding was in place. Weeks passed and little changed though Robinson seemed like a kid in a candy shop with his uncontrolled spending. Several calls to Hollywood confirmed my suspicions—Robinson had been involved in several shady production deals. Also, he had rewritten Steve Lodge's *Kingdom of the Spiders*, thus usurping writing credit and the bulk of the writer's residuals. Notably, every script submitted to him at FIFC received his declared, "It needs a rewrite!" Hell, that can be said about damn near every script ever written, but that was his ploy to receive a writer's credit.

After five weeks, FIFC now owed me $12,589 in back wages and enough was enough. I knew how to make pictures and didn't need any more unpaid practice. At the Orlando Airport, I called Robinson's wife, Gayle, notified her of the rental car's location and returned to California.

Gayle was a vivacious, busty blond with an exquisite body and completely subservient to her coked-up husband. A later story involved Robinson's gala party on a chartered cabin cruiser in an attempt to attract investors. He and Patty had an open marriage, so Robinson suggested she provide a little persuasive fun to a potential investor. Minutes later, Robinson saw the investor standing alone on the ship's bridge. Checking below deck, he found Gayle copulating a crewmember. Robinson cursed, and chased them until the Captain with several crewmembers subdued him. Evidently, when Robinson first pointed out the investor, Gayle mistook the lucky crewmember standing nearby for Mr. Moneybags.

Subsequently, FIFC was dissolved, but not before Robinson has squandered almost $100,000—much of it on nose candy. He died of a heart attack at 52, a few years later.

The Stuntmen's Association's Picnic was held annually at the Studio City Municipal Park. Many SAMP members were pissed because they had to "stake out" the park area at six a.m. picnic morning to prevent John Q. Public from homesteading. To prevent this problem and to provide a better picnic location, I suggested the Veterans of Foreign Wars facilities in Reseda. The VFW charge of $1.00 per person would be offset by the benevolent donations of hamburgers, hot dogs, ice cream, soda, candy and beer from merchants on behalf of our invited local orphanage children.

This spacious, six-acre, VFW facility was the ideal picnic location with a twenty-foot barbeque grill, a fully-equipped kitchen, a large community room with a juke box, tree-shaded picnic tables, an Olympic-size swimming pool, two baseball fields and parking for over 100 vehicles.

Touring the complex with SAMP's picnic chairman, George Wilbur, one of those born again fellows, he seemed pleased until he spied the VFW member's cocktail lounge. With a furrowed brow he blatantly stated, "We can't hold the picnic here, all the guys will get drunk!" I thought he was kidding, but he wasn't. This site epitomized the perfect family-oriented recreation center with every amenity imaginable, but this clown believed all the guys were going to get falling-down drunk. Had member intoxication ever been a problem at previous SAMP picnics? Never.

Hubie Kerns, Sr., *Batman* TV series stunt double for Adam West, knew my production background, called to say he needed me immediately in St. George, Utah. He was producing *Solo*, the story of a housewife lost on her first solo airplane flight. It was a Mormon-funded film directed by Lyman Dayton, noted for his low-budget film blockbusters.

For whatever reasons, on the second day into filming, the Boulder, Colorado, crew decided they preferred me the first assistant director. Kerns panicked. The production company was a Directors Guild of America signatory, but he didn't want to add another DGA member to the film's meager $644,000 budget.

I was not a DGA member, though the opportunity to join the Guild had availed itself on several previous occasions. My main reason for not joining, besides the exorbitant $5000 initiation fee, was that I didn't want to be another DGA member listed on the guild's out-of-work work roster. During this time, I was working more as a non-union assistant director than many of the DGA A.D.'s I had known for years.

A persistent Hubie persuaded me to take over the show with his promise to pay me under-the-table. To protect his ass from a DGA fine and reprimand our handshake swore me to secrecy.

Between shots I overheard the sound mixer, Jerry Wolfe, whispering to the script girl. Interrupting, I asked him to explain what I thought I had heard. Reluctantly, he admitted running out of recording tape during a previous shot and now, he was actually attempting to cover it up. How could he believe he'd get away with this? We would discover the missing sound track when the dailies returned from the lab. But the big question was how do you run out of tape when the Nagra sound recorder is twelve inches from your nose?

Wolf was from Hollywood and constantly complained, "I'm only getting a $1000 a week and that includes my equipment." Really, I thought, "Well Pal, you made the deal, so live with it." That evening, I confronted Hubie, asking where he had found this guy, "Oh, he's married to Barbara the makeup gal." Hubie figured to save an additional motel room cost, but offered to have another sound mixer on the set "by tomorrow." But I relented, believing my "people skills" could solve the problem. Wrong. Always get rid of the bad apples.

Back on the set, nothing changed—when I announced, "Standing by to roll," this bozo was fifty yards away playing Frisbee with his boom operator, when he should have been watching the cast rehearsals. Problems continued and, of the entire crew, he was the only individual to cause any problems during the entire twenty-one days of filming.

While readying to film at a woman's maternity clinic (there are many in Utah), Hubie was adamant that we complete the ten pages of script by 12:30pm, "The clinic opens for business at one o'clock and if we get out of there on time, the crew can have the rest of the day off to lounge by the pool," he said. I announced the situation to the crew and during the next five hours they busted their collective butts. We arrived at 7am and vacated the building at 12:45pm. This crew was remarkable, one of the best I have ever worked with.

The trucks were loaded to return to the motel when Hubie arrived, "Okay, now we're going to shoot at…" "Hold it," I said, taking him aside. "You're not going to make me out a liar. This crew gets the rest of the day off as you promised or I'm on the next plane out of here." Grudgingly, Kerns agreed.

Returning to Hollywood, film editor Tom Boutross and I commiserated over the sound mixer's antics. Tom then mentioned this jerk had run out of tape again on two other scenes. To quote porn star John Holmes, "There's no end to this prick."

The film recouped the producer's money, $644,000, in one month. Kerns proved to be a prevaricator once again when I later received an IRS Form 1099 for my wages paid.

Stories about Hubie's unsuccessful ventures have become legend; he got into the family trampoline business and became fraught with injured children lawsuits; he invested in an electronics company and they went belly-up; he produced a film north of the border and after a truck loaded with soldiers flipped, he was sued by the Canadian government; he invested in Florida lettuce and the biggest storm in 30 years wiped out the crops.

During the 1966 *Batman* TV series filming, Hubie confided that he had discussed a room addition to his Woodland Hills home with Roger Creed, my then brother-in-law. They had been friends for over 20 years and Roger had constructed countless homes and seven San Fernando Valley bowling alleys; so he was certainly a qualified contractor. "But," I said, "Friends are friends and business is business. Get it in writing." Hubie had agreed that Roger would perform stunt work on *Batman* in exchange for cut-rate costs on building materials and labor. Roger later became disgruntled when the *Batman* stunt work didn't materialize and walked away with only half of the construction completed. When I questioned Hubie about their written agreement, he sheepishly said, "I don't have one. I thought you only said that because Roger was your brother-in-law." Duh.

Solo's young assistant to director, Ric Swartzlander, performed his duties well, I asked about his future plans. My ears perked when he mentioned a CBS Page job offer, but he was dubious about accepting it. I quickly mentioned the great advantages of being a TV Page, especially for a network known for "hiring from within." I was visiting Universal a few years ago, I heard a voice call, "Jesse!" A smiling Ric greeted me with a career update; he had taken the CBS Page job. More importantly, Ric had become one of TV's top comedy writer-producers. As George Peppard said to his *A-Team* buddies, "I love it when it all comes together."

On Twentieth Century-Fox's *Johnny Dangerously*, I conversed with former *Saturday Night Live* member Joe Piscopo, and praised his impression of Frank Sinatra and others, then remarked that he was "a man of a thousand faces." A week later, an L.A. Times Calendar article labeled Piscopo as *The Man of a Thousand Faces*, written apparently by a youthful scribe, obliviously unaware that silent film legend Lon Chaney was the original titleholder.

CHAPTER 26

1984

After a couple of years away from the Stuntmen's Association, I discovered once again that some things never change, only the faces, especially at the SAMP monthly meetings, where the subjects and dialogue had remained the same since 1961.

Once again, I was elected as the Stuntmen's Association's secretary and with Dick Durock's adept computer knowledge; we created the first newsletter on a Commodore computer. I was hopeful a monthly SAMP bulletin would help unify the membership, increase participation and employment. Basically, I found that most stunt men lived in a vacuum and knew little about their fellow fall guys. One guy was amazed his buddy was a horseman, and they had known each other for over thirty years.

The newsletter, I believed, would relate the latest industry information regarding the stunt ranks, plus feature two member biographies a month. With so many varied backgrounds, it would be an excellent way to know your fellow members. A questionnaire was sent to the membership, but none were returned. Well, so much for unity. I contemplated submitting my autobiography, but believed it was too self-serving. However, it inadvertently might have caused others to submit their bios.

Later, after I had relinquished the newsletter editorial duties to Neil Summers, Lennie Geer asked me to have Summers give Everett Creach a newsletter mention for hiring him on *What Comes Around.* Summers replied, "Fuck Creach! He didn't hire me!" Editor, huh?

The infinite wisdom of SAMP's Board of Directors decreed a $25 assessment would be levied on any member not having a valid excuse for missing the monthly meeting. My contention, since SAMP's formation, was that if a member chose not to attend, so what? Every organization has the participants and the followers. If those members choose to stay away, fine, we have their dues payment. Besides, the members you saw rarely were inclined to create problems when they did attend. They usually complained about false information they had heard, which then had to be explained to them ad nauseam.

One evening SAMP's Board discussed a monthly dues hike. I interceded, suggesting that Treasurer Denver Mattson and I should first check SAMP's financial records to determine where we might eliminate any frivolous spending. The Board agreed.

While Denver and I checked the expenditures in an adjoining room, 20 minutes later we heard the vote called and passed, "To raise the SAMP dues." Certain Board members had an ulterior motive to raise the monthly dues and railroaded the vote. These folks always kept the moral compass spinning.

They cited the average age of a Stunts Unlimited member was much less than SAMPs. This fact caused much consternation and hand wringing among certain SAMP Board members and a dues hike would cause SAMP's older, inactive stuntmen, who were now working only a handful of days a year to resign. Supposedly, this move would make SAMP's stunt directory more youthfully appealing to those hiring.

Their ploy worked to a minor degree, but years later SAMP would institute a Lifetime Membership roster, giving the "old-timers" a place to settle. However, my decade-old question remained unanswered: What is SAMP giving each member for the dues they pay? The SAMP office provided coffee and a pool table, but how much coffee and pool can you handle? The original intent was for the office secretary to seek up and coming productions and their stunt opportunities. For many factors too numerous to mention this plan never achieved success.

Like many organizations, there were those in power who use their official position to further their own agendas. Often, the group's welfare was ignored, especially when a coordinator presented a motion. If you opposed him, he might not hire you on his next film project.

After a coordinator's motion passed, a certain Board member surreptitiously voiced his displeasure to me even though he had supplied a supporting vote, compeled me to ask, "In the past twenty years has this guy ever hired you? "No," he answered. I then countered, "Well, what makes you think he will now?"

Director Georg Fenady had me driving a Jaguar XKE roadster convertible for Universal's *Whiz Kids* TV series. I had spent the morning doing speedy chase run-bys, so by the time the show's stunt coordinator showed up, the car was part of me. Georg described the shot he wanted, a 90° slide ending with the Jag's nose framed between two bushes for camera. On the first take I overshot my mark by three feet, but on the second attempt the tires slid exactly to the pavement's chalk marks. Georg yelled, "Print it!" The arrogant stunt coordinator Roydon Clark snidely interjected, "I'll bet you couldn't do that again!" I yelled back, "I don't want to take your money, but let's see you do it." That ended the discussion. Usually, when doubling Jim Garner, Garner always did his own stunt driving, so I knew I'd win that bet.

John Thomas Lenox called from Disney Studios to say he was prepping *Splash*, Ron Howard's first major film starring Tom Hanks, John Candy and Daryl Hannah, and wanted me as his stunt coordinator again. The *Splash* script was impressive, but it was the underwater mermaid ballet finale that caught my attention, triggering visions of a spectacular underwater show I had enjoyed in 1969 at the Stardust Hotel on San Diego's Hotel Circle. The cocktail lounges wrap-around windows allowed a perfect underwater view of the swimming pool. The patrons were captivated by the sensuous, slow motion, movements of gorgeous ladies with long flowing manes, sheathed in mermaid tails and strategically placed seashells on their breasts – with nary an ounce of fat on these beautiful dolls. Lenox suggested I locate these underwater performers.

Lenox's glowing introduction would have made my mother proud, but, oddly, Ron Howard stared silently at my résumé, barely acknowledging my presence. I considered mentioning my doubling his brother Clint on the *Cowboys* TV pilot and also working with his dad, Rance, but his impassive stare wasn't inviting when he asked about stunt coordination. I simply stated my philosophy, "You tell me what you want and I'll get it for you." This was my modus operandi, developed over many years of working with the industry's greatest directors who knew what they wanted—and God help you if you didn't give it to them.

However, I goofed. I didn't realize how much the business was changing. Hollywood was now flooded with neo-directors who relied completely on their department heads to take the reins. A case in point: A costume gal interrupted Howard about an actress' dress, he responded, "I don't care. You handle it." Years ago, this comment would have proved disastrous when the wrong dress color might have clashed with another actor's wardrobe or even the set's wallpaper. But on this day color wasn't a consideration and neither was I.

You can't knock success. Ron Howard intelligently surrounded himself with talented artists and has become one Hollywood's most successful award-winning director/ producers.

Later, in the hallway, Lenox sensing my nervousness, asked about my "lean and hungry look" and I divulged my Internal Revenue Service problem. Obviously, my tension didn't inspire Howard's confidence.

Thanks to a lying, cheating, tax accountant, I now owed the Feds almost $13,000 and this infamous bootjack group had garnished my wages, including residuals from every studio in town. Sympathetic friends proclaimed, "They can't do that." Well, they can and they did—two days of work for Bill Couch on *Explorers* at Paramount brought earnings of over $1200, but I received a check for only $75.00.

During a visit to the local IRS office, the collection agent, a former California Highway Patrol officer, waved a form in my face, bragging, "With this piece of paper I can confiscate your car right now!" He asked if I had a safe deposit box. Regrettably, I wasn't recording our conversation when he offered to purchase my gun collection secured in the bank deposit box.

Lenox later rewarded my pre-production efforts to locate the underwater ballet swimmers with a day on the film. Arriving at the downtown

Los Angeles Grocery Market location the second assistant director pointed me to the portable dressing rooms. Changing into a workmen's wardrobe I exited my dressing room and met John Candy. We hit it off instantly. A kind, gentle man, John candidly expressed his concern about whether he had "made the right choice," moving his wife and children from Toronto, Canada. I assured him that Hollywood enjoyed everything he had done on the SCTV—Second City TV series, "Plus, there's no one else in the business like you." He appeared somewhat relieved.

At a special studio screening of *Splash*, I was anxious to see the completed version, figuring it embraced many elements conducive to make it a hit film. The plot was tight, the script well written and the underwater mermaid ballet was sure to be a spectacular hit. Well, it wasn't—the grand underwater finale sequence was completely omitted.

Interestingly, the film's opening scene was set-up in the standard 1.33:1 academy aperture; the square picture format used prior to the present day wide-screen picture format. It was also colored in a sepia tone, giving it a muted vintage appearance.

The next day, I phoned Lenox's office at Disney and when his secretary, Bobbi Kronowitz, answered, I remarked about the film's standard aperture and sepia opening scene. "Oh yes, that was John's idea," she said enthusiastically. "Yeah," I said, "Just like the opening scenes of my *Rip-Off* script." As with John, she had also read my script and the sound of her sucking wind, "Ohhhhhh," almost made me laugh.

The standard academy aperture in sepia or black & white is often used in a "flash back" to convey a time change, and I certainly didn't invent it. It's most notable presence is seen *Yankee Doodle Dandy*, *Casablanca* and in the opening and closing sequences of the *The Wizard of Oz*. John obviously realized that this fine cinematic element would enhance the *Splash* storyline and my script only served to remind him.

Kronowitz, however, epitomized the new caliber of people entering the film business. Arriving unemployed from New York, she accepted a friend's suggestion to become a studio script reader. Without any previous script writing or reading experience, she bragged, "If the first ten pages of a script didn't grab me," I'd reject it." Whoa. Granted, many scripts are vapid, some even a total waste of time. But, now a writer's blood, sweat and tears were now being reduced to the whims of an individual uneducated in cinematic storytelling. A know-nothing is making decisions that would affect countless individuals and their livelihoods. It was unconscionable, but indicative of what the business had become in the 1980s.

During my tenure with Dick Bartlett I learned how to read, analyze a script, and how to distinguish good from bad writing of characters, plots and storylines. Mainly, is the work salvageable? This gal had no conception of what "reading scripts" really entailed.

Even scarier were her aspirations to be a screenwriter. My blood boiled when she described her personal notebook full of plots, dialogue and characters procured from the scripts she had rejected. Without a conscience, her future goal was to pilfer someone else's life work. Perhaps, she should first purchase a dictionary and look up the word, *plagiarism.*

It was now June 1984 and since the production side of the business was always my first love, I was hired as the assistant director on *Tuff Turf.* This film was New World Pictures' 1984's answer to James Dean's *Rebel without a Cause.* The script's writing credit suspiciously listed "Jett Rink" as the author—Dean's character name in the George Stevens film, *Giant.*

Tuff Turf starred James Spader, Kim Richards and Robert Downey, Jr. The boys performed professionally and, in our many conversations between takes, I predicted a promising future for each of them.

Pat Kehoe, an assistant director I'd worked with at Disney when he was a second A.D., was the film's associate producer. But power changes some people. Pat figured he could generate greater work power from the cast and crew through the art of intimidation. Instead, he pissed everyone off. It was a side of him I had never seen and it didn't work on me. I had also read that book.

His abrasive, often abusive, domineering demeanor succeeded in propelling actress Kim Richards into massive crying jags. It then became my duty to comfort and get her in front of the camera. It was one hellava way to treat your lead actress.

It all began during pre-production's first day of rehearsal, when Kim arrived in her $60,000 Ferrari, and innocently parked next to Kehoe's battered Volkswagen bug. From that day on, Kehoe directed his demeaning, remarks regarding her tardiness, her boyfriend, and anything else he could find at Richards.

While I continued to comfort the actress, Kehoe never reprimanded the camera, hair or makeup departments who ignored my every effort to help them keep on schedule. While at the vacant school location, I watched the puzzled DP for 10 minutes as he studied a room with one window and a lone light bulb hanging from the ceiling. Checking my watch, I asked if there was a problem, he replied that he was trying to determine the "light source." Jezzz, I thought, there's only two, take your pick. If you show the window, that's it. If you show the bare light bulb, that's the one. But, his decision should have been made when we first scouted this location.

Kim appreciated my help and mentioned that she was going to produce her own film in North Carolina, and wanted me as her assistant director. (There's the Hollywood Kiss of Death again.) Kim went on to make her film and naturally, my phone calls to her were never returned.

Tuff Turf continued to be an uphill battle, what with Kehoe and his power-play. We were into the third week of principle photography when I was asked to be stunt coordinator on *French Quarter Undercover*, to be filmed in New Orleans. This was my escape route—at more than double the money. Los Angeles was hosting the 1984 Olympics in two weeks, so I welcomed the opportunity to avoid the predicted invading mass of humanity.

The Delta flight was perfect and I was delighted to once again visit New Orleans. This, however, was like leaping from the frying pan into the fire. *Tuff Turf* had its share of production problems, but *French Quarter Undercover* presented a new dilemma; amateur filmmakers. What these folks didn't know about picture making could fill volumes—and does. Check your local library.

Conversely, reading the *Undercover* script on the New Orleans flight was one of the best screenplays I had ever read. The scriptwriter was a local nightclub entertainer-actor, Bill Holliday. He was offered a production deal from Twentieth Century-Fox, but decided to stay with his friends in Louisiana to finance and produce the project themselves. During the filming a very disappointed Billy confided to me that this entire venture was a mistake he would never make again. How right he was.

My buddy, Roy Downey, was again handling the special effects. Viewing the situation, we decided early on, that with our combined alliance, we'd struggle through this production. With a crew of forty there were possibly only three experienced film professionals. In every motion picture production there are inherent problems. But with these neophyte "geniuses" the situation soon went from bad to worse.

As the film commenced, the *French Quarter Undercover* script had two N.O.P.D. cops tracking down foreign terrorist's intent on bombing the 1984 World's Fair in New Orleans. Actor Michael Parks received a flat $30,000 to co-star with Holliday. His demands were constant as he exerted his "power" at every opportunity. To the uninformed Hollywood outsider, he was the prime cause his *Then Came Bronson* TV series was canceled after one season. Lightning strikes twice. The filming inside a Mississippi River waterfront warehouse came to an abrupt halt one night when Parks decided he disliked the scripted scenes. He had the script in his hands for two months and "now" he didn't like the dialogue. For almost three hours, the entire crew lingered and watched as an obedient production secretary, with her portable typewriter, precariously wobbling on an apple box, punched out revisions dictated by Parks.

I didn't have a call this day for the filming of the re-enactment of an actual New Orleans hold up at an open-market poultry shop. This required Holliday and Parks to apprehend two young black thugs as they ran from a store. Arriving, just as the director called "Action," I strained to look past the roped-off crowd of spectators. Billy fired his shotgun at one of the escaping bandits according to the script. Rushing to the black boy's prone body, he said, "Hey, this kid's really hurt!" His statement grabbed me. I knew the script forwards and backwards, but I didn't recall this line of dialogue. Why would he ad-lib that line? It didn't fit the two rogue cops pursuing a couple of thieves. Pushing through the crowd, I could now clearly see Billy kneeling over the boy's lifeless form. Suddenly, a puddle of blood two feet across appeared. Cradling the lifeless boy's head, Billy continued to scream for help. My stomach churned. Turning away, I almost vomited as only one thought crossed my mind, "Oh God, not again!"

Minutes later, I again found myself at the Vieux Carré Hotel Bar for a double glass of diversion; only this time it was vodka on the rocks. I kept asking, "Why is it, every time I hit this town, a black kid is killed?" A distraught Roy appeared unexpectedly at my side and also ordered a drink. We both just looked at each other. The boy was alive, he said. The shotgun blast had ripped open the right side of the boy's jaw and cheek—all because one of the actors didn't point the shotgun to one side. A plastic surgeon had been called in, and the prognosis deemed the boy would recover fully. That evening Billy and Parks kept a night-long vigil at the hospital.

French Quarter Undercover turned out as I predicted; a box-office bomb. This completed celluloid abortion bared no resemblance to the wonderful script I had read on my flight from Los Angeles. This production team of know-nothings deviated completely from Billy Holliday's original writings—so oblivious of what a fine script really they had.

Fortunately or unfortunately, a prophetic Billy Holliday missed the picture's premiere in New Orleans. Less than two months after filming was completed on the *French Quarter Undercover*, Billy died of a massive heart attack.

Stunt man Bill Couch had called me for Paramount's *Explorers* to double a kid as a space capsule crashes into a crowded drive-in movie snack bar. Suspended from a thirty-foot track, the capsule was rigged to plow through the scored wall, traveling the twenty-foot snack bar counter length at 25 mph. I stood at the counter's far end, ready to leap out of its careening path. On "Action" there was a dull thud, then a whirring sound – the space capsule couldn't get through the wall. The effects guy again scored the wall, almost to the point where a sneeze would collapse it. With great anticipation, on Take Two, I watched the capsule come through the wall at three miles per hour. It was so laughable the kid actors ended up doing their own dodging of this runaway space capsule.

Stunt man Bob Herron, also a frustrated comedian, always had a joke to tell and, in the first-person, related a New York City experience of picking up a lady, taking her to his room. In the sack, he was doing his stuff when she remarked, "Oh, you're sooo big." Flattered, he replied, "Well, thank you." "Oh no," she replied, "I mean you're so big I can't get my arms around you." I said, "Bobby, I don't think I'd tell that story, joke or not."

Stunt man Dick Warlock made an initial visit to a physician for his annual medical checkup and assumed "the position" for the dreaded digital prostate examination. "Relax," said the doctor, "I said relax," who then forced the issue. Involuntary or not, Dick backhanded the sawbones, propelling him across the room into the wall and to the floor. Dazed, the doctor struggled to his feet and made a hasty exit. Moments later a nurse appeared to suggest that Warlock find another medic.

Five years had passed since the last Stuntmen's Association TV stunt special and now, the Beverly Hills mega-talent agency, Creative Artists Associates, was beckoning. SAMP President Max Kleven, several Board members and I (as Secretary) were invited to evaluate the program proposal. Everything appeared legitimate and Lee Marvin was signed to host the show, but Kleven quickly grabbed control of the production reins. At the next SAMP board and general membership meetings Kleven vowed that each and every association member would receive one day of work on the stunt special. Unanimously, of course, the membership voted to accept the production proposal. However, in addition to his stunt coordinator duties, Kleven also wrangled his way into scripting the show, allowing him to join the Writer's Guild of America, West. For his involvement, Kleven reputedly received $4500 a week for the production's duration.

When the smoke cleared it was quite evident Kleven didn't walk like he talked. Every SAMP member did not receive one day of work on the show. In fact, only a handful of SAMP members worked the show, as Kleven hired several non-SAMP performers, including those from Stunts Unlimited. There was no excuse; he made a promise and didn't keep it.

This was the straw that broke the camel's back and I resigned as Secretary, the first SAMP officer ever to resign in office. Ultimately, the

CAA packaged production paid production fees of $50,000 to SAMP.

Everett Creach, the stunt coordinator on Jerry Reed's *What Comes Around* in Nashville, Tennessee, called... the film's money man had requested me. What a thrill to visit Music City, U.S.A. But I was bowled over the next day when crossing the street; everyone made eye contact and one said, "Good morning." This was as it used to be in L.A. Life is too short to have it any other way.

Everett was intense and, seemingly, paranoid, which the other stunt guys always found humorous, joking about "Why Everett doesn't go to football games? Because, when the teams go into a huddle, he thinks they're talking about him." Everett and I were not close, but on several occasions our conversations gave me a temporary feeling of true friendship. But never, for the life of me, could I understand his problem. He rose through the ranks from an extra, to a fine stunt man, to a talented second unit action director. He had no reason to feel insecure.

My ol' buddy Lennie Geer candidly remarked that he was surprised as hell—"I never thought you'd make it as a stunt man." I wasn't surprised. That was par for the course. We all met a lot of stunt wannabees and 99.9% of them didn't make it. So, with my 500 TV and motion picture credits, I guess it did surprise him.

Filming in Gallatin, Tennessee, we performed a saloon donnybrook, and then crashed through a window. The second morning I decided to drive the stunt van to the location causing Lennie Geer to quip, "By tomorrow, Jesse will be producing this film." Of course, there was the obligatory car chase and, in contrast to L.A. filming, Nashville's police escorted our caravan of picture vehicles from one side of Nashville to the other in ten minutes.

Everett had five young guys in the bar fight who I figured were local hires. They were, but in fact were a group of Tucson stunt wannabees, created by Dave Cass. Traveling to each film location by car, they would live in one motel room, and hire on as film extras. When the action started Cass and Everett would convert these guys to SAG stunt contracts while legitimate stunt men sat at home.

Contrary to California, where all structures are susceptible to demolition every twenty years or by earthquake—whichever comes first—I marveled at the South's historical preservation. Beneath each footstep was a record of the past dating back to our nation's origins and before. Piquing my life-long study of the War for Southern Independence, I drove to Franklin, 18 miles south of Nashville, the site of the five-hour tragic Battle of Franklin, which many consider it to be "The Gettysburg of the South." I stood on Winstead Hill where Confederate General John Bell Hood watched as the battle consumed over 7500 soldiers, including six Confederate Generals.

A mile east of the Battlefield, I sat on the rear veranda steps of The Carnton Plantation. The feeling of contentment was exhilarating, like I had come home. Then and there I decided Tennessee was where I wanted to be.

Returning to Hollywood, I described my feelings to my Mom, who concurred, "If you're that unhappy living here, then you should move, otherwise you won't be doing yourself or anyone else any good." Mom always had a way of cutting to the chase.

CHAPTER 27

1985

Once again, I was "between pictures" and agreed to do a "freebie" as the first assistant director-stunt coordinator on a 10-minute horror film presentation. I believed the basic story concept had merit; a vintage mirror inhabited by a creature, who snatches its victims while they shave, bathe or apply makeup.

The wannabe, pseudo-director, sported a $500 director's viewfinder, sat in his personalized, silk-screened, director's chair he brought from home. Judging by his previous comments of having "read all about Hollywood," I expected him to wear a beret, ascot and puttees. He sat coma-like, agonizing about the shot, or that's what I thought he was doing. Actually, he had only a vague idea of what he wanted to film, all without a shot list. Historically, the conversation between the director, assistant director and the director of photography is the first step in on-set filming. However, to this crew, his indecision became the equivalent of a pack of hungry wolves thinning the herd—they go for the weakest and the slowest. Suddenly, everyone on the set had a suggestion, including the craft service gal. Finally, I cleared the set, set the shot and we began filming.

While awaiting the next set-up, a ballet sequence, I mentioned to the twenty year-old prima ballerina that the best dancers in films were men; Fred Astaire, Gene Kelly, and Cyd Charisse. She just stared at me, obviously unaware that Ms. Charisse was one of the most beautiful and talented ladies to ever appear on the silver screen.

Today, everybody's in show biz. Decades ago, there was a mystical aura surrounding the cinema. Now, with *Entertainment Tonight, Access Hollywood,* E! Entertainment Television, *Inside Edition* and talk shows ad nauseam, the world knows everything there is to know about Tinseltown, often instantly. Audiences now include not only the non-participants, but those serious enough to establish a show biz career.

Fifty years ago, only a handful of United States colleges and universities maintained a cinema arts department, most predominately was the University of Southern California and the University of California at Los Angeles. Today, half a million show biz hopefuls graduate annually, nationally. Woe to the institute of higher learning that lacks a communications or cinema arts curriculum.

Having experienced the New Orleans filmmaking scene, I decided to change my San Francisco script location to the Crescent City. A call to my buddy, Phil Seifert, Louisiana Film Commission Director, allowed a gratis room at the St Louis Hotel in the French Quarter. For ten days I adapted the script to include the charm and history of the Southern city. Returning to Hollywood, I again proceeded to seek a film production deal, while still pursuing stunts.

Testament Producer Jonathan Bernstein recommended me for stunt coordinator on *The Naked Cage.* The tenth floor elevator doors opened and I immediately contemplated pushing the down button when I saw the Cannon Films logo. This company was the scourge of Hollywood, known for bounced checks and any other violation they could get away with, but I was curious and decided to hear them out.

The Naked Cage was of the women-in-prison genre. Director Paul Nicholas proudly said the entire fight scene would be filmed differently – shot with a hand-held camera. I imagine my facial expression gave me away. The longer I stared at him the more animated he became, trying to explain his new revelation in filmmaking. Finally, I exited with Nicholas on my heels, all the way back to the elevator, attempting to justify his cinematic genius.

I wasn't opposed to hand-held camera use, as this filming form had been used to shoot fight scenes for decades. However, these shots must be used judiciously. *Daily Variety*'s first sentence of *The Naked Cage* film review stated the cell block fight was one of the worst ever shot in the annals of Hollywood.

I'm forever amazed at the neophytes arriving at Hollywood's door who attempt to reinvent the wheel. Disregarding today's high-tech computer imagery, virtually everything was done cinematically by 1930. Most of what you see today is a modern variation of those techniques.

Still pursuing my love of Dixieland Jazz, I invited a buddy and his lawyer girlfriend to the Beef & Barrel restaurant in Northridge to hear *The Great Pacific Jazz Band*, headed by Bob Ringwald, Molly's dad. The lawyer smiled when I mentioned my desire to date an attorney, and then became offended when I said "I want to do to her what they've been doing to me for years."

Again, I would run away to Ventura's Pierpont Inn to transform my script ideas to a script and decided a quiet drive to the quaint nearby town of Ojai would stimulate my creative juices. Lake Cachuma was beautiful as I traveled a desolate country back road to Ventura. Cresting a hill, I saw a young female backpacker with her thumb out. I had never picked up a hitchhiker, but we were in the middle of nowhere and I figured this gal definitely needed a ride.

She looked about sixteen, had acne blemishes and I almost drove off the road when the knapsack on her lap exposed a month old infant. Our small talk revealed she was from San Francisco, visiting her brother in Ventura. We hadn't gone a mile before she asked if I messed around with girls, "Every chance I get," I answered. "Would you like some head for five bucks? Her question produced more than a twinge of excitement where it counted. However, the national AIDS scare had just peaked, especially in the City by the Bay, and that alone killed all my carnal thoughts. We finally arrived in Ventura and I wished her luck with a $5.00 bill. Personally, I believed she was working the old road and figured she would be safe carrying her bundle of joy. Additionally, I was also suspicious of a small motor home that refused to pass us.

Former Teamster John Reade, now heading up Disney's Location Services Department, called to ask if I would set up a stunt show for the studio's executive picnic. Immediately, I figured this was a great opportunity to get back into the studio since Michael Eisner's regime had taken over. A meeting with production exec Marty Katz hashed out the details and we were set. With eight fellow stunt guys at Disney's Golden Oak Ranch, we performed a 10-minute program that included gunfights, high falls and a Western Street brawl. The elite Disney families enjoyed the show and we joined them for barbequed hamburgers and hot dogs. While we mingled, Marty Katz shouted from his chaise lounge, "Jesse, I'm not going to forget this." I smiled, turned to the other stunt guys, "Well guys, that's the kiss of death. We'll never work at this studio again." And, to this day, none of us ever have. Once again, when a producer says "You'll be there," you can bet your ass you won't.

Simon & Simon and *MacGyver* kept me busy. On *Amazing Stories* it was especially fun to work again with Kelly Reno, whom I hadn't seen since 1977 on *The Black Stallion.* In eight years he had grown to be a delightful young man.

Producer Hal Klein called me for *Acceptable Risks*, starring Brian Dennehy and Cicely Tyson, suggested I join the director for lunch "to discuss the action he has in mind." When the director said, "Oh, I don't know," my reaction of "Well, why don't we try what's in the script?" seemed to pacify him. To me, this was just another example of the business going to hell: another wannabee director without a vision or an inclination to understand what he read in the script.

Reading the Hollywood trade paper ads early often proved advantageous. A celebrity TV interview show needed a soundman immediately and I got the job by phoning the producer at 7am. The guests were videotaped dining at their favorite restaurant. Comic Jackie Vernon was the guest celebrity and my favorite from *The Ed Sullivan Show*; recalling his sad sack expression, deadpan comments as he pressed a clicker to an imaginary slide show. Off camera, I adjusted my headset as Vernon chatted between bites. Evidently, he heard me chuckle as I monitored the recorder's view meters. A comedian needs an audience and now, to the host's consternation, Jackie was ignoring him and playing his hilarious comments directly to me.

Conversing afterward, Jackie and I discovered that we had a mutual TV producer friend and later enjoyed several lunches together. He was a gentle guy and passed away the following year.

CHAPTER 28

1986

The year started off promising with stunt jobs on *MacGyver* and *Remington Steele*. Vince Deadrick, Jr. was coordinating the anti-gun *MacGyver* TV series. In Griffith Park, on a winding road east from the famous Greek Theater, we filmed in a dense forest of tall pine trees. I was astounded. As a Los Angeles native I never knew of this acreage, a scant three miles from where I was born and raised. It was like being in the wooded Alps, which was exactly what the script demanded, reminding me of Sam Goldwyn's old Hollywood adage, "A tree's a tree and a rock's a rock—shoot it in Griffith Park."

MacGyver's Richard Dean Anderson, with barking dogs on his trail, ran through the woods as the camera trucked with him. Passing the camera dolly, he yelped in pain and grabbed his right pinkie finger, now at an opposing right angle to his hand. He had struck his finger on the dolly grip's tool belt. Immediately, he was rushed to the nearest hospital, the Children's Hospital at Sunset and Vermont.

It was a freak accident and, as a stunt performer or A.D., you're constantly looking for anything on the set that can prove hazardous. Basically, it's an expanded version of Murphy's Law—"If anything can go wrong, it will… Ten Fold."

On *Remington Steele*, Ernie Orsatti was the stunt coordinator and I had complete faith in his proven abilities. For my ten-foot drop through a skylight window, he and Lane Leavitt, a stunt equipment supplier, set the fall pad in place. For whatever reason, Leavitt found his way to my perch and suddenly jumped the ten feet to the pad. Ernie was pissed—knowing it's difficult to command a stunt adjustment if some yahoo attempts what the stunt performer is hired to do.

In the shot, I leaped with my arms outspread to take the shattered skylight window with me. Amidst the raining debris, I hit the pad feet first and stuck—and heard the ominous "snap." My left ankle was fractured. Hobbling to a chair, Ernie was troubled that no one had ever been injured on his shows. Immediately, I searched for the cause of my injury. Simply, when Ernie and Leavitt set the pad, they double folded it back and underneath. Later, when I mentioned prop man Bill Petrotta's eight-inch foam composition pad, which I had fallen into from twenty feet on Blake Edwards' *The Ferret* TV pilot, Leavitt said, "Oh, I have one of those outside, leaning against the sound stage wall." All I could say was "Then why the hell didn't you say so?"

I trusted Ernie implicitly, but I still should have checked out the fall pad myself. It was another one of those times I neglected to follow my own advice: Check everything out.

Pierce Brosnan was concerned as my ankle began to swell and throb. Stephanie Zimbalist also checked on me, but neither of these stars visited me together. When each scene was over they were like fighters in the ring—they went to their respective corners. Acting in an intimate scene, then at "Cut and Print," each would turn and ignore the other. With their own entourage in tow, Pierce sat at one end of the sound stage and Stephanie at the other.

Obviously, this feud was not as enduring as the Hatfield's and the McCoy's—on an E! Channel interview years later, Stephanie spoke compassionately of Pierce and his talents.

For six weeks I wore a plaster ankle cast and to this day have never heard from Ernie Orsatti. Thoughts of moving to Nashville now became my foremost desire.

John "Bear" Hudkins and I discussed a few of the stunt guys we had worked with through the years. Chomping on his cigar, Bear mentioned his many locations and friendship with veteran stunt man Jack Williams,

"Jack's a brilliant guy, speaks six languages and was always reading a book. One day he asked, 'Bear, why don't the other stunt guys like me? Is it because I'm so intelligent?' I said, 'No, Jack, it's because you're a prick!'" Bear loved telling this story.

Born into a rodeo family, Jack William's mother was a trick rider and his father, Jack, Sr., was one of the top horse fall stunt men in Hollywood's silent era. Jack Williams worked his first film when he was 12 in 1932, and performed more horse falls than any other stunt man. He was the best—Westerns would not have been same without him.

Mickey Rooney's son, Tim, called me for a TYBY yogurt commercial. Evidently, Mickey had visited his Westlake Village neighbor, former MGM studio head James Aubrey, that morning. Greeted by Aubrey and his Doberman Pincher, Mickey got down on all fours, face to face with the pooch, and the bitch latched on to his cheek. Unable to appear with a swollen puss, I once again doubled Mick. On the set, Tim confided that when he suggested me, Mick replied, "He doesn't look like me." Tim seemingly went ballistic, "What the fuck do you mean he doesn't look like you? Jesse looks more like you than we do," referring to himself and Mickey, Jr. I'll chalk up Mick's inane comment to his pain medication.

Tim rewrote the TYBY yogurt commercial ad with me, as Mick, seated at a dressing room table applying makeup, slightly out of focus, as he calls, "Dad, we're ready." I answered, "Be right there, Tim," and, to my surprise, they used my voice in the TV ad.

This day ended an era. I had doubled Mickey since 1959 and now, twenty-seven years later, this day would be my last.

As I said, the business in general had changed and my employment had dwindled to about five to 10 days a year, a vast contrast from the 125 to 200 days in previous years. My contacts in production had vanished in one form or another. The producers, directors, production managers and assistant directors I knew had either died, retired or couldn't get a job themselves. As for the reigning stunt coordinators, unless you were a member of their cliques, you would not be considered, much less hired on their films.

Producer Bob Manning recommended me to stunt coordinate Fred

"The Hammer" Williamson's *The Messenger*, one of several film attempts to generate the former football player into an action hero.

Traveling down a Palmdale desert road, I had Chuck Hicks and Jim Winburn confront Williamson by the continuous sideswiping of their car into his vehicle. Directing from the camera car, I watched Williamson as he nonchalantly drove, but disregarded the banging and crunching. How the hell do you ignore another vehicle slapping into your car door? I cut the shot and explained to Williamson how ludicrous he appeared. We went for another take and again, Williamson drove along like he was going to a Sunday picnic. I waved the guys to slap him hard again, accelerate out of the shot and that was it. I figured; let the editor try to make something of the shots. Special effects man John Hartigan and I just shook our heads in disbelief.

While Williamson directed a scene in a nearby diner, I staged and rehearsed a fight scene with Hicks in the parking lot. In a traditional good versus evil duel, Hicks pummels Williamson, but then the worm turns and Williamson gets the advantage, plows Hicks into the ground. Williamson didn't like the routine and, one by one, eliminated Hick's punches. In the ridiculous final cut, Chuck Hicks never throws a punch and is beaten to a pulp by Williamson. Hell, even Superman took a punch.

Since my infancy, ringing in the New Year was a Wayne Family tradition, especially in the early fifties, when Guy Lombardo and His Royal Canadians began their New Year's Eve telecasts from New York's Waldorf-Astoria Hotel. Sadly, Guy passed away November 5, 1977 and once kidded, "When I go, I'm taking New Year's Eve with me." Well, for me and millions of other viewers, he did. New Year's Eve hasn't been the same without his orchestra's famous rendition of "Auld Lang Syne."

Motivated by the lack of a New Year's Eve celebration, I created a TV show that I wanted to see—featuring entertainers I had enjoyed all my life. A Live-by-Satellite television tribute, *New Year's Eve in New Orleans*, hosted by Mel Tormé, and featuring Steve Lawrence and Edie Gorme, Vic Damone and Diahann Carroll, the McGuire Sisters, Al Hirt, Pete Fountain, Lionel Hampton, Tony Randall, John Byner and Soupy Sales. I even had a 30 minute segment from Nashville starring Crystal Gayle.

Projected were ten-second bumper greetings from Steve Allen and Jayne Meadows, Alice Faye and Phil Harris, Roy Rogers and Dale Evans, Billy Dee Williams, Carl Reiner, Mickey Rooney, Jerry Lewis, Butterfly McQueen, June Allison and Van Johnson, Karl Malden and Jonathan Winters. Topping it off, of course, was a musical tribute featuring the original Guy Lombardo Orchestra. For over ten exhaustive years I approached television's leading programmers and syndicators, only to be rebuked with, "There's no audience for this type of show, but do you have something for the 18-34 age group with rock music?" No, I didn't and wouldn't even consider it. Their theory: Everyone over 50 goes to bed at 10pm New Years Eve.

It was fun to work the *Gavilan* TV series Malibu location, starring Robert Urich, with buddy director Don Chaffey again, whom I hadn't seen since 1979 on Urich's *Vega$* show. Bob pulled the rug out from under me, literally, as I played a henchman. It's one of those gags where the slick hardwood floor offered no resistance to his quick jerk and you're just a passenger – instantly on your face.

After we wrapped, Don and I had drinks at Paradise Cove's *The Sand Castle*, most memorable as the restaurant next to James Garner's house trailer on *Rockford Files*. Mentioning my *San Francisco Rip-Off* script, Don was anxious to read it. A week later, Don graciously called to say how much he liked the story and wanted to direct the comedy-action script. Again, the trick now was to find the financing.

CHAPTER 29

1987

January began with a rush when Dick Warlock summoned me to MGM for *Spaceballs* to double Mel Brooks. Nick McLean, an old buddy I had known since the sixties, and watched rise through the camera ranks, was the Director of Photography.

Mel Brooks became my favorite comedy picture maker the moment I saw his first film, *The Producers*, and can't recall laughing as hard while viewing *Blazing Saddles*. Having worked on *Young Frankenstein* and *Silent Movie*, I eagerly looked forward to participating in his latest cinematic zaniness, *Spaceballs*.

In this *Star Wars* parody, John Candy played a Chewbacca-type role. I looked forward to seeing him again, and maybe do an "I told you so." But, unfortunately, his scenes had been completed before I arrived.

Mike Tillman and Jack West doubled George Wyner and Rick Moranis, respectively. While quietly conversing on the sound stage, we suddenly heard a brash voice commanding, "Put it out! PUT IT OUT!" Looking in all directions around the now silenced set, we discovered a steely-eyed Mel Brooks, seated 40 feet away, glaring at us. "Mike, I think it's your cigarette," I said. Immediately, he ground it into the stage floor. The rehearsal continued as we wondering why Brooks had made a scene, rather than have an assistant make a quiet request to Mike. We all later learned Brooks' arrogance had no bounds.

The production's edgy tension continued with several department heads not speaking to each other. Now, that's a hellava way to make a film, but then, like a ship's captain, it's the director who sets the tone on the set. I could only think about Hollywood's bygone days when this behavior would not have been tolerated for a moment.

Spaceballs great finale was the spaceship's evacuation, and it did read "funny" on paper. In addition to the spaceship's personnel, the exodus included a parade of circus trapeze artists —clowns, jugglers, stilt-walkers, fire-eaters, acrobats, elephants and a bearded lady, portrayed by Matilda the Hun, a 6'3", 300 lb. professional lady wrestler named Deana Booher. Playing a spaceship technician I was to bump into her, and said, "Just walk the line and I'd find you in the crowd." On "Action" I rushed in and Bam!!! Suddenly, my feet were over my head as I crashed to the floor on my back. Deena was right on the button. Jumping up, I ran out of the scene as the crew applauded. However, in a Brooks' film, God only knows why this shot and many others that day never made it to the film's final cut. Too bad, because that finale really *was* funny.

Another shot had Warlock in a bear suit escaping, crawling, on his hands and knees. He looked ridiculous, so I suggested he stand upright and slowly sneak "suspiciously" along the spaceship wall. Dick conferred with Brooks, who agreed.

Mike Tillman was a nice, quiet guy and one fine stunt man. Few stunt men performed as many pipe ramp car crashes as he (750 at last count), and as a result of a head injury passed away long before his time. He was a sweetheart, truly one of the good guys.

Filming was completed on *Spaceballs* and I jumped over to Universal for their *Outlaws* TV series starring Rod Taylor. We wrapped and I was ready to leave my illustrious hometown.

On February 14, 1987, I made my promised move to Nashville and spent my first night at Music Row's Shoney's Inn, witnessing my first snowfall. The next morning, I met one of my favorite Country Music legends, Merle Haggard in the hallway, "Hi Merle, I haven't seen you since we worked together in Boise on Clint Eastwood's *Bronco Billy*. I was one of the stunt-men." He quickly smiled, "Yeah, good to see you again," and discussed his appearance later that night on The Nashville Network's Ralph Emery's *Nashville Now* TV show.

Moving to Music City USA was exciting and definitely not the traumatic experience psychologists would have you believe—equating moving to a divorce or death in the family. Los Angeles had been the only place I had ever resided, but I was eager to begin a new life and a new job. Almost immediately, I entered Nashville's film and video arena, working as a director, stunts coordinator and/or videographer on music videos and commercials.

On my way to Nashville, an incident in Arkansas on Highway 40 still has me chuckling. Four 20-somethings in a van seemed to be enjoying themselves. They were all over the highway. On I-40's right shoulder a bright orange vinyl sign on a large tripod read: "DEA Drug Inspection Ahead with Drug sniffing Dogs – 1 Mile." A quarter of a mile ahead loomed an off-ramp—and the van quickly exited. When I peered down the ramp, two police cars, and two dogs were waiting to greet the van.

When I related this tale to a cop buddy, he said it was a common drug enforcement tactic—a desolate off-ramp, with no service stations, restaurants or residents, makes it difficult for the evading suspects to conjure up an excuse.

Aided by Nashville Police detective Mark Garafola, whom I'd met on *What Comes Around*, I rented a spacious two-bedroom, two-bath for $425, cheap by L.A.'s inflated rental rates, where I was paying $500 for a small one-bedroom, one-bath apartment. Today, a decent L.A. one-bedroom apartment in Studio City will start at $1500 a month.

Of the four hundred mailed announcements relating my move to Nashville, only producer Mac Harding responded; wishing he could leave Hollywood, too. However, SAMP's Board of little old ladies latched onto my notice like a bulldog. My Charter Member status was questioned, as a lengthy debate ensued regarding the definition of a Charter Member. Seems no one knew its meaning and eventually my validity as a 1961 SAMP Charter Member was resolved.

Again, Jealousy, Ego and Greed had reared its ugly head by those who figured I might take a job from them two thousand miles way. As usual, this inquisition wasted time that would have been better-served seeking employment and better benefits for the organization's membership.

CHAPTER 30

1988

Eventually, I allowed my Nashville subscriptions to *Daily Variety* and *The Hollywood Reporter* to expire when I didn't recognize any names mentioned, contrary to when every name rang a bell. So it was, "Austa-lavista baby."

Ironically, a final issue of the *Reporter* detailed Victor Kingery, a Colorado oil millionaire's Tinseltown arrival with high hopes of becoming the next movie mogul. A Hollywood buddy knew the director on Kingery's Nashville project, put us together, and I flew out to their spacious, but ominously vacant Century City suite of ten offices. Only Kingery's office was luxuriously furnished with an antique desk, augmented with a hundred framed photographs of him schmoozing with Hollywood celebrities. Oddly, I noted how all the pictures were taken at one location, and during one party; a soirée that his expensive publicity agency had arranged.

Kingery was evasive about the film's budget, and then reluctantly admitted he would finance the production with his own money. Returning to Nashville, I regretted the meeting was not all I had hoped it to be. I'd been involved in many projects under similar conditions and experience usually influenced my view, and something here was amiss. Regardless, I discounted my feelings and figured—well, at least the guy is a millionaire.

The *Music City Blues* script was the ubiquitous Nashville saga—a guitar-playing singer, struggling to hit the big time in Country Music.

Regardless, Kingery arrived in Nashville with a fanfare and hired me as the production manager at a pre-production rate of $1500 week, with an increase to $2500 week during principle photography. He paid my salary with his personal check, not an uncommon practice on independent productions, and often used until the production company bank accounts were set.

Selecting the crew was my responsibility as I waited for the funding, but Kingery was "playing producer" and hired a local art director and a set dresser. The set dresser had quit his steady job at a local TV station because he wanted to "move into film."

Constant unexplained delays and promises prevented my setting up the bank accounts, production insurance and the Screen Actors Guild contracts, though Kingery and the director enjoyed their lavish hotel suites and drove leased Lincoln Town Cars. I completed the script breakdown, schedule and budget, but Kingery still avoided discussing any financial details.

Unexpectedly, a Hollywood production designer arrived, receiving an unknown salary paid by Kingery. My suspicions continued to grow as we discussed his art department's budget. At Kingery's request, I had painstakingly recalculated the budget several times and knew where every dime was placed. But when the designer said, "I can't do it for that amount," I emphatically declared, "That's all you're getting." He then matter-of-factly replied, "Oh, okay." Hollywood is much like our government—the more you give them, the more they will spend.

Kingery's meetings continued as he become desperate in his quest to fund the film through Nashville sources. My local contacts warned me, "No one in Nashville will finance a movie. They've been screwed too many times."

We were two weeks into preproduction when Kingery said he now wanted me to be the first assistant director, "Because your on-set experience is invaluable to the director." Suddenly, a mustached, dressed in black, so-called, "money-man", formerly with Dick Clark Productions, arrived from Hollywood. All I could think was that I wouldn't want to buy a used car from this guy. It was obvious Kingery didn't want me involved in the financial dealings and then hired a production manager I recommended out of Atlanta, whom I had previously met on *Hopscotch*, when she was the assistant production coordinator. She now had daily meetings with the man in black, but she would never divulge their discussions with me. Her panicked expression was priceless when I asked about my elusive third week paycheck.

At the end of the fourth week I was now owed $3000, as was she, too, was unpaid for her two weeks. However, one morning I laughed when I entered the disserted hotel production offices to find Kingery had flown the coop. He abandoned a closet full of clothes, a portable computer, two cell phones and suitcases, leaving no clue as he exited the hotel lobby that would suggest he was leaving. In his wake, he left owing Bell South, Budget Car Rentals, Ramada and Rodeway Inns, copier rental and office supplies, weeks of salaries for the director of photography, production designer, production manager, art director, set dresser, and myself, totaling over $75,000.

I didn't appreciate getting screwed again, recalling the Florida debacle and phoned an old friend, Ronny Van Gompel, a Los Angeles private investigator. He called his buddy, the Chief Investigator for the L.A. District Attorney's office, and two of his agents visited Kingery at his leased ($3500 a month) Sunset Boulevard mansion, next door to Barbra Streisand. Two days later, $3000 was waiting for me at my local Western Union office. The other personnel never received a dime and felony arrest warrants for fraud awaits Kingery should he ever return to Tennessee.

Exiting a Nashville Chinese restaurant I met Conway Twitty and his wife, Dee, and mentioned we had both "worked in my first film, Mickey Rooney's *Platinum High School*." Grinning, Conway confessed, "Yeah. That was my first... *and* last film!"

Hee Haw television director Bob Boatman died from an accidental wound in 1989. Supposedly, he pulled out a dresser drawer—it fell to the floor, causing an antique .22 caliber pistol to discharge, sending a bullet into a femoral artery in his groin. Bleeding, he staggered from the bedroom through the kitchen to the garage. A neighbor later found his slumped body beside his silver 450 SL Mercedes Benz, dead. He was 59 years old.

Bob and I first met at KTLA in 1954, later worked together at the station in 1958-59, and remained good friends. A year prior to my move to Nashville he asked if I could get his son, Bill, an assistant cameraman's job. In Nashville, over lunch two years later, I inquired how Bill was doing. "Oh, he hasn't stopped working since you introduced him to that producer." Bob smiled, "The phone call you made did the trick." As pleased as I was to help the then twenty-one year old, I was equally disappointed that Bill never called to tell me the results, much less, say thank you.

A year later, when I asked Bob about work as a TV cameraman at *The Nashville Network* he replied, "Anything you do in this town, you'll have to do on your own." His wife, Ann, was a production executive for TNN (third in command) and I suspect a quick phone call could have opened a door somewhere. Then again, what's that about no good deed going unpunished?

Okay, so much for my friends and their acute cases of amnesia. This malady has now grown to epidemic proportions and has affected everyone who has ever worked in Hollywood.

In a town where you change jobs as often as your lover, the greatest percentage of work – in all phases of the business—comes from refer-rals. One guy advised, "You gotta have someone spreading the word about your talent and abilities." How very true. Through the years certain individuals boasted, "I'm the greatest stunt man," only to be regarded as boisterous buffoons by their peers. But, as the guy said, "A lie is as good as the truth if you can get someone to believe it" confirmed their lip service paid off when they were hired by unsuspecting new producers. I was taught bragging wasn't necessary, much less appropri-ate; if you were good at your job your talent would speak for itself.

Billionaire Donald Trump evidently disagrees, stating that you should "Brand Yourself and Toot Your Horn. If you don't tell people about your success, they probably won't know about it. Subtlety and modesty are appropriate for nuns and therapists." I do believe he might be right.

A Nashville news broadcast described the Lyme Tick Disease and the numbing ache in my left elbow fit the symptom, so I ran to the nearest doctor. A blood test proved negative for LTD, but the doctor couldn't diagnose what caused the pain. A nurse friend suggested spraying my elbow with WD-40 and the pain vanished almost immediately. A week later, the checkout stand rag sheet, *The Globe*, obsessed about the healing effects of WD-40. That's the only time I have ever believed anything they ever printed.

CHAPTER 31

1990

I was firmly rooted and contented living in Nashville, when I received a work call for *Blind Vengeance*, a TV movie starring Gerald McRaney filming in Hernandez, Mississippi, 25 miles south of Memphis, Tennessee. Mitch Herron, a local Memphis stunt man, was to fall from the town square's majestic courthouse into cardboard boxes and mattresses. Immediately, David McCarty, the panicked location manager from New Orleans, (I had met him on *French Quarter Undercover*) began shouting for grips to dig up a ten by thirty foot Iris flower garden, asserting the flowerbed would be replanted later. "Wait a minute," I said, asking the key grip, "Do you have any parallels (sections of scaffolding) in the grip truck?" They did and twenty minutes later the boxes and pads were securely suspended over the garden and not a flower blossom had been disturbed.

At day's end, the second A.D., Todd Corman, whom I had hired in 1980 as a location manager on *Boxoffice*, said I would be paid for only one day, since I wasn't "photographed the first day." I laughed knowing this edict wasn't coming from him, but from the production manager Albert Salzer. "Todd, go tell Al to pay for the three days I'm here or the next voice he hears will be from SAG." I received full payment for the three days.

Back in Nashville, I enjoyed plying my video experience on productions with many Music City greats, including directing a TV series, "A

Date with Dale," starring Dale Evans. Other productions would feature Willie Nelson, Jeanne C. Riley (What a doll!), Travis Tritt, Marty Stuart, Hoyt Axton, Randy Travis, Jessie Colter, Skeeter Davis, Becky Hobbs, Tanya Tucker, Trisha Yearwood, Billy Walker and Little Jimmy Dickens.

I even worked as a song plugger for Billy Strange. It was said this if you wanted your song to become a hit, just take it to a particular record executive, slap the song and $50,000 cash on his desk and say "Here's the song *WE* wrote!" and your song would become a Top 10 hit.

But the real shocker was, as the director and videographer, on a railroad music cassette TV commercial in Chattanooga—the video scenes appeared as if they had been shot on film stock. During taping, "the film look" wasn't discernible through the camera's viewfinder or the 5-inch producer's monitor, but on a large editing suite monitor the shots were spectacular and overwhelming. My combination of low-key lighting and the development of Sony's new Digital Betacam SP video camera made it appear the TV ad was shot on film.

Today, the film industry is once again in transition as high definition digital video technology continues to the next levels in presenting a spectacular image.

Three and a half years had passed since *Spaceballs*, when I heard about Mel Brooks' new film project, *Life Stinks*. Mitchell Block, his longtime assistant director, ran interference for me to secure the stunt coordinator duties, but other production forces interceded, relegating me as just Brooks' stunt double.

Regardless, I returned to Hollywood in June 1990 to work on my fourth Mel Brooks film and bunked in with my former Parisian dancer girlfriend, Michele Martel. It was nice to see her again, but I had forgotten about her smoking addiction to Gauloises, the powder blue packaged French cigarettes with the putrid aroma of a burning rope. Her three-pack-a-day habit was blazing up $150 a month and a mere suggestion that she stop smoking made me thankful I didn't speak French.

Regardless, she was a great lady and one fantastic cook, especially her Hungarian Goulash. One day, with complete disregard for our American-French diplomatic relations, I asked, "Why do Parisians hate

Americans?" With her ladle waving, "What do you mean we hate Americans? We hate each other—we hate our next door neighbor!" I doubled up in laughter, as she explained the French countryside residents' friendliness versus the major city folk, which, I thought, probably pertains to any nation.

Back on the set, Director of Photography Steve Poster greeted me, we reminisced about last working on *Testament* for director Lynn Littman. We had contemplated she would become the town's most notable lady director, but she was a one-shot-wonder. Too bad, I believed she could have done very well.

I soon learned "Life Stinks" personified Brooks' own jaundiced view of humanity. During my pre-production rehearsal he entered the sound stage ceremoniously without a greeting. He stared angrily at my multi-pocket photographer's vest, and barked, "Is that 'wardrobe'?" Sensing his rancor, I replied, "Yeah, mine." That should have been a warning of future events.

With cataracts in both eyes, my Ray-Ban Balorama wrap-around sunglasses were priceless. The bright sunlight so blurred my vision I couldn't recognize anyone beyond five feet. Bear Hudkins suggested I visit the Motion Picture Country Home and Hospital for an eye checkup.

While in the waiting room, veteran, award-winning director of photography, Joseph Biroc (*It's a Wonderful Life, Towering Inferno, Airplane!*) entered. We had worked together on many films, including Robert Aldrich's *The Grissom Gang*. But when I mentioned Mel Brooks, Joe became outraged, relating *Blazing Saddles,* and how he had asked to be replaced after the first week of filming. Ultimately, he said the Warner Bros. studio chief Bob Daley's pleas and a hefty salary increase convinced Joe to complete the film.

Immediately, the Country Home/Hospital referred me to Dr. Samuel Masket, the premiere eye surgeon, teacher of laser cataract procedures to Ophthalmologists the world over. A date was tentatively set for surgery, pending my *Life Stinks* stunt schedule.

Producer-production manager Hal Klein said, "A fish stinks from the head down," and this truism certainly applied to Mel Brooks. In all my years, I had never witnessed such disharmony and dissension as on the

Life Stinks film set. Brooks ruled with an intimidating, condescending iron hand, making everyone a daily candidate as his "Whipping Boy." Several crew members wanted to quit, but without another show lined up, they grudgingly stayed. Finally, in desperation and disgust, the hairdressing department did quit en mass.

While doubling Brooks in a rehearsal, being chased by two homeless heavies, a wardrobe gal Brooks had promoted to costume designer, said that my shoestrings weren't tied to match Brooks' shoe lacings. Again, this was a video assist rehearsal for Brooks to view his scene. He was going to do the running himself, but I couldn't believe what I'd heard from this know-nothing idiot. I looked into her eyes, and said, "Get the fuck away from me." Men's costumer Norm Bursa, whom I'd known since 1960 at MGM, almost busted out laughing. It worked—she never came near me again. This bimbo was another blatant example of the incompetents now inhabiting the business.

Brooks met his match when he tried his bullying tactics on my old buddy, camera operator George Kohut. George and I first worked on *Return to Macon County* (1975) and on *Hopscotch* (1979). He would answer Brooks with "Yes, SIRRR" and "No, SIRRR," to the entire crew's amusement. Egomaniac Brooks was so into himself, he never realized he was being mocked.

With a daily 7am crew call, the set was ready to film when Brooks would make his grand entrance around 9am. After makeup and wardrobe, he would arrive on the set by 10 or 11am with no idea of what was to be filmed that day. Most often, it was noon before the first shot was in the can.

A crew likes to anticipate what they are to do so there are no surprises. Brooks had no shot list and while Mitch attempted to have the first setup ready to shoot, Brooks would invariably change it. Notably, 99.9% of the time, Mitch's staged version was better than Brooks and everyone knew it. Mitchell Bock would later become a successful television series director.

While waiting a cataract surgery date, I worked at Fifth and Spring Streets in L.A.'s 95° July heat. The bright sunlight was a killer to my eyes and with the exception of the film's last day, I performed all the stunt action with impaired vision.

This particular scene with actor Danny Wells (bartender on *The Jefferson's*) in a Mercedes had me doubling Brooks with my right hand stuck in his car window—running the hundred yards to Fourth Street at a car speed of 15mph, then a climatic scene with he and Brooks.

Receiving no directions from Brooks, I waved my cleaning rag in my left hand (my idea) to create an antimated greater sense of comedic action. Brooks sat comfortably in his tall director's chair viewing the video playback, suggested another take—"Place 'B' camera next to 'A' camera and zoom with Jesse." We did the shot again and Mitchell Bock interjected, "Okay, we've got three takes, how many times are we going to do this shot?" Brooks turned and glared at me, "We're going to keep doing it until Jesse gets hurt." Shocked, that he would make such a comment, I retorted, "Well Pal, you'd better get more film because we're going to be here all day—because I don't intend to get hurt." What an asinine comment to make to any stunt performer. The sonofabitch then stammered, "Uh, uh, one more take." I did the run again, and in the film's final cut I can be seen running about thirty feet and it's a dissolve, eliminating Well's car scene completely.

Dr. Sam Masket's performing 4-5 cataract operations per day put me at ease, in contrast to the guy who operates once a week and must refer to his medical manual. Finally, surgery for each eye was set a week a part—each procedure took forty minutes and I never experienced an iota amount of pain. When Dr. Sam removed the eye patch, it was reminiscent of the movie scene when the joyous patient shouts, "I can see! I can SEE!"

While waiting to work *Life Stinks* again, I'd meet Bear Hudkins, Richard Farnsworth, Al Wyatt, Buddy Van Horne, Pat Buttram and director Bob Totten for morning coffee at Charles in Studio City. Al Wyatt, now remarried to a Philippina, suggested a plan—his wife had Philippine lady friends who would pay $7500 to become an Ameri-can/wife/citizen. All I had to do was to wait until the bride received her emigration documents and then file for divorce. Bear took me aside and mentioned a guy who had accepted the $7500 offer, "But it later cost him twenty thousand when the gal became ill." I told Al my marriage fee was $25,000 and he never mentioned it again.

I ran into a production manager, we discussed the biz changes; especially the apparent DGA cloning of female assistant directors – all five-foot-two, with asses two axe handles wide—a common sight on every set, while male A.D.s with thirty years of experience at home waiting for the phone to ring. He admitted, "They work for scale and they do everything I tell them to do."

Back on the *Life Stinks* set, Brooks, lounged under the canopy with bullhorn in hand, viewing a rehearsal on the TV monitor, bellowed his demands to veteran character actor Jeffery Tambor, seventy-five yards away, riding a gigantic Caterpillar earthmover. Tambor obviously had his fill and screamed, "Fuck you! If you want to talk to me get your ass down here." Brooks jumped from his perch and ran to Tambor, once again to the crew's amusement.

The ubiquitous video assist playback undoubtedly has Hollywood's greatest directors, John Ford, Frank Capra, and Michael Curtiz, et al, spinning in their graves. These gentlemen stood near the camera, peering over the camera operator's shoulder, in close proximity to the actors and knew exactly what they wanted to appear on that piece of celluloid. Conversely, Brooks directed by committee—he and his entourage viewed each videotaped shot and would then discuss it for ten minutes. Even after reviewing a take, Brooks still didn't know if what he had just seen was what he wanted. He muttered after the third take of my tackling another stunt man in the street, "What if Jesse's foot was six inches to the left?" We did a fourth take with our ankles scraped and bleeding through shredded socks. This was ridiculous—as soon as we hit the pavement the editor would cut to a close up of Brooks anyway.

Brooks bellowed a similar order when stuntwoman Denise Lynn Roberts and I jumped into a 6'x 6'x 6' cardboard box during his and Lesley Ann Warren's "Fred & Ginger" dance number. Stunt coordinator David Ellis had placed one layer of cardboard boxes inside the tall box, covered them with a flattened piece of cardboard. I questioned him about the boxes, but he maintained it was the perfect "catcher." Hand-in-hand, Denise and I did the old Texas-switch, when Brooks and Warren passed behind a warehouse pillar; we jumped ten feet into the box. The cardboard layer exploded as our feet sliced through it like a knife.

Denise and I ended up in a seated position on the uncrushed boxes, "Are you okay?" Through watery eyes, she said, "Fine."

Brooks, naturally, wanted another take "with Jesse slightly in front of Denise." We did the jump again and Brooks seemed satisfied. Ellis asked what we wanted for the stunt adjustment. I said $400 each; and he agreed. We changed out of wardrobe and Denise admitted she had sprained her ankle on our first jump. What a tough, talented stunt gal.

A week later our checks arrived and the stunt adjustment was $200, not the $400 Ellis had promised. Phoning him, he said the production manager thought the adjustment was too much. The stunt coordinator controls the stunt budget and it was obvious Ellis lied and had made the decision to reduce our adjustment. I told him he was full of shit.

Initially, Ellis had tipped off his lack of integrity and gutless behavior, when he admitted that whenever Brooks suggested a shot, he went along with it because he didn't want to run the risk of Brooks' rage.

Stunt adjustment tampering? This was the second time since November 8, 1963, on *The Adventures of Jamie McPheeter's*, doubling Kurt Russell, when Paul Baxley had agreed to a stunt adjustment, and then reneged four days later. Both of these sleazy sonofabitches were cut from the same bolt of cloth.

A few days later, a *Life Stinks* second A.D. called me to double the egomaniac again. I declined, having had made my return flight reservations to Tennessee. Twenty minutes later Mitch called and, after hearing about the stunt adjustment was deeply apologetic. He promised to make up the missing stunt adjustments and I agreed.

The final shot had Brooks snoozing on a loading dock – a door opens and he is scraped off into a dumpster. Ellis said, "You're his double, you talk to him." Ol' chickenshit Ellis was still playing the Caine Mutiny's Ensign Pulver—hiding from the Captain.

Brooks moved into the prone position for the close-up and I adamantly advised him to place his back up against the door so it wouldn't slap him when it swung open. He did the shot then complained the door had struck his back. I just grinned and walked away. What a dumb bastard!

That was the last shot of the film, a wrap—as I watched Ellis run from the set without saying a word. He epitomized the no-class breed that had infiltrated the film business in recent years. He wouldn't have lasted ten minutes with the old timers.

In 1997, Lynn was diagnosed with a rare form of adrenal cancer. In the ensuing six years, this brave young lady would endure 33 surgeries, eight rounds of chemotherapy and radiation. Denise Lynn Roberts was one of the finest stunt gals I ever worked with. She passed away on March 22, 2003.

As for Brooks, it just continues to prove that good things do happen to bad people. His 2001 Broadway production of *The Producers*, based on his 1968 film, became an unbridled success and garnered 12 Tony Awards. Later, a remake of his original film again made him millions.

The prolific, astute writer-producer-director Joseph L. Mankiewicz defined him perfectly: "The death of Hollywood is Mel Brooks and special effects. If Mel Brooks had come up in my day he wouldn't have qualified to be a busboy."

During this three-month *Life Stinks* ordeal, I enjoyed several lunches with Director Don Chaffey at the Smoke House. We remained optimistic that funding for my *San Francisco Rip-Off* script would be found. Don's gracious invitation to his yearly Hollywood Christmas Eve party would coincide with my December visit to see my Mom, but he suffered a fatal heart attack at his other home on New Zealand's Kawau Island on November 13, 1990. Don was the quintessential English gentleman.

Back in Tennessee, I phoned Greg Amsterdam and described my latest Brooks episode. Candidly, he related Brooks' ace card—agent Michael Ovitz of Creative Artists Agency (in 1990, Hollywood's most powerful movie mogul). "The studios would not refuse an Ovitz-Brooks project," he said, "for fear they might need another Ovitz/CAA client— six months down the road."

When Brooks was prepping *Robin Hood: Men in Tights*, someone asked if I was going to work the film. 'No way in hell! After four Brooks films, I'd had enough—a decision that now placed me in the great fraternity of those who worked with Brooks and never wanted to do so again. To put it graphically, working with Brooks is like taking a shit—as soon as it's over you want to get as far away as possible.

On *Men in Tights* it became known that Brooks considered stunt performers to be nothing more than extras and, to prove his point—the stunt performers were not invited to the film's wrap party. On the film's final day, Brooks exited toward the stage door as veteran stunt man Vince Deadrick, Sr. yelled, "Hey Mel." Brooks turned to see Vince fronting the group of glaring stuntmen: "See ya at the wrap party." Brooks angrily stomped away. When the stunt film credits for *Robin Hood: Men in Tights,* rolled—the only name missing was Vince Deadrick, Sr. What a petty, vindictive, despicable asshole.

I was happy to be back in Nashville, far away from this Hollywood madness. Veteran stunt man Chuck Courtney called to say he had recommended me to play "Shorty Waddle" the killer of the week on *In the Heat of the Night,* filming in Conyers, Georgia, 20-miles east of Atlanta. Gratefully, I thanked Chuck for the three-day job, then thought—this show could set my career back twenty years – Hopefully!!!

The special effects man wired the squibs to my chest and we proceeded as a Sparta cop blows me away. While lying on the damp sod, with the actor standing over me, I noticed his automatic pistol was cocked and pointed at my crotch. Calmly, I told him not to move a muscle and called "Props." The assistant prop man was at first perturbed at the interruption, but when he spied the cocked firearm; his eyes looked like pie tins—as he carefully unloaded the gun.

After the scene, the assistant effects guy called me aside, mentioned the "shotgun" house had no bathroom and suggested I wash my hands, "You've been lying where they empty their pee cans every morning." Later, back at the hotel after a long hot shower, I relaxed with a double Scotch with dinner and a substantial dose of aspirin as an illness preventative.

A month later, I was shocked and saddened to hear that Chuck Courtney had suffered an incapacitating stroke.

CHAPTER 32

1991

The following appeared in Nashville's, The Tennessean May 14, 1991

REVIEWING MICKEY
A Former Stunt Double Stops to Reflect
on working with a Hollywood Legend

A recent review of Mickey Rooney's autobiography, *Life Is Too Short,* caused me to reflect on my personal experiences with him.

I'm a former member of the Hollywood film community and was Rooney's stunt double from 1959, in *Platinum High School,* to *Leave 'Em Laughing,* to a *TCBY* commercial in 1986.

I found the book to be mostly accurate, and also very enlightening, especially about his lack of a strong father figure. This first caught my attention in 1961 while visiting Mickey during the TV filming of a *Pete & Gladys* episode. I watched as veteran director Jack Donohue, Mick's old friend from MGM, an imposing, gentle man, placed his arm around Rooney's shoulders, pulled him close, and said, "Now son, you go in there and..."

Mick was then forty, but this was as if Judge Hardy was giving advice to Andy. To my amazement, Rooney immediately became subservient, like a puppy wanting to please his master. This was indeed contrary to the always-on, opinionated and forceful Mickey Rooney, we all knew.

I must disagree with Diane White of the Boston Globe for her review of April 14. With her obvious bias, it's too bad she lashed into her personal, name-calling tirade without considering the book for its worth.

White is perturbed that Rooney doesn't delve into self-analysis for an "insight into his own disturbed, driven, obnoxious personality." I don't believe he is perceived as such in this book. But, if he were, would we really want to hear an amateur's theory regarding their life? White also contends "that Rooney might have written an interesting story about his life if he'd had some help from a professional writer". Well, knowing Mick's academic background, I would say he had one, or maybe five - all too young to know that the Palomar Ballroom, which burned down in 1939 was located at Third and Vermont, not Third and Western. Also, Herbert J. Yates headed up Republic Studios, not Columbia Pictures (Harry Cohn).

White mentions Rooney's diatribe "against Hollywood and the people who run the business." Mick's been at it for seventy years. Who has a better right to evaluate the condition of the business than he does? Personally, having been in the TV and film industry since I was eight years old, I find that the forty-two years I've experienced, I tend to agree with about 99.9% of Rooney's evaluation.

Overall, I found the book hard to put down. There were a couple of items I would have preferred not to know about Ava Gardner, though these might prove titillating to some. But, having "been there," it brought back some memories, answered some questions and provoked a few.

For instance, why wasn't Red Skelton mentioned? It was Rooney who first spotted him and brought him to the attention of MGM's L.B. Mayer in the late 30's. In turn, when Rooney had lean earnings in the 1960s, it was Red who kept him busy guest starring on the *Red Skelton Show*.

That's Mickey Rooney. I also want to mention someone who is in all our prayers. Michael Landon is genuinely one of the true gentlemen and nice guys of the industry. I first met Mike in May, 1959, during the filming of the *Bonanza* TV pilot at Paramount. During the course of the show's fourteen year run, I worked on about 20 episodes. Mike has never changed, but just grew more talented. God bless you, Mike, and get well soon.

Initially, upon my arrival in Nashville in 1987, intent to establish myself as a working stunt man/stunt coordinator, I arranged a meeting with Dancy Jones, the newly governor-appointed Director of the Tennessee State Film Commission. Subsequently, my 1991 Nashville Scene Letter to the Editor explained what happened at that meeting.

October 18, 1991

Clark Parsons
The Nashville Scene
301 Broadway
Nashville, TN 37201
LETTER TO THE EDITOR

Dear Mr. Parsons:

Thank you for your well researched article, 'Where have all the movies gone?' on Tennessee's Film, Entertainment and Music Commission and its director, Dancy Jones. You have stated what most of us in the film and video community have been muttering for over four years.

On June 1, 1987, two months after Ms. Jones took her appointed position, I met with her to introduce myself. Having moved to Nashville six months earlier, I related my Hollywood experience as a stunt man, with over 500 TV and motion picture credits, and also my behind-the-camera tenure as an assistant director and production manager.

In our conversation, spanning an hour, I, too, agree, with AFCI's Leigh Von der Esch, that Ms. Jones is a 'first class professional and a true Southern lady.' However, during our chat, many of Ms. Jones' comments toward Hollywood were tantamount to 'They put their pants on one leg at a time.' She's right, but it appeared she was trying to convince herself that it really was true.

Concluding, I mentioned the 400 announcements to former Hollywood employers and associates (i.e. producers, directors, assistant directors, production and location managers), I mailed to report my new Nashville location—explained that these folks were in the 'mainstream of production' and were not idly sitting on their hands. Presenting a set of duplicate Avery mailing labels, she politely pushed them back toward me, saying, 'We'll handle it our way.' I then realized the Tennessee film industry was in deep manure.

As a Los Angeles native, my knowledge of locations and permits was established many years ago while working on low-budget films, where we all wore several hats. As a production manager and/or assistant director, I very often negotiated location rates and permits. On *Godfather II*, I took over for location manager Jack English, while he handled the Dominican Republic location sites.

My production experience was a prime reason Los Angeles Mayor Sam Yorty appointed me, along with Actor Jock Mahoney and Toni Kimmel to establish L.A.'s ONE-STOP PERMIT OFFICE in October 1971. For a token $1.00 a year, our creation continues today to facilitate the needs of the Hollywood motion picture community.

For Ms. Jones to refuse an offer of assistance is unconscionable. Every successful business entrepreneur knows that it's wise to surround oneself with qualified advisors. Universal Studios/MCA's Lew Wasserman admitted his 'genius' was derived by surrounding himself with those who knew more than he did. This would apply especially to the FEMC, who is attempting to service an industry they've only read about in fan magazines.

The FEMC has seemingly invoked an 'us and them' attitude since Jones' April 1, 1987 appointment. All other state film commissions are free and open with information regarding pending productions coming to their area. Conveniently, many offer 24-hour telephone recording systems, listing future projects, including the production company addresses and phone numbers to contact. In Tennessee, by the time the FEMC finally decides to divulge any vital information on an incoming production, most of the jobs on the film have already been filled. Many producers have complained that had they known what was available in Tennessee, they wouldn't have had to bring 'it' from Hollywood. Never are they apprised of what we really have in our state. But, what can you expect when the FEMC doesn't speak the language of a film production executive. Never having been involved in filmmaking, how can the FEMC know the particular requirements of the film industry? And most definitely, you don't learn it overnight.

Astonished can only describe my reaction to Ms. Jones' comments to the *I'll Fly Away* TV series producer that a film crew could not be staffed in Nashville. So, off he went to film in Atlanta.

While freelancing, I resumed my videographer chores and directed several music videos and commercials. Nashville's pace was slower and so enjoyable.

In May 1988, I was hired as the production manager on *Music City Blues*. This film was never fully financed and eventually folded. However, during the film's six weeks of pre-production, I received phone calls from experienced crew people in Nashville, and from those in Atlanta, Chicago, Los Angeles and Orlando. I subsequently amassed a four-inch stack of resumes from skilled professionals who wanted to work in our city. Interestingly, many of the out-of-towners contended they would stay with Nashville friends or rent a room at their own expense if they were hired.

Never was there a problem finding competent crew members in Nashville. To say that our city is unable to supply a crew, once again reflects the FEMC's lack of knowledge of the motion picture industry and of Nashville.

As for the FEMC board and advisory committee—it's inundated with members of the music sector. The new board chairman, Dave Skepner, is obliviously out of touch to ask, 'If there are so many critics of the FEMC, why haven't they spoken up?' Those I've met in our film/video community have been very vocal, but not one person will comment 'aloud' for fear of reprisal. Generally, they're all hopeful that maybe someday a production just might come to our beloved Nashville. But they're not about to say anything that may offend the FEMC for fear that it might cost them their livelihood down the road.

Unfortunately, in addition to the unemployed ranks within the film/video community, the real loser is the Tennessee taxpayer. I don't know the financial breakdown of the FEMC budget or what portion of the state funding is allocated specifically for the procurement of film production. But, regardless the amount, we're not getting our money's worth. I do know, however, that the Louisiana Film Commission's fiscal budget does not exceed $190,000 and their film production schedule, as are many of our other surrounding states, is consistently booked. Then again, their film commissions know the requirements of the filmmakers.

JESSE WAYNE
Nashville, TN"

In the eight years Ms. Jones held her Governor-appointed position, she did not entice one Hollywood-based production to Tennessee. The small two or three productions that found its way to Tennessee did so by its own volition and necessity.

Fortunately, in Nashville, I was again directing TV shows, commercials, country music videos, also functioning often as the videographer. Again, the creative satisfaction of doing what you love is exhilarating and, in my case, definitely easier on the body.

In Music City, I received a call to be stunt coordinator and also crash through a breakaway table on a Marty Stuart-Travis Tritt music video, *"The Whiskey Ain't Working."* I needed two additional stuntmen, so I called a Memphis guy I'd met on Jerry Reed's 1984 film, *What Comes Around*. He arrived in Nashville and we commenced filming at a local bar for a shot of this 6'3" moose being knocked through the bar's front door. Special effects supplied two balsa wood breakaway doors. With most stunt guys, crashing through a breakaway door is your basic gag. I carefully explained how I wanted him to get airborne like Superman, crash through the door and land in the king size mattress. His eyes widened and you'd have thought I'd asked this bozo to leap off a ten-story building into a wet sponge. Take one was lousy, and two was even worse. This guy had no body control, and you definitely can't teach it in two minutes, and to some, never. Maybe, I thought, a quick cut away could save the shot in editing. It did.

He had also brought along a buddy, John Steinriede, a former

U.S.M.C. Vietnam veteran, for the saloon donnybrook. During the melee the bozo was too stiff, threw a girly punch while Steinriede's every punch was picture perfect. When I later asked John if he'd ever done a fight before, he said, "Not in front of a camera." I roared.

We then moved to an exterior shot of the moose and a gal in skin-tight jeans seated in a convertible. The camera was set at the car's back bumper as he was to speed away. On "Action," in the wrong gear, he stupidly accelerated in reverse—almost backing over the camera, tripod and the cameraman. What a loose cannon. This clown personified the stunt wannabees that are now found in every state of our nation.

Through the years, I offered encouragement and, often, personal assistance to those who expressed a sincere desire to become a stunt performer. But no more will I be responsible for anyone wasting a day or a year of his or her life for a dream that will not happen. Today's stunt field is over-populated, with current estimates of three thousand stunt performers in the Los Angeles area alone. Do the math. The numbers suggest it is virtually impossible to find a stunt gig when you have a hundred individuals vying for each job.

Exacerbating this futile job-hunt has been the demise of television's 30, 60 and 120-minute weekly action shows – as most all now have been replaced by sitcoms, news magazine and reality shows. Additionally, global runaway TV and film productions from Hollywood now prevent most stunt performers from ever amassing the hundreds of screen credits their predecessors accumulated.

A producer I had met in Nashville called—he wanted me on the next plane to Eureka Springs, Arkansas, to be his production manager for *Bigfoot: The Movie*. Pleased he remembered me I met his buddy, a wannabee writer/director and immediately, a warning signal appeared; another genius in the making. Normally, a script for a low-budget film of this genre seldom exceeds 90 to 100 pages, but this phonebook-sized epic was over 150 pages, and growing.

Later at dinner the producer confided that he and his director were trying to appease their oil multi-millionaire financier in Tulsa. Apparently Mr. Money Bags constantly suggested sub-plots, and had also demanded a film role for his younger boyfriend.

After scanning the script, I suggested a rewrite to reduce the page count. Then the warning bells chimed louder when the producer wouldn't allow me to do the basics; open a film production account, arrange insurance or become a Screen Actors Guild signatory. It grew worst daily, but without a completed script and a budget breakdown you were playing self-diggy-doo. After two weeks I had had enough, and asked them to call me if and when they were serious about making the picture. Six months later the producer called to say the film had tanked, but he and his had buddy walked [or ran] away with about $160,000 from Mr. Tulsa's Money Bags.

In October 1983, I returned to Los Angeles to care for my Mom, who was now experiencing dementia. My first reaction was denial, then anger, as I vowed to never place her in a convalescent home, but when she fell in her apartment, I discovered I had no choice.

During this time I realized how unprepared I was for Mom's debilitating condition. If only there had been prior information, even a high school class to inform us that our parents could suffer from this and/or other conditions. This might have alleviated some of the shock. I was devastated as emotions ran wild as I watched helplessly until Mom passed away Thanksgiving Day 1998 at 90 years old.

In the mid-eighties, stunt man Rick Barker and I made different career choices. I disliked what was happening to the industry, but as Rick adapted to the changing business, I did not.

In late 1999, a chance meeting at the SAMP office got us together again. Happily, Rick had not succumbed to Hollywood amnesia and hired me on a NIKE commercial—*Y2K: The Day After*. The residuals paid very well for the one-day shoot – $10,000.

After settling my Mom's affairs, I returned to Nashville in January 2000, but soon learned for the second time what Thomas Wolfe had said, "You can't go home again."

Music City had changed drastically in the seven years I was gone. The official estimate was that 125,000 illegal aliens had now invaded the Nashville Metropolitan area, and were employed at every hotel, restaurant and construction site.

In a discussion with Nashville's Chief of Police Robert Kirchener, "Do you want a firearm, Jess? Go to any corner on South Lafayette, mention your choice firearm, and you'll have it in an hour for $50 [1990 price]." Additionally, *The Crips* and *The Bloods* now controlled their own drug cartel, where violent gangland activities had now become weekly crime incidents. Nashville had become another Los Angeles.

In 2003, I made a decision to move to Cody, Wyoming. With a state population of half a million, and 8000 in Cody, it was a joy to travel from one side of town to the other in five minutes. Only 53 miles from Yellowstone National Park's East Gate, I delved into Wild Bill Cody's town and our Nation's first national park's history. Most notable was John Colter, a member of the Lewis & Clark expedition, who ventured off to become the first white man in Yellowstone in 1807.

Still yearning to work in the business I loved, I believed this story would make a fine film and immediately sent a book of John Colter's adventures to director Georg Fenady. Happily, he agreed to direct this film, with a low $2-3,000,000 budget and a 30-day shooting schedule. It would be fun, we agreed, working again with our closest filmmaking friends. Calls to director of photography Nick McLean, gaffer Mike Katz and special effects guru Roy Downey started our family crew list. We all figured this would be our final film effort to make "one for the Gipper."

Now, the trick was to find funding for this project; and my being 1600 miles out of the Hollywood "loop," I knew I would have to rely on Georg and his film contacts. Then Georg called one day. "Jess, I'm 77 and going into these offices I'm sure these youngsters are thinking, 'What's this old fart doing here?' Forty years ago, I probably would have said the same thing. I think we're fighting an uphill battle." I had to agree. The ship had sailed. Most everyone else we knew was either retired; a resident of the Motion Picture Country Home or dead.

That ended our moviemaking endeavor. With the 30 to 40 year old studio production heads now basing their filmmaking concepts on comic books, cartoons and video games, we had no way to fight, much less win this battle.

Georg Fenady passed away May 29, 2008 from pancreatic cancer. Georg was the best. As a producer I knew I would have had a fine film with Georg at the helm. I dearly miss him.

In 2015, Leonardo DiCaprio would star in a magnificent, Academy award winning film, *The Ravenant*, extolling the combined adventures of John Colter, John Bridger and other mountain men of the early 1800s.

Epilogue

Being a Los Angeles native allowed me to witness firsthand the vast changes in the City of the Angels, the people and the film industry. Many actors, producers, directors and stunt performers, those I thought were in for the long haul, disappeared, and those with seemingly little to offer are still riding high.

Gone are the days when an individual established a firm foundation in their craft and paid their dues accordingly. The when opportunity knocked, you were ready, willing and able. Today, many of Tinseltown's inhabitants—in front and behind the camera—are not proficient at their job and won't ask for help, fearing, "Everyone will realize I don't know what I'm doing." Instead, it's, "If you can't dazzle'em with brilliance, baffle 'em with Bull Shit."

Years ago, via the studio system, ninety-nine percent of these wannabees would have been run out of town. Today, if you want to be a director, producer, or virtually any job on the set, simply attend a $295 weekend seminar and then have your business cards printed on Monday. Quite possibly, no one will question your qualifications because they have all traveled this same route.

Hollywood screenwriter Robert Port summed it up: "L.A.'s like the Foreign Legion. You come in with one identity and if you survive, you get out with a whole new one."

Overall, there was never a great abundance of integrity among the Hollywoodites, but the inhabitants of yesterday did regard the industry with a certain sense of admiration. Today, the players consider the film business a bottomless money pot, where lawyers, bean counters and mega-corporations with no love or knowledge of filmmaking are in control.

Above all else, today's greatest enemy to stunt performers is *Computer Generated Imaging*. CGI technology has advanced incrementally and can now create virtually any film imagery imaginable. No longer will a Dar Robinson need to fall from Toronto's CN Tower at risk to life and limb. A CGI artist now moves the computer mouse to exact the action—and a producer will never again pay one cent in Screen Actors Guild stunt performer residuals. More so, a production crew will cease to travel to a distant location, when the site can be created at a computer console at a fraction of the cost. Most likely created by someone in India, Japan or Korea.

Change is constant as evidenced by James Cameron's *Avatar,* created in his new 3D process. Like previous carnations it has revolutionized and enhanced the audience viewing experience as much as color, surround sound, and the widescreen did decades ago.

To the often-asked question, Yes, I do miss stunt work. Walking on the set and being afforded more respect than most actors was a gratifying sense of recognition and accomplishment. Traveling worldwide was rewarding and educational, but I never understood why we called it work—if you do something you love, it's not work, but a joyful passion.

In 1992 I was surprised with a Stuntmen's Association engraved plaque proclaiming, "A Lifetime Membership in recognition of your accomplishments and dedication." This gesture was heartwarming, but the thrill soon vanished when I discovered the previous recipients were no longer performing stunts. Consciously, I had never retired from the stunt ranks, though the scarcity of work involuntarily suggested it. Now, the walnut-framed plaque had placed me outside looking in and was tantamount to being in the Stuntmen's Witness Protection Program.

Upon retiring, Sean Connery said, "Making a film is either utopia or like shoveling shit uphill." Indeed. Often it was the greatest experience imaginable, but at later times I'd wonder, "What the hell are we doing here?" However, as Director Georg Fenady said, "It's the best damn business in the world," and, without a doubt, it was a wonderful trip, like riding a rocket—constantly on the cutting edge of technology, trends and current events—everything relevant to the human condition. Each new assignment was an exciting adventure and a challenge to the mind and body. I couldn't wait to get to my next set—unlike our nation's present working majority who seemingly hate their jobs.

There was no other business where you could have as much fun – I loved every moment (well, almost), the burns, bruises and a couple of broken bones – not too bad for a forty-year run. Plus, I helped several folks to become millionaires, but more importantly, I cherish the friendship of a few best friends and working with the greatest talent Hollywood and the World has ever known.

To the very few of us remaining stunt guys and gals who worked within the Hollywood studio system—we enjoyed the best of it— meeting and working with the greatest entertainers of the 20th Century. Sure, we reminisce about those magnificent bygone "Old days," but the Hollywood we knew is long gone. But I still feel honored to have been a part of it.

Virtually every dream I envisioned manifested itself into reality. I only regret I wasn't a bit nicer to couple of my lady friends. (No, I'm not referring to the ex-wives.) But like the guy said, "Don't cry because it's over; smile because it happened." Overall, Irving Berlin said it best, "There's no business like show business."

Lastly, reports that the movie business lacks the fun of years past may be premature, and Mel Gibson may be the exception. On a recent film, Mel toasted a glass high, proclaimed the ultimate liquid to promote excellent health and longevity—Drink your own urine! The next day his kiss-ass entourage sipped their own urine as Mel declared, "Hey guys, I was only drinking apple juice."

Short Takes

…My Mom once suggested that it was better to raise pigs instead of children. Reasoned that if the pigs ever got out of hand you can always slaughter them and eat them. For eighteen years I slept with one eye open.

…The adored, Oscar-winning actress, learning of the oral expertise of another actress to get a role, remarked to her studio hairdresser, "Thank God I don't have to do *that* anymore."

…The Dirtiest Words Ever Said on Television: "Ward, you were a little hard on the Beaver last night," on *Leave it to Beaver*.

…Veteran stunt man Davy Sharpe, wearing a two-gun belt & holster, could draw the Colt .45s while doing a backward flip and fire both as he landed.

…A stunt man returned from location to the apartment he shared with his blonde model live-in and was greeted by his amour and Wilt "The Stilt" Chamberlain coming from the bedroom.

…Robin Williams on TV's *Mork & Mindy*, making their move from Colorado to California, remarked, "Oh Min, we'll be closer than Karen Black's eyes."

…A few stunt guys were discussing high falls and the current rate of $15.00 per foot. Roydon Clark, with a distain for high work, brought laughter when he quipped, "I'll take one foot of that!"

…A stunt guy's eyes went blank when reminded of a $4000 stunt coordinating job I gave him on Producer Mark Carliner's *The Phoenix* two years before. His "speed medication" had erased any recollection of the job. At least his "amnesia" was drug induced.

…Debonair actor George Sanders left a final note: "Dear World, I am leaving because I am bored. I feel I have lived long enough. I am leaving you with your worries in this sweet cesspool. Good luck." Zsa Zsa Gabor said of her former husband, "George was the only one I really loved." Too bad her amorous feelings were not enough to keep him from suicide, but should give her other 28 ex-husbands a thought to ponder.

…To initiate a new female second assistant director, a crewmember would phone the set from an adjoining sound stage and ask for Mike Hunt. The rest of the crew howled as the unaware A.D. screamed "Mike Hunt" to no avail.

…Rumor had it that on Oliver Stone's *Born on the 4th of July* film the famed director suggested that Tom Cruise take a paralyzing drug to fully capture the debilitating effects of an injured Vietnam soldier. Cruise actually considered taking the drug until a doctor mentioned there was a 10-15% possibility of permanent disability. DUH! When you're in front of the camera I think it's called *ACTING*!

…Then there was the stunt guy who made $150,000 the first year jumping cars on the high-rated action "Dukes of Hazzard" TV series—shoved it all up his nose. His action substantiated Robin Williams' astute observation, "Cocaine is God's way of saying you have too much money."

…Mucho handsome Klinton Spillsbury was chosen to reprise Clayton Moore's role in a 1981 *The Legend of the Lone Ranger* remake. Spillsbury evidently made John Gilbert sound like Sir Laurence Olivier causing the studio to re-dub the entire film with a voice befitting the beloved "Masked Man."

…Director Michael Curtiz relaxed in his open-top dressing room as a young starlet performed her oral expertise, laid his head back in enjoyment to see two grips watching from the sound stage catwalk, pushed her aside, screamed "Git away, git away, you filthy thing."

…The Golden Rule, "He, who has the gold, rules," becomes most apparent when you're running a show. You're the center of attention to the stunt performers you've hired as they hang on your every word.

…The importance of checking your equipment became extremely evident when I road tested a car chase vehicle. When I accelerated to 40mph the Jeep began to shake; the lug nuts on all four wheels were finger-loose.

…Premier veteran stunt man Davy Sharpe was usually seen chomping on an unlit cigar. This protruding object became his ubiquitous trademark after he was asked to "rehearse" a stunt, only to have the producer suddenly declare, "They wrote out the stunt." Later, when viewing the completed film, the stunt he "rehearsed" was in the final cut. From that point on, Davy always had a cigar between his clinched teeth whenever he "rehearsed" a stunt.

…It's been reported that all thoroughfares in Beverly Hills are Drives, no Avenues, Boulevards or Streets.

…Larry Duran played the high jacking pilot in Ross Hunter's 1973 remake of Frank Capra's *Lost Horizon* pix as his father did in 1937. Wrong, it was just a press agent's dream.

…A smart 1960s-70s leading actor starred in three Universal Studios TV series drew pay advances greatly exceeding his weekly salary. To recoup their investment the studio kept him employed. That's one way to guarantee job security.

…The funniest line heard on *Saturday Night Live*: "Kunta Kinte spells his name with a 'C.'"

…The Starlite Room just paid North Hollywood TV $100 to repair the Zenith TV set, the bartender cussed because the channels kept flipping from one to another. He never knew I was triggering the set with my own Zenith remote control in my pocket.

…Stunt man Jerry Summers, working on Blake Edwards' *Darling Lili* in 1970, ran and latched onto a biplane wing as it took off. Thanks to Blake, he did 28 takes at a $1000 a shot—making Jerry the highest paid stunt man at the time, for one day, for one stunt.

…During the 1964 Presidential election campaign, LBJ Democrats warned that a vote for Barry Goldwater would cause an escalation of the Vietnam police action into a full blown war, resulting in mass civil unrest in America. Sure enough, I voted for Goldwater and that's exactly what happened.

…Housekeeping while he was on a foreign movie location, a stunt man's wife pried opened his locked briefcase and found explicit Polaroid pictures of his amorous extramarital adventures. Yes, in the divorce settlement she got to keep the house.

…A wag mentioned his recent viewing of Disney's *103 Dalmatians*, only to be corrected: "You mean 102 Dalmatians." He replied, "I was counting Glenn Close."

…When David Lean's roadshow epic film, *Doctor Zhivago*, was released in 1968, comedian Henny Youngman commented on the film's record high $3.50 admission price, "What is he… a Specialist?"

…After receiving his late 1960's Army induction letter, a future stunt guy downed a bottle of Jack Daniels for courage and a shotgun to blow away his big toe. Had he merely suggested his intentions to the Draft Board, he undoubtedly would have been excused on a Section 8.

…An extra on *There was a crooked man…*, later a stunt performer, enhanced the Indio motel's window flower boxes with marijuana seeds, later had his ass nailed during the police stakeout.

…From October 1962, Troy Melton complained daily about his purchase of The Playboy restaurant and bar at Bronson and Melrose, but thirty years later walked away with $750,000 when Paramount Pictures purchased the property.

…An inebriated Donald O'Connor came into the Starlite Room with his driver. Introducing myself as Mickey Rooney's stunt man, Donald smiled "Hi Mick, you're looking good." Don was one of my all-time favorite entertainers.

…An LAPD buddy and his partner checking on a lover's lane parked car, peered in to see a boy and girl about sixteen, locked in a 69 position. The boy's mouth was near the girl's vagina; with a pocketknife he was cutting her pubic hair; which were caught on his braces. The cops figured the kid had enough problems and moved on.

…The Universal cast and crew awaited the arrival of the husband and wife actors John Cassavetes and Gena Roland. Cassavetes pulled on to the backlot set without Gena. Seems they had an argument on the

Ventura Freeway and she got out. The panicked A.D. sent a driver in search. Two hours later Gena arrived after hitching a ride. They're still trying to locate the studio driver.

...Wrong place at the wrong time: Lorne Greene, the *Bonanza* patriarch, had a makeup artist fired because he "entered before knocking," catching Ben Cartwright without his hairpiece.

...A sleep-starved buddy almost belted me when I suggested a new cure for his insomnia, "Get plenty of sleep!" Hey, it was funny when W.C. Fields said it.

...On a distant location the black stunt coordinator on a major gangster film was arrested for drug possession with intent to sell was bailed out of jail by the studio.

...A 1950's NBC live broadcast of the *Today Show* received a notice from the network's Standards & Practices office when a very pregnant Big Band singer Helen O'Connell sang, "Give me something to remember you by."

...From his lofty camera boom perch, director Cecil B. DeMille spied a female extra talking, bellowed into his bullhorn, "If what you have to say is so important, why don't you share it with all of us?" She smiled, "I said, 'I wonder when that bald-headed bastard is going to call lunch?'" DeMille paused a moment, then announced, "Lunch, one hour."

...While walking to the Rickshaw Boy's restaurant pay phone, I passed Cary Grant cuddling in a back booth with a stunning blond.

...To prevent the patter of little feet an amorous lady and I couldn't find a condom and substituted Saran Wrap.

...Then there was a TV producer's effort to eliminate future problems with his lead actors by filming each of their death scenes the first day of the series.

...While in KTLA's guard gate, a dilapidated car pulled up, the driver said he had a meeting with Jim Schulke, the station's vice president/general manager. The guard took another look at the car and pointed to the farthest end of the parking lot park. The gent made the long hike to the executive offices and fifteen minutes later the guard was fired. Seems the visitor was an NBC network president and driving a loaner while his vehicle was being repaired. Presumably, there's a moral here pertaining to never judging a book by its cover.

…A producer needed a copy of John Wayne's film, *The Three Godfathers*, asked his neophyte assistant to locate a DVD copy and he returned with the three *Godfather* films made by Francis Ford Coppola.

…Gaffer Mike Katz constantly suggested a ménage à trois to his beautiful wife, Bonnie, until she finally conceded, "Okay, who's the guy?" Mike never mentioned the subject again.

…Art department painters continued to amaze me when they transformed plywood flats into prison walls by adding a craggy horizontal bead of caulking to simulate cement blocks, and sawdust to the gray paint to create the course surface.

… At the Foxfire Room, Teamster brothers Jim and Jack Grant's arm wrestling bout ended with a loud crack, when Jim's arm broke between his shoulder and elbow.

…I couldn't afford the pay cut and declined the $350 a week first assistant director job on the non-DGA TV series, *Life and Times of Grizzly Adams*, filming in Utah. "I need $500 a week," but the producer retorted, "You're kidding, the director's only getting $600."

… Doubling Peter Falk on *Columbo*, Jerry Summers was hanging from a tree limb with his feet three feet from the ground. Dropping, he broke an ankle—a compound fracture. It was just a freak accident.

…When Robert Morse on *Where were you when the lights went out?* questioned his key light placement, veteran Director of Photography Ellingsworth Fredricks asked him, "How many films have you lighted?

…In the mid-60s, when a local L.A. KTTV kiddie show host dated the estranged wife of actor Rory Calhoun, the actor's stunt double Reg Parton ambushed the fellow, rendering him a thorough bone-breaking beating.

…Every five-year-old daughter should be enrolled in modeling school to teach her poise, confidence, carriage and, especially, how to take a seat. Watch the talk shows as the famous female guests plop down next to the host like a sack of potatoes.

…At Laurel Canyon and Moorpark (backwards it's Krap Room) stop light, actor Gig Young stopped his Rolls Royce beside my 1967 Mustang convertible and asked the time. "Three-twenty, but don't tell me your

Rolls clock is busted?" He just smiled his famous grin and drove away.

...While sport coat shopping Dorman's in Studio City, I said to a buddy, "You know, I'm a real clothes horse." He replied, "Pony, Jess, Pony."

...In Florida's grassland swamp, special effects concealed the airboat stirring mechanism beneath the driver's high-mounted seat. While driving the speedy boat to location, residents called the local police and the Coast Guard to report a runaway airboat racing through the Everglades.

...A famed cowboy hero film star won his stand-in's gratitude and admiration when he insisted the production company keep his buddy on the clock until wrap daily to earn overtime. The benevolent actor would then go to the stand-in's home and bang his wife.

...A curled carrot ribbon adorned each backstage lunch entrée and I'd remark to Nadine, the matronly waitress, "Hey, this bacon isn't cooked," and every time she'd reply, "That's not bacon!" This repartee went on for years and every time she was dead serious.

...Set Rule #13: Never shit where you eat. The beautiful ladies on the movie set didn't just walk in off the street. Someone placed them there. Don't fraternize if you want to stay employed.

...A costumer mentioned numerous occasions when he entered an actor's dressing room to find a lady visitor performing orally. Without blinking an eye, "Excuse me, I've seen it all, just like a doctor," as the lady continued her manipulations without missing a beat.

...Mr. T's character name on *The A-Team* was shortened to "B.A." from the original scripted handle, "Bad Ass Baracus."

...During filming, the producer honored his famous singer/actor's request for a blowjob in the morning and another in the afternoon, each time with a different lady.

...To get the best Mercury car deal, a frugal stunt man got the salesman into the stunt business, and later complained when the guy began getting his jobs.

...Billy "Sailor" Vincent, former stunt double for W.C. Fields and Charles Laughton, was an extra on *Bonanza* in his twilight years. The five visiting nuns were startled when "Sailor" tripped and fell face first at their feet. Slowly, painfully, rising to his feet, Sailor pointed at the priest, "He tripped me." The priest and the glaring nuns were shocked speechless by Sailor's accusation, as the white-haired old man brushed himself off and limped away without a backward glance.

…Reel Hollywood Class. Those invited to Jack Warner's home for tennis and a Sunday barbeque were treated to hamburgers made of ground filet mignon.

…One day Veteran stunt man Saul Gorss' seven year old kid said, "Hi Roger, ya old codger!" and threw a right cross striking Roger Creed in the balls.

…On *The Californians* TV series, the director was screaming about "losing the light," had Wally Rose, in a fight with Alex Sharp, was supposed to leap from a speeding wagon. After two passes Alex finally grabbed Wally by his collar and seat of the pants and yelled, "You're going," heaving him from the wagon.

…History's five most famous men shot in the back of the head: Abe Lincoln, Jesse James, Wild Bill Hickock, John F. Kennedy, and the guy sitting in front of Pee Wee Herman.

…A stunt coordinator complained to the female producer that he witnessed a grip dealing drugs on the set. Unbeknownst to him, the grip was the producer's lover and the stunt man never worked another film for her.

…A 12-year-old buddy was selling newspapers in Hollywood as Bela Lugosi's limousine stopped at his corner. A devoted *Dracula* fan, he yelled into the open window, "Hoowww dooo you dooooo? Let me suck your blood," as Bela Lugosi flipped him the finger.

…*The Big Valley* TV series was the first network program to use "bastard," referring to Lee Majors as Barbara Stanwick's son.

…While cleaning props, Paramount prop man Penny left a bottle of rubbing alcoholon a work table. A former pugilist-film extra quickly grabbed it and took a healthy swig. Penny yelled and the guy ran like hell. Whoa, Nellie.

…During the 1960 Writers Guild West strike, Warner Brothers reworked one series script to another show crediting: *Written by W. Hermanos*. Hermanos is Spanish for Brothers. In the ensuing years the producers would enact a plan to hire writers as producers -- at a higher pay rate, thus making their allegiance to the studio proprietary. This practice continues today.

…Malibu Colony residents were enraged when Martin Sheen, their newly appointed Honorary Mayor, invited the homeless to their sunny shores. The next day a destitute individual basking in his new found shelter under the Malibu Pier held a sign: "Tell Martin I'm here."

…When the *Police Story* TV series filming permits for L.A.'s Chinatown were suddenly cancelled, Director Virgil Vogel called stunt man/actor George Cheung for help. Securing a letter from the San Francisco's Tong (club) leader, George presented it to the L.A. Tong and filming commenced immediately.

…Veteran Stunt man Davy Sharpe and Director Dick Bartlett were having a drink at Bill Story's near Universal as a newly-wed couple settled into a corner booth. "Let's give 'em some excitement," said Davy. Bartlett threw a picture punch. Davy flipped backward and landed on the couple's table. A man seated at the bar yelled, "Free for all" and knocked the guy next to him off the stool.

…David Janssen, returning from his *Fugitive* TV series hiatus, was asked about his lengthy Caribbean vacation, he replied, "A bar is a bar is a bar."

…Bear Hudkins mentioned Classic Bob's, a Van Nuys gentlemen's strip club a friend had visited. The bouncer asked where he preferred to be seated, "I want to sit so close I can smell 'it'" and was promptly ejected. Then I asked, "That was really you, wasn't it?" Bear only grinned.

…I was to be wrapped and bound with barbed wire and wondered how special effects would accomplish this fete without a bloodletting. Ingeniously, they had cut and tied rubber bands every two inches along a coil of wire. After applying metallic paint you couldn't tell the difference.

…In the course of a male-female romantic relationship, when the lady says, "I never want to hurt you," take immediate notice that you're going to get hurt big, really big.

…Proving once again a Johnson has no conscience; a stunt guy's repeated phone calls to meet a fourteen year old was greeted at the secret rendezvous by her stunt man dad and professional boxer brother, and was promptly beaten to a bloody pulp.

…Question to a newspaper column, "What ever happened to actress Ida Lupino's brother, Phil?" Answer: "Last we heard he was in Manila making envelopes."

…Transportation Captain Steve Boyd waited until his honey wagon driver took a coffee break, entered a men's room stall, pulled a warmed Hershey chocolate bar from his pocket and smeared it on the walls. Steve watched as the driver returned and heard him cussing a blue streak, "Look what some sonofabitch did!" Steve approached the wall, took a finger swipe through the brown mass, tasted his finger, he exclaimed, "It's Harry! He's been eating those refried beans again!"

…Errol Flynn, guest starring on *The Red Skelton Show*, remarked to TV floor director Ken McManus, "I just received the best blow job of my life," then pointed to his smiling 16-year old companion, Beverly Aadland.

…Stunt man Roger Creed warned of an England-to-Hollywood stunt guy emigrant, "Don't introduce him to your film's director at lunch or he'll have dinner with him that evening and your job by the next morning."

…So evident of their personal character and gratitude: both Gary Cooper and Frank Sinatra purchased homes for their stunt doubles.

…When Tinseltown beckoned Film and Radio star Fred Allen, he aptly added his two cents: "You can take all the sincerity in Hollywood, place it in the navel of a fruit fly and still have room enough for three caraway seeds and a producer's heart."

THE END

For a complete list of my film credits please check
www.IMDB.com

JESSE WAYNE

Director – **A DATE WITH DALE** – starring Dale Evans – 12 episodes –
3-camera
  Trinity Broadcasting Network

Director – **KIDS IN HARMONY**—3-Camera—Taped TV Pilot
  Ramdom Entertainment—North Hollywood, CA

Writer / Producer – **NEW YEARS EVE IN NEW ORLEANS** (TV
Synd.)
  Diamond J Entertainment (in development)

Writer/Producer – **San Francisco RIP-OFF** (Feature)
  Diamond J Entertainment (in developement)

Co-Prod/Dir/Videographer – **VALLEY VIDEO SHOPPER** (TV
Series)
    Random Entertainment—North Hollywood, CA

Videographer, Floor Dir. Freelance—Los Angeles & Nashville
  Technical Dir. & Lighting Nashville—WDCN/Channel 8, Gospel
  Christian Network, Trinity Broadcasting Network

Camera Operator Video: Sony Betacam Sp, RCA TKs, Ikegami, etc.
  Motion Picture Film Cameras: 16mm & 35mm

Writer—Featured Essays – The Tennessean & The Nashville Scene
Nashville, TN (Copies on Request)

Still Photographer Portrait—Product—Commercial—Boudior---Real Estate

Actor's Gun Coach Fast Draw & Fancy Gun Handling Instruction

Production Manager – Movie Magic™ Production Software
Production Manager – MUSIC CITY BLUES—Thom Keith, Director
  Kingery Entertainment Corp.—Los Angeles, CA
Production Manager (USA) – TICKET TO HEAVEN (Canadian) San
Francisco, CA
Production Manager – BIGFOOT: THE MOVIE—Eureka Springs, AR

1st Asst. Director – TUFF TURF—Fritz Kiersch, Director
  New World Pictures—Hollywood, CA
1st Asst. Director – SOLO—Lyman Dayton, Director
  Dayton/Stewart Productions—St.George, Utah location
1st Asst. Director – CHASTITY & THE STARLETS—Dan Symmes,
Director
  John Lamb, Producer—Rainbow Video, Hollywood, CA
1st Asst. Director – THE GHOST TEAM—Maury Monroe, Producer
  Hollywood, CA
1st Asst. Director —BLINDSIDE—Rod Cavin, Producer
  Florida International Film Corporation—Orlando, FL
1st Asst. Director – REFLECTIONS (3-D)—Dan Symmes, Director
  Robert Crawford, Producer—Hollywood, CA
1st Asst. Director – BOXOFFICE—Josef Bogdanovitch, Director
  Bee Movies, Inc.—Hollywood, CA
1st Asst. Director – EVERY GIRL SHOULD HAVE ONE—Bob Hyatt,
Dir.
  Robert Fridley Productions—Hollywood, CA
1st Asst. Director (2nd Unit) – RACKET (Stunt Action
  David Winters, Producer—Hollywood, CA

Assoc. Prod./1st A.D. – THE WILD RIDE (3-D) Dan Symmes, Director
   Chris Condon, Producer—Stereovision, Inc.—Hollywood, CA
Assoc. Prod./1st – ANY AFTERNOON—John Woodbridge, Director-Hollywood, CA

Location Manager – GODFATHER II—Gray Frederickson, Producer—Hollywood, CA
   Subbed for Location Manager—Jack English for 2 weeks.

Videographer – BILLY WALKER'S 20 GREATEST HITS—TNN Commercial
   Hendersonville, TN
Videographer – GREAT AMERICAN TRAIN SONGS—TNN Commercial
   TVA Railroad—Chattanooga, TN
Videographer – HOLLYWOOD BEACH MURDERS—Add'l. Photography
   Cecil Scaife, Producer—Nashville, TN

Cinematographer PAPER HERO—Robt. Kraft, Producer/Director—L.A., CA
Cinematographer – CALIFORNIA CONNECTION—Frank Q. Dobbs, Dir.
   Terlingua, Texas

Writer/Dir./Cinematographer – L.A.: THE ECOLOGICAL CITY—City of Los Angeles

Oct. 1971- Jan. 1973 – ONE STOP FILM PERMIT OFFICE—City of L.A.
   With Jock Mahoney we were appointed to formulate this office by Mayor Sam Yorty

Announcer/Newscaster – KCSN – 88.5 FM—AM News—CAL State Northridge

1965-1967 Asst. to Prod / Dir RICHARD BARTLETT (Wagon Train, Laredo, etc.)
Hollywood, CA

2nd Unit Director – MEN OF THE GREEN BERET—Earl Lyon, Producer
United Pictures, Inc.—Kern River, CA location

Publicity Director – MISS SAN FERNANDO VALLEY BEAUTY PAGEANT
1965 & 1966—Sportsmen's Lodge—Studio City, CA

1961-1984 – STUNTMEN'S ASSN. Charter/Life Time Member—Former
Board of Director—Secretary & Treasurer—Publicity Director

1959 MGM STUDIOS—"PLATINUM HIGH SCHOOL"—Feature
Became Mickey Rooney's Stunt Double

1958-1959 KTLA CHANNEL 5—Los Angeles, CA—Production & Talent
Coordinator, Camera Operator, Publicity Dept., Newsroom, Stage Crew & Page.

1958 HESPERIA, CALIFORNIA WILD WEST DAYS—Producer,
Writer & Director—Live Stunt Show & Fast Draw Contest

1957-1959 STUNT MAN/ACTOR—Live Western Shows—Calico Ghost Town *(Barstow, CA)*, Corriganville Movie Ranch *(Simi Valley, CA)*
Conventions, Market Openings & Stage Shows.

1949-1951 – CHILD ACTOR—Local Live TV -Los Angeles, CA

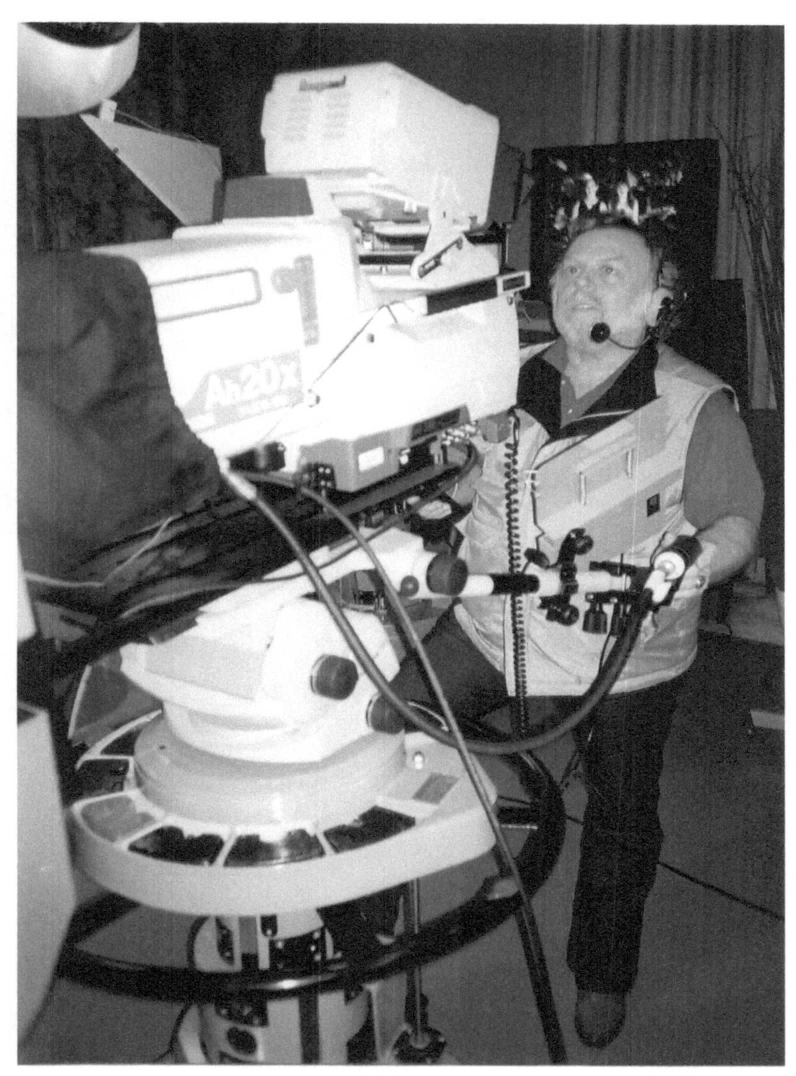